T0191524

Lecture Notes in Computer Science 11503

Commenced Publication in 1973
Founding and Former Series Editors:
Gerhard Goos, Juris Hartmanis, and Jan van Leeuwen

Pascal Hitzler · Miriam Fernández ·
Krzysztof Janowicz · Amrapali Zaveri ·
Alasdair J. G. Gray · Vanessa Lopez ·
Armin Haller · Karl Hammar (Eds.)

The Semantic Web

16th International Conference, ESWC 2019
Portorož, Slovenia, June 2–6, 2019
Proceedings

 Springer

Editors
Pascal Hitzler ⓘ
Wright State University
Dayton, OH, USA

Miriam Fernández ⓘ
KMi, The Open University
Milton Keynes, UK

Krzysztof Janowicz
University of California
Santa Barbara, CA, USA

Amrapali Zaveri
Maastricht University
Maastricht, The Netherlands

Alasdair J. G. Gray ⓘ
Heriot-Watt University
Edinburgh, UK

Vanessa Lopez
IBM Research
Dublin, Ireland

Armin Haller ⓘ
The Australian National University
Canberra, ACT, Australia

Karl Hammar ⓘ
Jönköping University
Jönköping, Sweden

ISSN 0302-9743   ISSN 1611-3349   (electronic)
Lecture Notes in Computer Science
ISBN 978-3-030-21347-3   ISBN 978-3-030-21348-0   (eBook)
https://doi.org/10.1007/978-3-030-21348-0

LNCS Sublibrary: SL3 – Information Systems and Applications, incl. Internet/Web, and HCI

This Springer imprint is published by the registered company Springer Nature Switzerland AG
The registered company address is: Gewerbestrasse 11, 6330 Cham, Switzerland

Preface

This volume contains the main proceedings of the 2019 edition of the Extended Semantic Web Conference (ESWC 2019). ESWC is established as a yearly major venue for discussing the latest scientific results and technology innovations related to the Semantic Web and linked data. At ESWC, international scientists, industry specialists, and practitioners meet to discuss the future of applicable, scalable, user-friendly, as well as potentially game-changing solutions. The 16th edition took place during June 2–6, 2019, in Portoroz, (Slovenia). Building on its past success, ESWC is also a venue for broadening the focus of the Semantic Web community to span other relevant research areas in which semantics and Web technology play an important role, as well as for experimenting with innovative practices and topics that deliver extra value to the community and beyond. This year's conference introduced some novelties compared with the past, particularly a new call for research tracks, enabling the community to more actively participate in the selection of emerging and relevant topics. This call led to the creation of three new research tracks this year: (1) Distribution and Decentralisation, (2) Velocity on the Web, and (3) Research of Research. The addition of these novel tracks complemented six well-established research tracks, including: (1) Ontologies and Reasoning, (2) Linked Data, (3) Natural Language Processing and Information Retrieval, (4) Semantic Data Management and Data Infrastructures, (5) Social and Human Aspects of the Semantic Web and, (6) Machine Learning. Aside from these nine research tracks, the conference features the In-Use, Industry, and Resources tracks, showing the diversity of topics, the research and development activity, the services and applications, and the industry outreach of the Semantic Web community.

The Research, Resource and In-Use tracks follow an Open and Transparency Review Policy established by the conference in 2018. Under this policy, papers, reviews, meta-reviews, and decisions are made Web-available. Senior Program Committee (PC) members sign their meta-reviews and PC members are given the option to sign their reviews. Under GDPR regulations, authors are provided with an option for their papers to be removed from the website. This model follows the successful reviewing policy applied by the *Semantic Web* journal.

These 11 tracks, including the nine Research tracks, Resources, and In-Use, constitute the main scientific program of ESWC 2019. This program contains 39 papers: 26 Research, eight Resources, and five In-Use, selected out of 134 full paper submissions. This corresponds to a total acceptance rate of 29% (28% for Research, 31% for Resources, and 33% for In-Use). The Industry track included three presentations out of ten submissions from companies that have adopted Semantic Web technologies.

In addition to these tracks, the conference offered many opportunities for participation, including: a poster and demo session, workshops and tutorials, a PhD symposium, and a project networking session.

The poster and demo session accepted 18 posters and 20 demos. In this session, researchers had the chance to present their latest results and advances in the form of live demos or face-to-face presentations.

The PhD symposium program received and accepted five contributions. These high-quality papers covered a broad range of topics related to the themes of ESWC, including federated querying, natural language processing, and semantics and ontology matching. The authors, who are both early or mid-to-late stage PhD students, were mentored by senior Semantic Web researchers both before and during the conference.

The conference program contained five workshops, seven tutorials. These included both full-day and half-day events. The main topics of the workshops focused on sentiment analysis and opinion mining, deep learning, and large-scale analytics, building knowledge graphs, and semantic technologies for Industry 4.0. The tutorials addressed a wide range of semantic topics relevant for both experts and novice researchers. The topics offered include data lakes, semantic data enrichment, question-answering systems, ontology engineering, querying linked data and knowledge graphs, and analytics on linked data streams.

ESWC also offers an exciting opportunity for EU-funded projects to network during a special session organized at the conference.

These associated events created an even more open, multidisciplinary, and cross-fertilizing environment at the conference, allowing for work-in progress and practical results to be discussed. Proceedings from these satellite events are available in a separate volume. The program also included three exciting invited keynotes.

The general and program chairs would like to thank the many people who were involved in making ESWC 2019 a success. First of all, our thanks go to the 22 co-chairs of the Research, In-Use and Resources Tracks and the 352 reviewers for all tracks, for ensuring a rigorous and open review process that led to an excellent scientific program. The scientific program was completed by an exciting selection of posters and demos chaired by Sabrina Kirrane and Olaf Hartig. Special thanks go to the PhD symposium chairs, Victor de Boer and Maria-Esther Vidal, who managed one of the key events at ESWC. The PhD students may become the future leaders of our field, and deserve both encouragement and mentoring. We also had a great selection of workshops and tutorials, as mentioned earlier, thanks to the commitment of our workshop and tutorial chairs, Maria Maleshkova and Stefan Schlobach. Thanks to our EU project networking session chairs, Ioanna Lytra and Laura Koesten, we had the opportunity to facilitate meetings and exciting discussions between leading European research projects. Networking and sharing ideas between projects is a crucial success factor for such large research projects. We are additionally grateful for the work and commitment of Katja Hose and Ruben Verborgh, who established a challenge track. Thanks to Nelia Lasierra and Steffen Stadtmüller for the organization of the industry track, and to Laura Hollink and Anna Tordai for playing the ever-challenging sponsor chair role. We thank STI International for supporting the conference organization. Stefano Borgo and Marija Komatar in particular deserve special thanks for the professional support of the local conference organization and for solving all practical matters. Further, we are very grateful to Agnieszka Ławrynowicz and Jędrzej Potoniec, our publicity and Web presence chairs, who kept our community informed throughout the year and to Blake Regalia, our Semantic Technologies Coordinator. Special thanks to our proceedings chair, Karl Hammar, for all his work in preparing this volume with the kind support of Springer. We finally thank our sponsors, listed on the next pages, for their vital support of this edition of ESWC. The general chair would like to close the preface with his warm thanks to the program chairs, Miriam Fernandez and Krzysztof Janowicz, for their rigorous commitment to selecting an exciting ESWC 2019 scientific program.

April 2019

Pascal Hitzler
Miriam Fernandez
Krzysztof Janowicz
Amrapali Zaveri
Alasdair J. G. Gray
Vanessa Lopez
Armin Haller
Karl Hammar

Organization

General Chair

Pascal Hitzler   Wright State University, USA

Research Track Program Chairs

Miriam Fernandez   The Open University, UK
Krzysztof Janowicz   University of California, Santa Barbara, USA

Resource Track Program Chairs

Amrapali Zaveri   Maastricht University, The Netherlands
Alasdair J. G. Gray   Heriot-Watt University, UK

In-Use Track Program Chairs

Vanessa Lopez   IBM Research, Ireland
Armin Haller   The Australian National University, Australia

Industry Track Program Chairs

Nelia Lasierra   F. Hoffmann-La Roche AG, Switzerland
Steffen Stadtmüller   Robert Bosch GmbH, Germany

Poster and Demo Chairs

Sabrina Kirrane   Vienna University of Economics and Business, Austria
Olaf Hartig   Linköping University, Sweden

PhD Symposium Chairs

Victor de Boer   Vrije Universiteit Amsterdam, The Netherlands
Maria-Esther Vidal   TIB Leibniz Information Centre for Science
                             and Technology, Germany, and Universidad Simon
                             Bolivar, Venezuela

Workshops and Tutorials Chairs

Maria Maleshkova   University of Bonn, Germany
Stefan Schlobach   Vrije Universiteit Amsterdam, The Netherlands

Challenge Chairs

Katja Hose   Aalborg University, Denmark
Ruben Verborgh   Ghent University – imec, Belgium, and Massachusetts
                           Institute of Technology, USA

Sponsoring Chairs

Laura Hollink   Centrum Wiskunde & Informatica, The Netherlands
Anna Tordai   Elsevier, The Netherlands

EU Project Networking Chairs

Ioanna Lytra   University of Bonn, Germany
Laura Koesten   University of Southampton, UK

Publicity and Web Presence Chairs

Agnieszka Ławrynowicz   Poznań University of Technology, Poland
Jędrzej Potoniec   Poznań University of Technology, Poland

Semantic Technologies Coordinator

Blake Regalia   University of California, Santa Barbara, USA

Proceedings Chair

Karl Hammar   Jönköping University, Sweden

Local Organizers

Stefano Borgo   ISTC-CNR, Italy
Marija Komatar   PITEA d.o.o., Slovenia

Subtrack Chairs

Ontologies and Reasoning

Mari Carmen   Universidad Politécnica de Madrid, Spain
  Suárez-Figueroa
Markus Stocker   TIB Leibniz Information Centre for Science
                           and Technology, Germany

Linked Data

Ricardo Usbeck   Fraunhofer IAIS, Germany
Aidan Hogan   Universidad de Chile, Chile

Natural Language Processing and Information Retrieval

Serena Villata	Université Côte d'Azur, CNRS, Inria, I3S, France
Harald Sack	FIZ Karlsruhe – Leibniz Institute for Information Infrastructure, Germany

Machine Learning

Stefan Dietze	GESIS - Leibniz Insitute for the Social Sciences, Germany and Heinrich Heine University Düsseldorf, Germany
Claudia d'Amato	Università degli Studi di Bari, Italy

Semantic Data Management and Data Infrastructures

Oscar Corcho	Universidad Politécnica de Madrid, Spain
Axel Polleres	Vienna University of Economics and Business, Austria

Social and Human Aspects of the Semantic Web

Anna Lisa Gentile	IBM Research, USA
Lora Aroyo	Google

Distribution and Decentralization

Maria Maleshkova	University of Bonn, Germany
Ruben Verborgh	Ghent University – imec, Belgium, and Massachusetts Institute of Technology, USA

Velocity on the Web

Emanuele Della Valle	Politecnico di Milano, Italy
Stefan Schlobach	Vrije Universiteit Amsterdam, The Netherlands

Research of Research

Alejandra Gonzalez-Beltran	University of Oxford, UK
Francesco Osborne	The Open University, UK
Sahar Vahdati	University of Bonn, Germany

Program Committee

Karl Aberer	Ecole polytechnique fédérale de Lausanne (EPFL), Switzerland
Maribel Acosta	Karlsruhe Institute of Technology, Germany
Alessandro Adamou	Data Science Institute, National University of Ireland Galway, Ireland
Nitish Aggarwal	Roku Inc., USA
Mehwish Alam	FIZ Karlsruhe, Germany
Panos Alexopoulos	Textkernel B.V., The Netherlands

Marjan Alirezaie   Örebro University, Sweden
Renzo Angles   Universidad de Talca, Chile
Mihael Arcan   Insight Centre for Data Analytics, Ireland
Natanael Arndt   AKSW, Institute for Applied Informatics (InfAI),
                           Leipzig University, Germany
Lora Aroyo   Google
Maurizio Atzori   University of Cagliari, Italy
Franz Baader   TU Dresden, Germany
Sebastian Bader   Fraunhofer IAIS, Germany
Andrea Ballatore   Birkbeck, University of London, UK
Payam Barnaghi   University of Surrey, UK
Valerio Basile   University of Turin, Italy
Zohra Bellahsene   University of Montpellier, France
Socorro Bernardos-Galindo Universidad Politécnica de Madrid, Spain
Leopoldo Bertossi   RelationalAI Inc. and Carleton University, Canada
Aliaksandr Birukou   Springer, Germany
Fernando Bobillo   University of Zaragoza, Spain
Katarina Boland   GESIS - Leibniz Institute for the Social Sciences,
                           Germany
Andrea Bonaccorsi   University of Pisa and IRVAPP-Fondazione Bruno
                           Kessler, Italy
Pieter Bonte   Ghent University – imec, Belgium
Alessandro Bozzon   Delft University of Technology, The Netherlands
Adrian M. P. Brasoveanu   Modul Technology GmbH, Austria
Carlos Buil Aranda   Universidad Técnica Federico Santa María, IMFD,
                           Chile
Gregoire Burel   The Open University, UK
Davide Buscaldi   LIPN, Université Paris 13, France
Anila Sahar Butt   CSIRO, Australia
Elena Cabrio   Université Côte d'Azur, France
Jean-Paul Calbimonte   University of Applied Sciences and Arts Western
                           Switzerland, Switzerland
Nicholas John Car   CSIRO, Australia
David Carral   TU Dresden, Germany
Irene Celino   Cefriel, Italy
Federica Cena   University of Turin, Italy
Davide Ceolin   Vrije Universiteit Amsterdam, The Netherlands
Pierre-Antoine Champin   Université Claude Bernard Lyon 1, France
Thierry Charnois   Université Paris 13, France
Gong Cheng   Nanjing University, China
Pieter Colpaert   Ghent University – imec, Belgium
Simona Colucci   Politecnico di Bari, Italy
Oscar Corcho   Universidad Politécnica de Madrid, Spain
Francesco Corcoglioniti   Fondazione Bruno Kessler, Italy
Philippe Cudre-Mauroux   University of Fribourg, Switzerland
Edward Curry   Insight Centre for Data Analytics, Ireland

Enrico Daga	The Open University, UK
Victor de Boer	Vrije Universiteit Amsterdam, The Netherlands
Daniel de Leng	Linköping University, Sweden
Stefan Decker	RWTH Aachen University, Germany
Thierry Declerck	DFKI, Germany
Emanuele Della Valle	Politecnico di Milano, Italy
Daniele Dell'Aglio	University of Zurich, Switzerland
Gianluca Demartini	The University of Queensland, Australia
Elena Demidova	L3S Research Center, Germany
Angelo Di Iorio	University of Bologna, Italy
Giorgio Maria Di Nunzio	University of Padua, Italy
Dennis Diefenbach	Université Jean Monet, France
Stefan Dietze	GESIS - Leibniz Insitute for the Social Sciences, Germany and Heinrich Heine University Düsseldorf, Germany
Dimitar Dimitrov	GESIS - Leibniz Institute for the Social Sciences, Germany
Anastasia Dimou	imec – IDLab, Ghent University, Belgium
Milan Dojchinovski	AKSW, Institute for Applied Informatics (InfAI), Leipzig University, Germany, and Czech Technical University in Prague, Czech Republic
Mauro Dragoni	Fondazione Bruno Kessler, Italy
Anca Dumitrache	FD Mediagroep, Amsterdam, The Netherlands
Michel Dumontier	Institute of Data Science, Maastricht University, The Netherlands
Claudia d'Amato	Università degli Studi di Bari, Italy
Aaron Eberhart	Wright State University, USA
Kemele M. Endris	L3S Research Center, Germany
Vadim Ermolayev	Zaporizhzhia National University, Ukraine
Pavlos Fafalios	L3S Research Center, Germany
Nicola Fanizzi	Università degli studi di Bari, Italy
Stefano Faralli	University of Rome Unitelma Sapienza, Italy
Catherine Faron Zucker	Université Nice Sophia Antipolis, France
Alberto Fernandez	Universidad Rey Juan Carlos, Spain
Miriam Fernandez	The Open University, UK
Javier D. Fernández	Vienna University of Economics and Business, Austria
Mariano Fernández López	Universidad San Pablo CEU, Spain
Jesualdo Tomás Fernández-Breis	Universidad de Murcia, Spain
Sébastien Ferré	Université de Rennes 1, France
Besnik Fetahu	L3S Research Center, Germany
Valeria Fionda	University of Calabria, Italy
George Fletcher	Eindhoven University of Technology, The Netherlands
Fred Freitas	Universidade Federal de Pernambuco, Brazil
Irini Fundulaki	FORTH-ICS, Greece
Adam Funk	University of Sheffield, UK

Kjetil Kjernsmo	Inrupt Inc.
Matthias Klusch	German Research Center for AI (DFKI), Germany
Haridimos Kondylakis	FORTH-ICS, Greece
Roman Kontchakov	Birkbeck, University of London, UK
Manolis Koubarakis	National and Kapodistrian University of Athens, Greece
Maria Koutraki	L3S Research Center, Germany
Ralf Krestel	Hasso Plattner Institute, Germany
Adila Krisnadhi	Universitas Indonesia, Indonesia
Tobias Käfer	Karlsruhe Institute of Technology, Germany
Patrick Lambrix	Linköping University, Sweden
Christoph Lange	University of Bonn and Fraunhofer IAIS, Germany
Danh Le Phuoc	TU Berlin, Germany
Freddy Lecue	CortAIx @Thales and Inria, Canada
Jens Lehmann	University of Bonn and Fraunhofer IAIS, Germany
Maurizio Lenzerini	Sapienza University of Rome, Italy
Yuan-Fang Li	Monash University, Australia
Alejandro Llaves	Fujitsu Laboratories of Europe, Spain
Steffen Lohmann	Fraunhofer IAIS, Germany
Nuno Lopes	TopQuadrant, Inc.
Vanessa Lopez	IBM Research, Ireland
Ismini Lourentzou	University of Illinois at Urbana - Champaign, USA
Thomas Lukasiewicz	University of Oxford, UK
Gengchen Mai	University of California, Santa Barbara, USA
Maria Maleshkova	University of Bonn, Germany
Andrea Mannocci	ISTI-CNR, Italy
Ioana Manolescu	Inria and Ecole Polytechnique, France
Alessandro Margara	Politecnico di Milano, Italy
Claudia Marinica	ETIS UMR 8051, University of Paris-Seine, University of Cergy-Pontoise, ENSEA, CNRS, France
Miguel A. Martinez-Prieto	University of Valladolid, Spain
Tobias Mayer	Université Côte d'Azur, France
Diana Maynard	The University of Sheffield, UK
Kenneth McLeod	Heriot-Watt University, UK
Alessandra Mileo	Insight Centre for Data Analytics, Ireland
Dunja Mladenic	Jozef Stefan Institute, Slovenia
Pascal Molli	University of Nantes, France
Gabriela Montoya	Aalborg University, Denmark
Raghava Mutharaju	IIIT-Delhi, India
Lionel Médini	LIRIS lab., Université de Lyon, France
Ralf Möller	University of Lübeck, Germany
Sebastian Neumaier	Vienna University of Economics and Business, Austria
Matthias Nickles	National University of Ireland, Ireland
Andriy Nikolov	metaphacts GmbH, Germany

Terhi Nurmikko-Fuller	Australian National University, Australia
Femke Ongenae	Ghent University – imec, Belgium
Sergio Oramas	Pandora, Spain
Francesco Osborne	The Open University, UK
Raul Palma	Poznan Supercomputing and Networking Center, Poland
Matteo Palmonari	University of Milano-Bicocca, Italy
Jeff Z. Pan	University of Aberdeen, UK
Harshvardhan Jitendra Pandit	Trinity College Dublin, Ireland
Tassilo Pellegrini	University of Applied Sciences St. Pölten, Austria
Silvio Peroni	University of Bologna, Italy
Catia Pesquita	LASIGE, Universidade de Lisboa, Portugal
Guangyuan Piao	Bell Labs, Ireland
Reinhard Pichler	TU Wien, Austria
Emmanuel Pietriga	Inria, France
Giuseppe Pirrò	Sapienza University of Rome, Italy
Dimitris Plexousakis	FORTH-ICS, Greece
Axel Polleres	Vienna University of Economics and Business, Austria
María Poveda-Villalón	Universidad Politécnica de Madrid, Spain
Freddy Priyatna	Universidad Politécnica de Madrid, Spain
Cédric Pruski	Luxembourg Institute of Science and Technology, Luxembourg
Jorge Pérez	Universidad de Chile and IMFD Chile, Chile
Héctor Pérez-Urbina	Google, USA
Alessandro Raganato	University of Helsinki, Finland
Dnyanesh Rajpathak	General Motors, USA
Jose Luis Redondo Garcia	Amazon Alexa, UK
Blake Regalia	University of California, Santa Barbara, USA
Georg Rehm	DFKI, Germany
Achim Rettinger	Trier University, Germany
Juan L. Reutter	Pontificia Universidad Católica de Chile
Martin Rezk	DMM.com, Japan
Mariano Rico	Universidad Politécnica de Madrid, Spain
Petar Ristoski	IBM Research, USA
Giuseppe Rizzo	LINKS Foundation, Italy
Mariano Rodríguez Muro	Google
Ana Roxin	University of Burgundy, France
Edna Ruckhaus	Universidad Politécnica de Madrid, Spain
Sebastian Rudolph	TU Dresden, Germany
Anisa Rula	University of Milano-Bicocca, Italy
Marta Sabou	TU Wien, Austria
Harald Sack	FIZ Karlsruhe – Leibniz Institute for Information Infrastructure, Germany

Sherif Sakr	The University of New South Wales, Australia
Angelo Antonio Salatino	The Open University, UK
Muhammad Saleem	University of Leizpig, Germany
Cristina Sarasua	University of Zurich, Switzerland
Felix Sasaki	Cornelsen Verlag GmbH, Germany
Bahar Sateli	Concordia University, Canada
Kai-Uwe Sattler	TU Ilmenau, Germany
Marco-Luca Sbodio	IBM Research, Ireland
Simon Scerri	Fraunhofer IAIS, Germany
Johann Schaible	GESIS - Leibniz Institute for the Social Sciences, Germany
Stefan Schlobach	Vrije Universiteit Amsterdam, The Netherlands
Patrik Schneider	TU Wien and Siemens AG, Austria
Giovanni Semeraro	Università degli studi di Bari, Italy
Barış Sertkaya	Frankfurt University of Applied Sciences, Germany
Saeedeh Shekarpour	University of Dayton, USA
Gerardo I. Simari	Universidad Nacional del Sur and CONICET, Argentina
Hala Skaf-Molli	University of Nantes, France
Monika Solanki	University of Oxford, UK
Dezhao Song	Thomson Reuters, USA
Adrián Soto	Pontificia Universidad Católica de Chile, Chile
Marc Spaniol	Université de Caen Normandie, France
Steffen Staab	University Koblenz-Landau, Germany and University of Southampton, UK
Nadine Steinmetz	TU Ilmenau, Germany
Armando Stellato	University of Rome Tor Vergata, Italy
Markus Stocker	TIB Leibniz Information Centre for Science and Technology, Germany
Audun Stolpe	Norwegian Defence Research Establishment, Norway
Umberto Straccia	ISTI-CNR, Italy
Martin Strohbach	AGT International, Germany
Heiner Stuckenschmidt	University of Mannheim, Germany
Mari Carmen Suarez-Figueroa	Universidad Politécnica de Madrid, Spain
York Sure-Vetter	Karlsruhe Institute of Technology, Germany
Vojtěch Svátek	University of Economics, Prague, Czech Republic
Pedro Szekely	Information Sciences Institute, USA
Ruben Taelman	Ghent University – imec, Belgium
Kia Teymourian	Boston University, USA
Harsh Thakkar	University of Bonn, Germany
Andreas Thalhammer	F. Hoffmann-La Roche AG, Switzerland
Allan Third	The Open University, UK
Ilaria Tiddi	Vrije Universiteit Amsterdam, The Netherlands

Thanassis Tiropanis	University of Southampton, UK
Konstantin Todorov	University of Montpellier - LIRMM - CNRS, France
Riccardo Tommasini	DEIB, Politecnico di Milano, Italy
Sebastian Tramp	eccenca GmbH, Germany
Raphael Troncy	EURECOM, France
Jürgen Umbrich	Vienna University of Economics and Business, Austria
Jacopo Urbani	Vrije Universiteit Amsterdam, The Netherlands
Ricardo Usbeck	Fraunhofer IAIS, Germany
Sahar Vahdati	University of Bonn, Germany
Marieke van Erp	KNAW Humanities Cluster, The Netherlands
Miel Vander Sande	Ghent University – imec, Belgium
Ruben Verborgh	Ghent University – imec, Belgium, and Massachusetts Institute of Technology, USA
María-Esther Vidal	TIB Leibniz Information Centre for Science and Technology, Germany, and Universidad Simon Bolivar, Venezuela
Serena Villata	Université Côte d'Azur, CNRS, Inria, I3S, France
Fabio Vitali	University of Bologna, Italy
Piek Vossen	Vrije Universiteit Amsterdam, The Netherlands
Domagoj Vrgoc	Pontificia Universidad Católica de Chile
Kewen Wang	Griffith University, Australa
Zhichun Wang	Beijing Normal University, China
Cord Wiljes	Bielefeld University, Germany
Gregory Todd Williams	The J. Paul Getty Trust, USA
Peter Wood	Birkbeck, University of London, UK
Josiane Xavier-Parreira	Siemens AG, Austria
Jie Yang	Amazon Research, USA
Fouad Zablith	American University of Beirut, Lebanon
Ondřej Zamazal	University of Economics, Prague, Czech Republic
Benjamin Zapilko	GESIS - Leibniz Institute for the Social Sciences, Germany
Amrapali Zaveri	Institute of Data Science, Maastricht University, The Netherlands
Lei Zhang	FIZ Karlsruhe, Germany
Ziqi Zhang	Sheffield University, UK
Rui Zhu	University of California, Santa Barbara, USA
Antoine Zimmermann	École des Mines de Saint-Étienne, France
Arkaitz Zubiaga	Queen Mary University of London, UK
Hanna Ćwiek-Kupczyńska	Institute of Plant Genetics, Polish Academy of Sciences, Poland

Additional Reviewers

Angelidis, Iosif
Atzeni, Mattia
Bhardwaj, Akansha
Bianchi, Federico
Borgwardt, Stefan
Collarana, Diego
Du, Jianfeng
Fawei, Biralatei
Flouris, Giorgos
Gottschalk, Simon
Gutiérrez Basulto, Víctor
Halvorsen, Jonas
Heling, Lars
Kondylakis, Haridimos
Kulbach, Cedric
Kľuka, Ján
Leskinen, Petri

Li, Ningxi
Luggen, Michael
Mami, Mohamed
Meilicke, Christian
Mihindukulasooriya, Nandana
Narducci, Fedelucio
Repke, Tim
Risch, Julian
Rodrigues, Cleyton
Smeros, Panayiotis
Tempelmeier, Nicolas
Thoma, Steffen
Troullinou, Georgia
Wang, Zhe
Westphal, Patrick
Wiens, Vitalis
Zhuang, Zhiqiang

Sponsors

Diamond Sponsors

STI International is a global network engaging in research, education, innovation, and commercialization activities on semantic technologies working to facilitate their use and applicability within industries and society as a whole. Launched in Berlin in January 2007, STI international designs its unique research infrastructure and implements public and internal services that support the individual partner organizations in their research collaboration, standardization, dissemination, and exploitation activities. ESWC is one of a number of events that STI International organizes.

 Jožef Stefan Institute

Gold Sponsors

QualiChain targets the creation, piloting, and evaluation of a decentralized platform for storing, sharing, and verifying education and employment qualifications and focuses on the assessment of the potential of blockchain technology, algorithmic techniques, and computational intelligence for disrupting the domain of public education, as well as its interfaces with private education, the labor market, public sector administrative procedures, and the wider socioeconomic developments.

The project focuses more specifically on the assessment of the implications (technical, political, socioeconomic, legal and cultural) as well as the impact – in terms of benefits and risks – of the prescribed solution's utilization, whose disruptive potential lies both in the exploitation of the innovative features of the aforementioned individual technologies, as well as in their unique combination in a new territory for the provision of a set of baseline services (Awards/Qualifications Archiving; Awards/ Qualifications Verification; Qualifications Portfolio Management) and a number of value-adding services (Career Counselling and Intelligent Profiling and Competency Management including Recruitment; Competencies Evaluation and Development; Consulting and Decision Support).

The proposed solution will be piloted through four representative scenarios, including: (1) cross-university degree equivalence verification; (2) smart curriculum design; (3) staffing the public sector; (4) providing HR consultancy and competency management services.

Springer is a global publishing company that publishes books, e-books, and peer-reviewed journals in science, humanities, technical, and medical (STM) publishing. Springer also hosts a number of scientific databases, including SpringerLink, Springer Protocols, and SpringerImages. Book publications include major reference works, textbooks, monographs and book series; more than 168,000 titles are available as e-books in 24 subject collections. Springer has major offices in Berlin, Heidelberg, Dordrecht, and New York City.

STI Innsbruck is a research group at the University of Innsbruck engaged in research and development to bring information and communication technologies of the future into today's world.

Silver Sponsors

ELSEVIER

Elsevier is a global information analytics business that helps scientists and clinicians to find new answers, reshape human knowledge, and tackle the most urgent human crises. For 140 years, we have partnered with the research world to curate and verify scientific knowledge. Today, we are committed to bringing that rigor to a new generation of platforms. Elsevier provides digital solutions and tools in the areas of strategic research management, R&D performance, clinical decision support, and professional education; including ScienceDirect, Scopus, SciVal, ClinicalKey, and Sherpath. Elsevier publishes over 2,500 digitized journals, including *The Lancet* and *Cell*, 39,000 e-book titles and many iconic reference works, including *Gray's Anatomy*. Elsevier is part of RELX Group, a global provider of information and analytics for professionals and business customers across industries.

IBM Research

We live in a moment of remarkable change and opportunity. Data and technology are transforming industries and societies, ushering in a new era of artificial intelligence. IBM Research is a leader in this worldwide transformation, building on a long history of innovation. For more than seven decades, IBM Research has defined the future of technology. Our scientists, among them six Nobel Laureates and six Turing Award winners, have produced ten U.S. National Medals of Technology and five U.S. National Medals of Science. Along the way we helped put a man on the moon, defeated Kasparov at chess, and built a Jeopardy! champion named Watson.

SIEMENS

Siemens AG (Berlin and Munich) is a global technology powerhouse that has stood for engineering excellence, innovation, quality, reliability, and internationality for more than 170 years. The company is active around the globe, focusing on the areas of electrification, automation, and digitalization. One of the largest producers of energy-efficient, resource-saving technologies, Siemens is a leading supplier of efficient power generation and power transmission solutions and a pioneer in infrastructure solutions as well as automation, drive, and software solutions for industry. With its publicly listed subsidiary Siemens Healthineers AG, the company is also a leading provider of medical imaging equipment – such as computed tomography and magnetic resonance imaging systems – and a leader in laboratory diagnostics as well as clinical IT. In the fiscal year 2018, which ended on September 30, 2018, Siemens generated revenue of €83.0 billion and a net income of €6.1 billion. At the end of September 2018, the company had around 379,000 employees worldwide. Further information is available on the Internet at http://www.siemens.com.

Bronze Sponsors

Information (ISSN 2078-2489; CODEN: INFOGG) is a scientific peer-reviewed open access journal of information science and technology, data, knowledge, and communication, and is published monthly online by MDPI. It is indexed by EI Compendex, Scopus (Elsevier), Emerging Sources Citation Index (ESCI - Web of Science), and other databases. Manuscripts are peer-reviewed and a first decision provided to authors approximately 16.5 days after submission; acceptance to publication is undertaken in 4.8 days: http://www.mdpi.com/journal/information.

metaphacts is a Germany-based company empowering customers to build and manage their own knowledge graphs and extract the most value out of their data, enable transparency, and reach smarter business decisions. We provide the expertise, products, and services to create thematically specialized knowledge graphs in areas such as business, finance, engineering and manufacturing, life sciences, cultural heritage, and more. Built entirely on open standards and technologies, our platform metaphactory covers the entire lifecycle of dealing with knowledge graphs, and makes authoring, curating, editing, linking, searching, and visualizing graph data easy, fast, and affordable.

Onlim specializes in automating customer communication for customer service, marketing and sales via chatbots and voice assistants. The Austrian high-tech company offers a multi-channel platform to create, manage, and distribute content for customer interactions via text- and voice-based conversational interfaces and serves clients such as the University of Vienna, Vienna Stock Exchange, Wien Energie, Olympiaregion Seefeld, Energienetze Steiermark, and more. As a spin-off of the University of Innsbruck Onlim's advanced technology is based on state-of-the-art research. Since 2015, Onlim's team has grown to over 25 experts in AI, machine learning, and semantics.

Semantic Web Company (SWC) is the leading provider of graph-based knowledge technologies and the vendor of PoolParty Semantic Suite, an innovative and enterprise-ready technology platform which helps organizations to build and manage knowledge graphs as a basis for various AI applications. Semantic Web Company has been consistently awarded KMWorld's "company that matters in knowledge management," and according to Gartner, PoolParty Semantic Suite is a "representative product" for "Hosted AI Services." With Credit Suisse, Roche, Philips and Asian Development Bank (ADB) among their customer base of Global 2000 companies, Semantic Web Company is continuously helping customers to roll out their knowledge management and AI strategy within their organizations.

Contents

Research Track

A Decentralized Architecture for Sharing and Querying Semantic Data   3
 Christian Aebeloe, Gabriela Montoya, and Katja Hose

Reformulation-Based Query Answering for RDF Graphs
with RDFS Ontologies.   19
 *Maxime Buron, François Goasdoué, Ioana Manolescu,
 and Marie-Laure Mugnier*

A Hybrid Graph Model for Distant Supervision Relation Extraction   36
 Shangfu Duan, Huan Gao, Bing Liu, and Guilin Qi

Retrieving Textual Evidence for Knowledge Graph Facts.   52
 Gonenc Ercan, Shady Elbassuoni, and Katja Hose

Boosting DL Concept Learners.   68
 Nicola Fanizzi, Giuseppe Rizzo, and Claudia d'Amato

Link Prediction in Knowledge Graphs with Concepts
of Nearest Neighbours.   84
 Sébastien Ferré

Disclosing Citation Meanings for Augmented Research
Retrieval and Exploration.   101
 Roger Ferrod, Claudio Schifanella, Luigi Di Caro, and Mario Cataldi

Injecting Domain Knowledge in Electronic Medical Records
to Improve Hospitalization Prediction   116
 *Raphaël Gazzotti, Catherine Faron-Zucker, Fabien Gandon,
 Virginie Lacroix-Hugues, and David Darmon*

Explore and Exploit. Dictionary Expansion with Human-in-the-Loop.   131
 Anna Lisa Gentile, Daniel Gruhl, Petar Ristoski, and Steve Welch

Aligning Biomedical Metadata with Ontologies Using
Clustering and Embeddings   146
 Rafael S. Gonçalves, Maulik R. Kamdar, and Mark A. Musen

Generating Semantic Aspects for Queries.   162
 *Dhruv Gupta, Klaus Berberich, Jannik Strötgen,
 and Demetrios Zeinalipour-Yazti*

A Recommender System for Complex Real-World Applications
with Nonlinear Dependencies and Knowledge Graph Context   179
    Marcel Hildebrandt, Swathi Shyam Sunder, Serghei Mogoreanu,
    Mitchell Joblin, Akhil Mehta, Ingo Thon, and Volker Tresp

Learning URI Selection Criteria to Improve the Crawling
of Linked Open Data   194
    Hai Huang and Fabien Gandon

Deontic Reasoning for Legal Ontologies   209
    Cheikh Kacfah Emani and Yannis Haralambous

Incorporating Joint Embeddings into Goal-Oriented Dialogues
with Multi-task Learning   225
    Firas Kassawat, Debanjan Chaudhuri, and Jens Lehmann

Link Prediction Using Multi Part Embeddings   240
    Sameh K. Mohamed and Vít Nováček

Modelling the Compatibility of Licenses   255
    Benjamin Moreau, Patricia Serrano-Alvarado, Matthieu Perrin,
    and Emmanuel Desmontils

GConsent - A Consent Ontology Based on the GDPR   270
    Harshvardhan J. Pandit, Christophe Debruyne, Declan O'Sullivan,
    and Dave Lewis

Latent Relational Model for Relation Extraction   283
    Gaetano Rossiello, Alfio Gliozzo, Nicolas Fauceglia,
    and Giovanni Semeraro

Mini-ME Swift: The First Mobile OWL Reasoner for iOS   298
    Michele Ruta, Floriano Scioscia, Filippo Gramegna, Ivano Bilenchi,
    and Eugenio Di Sciascio

Validation of SHACL Constraints over KGs with OWL 2 QL
Ontologies via Rewriting   314
    Ognjen Savković, Evgeny Kharlamov, and Steffen Lamparter

An Ontology-Based Interactive System for Understanding User Queries   330
    Giorgos Stoilos, Szymon Wartak, Damir Juric, Jonathan Moore,
    and Mohammad Khodadadi

Knowledge-Based Short Text Categorization Using Entity
and Category Embedding   346
    Rima Türker, Lei Zhang, Maria Koutraki, and Harald Sack

A Hybrid Approach for Aspect-Based Sentiment Analysis Using
a Lexicalized Domain Ontology and Attentional Neural Models   363
  Olaf Wallaart and Flavius Frasincar

Predicting Entity Mentions in Scientific Literature.   379
  Yalung Zheng, Jon Ezeiza, Mehdi Farzanehpour, and Jacopo Urbani

Resources Track

AYNEC: All You Need for Evaluating Completion Techniques
in Knowledge Graphs   397
  Daniel Ayala, Agustín Borrego, Inma Hernández, Carlos R. Rivero,
  and David Ruiz

RVO - The Research Variable Ontology   412
  Madhushi Bandara, Ali Behnaz, and Fethi A. Rabhi

EVENTSKG: A 5-Star Dataset of Top-Ranked Events in Eight
Computer Science Communities   427
  Said Fathalla, Christoph Lange, and Sören Auer

CORAL: A Corpus of Ontological Requirements Annotated
with Lexico-Syntactic Patterns   443
  Alba Fernández-Izquierdo, María Poveda-Villalón,
  and Raúl García-Castro

MMKG: Multi-modal Knowledge Graphs   459
  Ye Liu, Hui Li, Alberto Garcia-Duran, Mathias Niepert,
  Daniel Onoro-Rubio, and David S. Rosenblum

BeSEPPI: Semantic-Based Benchmarking of Property
Path Implementations.   475
  Adrian Skubella, Daniel Janke, and Steffen Staab

QED: Out-of-the-Box Datasets for SPARQL Query Evaluation.   491
  Veronika Thost and Julian Dolby

ToCo: An Ontology for Representing Hybrid
Telecommunication Networks.   507
  Qianru Zhou, Alasdair J. G. Gray, and Stephen McLaughlin

A Software Framework and Datasets for the Analysis of Graph
Measures on RDF Graphs   523
  Matthäus Zloch, Maribel Acosta, Daniel Hienert, Stefan Dietze,
  and Stefan Conrad

In-Use Track

The Location Index: A Semantic Web Spatial Data Infrastructure   543
   Nicholas J. Car, Paul J. Box, and Ashley Sommer

Legislative Document Content Extraction Based on Semantic Web
Technologies: A Use Case About Processing the History of the Law   558
   Francisco Cifuentes-Silva and Jose Emilio Labra Gayo

BiographySampo – Publishing and Enriching Biographies on the Semantic
Web for Digital Humanities Research   574
   Eero Hyvönen, Petri Leskinen, Minna Tamper, Heikki Rantala,
   Esko Ikkala, Jouni Tuominen, and Kirsi Keravuori

Tinderbook: Fall in Love with Culture   590
   Enrico Palumbo, Alberto Buzio, Andrea Gaiardo, Giuseppe Rizzo,
   Raphael Troncy, and Elena Baralis

Using Shape Expressions (ShEx) to Share RDF Data Models
and to Guide Curation with Rigorous Validation   606
   Katherine Thornton, Harold Solbrig, Gregory S. Stupp,
   Jose Emilio Labra Gayo, Daniel Mietchen, Eric Prud'hommeaux,
   and Andra Waagmeester

Correction to: Using Shape Expressions (ShEx) to Share RDF Data Models
and to Guide Curation with Rigorous Validation C1
   Katherine Thornton, Harold Solbrig, Gregory S. Stupp,
   Jose Emilio Labra Gayo, Daniel Mietchen, Eric Prud'hommeaux,
   and Andra Waagmeester

Author Index   621

Research Track

A Decentralized Architecture for Sharing and Querying Semantic Data

Christian Aebeloe$^{(\boxtimes)}$, Gabriela Montoya , and Katja Hose

Aalborg University, Aalborg, Denmark
{caebel,gmontoya,khose}@cs.aau.dk

Abstract. Although the Semantic Web in principle provides access to a vast Web of interlinked data, the full potential remains mostly unexploited. One of the main reasons for this is the fact that the architecture of the current Web of Data relies on a set of servers providing access to the data. These servers represent bottlenecks and single points of failure that result in instability and unavailability of data at certain points in time. In this paper, we therefore propose a decentralized architecture (PIQNIC) for sharing and querying semantic data. By combining both client and server functionality at each participating node, and introducing replication, PIQNIC avoids bottlenecks and keeps datasets available and queryable although the original source might not be available. Our experimental results, using a standard benchmark of real datasets, show that PIQNIC can serve as an architecture for sharing and querying semantic data, even in the presence of node failures.

1 Introduction

More and more datasets are being published in RDF format. These datasets cover a broad range of topics, such as geography, cross-domain knowledge, government, life sciences, etc. Access to these datasets is offered in different ways, e.g., they can be downloaded as data dumps, they can be queried via SPARQL endpoints, or they can be "browsed" via dereferencing URIs.

Once published, however, we are often in a situation where the datasets, or rather the interfaces to access them, are not available when needed. In fact, studies found that over half of the public SPARQL endpoints have less than 95% availability [2]. The reason often simply is that maintaining these interfaces requires considerable resources from the data providers. In practice, this means that the data necessary to answer a certain query might not be available at a specific time so that the answer might be incomplete – or in general, the same query might have different answers at different points in time.

Hence, despite the great potential of the Semantic Web, accessing RDF datasets today entirely relies on the services offered by the data providers, e.g., web interfaces with downloadable datasets, SPARQL endpoints, or dereferenceable URIs. Especially SPARQL endpoints often require huge amounts of resources for query processing, which further increases the burden on the data

© Springer Nature Switzerland AG 2019
P. Hitzler et al. (Eds.): ESWC 2019, LNCS 11503, pp. 3–18, 2019.
https://doi.org/10.1007/978-3-030-21348-0_1

providers [9,22]. Despite recent efforts that proposed to implement monetary incentives to solve this problem [8], we argue that we can achieve availability by applying decentralization instead of relying on the availability of single servers and their functionality. This not only better reflects the nature of the World Wide Web but also avoids dependencies and single points of failure.

In this paper, we therefore propose PIQNIC (a P2p clIent for Query processiNg over semantIC data). PIQNIC introduces decentralization as a key concept by building on the Peer-to-Peer (P2P) paradigm and replication. PIQNIC functions as a P2P network of homogeneous nodes that can be queried by any node in the network. By combining both client and server functionality at each peer and introducing replicas, we avoid single points of failure as (sub)queries can be processed by multiple alternative peers and the data is still available even though the original source is not. In doing so, PIQNIC offers a solution to one of the main problems that the current Semantic Web is suffering from: availability of datasets [2]. It is therefore not our main goal to enable load sharing among nodes to enhance query processing performance and outperform existing systems. In summary, this paper makes the following contributions:

– A P2P-based architecture for publishing and querying RDF data (PIQNIC)
– A customizable scheme for replicating and fragmenting datasets
– Query processing strategies in PIQNIC networks with replicated and fragmented data
– An extensive evaluation of the proposed approaches

This paper is structured as follows. While Sect. 2 discusses related work, Sect. 3 presents the PIQNIC framework and its main concepts. Section 4 then describes how to process queries in PIQNIC. Section 5 then presents the results of our evaluation and Sect. 6 concludes the paper with a summary and an outlook to future work.

2   Related Work

Recent developments in privacy and personal data on the social Web has inspired interesting new applications and use cases. The Solid project [14], for instance, uses a decentralized architecture and Semantic Web technologies to enable personal online datastores (pod) to be stored separately from applications. In fact, users decide themselves where a pod is hosted, giving them control over their data. While the idea of storing Linked Data in multiple locations is central to our work, Solid focuses on privacy protection of personal data whereas we focus on the availability of open datasets.

Federated query processing over SPARQL endpoints, e.g., [19], is a widely used approach to query over distributed Linked Open Data. To lower the computational load at the servers hosting the SPARQL endpoints, recent proposals, such as Triple Pattern Fragments (TPF) [22] and Bindings-Restricted Triple Pattern Fragments (brTPF) [9], propose to shift part of the load to the client issuing the query [18]. This, in turn, increases the availability of the servers.

Nevertheless, TPF/brTPF servers still represent a single point of failure; if the server is not available, the hosted datasets are not available either, which is the problem we are targeting in this paper.

To further share the computational load in a TPF setting, processing SPARQL queries in networks of browsers has been proposed [6,7,17]. The key principle is to share the computational load among a set of clients based on the functionality offered by their browsers and caching of recently used datasets using a collaborative caching system based on overlay networks [5]. However, browsers are relatively unstable nodes, with very limited processing power and storage capacity, which naturally limits the general applicability. In contrast, we aim at a relatively stable network with more powerful nodes and datasets split into smaller fragments that are replicated.

Replication of triple pattern fragments has been considered in [16], where fragments are replicated at multiple servers to allow for balancing the server loads and providing fault tolerance. While [16] considers a fixed set of servers that provide access to a fixed set of replicated fragments, and clients that are aware of the allocation of fragments to servers, PIQNIC has a fault-tolerant P2P-based architecture where clients also serve replicated fragments to other clients, which naturally allows for handling dynamic behavior of the clients.

P2P systems in general vary in their level of decentralization. Structured P2P systems organize their peers in an overlay network using, for instance, Distributed Hash Tables (DHTs) to decide were to store and find particular data items. Some of these systems were proposed to support RDF data [3,11,12]. The key principle of these systems is that the connections between peers, i.e., the layout of the network, and the data placement is imposed on the participating peers, restricting their autonomy. As a consequence, such systems are vulnerable to situations where many peers leave and join the network as this might require major reorganizations of structure and data placement in the network.

Unstructured P2P systems, on the other hand, retain a high degree of peer autonomy, i.e., there is no globally enforced network layout or data placement. The basic way of processing queries in such networks is flooding, i.e., a request is flooded through the network along the connections between neighboring peers until an answer has been found. These systems are therefore more reliable with respect to dynamic behavior, i.e., nodes joining and leaving the network. The prospects of unstructured P2P techniques as a decentralized architecture for Linked Data have also been recognized in recent vision papers [15,20]. While these papers provide interesting insights in the benefits of decentralization and replication, we propose a concrete system and implementation for query processing over an unstructured network of P2P nodes.

3   PIQNIC

PIQNIC builds upon basic principles of P2P systems; a client software is running at each participating peer that (i) provides access to a network of clients without central authority and (ii) offers access to datasets stored locally at other nodes in the network. To minimize local space consumption at a node, we use HDT [4] files. As common in P2P networks, nodes do not have global knowledge of all the peers in the network and their connections. Hence, PIQNIC nodes always maintain a partial view of the entire network. This partial view consists of (i) nodes with related data, i.e. data that uses common URI/IRIs, to ensure that queries over multiple datasets can be completed efficiently and (ii) random neighbors to ensure connectivity of the entire network.

Before going into details on query processing (Sect. 4), this section first introduces the notion of datasets and data fragments (Sect. 3.1). Afterwards, Sect. 3.2 outlines PIQNIC's network architecture. Last, Sect. 3.3 describes the dynamic behavior of PIQNIC nodes, maintaining a partial view over the network, and data replication.

3.1   Data Fragmentation

Since RDF datasets can be quite large (e.g., YAGO3 [13] with over 100 million triples), replicating entire RDF datasets at another node might not always be possible or useful. Hence, inspired by the TPF style of accessing data, we propose a customizable approach for fragmenting large datasets.

Consider the infinite and disjoint sets U (the set of all URIs/IRIs), B (the set of all blank nodes), L (the set of all literals), and V (the set of all variables). An RDF *triple t* is a triple s.t. $t \in (U \cup B) \times U \times (U \cup B \cup L)$, and a *triple pattern* tp is a triple s.t. $tp \in (U \cup B \cup V) \times (U \cup V) \times (U \cup B \cup L \cup V)$. A knowledge graph $\mathcal{G}$ is a finite set of RDF triples.

Definition 1 (Fragment). *Let $\mathcal{G}_N$ be a knowledge graph that includes all RDF triples in a PIQNIC network. A fragment f is a 4-tuple $f = \langle T, N, u, i \rangle$ with the following elements:*

- *T is a finite set of RDF triples, and $T \subseteq \mathcal{G}_N$,*
- *N is a set of PIQNIC nodes storing the fragment,*
- *u is a URI/IRI that identifies the fragment, and*
- *i is an identification function that determines whether the fragment contains triples matching a given triple pattern.*

Identification functions are mainly used during query processing to determine whether or not a triple pattern should be evaluated over a fragment.

Following the principle that a data provider uploads a dataset using a local PIQNIC node, we say that datasets are "owned" by a specific node. The owner node manages the allocation of replicas to other nodes in the network (details in Sect. 3.3). We then define a dataset as a set of fragments:

Definition 2 (Dataset). *A dataset D is a triple $D = \langle F, u, o \rangle$ with the following elements:*

- *F is a set of fragments,*
- *u is a URI/IRI that identifies the dataset, and*

- o is an identifier of the "owner" node, i.e., the node that uploaded F to the network.

A fragmentation function $\mathcal{F}$ is then defined as follows.

Definition 3 (Fragmentation function). *A fragmentation function $\mathcal{F}$ is a function that, when applied to a knowledge graph $\mathcal{G}$, creates a set of fragments $F = \mathcal{F}(\mathcal{G})$, i.e., $\mathcal{F}(\mathcal{G}) : \mathcal{G} \mapsto 2^{\mathcal{G}}$.*

Concrete fragmentation functions can result in different levels of granularity. For example, a fragmentation function $\mathcal{F}_C$ that results in $\mathcal{F}_C(\mathcal{G}) = \{\mathcal{G}\}$ is a very coarse-granular fragmentation function that does not split up the original knowledge graph $\mathcal{G}$. On the other hand, a fragmentation function $\mathcal{F}_F$ that results in $\mathcal{F}_F(\mathcal{G}) = \{\{t\} \mid t \in \mathcal{G}\}$, creates a separate fragment for each individual triple and is very fine-granular. PIQNIC uses a predicate-based fragmentation function $\mathcal{F}_P$ as defined in Definition 4.

Definition 4 (Predicate-based fragmentation function). *Let p_t denote the predicate of a triple t. A predicate-based fragmentation function $\mathcal{F}_P(\mathcal{G}) = \{F_p \mid \exists t \in \mathcal{G} : p_t = p \land (\forall t' \in \mathcal{G})[p_{t'} = p] : t' \in F_p\}$ defines one fragment for each unique predicate in the knowledge graph $\mathcal{G}$.*

Naturally, more complex fragmentation functions can be defined. However, in its current implementation PIQNIC uses $\mathcal{F}_P$ because it has a straightforward implementation and is guaranteed to generate pairwise disjoint fragments as each triple has exactly one predicate, i.e., for any two fragments $f_i, f_j \in \mathcal{F}_P(\mathcal{G})$ it holds that $f_i \cap f_j = \emptyset$.

Example 1 (Fragmentation). Consider example knowledge graph $\mathcal{G}_E$ in Table 1a. Applying $\mathcal{F}_P$ to $\mathcal{G}_E$ results in the set of fragments $f_1, f_2, f_3\ f_4$, and f_5 shown in Table 1b; one fragment for each unique predicate p_1, p_2, p_3, p_4, and p_5.

Table 1. Applying $\mathcal{F}_P$ to a knowledge graph $\mathcal{G}_E$

(a) Knowledge graph $\mathcal{G}_E$

Knowledge graph $\mathcal{G}_E$		
$\langle a\ p_1\ b\rangle$	$\langle a\ p_2\ c\rangle$	$\langle a\ p_3\ d\rangle$
$\langle b\ p_2\ e\rangle$	$\langle b\ p_1\ d\rangle$	$\langle b\ p_3\ d\rangle$
$\langle c\ p_3\ d\rangle$	$\langle d\ p_1\ c\rangle$	$\langle c\ p_2\ a\rangle$
$\langle f\ p_4\ d\rangle$	$\langle d\ p_4\ f\rangle$	$\langle e\ p_5\ g\rangle$

(b) $\mathcal{F}_P(\mathcal{G}_E)$

f_1	f_2	f_3	f_4	f_5
$\langle a\ p_1\ b\rangle$	$\langle a\ p_2\ c\rangle$	$\langle a\ p_3\ d\rangle$	$\langle f\ p_4\ d\rangle$	$\langle e\ p_5\ g\rangle$
$\langle b\ p_1\ d\rangle$	$\langle b\ p_2\ e\rangle$	$\langle b\ p_3\ d\rangle$	$\langle d\ p_4\ f\rangle$	
$\langle d\ p_1\ c\rangle$	$\langle c\ p_2\ a\rangle$	$\langle c\ p_3\ d\rangle$		

3.2 Network Architecture

A PIQNIC network consists of a set of interconnected nodes, each maintaining a local data/triple store to manage a set of fragments. A node is defined as follows.

Definition 5 (Node). *A node n is a triple* $n = \langle \Gamma, \Delta, N \rangle$ *where*

- Γ *is the set of fragments located on the node,*
- Δ *is a set of datasets owned by the node, and*
- N *is a set of so-called neighbor nodes in the network.*

Each node n maintains a set $n.N$ of neighbor nodes representing a partial view over the network. In order to ensure that (i) related data is close in the network to increase the completeness of query answers, and (ii) all data and nodes can be reached (connectivity of the network), $n.N$ contains nodes with related fragments as well as random nodes in the network.

To account for changes in the network, PIQNIC uses periodic shuffles [23] between pairs of nodes. A node n selects a random node n' in $n.N$, which it sends a subset of its neighbors, removing them from its own partial view. This subset consists of the least related neighbors based on the "joinability" of the nodes' fragments.

Definition 6 (Fragment Joinability). *Let s_t and o_t be the subject and object of triple t, $\mathcal{G}_N$ the knowledge graph containing all RDF triples in a network, and $f_1, f_2 \in \mathcal{F}_P(\mathcal{G}_N)$. f_1 and f_2 are said to be "joinable", denoted $f_1 \perp\!\!\!\perp f_2$, iff for at least one triple $t_1 \in f_1$, there exists a triple $t_2 \in f_2$, s.t. $\{s_{t_1}, o_{t_1}\} \cap \{s_{t_2}, o_{t_2}\} \neq \emptyset$.*

We observe that the binary relation $\perp\!\!\!\perp$ is symmetric and reflexive. It is symmetric since if t_1 has a subject or object in common with t_2, t_2 has the same subject or object in common with t_1. It is reflexive since any triple t has its own subjects and objects in common with itself.

Fragment joinability only considers *if* two fragments are joinable, and does not consider the rate of overlap between them. This is to avoid favoring large fragments where the absolute number of joint subjects and objects is likely to be higher than for small fragments because of the higher number of triples. The relative number of overlapping subjects and objects is not a good alternative either as fragments with a small overlap might still be important to achieve complete query results.

Based on Definition 6, we can now define a relatedness metric to rank a node's neighbors. We consider only non-identical joinable fragments. Hence, given a node n the goal is to select the k least related nodes R, where $R \subseteq n.N$ s.t. we minimize the objective function in Eq. 1.

$$Rel(n) = \operatorname*{arg\,min}_{R \subseteq n.N} \sum_{n_i \in R} \frac{|Join(n, n_i)|}{|n.\Gamma|} \quad s.t. \ |R| = k \qquad (1)$$

where $Join(n, n_i)$, as defined in Eq. 2, is the set of fragments in n that are joinable with one of node n_i's fragments that does not have the same fragment identifier.

$$Join(n_1, n_2) = \{f_1 \in n_1.\Gamma \mid \exists f_2 \in n_2.\Gamma : f_1 \perp\!\!\!\perp f_2 \land f_1.u \neq f_2.u\} \qquad (2)$$

Example 2 (Neighbor Ranking). Consider the fragments in Table 1b and their assignment to the 4 nodes in Fig. 1a. Note that f_1, f_2, and f_3 are pairwise joinable. We observe that $f_4 \perp\!\!\!\perp f_1$, $f_4 \perp\!\!\!\perp f_3$, and $f_5 \perp\!\!\!\perp f_2$. Assuming we would like to select the least related neighbor of n_4 to shuffle, we apply Eq. 1 and obtain:

- n_1: Since $f_4 \perp\!\!\!\perp f_1$ and $f_5 \perp\!\!\!\perp f_2$, then $r_1 = 2/2 = 1$
- n_2: Since $f_4 \perp\!\!\!\perp f_3$ and $f_5 \perp\!\!\!\perp f_2$, then $r_2 = 2/2 = 1$
- n_3: Since $f_4 \perp\!\!\!\perp f_1$, $f_4 \perp\!\!\!\perp f_3$, $f_5 \not\perp\!\!\!\perp f_1$ and $f_5 \not\perp\!\!\!\perp f_3$, then $r_3 = 1/2 = 0.5$

This results in n_3 being the least related neighbor, and as such it is removed after the shuffle and replaced by a new neighbor n_5 (Fig. 1b).

To compute relatedness in a running system, the nodes exchange the sets of objects and subjects in a compressed representation, such as bitvectors, which can be stored locally for future use.

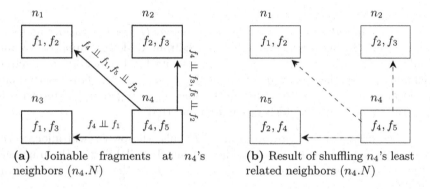

(a) Joinable fragments at n_4's neighbors ($n_4.N$)

(b) Result of shuffling n_4's least related neighbors ($n_4.N$)

Fig. 1. Computing the relatedness of n_4's neighbors and shuffling. *Solid arrows denote a connection to a neighbor in list $n_4.N$, and dashed arrows neighbors after a shuffle.*

3.3 Replication of Datasets

Any node participating in a PIQNIC network can upload a dataset and become its owner node. When uploading a knowledge graph $\mathcal{G}$, a fragmentation function ($\mathcal{F}_P(\mathcal{G})$) is applied to obtain a set of fragments. This set of fragments is then used to create a dataset D.

Allocation of fragments in a PIQNIC network follows a chaining approach, i.e., the owner node passes the fragment on to one of its neighbors, which inserts the fragment into its own local data store and forwards the fragment to one of its neighbors. This continues for a certain number of steps, referred to as *replication factor* (r_f). If a node cannot insert a fragment (for instance because of too little available storage space), it passes the request to one of its neighbors. Lastly, the set of nodes at which the fragment has been inserted is returned to the owner node.

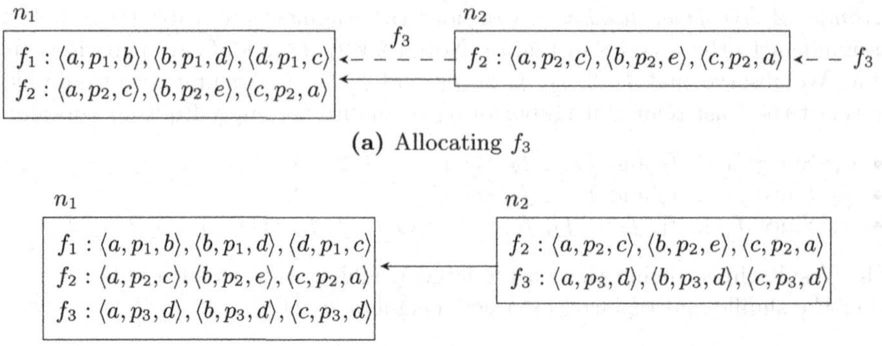

n_1 $\qquad\qquad\qquad\qquad\qquad\qquad$ n_2

$$\boxed{\begin{array}{l} f_1 : \langle a, p_1, b\rangle, \langle b, p_1, d\rangle, \langle d, p_1, c\rangle \\ f_2 : \langle a, p_2, c\rangle, \langle b, p_2, e\rangle, \langle c, p_2, a\rangle \end{array}}$$

$\xleftarrow{\ \ f_3\ \ }$ $\boxed{f_2 : \langle a, p_2, c\rangle, \langle b, p_2, e\rangle, \langle c, p_2, a\rangle}$ $\xleftarrow{\ f_3}$

(a) Allocating f_3

n_1 $\qquad\qquad\qquad\qquad\qquad\qquad$ n_2

$$\boxed{\begin{array}{l} f_1 : \langle a, p_1, b\rangle, \langle b, p_1, d\rangle, \langle d, p_1, c\rangle \\ f_2 : \langle a, p_2, c\rangle, \langle b, p_2, e\rangle, \langle c, p_2, a\rangle \\ f_3 : \langle a, p_3, d\rangle, \langle b, p_3, d\rangle, \langle c, p_3, d\rangle \end{array}}$$

$\longleftarrow$ $\boxed{\begin{array}{l} f_2 : \langle a, p_2, c\rangle, \langle b, p_2, e\rangle, \langle c, p_2, a\rangle \\ f_3 : \langle a, p_3, d\rangle, \langle b, p_3, d\rangle, \langle c, p_3, d\rangle \end{array}}$

(b) States of n_1 and n_2 after allocation

Fig. 2. Allocating fragment f_3 at node n_2 with $r_f = 2$. *Dashed lines denote the allocation of a fragment, solid lines denote a neighbor relation.*

Example 3 (Allocation and replication of a fragment). Let us consider nodes n_1 and n_2 in Fig. 2a and fragments f_1, f_2, and f_3 from Table 1b. Suppose n_2 wants to allocate f_3 with $r_f = 2$. n_2 inserts f_3 into its local datastore, and selects neighbor n_1. f_3 is then forwarded to n_1 with $r_f = r_f - 1 = 1$. f_3 is inserted into n_1's local data store, resulting in Fig. 2b. Since $r_f = 1$, $\{n_1, n_2\}$ is returned to n_2 as the set of nodes in which f_3 has been inserted.

If a node containing a fragment from $D.F$ fails, the owner will allocate the fragment to another node, ensuring the continued availability of the fragment. If the owner itself fails, another node can take over the task of maintaining availability.

Besides making sure fragments are always available, PIQNIC exposes the following operations, which the owner of a dataset D can execute: (i) add triples to fragments in D, (ii) remove triples from fragments in D, (iii) allocate fragments to further nodes, and (iv) revoke an allocation of a fragment from a node. This update is executed locally on the owner node, after which it forwards the updated fragment to the nodes it is allocated to.

Joining a PIQNIC network can be achieved by knowing an arbitrary node and making it a neighbor. Consider, for instance, a node n_1 wants to join the network via node n_2; n_1 therefore sends a message to n_2, which replies with its neighbors. n_1 will then take over some replicas of these neighbors and gradually become a full member of the network.

4   Query Processing

Any node in a PIQNIC network can issue queries. Query processing follows the basic principle of flooding that is employed in P2P systems [1], i.e., a query is forwarded to a peer's neighbors, which in turn forward it to their neighbors, until a certain Time-To-Live (TTL) value/distance is reached. A query is executed at the node that issued the query, while individual triple patterns may be processed by the node's neighbors, i.e., SPARQL operators, such as UNION, are evaluated at the query issuer. In PIQNIC, a SPARQL query q at a node n_i is processed in the following steps:

1. Estimate the cardinality of each triple pattern in q using variable counting. The order in which triple patterns are processed is determined by this estimation, i.e., more selective triple patterns are evaluated first.
2. Evaluate q's triple patterns, starting from n_i's local datastore, over the data accessible via n_i's neighbors by flooding the network using a specified TTL value.
3. Receive partial results from the queried nodes in the network (nodes with no result answer with an empty reply). Partial results are sent directly to the querying node.
4. Compute the final query result by combining the intermediate results of the triple patterns and the remaining operations necessary to complete q.

We use fragment identifiers to avoid querying the same fragment twice on different nodes, i.e., if a fragment with the same identifier has already been queried by a previous node, it will not be queried again. Moreover, if a fragment is available locally, we use that and do not query it again on another node.

Obviously, step 2 can be implemented in different ways. However, before going into details on this aspect, let us first define an identification function (i in the Definition 1) to decide whether a fragment is relevant for a particular triple pattern or not. As fragmentation is defined on predicates, we use a predicate-based identification function.

Definition 7 (Predicate-based identification function). *Let $\mathcal{F}_P(\mathcal{G}_N)$ be a the set of fragments in a network, $f \in \mathcal{F}_P(\mathcal{G}_N)$ be a fragment, tp be a triple pattern and p_{tp} the predicate of tp. A predicate-based identification function $\mathcal{F}_{IP}(f, tp)$ returns true iff $\forall t \in f : p_t = p_{tp}$ or p_{tp} is a variable.*

A triple t is said to be a matching triple for a triple pattern tp iff there exists a solution mapping μ s.t. $t = \mu[tp]$, where $\mu[tp]$ is the triple obtained by replacing variables in tp according to μ.

Definition 8 (Solution mappings [22]). *Let U, B, L, V be the set of all URIs, blank nodes, literals, and variables. Then the answer S to a SPARQL query is a set of solution mappings s.t. a solution mapping is a partial mapping $\mu : V \mapsto (U \cup B \cup L)$.*

We implemented and evaluated three query processing strategies that differ in step 2 of the above description: Single, Bulk, and Full.

Single Strategy. The Single approach is inspired by query processing in TPF [22] and Jena ARQ[1]. The triple patterns of a query q are processed sequentially. To process the current triple pattern we use the intermediate results from

---

[1] https://jena.apache.org/documentation/query/index.html.

the node's local fragments (step 1) and previously computed triple patterns. We instantiate the triple pattern with the already known result mapping and send it to the neighbors. This is done for each known solution mapping separately, hence the name of this strategy: Single.

Bulk Strategy. Obviously, the Single strategy can be improved by sending sets of solution mappings along with a triple pattern throughout the network, instead of individual solution mappings. This is a similar optimization as proposed in [9] to improve TPF query processing. Hence, using the Bulk strategy we expect that considerably fewer messages are sent throughout the network. Ideally, all bindings are sent along in a single message. However, for some triple patterns there is a high number of intermediate solution mappings, e.g., query L1 in our evaluation has more than $232,000$ solution mappings for variable ?results. Propagating such a large number of bindings through the network might easily become a problem because of the message size. Hence, in such cases, we send the bindings in groups of up to s_m bindings. In our current implementation, we use a default value of $s_m = 1,000$ (empirically determined based on the data and queries used in our experiments).

Full Strategy. In contrast to the other strategies, the Full strategy does not include the results of already computed solution mappings in the queries sent throughout the network. Instead, it forwards the triple patterns as defined in the original input query to the neighbors and exploits the fact that this can be done in parallel (instead of sequentially as in the other strategies). However, as this strategy cannot exploit the selectivity of triple patterns if instantiated with solution bindings, in general more data has to be sent through the network. Likewise, more data has to be processed locally at the querying node to compute the final result.

5   Evaluation

We implemented a prototype PIQNIC node[2] in Java 8, using the HDT Java library[3] for the local datastore and extended Apache Jena[4] to support the three query processing approaches discussed in Sect. 4.

Experimental Setup

We ran our experiments on a server with 4xAMD Opteron 6376, 16 core processors at 2.3 GHz, 768 KB L1 cache, 16 MB L2 cache and 16 MB L3 cache each (64 cores in total), and 516 GB RAM. To evaluate our approach we used extended LargeRDFBench [10]. LargeRDFBench comes with 13 datasets with altogether

---

[2] The source code is available at https://github.com/Chraebe/PIQNIC.
[3] https://github.com/rdfhdt/hdt-java.
[4] https://jena.apache.org/.

over 1 billion triples and was designed to evaluate federated SPARQL query processing engines. LargeRDFBench provides a total of 40 queries divided into four distinct sets: simple (S), complex (C), large data (L), and Complex and large data (CH). However, to enable a more fine-granular analysis, we distinguish the two subsets of S that were originally defined in FedBench [21] but merged together in LargeRDFBench: cross domain (CD) and life sciences (LS).

In our experiments, we varied a broad range of parameters. However, due to space restrictions we do not show all experimental results in this paper but focus on a subset. Results of additional experiments are available on our website[5]. For each experiment, we measured the following metrics:

- *Query Execution Time* (QET) is the amount of time it takes to answer a query, i.e., the time elapsed between issuing the query and obtaining the final answer.
- *Completeness* (COM) measures how complete the computed set of answers for a query is; expressed as the percentage of computed answers in comparison to the complete set of answers.
- *Number of Transferred Bytes* (NBT) is the total number of bytes transferred between nodes during query execution.
- *Number of Messages* (NM) is the total number of messages exchanged between nodes during query execution.

Each experiment was run as follows: all queries in the query load were executed 3 times at randomly chosen nodes in the network – the reported measurements represent the averages of the 3 executions.

Experimental Results

Unless stated otherwise, we use the following default values: #Nodes: 200, TTL: 5, Replication: 5%, #Neighbors: 5. We used a timeout of 1200 s, i.e., 20 min, and the experiments were executed without shuffles during. The average storage space used per node was 1.1 GB with 18.1 million triples. The test dataset's size is 61 GB with 1 billion triples.

Performance of Query Execution Strategies. Full timed out for all queries in groups L and CH, and all but a few queries in C, while Single timed out for most queries in the aforementioned groups. Moreover, the queries that timed out for all approaches have a very large number of intermediate results (up to 50 million triples). Such queries are also not supported by state-of-the-art federated query processing approaches [10] and is therefore a general problem that is considered out of the scope of this paper. Therefore, the following discussion focuses on query groups CD and LS – the omitted results can be found on our website (see Footnote 5). The corresponding query execution times (QET) are shown in Fig. 3.

---

[5] http://relweb.cs.aau.dk/piqnic/.

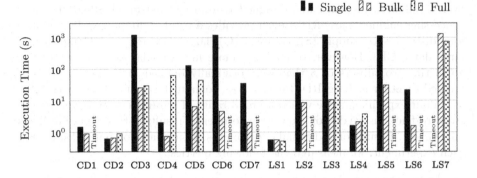

Fig. 3. QET for `Single`, `Bulk`, and `Full` over queries CD and LS. *Note that the y-axis is in log scale.*

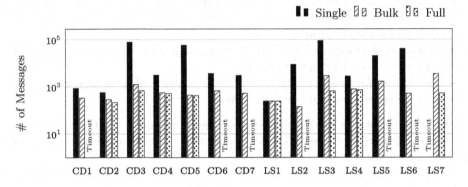

Fig. 4. NM for `Single`, `Bulk`, and `Full` over queries CD and LS. *Note that the y-axis is in log scale.*

As we can clearly see, generally `Bulk` performs much better than the other two approaches with respect to execution time. It is not surprising that `Bulk` in general performs better than `Single`, as sending groups of bindings instead of sending each binding separately, considerably reduces communication and computational overhead. While `Full` does perform quite poorly in most cases, it is faster than both `Bulk` and `Single` in rare cases, e.g., LS7. This is due to the fact that some triple patterns have a very low selectivity. In such cases, almost all triples in a fragment are relevant and it is therefore more efficient to download the entire fragment instead of exchanging multiple rounds of messages with large amounts of data.

This is evident from Fig. 4, which shows the number of messages sent through the network. Not surprisingly, in all cases `Single` sends more messages throughout the network than the two other approaches. While, expectedly, `Full` is better in this regard than `Bulk`, they are still quite similar in most cases. This is due to the cardinalities of most triple patterns being lower than 1,000, and thus only one message is sent. The queries that did not time out all delivered complete query results (100% completeness).

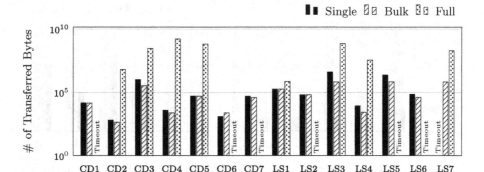

Fig. 5. NTB for Single, Bulk, and Full over queries CD and LS. *Note that the y-axis is in log scale.*

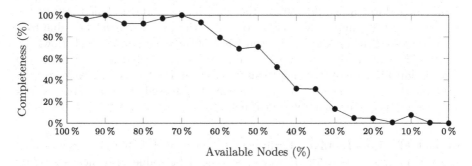

Fig. 6. COM for queries when varying the number of nodes failures (Bulk strategy, no recovery time)

Figure 5 shows the number of transferred bytes (NTB) for queries in groups CD and LS. Again, we leave out queries that timed out. Not surprisingly, Full transfers the most amount of data in all cases. For most queries Single and Bulk are comparable and the differences negligible.

Robustness of the Network. We also evaluated how PIQNIC networks perform in the presence of node failures. To test robustness and availability of data, we focused on the Bulk strategy and the query sets CD and LS. Figure 6 shows the average completeness of queries with a varying number of failing nodes. In the experiment, we executed all the queries and noted the completeness, i.e., we gradually killed a randomly selected number of nodes until no nodes were left in the network. The network was given no recovery time after nodes had been killed. The results show the robustness of PIQNIC against node failures; the results start with a completeness of 100% and stayed above 90% until less than 60% of the nodes were running. Afterwards, the completeness gradually decreased.

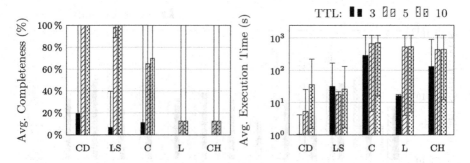

Fig. 7. Average COM and QET `Bulk` strategy and TTL 3, 5, and 10 (QET log scale)

When giving the network recovery time between each run, i.e., allowing all nodes to perform 3 shuffles before the next set of nodes is killed, PIQNIC is able to keep the completeness close to 100% (the lowest was 94,44% due to a single query not being answered) even when 50% of the nodes failed. However, we should mention that query execution time was affected as each node had more fragments to look through. This shows that PIQNIC is able to keep data available through replication at the tradeoff of increased execution time as it is more expensive to find the relevant fragment.

Impact of Time-To-Live. Intuitively, a higher TTL value gives access to a larger part of the network. However, a large TTL value also means sending messages to more nodes. In fact, since we use a flooding technique, the amount of sent messages increases exponentially with the TTL value. To systematically analyze the impact of the TTL value, we compare *COM* and *QET* for three TTL values; 3, 5, and 10. Figure 7 shows average completeness and execution time for each of the 5 groups of queries in our query load, using the `Bulk` strategy. Even though many of the queries in groups L and CH timed out, they still provided some results before timing out. In general, a TTL value of 3 results in incomplete results for all query groups. We observe that even though a TTL value of 10 gives in total more complete results, the additional query execution time indicates that this might not necessarily be a good tradeoff. Instead, a TTL value of 5 shows almost as complete results with lower execution times.

6 Conclusions

In this paper, we proposed PIQNIC (a P2p clIent for Query processiNg over semantIC data), to process queries over semantic datasets. PIQNIC is inspired by recent advances in decentralized Semantic Web systems as well as P2P systems in general, and provides an implementation that, in addition to providing query access to vast amounts of data as a client, functions as a server maintaining a local datastore. We presented a general architecture for sharing and processing RDF data in a decentralized manner and customizable approaches for data fragmentation and query processing over a network of nodes. Our experiments show that the `Bulk` strategy provides the best performance on average and that PIQNIC is able to tolerate node failures. As highlighted by one of our experiments, it is not straightforward to find a good balance between completeness, TTL, and query execution time. Moreover, the lack of global knowledge makes it difficult to assess the completeness of a query answer. We will therefore investigate this problem in our future work. Studying the impact of alternative methods for fragmentation and relatedness methods is also part of our future work, as well as processing queries with a high number of intermediate results efficiently.

Acknowledgments. This research was partially funded by the Danish Council for Independent Research (DFF) under grant agreement no. DFF-8048-00051B & DFF-4093-00301B and Aalborg University's Talent Programme.

References

1. Adar, E., Huberman, B.A.: Free riding on Gnutella. First Monday **5**, 10 (2000). https://doi.org/10.5210/fm.v5i10.792
2. Buil-Aranda, C., Hogan, A., Umbrich, J., Vandenbussche, P.-Y.: SPARQL web-querying infrastructure: ready for action? In: Alani, H., et al. (eds.) ISWC 2013. LNCS, vol. 8219, pp. 277–293. Springer, Heidelberg (2013). https://doi.org/10.1007/978-3-642-41338-4_18
3. Cai, M., Frank, M.R.: RDFPeers: a scalable distributed RDF repository based on a structured peer-to-peer network. In: WWW, pp. 650–657 (2004). https://doi.org/10.1145/988672.988760
4. Fernández, J.D., Martínez-Prieto, M.A., Gutiérrez, C., Polleres, A., Arias, M.: Binary RDF representation for publication and exchange (HDT). J. Web Semant. **19**, 22–41 (2013)
5. Folz, P., Skaf-Molli, H., Molli, P.: CyCLaDEs: a decentralized cache for triple pattern fragments. In: Sack, H., Blomqvist, E., d'Aquin, M., Ghidini, C., Ponzetto, S.P., Lange, C. (eds.) ESWC 2016. LNCS, vol. 9678, pp. 455–469. Springer, Cham (2016). https://doi.org/10.1007/978-3-319-34129-3_28
6. Grall, A., et al.: Ladda: SPARQL queries in the fog of browsers. In: Blomqvist, E., Hose, K., Paulheim, H., Ławrynowicz, A., Ciravegna, F., Hartig, O. (eds.) ESWC 2017. LNCS, vol. 10577, pp. 126–131. Springer, Cham (2017). https://doi.org/10.1007/978-3-319-70407-4_24
7. Grall, A., Skaf-Molli, H., Molli, P.: SPARQL query execution in networks of web browsers. In: DeSemWeb@ISWC (2018)
8. Grubenmann, T., Bernstein, A., Moor, D., Seuken, S.: Financing the web of data with delayed-answer auctions. In: WWW, pp. 1033–1042 (2018)
9. Hartig, O., Buil-Aranda, C.: Bindings-restricted triple pattern fragments. In: Debruyne, C., et al. (eds.) OTM 2016. LNCS, vol. 10033, pp. 762–779. Springer, Cham (2016). https://doi.org/10.1007/978-3-319-48472-3_48
10. Hasnain, A., Saleem, M., Ngomo, A.N., Rebholz-Schuhmann, D.: Extending LargeRDFBench for multi-source data at scale for SPARQL endpoint federation. In: SSWS (2018)

11. Kaoudi, Z., Koubarakis, M., Kyzirakos, K., Miliaraki, I., Magiridou, M., Papadakis-Pesaresi, A.: Atlas: storing, updating and querying RDF(S) data on top of DHTs. J. Web Semant. **8**(4), 271–277 (2010). https://doi.org/10.1016/j.websem.2010.07.001

12. Karnstedt, M., et al.: UniStore: querying a DHT-based universal storage. In: ICDE, pp. 1503–1504 (2007). https://doi.org/10.1109/ICDE.2007.369054

13. Mahdisoltani, F., Biega, J., Suchanek, F.M.: YAGO3: a knowledge base from multilingual Wikipedias. In: CIDR (2013)

14. Mansour, E., et al.: A demonstration of the solid platform for social web applications, In: WWW Companion, pp. 223–226 (2016). https://doi.org/10.1145/2872518.2890529

15. Marx, E., Saleem, M., Lytra, I., Ngomo, A.N.: A decentralized architecture for SPARQL query processing and RDF sharing: a position paper. In: ICSC, pp. 274–277 (2018). https://doi.org/10.1109/ICSC.2018.00049

16. Minier, T., Skaf-Molli, H., Molli, P., Vidal, M.-E.: Intelligent clients for replicated triple pattern fragments. In: Gangemi, A., et al. (eds.) ESWC 2018. LNCS, vol. 10843, pp. 400–414. Springer, Cham (2018). https://doi.org/10.1007/978-3-319-93417-4_26

17. Molli, P., Skaf-Molli, H.: Semantic web in the fog of browsers. In: DeSemWeb@ISWC (2017)

18. Montoya, G., Aebeloe, C., Hose, K.: Towards efficient query processing over heterogeneous RDF interfaces. In: DeSemWeb@ISWC (2018)

19. Montoya, G., Skaf-Molli, H., Hose, K.: The *Odyssey* approach for optimizing federated SPARQL queries. In: d'Amato, C., et al. (eds.) ISWC 2017. LNCS, vol. 10587, pp. 471–489. Springer, Cham (2017). https://doi.org/10.1007/978-3-319-68288-4_28

20. Polleres, A., Kamdar, M.R., Fernández, J.D., Tudorache, T., Musen, M.A.: A more decentralized vision for linked data. In: DeSemWeb@ISWC (2018)

21. Schmidt, M., Görlitz, O., Haase, P., Ladwig, G., Schwarte, A., Tran, T.: FedBench: a benchmark suite for federated semantic data query processing. In: Aroyo, L., et al. (eds.) ISWC 2011. LNCS, vol. 7031, pp. 585–600. Springer, Heidelberg (2011). https://doi.org/10.1007/978-3-642-25073-6_37

22. Verborgh, R., et al.: Triple pattern fragments: a low-cost knowledge graph interface for the web. J. Web Semant. **37–38**, 184–206 (2016). https://doi.org/10.1016/j.websem.2016.03.003

23. Voulgaris, S., Gavidia, D., van Steen, M.: CYCLON: inexpensive membership management for unstructured P2P overlays. J. Netw. Syst. Manage. **13**(2), 197–217 (2005). https://doi.org/10.1007/s10922-005-4441-x

Reformulation-Based Query Answering for RDF Graphs with RDFS Ontologies

Maxime Buron[1,2(✉)], François Goasdoué[3(✉)], Ioana Manolescu[1,2(✉)], and Marie-Laure Mugnier[4(✉)]

[1] Inria Saclay, Palaiseau, France
{maxime.buron,ioana.manolescu}@inria.fr
[2] LIX (UMR 7161, CNRS and Ecole polytechnique), Palaiseau, France
[3] Univ Rennes, CNRS, IRISA, Lannion, France
fg@irisa.fr
[4] Univ. Montpellier, LIRMM, Inria, Montpellier, France
mugnier@lirmm.fr

Abstract. Query answering in RDF knowledge bases has traditionally been performed either through graph saturation, i.e., adding all implicit triples to the graph, or through query reformulation, i.e., modifying the query to look for the explicit triples entailing precisely what the original query asks for. The most expressive fragment of RDF for which Reformulation-based query answering exists is the so-called database fragment [13], in which implicit triples are restricted to those entailed using an RDFS ontology. Within this fragment, query answering was so far limited to the interrogation of data triples (non-RDFS ones); however, a powerful feature specific to RDF is the ability to query data and schema triples together. In this paper, we address the general query answering problem by reducing it, through a pre-query reformulation step, to that solved by the query reformulation technique of [13]. We also report on experiments demonstrating the low cost of our reformulation algorithm.

Keywords: Query answering · Query reformulation · RDF · RDFS

1 Introduction

RDF is the standard model for sharing data and knowledge bases. The rapid increase in number and size of RDF graphs makes efficient query answering on RDF quite a challenging task. *Reasoning* raises a performance challenge: query answering on an RDF graph no longer reduces to *evaluating* the query on the graph (by finding all the homomorphisms, or embeddings, of the query in the graph). Instead, it requires taking into account also the possible ontology (or knowledge) rules, which specify how different classes and properties of an RDF graph relate to each other, and may lead to query answers that evaluation alone cannot compute. Moreover, SPARQL, the standard query language of RDF, allows *querying the data and the ontology together*. This is a radical departure

© Springer Nature Switzerland AG 2019
P. Hitzler et al. (Eds.): ESWC 2019, LNCS 11503, pp. 19–35, 2019.
https://doi.org/10.1007/978-3-030-21348-0_2

both from relational databases, and from Description Logics (DL)-style models for RDF data and queries.

For what concerns reasoning, two main methods have been explored: graph saturation, which injects the ontology knowledge into the graph, and query reformulation, which pushes it into the query. Saturation adds to the graph all the triples it entails through the ontology. Evaluating a query on a saturated graph can be quite efficient; however, saturation takes time to compute, space to store, and needs to be updated when the data and/or ontology rules change. Reformulation leaves the graph unchanged and builds a reformulated query which, evaluated on the original graph, computes all the answers, including those that hold due to entailed triples. Each query reformulation method, thus, targets a certain ontology language and a query dialect. The most expressive RDF fragment for which sound and complete reformulation-based query answering exists is the so-called database fragment [13], in which RDF Schema (RDFS, in short) is used to describe the ontology, while queries only carry over the data triples.

In this work, we present a novel *reformulation-based query answering* under *RDFS* ontologies for *Basic Graph Pattern (BGP) queries over both the data and the ontology*. This goes beyond the closest algorithm previously known [13] which is restricted to queries over the data only (not over the ontology). The algorithm we present here also goes beyond those of RDF platforms such as Jena, Virtuoso or Stardog, which we found experimentally to be incomplete when answering through reformulation queries over the data and the ontology of an RDF graph. Below, we recall some terminology (Sect. 2) and discuss the state of the art (Sect. 3). Then, Sect. 4 introduces our novel query reformulation algorithm, which we implemented in the platform used in [10,13], leveraging an efficient relational database (RDBMS) engine for query answering. Our experiments (Sect. 5) demonstrate the practical interest of our reformulation approach. Detailed proofs are available in [9].

2   Preliminaries

We present the basics of the RDF graph data model (Sect. 2.1), of RDF entailment used to make explicit the implicit information RDF graphs encode (Sect. 2.2), as well as how they can be queried using the widely-considered SPARQL Basic Graph Pattern queries (Sect. 2.3).

2.1   RDF Graph

We consider three pairwise disjoint sets of values: $\mathscr{I}$ of IRIs (resource identifiers), $\mathscr{L}$ of literals (constants) and $\mathscr{B}$ of blank nodes modeling unknown IRIs or literals, a.k.a. to *labelled nulls* [4]. A *well-formed triple* belongs to $(\mathscr{I} \cup \mathscr{B}) \times \mathscr{I} \times (\mathscr{L} \cup \mathscr{I} \cup \mathscr{B})$, and an *RDF graph* G is a set of well-formed triples. A triple $(\mathsf{s}, \mathsf{p}, \mathsf{o})$ states that its *subject* s has the *property* p with the *object* value o [1]. We denote by $\mathrm{Val}(G)$ the set of all values (IRIs, blank nodes and literals) occurring in an RDF graph G, and by $\mathrm{Bl}(G)$ its set of blank nodes.

Table 1. RDF statements.

RDF assertions	Triple notation
Class assertion	$(\mathbf{s}, \tau, \mathbf{o})$
Property assertion	$(\mathbf{s}, \mathbf{p}, \mathbf{o})$ with $\mathbf{p} \notin \{\tau, \prec_{sc}, \prec_{sp}, \hookleftarrow_d, \hookrightarrow_r\}$
RDFS constraints	Triple notation
Subclass	$(\mathbf{s}, \prec_{sc}, \mathbf{o})$
Subproperty	$(\mathbf{s}, \prec_{sp}, \mathbf{o})$
Domain typing	$(\mathbf{s}, \hookleftarrow_d, \mathbf{o})$
Range typing	$(\mathbf{s}, \hookrightarrow_r, \mathbf{o})$

Within an RDF graph, triples model either factual *assertions* for unary relations called *classes* and binary relations called *properties*, or *RDFS ontological constraints* between classes and properties. The RDFS constraints are of four flavours: **subclass** constraints, **subproperty** constraints, typing of the **domain** (first attribute) or of the **range** (second attribute) of a property. The triple notations we adopt for RDF assertions and constraints are shown in Table 1. In a triple, we use _:b (possibly with indices) to denote blank nodes, and strings between quotes to denote literals.

We consider RDF graphs with *RDFS ontologies*, i.e., constraints of the four flavors above, excluding constraints which would alter the commonly-accepted RDFS semantics. For instance, $(\hookleftarrow_d, \prec_{sp}, \hookrightarrow_r)$ is not allowed as it would make domain typing a particular case of range typing. Let RDFS(G) denote the RDFS constraints of a graph G. We define:

Definition 1 (RDF graph with an RDFS ontology). *An RDFS ontology (or ontology in short) is a set of RDFS constraints, whose subjects and objects are either IRIs (other than $\prec_{sc}, \prec_{sp}, \hookleftarrow_d, \hookrightarrow_r, \tau$) or blank nodes.*

An RDF graph G with ontology O is such that: RDFS$(G) = O$.

Example 1 (Running example). Consider the following RDF graph:

$G_{\text{ex}} = \{$(:worksFor, $\hookleftarrow_d$, :Person), (:worksFor, $\hookrightarrow_r$, :Org), (:PubAdmin, $\prec_{sc}$, :Org)

(:Comp, $\prec_{sc}$, :Org), (_:b_C, $\prec_{sc}$, :Comp), (:hiredBy, $\prec_{sp}$, :worksFor)

(:ceoOf, $\prec_{sp}$, :worksFor), (:ceoOf, $\hookrightarrow_r$, :Comp),

(:p$_1$, :ceoOf, :c), (:c, τ, _:b_C), (:p$_2$, :hiredBy, :a), (:a, τ, :PubAdmin)$\}$

The ontology of G_{ex}, i.e., the first eight triples, states that persons are working for organizations, some of which are public administrations or companies. Further, there exists a special kind of company (modeled by _:b_C). Being hired by or being CEO of an organization are two ways of working for it; in the latter case, this organization is a company. The assertions of G_{ex}, i.e., the four remaining triples, states that :p$_1$ is CEO of :c, which is a company of the special kind _:b_C, and :p$_2$ is hired by the public administration :a.

Table 2. RDFS entailment rules.

Rule [2]	Entailment rule
rdfs2	$(p, \hookleftarrow_d, o), (s_1, p, o_1) \rightarrow (s_1, \tau, o)$
rdfs3	$(p, \hookrightarrow_r, o), (s_1, p, o_1) \rightarrow (o_1, \tau, o)$
rdfs5	$(p_1, \prec_{sp}, p_2), (p_2, \prec_{sp}, p_3) \rightarrow (p_1, \prec_{sp}, p_3)$
rdfs7	$(p_1, \prec_{sp}, p_2), (s, p_1, o) \rightarrow (s, p_2, o)$
rdfs9	$(s, \prec_{sc}, o), (s_1, \tau, s) \rightarrow (s_1, \tau, o)$
rdfs11	$(s, \prec_{sc}, o), (o, \prec_{sc}, o_1) \rightarrow (s, \prec_{sc}, o_1)$
ext1	$(p, \hookleftarrow_d, o), (o, \prec_{sc}, o_1) \rightarrow (p, \hookleftarrow_d, o_1)$
ext2	$(p, \hookrightarrow_r, o), (o, \prec_{sc}, o_1) \rightarrow (p, \hookrightarrow_r, o_1)$
ext3	$(p, \prec_{sp}, p_1), (p_1, \hookleftarrow_d, o) \rightarrow (p, \hookleftarrow_d, o)$
ext4	$(p, \prec_{sp}, p_1), (p_1, \hookrightarrow_r, o) \rightarrow (p, \hookrightarrow_r, o)$

A *homomorphism between RDF graphs* allows characterizing whether an RDF graph *simply entails* another, based on their explicit triples only:

Definition 2 (RDF graph homomorphism). *Let G and G' be two RDF graphs. A homomorphism from G to G' is a function φ from $\mathrm{Val}(G)$ to $\mathrm{Val}(G')$, which is the identity on IRIs and literals, such that for any triple (s, p, o) in G, the triple $(\varphi(s), \varphi(p), \varphi(o))$ is in G'.*

Note that, according to the previous definition, a G blank node can be mapped to any G' value. A graph G' simply entails a graph G if there is a homomorphism φ from G to G', which we denote by $G' \models^{\varphi} G$.

2.2   RDF Entailment Rules

The semantics of an RDF graph consists of the explicit triples it contains, and of the implicit triples that can be derived from it using *RDF entailment rules*.

Definition 3 (RDF entailment rule). *An RDF entailment rule r has the form $body(r) \rightarrow head(r)$, where $body(r)$ and $head(r)$ are RDF graphs, respectively called* body *and* head *of the rule r.*

The standard RDF entailment rules are defined in [2]. In this work, we consider the rules shown in Table 2, which we call *RDFS entailment rules*; all values except the τ, $\prec_{sc}$, $\prec_{sp}$, $\hookleftarrow_d$, $\hookrightarrow_r$ properties are blank nodes. These rules are the most frequently used for RDFS entailment; they produce implicit triples by exploiting the RDFS ontological constraints of an RDF graph. For example, the rule rdfs9, which propagates values from subclasses to their superclasses, is defined by $body(\mathtt{rdfs9}) = \{(s, \prec_{sc}, o), (s_1, \tau, s)\}$ and $head(\mathtt{rdfs9}) = \{(s_1, \tau, o)\}$. The *direct entailment* of an RDF graph G with a set of RDF entailment rules

$\mathcal{R}$, denoted by $C_{G,\mathcal{R}}$, characterizes the set of implicit triples resulting from rule applications that use solely the explicit triples of G. It is defined as:

$$C_{G,\mathcal{R}} = \{\varphi(\text{head}(r)) \mid r \in \mathcal{R}, G \models^{\varphi} \text{body}(r)\}$$

For instance, the rule rdfs9 applies to the graph G_{ex}: $G_{\text{ex}} \models^{\varphi}$ body(rdfs9) through the homomorphism φ defined as $\{s \mapsto \_{:}b_C, o \mapsto :\text{Comp}, s_1 \mapsto :c\}$, hence allows deriving the implicit triple $(:c, \tau, :\text{Comp})$.

The *saturation* of an RDF graph allows materializing its semantics, by iteratively augmenting it with the triples it entails using a set $\mathcal{R}$ of RDF entailment rules, until reaching a fixpoint; this process is finite [2]. Formally:

Definition 4 (RDF graph saturation). *Let G be an RDF graph and $\mathcal{R}$ a set of entailment rules. We recursively define a sequence $(G_i^{\mathcal{R}})_{i\in\mathbb{N}}$ of RDF graphs as follows: $G_0^{\mathcal{R}} = G$ and $G_{i+1}^{\mathcal{R}} = G_i^{\mathcal{R}} \cup C_{G_i^{\mathcal{R}},\mathcal{R}}$ for $0 \leq i$. The saturation of G w.r.t. $\mathcal{R}$, denoted by $G^{\mathcal{R}}$, is $G_n^{\mathcal{R}}$ for n the smallest integer such that $G_n^{\mathcal{R}} = G_{n+1}^{\mathcal{R}}$.*

Example 2. The saturation of G_{ex} w.r.t. the set $\mathcal{R}$ of RDFS entailment rules shown in Table 2 is attained after the following *two* saturation steps:

$$(G_{\text{ex}})_1^{\mathcal{R}} = G_{\text{ex}} \cup \{(\_{:}b_C, \prec_{sc}, :\text{Org}), (:\text{hiredBy}, \hookleftarrow_d, :\text{Person}), (:\text{hiredBy}, \hookrightarrow_r, :\text{Org}),$$
$$(:\text{ceoOf}, \hookleftarrow_d, :\text{Person}), (:\text{ceoOf}, \hookrightarrow_r, :\text{Org}),$$
$$(:p_1, :\text{worksFor}, :c), (:c, \tau, :\text{Comp}), (:p_2, :\text{worksFor}, :a), (:a, \tau, :\text{Org})\}$$
$$(G_{\text{ex}})_2^{\mathcal{R}} = (G_{\text{ex}})_1^{\mathcal{R}} \cup \{(:p_1, \tau, :\text{Person}), (:p_2, \tau, :\text{Person}), (:c, \tau, :\text{Org})\}$$

Simple entailment between RDF graphs, which is based on their explicit triples only, generalizes to *entailment between RDF graphs w.r.t. a set of RDF entailment rules*, to also take into account their implicit triples.

A graph G entails a graph G' w.r.t. a set of rules $\mathcal{R}$, noted $G \models_{\mathcal{R}}^{\varphi} G'$, whenever there is a homomorphism φ from G' to $G^{\mathcal{R}}$. Of course, simple entailment and entailment between RDF graphs coincide when $\mathcal{R} = \emptyset$. For simplicity, we will just write $G \models_{\mathcal{R}} G'$ whenever φ is not needed for the discussion.

In this work, unless otherwise specified, $\mathcal{R}$ denotes the rules from Table 2.

2.3 Basic Graph Pattern Queries

A popular fragment of the SPARQL query language consists of conjunctive queries, also known as basic graph pattern queries. Let $\mathscr{V}$ be a set of variable symbols, disjoint from $\mathscr{I} \cup \mathscr{B} \cup \mathscr{L}$. A *basic graph pattern* (BGP) is a set of *triple patterns* (triples in short) belonging to $(\mathscr{I} \cup \mathscr{B} \cup \mathscr{V}) \times (\mathscr{I} \cup \mathscr{V}) \times (\mathscr{I} \cup \mathscr{B} \cup \mathscr{L} \cup \mathscr{V})$. For a BGP P, we denote by $\text{Var}(P)$ the set of variables occurring in P, by $\text{Bl}(P)$ its set of blank nodes, and by $\text{Val}(P)$ its set of values (IRIs, blank nodes, literals and variables).

Definition 5 (BGP query). *A BGP query (BGPQ) q is of the form $q(\bar{x}) \leftarrow P$, where P is a BGP also denoted by body(q) and $\bar{x} \subseteq \text{Var}(P)$ is the set of q's answer variables. The arity of q is that of $\bar{x}$, i.e., $|\bar{x}|$.*

Partially instantiated BGPQs generalize BGPQs and have been used for reformulation-based query answering [13]. Starting from a BGPQ q, partial instantiation replaces *some* variables and/or blank nodes with values from $\mathscr{I} \cup \mathscr{L} \cup \mathscr{B}$, as specified by a substitution σ; the partially instantiated query is denoted q_σ. Observe that when $\sigma = \emptyset$, q_σ coincides with q. Further, due to σ, and in contrast with standard BGPQs, some answer variables of q_σ can be bound:

Example 3. Consider the BGPQ asking for *who is working for which kind of company*: $q(x, y) \leftarrow (x, :\text{worksFor}, z), (z, \tau, y), (y, \prec_{sc}, :\text{Comp})$, and the substitution $\sigma = \{x \mapsto :\text{p}_1\}$. The partially instantiated BGPQ q_σ corresponds to $q(:\text{p}_1, y) \leftarrow (:\text{p}_1, :\text{worksFor}, z), (z, \tau, y), (y, \prec_{sc}, :\text{Comp})$.

The semantics of a (partially instantiated) BGPQ on an RDF graph is defined through homomorphisms from the query body to the saturation of the queried graph. The homomorphisms needed here are a straightforward extension of RDF graph homomorphisms (Definition 2) to also take variables into account.

Definition 6 ((Non-standard) BGP to RDF graph homomorphism).
A homomorphism from a BGP q to an RDF graph G is a function φ from $\text{Val}(body(q))$ to $\text{Val}(G)$ such that for any triple $(s, p, o) \in body(q)$, the triple $(\varphi(s), \varphi(p), \varphi(o))$ is in G. For a standard homomorphism, as per the SPARQL recommendation, φ is the identity on IRIs and literals; for a non non-standard one, φ is the identity on IRIs, literals and *on blank nodes.*

We distinguish *query evaluation*, whose result is just based on the explicit triples of the graph, i.e., on BGP to RDF graph homomorphisms, from *query answering* that also accounts for the implicit graph triples, i.e., based on both BGP to RDF graph homomorphisms *and* RDF entailment. In this paper, we use two flavors of query evaluation and of query answering, which differ in relying either on standard or on non-standard BGP to RDF graph homomorphisms.

Definition 7 ((Non-standard) evaluation and answering). *Let q_σ be a partially instantiated BGPQ q_σ obtained from a BGPQ q and a substitution σ. The standard answer set to q_σ on an RDF graph G w.r.t. a set $\mathcal{R}$ of RDF entailment rules is: $q_\sigma(G, \mathcal{R}) = \{\varphi(\bar{x}_\sigma) \mid G \models_{\mathcal{R}}^\varphi body(q)_\sigma\}$ where $\bar{x}_\sigma$ and $body(q)_\sigma$ denote the result of replacing the variables and blank nodes in $\bar{x}$ and $body(q)$, respectively, according to σ.*

If $\bar{x} = \emptyset$, q_σ is a Boolean query, in which case q_σ is false when $q_\sigma(G, \mathcal{R}) = \emptyset$ and true when $q_\sigma(G, \mathcal{R}) = \{\langle\rangle\}$, i.e., the answer to q_σ is an empty tuple.

We call $q_\sigma(G, \emptyset)$ the standard evaluation of q_σ on G, written $q_\sigma(G)$ for short, which solely amounts to standard BGP to RDF graph homomorphism finding.

The non-standard answer set, denoted $\widetilde{q_\sigma(G, \mathcal{R})}$, and non-standard evaluation $\widetilde{q_\sigma(G)}$ of q_σ on G w.r.t. $\mathcal{R}$ only differ from the standard ones by using non-standard BGP to RDF graph homomorphisms.

These notions and notations naturally extend to *unions* of BGPQs.

Example 4. Consider again the BGPQs from the preceding example. Their standard evaluations on G_{ex} are empty because G_{ex} has no explicit :worksFor assertion, while their standard answer sets on G_{ex} w.r.t. $\mathcal{R}$ are $\{\langle :p_1, \_:b_C \rangle\}$ because :p_1 being CEO of :c, :p_1 implicitly works for it, and :c is explicitly a company of the particular unknown type $\_:b_C$.

Consider now the BGPQ $q(x) \leftarrow (x, :\text{worksFor}, y), (y, \tau, \_:b_C)$. Under standard query answering, it asks for *who is working for some kind of organization* and its answer set is $\{\langle :p_1 \rangle, \langle :p_2 \rangle\}$; by contrast, under non-standard query answering, it asks for *who is working for an organization of the particular unknown type* $\_:b_C$ in G_{ex} and its answer set is just $\{\langle :p_1 \rangle\}$.

3   Prior Related Work

Two main techniques for answering BGPQs on RDF graphs have been investigated in the literature.

Saturation-Based Query Answering. This technique directly follows from the definition of query answers in the W3C's SPARQL recommendations [3], recalled in Sect. 2.3 for BGPQs. Indeed, it trivially follows from Definition 7 that $q(G, \mathcal{R}) = q(G^{\mathcal{R}})$ (resp. $\overbrace{q(G, \mathcal{R})} = \overbrace{q(G^{\mathcal{R}})}$), i.e., query answering reduces to query evaluation on the *saturated* RDF graph. Saturation-based query answering is typically fast, because it only requires query evaluation, which can be efficiently performed by a data management engine. However, saturation takes time to be computed, requires extra space to be stored, and must be recomputed or maintained (e.g., [7,8,13]) upon updates. Many RDF data management systems use saturation-based query answering. They either allow computing graph saturation, e.g., Jena and RDFox, or simply assume that RDF graphs have been saturated before being stored, e.g., DB2RDF.

Reformulation-Based Query Answering. This technique also reduces query answering to query evaluation, however, the reasoning needed to ensure complete answers is performed on the query and not on the RDF graph. A given query q, asked on an RDF graph G w.r.t. $\mathcal{R}$ is *reformulated* into a query q' such that $q(G, \mathcal{R}) = q'(G)$ or $q(G, \mathcal{R}) = \overbrace{q'(G)}$ holds. Standard or non-standard query evaluation is needed on the reformulated query, depending on the considered RDF fragment: when blank nodes are allowed in RDFS constraints, non-standard evaluation is used [13], while standard evaluation is sufficient otherwise [5,12]. Different SPARQL dialects have been adopted for BGPQ reformulation in more limited settings than the one considered in this paper, i.e., the database fragment of RDF and unrestricted BGPQs. *Unions of BGPQs (UBGPQs in short)* have been used in [5,12,13]. However, these works are restricted to input BGPQs that must be matched on *RDF assertions* only. BGPQs aiming at interrogating solely the RDFS ontology, or the ontology *and* the assertions are not considered, even though such joint querying is a major novelty of RDF and SPARQL. The techniques adopt unions of BGPQs [5] or of *partially instantiated* BGPQs [12,13], depending on whether variables can be used in class and property positions in queries, e.g., whether a query triple (x, τ, z) or (x, y, z) is allowed. Reformulation-based query answering in the DL fragment of RDF, which is strictly contained in the database fragment of RDF, has been investigated for relational conjunctive queries [5,11], while the slight extension thereof considered in [6,12,14,18] has been investigated for one-triple BGPQs [14,18], BGPQs [12], and SPARQL queries [6]. In [6], SPARQL queries are reformulated into *nested* SPARQL, allowing nested regular expressions in property position in query triples. These reformulations allow sound and complete query answering on restricted RDF graphs with RDFS ontologies: these graph *must not contain blank nodes*. While such nested reformulations are more compact, the queries we produce are more practical, since their evaluation can be delegated to any off-the-shelf RDBMS, or to an RDF engine such as RDF-3X [17] even if it is unaware of reasoning; further, we do not impose restrictions on RDF graphs.

In Sect. 4, we devise a reformulation-based query answering technique for the entire database fragment of RDF and unrestricted BGPQs.

Reformulation-based query answering is well-suited to frequently updated RDF graphs, because it uses the queried RDF graph at query time (and not its saturation). However, reformulated queries tend to be more complex than the original ones, thus costly to evaluate. To mitigate this, [10] provides an *optimized reformulation framework* whereas an incoming BGPQ is reformulated into a *join of unions of BGPQs (JUBGPQ in short)*. This approach being based on a database-style *cost model*, JUBGPQ reformulations are very efficiently evaluated.

Some available RDF data management systems use reformulation-based query answering but return incomplete answer sets in the RDF setting we consider[1], e.g., AllegroGraph[2] and Stardog[3] miss answers because they cannot evaluate triples with a variable property on the schema, while Virtuoso[4] only exploits subclass and subproperty constraints, but not domain and range ones. Finally, *Hybrid* approaches have also been studied, e.g., in [19], where some one-triple queries are chosen for materialization and reused during reformulation-based answering.

4 Extending Query Reformulation to Queries over the Ontology

We now present the main contribution of this paper: a reformulation-based query answering (QA) technique able to compute all answers to a BGPQ against *all* the explicit and implicit triples of an RDF graph, i.e., its RDF assertions *and* RDFS constraints, as per the SPARQL and RDF recommendations [2,3]. The central idea is to *reduce* this full QA problem to an *assertion-level* QA, i.e., where the query is confined to just the explicit and implicit RDF assertions.

---

[1] See discussion at https://team.inria.fr/cedar/rdfs-reasoning-experiments/.

[2] https://franz.com/agraph/support/documentation/current/reasoner-tutorial.html.

[3] https://www.stardog.com/docs/#_owl_rule_reasoning.

[4] http://docs.openlinksw.com/virtuoso/rdfsparqlruleimpl.

To this aim, we divide query reformulation in two steps: the first reformulation step implements the reduction, while the second step relies on the reformulation technique of [13], which considers assertion-level QA.

4.1 Overview of Our Query Reformulation Technique

Let us first notice that the body of any BGPQ q can be divided into three disjoint subsets of triples (s, p, o), according to the nature of term p: the set b_c of RDFS triples where p is a built-in RDFS property ($\prec_{sc}$, $\prec_{sp}$, $\hookleftarrow_d$, $\hookrightarrow_r$); the set b_a of assertion triples where p is τ or a user-defined property; and the set b_v where p is a variable. We denote by q_c, q_a and q_v the subqueries respectively associated with these bodies. If b_v is not empty, q can be reformulated as a union of BGPQs, say $\mathcal{Q}$, composed of all BGPQs that can be obtained from q by substituting some (possibly none) variables occurring in q_v with one of the four built-in RDFS properties. We assume this preprocessing step to simplify the explanations, even if in practice it may not be performed. Then, the answers to any BGPQ $q' \in \mathcal{Q}$ can be computed in two steps:

1. compute the answers to the subquery q'_c, i.e., with body restricted to the RDFS triples; if q'_c has no answer, neither has q'. Otherwise, each answer to q'_c defines a (partial) instantiation σ of the variables in q'.
2. compute the assertion-level answers to each partially instantiated query $(q'_{a,v})_\sigma$, where $q'_{a,v}$ is the subquery with body $b'_a \cup b'_v$, and return the union of all the obtained answers.

To summarize, Step 1 computes answers to RDFS triples, which allows one to produce a set of partially instantiated queries that no longer contain RDFS triples. Hence, these queries can then be answered using RDF assertions only, which is the purpose of Step 2. Our two-step query reformulation follows this decomposition. It furthermore considers a partition of the set $\mathcal{R}$ of RDFS entailment rules (recall Table 2) into two subsets: the set of rules $\mathcal{R}_c$ that produces *RDFS constraints* and the set of rules $\mathcal{R}_a$ that produces *RDF assertions*:

- $\mathcal{R}_c = \{\texttt{rdfs5}, \texttt{rdfs11}, \texttt{ext1}, \texttt{ext2}, \texttt{ext3}, \texttt{ext4}\}$;
- $\mathcal{R}_a = \{\texttt{rdfs2}, \texttt{rdfs3}, \texttt{rdfs7}, \texttt{rdfs9}\}$.

The reason of this decomposition is that query answering remains complete if, on the one hand, only $\mathcal{R}_c$ is considered to answer queries made of RDFS triples (Step 1: for any graph G, $q'_c(G, \mathcal{R}) = q'_c(G, \mathcal{R}_c)$), and, on the other hand, only $\mathcal{R}_a$ is considered to answer queries on RDF assertions only, as shown in [13].

Query reformulation does not directly work on the entailment rules as classical backward-chaining techniques would do. Instead, a set of so-called *reformulation rules* is specifically associated with $\mathcal{R}_c$ (resp. $\mathcal{R}_a$). We can now outline the two-step query reformulation algorithm:

Step 1. Reformulation w.r.t. $\mathcal{R}_c$: The input BGPQ q is first reformulated into a union $\mathcal{Q}_c$ of partially instantiated BGPQs, using the set of reformulation rules associated with $\mathcal{R}_c$ (see Fig. 1). This reformulation step is sound and complete for query answering w.r.t. $\mathcal{R}_c$, i.e., for any graph G, $q(G, \mathcal{R}_c) = \overset{\frown}{\mathcal{Q}_c(G)}$; furthermore, it preserves the answers with respect to the set $\mathcal{R}$, i.e., $q(G, \mathcal{R}_c \cup \mathcal{R}_a) = \overset{\frown}{\mathcal{Q}_c(G, \mathcal{R}_c \cup \mathcal{R}_a)}$ (see Theorem 1).

Step 2. Reformulation w.r.t. $\mathcal{R}_a$: We recall that $\mathcal{Q}_c$ consists of queries that do not contain RDFS triples. It is given as input to the query reformulation algorithm of [13], which relies on a set of reformulation rules associated with $\mathcal{R}_a$ to output a union $\mathcal{Q}_{c,a}$ of partially instantiated BGPQs. This reformulation step being sound and complete for query answering on the RDF assertions of an RDF graph, we obtain the soundness and completeness of the two-step reformulation, i.e., $q(G, \mathcal{R}_c \cup \mathcal{R}_a) = \overset{\frown}{\mathcal{Q}_c(G, \mathcal{R}_a)} = \overset{\frown}{\mathcal{Q}_{c,a}(G)}$ (see Theorem 2).

4.2   Reformulation Rules Associated with $\mathcal{R}_c$

We now detail reformulation rules associated with $\mathcal{R}_c$, see Fig. 1. Each reformulation rule is of the form $\frac{input}{output}$, where the input is composed of a triple from a partially instantiated query q_σ and a triple from O and the output is a new query obtained from q_σ by instantiating a variable, removing the input triple, or replacing it by one or two triples. The notation *old triple/new triple(s)* means that *old triple* is replaced by *new triple(s)*. The specific case where *old triple* is simply removed is denoted by *old triple/−*. The notations for the triples themselves are the following:

- a bold character like c, p, s or o represents an IRI or a blank node
- a v character represents a variable of the query
- s and o characters represent either variables, IRIs or blank nodes, in subject and object positions respectively.

The four rules (1) substitute a variable in a property position by one of the four built-in RDFS properties. All the other rules take as input query triples of the form $(s, \mathbf{p}, o)$, where $\mathbf{p}$ is a built-in RDFS property. Rule (2) simply removes from q_σ an (instantiated) input triple found in O.

Query triples with a domain ($\hookleftarrow_d$) or range property ($\hookrightarrow_r$) are processed by Rules (3)–(11). Given a triple $(\mathbf{p}, \hookleftarrow, \mathbf{c})$ in O (where $\hookleftarrow$ stands for $\hookleftarrow_d$ or $\hookrightarrow_r$), Rule (3) replaces a query triple of the form $(v_1, \hookleftarrow, v_2)$ by two triples $(v_1, \prec_{sp}, \mathbf{p})$ and $(\mathbf{c}, \prec_{sc}, v_2)$. This rule relies on the fact that a triple $(\mathbf{p}', \hookleftarrow, \mathbf{c}')$ belongs to the saturation of the RDF graph by $\mathcal{R}_c$ if and only if $\mathbf{p}'$ is a subproperty of $\mathbf{p}$ (including $\mathbf{p} = \mathbf{p}'$) and $\mathbf{c}$ is a subclass of $\mathbf{c}'$ (including $\mathbf{c} = \mathbf{c}'$), see Lemma 1 in Sect. 4.3. However, we do not assume that the ontology ensures the reflexivity of the subclass and subproperty relations, hence Rules (4)–(7), whose sole purpose is to deal with the cases $\mathbf{c} = \mathbf{c}'$ and $\mathbf{p} = \mathbf{p}'$. Should the ontology contain axiomatic triples ensuring the reflexivity of subclass and subproperty, these four rules would be useless. Note that a natural candidate rule to deal with the case where $\mathbf{c} \neq \mathbf{c}'$ and $\mathbf{p} \neq \mathbf{p}'$ would have been the following:

$$\frac{(\mathbf{p}', \hookleftarrow, \mathbf{c}') \in q_\sigma, (\mathbf{p}, \hookleftarrow, \mathbf{c}) \in O}{q_\sigma[(\mathbf{p}', \hookleftarrow, \mathbf{c}')/(\mathbf{p}', \prec_{sp}, \mathbf{p}), (\mathbf{c}, \prec_{sc}, \mathbf{c}')]} \tag{17}$$

$$\frac{(s,v,o) \in q_\sigma}{q_{\sigma \cup \{v \to \prec_{sc}\}}}, \frac{(s,v,o) \in q_\sigma}{q_{\sigma \cup \{v \to \prec_{sp}\}}}, \frac{(s,v,o) \in q_\sigma}{q_{\sigma \cup \{v \to \hookleftarrow_d\}}}, \frac{(s,v,o) \in q_\sigma}{q_{\sigma \cup \{v \to \hookleftarrow_r\}}} \tag{1}$$

$$\frac{(\mathbf{s},\mathbf{p},\mathbf{o}) \in q_\sigma, (\mathbf{s},\mathbf{p},\mathbf{o}) \in O}{q_\sigma[(\mathbf{s},\mathbf{p},\mathbf{o})/-]} \tag{2}$$

$$\frac{(v_1,\hookleftarrow,v_2) \in q_\sigma, (\mathbf{p},\hookleftarrow,\mathbf{c}) \in O}{q_\sigma[(v_1,\hookleftarrow,v_2)/(v_1,\prec_{sp},\mathbf{p}),(\mathbf{c},\prec_{sc},v_2)]} \tag{3}$$

$$\frac{(v_1,\hookleftarrow,v_2) \in q_\sigma, (\mathbf{p},\hookleftarrow,\mathbf{c}) \in O}{q_{\sigma \cup \{v_1 \to \mathbf{p}\}}} \tag{4}$$

$$\frac{(v_1,\hookleftarrow,v_2) \in q_\sigma, (\mathbf{p},\hookleftarrow,\mathbf{c}) \in O}{q_{\sigma \cup \{v_2 \to \mathbf{c}\}}} \tag{5}$$

$$\frac{(v,\hookleftarrow,\mathbf{c}) \in q_\sigma, (\mathbf{p},\hookleftarrow,\mathbf{c}) \in O}{q_{\sigma \cup \{v \to \mathbf{p}\}}} \tag{6}$$

$$\frac{(\mathbf{p},\hookleftarrow,v) \in q_\sigma, (\mathbf{p},\hookleftarrow,\mathbf{c}) \in O}{q_{\sigma \cup \{v \to \mathbf{c}\}}} \tag{7}$$

$$\frac{(v,\hookleftarrow,\mathbf{c}) \in q_\sigma, (\mathbf{p},\hookleftarrow,\mathbf{c}) \in O}{q_\sigma[(v,\hookleftarrow,\mathbf{c})/(v,\prec_{sp},\mathbf{p})]} \tag{8}$$

$$\frac{(\mathbf{p},\hookleftarrow,v) \in q_\sigma, (\mathbf{p},\hookleftarrow,\mathbf{c}) \in O}{q_\sigma[(\mathbf{p},\hookleftarrow,v)/(\mathbf{c},\prec_{sc},v)]} \tag{9}$$

$$\frac{(s,\hookleftarrow,\mathbf{c}_1) \in q_\sigma, (\mathbf{c},\prec_{sc},\mathbf{c}_1) \in O, \mathbf{c} \neq \mathbf{c}_1}{q_\sigma[(s,\hookleftarrow,\mathbf{c}_1)/(s,\hookleftarrow,\mathbf{c})]} \tag{10}$$

$$\frac{(\mathbf{p},\hookleftarrow,o) \in q_\sigma, (\mathbf{p},\prec_{sp},\mathbf{p}_1) \in O, \mathbf{p} \neq \mathbf{p}_1}{q_\sigma[(\mathbf{p},\hookleftarrow,o)/(\mathbf{p}_1,\hookleftarrow,o)]} \tag{11}$$

$$\frac{(v_1,\prec,v_2) \in q_\sigma, (\mathbf{c}_1,\prec,\mathbf{c}_2) \in O}{q_{\sigma \cup \{v_1 \to \mathbf{c}_1\}}} \tag{12}$$

$$\frac{(v,\prec,\mathbf{c}_2) \in q_\sigma, (\mathbf{c}_1,\prec,\mathbf{c}_2) \in O}{q_{\sigma \cup \{v \to \mathbf{c}_1\}}} \tag{13}$$

$$\frac{(\mathbf{c}_1,\prec,v) \in q_\sigma, (\mathbf{c}_1,\prec,\mathbf{c}_2) \in O}{q_{\sigma \cup \{v \to \mathbf{c}_2\}}} \tag{14}$$

$$\frac{(\mathbf{c}_1,\prec,o) \in q_\sigma, (\mathbf{c}_1,\prec,\mathbf{c}_2) \in O, \mathbf{c}_1 \neq \mathbf{c}_2}{q_\sigma[(\mathbf{c}_1,\prec,o)/(\mathbf{c}_2,\prec,o)]} \tag{15}$$

$$\frac{(s,\prec,\mathbf{c}_2) \in q_\sigma, (\mathbf{c}_1,\prec,\mathbf{c}_2) \in O, \mathbf{c}_1 \neq \mathbf{c}_2}{q_\sigma[(s,\prec,\mathbf{c}_2)/(s,\prec,\mathbf{c}_1)]} \tag{16}$$

Fig. 1. Reformulation rules for a partially instantiated query q_σ w.r.t. an RDFS ontology O. For compactness, we factorize similar rules, using the symbol $\hookleftarrow$ to denote either $\hookleftarrow_d$ or $\hookleftarrow_r$, and $\prec$ to denote either $\prec_{sc}$ or $\prec_{sp}$.

However, such a rule is flawed: it would blindly consider all triples $(p, \hookleftarrow, c)$ from O, which causes a combinatorial explosion. Instead, we propose Rules (10) and (11), which use p' and c' as guides to replace $(p', \hookleftarrow, c')$ by other domain/range triples based on the subproperty-chains from p' and the subclass-chains to c'.

Query triples with a subclass ($\prec_{sc}$) or subproperty ($\prec_{sp}$) property are processed by Rules (12)–(16). Rules (12), (13), (14) instantiate a variable using an ontology triple of the form $(c_1, \prec, c_2)$. In Rule (12), which considers a query triple with two variables and instantiates one of these variables, we arbitrarily chose to instantiate the first variable. The two last rules allow to go up or down in the class and property hierarchies.

4.3 Reformulation Algorithm Associated with $\mathcal{R}_c$

The reformulation algorithm itself, denoted by Reformulate$_c$, is presented in Algorithm 1. The set of queries to be explored (named *toExplore*) initially contains q. Exploring a query consists of generating all new queries that can be obtained from it by applying a reformulation rule (lines 7–9). Newly generated queries are put in the set named *produced*. The algorithm proceeds in a breadth-first manner, exploring at each step the queries that have been generated at the previous step. When no new query can be generated at a step, the algorithm stops, otherwise the next step will explore the newly generated queries (line 11). Note the use of a set named *explored*, which contains all explored queries; the purpose of this set is to avoid infinite generation of the same queries when the subclass or subproperty hierarchy contains cycles (other than loops), otherwise it is useless. Importantly, not all explored queries are returned in the resulting set, but only those that no longer contain RDFS triples (lines 5–6). Indeed, on the one hand RDFS triples that contain variables are instantiated by the rules in all possible ways using the ontology, and, on the other hand, instantiated triples that belong to the ontology are removed (by Rule (2)). Finally, note that a variable v in a triple of the form (s, v, o) is replaced by a built-in RDFS property in some queries (by Rule (1)) and left unchanged in others as it may also be later mapped to a user-defined property in the RDF graph G.

A simple analysis of the reformulation rule behavior shows that the worst-case time complexity of algorithm Reformulate$_c$ is polynomial in the size of O and simply exponential in the size of q. More precisely:

Proposition 1. *The algorithm* Reformulate$_c$ *runs in time* $\mathcal{O}(|Val(O)|^{6|q|})$, *where $|q|$ is the number of triples in the body of q.*

The correctness of the algorithm relies on the following lemma, which characterizes the saturated graph $G^{\mathcal{R}_c}$ from the triples of G. We call $\prec_{sc}$-chain (resp. $\prec_{sp}$-chain) from s to o a possibly empty sequence of triples $(s_i, \prec_{sc}, o_i)$ (resp. $(s_i, \prec_{sp}, o_i)$) with $1 \leq i \leq n$, such that $s_1 = s$, $o_n = o$ and, for $i > 1$, $s_i = o_{i-1}$.

Algorithm 1. Reformulate$_c$

Input : BGPQ q and ontology O
Output: the reformulation of q with the rules from Fig. 1

1 $result \leftarrow \emptyset$; $toExplore \leftarrow \{q\}$; $explored \leftarrow \emptyset$
2 **while** $toExplore \neq \emptyset$ **do**
3 | $produced \leftarrow \emptyset$
4 | **for** each $q_\sigma \in toExplore$ **do**
5 | | **if** q_σ does not contain any RDFS triple **then**
6 | | |_ $result \leftarrow result \cup \{q_\sigma\}$
7 | | **for** each RDFS triple t in q_σ **do**
8 | | | **for** each q'_σ obtained by applying a reformulation rule to t **do**
9 | | | |_ $produced \leftarrow produced \cup \{q'_\sigma\}$
10 | |_ $explored \leftarrow explored \cup \{q_\sigma\}$
11 |_ $toExplore \leftarrow produced \setminus explored$
12 **return** $result$

Since we do not enforce the reflexivity of the subclass relation, a triple $(c, \prec_{sc}, c)$ belongs to $G^\mathcal{R}$ if and only if there is a non-empty $\prec_{sc}$-chain from c to c (which includes the case $(c, \prec_{sc}, c) \in G$). The same holds for the subproperty relation.

Lemma 1. *Let G be an RDF graph. It holds that:*

- $(c, \prec_{sc}, c') \in G^{\mathcal{R}_c}$ *iff G contains a non-empty $\prec_{sc}$-chain from c to c';*
- $(p, \prec_{sp}, p') \in G^{\mathcal{R}_c}$ *iff G contains a non-empty empty $\prec_{sp}$-chain from p to p';*
- $(p', \hookleftarrow_d, c') \in G^{\mathcal{R}_c}$ *iff G contains a triple $(p, \hookleftarrow_d, c)$, a (possibly empty) $\prec_{sp}$-chain from p' to p and a (possibly empty) $\prec_{sc}$-chain from c to c'. The case for $(p', \hookrightarrow_r, c') \in G^{\mathcal{R}_c}$ is similar (replace $\hookleftarrow_d$ by $\hookrightarrow_r$ in the statement above).*

Below, we assume *without loss of generality* that the input query does not contain blank nodes; if needed, these have been equivalently replaced by variables. Therefore, all blank nodes that occur in the output reformulation have been introduced by the reformulation rules, and specifically refer to unknown classes and properties they identify within the ontology at hand. This justifies the subsequent use of non-standard query evaluation and answering in the next theorems.

Theorem 1. *Let G be an RDF graph with ontology O and q be a BGP query without blank nodes. Let $\mathcal{Q}_c$ be the output of Reformulate$_c(q, O)$. Then:*

$$q(G, \mathcal{R}_c) = \overbrace{q(G, \mathcal{R}_c)} = \overbrace{\mathcal{Q}_c(G)} \tag{18}$$

$$q(G, \mathcal{R}_c \cup \mathcal{R}_a) = \overbrace{q(G, \mathcal{R}_c \cup \mathcal{R}_a)} = \overbrace{\mathcal{Q}_c(G, \mathcal{R}_c \cup \mathcal{R}_a)} \tag{19}$$

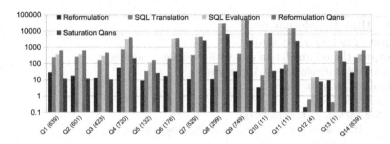

Fig. 2. Query answering times through reformulation and saturation.

Example 5. Consider the BGPQ asking for *how someone is related to some particular kind of company*: $q(x,y) \leftarrow (x,y,z), (z,\tau,t), (y, \prec_{sp}, :\text{worksFor}), (t, \prec_{sc}, :\text{Comp})$. Its answer set on G_{ex} w.r.t. $\mathcal{R}$, which can be easily checked using $(G_{\text{ex}})^{\mathcal{R}}$ provided in Sect. 2, is: $q(G_{\text{ex}}, \mathcal{R}) = \{\langle :\text{p1}, :\text{ceoOf}\rangle\}$.

The output of Reformulate$_c(q, \text{RDFS}(G_{\text{ex}}))$ is:

$$\mathcal{Q}_c = \{q'(x, :\text{ceoOf}) \leftarrow (x, :\text{ceoOf}, z), (z, \tau, \_:b_C),$$
$$q''(x, :\text{hiredBy}) \leftarrow (x, :\text{hiredBy}, z), (z, \tau, \_:b_C)\}$$

where q' and q'' are obtained by binding, using Rule (13), y to either :ceoOf or :hiredBy, and t to $\_:b_C$. Further, these bindings have also produced the fully instantiated RDFS constraints (:ceoOf, $\prec_{sp}$, :worksFor) and ($\_:b_C$, $\prec_{sc}$, :Comp) in q', as well as (:hiredBy, $\prec_{sp}$, :worksFor) and ($\_:b_C$, $\prec_{sc}$, :Comp) in q'', which have then been eliminated by Rule (2).

The *non-standard* answering of $\mathcal{Q}_c$ on G_{ex} w.r.t. $\mathcal{R}$, i.e., $\widetilde{q'(G_{\text{ex}}, \mathcal{R})} \cup \widetilde{q''(G_{\text{ex}}, \mathcal{R})}$ provides the correct answer set $\{\langle :\text{p1}, :\text{ceoOf}\rangle\}$, whose only tuple results from q'. Using *standard* answering, the incorrect answer $\langle :\text{p2}, :\text{hiredBy}\rangle$ would have also been obtained from q'', since under this semantics q'' asks for *who is hired by an organization of some type* (this is the case of :p2 who is hired by a public administration) and not *who is hired by an organization of the particular unknown type of company designated by* $\_:b_C$ *in* G_{ex}.

We now rely on the query reformulation algorithm, from [13], say Reformulate$_a$, which takes as input a partially instantiated BGPQ q *without RDFS triples*, and a graph G and, using a set of reformulation rules associated with $\mathcal{R}_a$, outputs a reformulation $\mathcal{Q}_a$ such that: $q(G, \mathcal{R}_c \cup \mathcal{R}_a) = q(G, \mathcal{R}_a) = \widetilde{\mathcal{Q}_a(G)}$. The adaptation of Reformulate$_a$ to an input UBGPQ instead of a BGPQ is straightforward. Furthermore, we notice that the algorithm would consider potential blank nodes in the input query as if they were IRIs. Hence, denoting by $\mathcal{Q}_{c,a}$ the output of Reformulate$_a(\mathcal{Q}_c, O)$, we obtain:

$$\widetilde{\mathcal{Q}_c(G, \mathcal{R}_c \cup \mathcal{R}_a)} = \widetilde{\mathcal{Q}_c(G, \mathcal{R}_a)} = \widetilde{\mathcal{Q}_{c,a}(G)} \qquad (20)$$

Putting together (20) and statement (19) in Theorem 1, we can prove the correctness of the global reformulation algorithm:

Theorem 2. *Let G be an RDF graph and q be a BGPQ without blank nodes. Let $\mathcal{Q}_{c,a}$ be the reformulation of q by the 2-step algorithm described in Sect. 4.1. Then: $q(G, \mathcal{R}_c \cup \mathcal{R}_a) = \widehat{\mathcal{Q}_{c,a}(G)}$ holds.*

5 Experimental Evaluation

We have implemented our reformulation algorithm on top of OntoSQL (https://ontosql.inria.fr), a Java platform providing efficient RDF storage, saturation, and query evaluation on top of an RDBMS [10,13]; we used Postgres v9.6. To save space, OntoSQL encodes IRIs and literals into integers, and a dictionary table which allows going from one to the other. It stores all resources of a certain type in a one-attribute table, all subject, object pairs for each data property in a table, and all schema triples in another table; the tables are indexed. Our server has a 2,7 GHz Intel Core i7 and 160 GB of RAM; it runs CentOs Linux 7.5.

We generated LUBM$^{\exists}$ data graphs [16] of 10M triples and restricted the ontology to RDFS, leading to 175 triples (123 $\prec_{sc}$, 5 $\prec_{sp}$, 25 $\hookleftarrow_d$ and 22 $\hookrightarrow_r$). We devised 14 queries having from 3 to 7 triples; one has no result, while the others have a few dozen to three hundred thousand results. Each has 1 or 2 triples which match the ontology (and must be evaluated on it for correctness), including (but not limited to) the generic triple (x, y, z), which appears 7 times overall in our workload. Some of our queries are not handled through reformulation by AllegroGraph and Stardog, nor by Virtuoso (recall Sect. 3).

Figure 2 shows for each query: the size of the UBGPQ reformulation (in parenthesis after the query name on the x axis), i.e., the number of BGPQs it contains; the reformulation time (with both $\mathcal{R}_c$ and $\mathcal{R}_a$); the time to translate the reformulation into SQL; the time to evaluate this SQL query; the total query answering time through reformulation, and (for comparison) through saturation. Note the logarithmic y axis. *Details of our experiments are available online* (see Footnote 1). The reformulation time is very short (0.2 ms to 55 ms). Unsurprisingly, the time to convert the reformulation into SQL is closely correlated with the reformulation size. The overhead of our approach is quite negligible, given that the answering time through reformulation is close to the SQL evaluation time.

As expected, saturation-based query answering is faster; however, saturating this graph took more than 1289 s, while the slowest query (Q9) took 46 s. As in [13], we compute for each query Q a *threshold* n_Q which is the smallest number of times we need to run Q, so that saturating G and running Q n_Q times on $G^{\mathcal{R}}$ is faster than n_Q runs of Q through reformulation; intuitively, *after n_Q runs of Q, the saturation cost amortizes.* For our queries, n_Q ranged from 29 (Q9) to 9648 (Q5), which shows that saturation costs take a while to amortize. If the graph or the ontology change, requiring maintenance of the saturated graph, reformulation may be even more competitive.

6   Conclusion

We have presented a novel reformulation-based query answering technique for RDF graphs with RDFS ontologies. Its novelty lies in its capacity to handle query triples over both the assertions and the ontology; such queries are not always handled correctly by existing RDF engines. In the future, we plan to integrate our reformulation technique in the cost-based optimized reformulation framework we introduced in [10] to improve its performance, and to an OBDA setting along the lines of [15].

Acknowledgements. This work is supported by the Inria Project Lab grant iCoda, a collaborative project between Inria and several major French media.

References

1. RDF 1.1 Concepts and Abstract Syntax. https://www.w3.org/TR/rdf11-concepts
2. RDF 1.1 Semantics. https://www.w3.org/TR/rdf11-mt/#rdfs-entailment
3. SPARQL 1.1 Query Language. https://www.w3.org/TR/sparql11-query/
4. Abiteboul, S., Hull, R., Vianu, V.: Foundations of Databases. Addison-Wesley, Reading (1995)
5. Adjiman, P., Goasdoué, F., Rousset, M.C.: SomeRDFS in the semantic web. JODS **8**, 158–181 (2007)
6. Arenas, M., Gutierrez, C., Pérez, J.: Foundations of RDF databases. In: Tessaris, S., Franconi, E., Eiter, T., Gutierrez, C., Handschuh, S., Rousset, M.-C., Schmidt, R.A. (eds.) Reasoning Web 2009. LNCS, vol. 5689, pp. 158–204. Springer, Heidelberg (2009). https://doi.org/10.1007/978-3-642-03754-2_4
7. Bishop, B., Kiryakov, A., Ognyanoff, D., Peikov, I., Tashev, Z., Velkov, R.: OWLIM: a family of scalable semantic repositories. Semant. Web **2**(1), 33–42 (2011)
8. Broekstra, J., Kampman, A.: Inferencing and truth maintenance in RDF schema. In: PSSS1 Workshop (2003). http://ceur-ws.org/Vol-89/broekstra-et-al.pdf
9. Buron, M., Goasdoué, F., Manolescu, I., Mugnier, M.L.: Reformulation-based query answering for RDF graphs with RDFS ontologies. Research report, Inria, March 2019. https://hal.archives-ouvertes.fr/hal-02051413
10. Bursztyn, D., Goasdoué, F., Manolescu, I.: Optimizing reformulation-based query answering in RDF. In: EDBT (2015)
11. Calvanese, D., Giacomo, G.D., Lembo, D., Lenzerini, M., Rosati, R.: Tractable reasoning and efficient query answering in description logics: the DL-Lite family. J. Autom. Reasoning (JAR) **39**(3), 385–429 (2007)
12. Goasdoué, F., Karanasos, K., Leblay, J., Manolescu, I.: View selection in semantic web databases. PVLDB **5**(2) (2011). https://hal.inria.fr/inria-00625090v1
13. Goasdoué, F., Manolescu, I., Roatis, A.: Efficient query answering against dynamic RDF databases. In: EDBT (2013). https://hal.inria.fr/hal-00804503v2
14. Kaoudi, Z., Miliaraki, I., Koubarakis, M.: RDFS reasoning and query answering on top of DHTs. In: Sheth, A., Staab, S., Dean, M., Paolucci, M., Maynard, D., Finin, T., Thirunarayan, K. (eds.) ISWC 2008. LNCS, vol. 5318, pp. 499–516. Springer, Heidelberg (2008). https://doi.org/10.1007/978-3-540-88564-1_32

15. Lanti, D., Xiao, G., Calvanese, D.: Cost-driven ontology-based data access. In: d'Amato, C., et al. (eds.) ISWC 2017. LNCS, vol. 10587, pp. 452–470. Springer, Cham (2017). https://doi.org/10.1007/978-3-319-68288-4_27

16. Lutz, C., Seylan, İ., Toman, D., Wolter, F.: The combined approach to OBDA: taming role hierarchies using filters. In: Alani, H., et al. (eds.) ISWC 2013. LNCS, vol. 8218, pp. 314–330. Springer, Heidelberg (2013). https://doi.org/10.1007/978-3-642-41335-3_20

17. Neumann, T., Weikum, G.: The RDF-3X engine for scalable management of RDF data. VLDB J. **19**, 91–113 (2010)

18. Urbani, J., van Harmelen, F., Schlobach, S., Bal, H.: QueryPIE: backward reasoning for OWL Horst over very large knowledge bases. In: Aroyo, L., et al. (eds.) ISWC 2011. LNCS, vol. 7031, pp. 730–745. Springer, Heidelberg (2011). https://doi.org/10.1007/978-3-642-25073-6_46

19. Urbani, J., Piro, R., van Harmelen, F., Bal, H.E.: Hybrid reasoning on OWL RL. Semant. Web **5**(6), 423–447 (2014)

A Hybrid Graph Model for Distant Supervision Relation Extraction

Shangfu Duan, Huan Gao, Bing Liu, and Guilin Qi[✉]

School of Computer Science and Engineering, Southeast University, Nanjing, China
{sf_duan,gh,liubing_cs,gqi}@seu.edu.cn

Abstract. Distant supervision has advantages of generating training data automatically for relation extraction by aligning triples in Knowledge Graphs with large-scale corpora. Some recent methods attempt to incorporate extra information to enhance the performance of relation extraction. However, there still exist two major limitations. Firstly, these methods are tailored for a specific type of information which is not enough to cover most of the cases. Secondly, the introduced extra information may contain noise. To address these issues, we propose a novel hybrid graph model, which can incorporate heterogeneous background information in a unified framework, such as entity types and human-constructed triples. These various kinds of knowledge can be integrated efficiently even with several missing cases. In addition, we further employ an attention mechanism to identify the most confident information which can alleviate the side effect of noise. Experimental results demonstrate that our model outperforms the state-of-the-art methods significantly in various evaluation metrics.

Keywords: Distant supervision · Relation extraction · Heterogeneous information · Hybrid graph

1 Introduction

Relation Extraction (RE) aims at extracting semantic relations from plain text. It plays a crucial role in a wide range of applications such as Knowledge Graph (KG) completion and question answering. For example, given the sentence #1 in Fig. 1, RE aims to identify the *FounderOf* relation between *Bill Gates* and *Bill & Melinda Gates Foundation*. Supervised approaches have achieved excellent performance in RE. However, they suffer from the lack of labeled data while manual annotation is very costly. Distant supervision (DS) [6,13,16] is a promising approach to solve this limitation. It can generate labeled data automatically by aligning KGs with text. As shown in Fig. 1, if the triplet <*Bill Gates, FounderOf, Bill & Melinda Gates Foundation*> exists in KG, then all the sentences containing *Bill Gates* and *Bill & Melinda Gates Foundation* are taken as the training instances of *FounderOf* relation.

© Springer Nature Switzerland AG 2019
P. Hitzler et al. (Eds.): ESWC 2019, LNCS 11503, pp. 36–51, 2019.
https://doi.org/10.1007/978-3-030-21348-0_3

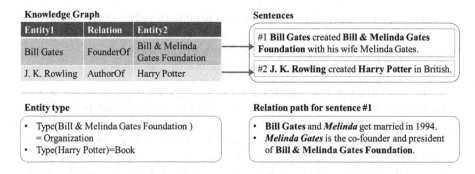

Fig. 1. Examples of DS.

Recently, various models based on Deep Neural Network (DNN) [14,23–25] have been proposed to improve Distant Supervision Relation Extraction (DSRE). These methods mainly focused on dealing with the noise problem brought by DS and have achieved a huge improvement. However, they still lacked sufficient background information for making predictions. For example, as shown in Fig. 1, there are two DS generated sentences and they describe different relations. It's hard to predict their relations exactly because they both use *"create"* to express corresponding relations. Recent studies have attempted to introduce more background information to enhance DSRE. Some methods proposed in [7,11] introduced the types and descriptions of entities which provide rich entity information to RE. Other researchers [5,22] carried out the representation learning of KG and the training of DS models jointly so as to introduce the knowledge in KG to the DS model. Zeng et al. [25] incorporated inference information that is hidden in extra text and proposed a path-based model to enhance DSER. These studies have shown the effectiveness of introducing background information. However, there are still two major problems remaining to be addressed.

On the one hand, the introduced background information is too sparse, especially for the long-tail relations. Previous methods only considered a single type of background information and it's not enough to cover the most cases. In addition, these methods always designed customized models to combine the corresponding knowledge which is limited to incorporate heterogeneous background information simultaneously. On the other hand, the previous studies did not consider alleviating the side effect of the introduced noise. For example, the methods [11] obtained the entity types with NLP tools and this inevitably brought some errors and hurt the RE performance.

To solve the above problems, we propose a novel graph-based model for DSRE, which can not only incorporate heterogeneous background information but also alleviate the side effect of introduced noisy information. We first transform different types of information into vectors with various encoders and treat each piece of information as a node in the graph. Then, we connect the related nodes and fuse all information with a Graph Convolutional Network (GCN). Notice that, our model is highly robust to the missing information and flexible to integrate various types of information. To alleviate the effect of the introduced noisy information, we further employ an attention mechanism over the graph, which can assign a higher weight to more confident information.

The contributions of our study can be summarized as follows:

- We propose a novel graph-based DS model, which can incorporate heterogeneous background information in a unified framework and is flexible to integrate various kinds of knowledge.
- We employ an attention mechanism over the graph which can alleviate the effect of the introduced noise.
- We conduct extensive experiments on a real-world DS dataset and the results demonstrate that our model outperforms state-of-the-art methods significantly via various evaluation metrics.

2   Background

In this section, we give a brief introduction of related background information and the Graph Convolutional Network.

2.1   Various Types of Background Information

Sentence Bag. We denote a DS generated data set as $\mathcal{D} = \{S_{(h_i,t_i)}|, i = 1, 2, \ldots\}$ and a sentence bag $S_{(h_i,t_i)}$ is a collection of sentences that each sentence mentions both entities h and t.

Entity Representation in KG. A Knowledge Graph (KG) is a collection of triples (h_i, r_i, t_i) and the representation learning of KG aims to learn a vector embedding of both entities and relations into a low-dimensional space. Translation-based model [2] was proposed by treating the labeled relation embedding $\mathbf{r_i}$ as a translation of the embeddings of $\mathbf{h_i}$ and $\mathbf{t_i}$, i.e. $\mathbf{h_i} + \mathbf{r_i} \approx \mathbf{t_i}$.

Entity Type. For any entity e, we can get its type y_{e_i} from a KG. Fine-grained entity types [13] provide powerful constraints between an entity pair and a relation. For example, as shown in Fig. 1, the type of *Harry Potter* is *book*. With this background knowledge, it's much easy to predict the relation between *J.K.Rowling* and *Harry Potter* from *FounderOf* and *AuthorOf*.

Relation Path. A relation path describes the flow of resource between multiple entities [4,12,15,20,21]. In DSRE, we define a relation path as a set of entities, $p = \{h, e_1, \ldots e_l, t\}$, which means the resource flows from h to t through l entities. More specifically, the path is represented as $h \xrightarrow{S_{(h,e_1)}} e_1 \xrightarrow{S_{(e_1,e_2)}} \ldots \xrightarrow{S_{(e_l,t)}} t$.

2.2   Graph Convolutional Network

Graph Convolutional Networks (GCN) [8,17] is an efficient variant of Convolutional Neural Networks (CNNs) and aims at dealing with the graph structure data. GCN can extract local graph structure and learn a better representation of each node. Given a graph with two inputs: A feature matrix $X \in \mathbb{R}^{N \times D}$ where N is the number of nodes and D denotes the size of node features and an adjacency matrix $A \in \mathbb{R}^{N \times N}$, a typical GCN outputs a node-level representation $Z \in \mathbb{R}^{N \times F}$ where F is the size of output features. Each neural network layer has the following form

$$H^{(l+1)} = f(H^{(l)}, A), \tag{1}$$

where $H^{(0)} = X$ and $H^{(L)} = Z$, L is the number of layers.

In each layer, the layer-wise propagation are shown in Eq. 2.

$$f(H^{(l)}, A) = \sigma(AH^{(l)}W^l) \tag{2}$$

To further solve the limitations of Eq. 2, Kipf et al. [8] uses a symmetric normalization and enforce a self-loops in the graph. In this paper, we will represent GCN as a transform function of X and A, as shown in Eq. 3, where $\hat{A} = A + I$, I is the identity matrix and $\hat{D}$ is the diagonal node degree matrix of $\hat{A}$.

$$GCN(X, A) = \sigma\left(\hat{D}^{-\frac{1}{2}} \hat{A} \hat{D}^{-\frac{1}{2}} X W\right) \tag{3}$$

3   Methodology

In this section, we present our hybrid graph model, which can fuse heterogeneous background information and alleviate the side effect of introduced noise.

3.1   Problem Definition

Given a DS generated dataset $D = \{S_{(h_i, t_i)}|, i = 1, 2, \ldots\}$, for each entity pair (h_i, t_i), we extend some background information from a KG, and denote the dataset as $\mathbb{I} = \{I_{(h_1, t_1)}, I_{(h_2, t_2)}, \ldots\}$. The label of each instance $I_{(h_i, t_i)}$ keeps same as the label of $S_{(h_i, t_i)}$. In this paper, our methods aim to predict the relation between an entity pair, and we finally learn a probability distribution $P(r_i|h_i, t_i; \theta)$ over all relations $r_i \in \mathcal{R}$, where θ denotes the parameters in our model.

3.2   Overview

The overview of our approach is shown in Fig. 2. When carrying out the RE task, our model not only considers the sentence bag generated by DS, but also introduces various types of background information, such as the entity type, the entity representation in KG, the entity graph context and the relation path. The whole process includes three stages. Firstly, these types of information are

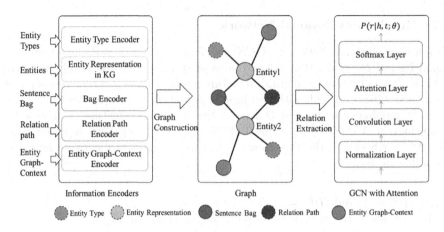

Fig. 2. Overview of our method.

converted into vector representations respectively using corresponding encoders. Then, we construct a hybrid graph by treating each piece of information as a node and connecting related information.

We utilize a graph convolutional methods to learn a more discriminative representation of each piece of information. Finally, an attention-based GCN model extracts features of the graph and outputs a probability distribution of relations. Notice that our model can fuse all types of information on the graph, even though some nodes may be missing.

3.3   Encoders

In this part, we will introduce different encoders that used for heterogeneous background information respectively.

Sentence Bag Encoder. For any sentence $s_i \in S_{(h,t)}$ with an entity pair (h,t), we apply a Bi-LSTM model [10] to obtain its vector representation $\mathbf{s}_i \in \mathbb{R}^{d_s}$ where d_s denotes the size of sentence embedding. It's also flexible to replace with other models as long as it can represent the semantics of the given sentence. Afterward, we get the sentence bag representation $\mathbf{S}_{(h,t)} \in \mathbb{R}^{d_s}$ by summing all sentence embeddings with different weight. There are plenty of methods to calculate the weigh and we follow the methods used in [25].

Entity Type Encoder. Given a entity e and its type $y_{e_i} \in \mathcal{T}$, where $\mathcal{T}$ denotes the type set of all entities. Here, we take the one-hot encoding as inputs. During the training process, we will learn a distribution representation of each entity type and update the representation matrix $\mathbf{M}_y \in \mathbb{R}^{|\mathcal{T}| \times d_t}$ dynamically, where d_t denotes the size of entity type embedding.

Entity Encoder. Each entity mention e_i will be mapped into a real-value vector $\mathbf{e}_i$ with dimension d_e. In which we use a pre-trained PTransE model [9] to get the embedding of all the entities. The reason why we adopt PTransE is that PTransE can capture the path information among the KG. In addition, most existing translation-based methods can be easily integrated into the framework.

Relation Path Encoder. We propose a relation path encoder to jointly inference among multiple paths with a selective attention. To represent the flow of information on a path, the entity embedding information also has been integrated into our relation path encoder.

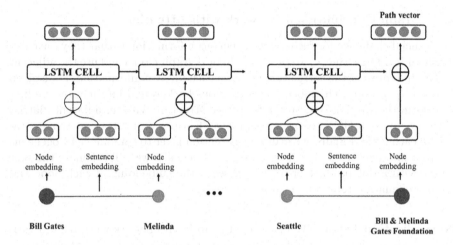

Fig. 3. The architecture of our path encoder.

As shown in Fig. 3, given an entity path $p = \{h, e_1, ..., e_l, t\}$ between an entity pair (h, t), we use the LSTM model to predict the relation by capturing the flows from h to t. For any LSTM cell at timestep k, we firstly concatenate corresponding entity embedding and sentence bag embedding, as shown in Eq. 4, where $W_e \in \mathbb{R}^{d_p \times (d_e + d_s)}$, $b_e \in \mathbb{R}^{d_p}$ are model parameters and the $\oplus$ means the concatenation operation. Here, d_p denotes the size of path embedding.

$$\mathbf{x}_k = W_e(\mathbf{e}_k \oplus \mathbf{S}_{(e_k, e_{k+1})}) + b_e, \tag{4}$$

Afterward, each process step is defined in Eq. 5, where $LSTM(x, h, c)$ denotes a standard LSTM cell [14], and at each timestep $k+1$, the hidden state h_{k+1} is a function of the current input embedding x_{k+1} with the last step's hidden status h_k and cell state C_k. We use the last hidden stages to represent the relation path vector $\mathbf{p} \in \mathbb{R}^{d_p}$.

$$h_{k+1} = LSTM(x_{k+1}, h_k, C_k) \tag{5}$$

Following the MIL framework [6,10], we use a selective attention over each path and get the embedding $\mathbf{P}_{(h,t)} \in \mathbb{R}^{d_p}$ which combines all information of relation paths.

Entity Graph-Context Encoder. For any entity e, we collect all entities that occur with it in a sentence as its graph-context N_e and encode the graph-context into a vector representation $\mathbf{N}_e \in \mathbb{R}^{d_e}$, as shown in Eq. 6.

$$\mathbf{N}_e = \sigma \left(\frac{1}{|N_e|} \sum_{e' \in N_e} e' \right) \tag{6}$$

3.4   Graph Convolutional Network with Attention

One crucial challenge for fusing heterogeneous information is that they have different embeddings. Hence, we propose a hybrid graph model and use the adjacent matrix to represent the correlation between each piece of information. For a given instance $I_{(h,t)}$ and each embeddings of various background information, we first transform the varying structure into a fixed structure with an adjacent matrix. Then, we apply a GCN to extract high-level features and get a new representation of each node. Finally, we utilize an attention layer to combine heterogeneous information together with different weights. Specially, we will calculate the similarity with a dot product operation between the embedding of each node and an approximation representation of relation r.

Normalization Layer. We propose an adaptive framework to transform various embeddings into a graph structure. More specifically, we represent our hybrid graph with a node matrix $\mathbf{X} = \{\mathbf{X}_1, \mathbf{X}_2, ..., \mathbf{X}_{d_g}\}$ and an adjacency matrix $\mathbf{A} \in \mathbb{R}^{d_g \times d_g}$. Here, each element in $\mathbf{X}$ denotes a kind of information and $\mathbf{A}_{i,j} = 1$ indicates the i_{th} and j_{th} information are correlated. In this paper, for an entity pair (h,t), we build the hybrid graph $\mathbf{X} = \{\mathbf{S}_{(h,t)}, \mathbf{P}_{(h,t)}, \mathbf{h}, \mathbf{y}_h, \mathbf{t}, \mathbf{y}_t, \mathbf{N}_h, \mathbf{N}_t\}$, where $\mathbf{h}$ and $\mathbf{t}$ are embeddings of the given entity pair, $\mathbf{y}_h$ and $\mathbf{y}_t$ are corresponding entity type embeddings, $\mathbf{N}_h$ and $\mathbf{N}_t$ are entity context embeddings. $\mathbf{S}_{(h,t)}$ and $\mathbf{P}_{(h,t)}$ are the sentence bag embedding and relation path embedding which connect both $\mathbf{h}$ and $\mathbf{t}$, $\mathbf{N}_h$ and $\mathbf{y}_h$ connect $\mathbf{h}$, $\mathbf{N}_t$ and $\mathbf{y}_t$ connect $\mathbf{t}$. In order to keep simplicity and convenient, we set the size of all embeddings as $d_i = d_s = d_p = d_e = d_t$, thus the node matrix can be denoted as $\mathbf{X} \in \mathbb{R}^{d_g \times d_i}$.

Convolutional Layer. We propose a variant of graph convolutional network [8, 17] which takes the inputs of the node matrix $\mathbf{X}$ and the corresponding adjacency matrix $\mathbf{A}$. The output is a matrix represents new features of each node. It's efficiently for our convolutional layer to capture the structure pattern with shared parameters. Specifically, we do not need to train large parameters over the whole graph and it's space-efficient and time-efficient. As shown in Eq. 7, the output matrix $\mathbf{G} \in \mathbb{R}^{d_g \times d_o}$ represents all background information, where d_o is the size of output features.

$$\mathbf{G} = GCN(\mathbf{X}, \mathbf{A}) \tag{7}$$

Attention Layer. It's straightforward that some extra knowledge may express irrelevant or noisy information on the given entity pair. Thus, we propose a graph attention layer to learn a discriminative representation among all background knowledge embeddings. Inspired by translation-based model, we use an approximation representation of the relation between entity pair (h, t), as shown in Eq. 8. Then, we calculate the similarity between each background knowledge embedding $\mathbf{G} = \{\mathbf{g}_1, ..., \mathbf{g}_{d_g}\}$ with the approximation relation representation $\mathbf{r}_{h,t}$, shown in Eq. 10.

Afterward, we apply a weighted sum operation overall features on the graph and assign a high weight to more relevant feature to alleviate the effect of noise, as shown Eq. 11:

$$\mathbf{r}_{h,t} = \mathbf{t} - \mathbf{h} \tag{8}$$

$$\mathbf{u}_j = tanh(\mathbf{W}_a \mathbf{g}_j + \mathbf{b}_a), \tag{9}$$

$$a_j = \frac{exp(\mathbf{r}_{h,t} \cdot \mathbf{u}_j)}{\sum_{k=1}^{d_g} exp(\mathbf{r}_{h,t} \cdot \mathbf{u}_k)}, \tag{10}$$

$$\mathbf{r}_g = \sum_{j=1}^{d_g} a_j \mathbf{g}_j, \tag{11}$$

where $\mathbf{W}_a \in \mathbb{R}^{d_i \times d_o}$ and $\mathbf{b}_a \in \mathbb{R}^{d_i}$ are the model parameters, a_j denotes the weight of each background feature.

Finally, we calculate the probability of each relation r in Eq. 12,

$$\mathbf{o} = \mathbf{M} \mathbf{r}_g, \tag{12}$$

where $\mathbf{M}$ is the score matrix to calculate the scores of each relation $r' \in \mathcal{R}$ and $\mathbf{o} \in \mathbb{R}^{d_r}$ denotes the probabilities of all relations, i.e. $\mathbf{o} = (o_{r_1}, o_{r_2}, ...)$. For a given entity pair (h, t) and the corresponding instance $I_{(h_1, t_1)}$, we conduct the conditional probability $P(r|h, t, I_{(h_1, t_1)})$ as shown in Eq. 13.

$$P(r|h, t, I_{(h_1, t_1)}) = \frac{\exp(o_r)}{\sum_{r' \in \mathcal{R}} \exp(o_{r'})} \tag{13}$$

3.5   Optimization

For an entity pair (h, r), the overall objective function is defined in Eq. 14, where θ denotes the parameters in our model.

$$\ell_\theta (r|h, t; \theta) = \log(P(r|h, t, I_{(h_i, t_i)})) \tag{14}$$

We use mini-batch stochastic gradient descent (SGD) to maximize our objective function.

$$\min_{\theta} \mathbb{E}\left[\sum_{(h_i,t_i)\in\mathbb{I}_{batch}} \frac{\ell_{\theta}\left(r_i|h_i,t_i,\theta\right)}{|\mathbb{I}_{batch}|}\right] \tag{15}$$

4   Experiments

Our experiments aim to measure (1) whether the introduction to additional background information can improve the prediction performance in DSRE, and (2) whether our model can reduce the effect of the introduced noisy data. Our source code and dataset are available at GitHub[1].

4.1   Dataset and Metrics

The most commonly used benchmark dataset for DSRE was proposed in [16], and this dataset was generated by aligning Freebase [1] relations with the New York Times (NYT) corpus. Due to the sparse and scattered connection of different entities, this dataset does not have enough relation paths to measure the effect of this type of information. Therefore, we apply an up-to-date dataset proposed in [25] which addresses the above issue by aligning Wikidata[2] relations with the NYT corpus. Compared to the Freebase dataset, this dataset contains more instances and the detailed statistics are shown in Table 1.

Table 1. Statistics of the benchmark dataset.

Set	#Sentences	#Entity pairs	#Facts
Train	647,827	266,118	50,031
Valid	234,350	121,160	5,609
Test	235,609	121,837	5,756

Following the previous work [13], we measure our model based on the held-out metric. This metric provides an approximation measurement of precision automatically by comparing the predicted relations with corresponding facts in Wikidata. We compare our model with the baseline methods and other approaches which employing part of background information. In addition, we also evaluate the robustness and capacity of different percentage of noisy data. To further demonstrate the effect of our hybrid graph model, we also report the Precision@N results and F1 score with different noise ratio.

---

[1] https://github.com/Apeoud/HG-DSRE.git.
[2] www.wikidata.org/.

4.2 Experimental Settings

We apply different combination of parameters in validation dataset and the optimal parameters are shown as follows. We use a pre-trained word embeddings on NYT corpus with different embedding size $d_w = \{50, \mathbf{100}, 200, 300\}$. For entity embedding, we train a PTransE model [9] with the dimension d_e among $\{\mathbf{50}, 100, 200, 300\}$. We select the learning rate λ for SGD among $\{\mathbf{0.01}, 0.1, 1.2\}$. For training, the best mini-batch size B is $\{30, \mathbf{50}, 100, 300\}$. We also apply dropout on the last layer to avoid overfitting with dropout rate 0.5. Other parameters have little effect and we follow the settings used in [25].

4.3 Precision-Recall Curve Comparison

To demonstrate the performance of our model, we compare it with other methods via the held-out evaluation. Figure 4(a) demonstrates the overall evaluation results which include our method with the comparison to three baseline approaches. (1) PCNN represents the Piecewise-CNN model with multi-instances learning used in [24]. (2) PCNN+path [25] incorporated relation path with PCNN model. (3) PCNN+KG [5] jointly learned an embedding of word in text and entity mention in KG. (4) HG is our method which introducing four additional information, the entity embeddings in KG, the entity type, the entity graph-context and the relation paths. Figure 4(b) introduce two variant of our method, HG(Path) and HG(KG). HG(Path) takes a limitation of the additional knowledge and only consider relation path information while HG(KG) only incorporate KG embeddings. From the aggregate precision/recall curves, we observe that:

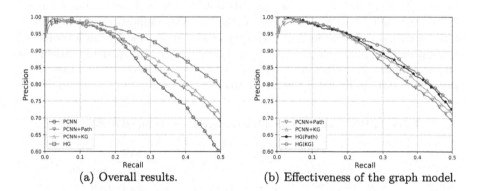

(a) Overall results.   (b) Effectiveness of the graph model.

Fig. 4. Aggregate PR curves upon the held-out evaluation. (a) shows the comparison between our methods and other baselines. (b) demonstrates the noise immunity when incorporating the same extra knowledge for our methods and others.

Overall Results. (1) When the recall is very small (0–0.1), all methods keep nearly equivalent performance. As the recall grows, the precision of PCNN drops rapidly. This observation indicates that only a small part of the instance contains reasonable information to make sufficient prediction and it's necessary to introduce external information to avoid this problem. (2) We also observe that the methods which utilize background information have a slow decay with the recall increase, this phenomenon indicates that incorporating background information can really improve the prediction accuracy. (3) Our methods (HG) outperform all methods and achieve the best performance with 20% improvement in precision to PCNN when recall equals 0.5 and 10% improvement to PCNN+Path. It indicates that our methods can take advantages of multiple background information.

Effectiveness of Our Hybrid Graph. While previous experiments demonstrate the effectiveness of incorporating multiple background information, there still lacks sufficient evidence to prove that our methods can reduce the effect of noisy information. Thus, we compare two variations of HG, named HG(Path) and HG(KG) which only take single background information (Path/KG) respectively. (1) Comparison between HG(path) and PCNN+Path as well as HG(KG) and PCNN+KG all indicate that even under the same background information, our methods still obtain at least 5% improvement at 0.5 recall. The main reason is that since our methods utilize the graph attention layer to filter out the effect of noisy information in relation path. (2) It seems that introducing KG information performs better than relation path information, either in our model or in PCNN. We observe that KG constructed by human usually contains few noisy data. Instead, the relation path is generated with an unsupervised way which may incorporate much more noise. (3) HG obtains the best performance among all HG variation, as shown in Fig. 4(a) and (b). This demonstrates that different information can complement each other and a fusion model can leverage all information to enhance the performance. Further more, our model is capable to fuse more information efficiently, such as entity description [7], we will take these information into account for the future work.

Table 2. P@N and F1 with different percentage of no-relation facts.

(Noise)	75%				85%				95%			
P@N (%)	10%	20%	50%	F1	10%	20%	50%	F1	10%	20%	50%	F1
PCNN	86.0	68.5	38.3	57.2	85.4	67.6	37.7	56.5	84.4	66.0	36.6	54.8
PCNN+Path	89.0	71.5	39.8	59.6	89.0	71.4	39.6	59.4	88.6	71.0	39.1	59.1
HG(Path)	88.9	73.5	41.2	58.4	88.8	72.9	41.0	57.8	87.9	71.5	40.7	57.1
HG(KG)	90.1	**77.8**	40.2	61.4	90.0	**76.9**	40.0	60.9	89.7	**76.4**	42.5	60.2
HG	**92.1**	76.5	**43.2**	**63.1**	**92.1**	76.4	**43.6**	**62.6**	**92.1**	76.2	**42.9**	**62.2**

4.4 Model Robustness

In DSRE, the generated dataset consists of plenty of noisy instances. More specifically, the instances labeled "NA" which means there exist no relation between two entities are viewed as a kind of noise and the RE models might not distinguish these noisy data very well. Following the settings proposed in [25], we evaluate those models with the same relational facts and different percentages of "NA" sentences to verify the robustness. There are three groups of experiments with noise percentages are 75%, 85%, and 95%. In each experiment, we extract top 20,000 predicting relational facts according to the predicting probabilities, and report the P@N for @top 10%, @top 20%, @top 50% and F1 score in Table 2.

Evaluations in Table 2 demonstrate: (1) Our model achieves the best performance among different noise percentage and has a very slow decay with the noise percentage increase. (2) In some special cases, the models that incorporating more knowledge worse that those methods with less knowledge. This phenomenon indicates that our model can not eliminate the effects of noise completely, and we leave this issue for future work.

4.5 Case Study

Table 3 shows two representative examples of testing dataset. In each case, we use the change of scores to demonstrate the effect of background information. The first case indicates that when the sentence lacks adequate information to make

Table 3. Representative cases in testing dataset.

ex#1	manhattan ?country_of America		Score
	sentence	...marked **America**...like downtown **manhattan**...	0.242
	path_1 path_2	...**manhattan** charged the garbage haulers in **new_york**... ...**new_york**... city in **America**...	0.564
	(inference)	$manhattan \xrightarrow{located\_in} new\_york \xrightarrow{captial\_of} America$	
	type	e_1 type: *location*, e_2 type: *country*	0.861
ex#2	new_south_wales ?located_in australia		score
	sentence	...in the **new_south_wales** in **australia**...	0.766
	path_1 path_2	in the southern alps of **victoria** and **new_south_wales** .. the_national_gallery of **australia** in **victoria**...	0.464
	(inference)	$new\_south\_wales \xrightarrow{shares\_border} victoria \xrightarrow{country} australia$	
	type	e_1 type: *state*, e_2 type: *country*	0.737

the prediction, incorporating various background information may enhance the performance significantly. For the second case, the sentence between the entity pair *new_south_wales* and *australia* includes sufficient evidence to predict the correct relation while the relation path underlies between the entity pair guide to the wrong direction and damage the capacity of classification. On the contrary, our model can capture the noise and utilize the constraints on the entity type to alleviate the effect of noisy information and correct to right relation. Generally, our method can learn a discriminative and powerful representation even with some noisy information.

5   Related Work

5.1   Distant Supervision

Distant Supervision (DS) was first proposed in [3] which focused on extracting binary relations by using a protein KG. With the development of DS, Mintz et al. [13] aligned Freebase [1] relations with New York Times (NYT) corpus to automatically generate the training data. Riedel et al. [16] proposed an assumption that there is at least one instance express the labeled relation among all sentences contains the entity pair. Following this *expressed-at-least-once* assumption, other researchers improved the original paradigm with kinds of methods. Surdeanu et al. [19] and Hoffmann et al. [6] utilized probabilistic graphics models to improve DSRE in MIL framework. Zheng et al. [26] built the inter information of aggregated inter-sentence to enhance DSRE performance. As these methods depend on the features obtained from NLP tools, so the errors derived from NLP tools will prorogate to DSRE system and effect their performance.

5.2   Neural Network Methods

With the great breakthrough of deep neural networks (DNNs), some researchers applied it for DSRE and obtained a promising result. Zeng et al. [24] firstly proposed a convolutional neural network (CNN) for relation classification. Zhou et al. [27] and Socher et al. [18] proposed to utilize bidirectional long short-term memory (Bi-LSTM) networks to model the sentence with sequential information with all words. Moreover, with the rise of attention mechanism, Lin et al. [10] employed sentence-level attention to reducing the weight of noisy data and achieves state-of-the-art. All theses methods only considered the sentence bag information and cannot deal with the case where all the sentences containing the same entities are wrongly labeled.

5.3   Methods with Background Information

The *expressed-at-least-once* assumption is often too strong in practice and previous methods are hard to deal with the cases when all sentences are not expressing the labeled relation. Therefore, some researchers introduced some background information to expand missing information. The types and descriptions of entities from additional corpus and KG have been introduced to DS in [7,11]. Other works [5,22] attempted to combine a human constructed KG into DSRE and propose a joint representation learning framework. In addition, Zeng et al. [25] built an inference chain between two target entities via intermediate entities from the text and proposed a path-based neural relation extraction model to encode the relational semantics from both direct sentences and inference chains. These methods all achieved promising success but also suffered the low coverage problem.

6   Conclusion and Future Work

In this paper, we proposed a novel graph-based model to fuse heterogeneous information for DSRE. Firstly, we converted various pieces of information into vector representations via corresponding encoders. Then, we constructed a hybrid graph and treated each piece of information embedding into a node and connected related node with an edge. In addition, an attention mechanism was proposed to alleviate the noisy information by incorporating structured triples in a KG. We evaluated our model on a real-world dataset and results demonstrated that our model achieves huge improvement both in enhancing accuracy with heterogeneous background information and reducing the side effect of noisy information.

Our hybrid graph model is convenient to capture the relevance of various types of data, including the unlabeled data. In the future, we will generalize our model to large unlabeled text and try to learn more confident knowledge in the unsupervised relation extraction task. Moreover, the effect of noisy knowledge has not been eliminated completely and we will consider designing a more efficient method to solve this problem.

Acknowledgement. This work was supported by National Natural Science Foundation of China Key (U1736204) and National Key R&D Program of China (2018YFC0830200).

References

1. Bollacker, K.D., Evans, C., Paritosh, P., Sturge, T., Taylor, J.: Freebase: a collaboratively created graph database for structuring human knowledge. In: Proceedings of SIGMOD, pp. 1247–1250 (2008)
2. Bordes, A., Usunier, N., García-Durán, A., Weston, J., Yakhnenko, O.: Translating embeddings for modeling multi-relational data. In: Proceedings of NIPS, pp. 2787–2795 (2013)
3. Craven, M., Kumlien, J.: Constructing biological knowledge bases by extracting information from text sources. In: Proceedings of ISMB, pp. 77–86 (1999)
4. Guu, K., Miller, J., Liang, P.: Traversing knowledge graphs in vector space. In: Proceedings of EMNLP 2015, pp. 318–327 (2015)

5. Han, X., Liu, Z., Sun, M.: Neural knowledge acquisition via mutual attention between knowledge graph and text. In: Proceedings of 8th AAAI and (EAAI-2018), pp. 4832–4839 (2018)
6. Hoffmann, R., Zhang, C., Ling, X., Zettlemoyer, L.S., Weld, D.S.: Knowledge-based weak supervision for information extraction of overlapping relations. In: Proceedings of ACL, pp. 541–550 (2011)
7. Ji, G., Liu, K., He, S., Zhao, J.: Distant supervision for relation extraction with sentence-level attention and entity descriptions. In: Proceedings of AAAI, pp. 3060–3066 (2017)
8. Kipf, T.N., Welling, M.: Semi-supervised classification with graph convolutional networks. In: Proceedings of ICLR (2016)
9. Lin, Y., Liu, Z., Luan, H., Sun, M., Rao, S., Liu, S.: Modeling relation paths for representation learning of knowledge bases. In: Proceedings of EMNLP, pp. 705–714 (2015)
10. Lin, Y., Shen, S., Liu, Z., Luan, H., Sun, M.: Neural relation extraction with selective attention over instances. In: Proceedings of ACL, pp. 2124–2133 (2016)
11. Liu, Y., Liu, K., Xu, L., Zhao, J.: Exploring fine-grained entity type constraints for distantly supervised relation extraction. In: Proceedings of COLING, pp. 2107–2116. ACL (2014)
12. McCallum, A., Neelakantan, A., Das, R., Belanger, D.: Chains of reasoning over entities, relations, and text using recurrent neural networks. In: Proceedings of EACL, pp. 132–141 (2017)
13. Mintz, M., Bills, S., Snow, R., Jurafsky, D.: Distant supervision for relation extraction without labeled data. In: Proceedings of ACL, pp. 1003–1011 (2009)
14. Miwa, M., Bansal, M.: End-to-end relation extraction using LSTMs on sequences and tree structures. In: Proceedings of ACL (2016)
15. Neelakantan, A., Roth, B., McCallum, A.: Compositional vector space models for knowledge base completion. In: Proceedings of ACL, pp. 156–166 (2015)
16. Riedel, S., Yao, L., McCallum, A.: Modeling relations and their mentions without labeled text. In: Proceedings of ECML PKDD, pp. 148–163 (2010)
17. Schlichtkrull, M.S., Kipf, T.N., Bloem, P., van den Berg, R., Titov, I., Welling, M.: Modeling relational data with graph convolutional networks. In: Proceedings of ESWC, pp. 593–607 (2018)
18. Socher, R., Huval, B., Manning, C.D., Ng, A.Y.: Semantic compositionality through recursive matrix-vector spaces. In: Proceedings of EMNLP-CoNLL, pp. 1201–1211 (2012)
19. Surdeanu, M., Tibshirani, J., Nallapati, R., Manning, C.D.: Multi-instance multi-label learning for relation extraction. In: Proceedings of EMNLP-CoNLL, pp. 455–465 (2012)
20. Toutanova, K., Chen, D., Pantel, P., Poon, H., Choudhury, P., Gamon, M.: Representing text for joint embedding of text and knowledge bases. In: Proceedings of EMNLP 2015, pp. 1499–1509 (2015)
21. Toutanova, K., Lin, V., Yih, W., Poon, H., Quirk, C.: Compositional learning of embeddings for relation paths in knowledge base and text. In: Proceedings of ACL, pp. 1434–1444 (2016)
22. Weston, J., Bordes, A., Yakhnenko, O., Usunier, N.: Connecting language and knowledge bases with embedding models for relation extraction. In: Proceedings of EMNLP, pp. 1366–1371 (2013)
23. Zeng, D., Liu, K., Chen, Y., Zhao, J.: Distant supervision for relation extraction via piecewise convolutional neural networks. In: Proceedings of EMNLP, pp. 1753–1762 (2015)

24. Zeng, D., Liu, K., Lai, S., Zhou, G., Zhao, J.: Relation classification via convolutional deep neural network. In: Proceedings of COLING, pp. 2335–2344 (2014)
25. Zeng, W., Lin, Y., Liu, Z., Sun, M.: Incorporating relation paths in neural relation extraction. In: Proceedings of EMNLP, pp. 1768–1777 (2017)
26. Zheng, H., Li, Z., Wang, S., Yan, Z., Zhou, J.: Aggregating inter-sentence information to enhance relation extraction. In: Proceedings of AAAI, pp. 3108–3115 (2016)
27. Zhou, P., Shi, W., Tian, J., Qi, Z., Li, B., Hao, H., Xu, B.: Attention-based bidirectional long short-term memory networks for relation classification. In: Proceedings of ACL, pp. 207–212 (2016)

Retrieving Textual Evidence
for Knowledge Graph Facts

Gonenc Ercan[1,2], Shady Elbassuoni[3(✉)], and Katja Hose[1]

[1] Aalborg University, Aalborg, Denmark
{gonenc,khose}@cs.aau.dk
[2] Informatics Institute Ankara, Hacettepe University, Ankara, Turkey
[3] American University of Beirut, Beirut, Lebanon
se58@aub.edu.lb

Abstract. Knowledge graphs have become vital resources for semantic search and provide users with precise answers to their information needs. Knowledge graphs often consist of billions of facts, typically encoded in the form of RDF triples. In most cases, these facts are extracted automatically and can thus be susceptible to errors. For many applications, it can therefore be very useful to complement knowledge graph facts with textual evidence. For instance, it can help users make informed decisions about the validity of the facts that are returned as part of an answer to a query. In this paper, we therefore propose FacTify, an approach that given a knowledge graph and a text corpus, retrieves the top-k most relevant textual passages for a given set of facts. Since our goal is to retrieve short passages, we develop a set of IR models combining exact matching through the Okapi BM25 model with semantic matching using word embeddings. To evaluate our approach, we built an extensive benchmark consisting of facts extracted from YAGO and text passages retrieved from Wikipedia. Our experimental results demonstrate the effectiveness of our approach in retrieving textual evidence for knowledge graph facts.

1 Introduction

Knowledge graphs, such as YAGO [23], DBpedia [1], and Google Knowledge Graph[1], have caused a revolution in information retrieval (IR). These knowledge graphs encode billions of facts, typically in the form of RDF triples[2]. For example, the following two facts from YAGO indicate that the late President John F. Kennedy died in Dallas on November 22, 1963:

> John_F._Kennedy diedIn Dallas
> John_F._Kennedy diedOnDate "1963-11-22"

The above set of facts, in the following referred to as a *knowledge subgraph*, provide very concise information about President Kennedy's place and date of

---

[1] https://developers.google.com/knowledge-graph/.
[2] https://www.w3.org/RDF/.

© Springer Nature Switzerland AG 2019
P. Hitzler et al. (Eds.): ESWC 2019, LNCS 11503, pp. 52–67, 2019.
https://doi.org/10.1007/978-3-030-21348-0_4

death. However, it lacks any context that a user might be interested in. In this paper, we therefore propose FacTify, an approach to complement knowledge subgraphs with *relevant* text passages extracted from a text corpus. For the above mentioned example, a relevant passage extracted from Wikipedia is:

> President Kennedy was assassinated in Dallas, Texas, at 12:30 pm Central Standard Time on Friday, November 22, 1963. He was in Texas on a political trip to smooth over frictions in the Democratic Party between liberals Ralph Yarborough and Don Yarborough (no relation) and conservative John Connally. Traveling in a presidential motorcade through downtown Dallas, he was shot once in the back, the bullet exiting via his throat, and once in the head.

Passages, such as the one above, serve many purposes. First, they provide evidence on the validity of the knowledge graph facts. This is particularly crucial in this era of "Alternative Facts", where misinformation and disinformation are flooding the Internet, and where there is a strong plea for providing more transparency in the way intelligent systems work. Second, the facts in many of the currently existing large-scale knowledge graphs are automatically constructed by making use of Information Extraction and NLP techniques. They are thus susceptible to errors and can have some invalid or inaccurate facts. Providing passages along with knowledge subgraphs allows the users to make informed decisions about the validity of the facts. Third, these passages will also contain additional information related to the knowledge subgraphs; information that might not even be present in the whole knowledge graph. For instance, from the passage shown above, the user can infer that President Kennedy was *assassinated*, and that he was shot twice.

Our task can be formulated as follows: given a knowledge graph and a text corpus, retrieve the *top-k most relevant passages* for a given knowledge subgraph consisting of one or *multiple* facts in the form of RDF triples. In this paper, we define passages as short ones consisting of *three* sentences. However, our approach is applicable to passages of any length. Since our goal is to retrieve short passages, we propose to combine exact matching using the Okapi BM25 model [22] with semantic matching using word embeddings. Word embeddings are distributed vector representations of words, which are capable of capturing semantic and syntactic relations between the words. To evaluate the effectiveness of our approach, we built a benchmark consisting of 56 knowledge subgraphs extracted from YAGO and a pool of passages retrieved from Wikipedia, which were assessed using Figure Eight crowdsourcing platform[3]. Our experimental results indicate that our approach, which combines exact and semantic matching, results in statistically significant improvements in IR effectiveness compared to using each type of matching on its own.

In summary, the contributions of this paper can be summarized as follows:

- A retrieval method that combines exact matching through the Okapi BM25 ranking model with semantic matching through word embeddings. Our method is general enough and can retrieve passages for one or multiple facts.

---

[3] https://www.figure-eight.com/.

– An extensive comparative study of multiple IR models for the above task. The created benchmark containing knowledge subgraphs from YAGO and passages retrieved from Wikipedia has been made publicly available (http:// relweb.cs.aau.dk/factify/).

The remainder of this paper is organized as follows. In Sect. 2, we discuss related work. Section 3 describes our approach to retrieve textual evidence for knowledge graph facts. In Sect. 4, we give an overview of our benchmark and then present our experimental results. Finally, we conclude and discuss future work in Sect. 5.

2   Related Work

Our work broadly falls in the area of fact checking. However, most approaches in this area either rely on the knowledge graph alone or utilize Web search engines or machine learning to perform fact checking. In this paper, our goal is to retrieve textual passages to verify knowledge graph facts and provide explanations and context for them. Our work is thus closely related to two different areas. The first one consists of IR models used to retrieve passages for knowledge graph facts and the second one consists of IR models that make use of word embeddings to rank search results. We discuss each one separately next.

2.1   Passage Retrieval for Knowledge Graph Facts

To the best of our knowledge, there are only a handful of approaches for the problem of retrieving text passages for knowledge graph facts [2,6,9,18]. All these approaches, with the exception of [6,18], operate on single facts only. For instance, the approach in [2] relies on language modeling to rank short passages for a given input fact. It assumes the presence of labels for the components of the facts and ranks the passages based on the passages' probabilities of generating the words in the concatenation of these labels. It then assumes independence between the words and smooths the passage probabilities with document and collection probabilities. This approach, however, operates only on the level of single facts. Moreover, it deploys only exact matching, i.e., semantically related words to those in the fact labels would not play any role in the ranking of passages unless a list of synonyms for terms is provided. In this paper, we experimentally compare our approach to [2] and show that our approach significantly outperforms this approach in terms of retrieving relevant passages for knowledge subgraphs.

DeFacto [9] retrieves webpages that are relevant for a given input fact by issuing several queries to a Web search engine. These queries are generated by verbalizing the fact using natural language patterns extracted by the BOA framework [10]. Once the webpages have been retrieved, they again use the BOA framework in addition to light-weight NLP techniques to determine whether a webpage contains useful evidence for the given fact. The approach then uses a set of classifiers to predict trustworthiness of the retrieved webpages as well as the fact itself. As can be seen, DeFacto relies heavily on external search engines, NLP, machine learning, and the BOA framework to retrieve textual evidence and estimate their trustworthiness as well as that of the fact. On the other hand, our approach is a general retrieval framework that can seamlessly operate on any knowledge graph and text corpus and does not rely on any external information that might not be available for certain knowledge graphs or corpora.

Similar to our approach, ROXXI [6,18] can be applied to knowledge sub-graphs containing multiple facts. However, it retrieves documents rather than passages as in our case. To do this, ROXXI makes use of textual patterns available in PATTY [20] to rank these documents using a language modeling based approach. Once retrieved, the documents are annotated to highlight the textual patterns of the given facts and a text snippet is generated using those textual patterns. However, ROXXI again relies on external textual patterns, which might not be available in general for many knowledge graphs.

Finally, ExFakt [7] is a framework that generates human-comprehensible explanations for knowledge graph facts from a given text corpus. It uses background knowledge encoded in the form of Horn clauses to rewrite a fact into a set of other easier-to-spot facts. The final output of the framework is a set of *semantic traces* for the fact generated from both the text corpus and the knowledge graph. However, ExFakt does not retrieve text passages for knowledge graph facts as in our case, and it can only support single facts.

2.2   Word Embeddings for Information Retrieval

As indicated above, our goal is to retrieve textual passage for a given set of facts. Vocabulary mismatch is a major challenge for many retrieval tasks, including ours. The semantic matching capability of latent models alleviates the vocabulary mismatch problem. Latent models, ranging from latent semantic models [16] to neural network based word embeddings [19], are used extensively in natural language processing and more recently in information retrieval tasks. Nevertheless, building effective document representations using word embeddings is an open research topic.

A basic method to build document vectors from word embeddings is to aggregate the word vectors by summation or averaging [24]. Different aggregation strategies including Fisher Vectors are also used to build document vectors [4,25]. As an alternative, the literature proposes methods that jointly learn the document representations (D2V) with word embeddings [17]. Document vectors are integrated into Skip-gram and CBOW methods [19] by adding an embedding layer for the documents.

While aggregation based methods provide a concise representation of documents, they do not fully take advantage of all pairwise similarities between the words in the documents. A method that makes use of pairwise similarities of words in the documents is the Word Mover's distance (WMD) [15]. WMD casts the similarity problem as a transportation problem, where the words in the first document produce items that should be transported to the second document's words and the cost of transportation is determined by the distance between the words in the embedding space. The production amount of words in the source document and the capacity of the words in the target document are determined by weights calculated using tf or tf-idf weights of the words. These weights control the amount of pairwise similarity taken into account. If the target words have infinite capacity, then transportation will take place between the most similar word pairs. This version of WMD is often referred to as Relaxed WMD. If the weights in the source document are large, then WMD uses all pairwise similarities.

Guo et al. [11] argue that both aggregate and WMD methods loosely match words in queries, thus causing a concept drift and degrading the performance of word embedding based IR methods. As a solution to this problem, they propose a non-linear scaling function depending on the inverse document frequency of the query word, allowing more strict matching for words with a high idf value, while retaining the ability to semantically match less discriminative words. Galke et al. [8] compare both aggregate and WMD based methods in an information retrieval task. The aggregate method using normalized tf-idf word weights achieves better results in a range of retrieval experiments compared to WMD and D2V methods. However, word embedding methods fail to beat the tf-idf baseline. Brokos et al. [3] use Relaxed WMD for document retrieval in question answering. They report better results using Relaxed WMD for re-ranking the results. Kenter and de Rijke [14] use Relaxed WMD and BM25 based weighting function as a feature in a sentence paraphrase classifier.

3   Retrieving Textual Evidence

As mentioned in the introduction, the problem we are targeting in this paper can be defined as follows. Given a knowledge graph and a text corpus, retrieve the top-k most relevant passages for a given input knowledge subgraph. A knowledge subgraph is a subgraph of the underlying knowledge graph that consists of one or more RDF triples, i.e., facts. A passage is defined as a short text excerpt, for instance consisting of three sentences extracted from the text corpus. Finally, a relevant passage is a passage containing textual evidence that verifies the facts in the knowledge subgraph.

Since knowledge subgraphs are in RDF while passages are in plain text, we use the *labels* (i.e., surface names) of resources in the knowledge graph to transform a knowledge subgraph into a keyword query. For instance, in YAGO, resource John_F._Kennedy is associated with the label *John F. Kennedy*. Similarly, the relation diedIn can be represented using the label *died in*. Our approach thus first transforms the knowledge subgraph for which passages are to be retrieved into a keyword query by replacing the RDF triples with their labels. For example, consider the knowledge subgraph

John_F._Kennedy diedIn Dallas
John_F._Kennedy diedOnDate "1963-11-22"

The corresponding keyword query for the above subgraph is *"John F. Kennedy died in Dallas John F. Kennedy died on date 1963-11-22"*. Note that the date "1963-11-22" is a literal and thus does not need to be substituted by a label.

Now, our original task of retrieving passages for a given knowledge subgraph is transformed into retrieving passages for the obtained keyword query representing the knowledge subgraph. We propose to combine two types of IR models to achieve this task. The first utilizes exact matching using term frequencies and the second employs semantic matching using word embeddings. Exact matching relies on term frequencies to rank query results. It thus assumes that the query terms will appear in some form in the documents. While this is an adequate assumption when retrieving long documents, short passages, such as the ones we are concerned with in this paper, might miss some of the query terms but can still be highly relevant. For example, the word "married" in a query might not appear at all in some of the relevant passages, which contain the words "wife" or "husband" instead.

A remedy to this vocabulary mismatch problem is to make use of word embeddings. Word embeddings are distributed vector representations of words, capable of capturing semantic and syntactic relations between them. They were successfully employed in various natural language processing tasks, such as question answering, document classification, and more recently in IR [8,15,17]. On the other hand, word embedding based approaches are susceptible to concept drift as a word can have a high similarity to collocated, hypernyms, meronyms as well as synonyms. Recent results hint at these challenges [8,11].

Hence, we propose a hybrid model that combines both exact and semantic matching to retrieve relevant passages for knowledge graph facts. This is inspired by the results from previous work on other IR tasks such as biomedical document retrieval for question answering [3] or monolingual and cross-lingual information retrieval [24], in which a hybrid approach, such as the one we propose, has been shown to achieve improvements in IR effectiveness. In the following subsections, we first explain each type of model separately, and then finally describe our hybrid model that combines both.

3.1 Exact Matching

For exact matching we use the OKAPI BM25 [22] retrieval model. Ad-hoc information retrieval experiments in early TREC shared tasks show that the BM25 retrieval model is one of the most effective IR models. The BM25 model uses term frequencies to estimate the relevance of passages as follows.

$$BM25(S,Q) = \sum_{i=0}^{|Q|} IDF(q_i) \frac{f(q_i,S)(k_1+1)}{f(q_i,S) + k_1(1 - b + b\frac{|S|}{avgsl})} \quad (1)$$

where $f(q_i, S)$ is the frequency of the query word q_i in passage S, $avgsl$ is the average passage length, and $IDF(q_i)$ is the inverse document frequency calculated using Eq. 2. The terms k_1 and b are free parameters weighing the normalization and frequency components of the scoring function.

$$IDF(q) = log\frac{N - df(q) + 0.5}{df(q) + 0.5} \tag{2}$$

3.2 Semantic Matching

Word embeddings represent words as d-dimensional dense vectors. The similarity or distance between the vectors of words in the embedding space measures the semantic relatedness between them. Pre-trained word embeddings are typically built from a large corpus and have a vocabulary formed of frequent words in that corpus. The vocabulary of the word embeddings can contain both the upper and lower case form of a word. In addition, word vectors for some common phrases might be available. In the following, we describe several embedding based models that can be used to rank passages given a knowledge subgraph.

IWCS. The IDF re-weighted word centroid similarity (IWCS) model [8] uses the word embedding vectors to construct a d-dimensional vector representing a passage. In the IWCS model, the word vectors of the given text are aggregated into a single vector using a linear weighted combination of its word vectors. The weight of each word is determined by the tf-idf weighting. Let $t(S, w)$ be the tf-idf weight for word w in the passage S normalized (L_2 norm) with respect to the other words in S and let $\overrightarrow{w}$ be the word vector. A single vector for passage S can then be computed as follows:

$$\overrightarrow{S} = \sum_{w \in S} \overrightarrow{w} t(S, w) \tag{3}$$

The centroid vector for the query $\overrightarrow{Q}$ can also be constructed in a similar manner. Finally, to rank a passage S with respect to a given query Q, we utilize the cosine similarity between these two centroids, i.e., $IWCS(S, Q) = cosine(\overrightarrow{S}, \overrightarrow{Q})$.

Average of Query IWCS. While the IWCS model was shown to be effective in some IR benchmarks [8], it is difficult to encode diverse relationships between word vectors in the d-dimensional space with simple aggregation. In order to test the validity of this hypothesis, we propose a model that unfolds the query and uses the average similarity of query words to the passage centroid as an estimate of relevance as follows.

$$QIWCS(S, Q) = \frac{1}{|Q|} \sum_{w \in Q} cosine(\overrightarrow{S}, \overrightarrow{w}) t(Q, w) \tag{4}$$

We refer to this model as QIWCS.

Pairwise Similarity. As a final word embedding based model, the average pairwise similarities between the query word vectors $\vec{q}$ and the passage word vectors $\vec{w}$ can be used as follows.

$$PairWise(S, Q) = \sum_{w \in S} \sum_{q \in Q} cosine(\vec{q}, \vec{w}) t(Q, q) t(S, w) \qquad (5)$$

We will refer to this model as PairWise in the remainder of this paper.

3.3 FacTify Model

Our approach combines both exact and semantic matching as follows. Given a knowledge subgraph transformed into a keyword query Q and a passage S, FacTify utilizes a hybrid model that ranks a passage S based on a linear combination of its score using BM25 and a word embedding based one as follows:

$$FT(S, Q) = \alpha BM25(S, Q) + (1 - \alpha)Embedding(S, Q) \qquad (6)$$

where $FT(S, Q)$ is the score of passage S for query Q using FacTify's hybrid model, $BM25(S, Q)$ is the BM25 score as computed using Eq. 1, $Embedding(S, Q)$ is an embedding based similarity (Sect. 3.2), and α is a weighting parameter. This results in three different hybrid models: FT-IWCS, FT-QIWS, and FT-PairWise, which result from combining BM25 with IWCS, QIWCS, and PairWise.

4 Evaluation

In this section, we present the results of experimentally comparing FacTify with its different hybrid models to each other and to several baselines. We start by describing the baselines and the evaluation setup, then we give an overview of our benchmark, and finally present our evaluation results.

4.1 Baselines

We compare FacTify to three different baselines. The first baseline is the plain BM25 model (see Eq. 1) without combining it with word embeddings. The second baseline is a recent approach proposed by Bhatia et al. [2], which is based on language models (LM). This model assumes that the words in a fact are conditionally independent and uses the probability $P(Q|S)$ to rank a passage S based on its probabilities of generating the knowledge subgraph query Q as in Eq. 8.

$$LM(Q, S) = P(Q|S) \propto \prod_{q \in Q} P(q|S) \qquad (7)$$

$$P(q|S) = \lambda_1 P(q|\theta_S) + \lambda_2 P(q|\theta_D) + \lambda_3 P(q|\theta_C) \qquad (8)$$

where q is a query keyword, λ_1, λ_2, and λ_3 are weighting parameters. The probability of a word given a passage $P(q|S)$ is defined as a mixture of three different language models. The first is the passage language model θ_S, the second is the language model of the document from which the passage was extracted θ_D, and the third is the collection language model θ_C, where the collection is the whole text corpus. The language models are estimated using maximum likelihood estimators with Laplacian smoothing, where V is the vocabulary, D is the document containing the passage S, and C refers to the collection.

$$P(q|\theta_S) = \frac{f(q,S) + 1}{|S| + |V|} \tag{9}$$

$$P(q|\theta_D) = \frac{f(q,D) + 1}{|D| + |V|} \tag{10}$$

$$P(q|\theta_C) = \frac{f(q,C)}{|C|} \tag{11}$$

Note that this model uses two smoothing methods, Laplacian and Jelinek-Mercer smoothing, where the latter is achieved through the collection language model. Since the length of passages $|S|$ is relatively small with respect to $|V|$ and $|D|$, the Laplacian smoothing often weakens the signal encoded in $P(q|\theta_S)$. As a third baseline, we propose a modification of the LM model that does not employ Laplacian smoothing, which we refer to as LM-noLap. Only Eqs. 9 and 10 are modified by removing the additive terms used for Laplacian smoothing.

4.2   Evaluation Setup

For the BM25 and the LM-based models, both the queries and the passages were tokenized, words were lower-cased and the passages were transformed into bags of words and indexed using Lucene[4]. For the hybrid models that make use of word embeddings, we used a Gazetteer approach to tokenize the text, by looking up entries from the word embedding, which can have upper and lower case letters as well as multiword entries. A Directed Acyclic Finite State Automata (DAFSA) was built for the vocabulary of the word embeddings using the construction algorithm of Daciuk et al. [5]. A word or phrase in the text was then mapped to a word vector with the closest form. Although any word embedding can be used, GloVe word embeddings pre-trained with 840 billion word corpora[5] and with word vector dimensions $d = 300$ was used [21].

The parameters of the Okapi BM25 were set as $k_1 = 1.2$, and $b = 0.75$, which are the default parameters optimized using the TREC dataset [13]. The linear weighted combination parameter α for the hybrid models in Eq. 6 was empirically set to 0.2, the linear weighted combination parameters for the language model approaches were set as follows $\lambda_1 = 0.6$, $\lambda_2 = 0.2$, and $\lambda_3 = 0.2$, as suggested by the authors of that model [2].

---

[4] http://lucene.apache.org/.
[5] https://nlp.stanford.edu/projects/glove/.

Table 1. Sample knowledge subgraphs and their corresponding keyword queries

Knowledge subgraph	Keyword query
Allianz_Arena isLocatedIn Munich	Allianz Arena is Located In Munich
Marie_Curie wasBornIn Warsaw	Marie Curie was born in Warsaw
Marie_Curie wasBornOn "1867-11-07"	Marie Curie was born on "1867-11-07"
Henri_Becquerel hasWonPrize Nobel_Prize	Henri Becquerel has Won Nobel Prize
Marie_Curie hasWonPrize Nobel_Prize	Marie Curie has Won Nobel Prize
Irene_Joliot-Curie hasWonPrize Nobel_Prize	Irene Joliot-Curie has Won Nobel Prize

4.3   Benchmark

To evaluate the effectiveness of FacTify (Sect. 3), we constructed a benchmark consisting of 56 different knowledge subgraphs extracted from the large knowledge graph YAGO [23]. The knowledge subgraphs are composed of both single and multiple facts. The average number of facts per knowledge subgraph in our benchmark is 1.41. Table 1 shows several sample knowledge subgraphs and their corresponding keyword queries. Our benchmark consists of 102 unique entities of various types, such as scientists, politicians, cities, writers, companies, and 19 unique relations overall.

For each knowledge subgraph in our benchmark, the top 20 passages using our three hybrid models and all the baselines were retrieved. Each passage was assessed using Figure Eight crowdsourcing platform (see Footnote 3), on a three-level scale: relevant, somehow relevant, or irrelevant. A passage was considered relevant if the annotator was capable to verify *all* the facts from the knowledge subgraph in the passage. If the annotator could only verify part of the knowledge subgraph, say a single fact for multi-fact subgraphs, or if the passage just implied the facts in the knowledge subgraph, the passage was marked as somehow relevant.

Overall, we had a pool of 4,145 unique passages for our 56 knowledge subgraphs. Each passage was annotated as described above by three different annotators. The inter-rater agreement between the three annotators was 0.39 using Fleiss' Kappa. The disagreement seems to be mainly attributed to passages that contain some sentences not directly related to the facts in the knowledge subgraph. Some annotators deem this to reduce the relevance of the passage, while others ignore it as long as the facts are verified in the passages. By eliminating those passages or acquiring more annotations for them, we believe the agreement would increase. A final relevance score for each passage was computed using a standard majority voting. For 329 passages, there was no consensus among the three annotators and these were thus assigned the mean of the three relevance levels (i.e., they were considered *somehow* relevant).

4.4   Results

To evaluate the effectiveness of our proposed models, we use the Normalized Discounted Cumulative Gain (NDCG) [12]. NDCG is a common metric for IR

Table 2. Average NDCG of the evaluated IR models

Model	NDCG@20	NDCG@10	NDCG@5	NDCG@1
FT-PairWise	**72.98**	**74.64**	**76.31**	**81.07**
FT-IWCS	71.90	73.01	75.00	80.00
FT-QIWCS	71.76	73.49	74.97	80.00
BM25	71.72	73.22	74.78	80.00
LM	31.59	32.55	35.05	31.07
LM-noLap	67.05	68.57	71.07	76.79

effectiveness that takes into consideration the rank of relevant results and allows the incorporation of different relevance levels. In addition, we also report the Mean Reciprocal Rank (MRR) and precision for the relevant passages. MRR and precision use binary relevance and allow us to evaluate the effectiveness of the different models in retrieving relevant passages that can *fully* verify all the facts in a knowledge subgraph (i.e, considering somehow relevant passages as irrelevant). Particularly, MMR evaluates whether the top-ranked results are relevant or not. Precision, on the other hand, measures the percentage of relevant results retrieved up to a particular rank.

In Table 2, we report the average NDCG at different ranks over all the knowledge subgraphs in our benchmark. Overall, the hybrid model FT-PairWise achieves the highest NDCG for all ranks. It significantly outperforms the plain BM25 model and LM-noLap model in ranks 5 to 20 (p-value < 0.05). When comparing the different hybrid models, the model that makes use of word embeddings without any aggregation, i.e., FT-PairWise, achieves the highest NDCG. Recall that FT-IWCS aggregates the word vectors of both the query and the passage, while FT-QIWCS aggregates only the words in the passage, and PairWise does not perform any aggregation. This result confirms our initial hypothesis that taking the sum of the word vectors results in information loss and can degrade the retrieval effectiveness. When the word embedding methods IWCS, QIWCS, and PairWise are used alone without combining them with the BM25 model, their performance was as low as 0.35 (NDCG@20).

Comparing the two language model baselines LM and LM-noLap, the LM model was significantly improved when the Laplacian smoothing was removed from the ranking model (i.e., the LM-noLap model). This result supports our intuition that using two smoothing techniques weakens the signal from the passage language model and gives more weight to the document one. Furthermore, having the document language model in the retrieval function improves the effectiveness for the top ranked passage, but tends to retrieve irrelevant passages from documents with high similarity to the query terms. The Okapi BM25 model achieved higher NDCG values compared to both the LM and LM-noLap models.

Table 3 shows the average MMR and precision of the evaluated IR models. MRR measures the average rank of relevant passages. Both FT-PairWise

Table 3. Average MRR and precision of the evaluated IR models

Methods	MRR	Precision@20	Precision@10	Precision@5	Precision@1
FT-PairWise	**75.97**	**50.03**	**54.82**	**58.93**	**66.07**
FT-IWCS	72.77	49.64	53.21	56.79	60.71
FT-QIWCS	72.75	49.29	53.93	56.43	60.71
BM25	72.80	49.38	53.57	55.71	60.71
LM	35.84	18.30	20.00	24.29	21.43
LM-noLap	74.96	46.25	52.14	57.50	**66.07**

and LM-noLap achieve higher MRR scores than BM25. On the other hand, the two other hybrid models FT-IWCS and FT-QIWCS did not show consistent improvements over BM25 when retrieving only relevant passages. We also report the precision for all models, and again the FT-PairWise and LM-noLap models were the most effective in retrieving a relevant passage in the top rank (i.e., Precision@1) for 66% of the knowledge subgraphs in our benchmark. When considering lower ranks, the precision of LM-noLap drops, even below that of BM25 when considering the top 10 passages. On the other hand, FT-PairWise was able to retrieve more relevant passages at all ranks. We conjuncture again that this is a consequence of relying on the document level language model, which limits the top ranking passages to only relevant documents, penalizing passages retrieved from documents that might not be entirely about the resources mentioned in the subgraph, but that might nonetheless contain relevant passages.

4.5   Discussion

When considering the results of the LM and LM-noLap models, our observation is that their performance is degraded mostly due to the document language model included in their ranking models. Especially when the Laplacian smoothing is used, the passage-level language model is smoothed more harshly as the length of the passages are relatively smaller compared to the vocabulary size. This gives significantly more weight to the document language model. Wikipedia contains articles listing information such as birth dates or various profiles grouped by an aspect (e.g., U.S. Presidents). These articles repeat certain words like *born* or numbers in dates with high frequencies, causing a high probability for generating these specific words. The original LM model is affected by this component and retrieves passages from these documents containing only a portion of the words with high frequencies. Removing the Laplacian smoothing alleviates this problem, as the passage-level language model will have more weight and the frequencies will be leveled out. Moreover, the document-level language model improves the ranking of passages extracted from relevant documents, for example for a subgraph about **Abraham_Lincoln**, the LM model retrieves passages from his Wikipedia article

Table 4. Top ranked passages retrieved by `FacTify` for some knowledge subgraphs

Query	Top ranking passage
Albert_Einstein graduatedFrom ETH_Zurich	ETH Zurich has produced and attracted many famous scientists in its short history, including Albert Einstein. More than twenty Nobel laureates have either studied at ETH or were awarded the Nobel Prize for their work achieved at ETH. Other alumni include scientists who were distinguished with the highest honours in their respective fields, amongst them Fields Medal, Pritzker Prize and Turing Award winners
Adolf_Hitler created Mein_Kampf	Mein Kampf (My Struggle) is a 1925 autobiographical book by Nazi Party leader Adolf Hitler. The work describes the process by which Hitler became antisemitic and outlines his political ideology and future plans for Germany. Volume 1 of Mein Kampf was published in 1925 and Volume 2 in 1926
Henri_Becquerel hasWonPrize Nobel_Prize Marie_Curie hasWonPrize Nobel_Prize	His grandparents, Marie and Pierre Curie together with Henri Becquerel won the Nobel Prize in Physics in 1903 for their study of radioactivity. Marie also won the Nobel Prize in Chemistry in 1911. Joliot's parents, Irène Joliot-Curie and Frédéric Joliot-Curie, won the Nobel Prize in Chemistry in 1935 for their discovery of artificial radioactivity

in the top ranks. While this strategy improves the accuracy of the top 1 result, it degrades the accuracy of the following passages in the result set as typically the same fact is not repeated in the same document multiple times.

On the other hand, since our proposed hybrid models do not rely on any document-level information, this allows them to retrieve passages from various Wikipedia articles that might not be strongly associated with one particular resource in the knowledge subgraph. For example, for the subgraph `BarackObama graduatedFrom ColumbiaUniversity` a relevant passage from the Wikipedia article titled "College Transfer" is retrieved stating that Barack Obama transferred from Occidental College to Columbia University. Similar observations can be made for all the knowledge subgraphs in our benchmark, as facts are usually repeated in different articles with different contextual information. We thus advocate that incorporating document-level information should be limited when retrieving passages to complement knowledge subgraphs.

As for BM25, it uses parameter k_1 to determine the saturation level of word frequencies, which is important for scoring passages containing only part of the subgraph with high frequency. LM on the other hand is linearly affected by word frequencies, a passage containing the word "born" but not the objects and subjects in the subgraph will have a higher score with LM than with BM25.

Finally, in Table 4, we display the top passages retrieved by our best-performing model, FT-PairWise, for several example knowledge subgraphs. As can be seen from the table, the top ranked passages are all relevant to the knowledge subgraphs. They provide textual evidence that verifies the facts in the knowledge subgraphs and in addition might provide additional contextual information. For instance, for the first knowledge subgraph in Table 4, one can verify that Albert Einstein graduated from ETH Zurich, but that also more than twenty Nobel laureates have either studied at ETH or were awarded the Nobel Prize for their work achieved at ETH. Similarly, for the last subgraph in Table 4, the top passage does not only confirm that Marie Curie and Henri Becquerel won the Nobel Prize in Physics but it also indicates that Curie later won another Nobel Prize in Chemistry, and that her daughter Irène Curie also won a Nobel prize in Chemistry. Note that this passage was retrieved from the Wikipedia article of Marie and Pierre Curie's grandson, Pierre Joliot. Similar interesting information can be deduced from the top retrieved passage for the third knowledge subgraph shown in Table 4.

To summarize, we have shown that our approach, FacTify, is effective in retrieving textual evidence for knowledge graph facts compared to various baseline approaches. Nonetheless, all the approaches have an upper limit of 72.98 NDCG@top-20. This indicates that there is room for improvement. One possible direction to explore is to use supervised learning approaches to learn how to rank the passages making use of both word embeddings and exact occurrences of the query words. Another direction worth exploring is to retrieve variable-length passages rather than ones that consist of three consecutive sentences as we did in this paper.

5 Conclusion

In this paper, we have proposed FacTify, a novel approach to retrieve textual passages for knowledge subgraphs consisting of one ore more facts. We proposed multiple IR models that combine exact matching through the Okapi BM25 model with semantic matching using word embeddings. We evaluated our approach using a benchmark consisting of 56 knowledge subgraphs extracted from YAGO and passages retrieved from Wikipedia, which were manually annotated for relevance through crowdsourcing. Our experimental results show that our approach outperforms the baselines and related work for retrieving relevant passages for knowledge graph facts. In future work, we plan to evaluate our approach on other knowledge graphs and text corpora. Furthermore, we plan to use our benchmark to train supervised deep-learning models to rank variable-length passages based on their relevance to knowledge subgraphs consisting of one or multiple facts.

Acknowledgments. This research was partially funded by the Danish Council for Independent Research (DFF) under grant agreement no. DFF-8048-00051B and Aalborg University's Talent Programme.

References

1. Auer, S., Bizer, C., Kobilarov, G., Lehmann, J., Cyganiak, R., Ives, Z.: DBpedia: a nucleus for a web of open data. In: Aberer, K., et al. (eds.) ASWC/ISWC -2007. LNCS, vol. 4825, pp. 722–735. Springer, Heidelberg (2007). https://doi.org/10.1007/978-3-540-76298-0_52
2. Bhatia, S., Dwivedi, P., Kaur, A.: Tell me why is it so? Explaining knowledge graph relationships by finding descriptive support passages. In: ISWC (2018)
3. Brokos, G.I., Malakasiotis, P., Androutsopoulos, I.: Using centroids of word embeddings and word mover's distance for biomedical document retrieval in question answering. In: ACL, p. 114 (2016)
4. Clinchant, S., Perronnin, F.: Aggregating continuous word embeddings for information retrieval. In: ACL, pp. 100–109 (2013)
5. Daciuk, J., Mihov, S., Watson, B.W., Watson, R.E.: Incremental construction of minimal acyclic finite-state automata. Comput. Linguist. **26**(1), 3–16 (2000)
6. Elbassuoni, S., Hose, K., Metzger, S., Schenkel, R.: ROXXI: Reviving witness dOcuments to eXplore eXtracted Information. PVLDB **3**(2), 1589–1592 (2010)
7. Gad-Elrab, M., Stepanova, D., Urbani, J., Weikum, G.: ExFaKT: a framework for explaining facts over knowledge graphs and text. In: WSDM (2019)
8. Galke, L., Saleh, A., Scherp, A.: Word embeddings for practical information retrieval. In: INFORMATIK (2017)
9. Gerber, D., et al.: Defacto - temporal and multilingual deep fact validation. Web Semant. **35**, 85–101 (2015)
10. Gerber, D., Ngomo, A.C.N.: Bootstrapping the linked data web. In: Workshop on Web Scale Knowledge Extraction (2011)
11. Guo, J., Fan, Y., Ai, Q., Croft, W.B.: Semantic matching by non-linear word transportation for information retrieval. In: CIKM, pp. 701–710 (2016)
12. Järvelin, K., Kekäläinen, J.: Cumulated gain-based evaluation of IR techniques. ACM TOIS **20**(4), 422–446 (2002)
13. Jones, K.S., Walker, S., Robertson, S.E.: A probabilistic model of information retrieval: development and comparative experiments: Part 2. Inf. Process. Manage. **36**(6), 809–840 (2000)
14. Kenter, T., De Rijke, M.: Short text similarity with word embeddings. In: CIKM, pp. 1411–1420 (2015)
15. Kusner, M., Sun, Y., Kolkin, N., Weinberger, K.: From word embeddings to document distances. In: ICML, pp. 957–966 (2015)
16. Landauer, T.K., Dumais, S.T.: A solution to Plato's problem: the latent semantic analysis theory of acquisition, induction, and representation of knowledge. Psychol. Rev. **104**(2), 211 (1997)
17. Le, Q., Mikolov, T.: Distributed representations of sentences and documents. In: ICML, pp. 1188–1196 (2014)
18. Metzger, S., Elbassuoni, S., Hose, K., Schenkel, R.: S3K: seeking statement-supporting top-K witnesses. In: CIKM, pp. 37–46 (2011)
19. Mikolov, T., Sutskever, I., Chen, K., Corrado, G.S., Dean, J.: Distributed representations of words and phrases and their compositionality. In: NIPS, pp. 3111–3119 (2013)
20. Nakashole, N., Weikum, G., Suchanek, F.: PATTY: a taxonomy of relational patterns with semantic types. In: EMNLP (2012)
21. Pennington, J., Socher, R., Manning, C.: Glove: global vectors for word representation. In: EMNLP, pp. 1532–1543 (2014)

22. Robertson, S.E., Walker, S., Jones, S., Hancock-Beaulieu, M., Gatford, M.: Okapi at TREC-3. In: TREC. vol. Special Publication 500–225, pp. 109–126. National Institute of Standards and Technology (NIST) (1994)
23. Suchanek, F.M., Kasneci, G., Weikum, G.: YAGO: a core of semantic knowledge. In: WWW, pp. 697–706 (2007)
24. Vulić, I., Moens, M.F.: Monolingual and cross-lingual information retrieval models based on (bilingual) word embeddings. In: SIGIR, pp. 363–372 (2015)
25. Zhou, G., He, T., Zhao, J., Hu, P.: Learning continuous word embedding with metadata for question retrieval in community question answering. In: ACL, vol. 1, pp. 250–259 (2015)

Boosting DL Concept Learners

Nicola Fanizzi, Giuseppe Rizzo[(⊠)], and Claudia d'Amato

LACAM – Dipartimento di Informatica & CILA,
Università degli Studi di Bari Aldo Moro, Bari, Italy
{nicola.fanizzi,giuseppe.rizzo1,claudia.damato}@uniba.it
http://lacam.di.uniba.it

Abstract. We present a method for boosting relational classifiers of individual resources in the context of the *Web of Data*. We show how weak classifiers induced by simple concept learners can be enhanced producing strong classification models from training datasets. Even more so the comprehensibility of the model is to some extent preserved as it can be regarded as a sort of concept in disjunctive form. We demonstrate the application of this approach to a weak learner that is easily derived from learners that search a space of hypotheses, requiring an adaptation of the underlying heuristics to take into account weighted training examples. An experimental evaluation on a variety of artificial learning problems and datasets shows that the proposed approach enhances the performance of the basic learners and is competitive, outperforming current concept learning systems.

1 Introduction and Motivation

The capability of assigning individual resources to their respective classes plays a central role in many applications related to the *Web of Data* [7] for carrying out tasks such as *completion* or *type* and *link prediction*. Indeed, these tasks can be regarded as relying on the classification of new individual resources, i.e. the prediction of their membership w.r.t. given classes (e.g. see [13]) or the fillers of given properties for fixed subjects [11,15]. Developing such a capability on the ground of sole semantic features ascertained via purely logic-based methods, can be computationally expensive and sometimes also scarcely effective, owing to the inherent incompleteness of the knowledge bases in such a context. Improvements in computational complexity, accuracy and predictiveness may be often obtained with a limited trade-off with the comprehensibility [3] of the classification model. To reach this compromise, a different approach can be pursued by *boosting* a simple (greedy) learner, that amounts to generate a sequence of weak classifiers for the target class(es) to form stronger classification models [16].

In the case of concept learning, weak learners can be derived from full-fledged conventional learners, such as those that search a space of hypotheses guided by some heuristics (e.g. DL-FOIL [5,6], CELOE or other algorithms in the DL-LEARNER suite [2]): the boosting process iterates the production of weak classifiers for the ensemble model adjusting the weights of the examples to drive

© Springer Nature Switzerland AG 2019
P. Hitzler et al. (Eds.): ESWC 2019, LNCS 11503, pp. 68–83, 2019.
https://doi.org/10.1007/978-3-030-21348-0_5

the focus towards covering *harder* examples. The induced classifiers will have the desirable property that the class assigned to an instance depends on the classifiers that cover it. This property makes classifications easier to understand, and is made possible by requiring: (a) suitable constraints from the adopted weak learner; (b) the use of a generalization of the basic boosting *meta-learning* schema [16]. The resulting classification model is simpler and formally better-understood than other ensemble models [3]. Even more so, it can scale better on large datasets and can be extremely effective.

In this work, we show how to apply a *constrained confidence-rated boosting* strategy to a weak learner extracted from existing concept learners, namely a simplified version of their core refinement-search routine, with a different heuristic function that takes into account the *hardness* of the examples to drive the search for refinements. The resulting solution can be regarded as a generalized framework allowing the application of the proposed boosting schema to any conventional learners, that is also those adopting different classification models, e.g. terminological decision trees [13]. Moreover this schema tends to produce more *stable* classifiers.

We performed an empirical evaluation of the proposed approach, applying the boosting schema to a weak learner, wDLF, derived from the latest release of DL-FOIL [6]. For a comparative evaluation, we also considered the conventional concept learners DL-FOIL [5] and CELOE [10], from the DL-LEARNER suite [2]. The experiments, carried out on artificial learning problems of varying difficulty with different datasets, confirmed empirically the expected enhancement of the ensemble models with respect to the weak classifiers induced by the basic learners and show an improved effectiveness also with respect to the conventional competitors. Interestingly, we observed that generally small numbers of iterations (hence of weak classifiers) were necessary to obtain accurate strong classifiers so that (efficiency and) comprehensibility of the resulting models is preserved to some extent.

The paper is organized as follows. In the next section, related works are reviewed. In Sect. 3 we recall the learning problem cast as an error minimization task. In Sect. 4 the basics of boosting are presented and we show how to apply it to the specific learning problem, while Sect. 5 shows how to adapt available (weak) concept learners as auxiliary routines for the presented boosting method. In Sect. 6 a comparative empirical evaluation with conventional systems on various datasets and related learning problems is reported. Further possible developments are suggested in Sect. 7.

2   Related Work

Ensemble methods use multiple learning algorithms to obtain better predictive performance than could be obtained from any of the constituent learning algorithms alone. Specifically, boosting refers to a family of algorithms that are able to convert weak learners to strong learners. The main principle is to fit a sequence of weak learners to weighted versions of the data. Examples that were misclassified by earlier rounds get their weight increased. The predictions made by weak hypotheses are then combined through a weighted majority vote to produce the final strong prediction. The most common implementation of boosting is ADABOOST_M1 [16].

One of the first rule-learning systems based on a generalized version of ADABOOST is SLIPPER [3]. It applied the ADABOOST scheme to weak learners based on a simple and efficient generate-and-prune rule construction method that produces rule-sets, where each propositional rule is labeled with a confidence value used in the final voting procedure determining the classification predicted by the whole model.

One of the first applications of the boosting approach to First-Order rule learners involved FOIL [12]. Another system, C^2RIB [8], produces strong binary classifiers in the form of clausal rule-sets, with each clause endowed with its confidence (and a single default clause for the negative case). The main difference to our proposal is that these algorithms are designed for a binary classification problem, where only positive and negative examples are available. We target ternary settings that can accommodate the case of uncertain-membership individuals w.r.t. the target concept which generally abound in the linked datasets due to the lack of disjointness axioms in the related vocabularies (ontologies).

A different trade-off between accuracy and comprehensibility of classifiers for semantically annotated resources was pursued through tree-based models (see below). A sort of bagging algorithm for the induction of *terminological random forests* has been devised [13] aiming at ensemble models to enhance accuracy and stability. This idea has been further developed in the algorithms for *evidential random forests* [14] as classification models that integrate uncertainty reasoning in prediction by resorting to the *Dempster-Shafer Theory*.

As regards concept learning, supervised approaches grounded on the idea of *generalization as search*, enacted by operators that are specifically designed for DL languages, have been proposed and implemented in learning systems like YINYANG [9], DL-FOIL [5,6] and DL-LEARNER [2]. YINYANG produces concept descriptions by resorting to the notion of *counterfactuals* [9] for specializing overly general concepts by ruling out negative examples for their extensions. DL-FOIL is grounded on a sequential covering strategy and exploits a (downward) refinement operator to traverse the search space and a heuristic, inspired by *information gain*, to select among the candidate specializations [5,6]. DL-LEARNER is a suite that collects the implementation of various concept learning algorithms which essentially differ in the heuristics adopted as scoring functions for candidate refinements. In particular CELOE [10] performs an accuracy-driven search for solutions biased towards (syntactically) simpler concept definitions.

Alternative classification models, such as logical decision trees, are targeted by different strategies. Specifically, *terminological decision trees* [13], i.e. decision trees with test-nodes containing DL concept descriptions, and procedures for their conversion into disjunctive descriptions, adopt a *divide-and-conquer* learning strategy (instead of the *separate-and-conquer* strategy embraced by most of the algorithms). Similarly, PARCEL and its extension SPACEL [17] adopt the *separate-and-conquer* strategy but it is based on the use of a set of workers generating partial solutions, which are subsequently combined to generate a complete concept description. Both PARCEL and SPaCEL use CELOE as a subroutine for building partial solutions, thus the quality of the final concept strictly depends on the quality of such class expressions.

Another related approach to concept learning is based on *bisimulation* [18], which amounts to a recursive partitioning of a set of individuals, similarly to terminological decision trees. However, instead of resorting to a refinement operator for producing partial solutions, the method exploits a set of pre-computed *selectors*, i.e. tests that are used to partition the set of individuals.

3   The Learning Problem

We consider knowledge bases (KBs) defined through representation languages adopted for the vocabularies in the Web of Data that can ultimately be mapped onto *Description Logics* (DLs) [1].

Basically, a KB can be regarded as a set $\mathcal{K} = \mathcal{T} \cup \mathcal{A}$ of inclusion axioms (in the *TBox* $\mathcal{T}$) in terms of *subsumption* ($\sqsubseteq$), and assertions (in the *ABox* $\mathcal{A}$) that describe, respectively, concepts (and relations) and individuals.

Given a limited set of training examples, i.e. individuals labeled with an intended membership w.r.t. a given target concept, the goal is to induce a function (*classification model* or *classifier*) that is able to predict the correct membership for further unseen individuals. More formally, the problem is:

Given:

- a knowledge base $\mathcal{K} = \mathcal{T} \cup \mathcal{A}$, with $\mathsf{Ind}(\mathcal{A})$ denoting the set of its individuals;
- a *target concept* C associated with an unknown classification function $f_C : \mathsf{Ind}(\mathcal{A}) \rightarrow \{+1, -1, 0\}$ such that, for each $a \in \mathsf{Ind}(\mathcal{A})$, the possible values (*labels*) correspond, respectively, to the cases $\mathcal{K} \models C(a)$, $\mathcal{K} \models \neg C(a)$, and uncertain membership (default);
- a set of classifiers, or *space of hypotheses*: $\mathcal{H} = \{h : \mathsf{Ind}(\mathcal{A}) \rightarrow \{+1, -1, 0\}\}$
- a *training set* $\mathbf{T} = \mathbf{Ps} \cup \mathbf{Ns} \cup \mathbf{Us}$ of examples, i.e. individual-label pairs, where each individual is associated with the unique known membership-label l for f_C, that corresponds to its intended classification (*ground truth*) w.r.t. C:
  - $\mathbf{Ps} = \{(a, +1) \mid a \in \mathsf{Ind}(\mathcal{A}),\ f_C(a) = +1\};$ *positive examples*
  - $\mathbf{Ns} = \{(b, -1) \mid b \in \mathsf{Ind}(\mathcal{A}),\ f_C(b) = -1\};$ *negative examples*
  - $\mathbf{Us} = \{(c, 0) \mid c \in \mathsf{Ind}(\mathcal{A}),\ f_C(c) = 0\}$ *uncertain-membership examples*

Learn: a classifier $H \in \mathcal{H}$ that minimizes the *empirical risk of error* $\hat{R}$ on $\mathbf{T}$:

$$H = \arg\min_{h \in \mathcal{H}} \hat{R}(h, \mathbf{T}) = \arg\min_{h \in \mathcal{H}} \frac{1}{n} \sum_{(x,l) \in \mathbf{T}} L(h(x), l)$$

where L is a *loss function* $L : \{-1, 0, +1\}^2 \rightarrow \mathbb{R}$, a cost function penalizing incorrect label assignments by the classifier. The accuracy of the induced classifier can be then assessed by measuring $\hat{R}(H, \mathbf{T}')$ on a separate *test set* $\mathbf{T}'$ of examples (i.e. $\mathbf{T} \cap \mathbf{T}' = \emptyset$).

Further constraints can be introduced on the set of solutions as preference criteria (e.g. specific loss functions or syntactic measures of complexity). Such constraints are aimed at avoiding hypotheses that overfit $\mathbf{T}$ remaining poorly predictive w.r.t. $\mathbf{T}'$ [4].

It is also important to note that the notion of negative example, say $(b, -1)$, corresponding to $\mathcal{K} \models \neg C(b)$, is stronger if compared to other settings, yet it is more coherent with the underlying open-world semantics that is adopted in the targeted setting. Other related approaches favour a weaker binary setting where positive and *non-positive* examples are considered, namely $\mathcal{K} \not\models C(b)$, which leads to targeting (extensionally) narrower concepts, hence classifiers that may turn out to be poorly predictive w.r.t. newly acquired instances as long as the KB population evolves.

Example 1 (simple problem). Given the following KB, suppose the goal is finding an hypothesis for classifying the individuals w.r.t. the concept Father.
$\mathcal{K} = \{$ Man $\sqsubseteq$ Person, Woman $\sqsubseteq$ Person, Artist $\sqsubseteq$ Person, Man $\sqsubseteq \neg$Woman$\} \cup$
      $\{$ Man(a), Man(b), Man(c), Woman(d), Woman(f), Artist(e), Robot(g),
        hasChild(a, d), hasChild$(b, e)\}$.
A training set $\mathbf{T}$ may include: $\mathbf{Ps} = \{a, b\}$ (instances of Man with a known child),
$\mathbf{Ns} = \{d, f\}$ (instances of Woman) and $\mathbf{Us} = \{c, e, g\}$.

4   Boosting a Concept Learner

In this section we present the proposed boosting-based framework. The framework is grounded on the application of a boosting-schema to concept learners. Specifically, boosting is used to create an ensemble classifier made up of class expressions. A *weak learner* is employed to find a single classifier (e.g. a rule, a clause or, as in our case, a single class expression), essentially by means of the same process used in the inner loops of the typical learning algorithms based on *sequential covering* (such as DL-FOIL or CELOE). The heuristics adopted to guide the construction of the classifier can be derived from the formal analysis of boosting-based learners.

4.1   Basics of Boosting

Boosting is a meta-learning method that is applicable to (weak) learners to get ensemble models that enhance the performance of the single classifiers. The original algorithm ADABOOST_M1 relies on a weak learner that is repeatedly invoked to get a series of *weak hypotheses* whose predictiveness is only required to be slightly better than random guessing. On each round, the weak learner generates a single classifier that determines changes in the distribution of the weights associated with the examples: the weights of misclassified examples get increased so that better classifiers can be produced in the next rounds knowing the harder examples to focus on. The weak hypotheses produced in various rounds are finally combined into a *strong hypothesis*, an ensemble that makes predictions via a majority vote procedure.

Algorithm 1. Generalized ADABOOST

1 **input** $\mathbf{T} = \{(e_i, l_i)\}_{i=1}^{N}$
2 **output** H: Hypothesis {*strong hypothesis*}
3 **for** $i = 1$ **to** N **do** $w_i^{(1)} = 1/N$ {*weight initialization*}
4 **for** $t = 1$ **to** T **do**   {*T is the number of iterations/hypotheses*}
5      $h_t \leftarrow$ WEAKLEARNER$(\mathbf{T}, \boldsymbol{w}^{(t)})$ {*next weak hypothesis*}
6   Choose $\alpha_t \in \mathbb{R}$
7   **for** $i = 1$ **to** N **do** $w_i^{(t+1)} \leftarrow w_i^{(t)} \exp(-\alpha_t l_i h_t(e_i))/Z_t$
8 $H \leftarrow \lambda x.\text{sign}\left(\sum_{i=1}^{T} \alpha_t h_t(x)\right)$
9 **return** H

A generalization of ADABOOST [16] produces models with a confidence value associated with each weak hypothesis that is used to weight their predictions (optionally even *declining* to vote/predict by assigning a null confidence to *uncovered* instances). The ensemble prediction takes into account the confidence values associated with each weak classifier. Formally, a set of examples $\mathbf{T} = \{(e_1, l_1), ..., (e_m, l_m)\}$ is given, where each instance e_i belongs to a domain $\mathbf{E}$ and each label l_i is in $\{-1, +1\}$. Also, a weak learning algorithm is assumed to require a distribution of weights $\boldsymbol{w}$ over the training examples (initially considered as uniform) indicating their *hardness*. In the generalized setting, the weak learner computes a weak hypothesis h_t of the form $h_t : \mathbf{E} \rightarrow \mathbb{R}$ where, given an instance x, the *sign* of $h_t(x)$ is interpreted as the predicted label while its *magnitude* $|h_t(x)|$ is interpreted as the amount of confidence in the prediction. The weak hypothesis may even abstain from predicting the label ($h_t(x) = 0$).

This boosting algorithm is described in Algorithm 1; here the constant Z_t ensures the normalization of each $\boldsymbol{w}^{(\cdot)}$ and parameter α_t depends on the weak learner. The returned strong hypothesis is indicated as a lambda abstraction $\lambda x.\text{sign}(\cdot)$.

4.2   Learning Confidence-Rated Hypotheses in DL

In related settings [3,8] the targeted strong hypothesis H is a set of hypotheses (rules/clauses), each associated with a confidence value. A single *default hypothesis* is associated with a negative confidence (i.e., the case when a prediction cannot be made confidently). To classify an individual, the sum of the confidences of all hypotheses covering it is computed, then the prediction is made according to the sign of this sum.

Our solution deviates from these settings to address the presented *ternary* classification problems: the (unique) label l_i associated with each $e_i \in \text{Ind}(\mathcal{A})$ is selected from $\{+1, -1, 0\}$. The targeted strong hypothesis H is an ensemble of concepts (i.e. class expressions) C_t, each associated with a confidence c_t.

Example 2 (confidence-rated ensemble model). Given the learning problem in Example 1, an induced ensemble model H may be:
        {Person [0.4], ¬Woman [0.8], Person [0.5], ∃hasChild.⊤ [0.9]}.

Algorithm 2. DL Concept Learner Boosting: BOOST(WEAKLEARNER,**T**): M

---

1 **input** WEAKLEARNER: Learning Function
2   **T** $= \{(e_i, l_i)\}_{i=1,\ldots,N}$ { *training set* }
3 **output** M: Classification Model {*list of concepts with their confidence*}
4 **for** $i = 1$ **to** N **do** $w_i^{(1)} = 1/N$
5 **for** $t = 1$ **to** T **do**
6      $C_t \leftarrow$ WEAKLEARNER(**T**, $\boldsymbol{w}^{(t)}$) {*concept learner*}
7   Let $\hat{c}_t$ be computed as in Eq. (2), using $\hat{\alpha}_t$ and h_t based on C_t
8   **for each** $i = 1$ **to** N **do** $w_i' \leftarrow w_i^{(t)} \exp(-\hat{c}_t)$ {*weights update*}
9      $Z_t \leftarrow \sum_{i=1}^{N} w_i'$
10   **for each** $i = 1$ **to** N **do** $w_i^{(t+1)} \leftarrow w_i'/Z_t$ {*weights normalization*}
11 **return** $\{C_t \, [\hat{c}_t]\}_{t=1,\ldots,T}$

The algorithm will generate only concepts associated with a positive confidence – that is, classifiers that can predict a definite membership w.r.t. the target class. Moreover, an implicit *default classifier* can be associated with a negative confidence (i.e., the case when a classification cannot be predicted confidently).

Coverage. As a consequence of representing hypotheses as DL concepts (with their semantics), the notion of *coverage* has to differ from the standard settings for binary problems (based on instances that trigger rules), namely:

Definition 1 (coverage). *A positive, resp. negative, example x is covered by a concept C when $\mathcal{K} \models C(x)$, resp. $\mathcal{K} \models \neg C(x)$. An uncertain-membership example is covered by C when both $\mathcal{K} \not\models C(x)$ and $\mathcal{K} \not\models \neg C(x)$ hold.*

This new notion has an impact on the setting of the confidence values: a positive confidence is assigned to covered examples whereas a negative one is assigned to uncovered examples. Therefore, denoting with h_t the classifier h_t : $\mathbf{E} \rightarrow \{-1, 0, +1\}$, that predicts a label based on concept C_t along with the entailments in Definition 1, the confidence associated to C_t can be defined as follows:

$$c_t = -\alpha_t \cdot (-1)^{I(l_i, h_t(e_i))}$$

where $I(\cdot, \cdot)$ denotes the indicator function for the *identity relation* (returning 1 in case of identity and 0 otherwise).

Hence the sign of c_t corresponds to the cases of instances e_i that are covered/uncovered by C_t (alternatively, uncovered examples may be assigned to a null confidence by h_t, similarly to the original setting).

The resulting boosting procedure is shown as Algorithm 2. Essentially it creates a model as a list of class expressions together with their confidence. This representation can be regarded as a generalization of a *Disjunctive Normal Form* adopted by many DL concept learners. The model can be made more compact by merging equivalent concepts in a single hypothesis whose confidence sums up the related confidence values:

Example 3 (compacted ensemble model). An ensemble model derived from the one presented in Example 2 is: {Person [0.9], ¬Woman [0.8], ∃hasChild.⊤ [0.9]}.

Algorithm 3. Strong Classifier: CLASSIFY$(M, x) : l_x$

---

1 **input** $\{C_t \ [\hat{c}_t]\}_{t=1,\dots,T}$: Classification Model
2   x: Ind($\mathcal{A}$) {*query individual*}
3 **output** $l_x \in \{-1, 0, +1\}$ {*predicted label*}
4 **for each** $l \in \{-1, 0, +1\}$ **do** $s_l \leftarrow 0$
5 **for** $t = 1$ **to** T **do**
6   **if** $\mathcal{K} \models C_t(x)$ **do** $s_{+1} \leftarrow s_{+1} + \hat{c}_t$ {*i.e. when* $h_t(x) = +1$}
7   **else if** $\mathcal{K} \models \neg C_t(x)$ **do** $s_{-1} \leftarrow s_{-1} + \hat{c}_t$ {*i.e. when* $h_t(x) = -1$}
8   **else** $s_0 \leftarrow s_0 + \hat{c}_t$ {*i.e. when* $h_t(x) = 0$}
9 **return** $\underset{l \in \{-1,0,+1\}}{\text{argmax}} \ s_l$

This represents a *strong classifier* that is used for classifying unseen instances. The related procedure is illustrated in Algorithm 3. Note that, differently from the original binary setting, to get a ternary classifier, the confidence values are collected separately per each label, with 0 as default case. The final classification is decided with a majority vote.

Optimization. In Algorithm 2, w is normalized using Z_t, that depends on c_t:

$$Z_t = \sum_{i=1,\dots,N} w_i^{(t)} \exp(-c_t) = \sum_{i=1,\dots,N} w_i^{(t)} \exp\left(-\left(-\alpha_t \cdot (-1)^{I(l_i, h_t(e_i))}\right)\right) \quad (1)$$

It was shown [3,16] that to minimize the training error, on each round the weak learner should pick the h_t and α_t which lead to the *smallest* value of Z_t. Thus, given a generated C_t, its confidence c_t, based on α_t and h_t, should be set to minimize Z_t. To this purpose the sum can be split up separating covered from uncovered examples. This simplifies the arguments of the exponential assigning opposite signs to the confidence magnitude α_t:

$$Z_t = \sum_{\substack{i=1,\dots,N \\ I(l_i, h_t(e_i))=1}} w_i^{(t)} \exp(-\alpha_t) + \sum_{\substack{i=1,\dots,N \\ I(l_i, h_t(e_i))=0}} w_i^{(t)} \exp(+\alpha_t).$$

Now letting

$$W_c = \sum_{i \mid I(l_i, h_t(e_i))=1} w_i^{(t)} \quad \text{and} \quad W_u = \sum_{i \mid I(l_i, h_t(e_i))=0} w_i^{(t)},$$

it can be further simplified as follows:

$$Z_t = W_c \exp(-\alpha_t) + W_u \exp(+\alpha_t)$$

The value that minimizes Z_t, obtained solving $\frac{\partial}{\partial \alpha_t} Z_t = 0$, is $\alpha_t = \ln(W_c/W_u)/2$ or, equivalently [16], its approximation $\hat{\alpha}_t$ obtained adding a *smoothing factor* s^{-1}, with $s = 2N$:

$$\hat{\alpha}_t = 0.5 \ln[(W_c + 1/s)/(W_u + 1/s)]. \quad (2)$$

Then the *smoothed* confidence $\hat{c}_t$ of any hypothesis is bounded from above by $0.5\ln(s)$ [3]. The analysis also suggests an objective function to be used by the weak learner [16]. Plugging the value of α_t in the equation above:

$$Z_t = 1 - \left(\sqrt{W_c} - \sqrt{W_u} \right)^2 .$$

As noted in [3], a hypothesis h_t minimizes Z_t iff it maximizes $|\sqrt{W_c} - \sqrt{W_u}|$. Such a h_t may be negatively correlated with the coverage, hence its confidence c_t is negative. Considering only positively correlated hypotheses, the objective function to be maximized by the weak learner searching for a suitable C_t is:

$$\sqrt{W_c} - \sqrt{W_u}$$

These considerations will be taken into account in the definition of the score function exploited by the weak learners.

5   Designing a Simple and Fast Weak Learner

In principle, any algorithm could be exploited as a weak learner for the presented ensemble schema, provided that it can return a hypothesis, in the form of a concept or any alternative classifier, based on a set of weighted training examples.

Considering an algorithm that adopts a sequential covering approach for the construction of concepts, one can simply detach and adapt the inner loop for the construction of a disjunct to get a weak learner straightforwardly.

Essentially, it should be required that the underlying search heuristic is adapted to focus towards covering the examples in accordance with their weight distribution, that has to be provided as an additional argument. We will showcase how to make this customization adopting the DL-FOIL specializing routine.

5.1   wDLF: A Weak Learner Derived from DL-FOIL

The original DL-FOIL algorithm [6] features a main routine based on sequential covering that produces a disjunctive concept made up of conjunctive partial descriptions, computed by the specialization procedure, that cover as many positives as possible while iteratively ruling out all of the negative examples. Each conjunctive description is provided by a downward refinement operator traversing the search space driven by a heuristic. Candidate refinements are scored by means of a measure inspired to the *information gain* (see below).

While the role of the main routine is intended to be played by the boosting meta-algorithm, the specialization procedure can be reused as a weak learner, provided that its heuristic biases the search towards concept descriptions that cover especially those examples indicated by the weight distribution as *harder*.

Algorithm 4 illustrates the adapted algorithm wDLF, that can be passed as a WEAKLEARNER to the boosting schema. Similarly to the mentioned original procedure that performs a (greedy) heuristic search aiming at (good) specializations of a general description of the target concept, wDLF seeks for proper

---

Algorithm 4. The Weak Learner WDLF($\mathbf{T}, \boldsymbol{w}$): C

```
1  {constant values set according to the configuration}
2  const ε: ℝ {minimal score threshold}
3         N_S: ℕ {number of specializations to be generated}
4  input T = Ps ∪ Ns ∪ Us: training set {i.e. labeled individuals}
5         w: Distribution of the examples {weights}
6  output C: Concept {best in terms of score (otherwise default)}
7  best ← 0
8  C ← INIT(T) {e.g. start with ⊤}
9  repeat
10     for i = 1 to N_S
11         repeat
12             C_ρ ← GETRANDOMREFINEMENT(ρ, C)
13             if (∃(p, +1) ∈ Ps : 𝒦 ⊨ C_ρ(p)) then
14             score ← SCORING(C, C_ρ, T, w)
15             if (score > best) then
16                 C ← C_ρ
17                 best ← score
18         until (best > 0)    {weakened constraint w.r.t. the original algo.}
19 until (best > ε)
20 return C    {⊤ as default classifier}
```

---

refinements (i.e. non equivalent concepts in a descending path through the subsumption hierarchy). Starting with the initialization of C with a general concept, the algorithm generates N_S candidate refinements by repeatedly invoking GETRANDOMREFINEMENT. This function randomly selects a specialization C_ρ from the set of the refinements computed by the operator ρ applied to C (see [6] for more details). The resulting concept description must cover at least a positive example and yield a minimal score fixed with a threshold. Note that for speeding up the induction of a weak classifier, unlike the case original more complex routine employed by DL-FOIL, in wDLF the incorrect coverage of some negative or null-labeled examples may be tolerated.

5.2   Heuristics

The heuristic employed in [6] to guide the search for good candidate concepts as possible refinement of the current concept was a *gain* g computed as follows:

$$g(C, C') = p' \cdot \left[\log \frac{p'}{p' + n' + u'} - \log \frac{p}{p + n + u} \right]$$

where p', n' and u' represent, respectively, the numbers of positive, negative and uncertain-membership examples covered by the refinement C', and p, n and u stand for the corresponding numbers of examples covered by C.

Following the previous discussion on optimization, a different heuristic is introduced to take into account the weights distribution:

$$s(C, C', \mathbf{T}, \boldsymbol{w}) = \left(\sqrt{W_c(C')} - \sqrt{W_u(C')} \right) - \left(\sqrt{W_c(C)} - \sqrt{W_u(C)} \right)$$

where $W_c(\cdot)$ and $W_u(\cdot)$ for the concepts C and C' are computed as illustrated in Sect. 4.2. The differences regarding a previous concept can be stored in a data structure for future use to save some computation.

Table 1. Facts concerning the ontologies employed in the experiments

Ontology	Language	#concepts	#object props	#datatype props	#individuals
BioPAX	$\mathcal{ALCHF}(\mathbf{D})$	28	19	30	323
NTN	$\mathcal{SHIF}(\mathbf{D})$	47	27	8	724
HDisease	$\mathcal{SHIF}(\mathbf{D})$	1499	10	15	639
Financial	$\mathcal{ALCIF}$	60	17	0	1000
Geoskills	$\mathcal{SHIF}$	596	23	0	2532

6   Empirical Evaluation

This section illustrates the design and the outcomes of a comparative empirical evaluation aimed at assessing the effectiveness of a boosted weak learner[1] against both the weak learner (see Sect. 4) and full-fledged algorithms. Details concerning the design and outcomes are provided in the following.

6.1   Design and Setup of the Experiments

In order to assess the effectiveness of the compared systems, the quality of the classifiers induced by each of them was evaluated against a baseline of target concepts. To this purpose, we considered publicly available Web ontologies featuring different expressiveness, numbers of individuals and numbers of concepts/roles. The salient characteristics are summarized in Table 1.

Each ontology was considered for producing 15 artificial problems/target concepts and related training & test sets, generated according to the randomized procedure described in [6]. A target concept description per problem was generated by randomly picking concepts/roles from the respective signatures and combining them through basic DL concept constructors: union, conjunction, complement, universal or existential restriction. All the available individuals were labeled as positive, negative, or uncertain-membership examples per target concept via the instance-checking service offered by a reasoner[2]. Note that this procedure a concept is picked only when both positive and negative examples are available. To allow the repetition of the experiments, a seed value can be set in the configuration for the internal pseudo-random generator: 1 in this case.

We adopted the weak learner wDLF described in Algorithm 4 as a baseline and compared the proposed approach against the latest releases of DL-Foil [6] and Celoe [10], that are based on a sequential covering algorithm. In the configuration of both wDLF and DL-Foil, the maximum number of candidate specializations to be evaluated per turn is a required parameter (N_S). This value was empirically set to 20.

---

[1] The source code, the datasets, the ontologies and supplemental material are publicly available at: https://bitbucket.org/grizzo001/DLbooster/src/master/.

[2] JFact was used: http://jfact.sourceforge.net.

BOOST(wDLF), the boosted version of wDLF, required the maximal number of weak hypotheses (T in Algorithm 2) as an additional parameter. It was set to 10, as larger values were observed not to produce significant improvements of the performance of the resulting strong learners. Throughout the experiments the performance of the ensemble classifiers was not significantly influenced by the value of the hyper-parameter T. A preliminary analysis (*grid search*) had been carried out to find out a good value for T testing the following values: 2, 5, 10, 20, and 30. Thus the increase of performance of the resulting ensembles w.r.t. the baseline of $T = 1$ was assessed in terms of average accuracy. As a result $T = 10$ was recognized as a reasonable tradeoff between ensemble complexity (efficiency) and effectiveness over the various problems and datasets.

As regards CELOE, a proper tuning of the refinement operator was also required. In particular, the operator was configured so that it could return concept descriptions obtained through all the available concept constructors, possibly also using the datatype properties available in the ontologies. Another required parameter is the time-out used to stop the training phase. This value was set to 10 s (larger values were also preliminarily tested but they brought no significant improvement while slowing down the learning process).

For a deeper insight in the cases of incorrect coverage, the following performance indices have been measured (on the test sets):

match rate (M%) cases of test examples with correct coverage;

commission error rate (C%) cases of incorrect coverage of test examples with definite membership: opposite class predicted;

omission error rate (O%) cases of incorrect coverage of test examples with definite membership: the model was unable to predict the membership;

induction rate (I%): cases of test examples with unknown membership: the model predicted a definite membership.

The *.632 bootstrap* resampling method was adopted to assess estimates of these indices with 30 runs of the experiment per problem, randomly varying the partitions of the available examples in training and test sets.

6.2 Aggregate Results and Discussion

The experiments showed interesting results. As an analytic *per problem* presentation would require a lot of space (a total of 75 problems) we report in Table 2 the outcomes (and standard deviations) averaged over the 15 learning problems.

As expected, BOOST(wDLF) produced accurate ensemble classifiers that significantly outperformed those induced by the weak learner. The performance was also equal or slightly superior compared to DL-FOIL and significantly better than CELOE, which tended to produce very simple and poorly predictive definitions often made up of a single (complemented) concept which erroneously covered many negative examples (see the next section for some examples).

Table 2. Aggregate outcomes of the experiments (averages and standard deviations)

Dataset	Index	wDLF	Boost(wDLF)	DL-Foil	Celoe
BIOPAX	M%	71.38 ± 20.42	**96.05 ± 01.59**	95.73 ± 03.74	94.53 ± 01.17
	C%	11.69 ± 09.07	01.59 ± 01.33	**00.13 ± 00.20**	03.24 ± 00.85
	O%	14.67 ± 17.20	**00.00 ± 00.00**	01.90 ± 03.31	01.62 ± 00.38
	I%	02.26 ± 00.40	02.36 ± 00.33	02.23 ± 00.40	**00.61 ± 00.18**
NTN	M%	95.84 ± 03.04	**98.89 ± 02.14**	97.78 ± 05.05	97.41 ± 00.15
	C%	01.61 ± 01.51	**00.00 ± 00.00**	00.05 ± 00.07	**00.00 ± 00.00**
	O%	00.06 ± 00.18	01.11 ± 02.14	02.17 ± 05.00	**00.00 ± 00.00**
	I%	02.49 ± 02.15	**00.00 ± 00.00**	00.01 ± 00.01	02.59 ± 00.15
HDISEASE	M%	77.18 ± 02.47	**90.33 ± 00.98**	88.75 ± 01.09	88.08 ± 01.09
	C%	00.07 ± 00.14	02.80 ± 01.10	00.04 ± 00.10	**00.00 ± 00.00**
	O%	22.18 ± 02.58	**03.25 ± 00.14**	03.64 ± 01.30	07.69 ± 00.90
	I%	**00.00 ± 00.01**	03.62 ± 01.15	07.57 ± 01.42	04.23 ± 00.16
FINANCIAL	M%	75.27 ± 10.05	93.42 ± 00.87	**93.52 ± 01.02**	87.40 ± 04.74
	C%	13.63 ± 05.18	00.32 ± 00.23	**00.22 ± 00.21**	06.33 ± 04.33
	O%	04.03 ± 10.76	**00.00 ± 00.00**	**00.00 ± 00.00**	00.00 ± 00.01
	I%	07.06 ± 01.80	06.26 ± 00.75	06.26 ± 00.88	**06.26 ± 00.52**
GEOSKILLS	M%	72.16 ± 15.36	**84.15 ± 03.15**	82.60 ± 04.69	50.20 ± 02.31
	C%	17.47 ± 14.24	02.00 ± 01.35	**00.00 ± 00.00**	23.66 ± 02.61
	O%	07.86 ± 02.67	11.33 ± 02.46	13.33 ± 04.43	**01.34 ± 00.12**
	I%	**02.52 ± 02.32**	**02.52 ± 02.32**	04.07 ± 04.09	24.80 ± 00.89

The classifiers induced by Boost(wDLF) showed more stability (a limited standard deviation) than those learned by DL-Foil and also by wDLF. The latter showed a worse performance in the experiments with all the KBs but NTN. In particular, it proved to be very sensitive to the distribution of the training data and, like Celoe, tended to induce simple descriptions that ended up misclassifying many test individuals. While commission was mainly due to induced concepts not overlapping with the targets, thus leading to misclassify positives, the omission cases were due to the simplicity of the induced concepts that made it difficult to predict a definite membership. Consequently, the match rate was lower w.r.t. the experiments with DL-Foil. Boost(wDLF) showed that the results could be improved both over all of the learning problems and also over the various runs of the boostrap procedure, i.e. different choices of training and test sets. Also, with the ensemble models, omission cases were totally avoided in the experiments with BIOPAX, or limited (with NTN, HDISEASE).

This was likely due to weak classifiers based on concepts that favored the prediction of a definite membership representing the majority class in the training set. Due to this bias, a limited increase of the commission rate w.r.t. DL-Foil and Celoe was also observed in the experiments. In the experiments with NTN,

HDISEASE and GEOSKILLS a lower induction rate was observed with ensemble classifiers compared to the rate observed with other classifiers.

While the larger induction rate marked in the experiments with DL-FOIL were due to the approximation of target concepts with a large number of uncertain-membership individuals in the training/test sets, BOOST(wDLF)'s strong models favored the prediction of an uncertain membership. This resembles the *vanishing gradient*, a phenomenon that affects neural networks training: this basically implies that weak models are initially induced with a considerable decrease of the weights for the correctly covered examples, hence the subsequent models have a negligible effect on these weights. As a result, the ensemble model quickly converges towards a solution that is sufficiently correct w.r.t. the available instances.

While it may represent a downside for the predictiveness of the classifiers, this aspect can enhance the readability of the ensemble models compared to the lengthy concept descriptions sometimes produced by DL-FOIL to fit the data.

BIOPAX

- BOOST(wDLF): {utilityClass [0.82], entity [14E-5]}
- DL-FOIL: (catalysis ⊔ pathwayStep) ⊓ ¬openControlledVocabulary ⊓ ¬protein ⊓ ∀STRUCTURE.sequenceInterval
- CELOE: ¬sequence

NTN

- BOOST(wDLF): { Man [3.41], Man ⊓ ∀ knows.⊤ [3.63], Man ⊓ ∀ ethnicityOf.⊤ [3.63],
  Man ⊓ ∀ parentOf.⊤ [3.63], Man ⊓ ∀ hasEnemy.⊤ [3.63] }
- DL-FOIL: Man ⊓ ((CitizenshipAttribute ⊓ ∃locationOf.⊤) ⊔ ∀spouseOf.Woman)
- CELOE: Man

HDISEASE

- BOOST(wDLF): { Lab_Tests [2.72], ¬Urine_specific_gravity_Class [0.99],
  Abnormal_findings_on_examination_of_other_body_fluids_substances_and_tissues_without_diagnosis_Class [3.35],
  Abnormal_findings_in_specimens_from_respiratory_organs_and_thorax_Abnormal_immunological_findings_Class [3.13]}
- DL-FOIL: Abnorma_findings_on_examination_of_other_body_fluids_substances_and_tissues_without_diagnosis_Class
  ⊔ (Acute_abdomen_Class ⊓ ¬Toxoplasma_oculopathy)
  ⊓ ¬Pseudomonas_aeruginosa_mallei_pseudomallei_as_the_cause_of_diseases_classified_to_other_chapters_Class))
- CELOE: NOT_CIE_Disease

Fig. 1. Some ensembles produced in the experiments

6.3   Examples of Induced Ensembles

For a simple qualitative evaluation, Fig. 1 reports some ensembles produced in the experiments: concepts (to be interpreted disjunctively) together with their confidence. Note that in these ensembles, BOOST(wDFL) was only able to induce classifiers made up of concepts names. Extremely short descriptions (such as those produced by CELOE or single runs of wDFL) often yielded larger commission error rates as they risk to cover negative examples. A final remark concerns the confidence values: they may exceed 1 (e.g. see the cases of NTN and HDISEASE) also as a consequence of the compaction of the ensemble models.

7 Conclusions and Outlook

We presented a methodology for boosting concept learners trading the comprehensibility of the classification model for accurate ensemble classifiers. In particular, a constrained confidence boosting schema was have applied taking an adapted version of the inner specializing routine in DL-FOIL as a weak learner. The underlying heuristic was modified to produce candidate concepts focused on covering hard examples. We have compared the boosted version of the algorithm with the weak learner, the original DL-FOIL and CELOE from the DL-LEARNER suite. The experiments showed that BOOST(wDLF) is able to better approximate target concepts, especially those with particularly complex definitions (e.g. featuring many nested sub-concepts).

We plan to investigate the implications of the method on efficiency and scalability. In particular, we intend to integrate a strategy for the *dynamic selection* of the ensemble size, even adopting a validation set to estimate an optimal value to ensure a good predictiveness of the strong classifier.

Also, we may apply the boosting strategy in combination to weak learners that adopt approximated inference mechanisms, like those built upon OCEL available in DL-LEARNER [2]. Another direction regards the investigation of different ensemble schemas and the exploitation of the inherent parallelism using frameworks for distributed data processing, such as APACHE SPARK.

References

1. Baader, F., Calvanese, D., McGuinness, D.L., Nardi, D., Patel-Schneider, P.F. (eds.): The Description Logic Handbook: Theory, Implementation and Applications, 2nd edn. Cambridge University Press, Cambridge (2007)
2. Bühmann, L., Lehmann, J., Westphal, P.: DL-Learner - a framework for inductive learning on the Semantic Web. J. Web Sem. **39**, 15–24 (2016)
3. Cohen, W.W., Singer, Y.: A simple, fast, and effective rule learner. In: Hendler, J., Subramanian, D. (eds.) AAAI 1999/IAAI 1999, pp. 335–342. AAAI/MIT Press, Menlo Park (1999)
4. De Raedt, L.: Logical and Relational Learning. Springer, Heidelberg (2008). https://doi.org/10.1007/978-3-540-68856-3
5. Fanizzi, N.: Concept induction in Description Logics using information-theoretic heuristics. Int. J. Semantic Web Inf. Syst. **7**(2), 23–44 (2011)
6. Fanizzi, N., Rizzo, G., d'Amato, C., Esposito, F.: DLFoil: class expression learning revisited. In: Faron Zucker, C., Ghidini, C., Napoli, A., Toussaint, Y. (eds.) EKAW 2018. LNCS (LNAI), vol. 11313, pp. 98–113. Springer, Cham (2018). https://doi.org/10.1007/978-3-030-03667-6_7
7. Heath, T., Bizer, C.: Linked Data: Evolving the Web into a Global Data Space. Morgan & Claypool, San Rafael (2011)
8. Hoche, S., Wrobel, S.: Relational learning using constrained confidence-rated boosting. In: Rouveirol, C., Sebag, M. (eds.) ILP 2001. LNCS (LNAI), vol. 2157, pp. 51–64. Springer, Heidelberg (2001). https://doi.org/10.1007/3-540-44797-0_5
9. Iannone, L., Palmisano, I., Fanizzi, N.: An algorithm based on counterfactuals for concept learning in the Semantic Web. Appl. Intell. **26**(2), 139–159 (2007)

10. Lehmann, J., Auer, S., Bühmann, L., Tramp, S.: Class expression learning for ontology engineering. J. Web Sem. **9**, 71–81 (2011)
11. Melo, A., Völker, J., Paulheim, H.: Type prediction in noisy RDF knowledge bases using hierarchical multilabel classification with graph and latent features. Int. J. Artif. Intell. Tools **26**(2), 1–32 (2017)
12. Quinlan, J.R.: Boosting first-order learning. In: Arikawa, S., Sharma, A.K. (eds.) ALT 1996. LNCS, vol. 1160, pp. 143–155. Springer, Heidelberg (1996). https://doi.org/10.1007/3-540-61863-5_42
13. Rizzo, G., d'Amato, C., Fanizzi, N., Esposito, F.: Tree-based models for inductive classification on the web of data. J. Web Sem. **45**, 1–22 (2017)
14. Rizzo, G., Fanizzi, N., d'Amato, C., Esposito, F.: Approximate classification with web ontologies through evidential terminological trees and forests. Int. J. Approx. Reason. **92**, 340–362 (2018)
15. Rowe, M., Stankovic, M., Alani, H.: Who will follow whom? Exploiting semantics for link prediction in attention-information networks. In: Cudré-Mauroux, P., et al. (eds.) ISWC 2012. LNCS, vol. 7649, pp. 476–491. Springer, Heidelberg (2012). https://doi.org/10.1007/978-3-642-35176-1_30
16. Schapire, R.E., Singer, Y.: Improved boosting algorithms using confidence-rated predictions. Mach. Learn. **37**(3), 297–336 (1999)
17. Tran, A.C., Dietrich, J., Guesgen, H.W., Marsland, S.: Parallel symmetric class expression learning. J. Mach. Learn. Res. **18**, 64:1–64:34 (2017)
18. Tran, T., Ha, Q., Hoang, T., Nguyen, L.A., Nguyen, H.S.: Bisimulation-based concept learning in description logics. Fundam. Inform. **133**(2–3), 287–303 (2014)

Link Prediction in Knowledge Graphs with Concepts of Nearest Neighbours

Sébastien Ferré[✉]

Univ Rennes, CNRS, IRISA, Campus de Beaulieu, 35042 Rennes, France
ferre@irisa.fr

Abstract. The open nature of Knowledge Graphs (KG) often implies that they are incomplete. Link prediction consists in inferring new links between the entities of a KG based on existing links. Most existing approaches rely on the learning of latent feature vectors for the encoding of entities and relations. In general however, latent features cannot be easily interpreted. Rule-based approaches offer interpretability but a distinct ruleset must be learned for each relation, and computation time is difficult to control. We propose a new approach that does not need a training phase, and that can provide interpretable explanations for each inference. It relies on the computation of Concepts of Nearest Neighbours (CNN) to identify similar entities based on common graph patterns. Dempster-Shafer theory is then used to draw inferences from CNNs. We evaluate our approach on FB15k-237, a challenging benchmark for link prediction, where it gets competitive performance compared to existing approaches.

1 Introduction

There is a growing interest for knowledge graphs (KG) as a way to represent and share data on the Web. The Semantic Web [1] defines standards for representation (RDF), querying (SPARQL), and reasoning (RDFS, OWL), and thousands of open KGs are available: e.g., DBpedia, Wikidata (formerly Freebase), YAGO, WordNet. The open nature of KGs often implies that they are incomplete, and a lot of work have studied the use of machine learning techniques to complete them.

The task of *link prediction* [16] consists in predicting missing edges or missing parts of edges. Suppose that film *Avatar* is missing a director in the KG, one wants to predict it, i.e. identify it among all KG nodes. The idea is to find regularities in the existing knowledge, and to exploit them in order to rank the KG nodes. The higher the correct node is in the ranking, the better the prediction is. Link prediction was originally introduced for social networks with a single edge type (a single *relation*) [12], and was later extended to multi-relational data and applied to KGs [16]. Compared to supervised classification, link prediction faces several challenges. First, there are as many classification problems as there are

This research is supported by ANR project PEGASE (ANR-16-CE23-0011-08).

© Springer Nature Switzerland AG 2019
P. Hitzler et al. (Eds.): ESWC 2019, LNCS 11503, pp. 84–100, 2019.
https://doi.org/10.1007/978-3-030-21348-0_6

relations, which count in the hundreds or thousands in KGs. Second, for each relation, the number of "classes" is the number of different *entities* in the range of the relation, which typically counts in the thousands for relations like *spouse* or *birthPlace*. Third, some relations can be multi-valued, like the relation from films to actors.

In this paper, we report on first experimental results on a novel approach to link prediction based on *Concepts of Nearest Neighbours (CNN)*, which were introduced in [5], and applied to *query relaxation* in [6]. This approach is a symbolic form of the k-nearest neighbours where numerical distances are replaced by graph patterns that provide an intelligible representation of how similar two nodes are. Our hypothesis is that the partitioning of the KG nodes into CNNs (see Sect. 4) provides a valuable basis for different kinds of inference. We here focus on link prediction, i.e. the inference of the missing node of an incomplete edge. The contribution of this work is a novel approach to link prediction that has the following properties:

1. it is a form of *instance-based learning*, i.e. it has no training phase;
2. it is a *symbolic approach*, i.e. it can provide explanations for each inference;
3. it shows *competitive performance* on a challenging link prediction benchmark.

The rest of the paper is organized as follows. Section 2 discusses related work on link prediction. Section 3 contains preliminaries about knowledge graphs and queries. Section 4 recalls the definition of CNNs, and their efficient computation. Section 5 presents our method to perform link prediction, using CNNs and Dempster-Shafer theory. Section 6 reports positive experimental results on benchmark FB15k-237 and two other datasets. Finally, Sect. 7 concludes and sketches future work.

2 Related Work

Nickel *et al.* [16] have recently written a "review of relational machine learning for knowledge graphs", where link prediction is the main inference task. They identify two kinds of approaches that differ by the kind of model they use: *latent feature models*, and *graph feature models*. The former is by far the most studied one. Before going into the details, it is useful to set the vocabulary as it is used in the domain. Nodes are called *entities*, edge labels are called *relations*, and edges are *triples* (e_i, r_k, e_j), where e_i is the *head* entity, e_j is the *tail* entity, and r_k is the relation that links the head to the tail.

Latent feature models learn *embeddings* of entities and relations into low-dimensional vector spaces, and then make inferences about a triple (e_i, r_k, e_j) by combining the embeddings of the two entities and the embedding of the relation. The existing methods vary by how they learn the embeddings, and how they combine them. Those methods are based on a range of techniques including: matrix factorization, tensor factorization, neural networks, and gradient descent. For example, one of the first method for KGs, TransE [2], models a relation as a translation in the embedding space of entities, and scores a candidate triple according to the distance between the translated head and the tail. Bordes *et al.* also introduced two datasets, FB15k and WN18, respectively derived from Freebase and Wordnet, which became references in the evaluation of link prediction methods. Toutanova and Chen [19] however showed that a very simple method was able to outperform previous methods because of a flaw in the datasets: many test triples have their inverse among the training triples. They introduced a challenging subset of FB15k, called FB15k-237, where all inverse triples are removed. Lately, performance was significantly improved on FB15k-237 by using convolutional architectures to learn embeddings [18] or to combine them in scoring functions [4]. The task of link prediction has also been extended with the embedding model RAE to *multi-fold relations* (aka. n-ary relations) and to *instance reconstruction* where only one entity of an n-ary relation is known, and all other entities have to be inferred together [20]. In this work, we limit ourselves to binary relations.

Graph feature models, also called *observed feature models*, make inferences directly from the observed edges in the KG. Random walk inference [11] takes relation paths as features, and sets the feature values through random walks in the KG. The feature weights are learned by logistic regression for each target relation, and then used to score the candidate triples. The method has shown improvement over Horn clause generation with ILP (Inductive Logic Programming) [15]. AMIE+ [8] manages to generate such Horn clauses in a much more efficient way by designing new ILP algorithms tailored to KGs. They also introduce a novel rule measure that improves the inference precision under the Open World Assumption (OWA) that holds in KGs. Both methods offer the advantage to produce intelligible explanations for inferences, unlike the latent feature models. However, they require a distinct training phase for each of the hundreds to thousands of target relations, whereas the latent feature models are generally learned in one phase. A fine-grained evaluation [14] has shown that rule-based approaches are competitive with latent-based approaches, both in performance and in running time.

A key difference of our approach is that there is no training phase, and all the learning is done at inference time. It is therefore an instance-based approach rather than a model-based approach. Given an incomplete triple $(e_i, r_k, ?)$ we compute Concepts of Nearest Neighbours (CNN) from the observed features of head entity e_i, where CNNs have a representation equivalent to the bodies of AMIE+'s rules. From there, we infer a ranking of candidate entities for the tail of relation r_k. In fact, as r_k is not involved in the computation of CNNs, many target relations can be inferred at nearly the same cost as a single relation. Indeed the main cost is in the computation of CNNs, which is easily controlled because the computation algorithm is any-time.

3   Preliminaries

A *knowledge graph* (KG) is defined by a structure $K = \langle E, R, T \rangle$, where E is the set of nodes, also called *entities*, R is the set of edge labels, also called *relations*,

$$E = \{\,Charles, Diana, William, Harry, Kate, George, Charlotte, Louis, male, female\}$$
$$R = \{\,parent, spouse, sex\}$$
$$T = \{(\{\,William, Harry\}, parent, \{\,Charles, Diana\}),$$
$$(\{\,George, Charlotte, Louis\}, parent, \{\,William, Kate\}),$$
$$(\,Charles, spouse, Diana),(\,Diana, spouse, Charles),$$
$$(\,William, spouse, Kate),(\,Kate, spouse, William),$$
$$(\{\,Charles, William, Harry, George, Louis\}, sex, male),$$
$$(\{\,Diana, Kate, Charlotte\}, sex, female)\}$$

Fig. 1. Example knowledge graph describing part of the British royal family.

and $T \subseteq E \times R \times E$ is the set of directed and labelled edges, also called *triples*. Each triple (e_i, r_k, e_j) represents the fact that relation r_k relates entity e_i to entity e_j. This definition is very close to RDF graphs, where entities can be either URIs or literals (or blank nodes) and relations are URIs called properties. It is also equivalent to sets of logical facts, where entities are constants, and relations are binary predicates. As a running example, Fig. 1 defines a small KG describing (part of) the British royal family (where the notation $(\{a, b\}, r, \{c, d\})$ is an abbreviation for $(a, r, c), (a, r, d), (b, r, c), (b, r, d)$).

Queries based on *graph patterns* play a central role in our approach as they are used to characterize the CNNs, and can be used as explanations for inferences. There are two kinds of *query elements*: triple patterns and filters. A *triple pattern* $(x, r, y) \in V \times R \times V$ is similar to a triple but with variables (taken from V) in place of entities. A *filter* is a Boolean expression on variables and entities. We here only consider equalities between a variable and an entity: $x = e$. A *graph pattern* P is a set of query elements. Equality filters are equivalent to allowing entities in triple patterns. There are two advantages in their use: (1) simplifying the handling of triple patterns that have a single form (var-var) instead of four (var-var, entity-var, var-entity, entity-entity); (2) opening perspectives for richer filters (e.g., intervals of values: $x \in [a, b]$). A *query* $Q = (x_1, ..., x_n) \leftarrow P$ is the projection of a graph pattern on a subset of its variables. Such queries find a concrete form in SPARQL with syntax SELECT ?x1...?xn WHERE { *graph pattern* }. Queries can be seen as anonymous rules, i.e. rules like those in AMIE+ [8] but missing the relation in the head. For example, the query $Q_{ex} = (x, y) \leftarrow (x, parent, u), (u, parent, v), (y, parent, v), (y, sex, s), s = male$ retrieves all (person, uncle) pairs, i.e. all pairs (x, y) where y is a sibling of a parent of x, and is male.

We now define the *answer set* that is retrieved by a query. A *matching* of a pattern P on a KG $K = \langle E, R, T \rangle$ is a mapping μ from variables in P to entities in E such that $\mu(t) \in T$ for every triple pattern $t \in P$, and $\mu(f)$ evaluates to true for every filter $f \in P$, where $\mu(t)$ and $\mu(f)$ are obtained from t and f by replacing every variable x by $\mu(x)$. In the example KG, a possible matching for the pattern of the above query is $\mu_{ex} = \{x \mapsto Charlotte, y \mapsto Harry, u \mapsto William, v \mapsto Diana, s \mapsto male\}$. A matching is therefore a homomorphism from the pattern to the graph. Term "matching" is taken from the evaluation of SPARQL queries. In logics, terms "grounding" and "instantiation" are used instead. The *answer set* $ans(Q, K)$ of a query $Q = (x_1, ..., x_n) \leftarrow P$ is the set of tuples $(\mu(x_1), ..., \mu(x_n))$ for every matching μ of P on K. In the running example, the pair $(Charlotte, Harry)$ is therefore an answer of query Q_{ex}. Note that several matchings can lead to a same answer, and that duplicate answers are ignored. In the following, we only consider queries with a single projected variable, whose sets of answers are assimilated to sets of entities.

4   Concepts of Nearest Neighbours (CNN)

In this section, we shortly recall the theoretical definitions underlying Concepts of Nearest Neighbours (CNN), as well as the algorithmic and practical aspects of computing their approximation under a given timeout. Further details are available in [5,6]. In the following definitions, we assume a knowledge graph $K = \langle E, R, T \rangle$.

4.1   Theoretical Definitions

Definition 1. *A* graph concept *is defined as a pair $C = (A, Q)$, where A is a set of entities and Q is a query such that $A = ans(Q)$ is the set of answers of Q, and $Q = msq(A)$ is the most specific query that verifies $A = ans(Q)$. A is called the* extension $ext(C)$ *of the concept, and Q is called the* intension $int(C)$ *of the concept.*

That most specific query $Q = msq(A)$ represents what the neighborhood of entities in A have in common. It is well-defined under graph homomorphism (unlike under subgraph isomorphism). It can be computed from A by using the categorical product of graphs (see PGP intersection $\cap_q$ in [7]), or equivalently Plotkin's anti-unification of sets of facts [17]. In the example KG, William and Charlotte have in common the following query that says that they have married parents: $Q_{WC} = x \leftarrow (x, sex, s), (x, parent, y), (y, sex, t), t = male, (x, parent, z), (z, sex, u), u = female, (y, spouse, z), (z, spouse, y)$. We have $A_{WC} = ans(Q_{WC}) = \{William, Harry, George, Charlotte, Louis\}$ so that $C_{WC} = (A_{WC}, Q_{WC})$ is a graph concept. A concept $C_1 = (A_1, Q_1)$ is more specific than a concept $C_2 = (A_2, Q_2)$, in notation $C_1 \leq C_2$, if $A_1 \subseteq A_2$. For example, by adding filter $y = William$ to the previous example, we get a more specific concept whose extension is $\{George, Charlotte, Louis\}$.

Definition 2. *Let $e_1, e_2 \in E$ be two entities. The* conceptual distance $\delta(e_1, e_2)$ *between e_1 and e_2 is the most specific graph concept whose extension contains both entities, i.e. $\delta(e_1, e_2) = (A, Q)$ with $Q = msq(\{e_1, e_2\})$, $A = ans(Q)$.*

For example, the above concept C_{WC} is the conceptual distance between William and Charlotte. The "distance values" have therefore a symbolic representation through the concept intension Q that represents what the two entities have in common. The concept extension A contains in addition to the two entities all entities e_3 that match the common query ($e_3 \in ans(Q)$). Such an entity e_3

can be seen as "between" e_1 and e_2: in formulas, for all $e_3 \in ext(\delta(e_1, e_2))$, $\delta(e_1, e_3) \leq \delta(e_1, e_2)$ and $\delta(e_3, e_2) \leq \delta(e_1, e_2)$. Note that order $\leq$ on conceptual distances is a partial ordering, unlike classical distance measures. A numerical distance $dist(e_1, e_2) = |ext(\delta(e_1, e_2))|$ can be derived from the size of the concept extension, because the closer e_1 and e_2 are, the more specific their conceptual distance and the smaller the extension. Dually, a numerical similarity $sim(e_1, e_2) = |int(\delta(e_1, e_2))|$ can be derived from the size of the concept intension (number of query elements), because the more similar e_1 and e_2 are, the more specific their conceptual distance and the larger the intension. For example, between William and Charlotte, the numerical distance is 5 and the numerical similarity is 9.

Definition 3. *Let $e \in E$ be an entity. A* Concept of Nearest Neighbours (CNN) *of e is a pair (S_l, δ_l) where S_l is the non-empty set of entities that are at the same conceptual distance δ_l from e. Therefore, a CNN verifies $S_l = \{e' \in E \mid \delta(e, e') = \delta_l\} \neq \emptyset$. It also verifies $S_l \subseteq ext(\delta_l)$, and S_l is called the* proper extension *of the CNN. We note $CNN(e, K)$ the collection of all CNNs of e in knowledge graph K.*

Here are the 6 CNNs of Charlotte in the running example.

l	S_l	$|ext(\delta_l)|$	$int(\delta_l)$	$\{l' \mid \delta_{l'} \leq \delta_l\}$
1	$\{Charlotte\}$	1	$x \leftarrow x = Charlotte$	-
2	$\{Diana, Kate\}$	3	$x \leftarrow (x, sex, s), s = female$	1
3	$\{George, Louis\}$	3	$x \leftarrow (x, sex, s), (x, parent, y), y = William, ...$	1
4	$\{William, Harry\}$	5	$x \leftarrow (x, sex, s), (x, parent, y), ...$	1, 3
5	$\{Charles\}$	8	$x \leftarrow (x, sex, s)$	1, 2, 3, 4
6	$\{male, female\}$	10	$x \leftarrow \emptyset$	1, 2, 3, 4, 5

The proper extensions of $CNN(e, K)$ define a partition over the set of entities E, where two entities are in the same cluster S_l if they are at the same conceptual distance to entity e. The intension of the associated graph concept δ_l provides a symbolic representation of the distance/similarity between every $e' \in S_l$ and e. The partial ordering over CNNs means that some CNNs are closer to e than others. As such, each CNN can be seen as a cluster of nearest neighbours of e, where the size of the extension of δ_l can used as a numerical distance.

Discussion. Given that $CNN(e, K)$ partitions the set of entities, the number of CNNs can only be smaller or equal to the number of entities, and in practice it is generally much smaller. This is interesting because, in comparison, the number of graph concepts is exponential in the number of entities in the worst case. Note that the search space of ILP approaches like AMIE+ is the set of queries, which is even larger than the set of all graph concepts. Computing the CNNs for a given entity is therefore a much more tractable task than mining frequent patterns or learning rules, although the space of representations is the same.

The pending questions that we start studying in this paper is whether those CNNs are useful for inference, and how they compare to other approaches.

Compared to the use of numerical measures, like commonly done in k-nearest neighbours approaches, CNNs define a more subtle ordering of entities. First, because conceptual distances are only partially ordered, it can be that among two entities none is more similar than the other to the chosen entity e. This reflects the fact that there can be several ways to be similar to something, without necessarily a preferred one. For instance, which is most similar to Charlotte? Diana because she is also a female (CNN S_2) or George because he is also a son of William (CNN S_3)? Second, because conceptual distances partition the set of entities, it can be that two entities are at the exact same distance, and are therefore undistinguishable in terms of similarity (ex. George and Louis in CNN S_3). Third, the concept intension provides an intelligible explanation of the similarity to the chosen entity.

4.2   Algorithmic and Practical Aspects

We here sketch the algorithmic and practical aspects of computing the set $CNN(e, K)$ of concepts of nearest neighbours of query entity e in a knowledge graph K. More details are available in [6]. The core principle of the algorithm is to iteratively refine a partition $\{S_l\}_l$ of the set of entities, in order to get an increasingly accurate partition converging to the partition induced by the proper extensions of CNNs. Each cluster S_l is associated to a query $Q_l = x \leftarrow P_l$, and a set of candidate query elements H_l. The relationship to CNNs is that when H_l is empty, (S_l, δ_l) with $\delta_l = (ans(Q_l), Q_l)$ is a CNN, i.e. S_l is the proper extension of a CNN whose conceptual distance has intension Q_l. When H_l is not empty, S_l may be an union of several proper extensions (lack of discrimination), and Q_l is not necessarily the most specific query that matches all entities in S_l (lack of precision in the conceptual similarity). In that case, one gets overestimates of conceptual distances for some entities in S_l.

Initially, there is a single cluster $S_0 = E$ with P_0 being the empty pattern, and H_0 being the *description* of e. The description of an entity e is a graph pattern that is obtained by extracting a subgraph around e and, for each entity e_i in the subgraph, by replacing e_i by a variable y_i, and by adding filter $y_i = e_i$. Here, we choose to extract the subgraph that contains all edges starting from e up to some depth.

Then at each iteration, any cluster S – with pattern P and set of candidate query elements H – is split in two clusters S_1, S_0 by using an element $h \in H$ as a discriminating feature. Element h must be chosen so that $P \cup \{h\}$ defines a connected pattern including variable x. In this work, this element is chosen so as to have a trade-off between depth-first and breadth-first exploration of the description of e but many other strategies are possible. The new clusters are defined as follows:

$$P_1 = P \cup \{h\} \qquad S_1 = S \cap ans(Q_1 = x \leftarrow P_1, K) \qquad H_1 = H \setminus \{h\}$$
$$P_0 = P \qquad\qquad S_0 = S \setminus S_1 \qquad\qquad\qquad H_0 = H \setminus \{h\}$$

The equations for S_1, S_0 ensure that after each split there is still a partition, possibly a more accurate one. The empty clusters ($S_i = \emptyset$) are removed from the partition. As a consequence, although the search space is the set of subgraphs of the description of e, which has a size exponential in the size of the description, the number of clusters remains below the number of entities at all time. In the running example, the initial cluster S_{1-6} (the union of clusters S_1 to S_6) is split with element $x = Charlotte$ into S_1 and S_{2-6}. Then cluster S_{2-6} is split with element (x, sex, s) into S_{2-5} and S_6. Then cluster S_{2-5} is split with element $s = female$ into S_2 and S_{3-5}. Next splits involve elements $(x, parent, y)$ and $y = William$ on S_{3-5}.

Discussion. The above algorithm terminates because the set H decreases at each split. However, in the case of large descriptions or large knowledge graphs, it can still take a long time. Runtime is easily controlled with a timeout because the algorithm is anytime. Indeed it can output a partition of entities at any time, along with an overestimate of conceptual distance for each cluster. Previous experiments indicate that the algorithm has the good property to output more than half of the concepts in a small proportion of the total runtime.

Actually, the above algorithm converges to an approximation of the CNNs, in the sense that the conceptual distance may be still be an overestimate at full runtime for some entities. This is because graph patterns are constrained to be subsets of the description of e. In order to get exact results, the duplication of variables and their adjacent edges should be allowed, which would considerably increase the search space.

Experiments on KGs with up to a million triples have shown that the algorithm can compute all CNNs for descriptions of hundreds of edges in a matter of seconds or minutes. In contrast, query relaxation does not scale beyond 3 relaxation steps, which is insufficient to identify similar entities in most cases; and computing pairwise symbolic similarities does not scale to large numbers of entities. A key ingredient of the efficiency of the algorithm also lies in a notion of *lazy join* for the computation of answer sets of queries. In short, the principle is to avoid the enumeration of all matchings of a query pattern by computing joins only as much as necessary to compute the set of query answers (see details in [6]).

5 Link Prediction

The problem of *link prediction* is to infer a missing entity in a triple (e_i, r_k, e_j), i.e. either infer the tail from the head and the relation, or infer the head from the tail and the relation. Because of the symmetry of the two problems, we only describe here the inference of the tail entity. In the following, we therefore consider e_i and r_k as fixed (we avoid them in indices), and e_j as variable. Our approach to link prediction is inspired by the work of Denœux [3], and adapted to our Concepts of Nearest Neighbours (CNNs). Denoeux defines a k-NN classification rule based on Dempster-Shafer (D-S) theory. Each k-nearest neighbour x_l of an instance to be classified x is used as a piece of evidence that supports the fact that x belongs to the class c_l of x_l. The degree of support is defined as a function of the distance between x and x_l, in such a way that the choice of k is less sensitive so that large values of k can be chosen. D-S theory enables to combine the k pieces of evidence into a global evidence, and to define a measure of *belief* for each class.

We adapt Denoeux's work to the inference of e_j in triple (e_i, r_k, e_j) in the following way. Given a computed partition of entities $\{(S_l, Q_l)$ with $Q_l = x \leftarrow P_l)\}_l$, as an approximation of $CNN(e_i, K)$, each cluster (S_l, Q_l) is used as a piece of evidence for the inference of the tail entity e_j relative to relation r_k. The degree of support depends on the *extensional distance* d_l between e_i and entities in S_l,

$$d_l = |ans(Q_l)|,$$

i.e. the number of answers of query Q_l, and on the *confidence* $\phi_{l,j}$ of the association rule $(x, r_k, e_j) \leftarrow P_l$, which is defined as

$$\phi_{l,j} = \frac{|ans(x \leftarrow P_l \cup \{(x, r_k, e_j)\})|}{|ans(Q_l)|},$$

i.e. the proportion of entities among the answers of Q_l that have an r_k-link to entity e_j. Because in KGs a head entity can be linked to several tail entities through the same relation, we consider a distinct classification problem for each candidate tail entity $e_j \in E$ with two classes c_j^1 (e_j is a tail entity) and c_j^0 (e_j is not a tail entity). For each cluster S_l and each candidate tail entity $e_j \in E$, the degree of support can therefore be formalized by defining a mass distribution $m_{l,j}$ over sets of classes as follows.

$$m_{l,j}(\{c_j^1\}) = \alpha_0 \, \phi_{l,j} \, e^{-d_l} \qquad m_{l,j}(\{c_j^0\}) = 0 \qquad m_{l,j}(\{c_j^1, c_j^0\}) = 1 - \alpha_0 \, \phi_{l,j} \, e^{-d_l}$$

$m_{l,j}(\{c_j^1\})$ represents the degree of belief for e_j being the tail entity, while $m_{l,j}(\{c_j^1, c_j^0\})$ represents the degree of uncertainty. $m_{l,j}(\{c_j^0\})$ is set to 0 to reflect the OWA (Open World Assumption) of KGs according to which a missing fact is not considered as false. Constant α_0 determines the maximum degree of belief, which can be lower than 1 to reflect uncertainty about known triples (e.g. 0.95). The degree of belief decreases exponentially with distance. Finally, we make the degree of belief proportional to the confidence of inferring entity e_j from Q_l. In [3], that confidence factor does not exist because it would be 1 for the class of the nearest neighbour, and 0 for every other class.

The Dempster's rule is then used to combine the evidence from all clusters of our partition $\{(S_1, Q_1), \ldots, (S_L, Q_L)\}$. It states that the joint mass distribution is defined for every non-empty set of classes $\emptyset \neq C \subseteq \{c_j^1, c_j^0\}$ by

$$m_j(C) = \frac{\sum_{C_1 \cap \ldots \cap C_L = C} m_{1,j}(C_1) \ldots m_{L,j}(C_L)}{1 - \sum_{C_1 \cap \ldots \cap C_L = \emptyset} m_{1,j}(C_1) \ldots m_{L,j}(C_L)}$$

Because $m_{l,j}(\{c_j^0\}) = 0$ for all l, j, it follows that the denominator equals 1, and $m_j(\{c_j^0\}) = 0$, and hence $m_j(\{c_j^1\}) = 1 - m_j(\{c_j^1, c_j^0\})$. Then, for $C = \{c_j^1, c_j^0\}$,

$C = C_1 \cap \ldots \cap C_L$ implies that $C_1 = \ldots = C_L = C$, and hence $m_j(\{c_j^1, c_j^0\}) = \prod_{l \in 1..L} m_{l,j}(\{c_j^1, c_j^0\})$. Finally, we arrive at the following equation for the belief of each candidate tail entity e_j.

$$Bel_j = m_j(\{c_j^1\}) = 1 - \prod_{l \in 1..L} (1 - \alpha_0 \, \phi_{l,j} \, e^{-d_l})$$

From the belief of each entity e_j, we can rank the entities by decreasing belief. Then, rankings of entities can be evaluated with measures such as Hits@N (the proportion of inference tasks where the correct tail entity appears in the first N entities) and MRR (Mean Reciprocal Rank, the average of the inverse of the rank of the correct entity).

Note that the above method can easily be generalized to the joint inference of the relation r_k and the tail entity e_j. It suffices to use indices k, j everywhere index j is used: $\phi_{l,k,j}$ would be the confidence of inferring relation r_k and tail entity e_j from Q_l, $c_{k,j}^1$ would be the class of entities linked to e_j through r_k, and $Bel_{k,j}$ would be the belief of inferring such a link.

6   Experiments

We here report on experiments comparing our approach to other approaches on several datasets. We first present the methodology, then we report the main performance results before an in-depth analysis, and examples of inferences and explanations. The companion page[1] provides links to the source code, the datasets, and the output logs.

6.1   Methodology

Datasets. We use three datasets to evaluate our approach. Table 1 provides statistics about them (numbers of entities, relations, train edges, validation edges (if any), and test edges). The main dataset is FB15k-237, introduced by Toutanova and Chen [19] as a challenging subset of dataset FB15k, which was formerly introduced by Bordes et al. [2] for link prediction evaluation. It is a set of triples derived from the Freebase KG. FB15k-237 is more challenging than FB15k because relations that are almost equivalent to another relation or to the

Table 1. Statistics of datasets.

Dataset	Entities	Relations	Train edges	Valid. edges	Test edges
FB15k-237	15,541	237	272,115	17,535	20,466
JF17k	28,645	322	171,559	-	66,615
Mondial	2,473	20	7,979	778	970

---

[1] Companion page: http://www.irisa.fr/LIS/ferre/pub/link_prediction/.

inverse of another relation have been removed, and because (head, tail) entity pairs that exist in the train dataset have been removed from the validation and test datasets to avoid potential trivial inferences. The dataset also comes with textual mentions but we ignore them as we focus on knowledge graphs. The two other datasets are used to complement and confirm results. JF17k is another dataset extracted from Freebase, introduced by [10] and available at http:// github.com/lijp12/SIR. Although it was designed to go beyond binary relations, we here only consider binary relations, letting n-ary relations to future work. We introduce Mondial as a subset of the Mondial database [13], which contains facts about world geography. We simplified it to the task of link prediction by removing labelling edges and edges containing dates and numbers, and by unreifying n-ary relations. It is available from the companion page.

Task. We follow the same protocol as introduced in [2], and followed by subsequent work. The task is to infer, for each test triple, the tail entity from the head and the relation, and also the head entity from the tail and the relation. We call *test entity* the known entity, and *missing entity* the entity to be inferred. We evaluate the performance of our approach by using the same four measures as in [18]: MRR and Hits@{1,3,10}. Like in previous work, we use filtered versions of those measures to reflect the fact that, for instance, there may be several correct tail entities for a 1-N relation (e.g., the relation from awards to nominees). For example, if the correct entity is at rank 7 but 2 out of the first 6 entities form triples that belong to the dataset (and are therefore considered as valid), then it is considered to be at rank 5.

Method. Because our approach has no training phase we can use both train and validation datasets as examples for our instance-based inference. Our approach has only two (hyper-)parameters (and no parameter to learn) for the computation of CNNs: the *depth* of the description of the test entity, and the *timeout* (i.e. the allocated computation time). We study the sensitivity to those parameters. For the inference of a ranking of entities, we set $\alpha_0 = 0.95$ and use all computed CNNs (no selection of the k-nearest CNNs). The implementation of our approach has been integrated to SEWELIS as an improvement of previous work on the guided edition of RDF graphs [9]. A standalone program for link prediction is available from the companion page. We ran our experiments on Fedora 25, with CPU Intel(R) Core(TM) i7-6600U @ 2.60 GHz, and 16 GB DDR4 memory. So far, our implementation is simple and uses a single core, although our algorithm lends itself to parallelization. We have observed that in all our experiments the memory footprint remains under 1.5%, i.e. about 240 Mb.

Baselines. We compare our approach to latent-based approaches by choosing the same tasks and measures as in previous work because it was not possible for us to run them ourselves (no access to a GPU), and also because it allows for a fairer comparison (e.g., choice of hyper-parameters by authors). On FB15k-237, we use results from [4,18] to compare with TransE, DistMult, HolE, ComplEx, R-GCN, and ConvE. On JF17k, we use results from [20] to compare with mTransH and RAE. We also compare our approach to a rule-based approach,

Table 2. Results on FB15k-237 for *Freq*, latent-based approaches (TransE, DistMult, HolE, ComplEx, R-GCN, ConvE), a rule-based approach (AMIE+), and our approach (CNN) with three timeouts (0.01 s, 0.1 s, 1 s): *-results are from [18], **-results are from [4].

Approach	MRR	Hits@1	Hits@3	Hits@10
Freq	.236	.175	.253	.356
AMIE+	.143	.096	.155	.241
(from [14])	-	.174	-	.409
DistMult*	.191	.106	.207	.376
ComplEx*	.201	.112	.213	.388
HolE*	.222	.133	.253	.391
TransE*	.233	.147	.263	.398
R-GCN*	.248	.153	.258	.414
ConvE**	.325	.237	.356	.501
CNN 0.01s (ours)	.250	.186	.268	.377
CNN 0.1s (ours)	.264	.198	.284	.395
CNN 1s (ours)	.286	.215	.311	.428

AMIE+, which we ran with its default parameters[2]. As suggested by AMIE+'s authors (equation 8, [8]), we ranked entities e_j by aggregating their *PCA confidence* $\phi_{l,j}$ of each rule R_l that enables to infer triple (e_i, r_k, e_j): $\phi_j = 1 - \prod_l (1 - \phi_{l,j})$. We also report better results on FB15k-237 from [14], although we were not able to reproduce them. We add yet another baseline Freq that simply consists in ranking entities e_j according to their decreasing frequency of usage in r_k over the train+valid dataset, as defined by $freq_j = |ans(x \leftarrow (x, r_k, y), y = e_j)|$. It is independent of the test entity, and therefore acts as a default ranking.

6.2 Results

Table 2 compares the results of our approach (CNN) to other approaches presented above as baselines on dataset FB15k-237. CNN was run with timeouts that are compatible with user interaction (0.01 s, 0.1 s, 1 s), and description depth 10, which ensures that most if not all relevant graph features of the test entity are captured. The output logs of CNN predictions and explanations is available from the companion page. Except for ConvE that outperforms other approaches on FB15k-237, CNN outperforms all other approaches as soon as 0.01 s for the fine-grain measures (MRR, Hits@1, Hits@3), and as soon as 1 s for measure Hits@10. CNN-1s reaches MRR = 0.286, halfway between the two other best approaches, R-GCN (−3.8%) and ConvE (+3.9%).

It can also be observed that CNN outperforms the simple Freq baseline on all measures and for all timeouts, which implies that it learns something useful beyond global statistics. Note that this is not the case of other approaches except

---

[2] We also ran it with advanced parameters on a 8-core server under AMIE+'s authors guidance. That led to many more rules but did not improve the results.

Table 3. Results on JF17k and Mondial for baseline *Freq*, two latent-based approaches (mTransH, RAE), a rule-based approach (AMIE+), and our approach (CNN, timeout = 0.1 s). Results marked with * are from [20].

Approach	JF17k				Mondial			
	MRR	Hits@1	Hits@3	Hits@10	MRR	Hits@1	Hits@3	Hits@10
Freq	*.234*	*.170*	*.252*	*.355*	*.142*	*.069*	*.159*	*.309*
mTransH*	-	-	-	.497	-	-	-	-
RAE*	-	-	-	.504	-	-	-	-
AMIE+	.211	.139	.252	.360	.179	.127	.208	.281
CNN 0.1 s (ours)	.409	.334	.440	**.556**	.327	.271	.355	.433

Table 4. Results on FB15k-237 of CNN (depth = 10, timeout = 1 s) for all prediction tasks, for predicting tails only, and for predicting heads only.

predicting	MRR	Hits@1	Hits@3	Hits@10
all	.286	.215	.311	.428
tails	.391	.307	.428	.553
heads	.182	.123	.194	.303

ConvE, especially for fine-grain measures, MRR and Hits@1. Apart from CNN and ConvE, none improves Hits@1 over Freq.

Those positive results are confirmed on the two other datasets, as far as results are available (see Table 3). CNN results are significantly higher than Freq and AMIE+ in both datasets and for all measures, by an MRR margin of 17.5% on JF17k and 14.8% on Mondial. On JF17k, CNN also outperforms the latent-based approach RAE by a margin of 5.2% with measure Hits@10 = 0.556. Given that our approach tends to be better at fine-grain measures, as shown on FB15k-237, the latter result is very encouraging. Indeed, CNN's first ranked entity is correct 33% of the time on JF17k, which makes its predictions really effective.

6.3   In-Depth Analysis

Predicting Heads vs Tails. Table 4 details the results of CNN on FB15k-237, distinguishing between predicting tails and heads. It shows clearly that it is much easier to predict tails than heads. This is not surprising given that, in KGs, relations are generally oriented in the more deterministic direction. For example, the relation between films and genres is oriented from films to genres because each film has only one or a few genres, while for each genre there are many films. This behaviour is even stronger in Mondial (MRR-all = 0.327, MRR-tails = 0.584, MRR-heads = 0.057) but very small in JF17k (±0.004). The latter can be explained by the fact that binary relationships are derived from n-ary relations, and therefore do not have a privileged orientation.

Table 5. Results of tail prediction for some of the most frequent relations in FB15k-237. #heads (resp. #tails) is the number of unique heads (resp. tails) for that relation. The MRR of baseline Freq is also included for comparison.

Relation	#heads	#tails	MRR_{Freq}	MRR	Hits@1	Hits@3	Hits@10
profession	4245	150	.434	.601	.455	.694	.874
gender	4094	2	.882	.899	.798	1	1
nationality	4068	100	.720	.772	.662	.866	.941
award	3386	406	.080	.270	.154	.296	.511
type_of_union	3033	4	.971	.971	.942	1	1
place_of_birth	2613	704	.155	.183	.100	.235	.359
place_lived	2519	804	.172	.194	.108	.239	.344
film/genre	1875	123	.315	.380	.226	.429	.711
film/language	1735	59	.744	.759	.688	.790	.911
film/country	1708	61	.685	.701	.573	.809	.931

Table 6. Evolution of the number of concepts, the maximum belief, and MRR as a function of timeout on FB15k-237 (depth = 1).

Timeout	#concepts	max. belief	MRR
0.01	11.8	.467	.235
0.1	49.1	.795	.264
1	219.6	.943	.286

Results Per Relation. Table 5 details the results further for a selection of 10 of the most frequent relations in dataset FB15k-237, only considering tail prediction. In order to give an idea of the difficulty to predict tails for each relation, we give the number of unique heads and tails in the train+valid dataset, as well as the MRR for baseline *Freq*. The results show that MRR is significantly increased with our approach for all relations, except *type_of_union* whose baseline MRR is already very high at .971. For half of the relations, Hits@1 is greater than .5, which means that predicting the first entity would be more than 50% correct. This includes properties with large numbers of tails, e.g. relation *nationality* has 100 unique tails and Hits@1 = .668. In Mondial, the best predicted relations are the continent of a country, the category of a volcano or island, the neighbour sea/ocean of a place, the archipelago of an island or the range of a mountain, with MRR all above 0.500.

Influence of Timeout. Table 6 shows the influence of timeout on the resulting MRR, and also on the number of computed concepts and on the maximal belief achieved for predicted entities. It can be observed that with only 1% of the largest timeout, the MRR is already at 82% of the largest MRR, despite the fact that only 5% of the concepts have been computed. This indicates that early approximations of concepts of nearest neighbours are already informative. Furthermore, improving the approximation with more concepts does not only improve MRR but also increases confidence in predictions as indicated by the steadily increasing maximal beliefs.

Influence of Description Depth. The description depth has a huge impact on the size of descriptions from which edges are chosen to discriminate concepts of nearest neighbours. In FB15k-237, descriptions have on average 750 edges at depth 1, already 20,000 edges at depth 2, and 110,000 edges at depth 10, i.e. 38% of the train+valid edges. This has an impact on computation times but in a reasonable proportion: the runtime overhead relative to the computation of CNNs for timeout $= 0.1\,$s (i.e., loading triples, computing descriptions, triple inference), ranges from $0.03\,$s at depth 1 to $0.3\,$s at depth 10.

We now look at the impact of description depth on results. We can expect *a priori* that a greater depth provides more information to discriminate candidate entities but is computationally more demanding. However, by varying depth between 1 and 20 for timeout $= 1\,$s, we observed very small standard deviations for the four measures, all around ± 0.005. This shows that most of the useful information is already present at depth 1. Nonetheless, it is a good property that increasing depth does not deteriorate performance because it means that depth does not need to be learned and can be set to a large value safely. The explanation for that property is that the iterative partitioning algorithm starts with shallow triples, proceeds with triples of increasing depth, and is usually stopped by timeout rather than by maximum depth.

6.4   Example Inferences and Explanations

Finally, we illustrate our inference method by looking at a few examples in detail (all inferences are available as logs from the companion page). In FB15k-237, the language of film "Dragon Ball Z: Bojack Unbound" is correctly predicted to be "Japanese" with MRR $= 1$, compared to MRR $= 0.2$ for baseline Freq. CNN-1s generates 26 concepts, from which the best explanation (in terms of belief) for "Japanese" is that the film is from Japan and has Toshiyuki Morikawa as an actor. The living place of "Tabu" is correctly predicted to be "Mumbai" with MRR $= 1$, compared to MRR $= 0.059$ for baseline Freq. CNN-1s generates 32 concepts, from which the best explanation is that "Tabu" has been awarded with "Filmfare Award for Best Actress", indicating that many people who earned this award live in Mumbai. The next predicted places are other cities in India. In a more systematic way, we looked at all successful and non-trivial inferences of the nationality of people, i.e. inferences where the correct entity is ranked first by our method, and is not in the three most frequent nationalities ($\mathrm{MRR}_{Freq} < 0.333$). Over the 10 such inferences, the number of concepts generated by CNN-1s is remarkably consistent and small, between 22 and 37. The concept intents have 2 or 3 elements (the explanation query), and the concept extents contain between 2 and 29 entities (the similar entities that serve as examples). The best explanations tell that nationality can be inferred by either the living place, the death place, the spoken language, a film in which the person played, or a winned award.

In Mondial, the continent of Sweden is correctly predicted as Europe because it is a constitutional monarchy (3-elements query), similarly to Denmark. Matterhorn is correctly predicted to be located in Switzerland because it is a mountain in the Alps that is also located in Italy (5-elements query), similarly to Monte Rossa. Lagen is correctly predicted to be located in Norway because it is the estuary of a river located in Norway (4-elements query).

Our instance-based approach is able to find very specific explanations, as shown by the above illustrations, which a rule-based approach would be unlikely to produce given their huge number. However, a limitation of our inference method is that it cannot yet provide generalized explanations such as "if a person X lives in any city of country Y, then X has nationality Y", which are the main kind of explanations rule-based and path-based approaches rely on.

7 Conclusion

We have shown that a symbolic approach to the problem of link prediction in knowledge graphs can be competitive with state-of-the-art latent-based approaches. This comes with the major advantage that our approach can provide detailed explanations for each inference, in terms of the graph features. Compared to rule-based approaches, which can provide similar explanations, we avoid the need for a training phase that can be costly in runtime and memory (rule mining), while achieving superior performance. Our approach is analogous to classification with k-nearest neighbours but our distances are defined as partially-ordered graph concepts instead of metrics.

There are many tracks for future work. Extending graph patterns with n-ary relations or richer filters over numbers, dates, etc. Optimizing the computation of CNNs by finding good strategies to drive the partitioning process, or by parallelizing it. Extending the CNN-based inference procedure to mimick non-instantiated AMIE+'s rules (e.g., *the nationality is the country of the living place*). Evaluate our approach on other datasets, and other inference tasks.

Acknowledgement. I warmly thank Luis Galárraga for his support about AMIE+.

References

1. Berners-Lee, T., Hendler, J., Lassila, O.: The semantic web. Sci. Am. **284**(5), 34–43 (2001)
2. Bordes, A., Usunier, N., Garcia-Duran, A., Weston, J., Yakhnenko, O.: Translating embeddings for modeling multi-relational data. In: Advances in Neural Information Processing Systems, pp. 2787–2795 (2013)
3. Denœux, T.: A k-nearest neighbor classification rule based on Dempster-Shafer theory. IEEE Trans. Syst. Man Cybern. **25**(5), 804–813 (1995)
4. Dettmers, T., Minervini, P., Stenetorp, P., Riedel, S.: Convolutional 2D knowledge graph embeddings. In: McIlraith, S.A., Weinberger, K.Q. (eds.) Conference on Artificial Intelligence (AAAI), pp. 1811–1818. AAAI Press (2018)

5. Ferré, S.: Concepts de plus proches voisins dans des graphes de connaissances. In: Ingénierie des Connaissances (IC), pp. 163–174 (2017)
6. Ferré, S.: Answers partitioning and lazy joins for efficient query relaxation and application to similarity search. In: Gangemi, A., et al. (eds.) ESWC 2018. LNCS, vol. 10843, pp. 209–224. Springer, Cham (2018). https://doi.org/10.1007/978-3-319-93417-4_14
7. Ferré, S., Cellier, P.: Graph-FCA in practice. In: Haemmerlé, O., Stapleton, G., Faron Zucker, C. (eds.) ICCS 2016. LNCS (LNAI), vol. 9717, pp. 107–121. Springer, Cham (2016). https://doi.org/10.1007/978-3-319-40985-6_9
8. Galárraga, L., Teflioudi, C., Hose, K., Suchanek, F.: Fast rule mining in ontological knowledge bases with AMIE+. Int. J. Very Large Data Bases 24(6), 707–730 (2015)
9. Hermann, A., Ferré, S., Ducassé, M.: An interactive guidance process supporting consistent updates of RDFS graphs. In: ten Teije, A., et al. (eds.) EKAW 2012. LNCS (LNAI), vol. 7603, pp. 185–199. Springer, Heidelberg (2012). https://doi.org/10.1007/978-3-642-33876-2_18
10. Jianfeng, W., Jianxin, L., Yongyi, M., Shini, C., Richong, Z.: On the representation and embedding of knowledge bases beyond binary relations. In: International Joint Conference on Artificial Intelligence (IJCAI), pp. 1300–1307 (2016)
11. Lao, N., Mitchell, T., Cohen, W.W.: Random walk inference and learning in a large scale knowledge base. In: Conference on Empirical Methods in Natural Language Processing, pp. 529–539. Association for Computational Linguistics (2011)
12. Liben-Nowell, D., Kleinberg, J.: The link-prediction problem for social networks. J. Am. Soc. Inform. Sci. Technol. 58(7), 1019–1031 (2007)
13. May, W.: Information extraction and integration with FLORID: the MONDIAL case study. Technical report 131, Universität Freiburg, Institut für Informatik (1999). http://dbis.informatik.uni-goettingen.de/Mondial
14. Meilicke, C., Fink, M., Wang, Y., Ruffinelli, D., Gemulla, R., Stuckenschmidt, H.: Fine-grained evaluation of rule- and embedding-based systems for knowledge graph completion. In: Vrandečić, D., et al. (eds.) ISWC 2018. LNCS, vol. 11136, pp. 3–20. Springer, Cham (2018). https://doi.org/10.1007/978-3-030-00671-6_1
15. Muggleton, S.: Inverse entailment and Progol. New Gener. Comput. 13, 245–286 (1995)
16. Nickel, M., Murphy, K., Tresp, V., Gabrilovich, E.: A review of relational machine learning for knowledge graphs. Proc. IEEE 104(1), 11–33 (2016)
17. Plotkin, G.: Automatic methods of inductive inference. Ph.D. thesis, Edinburgh University, August 1971
18. Schlichtkrull, M., Kipf, T.N., Bloem, P., van den Berg, R., Titov, I., Welling, M.: Modeling relational data with graph convolutional networks. In: Gangemi, A., et al. (eds.) ESWC 2018. LNCS, vol. 10843, pp. 593–607. Springer, Cham (2018). https://doi.org/10.1007/978-3-319-93417-4_38
19. Toutanova, K., Chen, D.: Observed versus latent features for knowledge base and text inference. In: Workshop on Continuous Vector Space Models and Their Compositionality, pp. 57–66 (2015)
20. Zhang, R., Li, J., Mei, J., Mao, Y.: Scalable instance reconstruction in knowledge bases via relatedness affiliated embedding. In: Conference on World Wide Web (WWW), pp. 1185–1194 (2018)

Disclosing Citation Meanings
for Augmented Research Retrieval
and Exploration

Roger Ferrod[1], Claudio Schifanella[1(✉)], Luigi Di Caro[1], and Mario Cataldi[2]

[1] Department of Computer Science, University of Turin, Turin, Italy
roger.ferrod@edu.unito.it, {schi,dicaro}@di.unito.it
[2] Department of Computer Science, University of Paris 8, Saint-Denis, France
m.cataldi@iut.univ-paris8.fr

Abstract. In recent years, new digital technologies are being used to support the navigation and the analysis of scientific publications, justified by the increasing number of articles published every year. For this reason, experts make use of on-line systems to browse thousands of articles in search of relevant information. In this paper, we present a new method that automatically assigns meanings to references on the basis of the citation text through a Natural Language Processing pipeline and a slightly-supervised clustering process. The resulting network of semantically-linked articles allows an informed exploration of the research panorama through semantic paths. The proposed approach has been validated using the ACL Anthology Dataset containing several thousands of papers related to the Computational Linguistics field. A manual evaluation on the extracted citation meanings carried to very high levels of accuracy. Finally, a freely-available web-based application has been developed and published on-line.

Keywords: Citation semantics · Literature exploration ·
Natural Language Processing

1 Introduction

With more than a million scientific articles published each year, keeping abreast of research progress is becoming an increasingly difficult task. For this reason, an increasing number of scientists rely on digital technologies that can analyze thousands of publications in a short time and provide research support.

Over the last few years, numerous techniques have been developed to analyze large amounts of data: from petabytes produced by the Large Hadron Collider, to the hundreds of millions of bases contained in the human genome; but this vast collection of data has the advantage, unlike natural language, of being naturally represented by numbers which, it is well known, can be easily manipulated by computers. Research literature, on the other hand, seems to be immune to this type of analysis, as the articles are designed to be read by humans only.

© Springer Nature Switzerland AG 2019
P. Hitzler et al. (Eds.): ESWC 2019, LNCS 11503, pp. 101–115, 2019.
https://doi.org/10.1007/978-3-030-21348-0_7

Text Mining and Natural Language Processing techniques aim to break this barrier. Using the recent scientific developments of the last thirty years, programs are now learning to extract information from textual sources. This opens up the possibility for scientists to make new discoveries by analyzing hundreds of scientific articles looking for correlations. Among these objectives, there is certainly the discovery of hidden associations, such as links between topics or between authors. Usually, it is possible to search for documents through keywords, or with the use of complex information on a structured database. However, suggestions about articles related to specific studies are extremely helpful in the analysis of the literature.

Of particular interest is the analysis of the citational aspects, i.e., how an article is cited and for which purpose. For this reason, it might be useful to classify citations in classes so as to be able to provide research paths suggesting articles according to specific characteristics or aims.

This work aims at illustrating a novel method for the construction of a semantically-enriched citation graph that makes use of Natural Language Processing and Data Mining technologies to enable advanced retrieval and exploration of a scientific literature. We first tested the approach with a large collection of articles related to the Computational Linguistics field, making available a web-based application called *CitExp* at http://citexp.di.unito.it. Finally, we also made a manual evaluation of 900 randomly-selected citation meanings, obtaining very high accuracy scores.

2   Related Work

The idea of exploring text collections received huge attention since large datasets started to become available for research purposes. While there exist several approaches for generic navigation objectives, like [2,18,20] to name a few, the peculiarity of scientific articles enables further possibilities of semantic access, relying on domain-centered metadata such as citations, co-authoring information, year of publication, and a more rigorous and section-oriented formatting of the content.

In relation with our proposed method, we find that the existing works lie around three main perspectives: *(i)* metadata-based navigation and interactive visualization models [2,18], *(ii)* topic- or author-centered browsing and structuring techniques [23,24], and *(iii)* network-based approaches dealing with citations [11,12,27], co-authorships [17,19], and statistically-relevant links between research articles [15,22]. While we locate our work on the third case, it inherits features from the others while differing from all three on the semi-supervised extraction of semantically-enriched citation paths for an informed navigation of scientific articles.

In recent years, different works offering a navigational model to visually explore scholarly data have been proposed. Faceted-DBLP [5] introduced a facet-based search interface for the DBLP repository, while in PaperCUBE [3] the authors used citations and co-authorship networks to provide browsing functionalities of scientific publications. Similar approaches are proposed by CiteSeer [13], Elsevier Scival and Microsoft Academic Search: in all these proposals, visual interfaces are built on top of a navigational model created from the collaboration networks and the citations. Finally, in the Delve system [1] common browsing functionalities are implemented over a dynamic set of publications, moving the focus on dataset retrieval.

A work similar to ours, based however on the use of ontologies, has been proposed in [25], where the authors identified and formalized different types of citations in scientific articles. In spite of this, the ontology includes a wide set of complex cases, making it exclusively suitable for manual (and costly) annotations of individual references. In [9], it has been developed a graph of publications, grouped according to citation reports and accessible through tools such as CitNetExplorer [8] and VOSviewer [7], where users can perform bibliometric research. In [6], the authors proposed a comparison between various methodologies developed for the purpose of grouping citations into the network. [26] presented a specific semantic similarity measure for short texts such as abstracts of scientific publications. The measure of semantic similarity can be useful to deepen the knowledge on the network of articles to identify groups of publications dealing with similar issues.

3   Data and Preprocessing Tools

3.1   Data

To test the method we used the ACL Anthology Dataset[1], i.e., a corpus of scientific publications sponsored by the Association for Computational Linguistics. The corpus consists of a collection of articles from various conferences and workshops, as well as past editions of the Computational Linguistics Journal or events sponsored by ACL. The purpose of this anthology does not end with the simple collection of results and publications, but rather arises as an object of study and research platform. Thousands of articles have been digitized and assembled in PDF format, while titles and authors have been extracted from the text to compose the corpus metadata. The current version has 21,520 articles and 287,130 references, of which 91,931 (32%) refer to articles inside the corpus. The ACL anthology is composed of a set of XML files, divided into folders and corresponding to the output of the Parscit software [10].

3.2   Snippet Extraction

The basic unit of our work is the *snippet*. A snippet is a portion of text that contains the reference, enriched by other information such as, for example, the section of the article in which it appears. The first phase has the main objective of extracting the snippets from the corpus. Unfortunately, the XML files used as input are devoid of documentation and of a scheme that defines them. Furthermore, some XML elements raise exceptions during the parsing, and the absence of documentation has not facilitated the resolution of errors. For this reason, the

---

[1] https://acl-arc.comp.nus.edu.sg.

files causing problems have been deliberately discarded. However, they represent a minimal part of the total corpus (1.73%) and therefore do not compromise the validity of the results. The final result of the preprocessing phase is a single XML file. It is important to note that during the processing by Parscit, the text undergoes various modifications. On the basis of the information obtained from the Parscit source code, it was possible to identify the applied transformations. In particular the excess of white spaces and the hyphenation of the words were removed. If this standardization process were not taken into account, the references (position indexes) indicated by Parscit would not correspond to the actual text.

3.3   Snippet Linking

The citations refer, through a numeric id, to *reference* tags containing the details of the referenced article. Parscit is able to extract information such as title, authors, year of publication and other information where present, from the references section of the article. In order to build a graph of articles, however, it is necessary to find a correspondence between the title specified in the reference and the title of the article, since in 23% of the cases these two strings do not coincide. Consider the following example: the title reported by the reference *"an efficient adaptable system for interpreting natural language queries"* actually refers to the article whose title is *"an efficient and easily adaptable system for interpreting natural language queries"*. The two strings have the same semantic content, but show a different wording.

Although the human eye is easily able to identify a strong resemblance between them, a simple pattern matching algorithm encounters major difficulties. In addition, the size of the data must also be kept in mind. Considering the complexity of the problem, it was decided to examine only citations inside the corpus, therefore each title extracted from a reference has been compared with each title in the corpus metadata. Although there are several algorithms to compare strings, most of them are not scalable with large amounts of data. We used the *Sequence-Matcher* class provided by the *difflib* library which implements a variant of a pattern matching algorithm published in 1980 by Ratcliff and Obershelp [16]. It is based on the principle of finding the longest common sequence, free of undesired elements (called junk). SequenceMatcher also supports heuristics for the automatic identification of junk elements. This process takes place calculating how many times each element appears in the sequence. If the duplicates of an element (after the first one) represent more than 1% of the sequence and the sequence is at least 200 elements long, then the element is marked as "popular" and is considered as junk (the version proposed by Ratcliff and Obershelp did not foresee the existence of junk elements). The search for common sequences is then recursively repeated, thus producing judicious correspondences.

The complexity of SequenceMatcher is quadratic in the worst case and linear in the best case, differently from the original version (as proposed by Ratcliff-Obershelp) that presented a cubic complexity in the worst case and quadratic in the best case. Given the complexity of the calculation, *difflib* provides three variants to the calculation of similarity (ratio, quick-ratio, real-quick-ratio) which gradually return an approximation of the exact value. In our case we used *quick-ratio* which represents a good compromise between correctness and efficiency.

The risk of having few associations among articles due to a too high degree of requested similarity carried to the choice of a reasonable threshold. This was finally set to 92%, when, in 100 random matches identified, none turned out to be a false positive. In this way, the risk of associating different articles has been reduced.

4 Semantic Analysis

4.1 Text Transformation

As usually done when dealing with textual documents, it was necessary to convert them into vector-based distributional representations. We first created a dictionary containing the words contained in the documents (taken only once). Then, for each document i, we counted the number of occurrences of each word w. The value is stored in an array in position X $[i, j]$, where j is the w-index in the dictionary. For this operation, we used the implementation provided by the *scikit-learn* library[2].

The implementation of the vector transformation algorithm also includes the possibility of using n-grams instead of single words, filtering out the stopwords and customizing the dictionary creation function (using the *tokenizer* function which splits the text into tokens, later used as features). However, occurrences are known to be improvable numeric representations of a corpus since they are not normalized with respect to documents length and spreading of the words over the document collection. To avoid the problem, we employed the well-known Term Frequency - Inverse Document Frequency (tf-idf) weighting strategy.

4.2 Syntax-Based Snippet Tokenization

The terms are provided by the tokenizer function which splits a string into tokens composed of single words or, in our case, groups of words (n-grams). The choice of the tokens is particularly crucial in the proposed method, since one of the main objectives of the final graph is to differentiate the citations according to their intention, or meaning.

The proposed approach focusses on finding those words which are syntactically linked to the citation (dubbed *trigger words* from now on). To explain in detail the method, consider the following example: the sentence extracted from the snippet '*X compared the difference between citation terms extracted*', where X takes the place of the reference. The syntactic parser [14] returns the syntactic tree depicted in Fig. 1.

---

[2] http://scikit-learn.org/stable/.

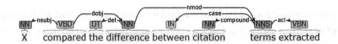

Fig. 1. Example of syntactic tree.

The first step is the identification of the words which are directly related to the citation, without taking into consideration the orientation and the type of the syntactic dependencies. Following the example, the tree visit begins with "*compared*". Afterwards, the process continues by only considering a specific set of dependencies[3] and following the orientation of the graph, up to a maximum depth of $d = 2$. In the example, the words extracted were "*compared*", "*difference*", and "*terms*".

Finally, since single words can carry little information, we proceeded to create n-grams by composing the trigger-words with all the words that separate them from the reference. In the example, we get:

- *compared*
- *compared the difference*
- *compared the difference between citation terms*

In order to generalize the obtained tokens, and therefore avoiding an excessively sparse matrix, a stemming[4] algorithm has been applied to the strings. By applying this on the previous example we obtain:

- *compar*
- *compar the differ*
- *compar the differ between citat term*

These three n-grams represent the tokens generated by our syntax-based tokenizer on the input snippet, and therefore the base units on witch the tf-idf computation works on. A maximum limit of 10K features (i.e. tokens generated as described above) has been set, taking the most frequent features only.

4.3   Dimensionality Reduction

It is often advisable to reduce the number of dimensions of a matrix before it is analyzed by a clustering algorithm. The reduction of the components is in fact part of the standard procedure applied to the study of large datasets and avoids numerous side effects (e.g., curse of dimensionality) that would compromise the results. In the specific case concerning our proposal, the matrix size was originally around 360K (snippets) × 10K (features). However, we reduced the number of snippets by 39% by removing 0-valued vectors, obtaining a final

---

[3] *nsubj, csubj, nmod, advcl, dobj.*
[4] The Porter Stemmer has been adopted.

matrix of 219K × 10K. Then, to reduce the number of dimensions, we used the well-known Latent Semantic Analysis [4], using the implementation provided by *scikit-learn*.

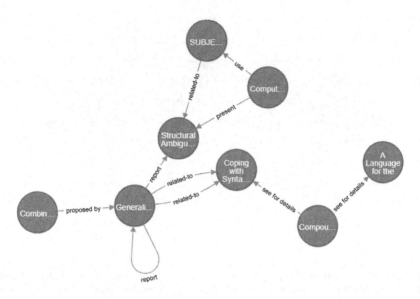

Fig. 2. Example of the citation graph of a publication: nodes represent publications, while edges express citations. Edge labels show extracted citation meanings.

5   Citation Meanings Extraction

5.1   Citation Clustering

For data with a large number of dimensions, such as text documents represented by tf-idf scores, the cosine similarity turned out to be a better metric than the Euclidean distance, as usual when dealing with textual data. We used KMeans in its minibatch variant with samples of 1000 elements. This way, the algorithm converges faster than the other tested methods (DBSCAN, hierarchical clustering) and produces results comparable, by quality, to the canonical version of KMeans. In addition, for this purpose, we made use of the initialization *k-means++* provided by *scikit-learn* which initializes the centroids maximizing the distance. Following numerous experiments, and considering the results provided by the analysis of the clustering silhouette, the value of K was set to 30. Figure 3 shows a small portion of the constructed graph.

The function provided by *scikit-learn* returns the spatial coordinates of the centroids, in the original data space (i.e., not reduced), and the cluster to which each sample belongs. Thanks to this information it was possible to obtain a top-terms ranking for each cluster, i.e., the features which were closer to the centroids and therefore more representative of that cluster.

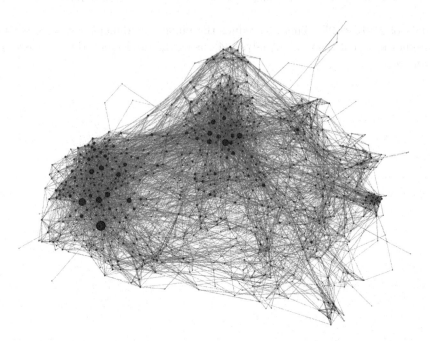

Fig. 3. Small portion of the graph, containing 947 nodes (4,5%) and 6267 relations (6,5%), visualized by the software Gephi, filtering the nodes according to their degree and highlighting, with different colors, the different classes of citations. (Color figure online)

Finally, starting from the clustering, the silhouette coefficient was calculated for each cluster. Since the implementation of *scikit-learn* does not provide the possibility of sampling the data and considering the large number of existing samples, it was necessary to implement our own version using a random sampling of 900 samples for each cluster. The results were then shown in a graph showing the average of the coefficient by means of a red line. Then, from the calculation of the silhouette, the cluster with the highest number of elements was excluded. In fact, it contained elements which were not semantically coherent with each other. The clustering phase ends by also producing an XML file containing the snippets (identified by an alphanumeric identifier) divided by associated cluster.

5.2   Cluster Labeling

The information gathered from the clustering phase has been subsequently analyzed and the classes corresponding to the clusters of particular interest have been assigned manually. The decision was taken by taking into account all the aspects highlighted by the clustering, in particular the silhouette values, the cardinality of each clusters, the top-terms and samples extracted from the clusters.

Classes

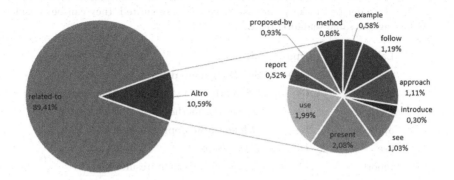

related-to	see	present	use	report	proposed-by	method	example	follow	approach	introduce
85428	984	1986	1906	501	886	819	557	1140	1060	284

Fig. 4. Citation meanings (or classes) and relative number of extracted citations.

Clusters that capture a particular aspect were labeled by storing this information in a *.json* file has been then used for the construction of the graph (see Fig. 2 for an example).

The largest cluster has been discarded a priori. In fact, alone, it represents the 67% of the data and contains very heterogeneous information, such as *('show')*, *('task')*, *('propos', 'in')* *('work')*, *('translat')*, *('word')*, etc. Some other clusters have been rejected for the same reason, showing also very low silhouette values. All these groups of citations have been labeled with the generic label *related-to*.

At the end of the selection process, 9 clusters (also called *citation meanings* from now on) were preserved and manually associated with labels. For example, one cluster having the top-terms: *('see'), ('for', 'detail'), ('see', 'X'), ('for', 'an', 'overview'), ('for', 'more', 'detail'), ('see', 'X', 'and'), ('detail', 'see'), ('for', 'discussed'), ('for', 'a', 'discussed'), ('for', 'further', 'detail')*, has been associated with the label: *see-for-details* as it captures a particular type of citation aimed at providing further details on the subject dealt with in the article. Examples of extracted snippets from the cluster are:

- *For a good discussion of the differences, see [X]*
- *See [X] for an overview and history of MUC6 and the Named Entity*
- *Actually, the extensions concern the use of tries (see [X]) as the sole storage device for all sorts of lexical information in MONA*
- *In (1) SMES is embedded in the COSMA system, a German language server for existing appointment scheduling agent systems (see [X], this volume, for more information).*

Table 1. Considered labels and relative meanings. A is the paper that mentions the paper B, while c represents something extracted from the snippet which is only relative to B (in that case, A has the only role of containing the relationship between B and c). Even if we decided to keep the last three labels separated, they can be considered as depicting the same semantic relation.

Label	Type	Meaning
see-for-details	$A \longrightarrow B$	See B for more details
follow	$A \longrightarrow B$	The authors of A followed what done in B
method	$B \longrightarrow c$	B uses the method c
approach	$B \longrightarrow c$	B follows the approach c
use	$B \longrightarrow c$	B makes use of c
report	$B \longrightarrow c$	B reports c (usually results)
present	$B \longrightarrow c$	B presents c
proposed-by	$B \longrightarrow c$	B proposes c
introduce	$B \longrightarrow c$	B introduces c

The entire set of identified labels are shown in Table 1, quantitatively distributed as in Fig. 4. Among the 9 identified citation meanings, we found that they belong to two different types:

$A \longrightarrow B$ - In this case, article A cites article B expressing some semantics about A and B, directly. This happens for labels *see-for-details* and *follow*.

$B \longrightarrow c$ - Citations of this type are contained in A, but express some semantics about article B only. The term c may refer to different concepts (methods, algorithms, results, etc.). The labels of this type are *method, approach, use, report, present, proposed-by,* and *introduce*.

It is important to note that in the latter case our method is able to extract (and use, for exploration purposes) semantic information about articles once cited in third-party articles. To the best of our knowledge, this is one of the first work following this approach. Differently from extracting information about papers directly within them, by doing it where they are referenced, there is some certainty about the recognized relevance of the extracted knowledge. Always in the $B \longrightarrow c$ case, we changed the $A \longrightarrow B$ label to *highly-related-to*.

A graph of 21,148 nodes (corresponding to the articles of the corpus) and 95,551 edges (representing the citations) was finally created. It has been observed that 8,416 nodes (around 40%) do not participate in any relation because they do not have citations to articles inside the corpus.

6   Model and Method Complexity

Starting from the snippets extracted in the preprocessing phase, 360,162 sentences were obtained, being then analyzed syntactically, according to the described method, creating a document-term matrix of $360,162 \times 10,000$. The operation required 4 h of processing on a computer equipped with an Intel Core i7 6500U, 12 GB of RAM, 1 TB HDD and 128 GB SSD. From the tf-idf matrix, 140,872 lines (39% of the total) were removed, composed exclusively of null values. The final matrix ($219,290 \times 10,000$) turned out to be more manageable by the reduction and clustering algorithms. The reduction through the truncatedSVD algorithm required the most memory consumption, quickly saturating the memory available from the machine and, for this reason, it took 84 min to produce the results. The 3,000-component reduction has preserved 83% of the variance. Thanks to the use of the minibatch variant, KMeans finished in just 15 s producing the 30 required clusters.

7 Evaluation

7.1 Application: Citation Explorer

In order to assess the effectiveness of the proposed method, we have developed a simple web application that allows the navigation of the literature through the extracted semantically-enriched citation paths. An online version is available at http://citexp.di.unito.it.

The collected and assembled data have been then stored in two csv files, containing the nodes and the edges of the graph respectively. A header is added to the csv document that specifies the structure. In this way, the elaboration of the ACL corpus ends, producing a result that is independent of the technology that can be used to visualize and analyze it. In our application, the data have been uploaded to a graph database (Neo4j[5]) on which basic queries were carried out to obtain statistics and validate the project objectives. The graph is constructed by composing information derived from the corpus metadata, the composition of the clusters, and the assigned labels. In the graph each node represents an article and stores information such as title, authors and, where present, the date of publication. The edges that connect the nodes represent the citations, characterized by the class (or label) and therefore by the type of reference. Unlabeled arches have been preserved, labeled with a generic *related-to* relation. Starting from a specific node it is in fact possible to navigate the graph following the path provided by the edges and filtering the nodes based on the information memorized by the database: title, authors and date of the article, class and section to which the reference belongs (see Fig. 5 for an example of interaction.).

In the application, the result of a standard search for papers includes several articles ordered by the weight (i.e., the rank) of the articles calculated with the PageRank algorithm [21]. Once an article of interest has been identified, the article details are shown together with a list of relevant articles filtered according to the citation classes. The selection algorithm is also based on PageRank and provides, in order of weight, both articles cited by the selected article and those that mention it. The application also includes several other interaction features

---

[5] https://neo4j.com.

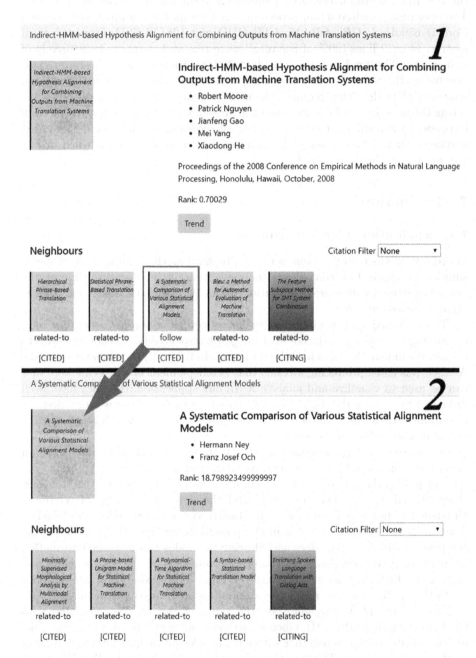

Fig. 5. Example of visualization and interaction (P1 *follow* ⟶ P2) with the developed web-based application, available at http://citexp.di.unito.it.

such as tooltips showing the sections and the sentences from which the citations were taken, the trend of citations over the years, and so forth. The trend is represented by the number of citations referring the article over the years and can be used, for example, to identify emerging articles or articles representing a foundation for ongoing research.

7.2   Reliability of the Extracted Citation Meanings

To give an overview of the reliability of the approach, we produced a validation dataset containing all citation texts with the automatically-associated citation meanings. In detail, we manually evaluated the correctness of 100 random instances for 9 citation meanings (i.e., 900 snippets)[6]. Table 2 reports the result of this evaluation. The resulting overall accuracy is 95.22%, demonstrating the high efficacy of the method in associating correct meanings to the citations[7].

Table 2. Accuracy of the manual validation. A set of 100 random snippets (for each extracted citation meaning) have been manually checked for correctness.

	see-for-details	proposed-by	introduce
Accuracy	98%	98%	93%
	follow	approach	method
Accuracy	96%	89%	96%
	report	present	use
Accuracy	97%	98%	92%

8   Conclusions and Future Work

We have introduced a new method for an advanced search and exploration of a large body of scientific literature, presenting a methodology comprising a pipeline and a set of tools for structuring and labeling citations.[8] Specifically, the proposed approach is based on a Natural Language Processing architecture and a semi-supervised clustering phase. To demonstrate the validity of the proposal, we first manually evaluated a random selection of the extracted knowledge on a large collection of scientific papers in the Computational Linguistics field (ACL Anthology). Then, we developed a freely-accessible web-based application, which will be maintained and further developed along the years for research purposes.

---

[6] We excluded from the evaluation the 10th cluster *related-to* since it included the remaining citations having a very broad scope.

[7] Since we did not have a complete labeled corpus with positive and negative examples, we could not compute standard Precision/Recall/F-measures.

[8] Both documentation and source code of the pipeline, as well as the complete set of citation snippets per category and the graph, are available at https://github.com/rogerferrod/citexp.

In particular, through the automatically-extracted citation meanings, it can be possible to browse the literature by following fine-grained types of citations, thus providing an enhanced retrieval process, with better at-a-glance overviews over the state of the art. In future work, we aim at applying the method on a broader domain, and at a larger scale.

A set of open issues emerged from this work. For example, in relation with the decomposition of the text in sentences, more effort should be spent since the used algorithms are not specific for scientific texts.

Finally, since the project dealt exclusively with the research of a methodology for the organization and storage of the scientific literature, it is reasonable to include tools to query the database for non-specialized users. Solutions of this kind include browser plugins, web platforms able to present the articles according to a narration (storytelling) dictated by the temporal evolution of the topics, or instruments related to bibliometric analyses of the articles.

References

1. Akujuobi, U., Zhang, X.: Delve: a dataset-driven scholarly search and analysis system. SIGKDD Explor. Newsl. **19**(2), 36–46 (2017). https://doi.org/10.1145/3166054.3166059. http://doi.acm.org/10.1145/3166054.3166059
2. Alexander, E., Kohlmann, J., Valenza, R., Witmore, M., Gleicher, M.: Serendip: topic model-driven visual exploration of text corpora. In: 2014 IEEE Conference on Visual Analytics Science and Technology (VAST), pp. 173–182. IEEE (2014)
3. Bergström, P., Atkinson, D.C.: Augmenting the exploration of digital libraries with web-based visualizations. In: 2009 Fourth International Conference on Digital Information Management, pp. 1–7, November 2009. https://doi.org/10.1109/ICDIM.2009.5356798
4. Deerwester, S., Dumais, S.T., Furnas, G.W., Landauer, T.K., Harshman, R.: Indexing by latent semantic analysis. J. Am. Soc. Inform. Sci. **41**(6), 391–407 (1990)
5. Diederich, J., Balke, W.T., Thaden, U.: Demonstrating the semantic GrowBag: automatically creating topic facets for facetedDBLP. In: Proceedings of the 7th ACM/IEEE-CS Joint Conference on Digital Libraries, JCDL 2007, p. 505. ACM, New York (2007). https://doi.org/10.1145/1255175.1255305. http://doi.acm.org/10.1145/1255175.1255305
6. Šubelj, L., van Eck, N.J., Waltman, L.: Clustering scientific publications based on citation relations: a systematic comparison of different methods. PLoS ONE **11**(4), e0154404 (2016)
7. van Eck, N.J., Waltman, L.: VOS: a new method for visualizing similarities between objects. In: Decker, R., Lenz, H.-J. (eds.) Advances in Data Analysis. SCDAKO, pp. 299–306. Springer, Heidelberg (2007). https://doi.org/10.1007/978-3-540-70981-7_34
8. van Eck, N.J., Waltman, L.: CitNetExplorer: a new software tool for analyzing and visualizing citation networks. J. Informetrics **8**(4), 802–823 (2014)
9. van Eck, N.J., Waltman, L.: Citation-based clustering of publications using CitNetExplorer and VOSviewer. Scientometrics **111**(2), 1053–1070 (2017)
10. Kan, M.-Y., Councill, I.G., Giles, C.L.: ParsCit: an open-source CRF reference string parsing package. In: Proceedings of the Language Resources and Evaluation Conference (LREC 2008), Marrakesh, Morrocco, May 2008

11. Kataria, S., Mitra, P., Bhatia, S.: Utilizing context in generative Bayesian models for linked corpus. In: AAAI, vol. 10, p. 1 (2010)
12. Kim, J., Kim, D., Oh, A.: Joint modeling of topics, citations, and topical authority in academic corpora. arXiv preprint arXiv:1706.00593 (2017)
13. Li, H., Councill, I.G., Lee, W.C., Giles, C.L.: CiteSeerx: an architecture and web service design for an academic document search engine. In: WWW (2006)
14. Manning, C.D., Surdeanu, M., Bauer, J., Finkel, J., Bethard, S.J., McClosky, D.: The Stanford CoreNLP natural language processing toolkit. In: Association for Computational Linguistics (ACL) System Demonstrations, pp. 55–60 (2014). http://www.aclweb.org/anthology/P/P14/P14-5010
15. McCallum, A., Nigam, K., Ungar, L.H.: Efficient clustering of high-dimensional data sets with application to reference matching. In: Proceedings of the Sixth ACM SIGKDD International Conference on Knowledge Discovery and Data Mining, pp. 169–178. ACM (2000)
16. Ratcliff, J.W., Metzener, D.E.: Pattern matching: the gestalt approach. Dr. Dobb's J. **13**(7), 46, 47, 59–51, 68–72 (July 1988)
17. Mutschke, P.: Mining networks and central entities in digital libraries. A graph theoretic approach applied to co-author networks. In: Berthold, M.R., Lenz, H.-J., Bradley, E., Kruse, R., Borgelt, C. (eds.) IDA 2003. LNCS, vol. 2810, pp. 155–166. Springer, Heidelberg (2003). https://doi.org/10.1007/978-3-540-45231-7_15
18. Nagwani, N.: Summarizing large text collection using topic modeling and clustering based on mapreduce framework. J. Big Data **2**(1), 6 (2015)
19. Newman, M.E.: Scientific collaboration networks. I. Network construction and fundamental results. Phys. Rev. E **64**(1), 016131 (2001)
20. Oelke, D., Strobelt, H., Rohrdantz, C., Gurevych, I., Deussen, O.: Comparative exploration of document collections: a visual analytics approach. In: Computer Graphics Forum, vol. 33, pp. 201–210. Wiley Online Library (2014)
21. Page, L., Brin, S., Motwani, R., Winograd, T.: The PageRank citation ranking: bringing order to the web. Technical report, Stanford InfoLab, November 1999. http://ilpubs.stanford.edu:8090/422/, previous number = SIDL-WP-1999-0120
22. Popescul, A., Ungar, L.H., Flake, G.W., Lawrence, S., Giles, C.L.: Clustering and identifying temporal trends in document databases. In: ADL, p. 173. IEEE (2000)
23. Rosen-Zvi, M., Chemudugunta, C., Griffiths, T., Smyth, P., Steyvers, M.: Learning author-topic models from text corpora. ACM Trans. Inf. Syst. (TOIS) **28**(1), 4 (2010)
24. Rosen-Zvi, M., Griffiths, T., Steyvers, M., Smyth, P.: The author-topic model for authors and documents. In: Proceedings of the 20th Conference on Uncertainty in Artificial Intelligence, pp. 487–494. AUAI Press (2004)
25. Shotton, S.P.D.: FaBiO and CiTO: ontologies for describing bibliographic resources and citations. Web Semant. Sci. Serv. Agents World Wide Web **17**, 33–43 (2012)
26. Strapparava, C., Mihalcea, R., Corley, C.: Corpus-based and knowledge-based measures of text semantic similarity. In: AAAI 2006 Proceedings of the 21st National Conference on Artificial Intelligence, vol. 1, pp. 775–780 (2006)
27. Tu, Y., Johri, N., Roth, D., Hockenmaier, J.: Citation author topic model in expert search. In: Proceedings of the 23rd International Conference on Computational Linguistics: Posters, pp. 1265–1273. Association for Computational Linguistics (2010)

Injecting Domain Knowledge
in Electronic Medical Records to Improve
Hospitalization Prediction

Raphaël Gazzotti[1,3]([⊠]) [iD], Catherine Faron-Zucker[1][iD], Fabien Gandon[1][iD],
Virginie Lacroix-Hugues[2], and David Darmon[2][iD]

[1] Université Côte d'Azur, Inria, CNRS, I3S, Sophia-Antipolis, France
{raphael.gazzotti,catherine.faron-zucker,fabien.gandon}@unice.fr
[2] Université Côte d'Azur, Département de Médecine Générale, Nice, France
vhugues@outlook.fr, david.darmon@unice.fr
[3] SynchroNext, Nice, France

Abstract. Electronic medical records (EMR) contain key information
about the different symptomatic episodes that a patient went through.
They carry a great potential in order to improve the well-being of patients
and therefore represent a very valuable input for artificial intelligence
approaches. However, the explicit knowledge directly available through
these records remains limited, the extracted features to be used by
machine learning algorithms do not contain all the implicit knowledge
of medical expert. In order to evaluate the impact of domain knowledge when processing EMRs, we augment the features extracted from
EMRs with ontological resources before turning them into vectors used
by machine learning algorithms. We evaluate these augmentations with
several machine learning algorithms to predict hospitalization. Our approach was experimented on data from the PRIMEGE PACA database
that contains more than 350,000 consultations carried out by 16 general
practitioners (GPs).

Keywords: Predictive model · Electronic medical record ·
Knowledge graph

1 Introduction

Electronic medical records (EMRs) contain essential information about the different symptomatic episodes a patient goes through. They have the potential
to improve patient well-being and are therefore a potentially valuable source
to artificial intelligence approaches. However, the linguistic variety as well as
the tacit knowledge in EMRs can impair the prognosis of a machine learning
algorithm.

In this paper, we extract ontological knowledge from text fields contained in
EMRs and evaluate the benefit when predicting hospitalization. Our study uses
a dataset extracted from the PRIMEGE PACA relational database [10] which

© Springer Nature Switzerland AG 2019
P. Hitzler et al. (Eds.): ESWC 2019, LNCS 11503, pp. 116–130, 2019.
https://doi.org/10.1007/978-3-030-21348-0_8

contains more than 350,000 consultations in French by 16 general practitioners (Table 1). In this database, text descriptions written by general practitioners are available with international classification codes of prescribed drugs, pathologies and reasons for consultations, as well as the numerical values of the different medical examination results obtained by a patient.

Our initial observation was that the knowledge available in a database such as PRIMEGE remains limited to the specificities of each patient and in particular that the texts found in there are based on a certain amount of implicit information known to medical experts. Moreover, the level of detail of the information contained in a patient's file is variable. Therefore, a machine learning algorithm exploiting solely the information at its disposal in an EMR will not be able to exploit this specific knowledge implicit in the documents it analyzes or, at best, it will have to relearn this knowledge by itself, possibly in an incomplete and costly way.

In that context, our main research question is: *Can ontological augmentations of the features improve the prediction of the occurrence of an event?* In our case study, we aim to predict a patient's hospitalization using knowledge from different knowledge graphs in the medical field. In this paper, we focus on the following sub-questions:

- How to integrate domain knowledge into a vector representation used by a machine learning algorithm?
- Is the addition of domain knowledge improving the prediction of a patient's hospitalization?
- Which domain knowledge combined with which machine learning methods provide the best prediction of a patient's hospitalization?

To answer these questions, we first survey the related work (Sect. 2) and position our contribution. We then introduce the proposed method for semantic annotation and knowledge extraction from texts and specify how ontological knowledge is injected upstream into the vector representation of EMRs (Sect. 3). Then, we present the experimental protocol and discuss the results obtained (Sect. 4). Finally, we conclude and provide our perspectives for this study (Sect. 5).

2   Related Work

In [12], the authors are focused on finding rules for the activities of daily living of cancer patients on the SEER-MHOS (Surveillance, Epidemiology, and End Results - Medicare Health Outcomes Survey) and they showed an improvement in the coverage of the inferred rules and their interpretations by adding 'IS-A' knowledge from the Unified Medical Language System (UMLS). They extract the complete sub-hierarchy of kinship and co-hyponymous concepts. Although their purpose is different from ours, their use of the OWL representation of UMLS with a machine learning algorithm improves the coverage of the identified rules. However, their work is based solely on 'IS-A' relationships without exploring the contributions of other kinds of relationships and they do not study the impact of this augmentation on different machine learning approaches: they used the AQ21 and the extension of this algorithm AQ21-OG to compare.

Table 1. Data collected in the PRIMEGE PACA database.

Category	Data collected
GPs	Sex, birth year, city, postcode
Patients	Sex, birth year, city, postcode
	Socio-professional category, occupation
	Number of children, family status
	Long term condition (Y/N)
	Personal history
	Family history
	Risk factors
	Allergies
Consultations	Date
	Reasons of encounter
	Symptoms related by the patient and medical observation
	Further investigations
	Diagnosis
	Drugs prescribed (dose, number of boxes, reasons of the prescription)
	Paramedical prescriptions (biology/imaging)
	Medical procedures

In [5], the authors established a neural network with graph-based attention model that exploits ancestors extracted from the OWL-SKOS representations of ICD Disease, Clinical Classifications Software (CCS) and Systematized Nomenclature of Medicine Clinical Terms (SNOMED-CT). In order to exploit the hierarchical concepts of these knowledge graphs in their attention mechanism, the graphs are transformed using the embedding obtained with Glove [15]. The results show that such a model better performs when identifying a pathology rarely observed in a training dataset than a recurrent neural network and it also better generalizes when confronted with less data in the training set. Again, this work also does not exploit other kinds of relationships, while we compare the impact of different kinds and sources of knowledge.

In [16] the authors extract knowledge from the dataset of [13] and structure it with an ontology developed for this purpose, then they automatically deduce new class expressions, with the objective of extracting their attributes to recognize activities of daily living using machine learning algorithms. The authors highlight better accuracy and results than with traditional approaches, regardless of the machine learning algorithm on which this task has been addressed (up to 1.9% on average). Although they exploit solely the ontology developed specifically for the purpose of discovering new rules, without trying to exploit other knowledge sources where a mapping could have been done, their study shows the value of structured knowledge in classification tasks. We intend here to study the same kind of impact but with different knowledge sources and for the task of predicting hospitalization.

3 Enriching Vector Representations of EMRs with Ontological Knowledge

3.1 Extraction of Ontological Knowledge from EMRs

Our study aims to analyze and compare the impact of knowledge from different sources, whether separately incorporated or combined, on the vector representation of patients' medical records to predict hospitalization. To extract domain knowledge underlying terms used in text descriptions written by general practitioners, we search the texts for medical entities and link them to the concepts to which they correspond in Wikidata, DBpedia and health sector specific knowledge graphs such as those related to drugs. Wikidata and DBpedia were chosen because general concepts can only be identified with general repositories. In this section, we describe how these extractions are performed but we do not focus on this step as it is only a means to an end for our study and could be replaced by other approaches.

Knowledge Extraction Based on DBpedia. To detect in an EMR concepts from the medical domain present in DBpedia, we used the semantic annotator DBpedia Spotlight [7]. Together with the domain experts, we carried out a manual analysis of the named entities detected on a sample of approximately 40 consultations with complete information and determined 14 SKOS top concepts designating medical subjects relevant to the prediction of hospitalization, as they relate to severe pathologies (Table 2).

For each EMR to model, from the list of resources identified by DBpedia Spotlight, we query the access point of the French-speaking chapter of DBpedia[1] to determine if these resources have as subject (property dcterms:subject) one or more of the 14 selected concepts.

In order to improve DBpedia Spotlight's detection capabilities, words or abbreviated expressions within medical reports are added to text fields using a symbolic approach, with rules and dictionaries (e.g., the abbreviation "ic" which means "heart failure" is not recognized by DBpedia Spotlight, but is thus correctly identified through this symbolic approach).

In the rest of the article, the $+s$ notation refers to an approach using the enrichment of representations with concepts from DBpedia according to the method previously described. The $+s*$ notation refers to an approach that does not exploit all text fields and extracts concepts from text fields related to the patient's personal history, allergies, environmental factors, current health problems, reasons for consultations, diagnoses, medications, care procedures, reasons for prescribing medications and physician observations. The $+s*$ approach focuses on the patient's own record, not on his family history and past problems. Note that the symptom field is used by doctors for various purposes and this is the reason why we excluded this field in the DBpedia concept extraction procedure for this approach.

---

[1] http://fr.dbpedia.org/sparql.

Table 2. List of manually chosen concepts in order to determine a hospitalization, these concepts were translated from French to English (the translation does not necessarily exist for the English DBpedia chapter).

Speciality	Labels
Oncology	Neoplasm stubs, Oncology, Radiation therapy
Cardiovascular	Cardiovascular disease, Cardiac arrhythmia
Neuropathy	Neurovascular disease
Immunopathy	Malignant hemopathy, Autoimmune disease
Endocrinopathy	Medical condition related to obesity
Genopathy	Genetic diseases and disorders
Intervention	Surgical removal procedures, Organ failure
Emergencies	Medical emergencies, Cardiac emergencies

Knowledge Extraction Based on Wikidata. Wikidata[2] is an open knowledge base that centralizes data from various projects of the Wikimedia Foundation. Its coverage on some domains differs from that of DBpedia. We extracted drug-related knowledge by querying Wikidata's endpoint.[3] More precisely, we identified three properties of drugs relevant to the prediction of hospitalization: 'subject has role' (property wdt:P2868), 'significant drug interaction' (property wdt:P2175), and 'medical condition treated' (property wdt:P769).

In Wikidata, we identify the drugs present in EMRs using the ATC code (property wdt:P267) of the drugs present in the PRIMEGE database. The CUI UMLS codes (property wdt:P2892) and CUI RxNorm (property wdt:P3345) have been recovered using medical domain specific ontologies. Indeed, the codes from these three representations are not necessarily all present to identify a drug in Wikidata, but at least one of them allows us to find the resource about a given drug. From the URI of a drug, we extract property-concept pairs related to the drugs for three selected properties (e.g., 'Pethidine' is a narcotic, 'Meprobamate' cures headache, 'Atazanavir' interacts with 'Rabeprazole').

In the rest of the article, the notation $+wa$ refers to an approach using the enrichment of our representations with the property 'acts as such', $+wm$ indicates the usage of the property 'treated disease' and $+wi$ of the property 'drugs interacts with'.

Knowledge Extraction Based on Domain Specific Ontologies. We were interested in the impact of contributions from domain specific knowledge graphs especially for text fields containing international drug codes from the Anatomical, Therapeutic and Chemical (ATC) classification and codes related to the reasons for consulting a general practitioner with the International Classification of Primary Care (CISP-2). We thus extracted knowledge based on three OWL

---

[2] https://www.wikidata.org.
[3] https://query.wikidata.org/sparql.

representations specific to the medical domain: ATC[4], NDF-RT[5] and CISP2.[6] The choice of OWL-SKOS representations of CISP2 and ATC in our study comes from the fact that the PRIMEGE database adopts these nomenclatures, while the OWL representation of NDF-RT provides additional knowledge on interactions between drugs, diseases, mental and physical states.

We extracted from the ATC OWL-SKOS representation the labels of the superclasses of the drugs listed in the PRIMEGE database, using the properties `rdfs:subClassOf` and `member_of` on different depth levels thanks to SPARQL 1.1 queries with property paths[7] (e.g. 'meprednisone' (ATC code: H02AB15) has as superclass 'Glucocorticoids, Systemic' (ATC code: H02AB) which itself has as superclass 'CORTICOSTEROIDS FOR SYSTEMIC USE, PLAIN' (ATC code: H02)).

Similarly, we extracted from the OWL-SKOS representation of CISP2 the labels of the superclasses with property `rdfs:subClassOf`, however, given the limited depth of this representation, it is only possible to extract one superclass per diagnosed health problem or identified care procedure (e.g., 'Symptom and complaints' (CISP-2 code: H05) has for superclass 'Ear' (CISP-2 code: H)).

In the OWL representation of NDF-RT, we selected three drug properties relevant to the prediction of hospitalization: 'may_treat' property (e.g. 'Tahor', whose main molecule is 'Atorvastatin' (ATC code: C10AA05) can cure 'Hyperlipoproteinemias' (Hyperlipidemia), 'CI_with' (e.g. 'Tahor' is contraindicated in 'Pregnancy') and 'may_prevent' (e.g. 'Tahor' can prevent 'Coronary Artery Disease')). A dimension in our DME vector representation will be a property-value pair. Here is an example RDF description of the drug Tahor:

```
@prefix : <http://evs.nci.nih.gov/ftp1/NDF-RT/NDF-RT.owl> .
:N0000022046 a owl:Class; rdfs:label "ATORVASTATIN"; :UMLS_CUI "C0286651";
    owl:subClassOf [
        rdf:type owl:Restriction; owl:onProperty :may_prevent;
        owl:someValuesFrom :N0000000856 ];
    owl:subClassOf [
        rdf:type owl:Restriction; owl:onProperty :CI_with;
        owl:someValuesFrom :N0000010195 ];
    owl:subClassOf [
        rdf:type owl:Restriction; owl:onProperty :may_treat;
        owl:someValuesFrom :N0000001594 ].
:N0000000856 rdfs:label "Coronary Artery Disease [Disease/Finding]".
:N0000010195 rdfs:label "Pregnancy [Disease/Finding]".
:N0000001594 rdfs:label "Hyperlipoproteinemias [Disease/Finding]".
```

In the rest of the article, the notation $+c$ refers to an approach using the enrichment of vector representations with ATC and the number attached specifies the different depth levels used (e.g., $+c_{1-3}$ indicates that 3 superclass depth levels are integrated in the same vector representation). $+t$ indicates the enrich-

---

[4] Anatomical Therapeutic Chemical Classification,
https://bioportal.bioontology.org/ontologies/ATC.
[5] National Drug File - Reference Terminology,
https://bioportal.bioontology.org/ontologies/NDF-RT.
[6] International Primary Care Classification,
http://bioportal.lirmm.fr/ontologies/CISP-2.
[7] https://www.w3.org/TR/sparql11-query/.

ment of vector representations with CISP2. $+d$ indicates the enrichment of vector representations with NDF-RT, followed in indices by CI if property 'CI_with' is used, *prevent* if property 'may_prevent' is used, *treat* if property 'may_treat' is used. For example, $+d_{CI,prevent,treat}$ refers to the case where these three properties are used together in the same vector representation of DMEs.

3.2 Integrating Ontological Knowledge in a Vector Representation

It is crucial when using a domain-specific corpus to generate its own representation, since many terms may be omitted in a general representation or an ambiguous notion may be applied to a term when it has a very precise definition in a given sector. We opted for a model using a bag-of-words representation (BOW) for different reasons: (i) the main information from textual documents is extracted without requiring a large corpus; (ii) the attributes are not transformed, which makes it possible to identify which terms contribute to the distinction of patients to hospitalize or not, even if this implies to manipulate very large vector spaces; (iii) the integration of heterogeneous data is facilitated since it is sufficient to concatenate other attributes to this model without removing the meaning of the terms previously represented in this way.

Just like in the structure of the PRIMEGE database, some textual data must be distinguishable from each other when switching to the vector representation of EMRs, e.g. a patient's personal history and family history. To do this, we have introduced provenance prefixes during the creation of the bag-of-words to trace the contribution of the different fields.

Concepts from knowledge graphs are considered as a token in a textual message. When a concept is identified in a patient's medical record, it is added to a concept vector. This attribute will have as value the number of occurrences of this concept within the patient's health record (e.g., the concepts 'Organ Failure' and 'Medical emergencies' are identified for 'pancréatite aiguë', acute pancreatitis, and the value for these attributes in our concept vector will be equal to 1).

Similarly, if a property-concept pair is extracted from a knowledge graph, it is added to the concept vector. For example, in vectors exploiting the NDF-RT (vector representation d), we find the couple consisting of CI_with as a property - contraindicated with- and the name of a pathology or condition, for example 'Pregnancy'.

Let $V^i = \{w_1^i, w_2^i, ..., w_n^i\}$ be the bag-of-words obtained from the textual data in the EMR of the ith patient. Let $C^i = \{c_1^i, c_2^i, ..., c_n^i\}$ be the bag of concepts for the ith patient resulting from the extraction of concepts belonging to knowledge graphs after analysis of his consultations from semi-structured data such as text fields listing drugs and pathologies with their related codes, and unstructured data from free texts such as observations. The different machine learning algorithms exploit the aggregation of these two vectors: $x^i = V^i \oplus C^i$ (Fig. 1).

From the following sentence "prédom à gche - insuf vnse ou insuf cardiaque - pas signe de phlébite - - ne veut pas mettre de bas de contention et ne

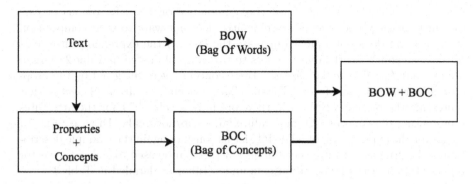

Fig. 1. Workflow diagram to generate vector representations integrating ontological knowledge alongside with textual information.

Table 3. Alternative concept vector representations of the EMR of a patient under Tahor generated using NDF-RT.

	C[1]: may_treat#Hyperlipoproteinemias	C[2]: CI_with#Pregnancy	C[3]: may_prevent#Coronary Artery Disease	...
+d_prevent	∅	∅	1	...
+d_CI	∅	1	∅	...
+d_treat	1	∅	∅	...
+d_CI,prevent,treat	1	1	1	...

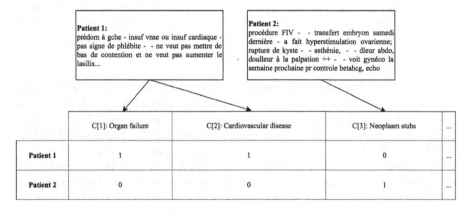

Fig. 2. Concept vectors generated for two EMRs with the bag-of-words approach under the +s configuration. The translation and correction of the texts are (a) for patient 1: "predom[inates] on the left, venous or cardiac insuf[ficiency], no evidence of phlebitis, does not want to wear compression stockings and does not want to increase the lasix". and (b) for patient 2: "In vitro fertilization procedure, embryo transfer last Saturday, did ovarian hyperstimulation, cyst rupture, asthenia, abdominal [pain], [pain] on palpation ++, will see a gyneco[logist] next week [for] a beta HCG, echo check-up".

veut pas augmenter le lasilix... -" (predom[inates] on the left, venous or cardiac insuf[ficiency], no evidence of phlebitis, does not want to wear compression stockings and does not want to increase the lasix...) the expression 'insuf cardiaque', meaning 'heart failure', refers to two concepts listed in Table 2: 'Organ failure' and 'Cardiovascular disease', these concepts were retrieved by the property dcterms:subject from DBpedia. The concept (occurrence) vector that represents the patient's EMR will therefore have a value of 1 for the attributes representing the concepts 'Organ Failure' and 'Cardiovascular Disease' (Fig. 2).

As for the exploitation of NDF-RT, let us consider again the example description of the drug Tahor introduced in Sect. 3.1. It can be used to enrich the vector representation of the EMR of patients under Tahor as detailed in Table 3.

4   Experiments and Results

4.1   Dataset and Protocol

We tested and evaluated our approach for enriching the vector representation of EMRs with ontological knowledge on a balanced dataset DS_B containing data on 714 patients hospitalized and 732 patients not hospitalized. When the observation field is filled in by general practitioners, it can go from 50 characters to 300 characters on average. The best filled in fields concern prescribed drugs and reasons for consultations, then come the antecedents and active problems.

Since we use non-sequential machine learning algorithms to assess the enrichment of ontological knowledge, we had to aggregate all patients' consultations in order to overcome the temporal dimension inherent in symptomatic episodes occurring during a patient's lifetime. Thus, all consultations occurring before hospitalization are aggregated into a vector representation of the patient's medical file. For patients who have not been hospitalized, all their consultations are aggregated. Thus, the text fields previously described (Table 1) are transformed into vectors.

We evaluated the vector representations by nested cross-validation [3], with an external loop with a K fixed at 10 and for the internal loop a K fixed at 3 with exploration of hyperparameters by random search [1] over 150 iterations.

The different experiments were conducted on an HP EliteBook 840 G2, 2.6 GHz, 16 GB RAM with a virtual environment under Python 3.6.3 as well as a Precision Tower 5810, 3.7 GHz, 64 GB RAM with a virtual environment under Python 3.5.4. The creation of vector representations was done on the HP EliteBook and on this same machine were deployed DBpedia Spotlight as well as domain-specific ontologies with Corese Semantic Web Factory [6],[8] a software platform for the Semantic Web. It implements RDF, RDFS, SPARQL 1.1 Query & Update, OWL RL.

---

[8] http://corese.inria.fr.

4.2   Selected Machine Learning Algorithms

We performed the hospitalization prediction task with different state-of-the-art algorithms available in the Scikit-Learn library [14]:

- *SVC*: Support vector machine (SVC stands for 'Support Vector Classification') whose implementation is based on the libsvm implementation [4]. The regularization coefficient C, the kernel used by the algorithm and the gamma coefficient of the kernel were determined by nested cross-validation.
- *RF*: The random forest algorithm [2]. The number of trees in the forest, the maximum tree depth, the minimum number of samples required to divide an internal node, the minimum number of samples required to be at a leaf node and the maximum number of leaf nodes were determined by nested cross-validation.
- *Log*: The algorithm of logistic regression [11]. The regularization coefficient C and the norm used in the penalization were determined by nested cross-validation.

We opted for a bag-of-words model and the above cited machine learning algorithms since it is possible to provide a native interpretation of the decision of these algorithms, thus allowing the physician to specify the reasons for hospitalizing a patient with the factors on which he can operate to prevent this event from occurring. Moreover, logistic regression and random forest algorithms are widely used in order to predict risk factors in EHR [9]. Finally, the limited size of our dataset excluded neural networks approaches.

4.3   Results

In order to assess the value of ontological knowledge, we evaluated the performance of the machine learning algorithms by using the $F_{tp,fp}$ metric [8]. Let TN be the number of negative instances correctly classified (True Negative), FP the number of negative instances incorrectly classified (False Positive), FN the number of positive instances incorrectly classified (False Negative) and TP the number of positive instances correctly classified (True Positive).

$$TP_f = \sum_{i=1}^{K} TP^{(i)} \qquad FP_f = \sum_{i=1}^{K} FP^{(i)} \qquad FN_f = \sum_{i=1}^{K} FN^{(i)}$$

$$F_{tp,fp} = \frac{2.TP_f}{2.TP_f + FP_f + FN_f}$$

Table 4 summarizes the results for each representation and method combination tested on the DS_B dataset:

- *baseline*: represents our basis of comparison where no ontological enrichment is made on EMR data i.e. only text data in the form of bag-of-words.
- *+s*: refers to an enrichment with concepts from the DBpedia knowledge base.

- $+s*$: refers to an enrichment with concepts from the DBpedia knowledge base, unlike $+s$, not all text fields are exploited, thus, concepts from fields related to the patient's personal history, allergies, environmental factors, current health problems, reasons for consultations, diagnoses, medications, care procedures followed, reasons for prescribing medications and physician observations are extracted.
- $+t$: refers to an enrichment with concepts from the OWL-SKOS representation of CISP-2.
- $+c$: refers to an enrichment with concepts from the OWL-SKOS representation of ATC, the number or number interval indicates the different hierarchical depth levels used.
- $+wa$: refers to an enrichment with Wikidata's 'subject has role' property (wdt:P2868).
- $+wi$: refers to an enrichment with Wikidata's 'significant drug interaction' property (wdt:P769).
- $+wm$: refers to an enrichment with Wikidata's 'medical condition treated' property (wdt:P2175).
- $+d$: refers to an enrichment with concepts from the NDF-RT OWL representation, $_{prevent}$ indicates the use of the may_prevent property, $_{treat}$ the may_treat property and $_{CI}$ the CI_with property.

4.4 Discussion

In general terms, knowledge graphs improve the detection of true positives cases, hospitalized patients correctly identified as such (Tables 5 and 6) and provide a broader knowledge of the data in patient files like the type of health problem with CISP-2 (Table 7).

Although the approach in combination with $+s*$ does not achieve the best final results, this approach achieves the best overall performance among all the approaches tested with 0.858 under logistic regression when using 8 K folds from the KFold during the training phase (Fig. 3). It also surpasses other methods under 3 K partitions by exceeding the *baseline* by 0.9% and at 4 K partitions by 0.7% $+t + s + c_2 + wa + wi$ which suggests an improvement in classification results if we enrich a small dataset with attributes from the enrichment provided by knowledge graphs.

Despite the shallow OWL-SKOS representation of CISP2, the $+t$ configuration is sufficient to improve a patient's hospitalization predictions, if we compare its results to those of the *baseline*. Surprisingly enough, a second level of super class hierarchy with $+c_2$ from the ATC OWL-SKOS representation provides better results while only one level of hierarchy with $+c_1$, seems to have a negative impact on them, this can be explained by the fact that the introduction of a large number of attributes ultimately provides little information, unlike the second level of hierarchy.

However the results show that applying DBpedia expansion to fields indirectly related to the patient's condition, such as family history, can lead machine learning algorithms to draw wrong conclusions even if prefixes have been added

Table 4. $F_{tp,fp}$ for the different vector sets considered on the balanced dataset DS_B.

Features set	SVC	RF	Log	Average
baseline	0.8270	**0.8533**	0.8491	0.8431
+t	0.8239	0.8522	**0.8545**	0.8435
+s	0.8221	0.8522	0.8485	0.8409
+$s*$	0.8339	0.8449	0.8514	0.8434
+c_1	0.8235	0.8433	0.8453	0.8245
+c_{1-2}	0.8254	0.8480	0.8510	0.8415
+c_2	0.8348	0.8522	0.8505	**0.8458**
+$d_{prevent}$	0.8254	0.8506	0.8479	0.8413
+d_{treat}	0.8338	0.8472	0.8481	0.8430
+d_{CI}	0.8281	0.8498	0.8460	0.8413
+wa	0.8223	0.8468	**0.8545**	0.8412
+wi	0.8149	0.8484	0.8501	0.8378
+wm	0.8221	0.8453	0.8458	0.8377
+$t + s + c_2 + wa + wi$	0.8258	0.8486	0.8547	0.8430
+$t + s* +c_2 + wa + wi$	0.8239	0.8494	0.8543	0.8425
+$t + c_2 + wa + wi$	0.8140	0.8531	**0.8571**	0.8414

Table 5. Confusion matrix of the random forest algorithm (on the left) and the logistic regression (on the right) on the *baseline* ('H' stands for Hospitalized and 'Not H' for 'Not Hospitalized').

	H	Not H
Predicted as 'H'	599	91
Predicted as 'Not H'	115	641

	H	Not H
Predicted as 'H'	588	83
Predicted as 'Not H'	126	649

Table 6. Confusion matrix of $+t + s* +c2 + wa + wi$ (on the left) and $+t + c2 + wa + wi$ (on the right) approaches under the logistic regression algorithm ('H' stands for Hospitalized and 'Not H' for 'Not Hospitalized').

	H	Not H
Predicted as 'H'	595	84
Predicted as 'Not H'	119	648

	H	Not H
Predicted as 'H'	597	82
Predicted as 'Not H'	117	650

Table 7. Patient profiles correctly identified as being hospitalized (true positives) after injecting domain knowledge (the comparison of these two profiles was made on the baseline and the $+t + s + c2 + wa + wi$ approaches with the logistic regression algorithm).

Patient profiles	Risk factors identified by knowledge graphs
Birth year: 1932 Gender: Female Without long-term condition 1 year of consultations before hospitalization No notes in the observations field	Usage of many antibacterial products noted by both ATC, and Wikidata (Amoxicil, Cifloxan, Orelox, Minocycline...) Different health problems affecting the digestive system noted by CISP2 (odynophagia 'D21', abdominal pain 'D06', vomiting 'D10')
Birth year: 1986 Gender: Male Without long-term condition 2 years of consultations before hospitalization	Within free text (contained in reasons of encounter and observations fields), daily chest pains are considered as 'Emergency' and a tongue tumor as 'Neoplasm stubs' by DBpedia

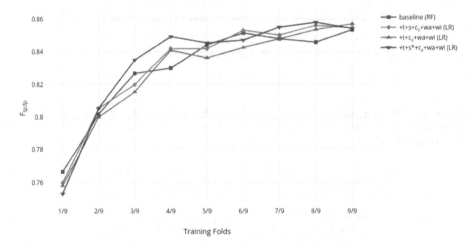

Fig. 3. Convergence curve obtained following the training on n (x-axis) KFold partitions for different configurations of the Table 4.

to distinguish provenance fields. The text field related to symptoms has been poorly filled in by doctors – as it was an 'observation' field – and the majority of the remarks thus detected by DBpedia Spotlight are mostly false alerts. Moreover, the qualitative analysis of the results showed cases involving negation ('pas de SC d'insuffisance cardiaque', meaning 'no symptom of heart failure') and poor consideration of several terms ('brûlures mictionnelles', related to bladder infection, are associated with 'Brûlure', a burn, which, therefore, has as subject the concept 'Urgence médicale', a medical emergency). Both cases are current limitations of our approach and we consider for our future work the need for handling negation and complex expressions.

5 Conclusion and Future Work

In this paper, we have presented a method for combining knowledge from knowledge graphs, whether specialized or generalist, and textual information to predict the hospitalization of patients. To do this, we generated different vector representations coupling concept vectors and bag-of-words and then evaluated their performance for prediction with different machine learning algorithms.

In the short term, we plan to identify additional concepts involved in predicting hospitalization of patients and to evaluate the impact of additional domain specific knowledge, as we focused mainly on drugs in our study. We also intend to propose an approach to automatically extract candidate medical concepts from DBpedia. Finally we plan to improve the coupling of semantic relationships and textual data in our vector representation, and support the detection of negation and complex expressions in texts.

Acknowledgement. This work is partly funded by the French government labelled PIA program under its IDEX UCAJEDI project (ANR-15-IDEX-0001).

Appendix

Among the three kernels tested for 'SVC' (RBF, linear and polynomial), the nested cross-validation selected RBF and a linear kernel equally. The ridge regression (L2 regularization) was overwhelmingly chosen by nested cross-validation for the logistic regression algorithm.

References

1. Bergstra, J., Bengio, Y.: Random search for hyper-parameter optimization. J. Mach. Learn. Res. **13**, 281–305 (2012)
2. Breiman, L.: Random forests. Mach. Learn. **45**(1), 5–32 (2001)
3. Cawley, G.C., Talbot, N.L.: On over-fitting in model selection and subsequent selection bias in performance evaluation. J. Mach. Learn. Res. **11**, 2079–2107 (2010)
4. Chang, C.C., Lin, C.J.: LIBSVM: a library for support vector machines. ACM Trans. Intell. Syst. Technol. (TIST) **2**(3), 27 (2011)
5. Choi, E., et al.: GRAM: graph-based attention model for healthcare representation learning. In: Proceedings of the 23rd ACM SIGKDD International Conference on Knowledge Discovery and Data Mining, pp. 787–795. ACM (2017)
6. Corby, O., Zucker, C.F.: The KGRAM abstract machine for knowledge graph querying. In: Web Intelligence and Intelligent Agent Technology (WI-IAT), vol. 1, pp. 338–341. IEEE (2010)
7. Daiber, J., Jakob, M., Hokamp, C., Mendes, P.N.: Improving efficiency and accuracy in multilingual entity extraction. In: Proceedings of the 9th International Conference on Semantic Systems (I-Semantics) (2013)

130   R. Gazzotti et al.

8. Forman, G., Scholz, M.: Apples-to-apples in cross-validation studies: pitfalls in classifier performance measurement. ACM SIGKDD Explor. Newsl. **12**(1), 49–57 (2010)

9. Goldstein, B.A., Navar, A.M., Pencina, M.J., Ioannidis, J.: Opportunities and challenges in developing risk prediction models with electronic health records data: a systematic review. J. Am. Med. Inform. Assoc. **24**(1), 198–208 (2017)

10. Lacroix-Hugues, V., Darmon, D., Pradier, C., Staccini, P.: Creation of the first french database in primary care using the ICPC2: feasibility study. Stud. Health Technol. Inform. **245**, 462–466 (2017)

11. McCullagh, P., Nelder, J.A.: Generalized Linear Models, vol. 37. CRC Press, Boca Raton (1989)

12. Min, H., Mobahi, H., Irvin, K., Avramovic, S., Wojtusiak, J.: Predicting activities of daily living for cancer patients using an ontology-guided machine learning methodology. J. Biomed. Semant. **8**(1), 39 (2017)

13. Ordóñez, F.J., de Toledo, P., Sanchis, A.: Activity recognition using hybrid generative/discriminative models on home environments using binary sensors. Sensors **13**(5), 5460–5477 (2013)

14. Pedregosa, F., et al.: Scikit-learn: machine learning in Python. J. Mach. Learn. Res. **12**, 2825–2830 (2011)

15. Pennington, J., Socher, R., Manning, C.: Glove: global vectors for word representation. In: Proceedings of the 2014 Conference on Empirical Methods in Natural Language Processing (EMNLP), pp. 1532–1543 (2014)

16. Salguero, A.G., Espinilla, M., Delatorre, P., Medina, J.: Using ontologies for the online recognition of activities of daily living. Sensors **18**(4), 1202 (2018)

Explore and Exploit. Dictionary Expansion with Human-in-the-Loop

Anna Lisa Gentile, Daniel Gruhl, Petar Ristoski[(✉)], and Steve Welch

IBM Research Almaden, San Jose, CA, USA
{annalisa.gentile,petar.ristoski}@ibm.com, {dgruhl,welchs}@us.ibm.com

Abstract. Many Knowledge Extraction systems rely on semantic resources - dictionaries, ontologies, lexical resources - to extract information from unstructured text. A key for successful information extraction is to consider such resources as evolving artifacts and keep them up-to-date. In this paper, we tackle the problem of dictionary expansion and we propose a human-in-the-loop approach: we couple neural language models with tight human supervision to assist the user in building and maintaining domain-specific dictionaries. The approach works on any given input text corpus and is based on the *explore and exploit* paradigm: starting from a few seeds (or an existing dictionary) it effectively discovers new instances (explore) from the text corpus as well as predicts new potential instances which are not in the corpus, i.e. *"unseen"*, using the current dictionary entries (exploit). We evaluate our approach on five real-world dictionaries, achieving high accuracy with a rapid expansion rate.

1 Introduction

Dictionary expansion [17] is one area where close integration of humans into the discovery loop has been shown to enhance task performance substantially over more traditional post-adjudication methods. This is not surprising, as dictionary membership is often a fairly subjective judgment (e.g., should a fruit dictionary include tomatoes?) [18]. Thus even with a system which finds "similar" terms (e.g., word2vec [14]) guidance is important to keep the system focused on the subject matter expert's notion of the lexicon.

In this work we propose a feature agnostic approach for dictionary expansion based on neural language models, such as word2vec and bidirectional Long Short Term Memory (BiLSTM) models [19]. To prevent semantic drift during the dictionary expansion, we effectively include human-in-the-loop. Given as input a text corpus and a set of seed examples, the proposed approach runs in two phases, *explore* and *exploit* (*EnE*), to identify new potential dictionary entries. After each iteration the subject matter expert adjudicates the proposed candidates by model, and resumes the next iteration. The *explore* phase identifies terms in the corpus that are similar to the seed entries: similarity is calculated using term vectors from the neural language model. The *exploit* phase constructs

© Springer Nature Switzerland AG 2019
P. Hitzler et al. (Eds.): ESWC 2019, LNCS 11503, pp. 131–145, 2019.
https://doi.org/10.1007/978-3-030-21348-0_9

additional complex multi-token terms based on all the current dictionary items. Identifying similar multi-token (or n-gram) terms is challenging for any word2vec style system, as they need to be "known" prior to model creation. A common solution to identify multi-token terms is to identify tokens that often appear together and therefore are probably a single term [14]: defining a threshold on their co-occurrence score can help identify valid n-grams. Once all valid terms are detected the term vector model can be built and while the vectors can be always updated, the terms themselves will always remain unchanged after the model is built. There are countless situations where having a static set of terms is not desirable. Dictionaries which have been automatically constructed are rarely complete - and it has been shown that even manually built dictionaries, that might be considered "complete", will inevitably evolve with time [12]. The most simple cause of incompleteness is that, when automatically constructing a dictionary from a corpus, valid terms may simply not occur. This is particularly true when considering multi-token terms, where the single different tokens might be present in the corpus but not in all their valid combinations - as an example, a medical corpus may contain the term *acute joint pain* but not the term *chronic hip pain*, which is however likely to occur in future texts from the same source. Including those "unseen" but valid terms in the dictionary is beneficial for all subsequent information extraction operations which are going to leverage it as a resource.

While the *explore* phase of our novel approach is similar in fashion to existing vector space models techniques, the combination of the *exploit* phase allows the dictionary extraction to go beyond the terms that actually occur in the input corpus. New phrases are generated by analyzing all the tokens (taken separately) from all the terms already in the dictionary. We generate new multi-token terms in two ways: (i) by *modification*, i.e. replacing certain tokens in an existing term with similar ones from the text corpus - e.g., "abnormal behavior" can be modified to "strange behavior"; (ii) by *extension*, i.e. concatenating additional tokens to an existing term, with related tokens from the text corpus, e.g., staring from the existing terms "abnormal blood count", "blood clotting" and "clotting problems" we can generate "abnormal blood clotting problems". The rationale is that many valid multi-token terms might not appear in a text corpus but there is enough statistical evidence to support their addition to the dictionary.

The main contribution of this work is the combination of the discriminative and the generative approaches (*explore* and *exploit*) in a highly interactive supervised model. Completely unsupervised, or even infrequently supervised models, are not particularly effective for dictionary generation. Without targeted and frequent adjudication of the extracted items many spurious results would be generated, thus requiring a heavy post-processing phase. We argue that close supervision results in a much more performant system. We show that high promptness of the human-in-the-loop (tighter computer/human partnership) results in nearly perfect performance of the system, i.e., nearly all the candidates identified by the system are valid entries in the dictionary. Specifically, we build targeted dictionaries and show that when requesting feedback every small batch of added terms (e.g. every 10 terms) we are able to construct much bigger valid dictionaries (more than double the size) as opposed to a single human post-processing evaluation of an automatically created dictionary.

We evaluate our approach on five real-world dictionaries, achieving high accuracy with a rapid expansion rate. Furthermore, we evaluate the importance of generating "future proof" dictionaries, i.e., we show that using a small subset of the entire text corpus can be used to generate dictionaries that have high coverage on the entire text corpus.

The rest of this paper is structured as follows. In Sect. 2, we give an overview of related work. In Sect. 3, we present our interactive dictionary expansion approach, followed by an evaluation in Sect. 4. We conclude with a summary and an outlook on future work.

2 Related Work

Dictionaries, ontologies and linguistic resources are the backbone of many NLP and information retrieval systems. The automatic construction of such resources has been the focus of research for many years. One of the first approaches to extract dictionaries from unstructured text is the one proposed by Riloff and Jones [17]: starting from a few seed terms it learns extraction patterns, which are then used to expand the seeds and iteratively repeat the process. Many similar approaches sprouted afterward [2,4,11,18]. Their main drawback is that they all require NLP parsing for feature extraction, and thus have a reliance on syntactic information for identifying quality patterns. Hence, such approaches underperform on less polished or grammatically incorrect text content, like user-generated text. Furthermore, completely automatic iterative methods can easily generate semantic drift - a few spurious extraction patterns can exponentially increase the inclusion of incorrect items in the dictionary.

A similar - and sometimes considered as preliminary - task is terminology extraction from text. Different from the dictionary extraction, *terminology extraction* aims at extracting the vocabulary that is specific of a certain domain, but extracted terms will belong to the several different concepts which are related to the domain. There are numerous solutions available that perform linguistic processing on a certain corpus and use various statistical techniques to understand which terms represent its domain-specific terminology. A comprehensive description (and implementation) of available techniques is available in [20,21]. In this work we compare to techniques based on term occurrence frequency [5]. A widely used example is the classic document-specific TFIDF (term frequency, inverse document frequency) [6] which has been adapted for this task [20]. The main reason for comparing with these methods is that they are (i) purely based on statistics and (ii) do not rely on external reference corpora apart from the input text. While terminology extraction can rightfully be considered as a preliminary step for dictionary extraction, we argue (and show with experiments) that performing initial candidate selection via terminology extraction can introduce unnecessary errors and limit the potential recall of the extraction, as opposed to performing the dictionary extraction directly on the raw corpus without any pre-processing. Removing the need of linguistic preprocessing can prove to be extremely beneficial when dealing with user-generated content, which is a valuable source of information for many domains. Even on technical domains such as pharmacovigilance, using a random Twitter stream as unlabeled training data has been proved successful for the recognition Adverse Drug Reaction [13].

Another challenge in the automatic creation of dictionaries is the fact that they can be highly dependent on the task at hand - one striking example is the creation of dictionaries of positive/negative words, which is highly influenced by the specific domain [9,16]. Many works tackle this hurdle by relying on machine learning techniques and tailor the algorithms to certain specific domains: these methods are in general expensive, requiring an annotated corpus and/or domain specific feature extraction (a comprehensive overview can be found in [15]). While it is clearly appealing to have completely automatic techniques, it comes at the expense of the need for annotations and fine-tuning for every new task/domain. We propose to mitigate the problem with a human-in-the-loop approach, where the "tuning" is an integral part of the process, i.e. the human works in partnership with the statistical method to drive the semantic of the task effectively and efficaciously.

Our work is closely related to *glimpse* [8], a statistical algorithm for dictionary extraction. The input is a large text corpus and a set of seed examples. Starting from these it evaluates the *contexts* (the set of words surrounding an item) in which the seeds occur and identifies "good" contexts. Contexts are scored retrospectively in terms of how many "good" results they generate. All contexts are kept which have a score over a given threshold and the candidates that appear in the most "good" contexts are provided first to the human-in-the-loop for adjudication. The approach has also been extended to *glimpseLD* [1], which is language agnostic and uses Linked Data to as a bootstrapping source. While both approaches have been proven to achieve high effectiveness for dictionary extension, both of the approaches can only identify new items that are present in the input text corpus. In this work, we adopt the *glimpse* computer/human partnership architecture and extend it with the *explore/exploit* algorithm for more effective dictionary expansion.

3   Approach

The input of the algorithm is a text corpus TC and a set of seed terms for the dictionary S. In the preprocessing step, we build a neural language model on the input text corpus TC. Our approach is based on the *explore and exploit* (*EnE*) paradigm to effectively discover new instances (explore) from the text corpus and generate new *"unseen"* instances based on human feedback (exploit). The approach is iterative: each iteration first runs the *explore* phase then the *exploit* one. After each iteration the subject matter expert performs adjudication on the proposed candidates. The *explore* phase uses all the terms currently in the dictionary to identify similar terms in the corpus (using the word2vec model), which are then accepted or rejected by the human-in-the-loop. All accepted terms are added to the dictionary and used in the *exploit* phase as well as all subsequent *explore* iterations. The *exploit* phase uses all terms in the dictionary and the neural language model to construct more complex terms that might be of interest for the user. The process stops once there are no more candidates to be discovered, or the user is satisfied with the results. The system architecture is shown in Fig. 1.

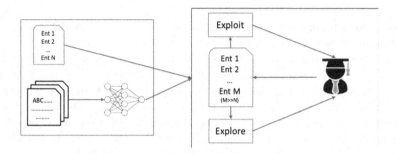

Fig. 1. EnE system architecture.

3.1   Explore

The *explore* phase uses all the terms currently in the dictionary to identify similar terms in the corpus (using the word2vec model). Word2vec is a computationally efficient two-layer neural network model for learning term embeddings from raw text. The output of the model is an embedding matrix W, where each term (single or multi token) from the corpus vocabulary V_{TC} is represented as an n-dimensional vector. When projecting this latent representations of words into a lower dimensional feature space, words which are semantically similar appear closer to each other. Therefore, the problem of calculating the similarity between two terms is a matter of calculating the distance between two instances in the given feature space. To do so we use the standard cosine similarity measure which is applied on the vectors of the instances. Formally, the similarity between two terms w_1 and w_2, with vectors V_1 and V_2, is calculated as the cosine similarity between the vectors V_1 and V_2:

$$sim(w_1, w_2) = \frac{V_1 \cdot V_2}{||V_1|| \cdot ||V_2||} \tag{1}$$

We calculate the similarity between the instances in the input dictionary and all the words in the corpus vocabulary V_{TC}. We sort the vocabulary in descending order using the cumulative similarity score, and choose the top-N candidates to present to the user. The accepted candidates are added in the input dictionary, which are then used in the *exploit* phase and the next iteration.

3.2 Exploit

In the *exploit* phase we try to identify more complex terms that don't appear in the corpus vocabulary, by analyzing the structure of the instances in the input dictionary. This is critical to help "future proof" a lexicon against new text. For a surveillance application (e.g., drug side effects mentioned on Twitter) it reduces how frequently a human needs to "tune up" the lexicon to make sure it is catching all relevant entity instances. We use two neural language models in this phase, i.e. word2vec [14] and bidirectional Long Short Term Memory (BiLSTM) models [19].

Exploit word2vec: Using the word2vec neural language model, we develop two phrase generation algorithms.

In the first approach, we first break each term in to a set of single tokens $T = \{t_1, t_2, \ldots, t_n\}$, then for each token t_i in T we identify a set of similar tokens $TS_{t_i} = \{ts_1, ts_2, \ldots, ts_s\}$ in the vocabulary V_{TC} using Eq. 1. In the next step, we build new terms by replacing t_i with a token ts_i from TS_{t_i}. The new terms are sorted based on the similarity score and the top-N are selected as candidates. For example, given the entry "abnormal behavior" the approach will identify "strange behavior", "abnormal attitude" and "strange attitude".

In the second approach, we generate new phrases by extending the instances with tokens from the text corpus that are related to the tokens in the instance. Related tokens are tokens that often share the same context, which means they often are surrounded by similar words. Given a word2vec model, we calculate the relatedness between two terms w_1 and w_2, as the probability $p(w_1|w_2)$ calculated using the softmax function,

$$p(w_1|w_2) = \frac{exp(v_{w_1}'^T v_{w_2})}{\sum_{w=1}^{V} exp(v_w'^T v_{w_2})}, \tag{2}$$

where v_w and v_w' are the input and the output vector of the word w, and V is the complete vocabulary of words.

As before, we first break each term in to a set of single tokens $T = \{t_1, t_2, \ldots, t_n\}$, then for each token t_i in T we identify a set of similar tokens $TR_{t_i} = \{tr_1, tr_2, \ldots, tr_r\}$ in the vocabulary V_{TC} using Eq. 2. In the next step, we build new multi-token term by appending a token tr_i from TR_{t_i} to each token t_i from T. The new phrases are sorted based on the relatedness score and the top-N are selected as candidates. For example, given the instance "clotting problems" in the input dictionary the approach first tries to identify related tokens in the text corpus for "clotting". For which the top word is "blood", because in many sentences "blood clotting" appears as a phrase, which can be used to generate new instances "blood clotting problems". In the next iteration the phrase can be further extended, by identifying new related words. For example, in the top-N related words for "blood" we will find "abnormal", which can be used to generate the instance "abnormal blood clotting problems".

Exploit BiLSTM: LSTM neural networks are special type of recurrent neural networks (RNN) [3] used in many NLP application. RNNs are able to model sequential data with temporal dependencies, like text. RNNs perform the same task for every element in a sequence, e.g., word in a sentence, conditioning the output of the model on the previous computations. One limitation of the basic RNN models is learning time-dependencies more than a few time-steps long [10]. LSTM networks solve this issue and are capable of learning long-term dependencies. Bidirectional LSTMs are an extension of the traditional LSTMs, which are able to capture the backwards dependences in the sequential data. Instead of training one LSTM model the BiLSTMs train two models, one for the data in the original direction, and one for the reversed copy of the input sequence. As the BiLSTM networks perform well on analyzing sequences of values and predicting the next one, they have been successfully applied for the task of text generation, i.e., given a sequence of words, the model can successfully predict the next word in the sequence. We use this capability for generating new multi-token dictionary candidates that are similar to the input seeds. To build such multi-token terms (phrases), we make use of the LSTM models in both directions, i.e., expanding existing terms in both forward and backward directions.

For the forward expansion, for each instance $T = \{t_1, t_2, \ldots, t_n\}$ in the input dictionary, we generate forward sub-sequences with size in the range $[1, n-1]$ starting from the first token t_1 till token t_{n-1}, resulting in a set of sequences $FS = \{t_1, t_1 - t_2, \ldots, t_1 - t_2 - \cdots - t_{n-1}, t_2 - t_3, \ldots, t_{n-1}\}$. Each of these sequences is then fed in the forward LSTM network to calculate the probability for each word in the corpus vocabulary V_{TC} to be the next word in the input sequence using the softmax function. For each input instance we select the top-100 generated new phrases, then we aggregate across all input instances, and select the top-N to present to the user.

For the backward expansion, for each instance $T = \{t_1, t_2, \ldots, t_n\}$ in the input dictionary, we generate backward sub-sequences with size in the range $[1, n]$ starting from the last token t_n to the first token t_1, resulting in a set of sequences $BS = \{t_n, t_n - t_{n-1}, \ldots, t_n - t_{n-1} - \cdots - t_1, t_{n-1} - t_{n-2}, \ldots, t_1\}$. Each of these sequences is then fed in the backward LSTM network to calculate the probability for each word in the corpus vocabulary V_{TC} to be the next word in the backward input sequence using the softmax function. For each input instance we select the top-100 generated new phrases, then we aggregate across all input instances, and select the top-N to present to the human-in-the-loop, which are reversed in the original order. In both modes, in cases where the phrases end with a stop-word (e.g. "a" and "the") we do a second forward pass in the network for the current sequence. Furthermore, rejected phrases that have high confidence value are copied in the next iteration, as many phrases might need multiple iterations to form a complete phrase.

For example, given the input instance "high blood pressure", the set of forward sequences will be $FS\{high, high\ blood, blood\}$ and the backwards sequences will be $BS = \{pressure, pressure\ blood, pressure\ blood\ high, blood, blood\ high, high\}$. Then each of these instances is fed in the forward and backward model, respectively.

For the forward sequence "high blood", the model proposes phrases like "high blood count", "high blood cell". While the phrase "high blood count" is a valid phrase, the phrase "high blood cell" although it has high confidence value it is not complete and cannot be accepted as valid. However, we can foresee that in the next iteration this phrase might result in a valid phrase with high confidence value. Therefore, in each iteration we keep a set of rejected phrases that have high confidence value, and we extend them once more in the next iteration. For example, the phrase "high blood cell" will be extended to a valid phrase "high blood cell count".

For the backward sequence "pressure blood", the backward model proposes phrases like "pressure blood low" and "pressure blood varying", which are then reversed to form human readable phrases, i.e., "low blood pressure" and "varying blood pressure".

4   Evaluation

To evaluate our approach we conduct three experiments, i.e., (i) count the number of newly discovered dictionary entries per iteration; (ii) the impact of the promptness of the human-in-the-loop on the system performance; (iii) capability of the system for identifying dictionary instances that are not present in the analyzed corpus, but might appear in future texts.

4.1   Dictionary Growth

We consider 3 different text corpora:

- *ADE*: A dataset from the healthcare domain, specifically tackling the problem of identifying Adverse Drug Events (ADE) in user generated data. The input text corpus consists of user blogs extracted from http://www.askapatient. com[1], containing a total of $1,384,716$ sentences. For this corpus we build a dictionary of ADE and the adjudication is performed by a medical doctor.
- *Twitter Food*: A dataset consisting of $4,203,922$ tweets, sampled from Twitter,[2] in the period of January 2017, filtered using an existing vocabulary of food items from [7]. For this corpus we build a dictionary of food items.
- *IBM Call Center*: A dataset from the IBM call center consisting of customer's surveys, containing a total of $6,004,804$ sentences. For this corpus we build 3 dictionaries containing terms expressing customers' satisfaction (*Satisfied*), terms expressing customers' being confused by the process (*Confusing*) and terms expressing customers' complaints about the phone connection (*Bad Connection*). The adjudication is performed by a team of subject matter experts that have many years experience working with costumer satisfaction data and maintaining call center systems.

---

[1] A forum where patients report their experience with medication drugs.
[2] https://twitter.com/.

Table 1. Accuracy of newly discovered dictionary instances per iteration and the average length, using W2V, EnE - W2V and EnE-BiLSTM approaches on 5 dictionaries.

Dataset	#sentences	#iter	W2V		EnE-W2V		EnE-BiLSTM	
			Acc.	Avg. Len.	Acc.	Avg. Length	Acc.	Avg. Len.
ADE	1,384,716	50	60.2	1.29	**80.3**	2.14	79.0	**2.66**
Twitter Food	4,203,922	20	67.5	1.74	**79.5**	2.34	58.3	**2.46**
Satisfied	6,004,804	20	61.3	2.39	**87.3**	3.26	75.0	**4.15**
Confusing	6,004,804	20	42.8	1.87	68.5	3.43	**71.5**	**3.79**
Bad Connection	6,004,804	10	66.0	2.26	**85.0**	2.85	81.5	**3.37**

We use the EnE approach to build the 5 dictionaries, using word2vec in the explore phase and word2vec (EnE-W2V) or BiLSTM (EnE-BiLSTM) in the explore phase. We use a standard word2vec model as a baseline, i.e., running only the explore phase of the EnE approach (W2V). For the baseline *W2V* approach in pre-processing we identify terms of maximum 3 tokens, using the phrase detection algorithm based on words co-occurrence proposed in [14]. We use the skip-gram algorithm with window size 10, 10 training iterations and 200 dimensional vectors.

The BiLSTM network has 4 stacked 256-unit LSTM layers, each followed by dropout layer with probability of 0.2 where the last layer is a fully connected Softmax layer. The models were implemented in TensorFlow,[3] and trained on Tesla P100 16 GB GPU.

We run the evaluation in 50 iterations for the *ADE* dictionary, 20 iterations for the *Twitter Food, Satisfied* and *Confusing* dictionary, and 10 iterations for the *Bad Connection* dictionary. In each iteration the algorithm proposes 20 candidates. The number of iterations was decided by the subject matter expert that is performing the adjudication, i.e., once the dictionary has sufficient number of entries the dictionary expansion stops. After each iteration we count how many new instances are discovered in the top 20 proposed candidates by the algorithm. The accepted instances are then added in the dictionary and used for the next iteration. For the *EnE* approach we run *explore* to identify 10 candidates, and *exploit* to identify another 10 candidates, while for the baseline *W2V* approach we propose directly 20 candidates. The accuracy results per iteration for each of the datasets are shown in Fig. 2, i.e., the fraction of accepted candidates by the adjudicator. The accuracy of all the approaches after the end of the process are shown in Table 1, including the average length of the discovered dictionary entries.

The results show that using the *EnE-W2V* and *EnE-BiLSTM* approach we are able to discover a steady number of instances in each iteration, significantly outperforming the baseline *W2V* approach. The *EnE-W2V* approach leads to better performance on most of the dataset, except the "IBM Call Center - Confusing" dataset where the *EnE-BiLSTM* app-

---

[3] https://www.tensorflow.org/.

a) *ADE*

b) *Twitter Food*

c) *IBM Call Center - Satisfied*

Fig. 2. Number of discovered new dictionary instances per iteration, using W2V, EnE - W2V and EnE-BiLSTM approaches on 5 dictionaries

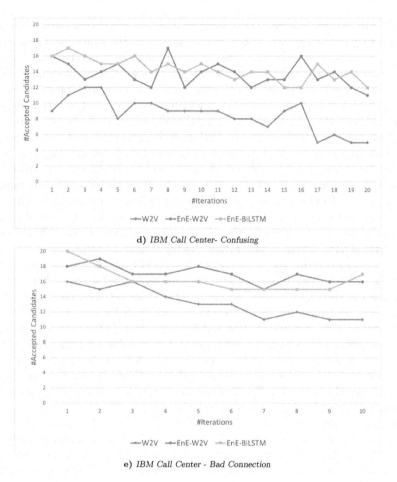

d) *IBM Call Center- Confusing*

e) *IBM Call Center - Bad Connection*

Fig. 2. (*continued*)

roach delivers higher accuracy. We can observe that on the *Twitter Food* dataset the *EnE-BiLSTM* approach performs poorly. There are two reasons for the low performance, i.e., the tweets are very short for the LSTM model to learn strong contexts for the words; (ii) the tweets contain a lot of syntactic irregularities, misspellings and incorrect grammar. We can observe that when using the *W2V* approach the number of newly discovered instances quickly decreases as the number of available instances in the whole corpus is decreasing in each iteration.

Furthermore, we can see that the *W2V* is able to identify only uni-grams and short phrases, while the *EnE* approaches can identify significantly longer phrases on all the datasets.

For the sake of completeness we compare our dictionary generation approach with fully automated terminology extraction methods. The two techniques are not directly comparable for the reason that while dictionary extraction aims at extracting terms that are cohesive and belong to the same specific semantic concept, terminology extraction aims at extracting the general vocabulary of a certain domain, but extracted terms will belong to the several different concepts. Nonetheless, given a corpus, all of terms extracted via terminology extraction would potentially contain all the terms which are specific to the corpus domain, in one big set. Therefore, one meaningful comparison that we can perform is the following: given a (validated) dictionary constructed with our approach, check how many are present in the set extracted with terminology extraction software. This would indicate if it is useful to perform terminology extraction as preliminary step and then extract all the single dictionaries for the domain.

We use the JATE software [20], which implements all state-of-the-art techniques for terminology extraction. Given that we are checking the recall of these techniques, we report results for the most comprehensive one, the TFIDF adaptation from JATE, which is generating the biggest set of terms.

We performed terminology extraction with JATE on the 5 dictionaries, with a very inclusive threshold i.e. considering any term with a score above zero as valid. For the IBM Call Center corpus, JATE extracted 118,176 terms. When considering the 3 dictionaries that we built with *EnE* for this corpus, only 17% from *Satisfied*, 10% from *Confusing* and 6% from *Bad Connection* are contained in the comprehensive JATE created terminology. Similarly for the *ADE* corpus, JATE extracted a set of 636,264 terms, and only 26% of the terms of the *ADE* dictionary built with *EnE* are present in this set. For the *Twiter food* corpus, JATE extracted a set of 1,164,329 terms, and only 43% of the terms of the *food* dictionary built with *EnE* are present in this set.

This experiment shows that although a fully automated terminology extraction method is able to generate a large number of lexicon entries, the coverage of relevant terms for specific tasks is very low. Therefore, using automatic approaches is not suitable for dictionary extension, rather a human-in-the-loop is required.

4.2   Impact of the Human-in-the-loop on the Dictionary Growth

In this experiment we show the importance of the interaction of the human-in-the-loop on the number of newly discovered instances, i.e., we evaluate if the user gives their feedback to the system sooner it will improve the performance of the system. To do so, we run the *EnE-W2V* approach with different feedback intervals on the *ADE* dataset. The feedback interval indicates how many candidates the system needs to identify before the user gives their feedback to the system. For example, when using feedback interval of 10, the user gives their feedback after 10 candidates are identified by the system. We evaluate feedback intervals of 10, 50, 100, 250 and 500. After each iteration we count the number of accepted candidates, and include them in the dictionary to be used for the next iteration. The results are shown in Fig. 3.

The results show that the tighter the human-in-the-loop integration is, the more quickly new instances are discovered. We see that with a large 500 examples

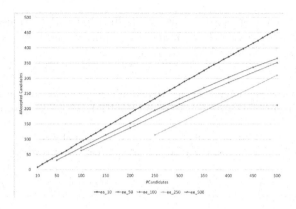

Fig. 3. Impact of the human-in-the-loop promptness on the number of newly discovered dictionary instances using EnE - W2V on the ADE dataset

feedback interval the human-in-the-loop system discovers 212 new instances, but requires the human to consider 500 candidates.

A more tightly integrated system with a 10 examples feedback interval finds 212 new instances in just 23 iterations, requiring the human to consider only 230 candidates. After 50 iterations the system discovered 460 new dictionary entries, compared to only 212 new entries when using 500 examples feedback interval. That yields 216% improvement in effectiveness of the system.

4.3   Generating "Future Proof" Dictionaries

In this experiment we evaluate if generating "unseen" instances to "future proof" a dictionary is useful. To do so, we take a small portion of the dataset to generate the vocabularies, and then we count how many of the newly generated instances that don't appear in the training set appear in the remaining text corpus that was not used for training. For the evaluation we use the 3 vocabularies from the *IBM Call Center* dataset. We randomly select 10% of the text corpus for training the neural language model and run both versions of the *EnE* algorithm to generate the vocabularies. Then we identify how many of the instances generated in the *Exploit* phase of the *EnE* approach don't occur in the training dataset, but occur in the remaining 90% of the text corpus.

The number of newly discovered entries that don't appear in the training set (#new entries), and the number of entries that appear in the future text (#future hits) on the 3 vocabularies are shown in Table 2. We can see that on the *Satisfied* dataset, both *EnE-W2V* and *EnE-BiLSTM* approaches identify a significant number of new entries that don't appear in the training dataset, but more than 50% of these entries appear in the remaining text corpus. The number of "future hits" slightly reduces on the other 2 vocabularies, but it is still significant.

These experiments prove that generating "future proof" dictionaries is useful, and it will certainly reduce how frequently a human needs to "tune up" the dictionaries in order to keep high coverage.

Table 2. Number of dictionary entries that don't occur in the training text corpus, but appear in a future text corpus. Tested on the IBM call center vocabularies.

Dataset	#iterations	EnE-W2V		EnE-BiLSTM	
		#new entries	#future hits	#new entries	#future hits
Satisfied	20	94	55 (58.51%)	83	44 (50.00%)
Confusing	20	79	32 (40.50%)	76	33 (43.42%)
Bad Connection	10	34	14 (41.17%)	52	19 (36.53%)

5   Conclusions

This paper proposes an interactive dictionary expansion tool using two neural language models. Our algorithm is iterative and purely statistical, hence does not require any feature extraction beyond tokenization. It incorporates human feedback to improve performance and control semantic drift at every iteration cycle. It does not require phrase detection prior building the model, but rather uses the neural language models to identify phrases with high confidence that might not appear in the input text corpus. This is critical to help "future proof" the dictionary to capture new terms in previously unseen text, thus reducing the how frequently the subject matter expert needs to "tune up" the dictionary. The evaluation shows that our approach is able to rapidly extend the input dictionaries with high accuracy. Furthermore, the experiments show the critical value of tight human-in-the-loop integration, which leads to higher efficiency and effectiveness for the task of dictionary expansion.

References

1. Alba, A., Coden, A., Gentile, A.L., Gruhl, D., Ristoski, P., Welch, S.: Multi-lingual concept extraction with linked data and human-in-the-loop. In: Proceedings of the Knowledge Capture Conference, p. 24. ACM (2017)
2. Ando, R.K.: Semantic lexicon construction: learning from unlabeled data via spectral analysis. Technical report, IBM Thomas J Watson Research Center, Yorktown Heights, NY (2004)
3. Bengio, Y., Simard, P., Frasconi, P.: Learning long-term dependencies with gradient descent is difficult. IEEE Trans. Neural Netw. **5**(2), 157–166 (1994)
4. Blohm, S., Cimiano, P.: Using the web to reduce data sparseness in pattern-based information extraction. In: Kok, J.N., Koronacki, J., Lopez de Mantaras, R., Matwin, S., Mladenič, D., Skowron, A. (eds.) PKDD 2007. LNCS (LNAI), vol. 4702, pp. 18–29. Springer, Heidelberg (2007). https://doi.org/10.1007/978-3-540-74976-9_6

5. Bourigault, D.: Surface grammatical analysis for the extraction of terminological noun phrases. In: Proceedings of the 14th Conference on Computational Linguistics - Volume 3, Stroudsburg, PA, USA, pp. 977–981 (1992)

6. Church, K., Gale, W.: Inverse document frequency (IDF): a measure of deviations from poisson. In: Armstrong, S., Church, K., Isabelle, P., Manzi, S., Tzoukermann, E., Yarowsky, D. (eds.) Natural Language Processing Using Very Large Corpora. Text, Speech and Language Technology, vol. 11, pp. 283–295. Springer, Dordrecht (1999). https://doi.org/10.1007/978-94-017-2390-9_18

7. Coden, A., Danilevsky, M., Gruhl, D., Kato, L., Nagarajan, M.: A method to accelerate human in the loop clustering. In: Proceedings of the 2017 SIAM International Conference on Data Mining, pp. 237–245. SIAM (2017)

8. Coden, A., Gruhl, D., Lewis, N., Tanenblatt, M., Terdiman, J.: SPOT the drug! An unsupervised pattern matching method to extract drug names from very large clinical corpora. In: Proceedings of the 2012 IEEE 2nd Conference on Healthcare Informatics, Imaging and Systems Biology, HISB 2012, pp. 33–39 (2012)

9. Hamilton, W.L., Clark, K., Leskovec, J., Jurafsky, D.: Inducing domain-specific sentiment lexicons from unlabeled corpora. In: Conference on Empirical Methods in Natural Language Processing, Austin, Texas, pp. 595–605 (2016)

10. Hochreiter, S., Bengio, Y., Frasconi, P., Schmidhuber, J., et al.: Gradient flow in recurrent nets: the difficulty of learning long-term dependencies (2001)

11. Igo, S.P., Riloff, E.: Corpus-based semantic lexicon induction with web-based corroboration. In: Proceedings of the Workshop on Unsupervised and Minimally Supervised Learning of Lexical Semantics, pp. 18–26. ACL (2009)

12. Kuriki, I., et al.: The modern Japanese color lexicon. J. Vis. **17**, 1 (2017)

13. Lee, K., et al.: Adverse drug event detection in tweets with semi-supervised convolutional neural networks (2017)

14. Mikolov, T., Sutskever, I., Chen, K., Corrado, G.S., Dean, J.: Distributed representations of words and phrases and their compositionality. In: Advances in Neural Information Processing Systems, pp. 3111–3119 (2013)

15. Pazienza, M.T., Pennacchiotti, M., Zanzotto, F.M.: Terminology extraction: an analysis of linguistic and statistical approaches. In: Sirmakessis, S. (ed.) Knowledge Mining. STUDFUZZ, vol. 185, pp. 255–279. Springer, Heidelberg (2005). https://doi.org/10.1007/3-540-32394-5_20

16. Pröllochs, N., Feuerriegel, S., Neumann, D.: Generating domain-specific dictionaries using Bayesian learning. In: ECIS 2015, pp. 0–14 (2015)

17. Riloff, E., Jones, R., et al.: Learning dictionaries for information extraction by multi-level bootstrapping. In: AAAI/IAAI, pp. 474–479 (1999)

18. Riloff, E., Wiebe, J., Wilson, T.: Learning subjective nouns using extraction pattern bootstrapping. In: HLT-NAACL 2003, pp. 25–32 (2003)

19. Schuster, M., Paliwal, K.K.: Bidirectional recurrent neural networks. IEEE Trans. Signal Process. **45**(11), 2673–2681 (1997)

20. Zhang, Z., Gao, J., Ciravegna, F.: JATE 2.0: Java automatic term extraction with apache solr. In: LREC 2016, Portorož, Slovenia (2016)

21. Zhang, Z., Gao, J., Ciravegna, F.: SemRe-Rank: Improving automatic term extraction by incorporating semantic relatedness with personalised pagerank. TKDD **12**(5), 57:1–57:41 (2018)

Aligning Biomedical Metadata with Ontologies Using Clustering and Embeddings

Rafael S. Gonçalves[(✉)], Maulik R. Kamdar, and Mark A. Musen

Center for Biomedical Informatics Research, Stanford University, Stanford, CA, USA
{rafael.goncalves,maulikrk,musen}@stanford.edu

Abstract. The metadata about scientific experiments published in online repositories have been shown to suffer from a high degree of representational heterogeneity—there are often many ways to represent the same type of information, such as a *geographical location* via its latitude and longitude. To harness the potential that metadata have for discovering scientific data, it is crucial that they be represented in a uniform way that can be queried effectively. One step toward uniformly-represented metadata is to normalize the multiple, distinct field names used in metadata (e.g., *lat lon, lat and long*) to describe the same type of value. To that end, we present a new method based on clustering and embeddings (i.e., vector representations of words) to align metadata field names with ontology terms. We apply our method to biomedical metadata by generating embeddings for terms in biomedical ontologies from the BioPortal repository. We carried out a comparative study between our method and the NCBO Annotator, which revealed that our method yields more and substantially better alignments between metadata and ontology terms.

Keywords: Biomedical metadata · Ontologies · Alignment · Embeddings

1 Introduction

Metadata are crucial artifacts to facilitate the discovery and reuse of data. Publishers and funding agencies require scientists to share research data along with metadata. Sadly, the quality of metadata published in online repositories is typically poor. In previous work, we identified numerous anomalies in metadata hosted in the U.S. National Center for Biotechnology Information (NCBI) BioSample metadata repository [1], which describe biological samples used in biomedical experiments [5]. For example, simple binary or numeric fields are often populated with inadequate values of different data types, and there are typically many ways to represent the same information in metadata fields (e.g., *lat lon, Lat-Long*, among dozens of other field names to represent a location via its latitude and longitude). This is not an idiosyncratic problem affecting just a

© Springer Nature Switzerland AG 2019
P. Hitzler et al. (Eds.): ESWC 2019, LNCS 11503, pp. 146–161, 2019.
https://doi.org/10.1007/978-3-030-21348-0_10

single database—it is a pervasive issue that affects nearly all data repositories, and that is detrimental to the ability to effectively search and reuse data.

To make data Findable, Accessible, Interoperable, and Reusable (FAIR) [22], it is necessary that the metadata that describe the data be of high quality. One step toward generating better quality metadata out of legacy metadata is to normalize the multiple field names that are used interchangeably in metadata to describe the same thing. By doing so, we can reduce the representational heterogeneity that currently hinders metadata repositories and thus improve the searchability of the associated data. In our study of the quality of BioSample metadata, we identified that metadata authors tend to use off-the-cusp field names to annotate their datasets even when there are standardized terms (specified by the repositories) to use for a particular type of value. Metadata field names are rarely linked to terms from ontologies or metadata vocabularies. While the use of ontology terms is encouraged in some fields, there is no mechanism to enforce or verify this suggestion. Ideally, the field names used in a metadata repository should be drawn from ontologies, and there should be one single field name, rather than many, to describe each distinct type of metadata value.

In this paper, we present a new method to semi-automatically align arbitrary strings with ontology terms using *embeddings*. Embeddings are representations of words or phrases (or other types of entities) as low-dimensional numeric vectors. Word embeddings are capable of capturing contextual information and relations between different words in a text corpus [4,14]. Our method works by clustering input strings according to a string distance metric, such as the Levenshtein edit distance, and then comparing embeddings for the input strings with embeddings computed for the human-readable labels of ontology terms. The term alignments are ranked by taking into account the cosine distance between embeddings, and the edit distance between input strings and ontology term labels. To show the efficacy of our method, we align a corpus of metadata field names taken from the BioSample metadata repository with terms from ontologies in BioPortal [12]. We compare three clustering methods over six different distance metrics to determine which combination works best for the BioSample corpus. Then, we carry out a comparative study of the alignments found by our method with those found by the NCBO Annotator [7]. Finally, we conduct semi-structured interviews with subject-matter experts to verify: (a) the quality of our alignments compared to those that the NCBO Annotator finds, and (b) the appropriateness of our alignments when the NCBO Annotator finds none.

2   Related Work

The NCBO Annotator is a reference service for annotating biomedical data and text with terms from biomedical ontologies. The service works directly with ontologies hosted in the BioPortal ontology repository. The NCBO Annotator relies on the Mgrep concept recognizer, developed at the University of Michigan, to match arbitrary text against a set of dictionary terms provided by BioPortal ontologies [17]. The NCBO Annotator additionally exploits is-a relations between terms to expand the annotations found with Mgrep and to rank the alignments.

There are several recent methods to generate embeddings for entities in an RDF graph or OWL ontology. These embeddings, often called knowledge graph embeddings, require triples of the form ⟨head entity, relation, tail entity⟩. Translation-based methods represent each *head* or *tail* entity as a point in a vector space, and the *relation* represents a vector translation function in a hyperplane (i.e., the *head* entity vector can be translated to the *tail* entity vector, using a geometrical function over the *relation* vector) [10,19,21]. Other methods to generate these knowledge graph embeddings are inspired by language modeling approaches, which rely on sequences of words in a text corpus—that is, random walks are carried out on an RDF graph to generate sequences of entities in nearby proximity, and these sequences can be used to generate latent numerical representations of entities [16]. While these methods have been effective for link prediction in knowledge graphs, triple classification, and fact extraction, they cannot be used to assess semantic similarity of different terms by examining how they are used in the context of literature.

Word embeddings can be generated from a corpus of textual documents through popular approaches such as skip-gram and continuous bag of words models [4,14]. Word embeddings generated from a corpus of biomedical abstracts have been shown to aid in the discovery of novel drug–reaction relations [15]. Embeddings can be computed for ontology term labels by using a weighted mean of word embeddings contained within the label. Such term embeddings have been used to align elements in the vocabularies of biomedical RDF graphs [8]. Such an approach does not require re-training the term embeddings (a shortcoming of phrase embedding approaches [13]), it can use domain-specific context (e.g., the biomedical significance behind the term *tumor region*, and similarity to other terms such as *cell region* or *site of cancer*), and it can enable similarity between terms with arbitrary word lengths.

The existing works to align biomedical text with ontology terms have the following shortcomings: they do not use vector space embeddings of terms [6]; they generate ontology term embeddings using the structure of the ontology rather than background knowledge from textual data [18]; and they perform alignments against only a few ontologies containing a small number of terms. Conventional syntactic similarity metrics (e.g., Levenshtein distance) do not capture the context where terms are used. Some techniques use embeddings computed with background knowledge from Wikipedia or other generic corpora. Such embeddings are not as appropriate for our case, because biomedical metadata field names consist of multi-word, domain-specific, and complex terms, which are not typically defined or mentioned together in generic corpora [20]. Using biomedical background knowledge is essential to improve the efficacy of alignments, since most terms are biomedicine-specific; and to provide textual contexts where the aligned terms are used, which is essential to help experts verify alignments.

3   Methods

The approach we designed to align a collection of arbitrary strings with ontology terms, shown in Fig. 1, consists of the following steps. (1) We cluster input

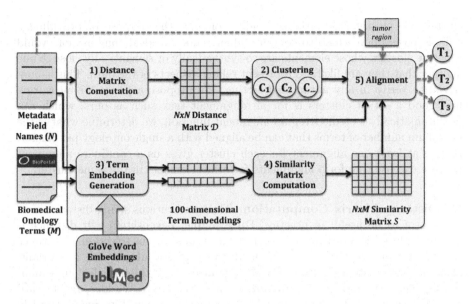

Fig. 1. Components of our metadata alignment method. In this figure, methods are colored in orange, metadata-related variables are colored in purple, and ontology-related variables are colored in blue. **(1) Distance Matrix Computation:** Our method uses a string distance metric to compare N metadata field names with each other, generating a distance matrix $\mathcal{D}$ of shape $N \times N$. **(2) Clustering:** A clustering function takes as input the distance matrix $\mathcal{D}$ and generates clusters of metadata field names. **(3) Term Embedding Generation:** Metadata field names and terms from biomedical ontologies are represented in a 100-dimensional vector space, using word embeddings generated from PubMed (https://www.ncbi.nlm.nih.gov/pubmed) abstracts. **(4) Similarity Matrix Computation:** Our method computes cosine similarity scores between term embeddings of N metadata field names and M ontology terms, generating an $N \times M$ similarity matrix $\mathcal{S}$. **(5) Alignment:** Given a metadata field name (e.g., *tumor region*), our method selects the cluster containing the field name, and then chooses the top metadata field names that have a minimal distance (using $\mathcal{D}$) from the given metadata field name. Using these highly similar field names, the distance matrix $\mathcal{D}$, and the similarity matrix $\mathcal{S}$, our method generates and ranks ontology alignments $\{T_1, T_2, T_3, \ldots\}$, shown on the right side of the figure as output. (Color figure online)

strings according to a distance metric (e.g., Levenshtein distance), which provides a grouping of syntactically similar strings. (2) We compare embeddings of input strings with ontology term embeddings trained on a corpus of biomedical ontologies. (3) We generate alignments between input strings and ontology terms by attending to the distance between the strings and the ontology terms.

For the purpose of human analysis, an ideal combination of a clustering function and a distance metric would yield relatively small clusters, for example, no bigger than 100 elements. We can test this automatically, by attending to observations such as the average size of the clusters, the size of the biggest cluster, the cluster size variance, and so on. For the purpose of providing a reliable basis upon which to compute alignments, an ideal combination would generate clusters whose elements are so syntactically or semantically close to one another that they are likely to represent related aspects of the data. This is non-trivial to verify in any automated setting. We propose a proxy for measuring how good a set of clusters is for an alignment task such as ours, which can be automatically tested. Given an alignment function, we determine what is the maximum number of terms that can be aligned with a single ontology per cluster. Having at least one alignment for each cluster gives us a candidate alignment that we can use to inform alignments for other elements in the same cluster.

(1) Distance Matrix Computation. There are various string distance metrics shown to be useful in practice. For example, Levenshtein edit distance is widely deployed in word processors to detect typos. In our selection of distance metrics, we included the Levenshtein distance metric along with its variant, Damerau-Levenshtein. We tested cosine distance as it is the basis for our semantic alignment. We also tested Jaro distance, its variant Jaro-Winkler, and Jaccard distance (set-based, with exact match), because they are well-known and widely used metrics. We use a distance metric to compare N metadata field names with each other, thus generating a distance matrix $\mathcal{D}$ of shape $N \times N$.

(2) Clustering. Clustering functions applicable to our method must not require an upfront specification of the number of clusters. This is intuitively necessary since we have no a priori knowledge of what the data are. When selecting clustering functions, we had prior knowledge that affinity propagation [3] worked well to cluster biomedical terms according to Levenshtein distance (see [5]). We compared affinity propagation with a highly common density-based algorithm–Density-Based Spatial Clustering of Applications with Noise (DBSCAN) [2], and with Hierarchical DBSCAN (HDBSCAN) [11], which is a hierarchical type of clustering that builds on DBSCAN. Each clustering function takes as input a distance matrix and assigns metadata field names to disjoint clusters.

(3) Term Embedding Generation. We describe the method we designed to represent metadata field names and ontology terms as high-dimensional numerical vectors, henceforth called *term embeddings*, based on the GloVe (Global Vectors for Word Representation) algorithm [14]. We generated word embeddings using a corpus of approximately 30 million PubMed abstracts from the MEDLINE database–a database of journal citations and abstracts for biomedical literature [9]. For this work, we used only the title and the abstract of each citation. We performed the same preprocessing steps to process biomedical publication abstracts (i.e., tokenization, medical entity normalization) from the PubMed repository as Percha et al. [15].

Word embeddings represent each word as a high-dimensional numerical vector based on co-occurrence counts of those words as observed in publications.

We used the GloVe algorithm to generate 100-dimensional word embeddings from the tokenized biomedical publications. The vectors are generated after a training phase of 20 iterations with an α learning rate of 0.75. These parameters (e.g., vector dimensions) are inspired by Percha et al. [15], who successfully used and evaluated biomedical word embeddings to discover novel drug–drug interactions.

We represent each metadata field name or ontology term in a high dimensional space using word embedding vectors. We generate a vocabulary of 2,531,989 words from 30 million PubMed biomedical publication abstracts. The words in our vocabulary appear in at least 5 distinct abstracts. We determined this threshold empirically, by identifying words that might be important for metadata field names (e.g., an unusual term such as **zymosterone**, which is a compound involved in the synthesis of cholesterol) and that are mentioned in only 5 abstracts. Subsequently, we represent each word in a 100-dimensional numerical space called the word embedding vector. We generate a term embedding vector by computing a weighted average of the words in the term label, with the weights being the Inverse-Document-Frequency (IDF) statistic for each word. We created a default embedding vector and IDF statistic (0.01) for any word not in the vocabulary. We show the equation to generate a term embedding vector below.

$$\mathbf{x}_{(term)} = \frac{\sum_{w_i \in \mathcal{L}(term)} idf_{(w_i)} * \mathbf{x}_{(w_i)}}{\sum_{w_i \in \mathcal{L}(term)} idf_{(w_i)}} \tag{1}$$

Here, $\mathbf{x}_{(w_i)}$ represents the 100-dimensional word embedding vector, and $\mathcal{L}(term)$ is the term label. For ontology terms, the term label $\mathcal{L}(term)$ is extracted from the values of annotations properties commonly used in biomedical ontologies to encode human-readable labels (i.e. *rdfs:label* and *skos:prefLabel*), whereas for metadata field names, the term label is the field name.

(4) Similarity Matrix Computation. We compute a cosine similarity matrix S for the N metadata field names and M ontology terms. Hence, the shape of matrix S is $N \times M$, and an individual cell in this matrix S_{ij} is the cosine similarity score $co\text{-}sim(N_i, M_j)$ between the metadata field name N_i and the ontology term M_j. We present the equation to compute $co\text{-}sim(N_i, M_j)$ below.

$$co\text{-}sim(N_i, M_j) = \frac{\mathbf{x}_{(N_i)} \cdot \mathbf{x}_{(M_j)}}{||\mathbf{x}_{(N_i)}|| ||\mathbf{x}_{(M_j)}||} = \frac{\sum_{k=1}^{n=100} x_{(N_i)k} * x_{(M_j)k}}{\sqrt{\sum_{k=1}^{n=100} x_{(N_i)k}^2} \sqrt{\sum_{k=1}^{n=100} x_{(M_j)k}^2}} \tag{2}$$

In the above equation, $\mathbf{x}_{(N_i)}$ and $\mathbf{x}_{(M_j)}$ are the 100-dimensional term embedding vectors for the metadata field name N_i and the ontology term M_j respectively.

(5) Alignment. We specify our approach to find alignments between strings and ontology terms in Definition 1.

Definition 1. *Let* $align_r$ (S, C_Ψ, D_m) *be a function that takes a set of strings S, a collection of clusters C computed according to a clustering function Ψ, and* *a matrix* D *of the pairwise distances between all strings in* S *computed according to a distance metric* m, *and returns an alignment map* $\mathcal{A} := $ S $\rightarrow$ $\mathcal{T}$ *that maps each input string in* S *to a list of recommended ontology terms* $\mathcal{T}$. *We say a string* $s \in S$ *is aligned with an ontology term* $t \in \mathcal{T}$ *if the average of the cosine similarity between the embeddings of* s *and* t, *denoted* $w(s)$ *and* $w(t)$ *respectively, and the edit similarity between* s *and* t *is above a threshold* r, *as follows.*

$$\mathcal{A} := \left\{ s \to t \mid s \in S \wedge \frac{\text{co-sim}(w(s), w(t)) + \text{edit-sim}(s, t)}{2} > r \right\} \tag{3}$$

We use both the cosine and edit similarities between strings to prevent false positive alignments between completely unrelated strings, which could result from aligning using cosine similarity alone. We have anecdotal evidence that the IDF ranking sometimes unduly attributes too much weight to certain words in metadata field names and throws off alignments. On the other hand, by taking both measures into account we run the danger of missing alignments between strings that are syntactically very different but semantically equivalent. We experimented with different weighting schemes between cosine and edit distance, and found the best compromise to be the average between *co-sim* and *edit-sim*.

Materials. The metadata in the NCBI BioSample are specified through fields that take the form of *name–value pairs*, for example, **geo location:** *Alaska*. Users of BioSample can use standard *field names* specified by BioSample, or they can (and often do) coin new names for their fields. We gathered all the fields names used across all metadata in BioSample. There are a total of 18,198 syntactically distinct field names in the BioSample metadata. We then normalized the metadata field names by replacing all non-alphabetic symbols with spaces, splitting words concatenated in CamelCase notation, converting all strings to lower case, and trimming all but one space between words. After removing duplicates, and strings which had fewer than 3 characters that we considered to be inappropriately short as metadata field names, we ended up with 15,553 unique field names. To generate embeddings, we used a corpus of ontologies from BioPortal composed of 675 ontologies, which was extracted on May 25, 2018.

4 Results

In this section we present the results of clustering and aligning the metadata field names from the BioSample repository with terms from ontologies in the BioPortal repository. We first carried out an exploratory study of clustering functions and distance metrics in order to identify a suitable combination for the BioSample corpus. Based on this experiment, described in Sect. 4.1, we hoped to draw a theory about selecting an ideal combination of a clustering function and distance metric that can be automated in the future. Subsequently, we performed a comparative study of the alignments found by our method and those found by the NCBO Annotator. We compare the two methods according to whether they found at least one alignment per cluster, and according to how many field names they were able to align. We describe this study in Sect. 4.2.

4.1 Clustering Metadata Field Names

In this experiment, we normalized the BioSample field names as described in Sect. 3, and then we evaluated combinations of clustering methods and distance metrics according to the following measures: number of clusters generated; average, median, and standard deviation of the number of field names in each cluster; number of field names in the biggest and smallest cluster; and number of clusters of the smallest size. We show the results in Table 1.

The HDBSCAN algorithm generated clusters that were of reasonable size for human analysis. The average cluster size across the board was around 20 field names, and the median cluster size was 10 or fewer. However, every distance metric we used resulted in at least one huge cluster with over 1,500 field names, and hundreds of tiny clusters with only 2 names each. Overall the clusters generated using HDBSCAN were not particularly suitable for human analysis.

Table 1. Results of clustering metadata field names. The table shows, from left to right, for each combination of clustering function and distance metric: the number of clusters; the average cluster size; the median cluster size; the standard deviation of the cluster size; the size of the biggest cluster; the size of the smallest cluster; and the number of clusters of the smallest size. The best results are shown in bold.

Clustering method	Distance metric	Nr. of clusters	Avg size	Median size	Std dev.	Biggest cluster	Smallest cluster	Nr. clusters of smallest size
HDBSCAN	Levenshtein	641	27	10	94	1671	2	140
	Damerau	712	24	8	85	1671	2	174
	Jaro	871	20	7	91	2232	2	230
	Jaro-Winkler	1053	16	6	80	2385	2	255
	Jaccard	721	24	9	81	1762	2	178
	Cosine	1381	12	6	89	3091	2	314
DBSCAN	Levenshtein	1191	14	2	279	8099	2	805
	Damerau	1178	14	2	280	8037	2	795
	Jaro	1623	10	2	192	7006	2	924
	Jaro-Winkler	941	18	2	345	10151	2	514
	Jaccard	1045	16	2	306	7660	2	755
	Cosine	1150	15	2	258	6844	2	702
AP	Levenshtein	2145	8	5	8	60	1	491
	Damerau	2146	8	5	8	58	1	495
	Jaro	1495	11	10	7	50	1	1
	Jaro-Winkler	**1387**	**12**	**10**	**9**	**61**	**2**	**13**
	Jaccard	1743	10	8	7	43	1	264
	Cosine	1415	12	7	32	1126	1	159

The results of clustering metadata field names using DBSCAN were very poor with all distance metrics. This method yielded extremely large clusters containing around 8,000 field names and over 500 clusters with only 2 field names. There is significant variability in the size of the clusters too, as illustrated by the high standard deviation of the size of clusters. Generally, the clusters generated using DBSCAN are even less suitable for human analysis than HDBSCAN.

Clustering metadata field names using affinity propagation resulted in seemingly high quality clusters in terms of size. There were on average 1,783 clusters across all distance metrics, which is higher than the other clustering methods. However, this means that the clusters are generally much smaller. On average there were 10 field names per cluster, and the median size was 8 field names. The sizes of the large clusters found by affinity propagation were especially encouraging; the largest cluster was found using the Jaro-Winkler distance metric and it has 61 field names. In comparison with the other methods, this is highly encouraging. The number of clusters of the smallest size varies between distance metrics. Clustering based on the Levenshtein, Damerau, or Jaccard distances results in many clusters with only one field name. Using the Jaro-Winkler distance as a basis for clustering seems to yield the best overall results—it results in a desirable number of metadata field names per cluster, it has low variability of cluster size, and it results in neither too big clusters nor too small clusters.

4.2   Alignments Between Field Names and Ontology Terms

In this experiment, we aimed to verify how well our approach can align clusters and their elements with ontologies and ontology terms, using different combinations of clustering methods and distance metrics. We compare the alignments obtained using our approach with those obtained using the NCBO Annotator. For each cluster in a set of clusters, we set out to find one ontology that provides the most alignments for the elements in that cluster—that is, an *ontology recommendation* for a cluster—and we record the number of field names aligned with that ontology. The alignments of our method are based on a minimum cosine similarity (threshold r in Definition 1) of 0.85 between the embeddings of field names and ontology terms. The results of this experiment are in Table 2.

Our method found an ontology with which to align cluster elements for over 90% of clusters, on average, across all combinations of clustering methods and distance metrics. On the other hand, the NCBO Annotator only found ontologies for less than 50% of clusters on average. The best coverage obtained using the NCBO Annotator is using affinity propagation and Jaro-Winkler distance, for which 69% of the clusters were aligned with ontologies. While this combination is not the best that our method found, if we take into account the average coverage of both our method and the NCBO Annotator, the combination just mentioned is still the best one, yielding 81% average coverage for both methods.

Using our method, we aligned 7 metadata field names per cluster with ontology terms across all combinations in Table 2, while the NCBO Annotator only aligned 2 field names, on average. Taking into account that the mean cluster size is 12 elements using affinity propagation and Jaro-Winkler, aligning 8 of those

Table 2. Comparison of alignments found by our approach and by the NCBO Annotator. The table shows for each combination of clustering method and distance metric: the number of ontology recommendations obtained for all clusters ("Nr. recs."); the percentage of clusters that have one ontology recommendation, i.e., coverage ("Cov."); the average/median number of field names in each cluster that were aligned with ontology terms. The best results are shown in bold.

Clustering method	Distance metric	Our approach			NCBO annotator		
		Nr. recs.	Cov.	Avg./median fields covered	Nr. recs.	Cov.	Avg./median fields covered
HDBSCAN	Levenshtein	625	98%	11/5	390	61%	3/1
	Damerau	695	98%	10/4	428	60%	3/2
	Jaro	853	98%	9/4	403	46%	3/2
	Jaro-Winkler	1027	98%	8/4	678	64%	2/1
	Jaccard	711	99%	10/4	441	61%	3/1
	Cosine	1355	98%	6/4	859	62%	2/1
DBSCAN	Levenshtein	1042	87%	7/2	309	26%	1/1
	Damerau	1031	88%	7/2	306	26%	2/1
	Jaro	1448	89%	6/2	642	40%	2/1
	Jaro-Winkler	821	87%	9/2	358	38%	2/1
	Jaccard	937	90%	7/2	375	36%	1/1
	Cosine	1037	90%	7/2	440	38%	1/1
AP	Levenshtein	1962	91%	5/4	773	36%	3/1
	Damerau	1961	91%	5/4	774	36%	3/1
	Jaro	1432	96%	7/6	867	58%	2/2
	Jaro-Winkler	**1295**	**93%**	**8/7**	**952**	**69%**	**2/2**
	Jaccard	1609	92%	6/5	1066	61%	2/2
	Cosine	1356	96%	7/5	913	65%	2/2

elements on average is a success. The most metadata field names aligned per cluster was achieved using the HDBSCAN algorithm. This is unsurprising, since HDBSCAN produces much larger clusters, and so it is more likely that it can find many more alignments per cluster and thus have better overall coverage.

Overall, using the NCBO Annotator we found alignments for 12,454 metadata field names, while using our method we found alignments for all terms. The average similarity score of the topmost alignments for all field names is 0.94 (where 1 means an exact match), which looks highly promising.

5   Evaluation by Expert Panel

To investigate the quality of the alignments found by our method, we designed an evaluation with a panel of subject-matter experts to verify the following two hypotheses. *(H1)* The ontology term alignments provided by our method are preferable to alignments provided by the NCBO Annotator for the same metadata field name. *(H2)* The ontology term alignments provided by our method are adequate to describe metadata field names even when the NCBO Annotator does not provide alignments for those field names. We continued to use a minimum similarity score (threshold r in Definition 1) of 0.85 between BioSample metadata field name and ontology terms, to ensure that our method provided good quality alignments.

5.1   Semi-structured Interview Design

We designed a semi-structured interview format to test our hypotheses, and we conducted interviews with four experts who are biomedical metadata experts. Our panel experts were specifically selected as they all have extensive experience in: engineering and working with metadata authoring and publishing software; constructing metadata forms for specific datasets and community standards; using ontologies and metadata vocabularies to annotate data; and working with users and developers to build infrastructure for describing scientific data. All experts have backgrounds and degrees in computer science.

We compiled one list of metadata field names to test each hypothesis. *List 1* to test *H1* was composed of 6 metadata field names randomly drawn from the set of metadata field names for which both our method and the NCBO Annotator found alignments. *List 2* to test *H2* was composed of 6 metadata field names randomly drawn from the set of metadata field names for which the NCBO Annotator did not find alignments. The selected metadata field names for the expert evaluation are listed in Table 3. The questions for each expert were randomly selected from List 1 and 2 in such a way that, for every metadata field name, we would have 3 responses from the experts.

Table 3. Lists of metadata field names used in the interviews. The table shows the metadata field names selected for *List 1* to test *H1*, and for *List 2* to test *H2*.

List 1		List 2	
Q1	sample depth m	Q7	scientific name
Q2	mapped reference genome	Q8	patientnumber
Q3	tissue source	Q9	participants
Q4	isolate id	Q10	stimuli
Q5	tumor region	Q11	cryptophytes
Q6	cardiovascular failure	Q12	relhumidityavg

In our study we asked the experts to discuss if and how each metadata field name is related to the ontology terms with which it is aligned. We use qualitative categories, which we describe in Table 4, to gather feedback from experts. We chose this style of scale since a typical Likert-style scale is unlikely to be informative as to precisely how a given term relates to a field name (according to the experts' understanding and interpretation of the text). For example, it is preferable to know, for a given metadata field name *bird species*, that the ontology term *species* is **more general** than *bird species*, or that *owl* is **more specific**, than it is to know that an ontology term is more or less appropriate to describe, or better or worse aligned with some field name.

Table 4. Expert response categories used in the interviews. The table shows the categories that we used to gather feedback about how metadata field names related to the recommended ontology terms. In the second column we show example recommended ontology terms for the input field name *"bird species"*.

Category	Examples for *"bird species"*
Unrelated	Mouse
Looks unrelated	Bird by species
May be related	Bird species identifier
More general	Species
More specific	Owl
Looks similar	Bird species name
Identical	Species of bird

The format of the interview was as follows:

1. We described the purpose of the study—to evaluate different algorithms for aligning metadata field names with ontology terms.
2. We described the challenge that our method meets—to normalize the many different field names used in metadata records to describe the same data.
3. We listed typical questions that experts could ask of the interviewer—to give example values for the metadata fields; to clarify the task or the questions; to clarify or give examples of the categories in Table 4.
4. We described the task that the experts were about to carry out—for each question out of 9 questions:
   (a) We showed the metadata field name, and asked the expert to describe her/his understanding of the field name. We ranked their understanding according to whether the meaning of the field name was *clear, roughly clear,* or *unclear.*
   (b) We showed a list of human-readable labels from the ontology terms that were aligned with the field name.
   (c) We asked the expert to discuss each ontology term along the categories described in Table 4 while voicing their reasoning.

5.2 Expert Panel Results

The results of testing *H1*, shown in Fig. 2, suggest that many of the alignments found by our approach were of very high quality—in the *identical* category. On the other hand, none of the alignments found by the NCBO Annotator were considered identical to the metadata field names. Among the alignments found by our method, none was considered *unrelated* to the corresponding field name, while the NCBO Annotator suggested 12 such *unrelated* alignments. For example, the NCBO Annotator suggested the term *mapped* for the field name *mapped reference genome* (Q2).

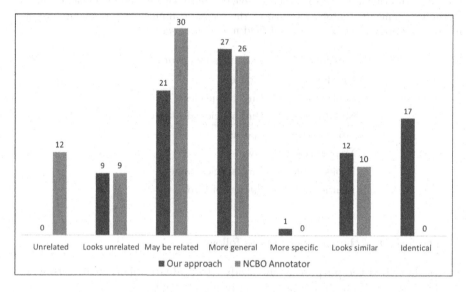

Fig. 2. Results of expert panel. Number of alignments that were considered to be in each of the categories along the *x*-axis, for both our method and the NCBO Annotator.

Both methods yielded 9 alignments that *looked unrelated* to the field names. One example of these is the ontology term *cardiovascular function* for the field name *cardiovascular failure* (Q6), as categorized by one expert. On the other hand, this expert considered the ontology term *cardiovascular* (given by the NCBO Annotator) to be *similar* to *cardiovascular failure*. One school of thought may consider *cardiovascular failure* to be *more specific* than *cardiovascular function*. In this case, the expert reasoning could also be that *cardiovascular function* indicates "heart is functioning well" and *cardiovascular failure* indicates "heart is not functioning well". In the future, we will show experts a small snippet of all descendants of the aligned ontology term (with definition) for more context.

The alignments found by the NCBO Annotator were often categorized as *more general* than the metadata field names. For example, for the field name *tissue source* (Q3) the NCBO Annotator suggested *tissue* and *source*, while our method suggested *tissue source site* and *source organ*. As expected, we found that when the metadata field names were syntactically identical or very similar to the labels of ontology terms, experts categorized them as *identical*. For example, experts categorized *depth of sample* as either identical or similar to the field name *sample depth m.* One expert observed that *depth of sample* is more generic, since it is missing the specification of the unit of measurement.

Interestingly, when answering Q8, two experts thought the meaning of the metadata field name *patientnumber* was clear—they saw the first ontology term recommended, which happened to be "patient number" and they said it was identical. When they saw the third term recommended, which was "number of patients", both experts revised their interpretation of the meaning of the field name. One expert lowered the alignment of both options to "similar", while the other expert admitted that the third option could be just as "identical" as the first option to align with the field name.

The results of testing *H2* demonstrate that most of the alignments found by our method were very precise, and categorized as either *similar* or *identical* by participants. The study showed that 39 (43%) ontology term alignments were considered *identical* matches to the metadata field names; 23 (26%) alignments were considered *similar*; 7 (8%) alignments *more specific* than the field name; 10 (11%) alignments *more general*; 8 alignments that *may be related*; 1 alignment that *looked unrelated*; and 2 alignments that were considered *unrelated*.

6   Conclusions

We developed a new method based on clustering and embeddings to align arbitrary strings with ontology terms. We applied our method to align metadata field names from NCBI BioSample metadata with terms from ontologies in the Bio-Portal repository. In our experiments we determined that clustering metadata field names using affinity propagation according to the Jaro-Winkler distance metric was the most suitable combination for our corpus. Using this combination as the basis of our alignment method, we were able to find high quality alignments between all metadata field names and at least one ontology term. Unlike existing ontology alignment or string similarity methods, we compute semantic similarity using a combination of background knowledge derived from biomedical publication abstracts and ontology term descriptions, and we can efficiently align strings against a corpus of 10 million terms from 675 ontologies.

We carried out a comparative study between our method and the NCBO Annotator, in which we discovered that our method found many more alignments overall. We also compared the two methods as part of an expert panel that we conducted via semi-structured interviews. We discovered that our method was able to find highly precise alignments even between strings that, while syntactically not the same, described the same thing. On the other hand, none of the alignments found by the NCBO Annotator were considered identical to the metadata field names. The overall results of our expert panel are illustrative of the efficacy of our method, and its potential for applications. In this work we tuned and applied our method to biomedical metadata, although in principle our approach can be applied to any domain that has a sufficiently rich source of textual knowledge and ontologies to generate embeddings from.

Our experiments show that our method is a suitable solution to align biomedical metadata with ontology terms. Aligning and replacing legacy field names in a metadata repository (or multiple repositories) with ontology terms can substantially improve the searchability of the metadata, and thus the discoverability of the associated data. The applications of our method are twofold: it can be used in metadata authoring software to give real-time suggestions for metadata field names, or to give suggestions for field values that should correspond to ontology terms; and it can be used to facilitate metadata cleaning, by equipping scientists with a means to align metadata field names with ontologies.

In future work, we will implement a generic metadata field recommendation service, and subsequently integrate it with the CEDAR metadata authoring tool for recommending (a) field names when users are building metadata templates, and (b) field values when users are filling in metadata templates. We will design a standalone tool that uses our method to: provide a visualization of clusters formed out of input metadata field names; recommend mappings between the field names and ontology terms; give users ranked options for the best terms for specific fields; and generate a new enriched dataset that materializes the selected field name mappings by replacing legacy field names with ontology terms.

Acknowledgments. This work is supported by grant U54 AI117925 awarded by the U.S. National Institute of Allergy and Infectious Diseases (NIAID) through funds provided by the Big Data to Knowledge (BD2K) initiative. BioPortal has been supported by the NIH Common Fund under grant U54 HG004028.

We thank the experts in our evaluation panel: John Graybeal, Josef Hardi, Marcos Martínez-Romero, and Csongor Nyulas (all of whom from the Center for Biomedical Informatics Research at Stanford University), for their participation.

References

1. Barrett, T., et al.: BioProject and BioSample databases at NCBI: facilitating capture and organization of metadata. Nucl. Acids Res. **40**, D57–D63 (2012)
2. Ester, M., et al.: A density-based algorithm for discovering clusters in large spatial databases with noise. In: Conference on Knowledge Discovery and Data Mining (1996)
3. Frey, B.J., Dueck, D.: Clustering by passing messages between data points. Science **315**(5814), 972–976 (2007)
4. Goldberg, Y., Levy, O.: Word2vec explained: deriving Mikolov et al.'s negative-sampling word-embedding method. arXiv preprint arXiv:1402.3722 (2014)
5. Gonçalves, R.S., Musen, M.A.: The variable quality of metadata about biological samples used in biomedical experiments. Sci. Data **6**, 190021 (2018)
6. Jiménez-Ruiz, E., Cuenca Grau, B.: LogMap: logic-based and scalable ontology matching. In: Aroyo, L., et al. (eds.) ISWC 2011. LNCS, vol. 7031, pp. 273–288. Springer, Heidelberg (2011). https://doi.org/10.1007/978-3-642-25073-6_18
7. Jonquet, C., et al.: NCBO annotator: semantic annotation of biomedical data. In: International Semantic Web Conference (2009)
8. Kamdar, M.R., et al.: An empirical meta-analysis of the life sciences (linked?) open data cloud (2018). http://onto-apps.stanford.edu/lslodminer
9. Koster, C., Seutter, M., Seibert, O.: Parsing the medline corpus. In: Recent Advances in Natural Language Processing (2007)

10. Lin, Y., et al.: Learning entity and relation embeddings for knowledge graph completion. In: AAAI Conference on Artificial Intelligence (2015)
11. McInnes, L., Healy, J., Astels, S.: HDBSCAN: hierarchical density based clustering. J. Open Source Softw. **2**(11), 205 (2017)
12. Noy, N.F., et al.: BioPortal: ontologies and integrated data resources at the click of a mouse. Nucl. Acids Res. **37**, W170–W173 (2009)
13. Passos, A., Kumar, V., McCallum, A.: Lexicon infused phrase embeddings for named entity resolution. arXiv preprint arXiv:1404.5367 (2014)
14. Pennington, J., Socher, R., Manning, C.: GloVe: Global vectors for word representation. In: Empirical Methods in Natural Language Processing (2014)
15. Percha, B., Altman, R.B., Wren, J.: A global network of biomedical relationships derived from text. Bioinformatics **1**, 11 (2018)
16. Ristoski, P., Paulheim, H.: RDF2Vec: RDF graph embeddings for data mining. In: Groth, P., et al. (eds.) ISWC 2016. LNCS, vol. 9981, pp. 498–514. Springer, Cham (2016). https://doi.org/10.1007/978-3-319-46523-4_30
17. Shah, N.H., et al.: Comparison of concept recognizers for building the open biomedical annotator. In: BMC Bioinformatics, vol. 10, p. S14. BioMed Central (2009)
18. Smaili, F.Z., Gao, X., Hoehndorf, R.: OPA2Vec: combining formal and informal content of biomedical ontologies to improve similarity-based prediction. arXiv preprint arXiv:1804.10922 (2018)
19. Socher, R., et al.: Reasoning with neural tensor networks for knowledge base completion. In: Advances in Neural Information Processing Systems (2013)
20. Wang, Y., et al.: A comparison of word embeddings for the biomedical natural language processing. J. Biomed. Inform. **87**, 12–20 (2018)
21. Wang, Z., Zhang, J., Feng, J., Chen, Z.: Knowledge graph embedding by translating on hyperplanes. In: AAAI Conference on Artificial Intelligence (2014)
22. Wilkinson, M.D., et al.: The FAIR Guiding Principles for scientific data management and stewardship. Sci. Data **3**, 160018 (2016)

Generating Semantic Aspects for Queries

Dhruv Gupta[1,2(✉)], Klaus Berberich[1,3], Jannik Strötgen[4],
and Demetrios Zeinalipour-Yazti[5]

[1] Max Planck Institute for Informatics, Saarbrücken, Germany
{dhgupta,kberberi}@mpi-inf.mpg.de
[2] Graduate School of Computer Science, Saarbrücken, Germany
[3] htw saar, Saarbrücken, Germany
[4] Bosch Center for Artificial Intelligence, Renningen, Germany
jannik.stroetgen@de.bosch.com
[5] University of Cyprus, Nicosia, Cyprus
dzeina@cs.ucy.ac.cy

Abstract. Large document collections can be hard to explore if the
user presents her information need in a limited set of keywords. Ambiguous intents arising out of these short queries often result in long-winded
query sessions and many query reformulations. To alleviate this problem, in this work, we propose the novel concept of semantic aspects (e.g.,
$\langle\{\text{michael-phelps}\}, \{\text{athens, beijing, london}\}, [2004, 2016]\rangle$ for the ambiguous query *olympic medalists*) and present the xFactor algorithm that
generates them from annotations in documents. Semantic aspects uplift
document contents into a meaningful structured representation, thereby
allowing the user to sift through many documents without the need to
read their contents. The semantic aspects are created by the analysis of
semantic annotations in the form of temporal, geographic, and named
entity annotations. We evaluate our approach on a novel testbed of over
5,000 aspects on Web-scale document collections amounting to more than
450 million documents. Our results show the xFactor algorithm finds relevant aspects for highly ambiguous queries.

1 Introduction

When querying large document collections or the Web, it is challenging to
guide the user to relevant documents. This is because short and ambiguous
keyword queries posed to information retrieval (IR) systems represent many
possible information needs [15]. This is a known acute problem; it has been
shown that around 46% users issue reformulated queries [22]. To assist users
in refining their search, existing approaches use related terms [31], named entities in knowledge graphs (KGs) [13] or hand-crafted knowledge-panels [24]. Still
with these aids, the user must read and consult individual documents in the
ranked list to check for their relevance. What is therefore needed is a way of
uplifting the unstructured text in documents to a structured representation that
exposes its key *aspects*. To this end, we propose the novel concept of *semantic*

© Springer Nature Switzerland AG 2019
P. Hitzler et al. (Eds.): ESWC 2019, LNCS 11503, pp. 162–178, 2019.
https://doi.org/10.1007/978-3-030-21348-0_11

aspects (e.g., ⟨{michael-phelps}, {athens, beijing, london}, [2004, 2016]⟩) that help users posing ambiguous queries (e.g., `olympic medalists`) explore document collections without reading their contents.

Table 1. Generated semantic aspects for the query `olympic medalists` from the New York Times document collection (covering 1987–2007). Each row in the table corresponds to one semantic aspect.

Time	Entities	Entity Type
	Query: `olympic medalists`	
[1980,1988]	`yago:sergei-grinkov, yago:maya-usova, yago:marina-klimova, yago:evgeni-platov, yago:oksana-grishuk, yago:sergei-ponomarenko, yago:ekaterina-gordeeva`	`wiki-category: olympic medalists in figure skating`
[1992,1992]	`yago:leroy-burrell, yago:jon-drummond, yago:dennis-mitchell, yago:michael-marsh-(athlete)`	`wiki-category: american sprinters`
[1996,1996]	`yago:dominique-dawes, yago:shannon-miller, yago:kerri-strug`	`wiki-category: olympic medalists in gymnastics`
[1998,1998]	`yago:jenni-meno, yago:kyoko-ina, yago:todd-eldredge, yago:todd-sand, yago:nicole-bobek`	`wiki-category: figure skaters at the 1998 winter olympics`

To generate semantic aspects for ambiguous keyword queries, we turn to natural language processing (NLP) tools that can help us enrich text with annotations. In particular, we make use of annotations in the form of named entities (persons and organizations), geographic locations, and temporal expressions. These are extremely important annotations in the domain of IR [20,36]: 71% of Web queries were found to mention named entities, while 30.9% of Web queries were either explicitly or implicitly temporal in nature. Generation of meaningful semantic aspects and their evaluation is challenging. To generate them, we must first model and interpret the semantics underlying the annotations. For example, temporal expressions can be highly uncertain (e.g., *90s*) and two locations or named entities in a KG can be related by many facts, e.g., 'Maria Sharapova lives in US but represents Russia in sports' [4]. Moreover, queries can signify different kinds of ambiguities: temporal ambiguity (e.g., `tokyo summer olympics` - 1964 or 2020), location ambiguity (e.g., `rome` - many US cities are named after European cities), or entity ambiguity (e.g., `spitz` - Mark or Elisa Spitz). Moreover, since semantic aspects are more than "related terms" or facts in KGs there currently exists no benchmark for their automatic evaluation.

Approach Outline. To solve the above challenges, we propose the following solutions in this work. To generate semantic aspects, we describe the xFactor algorithm (Sect. 4). xFactor takes as an input a large set of annotated documents retrieved for a keyword query and outputs a set of semantic aspects. xFactor generates the semantic aspects in three steps. First, it partitions the input document set by identifying salient sets of annotations in formal models that capture the semantics of an annotation type (e.g., named entities). Second, xFactor additionally considers salient co-occurrences of annotations with different semantics (e.g., named entities and temporal expressions) by virtue of them being present in the same document partition. Third, it outputs all possible ways of analyzing the initial ambiguity behind the query. This is done by permuting the order in which the annotations are considered for partitioning the initial set of documents. Table 1 shows examples of generated semantic aspects for the ambiguous query $olympic\ medalists$. To perform automated evaluation of the generated semantic aspects, we provide a novel evaluation benchmark compiled from Wikipedia with new measures to the research community (Sect. 6).

2 Preliminaries

We first cover the required terminology to describe our method.

Document Model. Consider, a large annotated document collection $\mathcal{D} = \{d_1, d_2, \ldots, d_{|\mathcal{D}|}\}$. Each document $d \in \mathcal{D}$ is processed with natural language processing (NLP) annotators that tag sequences of words in the document with annotations from a given type $\mathcal{X}$ (e.g., temporal expressions). Formally, let each document be represented by n bags-of-annotations:

$$d = \{d_{\mathcal{X}_1}, d_{\mathcal{X}_2}, \ldots, d_{\mathcal{X}_n}\}. \tag{1}$$

Specifically, for this work, we consider the following semantic annotations: temporal expressions, geographic locations, and other named entities (persons and organizations). Thus, our document model refers to the bags-of-annotations for entities ($d_{\mathcal{E}}$), locations ($d_{\mathcal{G}}$), and temporal expressions ($d_{\mathcal{T}}$): $d = \{d_{\mathcal{E}}, d_{\mathcal{G}}, d_{\mathcal{T}}\}$.

Aspect Model. Let an ambiguous query q reflect the *information need* of a user. An information retrieval (IR) method in response to the query q returns a set of pseudo-relevant documents $\mathcal{R} \subset \mathcal{D}$. The document set $\mathcal{R}$ conveys many implicit information needs. The user's information need may be a subset of those reflected by the documents [15]. Our aim is to extract an ordered set of semantic aspects $\mathcal{A}$ that make these implicit information needs explicit, thereby pointing the user to the relevant documents:

$$\mathcal{A} = \langle a_1, a_2, \ldots, a_{|\mathcal{A}|} \rangle. \tag{2}$$

An aspect a (e.g., $\langle\{$michael-phelps$\}, \{$athens, beijing, london$\}, [2004, 2016]\rangle$) is determined by considering the salience of annotations sharing the same semantics (e.g., temporal expressions) as well as co-occurrence with annotations of different semantics (e.g., temporal expressions and named entities). An aspect $a \in \mathcal{A}$ is modeled as: $a = \langle x_1, \ldots, x_n \rangle$, where x (e.g., time interval) corresponds to salient annotation(s) from type $\mathcal{X}$ (e.g., temporal expressions). For this work, the aspects are modeled as: $a = \langle a_{\mathcal{E}}, a_{\mathcal{G}}, a_{\mathcal{T}} \rangle$.

Annotation Models. For large-scale enrichment of text documents with semantic annotations we utilize two different NLP tools. First, we make use of a named entity recognition and disambiguation (NERD) tool Aida [26] to annotate and disambiguate mentions of named entities to canonical entries in KGs (i.e., Yago [34]). Second, to resolve expressions of time in text we leverage a temporal tagger HeidelTime [33] that can annotate them with high precision. We next explain the formal models for each of the annotation types.

Named Entities and Entity Model. Named entities in text are modeled as canonical entries of a KG (e.g., Yago [34]). These annotations are obtained by using NERD tools (e.g., Aida [26]). We differentiate between locations and other named entities, by the presence of geographic coordinates in their KG entry. Let, $\mathcal{G}$ and $\mathcal{E}$ denote the type information associated with locations and other entities, respectively. Named entities may share common relationships that convey a degree of their relatedness. For example, *tokyo* and *beijing* are related as they both lie in *asia*. These relationships in Wikipedia are encoded in the form of an explicit link structure. Concretely, each named entity mention disambiguated by Aida, is linked to its Wikipedia article. Each Wikipedia article contains links to other Wikipedia articles, indicating their semantic relatedness. We model each named entity by its Wikipedia link structure. Formally, each named entity e can be described by the links ℓ its article W_e has to other articles in Wikipedia W:

$$W_e = \{\ell_1, \ell_2, \ldots, \ell_{|W|}\}. \tag{3}$$

Temporal Expressions and Time Model. Temporal expressions in documents can be annotated using temporal taggers (e.g., HeidelTime [33]). Such annotators are able to identify and resolve explicit, implicit, relative, and underspecified temporal expressions using metadata such as publication dates [33]. Let, $\mathcal{T}$ denote the type information associated with temporal expressions. Each annotation in $\mathcal{T}$ (i.e., dates) is represented by their UNIX time epochs (i.e., number of milliseconds since 01-January-1970). Temporal expressions are challenging to analyze as they can be present at different levels of granularity, e.g., day, month, or year granularity. Furthermore, temporal expressions can indicate an uncertain time interval, e.g., *1990s*. In such cases, the begin and end of the time interval conveyed is not clear. An uncertain temporal expression can therefore refer to infinitely many time intervals. The uncertainty in temporal expressions can be modeled by analyzing when the time interval could have begun and ended [8]. That is, the temporal expression *1990s* can refer to any time interval that can begin (b) in [1990, 1999] and end (e) in [1990, 1999]. In other words, $b \in [b_\ell, b_u]$ and $e \in [e_\ell, e_u]$ (with $b \leq e$) giving the uncertainty-aware time model [8]:

$$T = \langle b_\ell, b_u, e_\ell, e_u \rangle. \tag{4}$$

For example, *1990s* can now be represented as: $\langle 1990, 1999, 1990, 1999 \rangle$.

3 Generating Factors

To generate semantic aspects for a given query, we first need to compute salience of annotations in models informed of their semantics. Thus, we are not simply counting annotations but rather considering the salience of entities, locations, and temporal expressions in their respective semantic models. We denote the methods that compute salience as **factor methods** and the resulting salient annotations as **factors** (e.g., sets of locations or time intervals). We next describe how to find factors associated with each annotation type $\mathcal{X}$ in a document set $\mathcal{R}$ by using its factoring method, factor($\mathcal{X}, \mathcal{R}$). Algorithm 1 outlines how factor methods use the salience computation for a given document partition and annotation type.

Factoring Named Entities - factor($\mathcal{X}_\mathcal{G}, \mathcal{R}$) and factor($\mathcal{X}_\mathcal{E}, \mathcal{R}$). The factor method for named entities outputs sets of entities and locations where each entity in the set is related to the others in highly relevant documents. Concretely, to create the factors (i.e., sets of locations and entities) we first compute: sim(e, e'), semantic relatedness between entities e and e'. This is done by calculating the Jaccard coefficient of links shared by the Wikipedia entries of e and e':

$$\text{sim}(e, e') = \frac{|W_e \cap W_{e'}|}{|W_e \cup W_{e'}|}, \tag{5}$$

We make use of Jaccard coefficient as entity relatedness measure, as it has shown good performance over other relatedness measures [14]. Second, we weight the entity-entity relatedness by the document relevance $s(d, \mathcal{R})$ (given by the IR method during retrieval) that contains them to compute entity salience $s(e, \mathcal{R})$. That is,

$$s(e, \mathcal{R}) = \sum_{d \in \mathcal{R}} s(d, \mathcal{R}) \cdot \sum_{e' \in d_\mathcal{E}} \text{sim}(e, e'). \tag{6}$$

Factoring Time - factor($\mathcal{X}_\mathcal{T}, \mathcal{R}$). Temporal expressions are challenging to analyze. For instance, uncertain temporal expressions such as *the 90s* can refer to an infinite number of time intervals. Thus, it becomes quite difficult to identify salient time intervals. To overcome these limitations, we use the approach by Gupta and Berberich [21] to generate factors for time. In brief, salient time intervals (time factors) in $\mathcal{R}$ (i.e., $s([b, e], \mathcal{R})$) can be found by generating overlaps of the temporal expressions in the uncertainty-aware time model and weighting them by the document's relevance, which contains the temporal expressions:

$$s([b, e], \mathcal{R}) = \sum_{d \in \mathcal{R}} s(d, \mathcal{R}) \cdot \text{sim}([b, e], d_\mathcal{T}), \tag{7}$$

where, $s(d, \mathcal{R})$ denotes the document relevance and sim($[b, e], d_\mathcal{T}$) denotes the salience of the time interval $[b, e]$ in the document's bag of temporal expressions $d_\mathcal{T}$. The value of sim($[b, e], d_\mathcal{T}$) is computed as follows:

$$\text{sim}([b, e], d_\mathcal{T}) = \frac{1}{|d_\mathcal{T}|} \cdot \sum_{T \in d_\mathcal{T}} \frac{\mathbb{1}([b, e] \in T)}{|T|}. \tag{8}$$

In Eq. 8, the cardinality $|T|$ denotes the number of time intervals T can generate and the indicator function $\mathbb{1}(\bullet)$ tests the membership of $[b, e]$ in T.

4 The xFactor Algorithm

In addition to annotation salience, we consider the co-occurrence salience of annotations from different types to generate semantic aspects. To this end, we propose the xFactor algorithm. Our xFactor algorithm is inspired by the Apriori algorithm for frequent itemset mining [6]. The Apriori algorithm, however, is not informed of annotation semantics. Thus, its direct application, will not capture any semantic co-occurrence among different annotation types.

Consider, a document set $\mathcal{R}$ and its n annotation types $\{\mathcal{X}_1, \mathcal{X}_2, \ldots, \mathcal{X}_n\}$. A set of salient aspects $\mathcal{A}$ can be derived by iteratively partitioning $\mathcal{R}$ for different annotation factors:

$$\text{Basis Step}: \{x_1\} = \text{factor}(\mathcal{X}_1, \mathcal{R}) \tag{9}$$

$$\text{Inductive Step}: \{x_k\} = \text{factor}(\mathcal{X}_k, \mathcal{R}^{(k-1)\ldots(1)}). \tag{10}$$

First and foremost, the salience of a factor (e.g., time interval) in each aspect is obtained by the factor method (Sect. 3) that considers a semantic model corresponding to its annotation type (e.g., temporal expressions). Second, each factor for an annotation type allows us to partition the document set $\mathcal{R}$ into documents that contain annotations that helped derive the factor and those documents which did not help. Thus, by iteratively applying the factor methods for the different annotation types, we can identify the salience between factors by virtue of their co-occurrence in the same partition. Mathematically given by:

$$\text{factor}(\mathcal{X}_1, \mathcal{R}): \{d_{\mathcal{X}_1} \in d \mid \forall d \in \mathcal{R}\} \rightarrow 2^{\mathcal{X}_1}, \tag{11}$$

$$\text{factor}(\mathcal{X}_k, \mathcal{R}^{(k-1)\ldots(1)}): \{d_{\mathcal{X}_k} \in d \mid \forall d \in \mathcal{R}^{(k-1)\ldots(1)}\} \rightarrow 2^{\mathcal{X}_k}. \tag{12}$$

Third and finally, we create a partition index that keeps track of factors that were generated by a particular partition of the pseudo-relevant set of documents $\mathcal{R}$. The partition index for iteration i of the recursive algorithm keeps track of:

$$\text{Partition Index}: \langle \{x_k\}_i, R_i^{(k-1)\ldots(1)} \rangle. \tag{13}$$

By concatenating the factors of different annotation types, from the same document partition, we can generate the aspects. Figure 1 exemplifies the recursive xFactor algorithm and how the aspects are generated. The xFactor algorithm thereby allows us to extract a subset of aspects that contain salient relationships among their factors from all possible combinations of different annotation types: $\mathcal{A} \subset 2^{\mathcal{X}_1 \times \mathcal{X}_2 \times \ldots \times \mathcal{X}_n}$. Algorithm 2 illustrates a tail-recursive version of the xFactor algorithm.

Minimum Salience and Aspect Ranking. The xFactor algorithm is still computationally expensive if we were to consider every factor for each annotation type. To prune the recursion depth, we utilize a minimum salience criteria. For a given value of minimum salience $\sigma \in [0, 1]$, a factor is deemed salient if and only if: $s(x, \mathcal{R}) \geq \sigma$. Using the salience we furthermore rank the aspects presented to the user as: $s(a, d) = \prod_{x_i \in a} s(x_i, d)$.

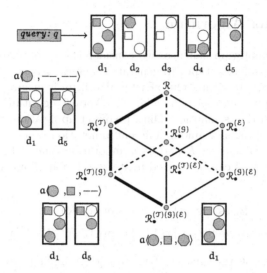

Fig. 1. The lattice structure for aspect generation by the xFactor algorithm is shown. Shapes in documents d represent annotation types. While colors represent different annotation values for same annotation type. Each element in the lattice corresponds to the partition of documents that arises by applying the factor method for that annotation type. For example, $\mathcal{R}_\bullet^{(\mathcal{T})}$ is generated by factoring $\mathcal{R}$ along time. The time factor $a = \langle \bullet, -, - \rangle$ is generated by documents $\{d_1, d_5\} \in \mathcal{R}_\bullet^{(\mathcal{T})}$. Continuing in this recursive manner over the geographic annotation type $\mathcal{G}$ we get $a = \langle \bullet, \blacksquare, - \rangle$. The sequence of factoring operations can be permuted to obtain different partitions; $\mathcal{R}_\bullet^{(\mathcal{T})(\mathcal{G})(\mathcal{E})}$ corresponds to time $\rightarrow$ geography $\rightarrow$ entity (traversing the bold edges).

Algorithm 1: Generate Factors.

Function factor$(\mathcal{X}, \mathcal{R}, \sigma)$
  $\bigcup\langle x, \mathcal{R}' \rangle \leftarrow$ generate pairs of: factors using the semantic model for $\mathcal{X}$ and the originating document partition.
  factors $\leftarrow \varnothing$
  foreach $(\langle x, \mathcal{R}' \rangle \in \bigcup\langle x, \mathcal{R}' \rangle)$ **do**
    if $(s(x, \mathcal{R}') \geq \sigma)$ **then**
      factors.add(x)
      PartitionIndex.put$(\langle x, \mathcal{R}' \rangle)$
  return factors

Algorithm 2: The xFactor Algorithm.

Function xFactor$(\mathcal{X}_1, \mathcal{X}_2, \ldots, \mathcal{X}_n, \mathcal{R}, \sigma)$
  // The set of aspects to return
  $\mathcal{A} \leftarrow \varnothing$
  x_nFactors $\leftarrow$ factor $(\mathcal{X}_n, \mathcal{R}, \sigma)$
  foreach $(x_n\text{Factor} \in x_n\text{Factors})$ **do**
    $\mathcal{R}' \leftarrow$ PartitionIndex.get$(x_n\text{Factor})$
    x_{n-1}Factors $\leftarrow$ factor$(\mathcal{X}_{n-1}, \mathcal{R}', \sigma)$
    $\ldots$
    foreach $(x_2\text{Factor} \in x_2\text{Factors})$ **do**
      $\mathcal{R}' \leftarrow$ PartitionIndex.get$(x_2\text{Factor})$
      x_1Factors $\leftarrow$ factor$(\mathcal{X}_1, \mathcal{R}', \sigma)$
      // Generate aspects
      foreach $(x_1\text{Factor} \in x_1\text{Factors})$ **do**
        $\mathcal{A} \leftarrow$
          $\mathcal{A} \cup \langle x_1\text{Factor}, \ldots, x_n\text{Factor} \rangle$
    $\ldots$
  return $\mathcal{A}$

5 Properties of the xFactor Algorithm

Structured Representation of Documents. The aspects which are assimilated from multiple documents can be used to transform the semi-structured documents with annotations (i.e., $d = \{d_{\mathcal{E}}, d_{\mathcal{G}}, d_{\mathcal{T}}\}$) into a structured representation of aspects (i.e., $d = \langle a_1, a_2, \ldots, a_n \rangle$). This structured representation of documents using aspects is then immediately useful for applications in search tasks, such as result diversification. To represent documents using aspects, we can obtain the inverse mapping of documents to aspects by looking for all $a \in \mathcal{A}$ associated with a particular document d in the partition index.

Query Pivoting. If the order in which the annotation types are factored are permuted then the xFactor algorithm will produce different sets of aspects. This is because the factor methods rely on a given document partition to generate the factors. For instance, for three annotation types, we can realize six different sets of aspects by permutation of the different factor methods. This in turn provides us different ways of analyzing three different kinds of initial ambiguity underlying the query: temporal ambiguity, e.g., *tokyo summer olympics*; geographical ambiguity, e.g., *springfield*; and named entity related ambiguity, e.g., *george bush*. If the sequence of factor methods is time → entity → geography, then the resulting set of aspects will be denoted by $\mathcal{A}_{\langle \mathcal{T}, \mathcal{E}, \mathcal{G} \rangle}$. The other five possibilities are: $\mathcal{A}_{\langle \mathcal{T}, \mathcal{G}, \mathcal{E} \rangle}$, $\mathcal{A}_{\langle \mathcal{G}, \mathcal{T}, \mathcal{E} \rangle}$, $\mathcal{A}_{\langle \mathcal{G}, \mathcal{E}, \mathcal{T} \rangle}$, $\mathcal{A}_{\langle \mathcal{E}, \mathcal{T}, \mathcal{G} \rangle}$, and $\mathcal{A}_{\langle \mathcal{E}, \mathcal{G}, \mathcal{T} \rangle}$. Using the illustration in Fig. 1, these six factor sequences can be obtained by following different paths in the lattice.

Summarizing Entity Sets. For each of the generated aspects, we can summarize the resulting factors (e.g., named entities) using background knowledge (e.g., KG) into broader semantic classification types (e.g., categories from Wikipedia). For instance, in Table 1, we have summarized all the named entities into categories from Wikipedia. Concretely, to arrive at the types for named entities, we look up all the types that an entity belongs to (following rdfs:type and rdfs:subClassOf links). Thereafter, we select the summary type as the one that covers most of the entities in the entity factor.

6 Evaluation

We next describe the setup and results of our experimental evaluation.

6.1 Annotated Document Collections

Document Collections. We test our algorithm on two different types of document collections. The first category of document collections consists of news articles. News archives have the benefit of being accompanied by rich metadata in the form of accurate publication dates and well-written text. This can aid NLP tools to provide more accurate annotations. For example, temporal taggers can resolve relative temporal expressions (e.g., yesterday) and implicit temporal expressions (e.g., good friday) with respect to the publication date. We consider two document collections in this category. One of them is a collection of approximately two million news articles published in the New York Times between 1987 and 2007. It is publicly available as the New York Times Annotated Corpus [5]. The other one is a collection of approximately four million news articles collected from various online sources during the period of 2013 to 2016, called Stics [25].

The second category of document collection consists of web pages. Web crawls unlike news articles have unreliable metadata and ill-formed language. This hampers us in obtaining high-quality semantic annotations for them. For example, we cannot resolve relative and underspecified temporal expressions, as the document creation time for Web pages may not reflect their true publication dates. We consider two web crawls [1,2] from 2009 and 2012, which are publicly available as ClueWeb'09 and ClueWeb'12 document collections, respectively. Statistics for the document collections are summarized in Table 2.

Annotating Documents. Semantic annotations are central to our approach. To obtain them, we utilize publicly available annotations for the document collections or automatically generate them using NLP tools. For the news archives and for ClueWeb'09, we utilized Aida [26], which performs named entity recognition and disambiguation. Each disambiguated named entity is linked to its canonical entry in the Yago KG and Wikipedia. As a subset of these named entities, we can obtain geographic locations. For ClueWeb'12, we utilized the FACC annotations [17] provided by Google. The FACC annotations contain the offsets of high precision entities spotted in the web pages. Temporal expressions for all the document collections were obtained using the HeidelTime temporal tagger [33]. In Table 2, we additionally report the average counts of the three types of semantic annotations found in at most 10,000 documents retrieved for each query in our testbed.

Table 2. Collection statistics.

Collection	#Documents	Avg. Time	Avg. Entities	Avg. Locations
New York Times	1,679,374	12.50	16.25	8.65
Stics	4,075,720	10.09	10.89	5.93
ClueWeb'09	50,220,423	30.59	8.23	9.49
ClueWeb'12	408,878,432	5.80	7.74	5.61

6.2 Ground Truth Semantic Aspects and Queries

To evaluate our system, we extracted 5,122 aspects from Wikipedia. This was done considering their diversity along annotation types of time, locations, and other named entities for a set of twenty-five keyword queries. The broad topics of the aspects along with the specific keyword queries and the number of aspects generated are listed in Table 4.

For each query, we constructed a set of ground-truth aspects by considering the table of events present on the Wikipedia page corresponding to the query [3,9]. For the table, we considered each row consisting of time, locations, and other entities as an aspect. If no locations or entities were mentioned, we extracted them from the associated event page of the row, by running Aida on the introductory paragraph of the event's Wikipedia page. For instance, consider Table 3 as an example Wikipedia table for Olympic medalists. Treating each row as a ground truth aspect, we look for temporal expressions, e.g., [2008, 2016] as a time factor; locations, e.g., Beijing, London, and Rio de Janeiro as a location factor; and other named entities, e.g., Usain Bolt as an entity factor. Similarly, for the second row in Table 3, the extracted aspect is: $\langle[2004, 2016], \{\mathsf{athens, beijing, london, rio\text{-}de\text{-}janeiro}\}, \{\mathsf{michael\text{-}phelps}\}\rangle$. The testbed is publicly available at the following URL: http://resources.mpi-inf.mpg.de/dhgupta/data/eswc2019/.

Table 3. An example table of events for generating ground truth.

Years	Description	Locations
2008 to 2016	Usain Bolt won total of 9 Olympic medals during the Summer Olympic games in the years he was active.	Beijing, London, and Rio de Janeiro
2004 to 2016	Michael Phelps has won a record number of 23 gold medals at various Olympic games during his career.	Athens, Beijing, London, and Rio de Janeiro

6.3 Measures

The two key characteristics for evaluating aspects are: their correctness with respect to a ground truth and their novelty with respect to other aspects in the set. These two characteristics taken together ensure that our aspect sets are meaningful and non-redundant. We next describe the measures of correctness and novelty.

Similarity computation between aspects is central to both the correctness and novelty. To compute the similarity between the two aspects, a (system generated) and b (ground truth), we consider their similarity dimension-wise:

$$\text{sim}(a, b) = \frac{1}{3}\left(\frac{|a_{[b,e]} \cap b_{[b,e]}|}{|a_{[b,e]}|} + \frac{|a_{\mathcal{E}} \cap b_{\mathcal{E}}|}{|a_{\mathcal{E}}|} + \frac{|a_{\mathcal{G}} \cap b_{\mathcal{G}}|}{|a_{\mathcal{G}}|}\right),$$

where, for temporal similarity we coarsen the time intervals at year granularity to make them comparable. The temporal overlaps are computed using the uncertainty-aware time model [8] by converting the time intervals to the four-tuple notation. While for the other two dimensions the similarity is akin to computing the overlap between bag-of-locations and bag-of-entities. Note that the similarity computation is done with respect to the system generated aspect

Table 4. Query categories with factor operation sequences and aspect counts (in brackets).

Entity - $\mathcal{A}_{\langle \mathcal{E}, \bullet, \bullet \rangle}$: *nobel prize* [114] |*oscars* [1,167] |*space shuttle missions* [155] |*olympic medalists* [48] |*paralympic medalists* [24]
Location - $\mathcal{A}_{\langle \mathcal{G}, \bullet, \bullet \rangle}$: *aircraft accidents* [513] | *avalanches* [56] | *epidemics* [211] | *famines* [133] | *genocides* [35] | *volcanic eruptions* [171] | *hailstorms* [39] | *landslides* [85] | *earthquakes* [39] | *nuclear accidents* [26] | *oil spills* [140] | *tsunamis* [88]
Time - $\mathcal{A}_{\langle \mathcal{T}, \bullet, \bullet \rangle}$: *assassinations* [130] | *cold war* [81] | *corporate scandals* [44] | *proxy wars* [34] | *united states presidential elections* [57] | *terror attacks* [316] | *treaties* [1,057] | *wars* [359]

(a in the denominator). This is done to avoid matching (and thereby not rewarding) those system aspects a with a very large time interval, bag-of-locations or bag-of-entities, to every ground truth aspect (b).

Correctness. Given a set of aspects $\mathcal{A}$ generated by our algorithm for a query q and the set of aspects $\mathcal{B}$ corresponding to the ground truth derived from Wikipedia page for the same query, correctness is given by:

$$\text{correctness}(\mathcal{A}, \mathcal{B}) = \frac{1}{|\mathcal{A}|} \sum_{a \in \mathcal{A}} \frac{1}{|\mathcal{B}|} \sum_{b \in \mathcal{B}} \text{sim}(a, b).$$

Novelty for the set of aspects $\mathcal{A}$ can be intuitively thought of measuring the dissimilarity with respect to $\mathcal{A}$ itself:

$$\text{novelty}(\mathcal{A}) = \frac{1}{|\mathcal{A}|} \sum_{a \in \mathcal{A}} \frac{1}{|\mathcal{A}|} \sum_{(a' \in \mathcal{A}/\{a\})} \left(1 - \text{sim}(a, a')\right).$$

We can additionally conform the correctness measure to the standard information retrieval measures such as **precision** and **recall** as follows:

$$\text{precision} = \frac{1}{|\mathcal{A}|} \sum_{a \in \mathcal{A}} \max_{b \in \mathcal{B}} \left(\text{sim}(a, b)\right) \quad \& \quad \text{recall} = \frac{1}{|\mathcal{B}|} \sum_{b \in \mathcal{B}} \max_{a \in \mathcal{A}} \left(\text{sim}(a, b)\right).$$

6.4   Evaluation Setup

Baselines and Systems. We consider two baselines to compare our proposed approach. As a naïve baseline, we treated each document in the pseudo-relevant set to represent an aspect. This is equivalent to presenting the user a ranked list of documents to satisfy her information need. The equivalent aspect for a document is constructed by considering the earliest and latest time point in the document as its time interval and bag-of-locations and bag-of-entities to represent the other two dimensions. As a second baseline, we consider latent Dirichlet allocation (LDA) [12]. With this baseline, we want to cluster together those documents that are semantically similar using only text. Using LDA, we discover k topics from the pseudo-relevant set of documents. From each topic's partition of documents,

Table 5. Results for news archives.

(a) Results for correctness (C) & novelty (N).

	New York Times			Stics		
	$\mu_{\mid\mathcal{A}\mid}$	C	N	$\mu_{\mid\mathcal{A}\mid}$	C	N
BM25	3,096	.0237	.4269	3,797	.0204	.4227
LDA-50	50	.0067	.2634	50	.0102	.2910
LDA-100	100	.0053	.2107	100	.0080	.2404
LDA-200	200	.0046	.1497	200	.0063	.1639
xFactor	2,261	.0161	.4201	503	.0190	.3862

(b) Results for precision (P) & recall (R).

	New York Times			Stics		
	$\mu_{\mid\mathcal{A}\mid}$	P	R	$\mu_{\mid\mathcal{A}\mid}$	P	R
BM25	3,096	.1577	.2749	3,797	.1414	.2828
LDA-50	50	.0471	.0160	50	.0634	.0311
LDA-100	100	.0432	.0102	100	.0483	.0207
LDA-200	200	.0400	.0070	200	.0456	.0129
xFactor	2,261	.2804	.1777	503	.2400	.1427

we derive the corresponding semantic aspect by considering the earliest and latest time point in the partition as its time interval and bag-of-entities and bag-of-locations to represent the two remaining dimensions. We refer to this baseline as LDA-k. For the xFactor algorithm, we considered the specific sequence of factor operations that were deemed meaningful for that query (as shown in Table 4). For instance, since the query *earthquakes* is oriented towards locations we considered the factor sequence operations $\mathcal{A}_{\langle \mathcal{G}, \mathcal{E}, \mathcal{T} \rangle}$ and $\mathcal{A}_{\langle \mathcal{G}, \mathcal{T}, \mathcal{E} \rangle}$.

Parameters. For each query in Table 4, we retrieve at most 10,000 documents with disjunctive operator using Okapi BM25 as the retrieval method. We used the standard parameters, $b = 0.75$ and $k_1 = 1.20$, for its configuration. For the LDA baseline, we followed Griffiths and Steyvers [19] for setting its parameters. Specifically, β was set to 0.1 and α was set to $50/\mid\text{topics}\mid$. We considered three topic set sizes for LDA namely, $\mid\text{topics}\mid \in \{50, 100, 200\}$ and the same number of top-k documents for each topic, e.g., for $\mid\text{topics}\mid = 50$, we picked top-50 documents for each topic as its generating partition. For our method, the minimum salience was set to $\sigma = 0.001$.

6.5 Results for Quality

Results for News Archives. We first consider the results of the systems in terms of correctness and novelty as reported in Table 5a. We additionally report the average number of aspects $\mu_{\mid\mathcal{A}\mid}$ for each system under comparison. Note that the Okapi BM25 baseline gives us an upper bound for the value of correctness that can be obtained against the ground-truth. As, ultimately we generate the LDA topics and aspect from this set of documents. For the New York Times collection, our method identifies the most correct aspects with respect to the ground truth as compared to the LDA baselines. Despite the observation that Okapi BM25 wins in terms of novelty by considering all pseudo-relevant documents, our method still achieves a high degree of novelty, thereby identifying the most non-redundant set of aspects and is able to partition the set of pseudo-relevant documents to the greatest degree. For the Stics news collection, our method outperforms the LDA baselines in terms of correctness and is close to the upper bound that can be achieved from the given set of pseudo-relevant documents. Okapi BM25 achieves a higher novelty value, however, the increase compared

Table 6. Results for web collections.

(a) Results for correctness (C) & novelty (N).   (b) Results for precision (P) & recall (R).

	ClueWeb'09			ClueWeb'12				ClueWeb'09			ClueWeb'12	
	$\mu_{|\mathcal{A}|}$	C	N	$\mu_{|\mathcal{A}|}$	C	N		$\mu_{|\mathcal{A}|}$	P	R	$\mu_{|\mathcal{A}|}$	P	R
BM25	9,580	.0155	.3958	9,742	.0266	.4531	BM25	9,580	.1151	.3595	9,742	.1494	.4018
LDA-50	50	.0123	.3275	50	.0177	.3478	LDA-50	50	.0734	.0999	50	.0930	.1049
LDA-100	100	.0092	.2880	100	.0126	.3025	LDA-100	100	.0560	.0808	100	.0718	.0770
LDA-200	200	.0064	.2441	200	.0097	.2554	LDA-200	200	.0433	.0502	200	.0585	.0500
xFactor	1,822	.0146	.4239	616	.0173	.4176	xFactor	1,822	.2218	.1880	616	.2433	.1648

to our method is not significant. Observing both correctness and novelty our method excels in providing both relevant and non-redundant sets of aspects when compared to the LDA baselines which can only achieve high novelty.

Now, consider precision and recall for the systems, as reported in Table 5b. For the New York Times, while considering precision, our system consists of more relevant aspects compared to the baselines. With respect to recall, the Okapi BM25 baseline wins by considering the entire pseudo-relevant set of documents. Note that the LDA baselines and our algorithm xFactor can not achieve this value as they discard many annotations, favoring precision over recall. Therefore, considering both precision and recall together, our system presents a balanced performance: high precision and recall. While the baselines achieve high recall only. For the Stics collection, when considering precision and recall, our method again shows significant improvements over the baselines. Thus, by taking all the four measures, correctness, novelty, precision, and recall, our method allows us to distill interesting aspects which can guide the user to navigate through a large number of documents.

Results for Web Collections. Web archives give us more challenging documents to test the effectiveness of our approach. Particularly, since they are not well-formed, they have a lower average number of annotations per document, the annotations in them are prone to more errors, and the size of the web archives is magnitudes larger than news archives. Hence, they present a challenging real-world scenario to test our methods. We first consider the results for the web archives when measuring correctness and novelty that are reported in Table 6a. For ClueWeb'09, our method outperforms both baselines in terms of novelty. In particular, for correctness our method comes close to the upper bound established by Okapi BM25. For ClueWeb'12 our method performs at par with baselines in terms of novelty. When considering the measures in isolation, for correctness the LDA baseline wins over our method and Okapi BM25 baseline has higher novelty than our method. However, when considering both correctness and novelty together, xFactor is consistent in providing more correct and novel aspects as opposed to the LDA baselines.

Next, we consider the second set of experimental results for web collections when measuring precision and recall that are reported in Table 6b. For ClueWeb'09, our method in terms of precision and recall outperforms the LDA

Table 7. Results for precision and recall at $k = \{10, 20, 50\}$.

(a) Results on news archives.

	New York Times			Stics		
	P@10	P@25	P@50	P@10	P@25	P@50
BM25	.1874	.1863	.1909	.1380	.1394	.1461
LDA-50	.0453	.0464	.0471	.0592	.0590	.0634
LDA-100	.0426	.0431	.0430	.0487	.0481	.0476
LDA-200	.0396	.0397	.0400	.0440	.0434	.0440
xFactor	**.2283**	**.2450**	**.2366**	**.1690**	**.1869**	**.1740**
	R@10	R@25	R@50	R@10	R@25	R@50
BM25	**.2593**	**.2672**	**.2510**	**.2732**	**.2834**	**.2700**
LDA-50	.0172	.0148	.0133	.0310	.0294	.0270
LDA-100	.0130	.0104	.0092	.0216	.0192	.0174
LDA-200	.0101	.0075	.0062	.0148	.0126	.0113
xFactor	.1729	.1691	.1633	.1274	.1295	.1237

(b) Results on Web collections.

	ClueWeb'09			ClueWeb'12		
	P@10	P@25	P@50	P@10	P@25	P@50
BM25	.1111	.1183	.1217	.1436	.1451	.1521
LDA-50	.0792	.0770	.0734	.0982	.0961	.0930
LDA-100	.0714	.0634	.0601	.0876	.0828	.0756
LDA-200	.0591	.0526	.0485	.0697	.0644	.0602
xFactor	**.1771**	**.1909**	**.1919**	**.1999**	**.1990**	**.2018**
	R@10	R@25	R@50	R@10	R@25	R@50
BM25	**.3632**	**.3973**	**.3380**	**.3867**	**.4357**	**.3727**
LDA-50	.1000	.1036	.0894	.0963	.1153	.0940
LDA-100	.0864	.0856	.0750	.0722	.0832	.0681
LDA-200	.0524	.0571	.0450	.0446	.0534	.0421
xFactor	.1523	.1649	.1532	.1469	.1607	.1362

baselines significantly. For ClueWeb'12, our method outperforms both baselines with respect to precision. However, in terms of recall Okapi BM25 outperforms our method when considering all the pseudo-relevant documents. Despite of this, our method provides a balanced performance with high precision and moderate recall as compared to the baselines which have high recall but very low precision.

6.6   Results for Ranking

Results for News Archives. The results of precision and recall at $k = \{10, 25, 50\}$ for the news archives are shown in Table 7a. As we can observe, the ranking provided by xFactor surpasses both the Okapi BM25 and LDA baselines in terms of precision for both the New York Times and Stics archives. While, our proposed algorithm provides a high level of recall for both the news archives when compared to LDA baseline.

Results for Web Collections. The results of precision and recall at $k = \{10, 25, 50\}$ for the Web collections are shown in Table 7b. Similar to the observations made in the case of news archives, we see that the aspects extracted by xFactor at increasing ranks result in higher precision than both the baselines. Our algorithm further provides high recall at increasing rank positions as compared to the LDA baselines, while the Okapi BM25, considering all the annotations in each document outperform our system and the LDA baseline.

Overall Summary

Our experiments on two large news archives show that annotations in the form of temporal expressions, locations, and other entities can be used to identify semantic aspects that are correct and novel for document exploration. On Web-scale corpora, where quality annotations are few, xFactor can also identify precise aspects for information consumption. Moreover, using annotation and co-occurrence salience, xFactor shows it can produce ranked list of highly-relevant aspects.

7 Related Work

Structuring Text for Search. [23] proposed TextTiling, an algorithm for identifying coherent passages (subtopics) in text documents. [28] utilized LDA to identify topics in documents for their structured representation. However, both approaches were not informed of semantic annotations, which we leverage to identify aspects for structuring text for search.

Faceted Search. Faceted Search systems allow a user to navigate document collections and prune irrelevant documents by displaying important features about them. [16,27] rely only on text to mine keyword lists present in pseudo-relevant documents for generating aspects. [7] discussed various algorithms that allowed business intelligence aggregations and advanced dynamic discovery of correlated facets across multiple dimensions. [29] leveraged semantic metadata present in Wikipedia such as entities and their associated category for automated generation of facets for exploring Wikipedia articles. [18] considered the use of named entities and their relationships in graphs for generating facets in DBpedia abstracts. Our approach, in contrast, considers the underlying semantics for each annotation during the generation of aspects. We additionally consider temporal expressions and geographic locations as additional annotations. Furthermore, we model the co-occurrences between different annotation types for generating aspects.

Temporal Search. [35] analyzed annotated documents for recommending related entities given an entity and an associated text. For this, the authors used temporal expressions, KGs and word embeddings. In a similar vein, [10] looked into incorporating temporal knowledge into embeddings for KGs. [11] on the other hand, analyze query logs to recommend time intervals for queries about events. In contrast, our approach models the uncertainty behind temporal expressions when generating query aspects. Our xFactor algorithm is additionally extensible to other annotation types (e.g., locations, numbers and sentiment). Moreover, xFactor allows query pivoting, thereby disambiguating query intent using different annotation types.

Entity Search. [30] leverage search-engine query logs to mine and suggest entities of relevance given an entity-oriented query. They consider metadata associated with the queries in the query log for their approach e.g., user clicks, user sessions, and query issue timestamps. [32] propose a method for recommending related entities for entity-centric queries using pseudo relevance feedback from retrieved documents and KGs. Their work, however, does not tap into the document contents or temporal expressions for generating aspects.

8   Conclusions

In this work, we discussed the xFactor algorithm that leverages semantic annotations such as temporal expressions, geographic locations, and other named
entities to generate semantic aspects. The xFactor algorithm consists of factor
methods that model the semantics of annotations in order to compute their
salience. xFactor additionally considers the co-occurrence salience of annotations
of different types to generate semantic aspects. Furthermore, the factor methods
can be applied in different orders to disambiguate different types of ambiguities
underlying the query and thereby identifying the most relevant set of semantic
aspects for it. Our experiments on two types of document collections that include
news archives and Web collections, show that the xFactor algorithm allows the
user to navigate through messy unstructured text in a structured manner.

References

1. The ClueWeb09 dataset. http://lemurproject.org/clueweb09/
2. The ClueWeb12 dataset. http://lemurproject.org/clueweb12/
3. List of lists of lists. https://en.wikipedia.org/wiki/List_of_lists_of_lists
4. Maria Sharapova. https://en.wikipedia.org/wiki/Maria_Sharapova
5. The New York Times Annotated Corpus. https://catalog.ldc.upenn.edu/
   LDC2008T19
6. Agrawal, R., Srikant, R.: Fast algorithms for mining association rules in large
   databases. In: VLDB 1994, pp. 487–499 (1994)
7. Ben-Yitzhak, O., et al.: Beyond basic faceted search. In: WSDM 2008, pp. 33–44
   (2008)
8. Berberich, K., Bedathur, S., Alonso, O., Weikum, G.: A language modeling approach for temporal information needs. In: Gurrin, C., et al. (eds.) ECIR 2010.
   LNCS, vol. 5993, pp. 13–25. Springer, Heidelberg (2010). https://doi.org/10.1007/
   978-3-642-12275-0_5
9. Bhagavatula, C.S., Noraset, T., Downey, D.: TabEL: entity linking in web tables.
   In: Arenas, M., et al. (eds.) ISWC 2015. LNCS, vol. 9366, pp. 425–441. Springer,
   Cham (2015). https://doi.org/10.1007/978-3-319-25007-6_25
10. Bianchi, F., Palmonari, M., Nozza, D.: Towards encoding time in text-based entity
    embeddings. In: Vrandečić, D., et al. (eds.) ISWC 2018. LNCS, vol. 11136, pp.
    56–71. Springer, Cham (2018). https://doi.org/10.1007/978-3-030-00671-6_4
11. Nguyen, T.N., Kanhabua, N., Nejdl, W.: Multiple models for recommending tem-
    poral aspects of entities. In: Gangemi, A., et al. (eds.) ESWC 2018. LNCS, vol.
    10843, pp. 462–480. Springer, Cham (2018). https://doi.org/10.1007/978-3-319-
    93417-4_30
12. Blei, D.M., et al.: Latent dirichlet allocation. J. Mach. Learn. Res. 3, 993–1022
    (2003)
13. Bordino, I., et al.: Beyond entities: promoting explorative search with bundles. Inf.
    Retr. J. 19(5), 447–486 (2016)
14. Ceccarelli, D., et al.: Learning relatedness measures for entity linking. In: CIKM
    2013, pp. 139–148 (2013)
15. Clarke, C.L.A., et al.: Novelty and diversity in information retrieval evaluation. In:
    SIGIR 2008, pp. 659–666 (2008)

16. Dou, Z., et al.: Finding dimensions for queries. In: CIKM 2011, pp. 1311–1320 (2011)
17. Gabrilovich, E., et al.: FACC1: freebase annotation of ClueWeb corpora, version 1 (release date 2013-06-26, format version 1, correction level 0), June 2013
18. Grau, B.C. et al.: SemFacet: faceted search over ontology enhanced knowledge graphs. In: ISWC 2016 (2016)
19. Griffiths, T.L., Steyvers, M.: Finding scientific topics. Proc. Natl. Acad. Sci. 101(Suppl. 1), 5228–5235 (2004)
20. Guo, J., et al.: Named entity recognition in query. In: SIGIR 2009, pp. 267–274 (2009)
21. Gupta, D., Berberich, K.: Identifying time intervals of interest to queries. In: CIKM 2014, pp. 1835–1838 (2014)
22. Hearst, M.A.: Search User Interfaces, 1st edn. Cambridge University Press, New York (2009)
23. Hearst, M.A., Plaunt, C.: Subtopic structuring for full-length document access. In: SIGIR 1993. pp. 59–68 (1993)
24. Henry, J.: Providing knowledge panels with search results, 2 May 2013. https://www.google.com/patents/US20130110825. US Patent App. 13/566,489
25. Hoffart, J., et al.: STICS: searching with strings, things, and cats. In: SIGIR 2014, pp. 1247–1248 (2014)
26. Hoffart, J., et al.: Robust disambiguation of named entities in text. In: EMNLP 2011, pp. 782–792 (2011)
27. Kong, W., Allan, J.: Extracting query facets from search results. In: SIGIR 2013, pp. 93–102 (2013)
28. Koutrika, G., et al.: Generating reading orders over document collections. In: ICDE 2015, pp. 507–518 (2015)
29. Li, C., et al.: Facetedpedia: Dynamic generation of query-dependent faceted interfaces for Wikipedia. In: WWW 2010, pp. 651–660 (2010)
30. Reinanda, R., et al.: Mining, ranking and recommending entity aspects. In: SIGIR 2015, pp. 263–272 (2015)
31. Santos, R.L.T., et al.: Search result diversification. Found. Trends® Inf. Retr. 9(1), 1–90 (2015)
32. Schuhmacher, M., et al.: Ranking entities for web queries through text and knowledge. In: CIKM 2015, pp. 1461–1470 (2015)
33. Strötgen, J., Gertz, M.: Multilingual and cross-domain temporal tagging. Lang. Resour. Eval. 47(2), 269–298 (2013)
34. Suchanek, F.M., Kasneci, G., Weikum, G.: YAGO: a large ontology from wikipedia and wordnet. Web Semant. 6(3), 203–217 (2008)
35. Tran, N.K., Tran, T., Niederée, C.: Beyond time: dynamic context-aware entity recommendation. In: Blomqvist, E., Maynard, D., Gangemi, A., Hoekstra, R., Hitzler, P., Hartig, O. (eds.) ESWC 2017. LNCS, vol. 10249, pp. 353–368. Springer, Cham (2017). https://doi.org/10.1007/978-3-319-58068-5_22
36. Zhang, R., et al.: Learning recurrent event queries for web search. In: EMNLP 2010, pp. 1129–1139 (2010)

A Recommender System for Complex Real-World Applications with Nonlinear Dependencies and Knowledge Graph Context

Marcel Hildebrandt[1,2(✉)], Swathi Shyam Sunder[1], Serghei Mogoreanu[1],
Mitchell Joblin[1], Akhil Mehta[1,3], Ingo Thon[1], and Volker Tresp[1,2]

[1] Siemens AG, Corporate Technology, Munich, Germany
{marcel.hildebrandt,swathi.sunder,serghei.mogoreanu,mitchell.joblin,
akhil.mehta,ingo.thon,volker.tresp}@siemens.com
[2] Ludwig Maximilian University, Munich, Germany
[3] Technical University of Munich, Munich, Germany

Abstract. Most latent feature methods for recommender systems learn to encode user preferences and item characteristics based on past user-item interactions. While such approaches work well for standalone items (e.g., books, movies), they are not as well suited for dealing with composite systems. For example, in the context of industrial purchasing systems for engineering solutions, items can no longer be considered standalone. Thus, latent representation needs to encode the functionality and technical features of the engineering solutions that result from combining the individual components. To capture these dependencies, expressive and context-aware recommender systems are required. In this paper, we propose *NECTR*, a novel recommender system based on two components: a tensor factorization model and an autoencoder-like neural network. In the tensor factorization component, context information of the items is structured in a multi-relational knowledge base encoded as a tensor and latent representations of items are extracted via tensor factorization. Simultaneously, an autoencoder-like component captures the non-linear interactions among configured items. We couple both components such that our model can be trained end-to-end. To demonstrate the real-world applicability of *NECTR*, we conduct extensive experiments on an industrial dataset concerned with automation solutions. Based on the results, we find that *NECTR* outperforms state-of-the-art methods by approximately 50% with respect to a set of standard performance metrics.

1 Introduction

In the context of recommender systems, collaborative filtering methods predict the interest of a user for items by considering past user-item interactions of similar users. Many popular collaborative filtering methods are based on the idea of learning latent representations for items and users. In that setting, the

P. Hitzler et al. (Eds.): ESWC 2019, LNCS 11503, pp. 179–193, 2019.
https://doi.org/10.1007/978-3-030-21348-0_12

recommendation task is solved by scoring user-item pairs via some function of the latent features. Popular approaches are based on matrix factorization (MF) and have been applied with great success in the past (e.g., in the Netflix challenge [1] and in Amazon's item-to-item collaborative filtering method [10]). Most factorization methods model the relation between users and items via dot products of the corresponding latent features. This implies, that – when either of the two latent factors is fixed – the recommendation engine becomes essentially linear. While this limited expressiveness suffices to capture the relations between the users and standalone items of similar type, MF-based methods are not well suited for dealing with heterogeneous (i.e., diverse in nature) items that interact with each other to form a complex system.

Nevertheless, such scenarios are commonplace when users configure modular products consisting of many different components (e.g., computers or IT infrastructure solutions). This setting imposes additional challenges on collaborative filtering systems. It is often the case that the functionality of the whole system depends on the technical properties of the individual components. Therefore, the need arises to model this context information explicitly. Moreover, instead of encoding preferences that the user has revealed in the past, latent features need to encode the functionality of the system that arises by combining the individual components. Depending on the complexity of the configured system, this may result in higher-order (i.e., non-linear) dependencies among the items.

Deep neural networks have proven to be highly effective in extracting hidden, non-linear representations from raw input data for a variety of tasks (e.g., natural language processing [16], computer vision [9], and speech recognition [8]). In particular, autoencoders are invaluable for learning efficient data representations in an unsupervised manner, and are often used for denoising, as generative models, as well as for producing latent representations that can be employed for further downstream tasks. Related to our use case, [15] and [6] describe architectures that integrate autoencoders into recommender engines. While these methods are capable of taking some context information into account, they only consider a setting with rather homogeneous items (books and movies, respectively) that all share the same (fairly small) set of features. The main challenge when dealing with highly modular, technical systems is, however, to find an efficient way to encode the numerous technical properties of items that belong to different device categories and thus have different feature sets. Moreover, this information must be channeled and merged with historical data efficiently to meet the requirements of real-world, industrial applications.

Present Work. In this work, we present *NECTR* (**N**eural **E**ncoders **C**ombined with **T**ensor Decompositions for **R**ecommendations) – a novel hybrid recommender system based on the combination of autoencoders and tensor factorizations. The basic idea is to form a graphical, multi-relational knowledge base, which contains technical information about items as well as historical user-item interactions. By factorizing the resulting adjacency tensor, one obtains semantically meaningful embeddings that preserve local proximity in the graph structure.

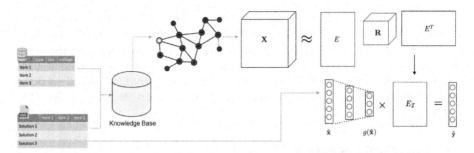

Fig. 1. The architecture of NECTR: We merge both historical data and technical information from industrial databases to form a joint multi-relational knowledge graph. Then we extract context-aware embeddings by factorizing the corresponding adjacency tensor. The resulting latent representations of items are employed in the output layer of an autoencoder-like neural network that is trained to score items based on the current configuration.

We leverage this information by coupling the tensor factorization with a deep learning autoencoder via a weight-sharing mechanism. The architecture of NECTR is illustrated in Fig. 1.

In order to demonstrate the practical benefits of *NECTR*, we conduct extensive, large scale experiments in a real-world industrial setting. The underlying data consists of around 50,000 engineering solutions (from the automation domain), 6,000 configurable items, and around half a million technical properties of items.[1] Our main findings are:

- *NECTR* outperforms all state-of-the-art methods that we considered by a large margin. In some of the most important metrics we achieve performance gains of more than 50%.
- *NECTR* can be efficiently trained in an end-to-end fashion. Moreover, recommendations can be executed in real time via a simple forward pass. This is crucial in real-world applications, since we require that the recommender system works in real time while the user is configuring a solution.

2   Background and Mathematical Notation

Before proceeding, we define the mathematical notations that we use for this paper and provide the necessary background on automation solutions and knowledge graphs.

2.1   Notation

Throughout this work, we use the following notation: Scalars are given by lowercase letters ($x \in \mathbb{R}$), column vectors by bold lowercase letters ($\mathbf{x} \in \mathbb{R}^n$), and

---

[1] The anonymized data along with implementations of all methods that we consider in this paper can be found under https://github.com/m-hildebrandt/NECTR.

matrices by uppercase letters ($X \in \mathbb{R}^{n_1 \times n_2}$). The i-th row and j-th column of matrix X are denoted as $X_{i,:} \in \mathbb{R}^{n_2}$ and $X_{:,j} \in \mathbb{R}^{n_1}$, respectively. Further, for $I \subset \{1, 2, \ldots, n_1\}$, $X_I \in \mathbb{R}^{|I| \times n_2}$ indicates the matrix formed by the rows of X indexed by elements in I. Third-order tensors are given by bold uppercase letters ($\mathbf{X} \in \mathbb{R}^{n_1 \times n_2 \times n_3}$). Slices of a tensor (i.e., two-dimensional sections obtained by fixing one index) are denoted by $\mathbf{X}_{i,:,:} \in \mathbb{R}^{n_2 \times n_3}$, $\mathbf{X}_{:,j,:} \in \mathbb{R}^{n_1 \times n_3}$, and $\mathbf{X}_{:,:,k} \in \mathbb{R}^{n_1 \times n_2}$.

2.2   Automation Solutions

Automation systems are closely related to control theory. Usually, the goal is that a set of variables in a system takes a prescribed value or varies in a prescribed way (a classical example is a heating unit with a thermostat and a controller). In this work we are concerned with industrial automation employed in manufacturing processes and machinery. Thereby, the employed solutions consist of a wide variety of components such as sensors, software, controllers, and human machine interfaces. Many of these components are general-purpose and can be applied in various industries, such as car manufacturing, bottling plants, pharmaceutical production, and oil refinery. However, the suitability of some components can also be heavily influenced by non-functional requirements, which arise in certain domains. Examples for such non-functional requirements may include environmental conditions, such as high temperatures and humidity, or legal requirements, as in food, pharmaceutical, or energy production. As an example, a cooling system in the food industry might contain the same functional components as the cooling of a nuclear power plant, however, in the latter case, fail-safe components are required. Selecting a consistent set of components is complicated as there are lots of interdependencies due to protocol standards or technical compatibility constraints. The large amount of such restrictions, the diversity of application domains, and in some cases, also the rather soft character of constraints prohibit the formulation of handcrafted, universally valid rules that are typically used in product configurators for less complex systems. Thus, in the context of automation solutions, recommender systems need to be sufficiently expressive to model the complex interplay of components while also taking technical properties into account.

2.3   Knowledge Graphs

In our approach, we make use of a knowledge graph to capture technical information describing configurable items and past solutions. All considered entities correspond to vertices in a directed graph with typed edges. We denote the indexed set of entities by $\mathcal{E}$ and the indexed set of binary relations by $\mathcal{R}$ with $r \subset \mathcal{E} \times \mathcal{E}$ for all $r \in \mathcal{R}$. Further, consider $n_E := |\mathcal{E}|$ and $n_R := |\mathcal{R}|$, i.e., the number of entities and relations, respectively. Figure 2 shows an excerpt of a knowledge graph in an industrial setting.

A triple of the form (e_i, r_k, e_j) with $(e_i, e_j) \in r_k$ is interpreted as a true fact. Given a relation $r_k \in \mathcal{R}$, the characteristic function $\phi_{r_k} : \mathcal{E} \times \mathcal{E} \to \{0, 1\}$

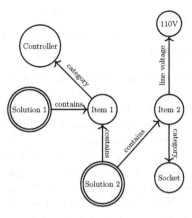

Fig. 2. An example of an industrial knowledge graph

indicates the truth value of triples. More concretely, $\phi_{r_k}(e_i, e_j) = 1\ (0)$ implies, that the corresponding triple (e_i, r_k, e_j) is interpreted as a true (unknown) fact. The entirety of all characteristic functions induces an adjacency tensor $\mathbf{X} \in \mathbb{R}^{n_E \times n_E \times n_R}$ with $\mathbf{X}_{i,j,k} = \phi_{r_k}(e_i, e_j)$.

Most knowledge graphs that are currently in use are far from being complete in the sense that they are missing many true facts about the entities at hand. Therefore, one of the canonical machine learning tasks applied to knowledge graphs consists of predicting new edges (i.e., facts) given the remaining connectivity pattern. This problem of link prediction is sometimes also referred to as knowledge graph completion.

One of the most popular knowledge graph completion methods is given by RESCAL [13]. RESCAL is based on factorizing the frontal slices of the adjacency tensor $\mathbf{X}$ as a product of the factor matrix $E \in \mathbb{R}^{n_E \times d}$ and the frontal slices of a core tensor $\mathbf{R} \in \mathbb{R}^{d \times d \times n_R}$. d is a hyperparameter that indicates the number of latent dimensions. This leads to

$$\mathbf{X}_{i,j,k} \approx E_{i,:}\mathbf{R}_{:,:,k}E_{j,:}^T .\tag{1}$$

The parameters of RESCAL are usually obtained by minimizing the sum of the squared residuals between the observed and the predicted entries of $\mathbf{X}$. Hence, the objective function is given by

$$\text{loss}(\mathbf{X}, E, \mathbf{R}) = \sum_{r=1}^{n_R} ||\mathbf{X}_{:,:,r} - E\mathbf{R}_{:,:,r}E^T||_F^2 ,\tag{2}$$

where $|| \cdot ||_F$ denotes the Frobenius norm. Usually this optimization problem is solved via alternating least squares. After fitting the model, the rows of E contain latent representations of the entities in $\mathcal{E}$. Similarly, each frontal slice of $\mathbf{R}$ contains the corresponding latent representations of the different relations in $\mathcal{R}$.

3   Related Methods

3.1   Recommender Systems

Most recommender systems are based on collaborative filtering (e.g., [1, 10]). These methods aggregate the preferences of users and generate recommendations based on user similarities in overall preference patterns. However, they sometimes suffer from the sparsity of data, i.e., the lack of adequate preference information. One of the ways to tackle this issue is to consider content information about the users/items as in content-based recommender systems. In their simplest form, content-based recommender systems are classifiers that map user and item information to the selection probability. Refer [11] for a survey of the related literature and state-of-the-art content-based recommender systems. Applying a purely content-based approach to our use case of industrial purchasing systems would ignore previous configuration patterns, which encode implicit requirements for automation solutions.

Hybrid recommender systems are those that use a combination of collaborative filtering and content-based approaches. They aim to balance the drawbacks of each individual approach and thereby achieve better performance. A detailed review of the various hybrid approaches is presented in [4]. [5] propose a hybrid recommender system where item categories are used as a means of determining user preferences. While this method is useful in domains involving homogeneous items, it is not well suited for complex industrial use cases, such as ours, where the customer preferences are guided by implicit requirements of the solution currently being built.

To tackle these use cases, [7] proposes RESCOM – a multi-relational recommender system, which combines historical data about solutions along with context information about items in a joint knowledge base. More concretely, RESCOM employs RESCAL (Sect. 2.3) to generate recommendations by projecting partial solutions into the corresponding low-dimensional space. However, RESCOM suffers from one shortcoming: while acting as a bilinear model for capturing interactions among items, RESCOM becomes linear in the recommendation step. Thus, it is not capable of capturing complex non-linear interactions among the items.

3.2   Autoencoders

Autoencoders (AE) are unsupervised neural networks wherein the output aims to reconstruct the input. While different versions of AE have been proposed [2, 12, 14], they all share two main building blocks: an encoder and a decoder. The encoder network $g : \mathbb{R}^n \to \mathbb{R}^d$, with $d \ll n$, takes a given input $x \in \mathbb{R}^n$ and maps it to a condensed representation $g(x)$. Subsequently, the decoder network $f : \mathbb{R}^d \to \mathbb{R}^n$ takes $g(x)$ as input and maps it to a reconstructed version of x. During training, the parameters of f and g are tuned such that $f\big(g(x)\big) \approx x$.

AE have also become a popular tool for collaborative filtering. [15] use AE to construct a hybrid recommender system. They incorporate side information by including item features at various layers of the AE. On a similar note, [6] propose a stacked AE that simultaneously encodes item and user features. It achieves good performance on two benchmark datasets with rather homogeneous items and relatively few features. In this sense, their use case significantly differs from ours: we consider items belonging to different categories (e.g., controllers, panels, and power supplies) and possessing category-specific features (e.g., resolution of a panel or the line voltage of a power supply). Combined with the sheer amount of technical attributes that we consider, encoding all these features and processing them directly via a neural network is not feasible.

4   Our Method – NECTR

In this paper, we propose *NECTR*, a recommender system consisting of two main components. One component is a knowledge graph that enables our model to structure context information about items. We make use of this information for recommendation purposes via a tensor factorization method described below. The second component consists of a neural network that acts as an encoder for solutions. We combine the two constituent components analogous to an AE structure resulting in a hybrid recommender engine. First, we introduce the problem setup in which *NECTR* was developed. Then, we proceed by describing the architecture of *NECTR*.

4.1   Problem Setup

This work evolved from a real-world industrial R&D project at Siemens. The project was centered around one of the major product configuration tools for automation solutions that has around 60,000 users per month. The purpose of the tool is to simplify the configuration process by providing intelligent selection wizards. Configuring an automation solution, however, is still not an easy task. As stated in Sect. 2, automation solutions can be very complex and be comprised of a wide range of subsystems and components, such as controllers, panels, and software. Each component is equipped with different features that must guarantee the operation of the overall system. Up to this point, without the help of experts, the configurator does not indicate to the user which components are relevant to the current solution. Hence, configuring a suitable solution requires domain expertise and a lot of effort. Our goal is to overcome this obstacle by either recommending a set of items that complement the users' current partial solutions or by reordering the list of all items based on their relevance (i.e., displaying the items that are most relevant first). Therefore, it is necessary to compute relevance scores for all items, such that the scores adjust dynamically depending on the components the user has already configured in the partial solution.

To reach this goal, we consider implicit feedback as training, validation, and testing data. For our purpose, a solution is represented as a vector $\mathbf{x} \in \mathbb{N}^{n_I}$, where n_I denotes the total number of configurable items. The i-th entry of $\mathbf{x}$

indicates the multiplicity of the corresponding item (i.e., the number of times an item has been added to the current solution). For training and testing purposes, a partial solution $\hat{\mathbf{x}} \in \mathbb{N}^{n_I}$ is obtained by randomly masking an observed solution by setting half of the positive entries to zero. A model is trained and evaluated with regards to its ability to recover the original solution $\mathbf{x}$ (i.e., to assign a high relative score to the masked items).

The predictive accuracy of a method is measured in terms of metrics that directly relate to our practical use case (see Sect. 5.2 for more details). In other words, the quality metrics, i.e., Mean Rank, Mean Reciprocal Rank, and Hits@k, measure the model's ability to accurately rank items. Furthermore, the scores obtained can be used either to explicitly recommend the highly ranked items or to sort the product list in decreasing order of scores, thereby placing the most relevant items on top. Hence, a model performing well with respect to the above mentioned metrics is also likely to be of practical use when integrated into a solution configurator.

4.2   Architecture

We merge both historical data concerning past automation solutions and technical information about components from an industrial database to form a joint multi-relational knowledge graph with entity set $\mathcal{E}$ and relation set $\mathcal{R}$ (recall Sect. 2.3). Moreover, we denote with $\mathbf{X} \in \mathbb{R}^{n_E \times n_E \times n_R}$ the corresponding adjacency tensor. In our use case, an entity can be a particular solution, a particular item, or a technical attribute (e.g., the category or the line voltage) describing an item (see Fig. 2 for an example). Relations are used to describe connections between entities. For example, solutions may be linked to items via the *contains*-relation, which indicates the items that are configured in a particular solution. Other relation types link items to their respective technical attributes (see the next Sect. 5 for more details about the data). To ease the notation, we denote with $\mathcal{I} \subset E$ the set of all entities that correspond to configurable items.

We use RESCAL (as described in Sect. 2.3) to generate embeddings for all entities contained in the factor matrix E. In particular, $E_{\mathcal{I}}$ contains the latent features of all configurable items. Hence, if items are similar from a technical point of view or if they are often configured together, they will be close to each other in the latent feature space. In RESCAL, we employ the modified loss function

$$\mathcal{L}_C = \sum_{\substack{(e_i, r_k, e_j) \\ (e_i, e_j) \in \phi_{r_k}^{-1}(\{1\})}} (1 - E_{i,:}\mathbf{R}_{:,:,k}E_{j,:}^T)^2 + (E_{i,:}\mathbf{R}_{:,:,k}E_{l,:}^T)^2 , \qquad (3)$$

where the second summand corresponds to a negative sample drawn from a contrastive distribution. Thereby, we draw the l-th entity in the negative sample uniformly at random from the set of entities that appear as object in an observed triple with respect to the k-th relation. This sampling procedure can be interpreted as an implicit type constraint which teaches the algorithm to discriminate between known triples on one side and unknown but plausible triples on the other side. The main advantage of this formulation is that we can deal with very high levels of sparsity since Eq. (3) balances positive and negative examples. Since our data is extremely sparse (in fact, only about $3 \cdot 10^{-6}\%$ of the entries in $\mathbf{X}$ are non-zero), we empirically found that minimizing the loss given by Eq. (2) results in fitting mostly the zeros in $\mathbf{X}$ leading to degenerate results.

In order to obtain embeddings for the automation solutions, we process the partial solutions $\hat{\mathbf{x}} \in \mathbb{R}^{n_I}$ (see Sect. 4.1) via a feed forward neural network. More concretely, we use a dense neural network $g : \mathbb{R}^{n_I} \to \mathbb{R}^d$ in order to extract high-level representations of solutions that capture non-linear interactions between the configured items. For simplicity, we constrain the output dimension of all hidden layers to be equal to d. Further, we employ ReLU activation functions in all hidden layers. No non-linearity is applied in the output layer.

Moreover, consider the binary version $\mathbf{y} \in \{0,1\}^{n_I}$ derived from $\mathbf{x}$ with $\mathbf{y}_i = \mathbb{1}_{\mathbf{x}_i > 0}$. That means each entry of $\mathbf{y}$ indicates whether or not the corresponding item is contained in the solution. *NECTR* is fitted such that it recovers the original, binary solution $\mathbf{y}$ from the partial solution $\hat{\mathbf{x}}$ containing the item counts. The underlying rationale behind this setup is that we want *NECTR* to learn whether an item is relevant in the context of a partial solution and in turn recommend this item to the user. Considering the actual counts in $\mathbf{x}$ as target variables would have resulted in an unwanted bias towards items that are frequently configured in large number (such as cables or sockets).

In a regular AE, one would employ a decoder network which mirrors the action of g in order to obtain a reconstruction of $\hat{\mathbf{x}}$. We, however, introduce a so-called context layer which induces side information into the AE architecture. This is realized by multiplying the latent representation of $\hat{\mathbf{x}}$ with the item embeddings obtained from the tensor factorization, followed by a non-linearity. More concretely, we obtain

$$\sigma(E_{\mathcal{I}} g(\hat{\mathbf{x}})) =: \tilde{\mathbf{y}}, \tag{4}$$

where $\sigma(\cdot)$ denotes the sigmoid function. Then *NECTR* is fitted such that the output approximates the original, binary solution, i.e., $\tilde{\mathbf{y}} \approx \mathbf{y}$. Entries of the reconstruction can be interpreted as scores indicating the relevance of an item for a given partial solution. They can be used to produce a ranked list and items that have the highest rank can be recommended to the user.

Equation (4) can be interpreted as an implicit similarity search in the latent feature space, where the discrepancy between solutions and items is measured in terms of the cosine distance. However, this might not be appropriate in a setting where the items are very heterogeneous and belong to different categories. Moreover, [7] find that after fitting the parameters of RESCAL, items of industrial automation solutions cluster in the latent feature space according to their categories. That is why it may not be appropriate to consider a single latent representation of a solution and compare it to all items across different categories. As a remedy to this problem, we propose category-specific transformations of the solution and compute the reconstructed version for each category separately.

To ease the notation, let $\mathrm{Cat}_i \subset \mathcal{I}$ denote the index set of items that belong to the i-th category. A category-specific reformulation of Eq. (4) is given by

$$\sigma(E_{\mathrm{Cat}_i} A_i g(\hat{\mathbf{x}})) =: \tilde{\mathbf{y}}_{\mathrm{Cat}_i}, \tag{5}$$

where $A_i \in \mathbb{R}^{d \times d}$ denotes a category-specific linear mapping. The reconstructed solution $\tilde{\mathbf{y}}$ is obtained by concatenating all $\tilde{\mathbf{y}}_{\mathrm{Cat}_i}$. Note that this alternative formulation does not lead to an increase in the computational complexity. We refer to the resulting method as $NECTR_{cat}$.

The parameters of the AE-like component are obtained by minimizing the recommendation loss given by

$$\mathcal{L}_R = -\sum_{i=1}^{n_S} \sum_{j=1}^{n_I} \mathbf{y}_j^{(i)} \log(\tilde{\mathbf{y}}_j^{(i)}) + (1 - \mathbf{y}_j^{(i)}) \log(1 - \tilde{\mathbf{y}}_j^{(i)}), \tag{6}$$

where n_S denotes the number of solutions in the training data. The index sets of the two sums are ranging over all solutions and all items, respectively. Further, after consulting domain experts in the field of industrial engineering solutions, we conjectured that nonlinear interactions between items are present, but not necessarily numerous. That is the reason for adding an additional L_1-regularizer on the weight matrices of g to induce sparsity.

The overall loss function of our recommender system is given by

$$\mathcal{L} = \mathcal{L}_R + \lambda \mathcal{L}_c + \text{regularization term}, \tag{7}$$

where $\lambda > 0$ balances the completion and the recommendation loss. This leads to the interpretation that the inclusion of the knowledge graph embeddings acts as a context-aware regularization. The whole model can be trained end-to-end by minimizing the loss given by Eq. (7) using stochastic gradient descent. Figure 1 summarizes the architecture of $NECTR$.

5   Real-World Experimental Study

5.1   Data

The evaluation has been performed on the real-world dataset collected in the context of an internal R&D project at Siemens. We distinguish between two sources of information: historical shopping data and product descriptions. Historical shopping data contains the specifications of 49,829 engineering solutions that have been configured by customers in the past. While some additional structural information is available, for the purposes of this study, we treat each engineering solution as a list of products used along with their respective quantities. Each of the 6,136 products that has been used in one of the historical solutions comes with a spec sheet, which summarizes its technical characteristics. Further, we distinguish between 5,062 possible attributes – with only a small part being relevant for any given item. One example of an attribute of particular importance is the product category. We distinguish between 8 categories, namely Industrial Communication, IPC, I/O System, Panel, Cables and Plugs, Software, Controller, and Industrial Control. In certain cases, a more granular categorization is available, e.g. Mobile Panel, Basic Panel, and Comfort Panel.

5.2 Evaluation

To guarantee a fair evaluation in a realistic setting, we follow the same experimental setup and evaluation scheme: First, we split the solutions in our dataset into training, validation, and test sets in the ratio 70-20-10. In particular, solutions that are assigned to the validation or test set are neither included in the knowledge graph nor are processed by the neural network g during training. Next, for each method, we perform cross-validation in order to choose the most suitable set of hyperparameters, i.e., the one yielding the highest mean reciprocal rank. The number of the latent dimensions for the embeddings is chosen from the range $\{10, 30, 50, 70, 90\}$. For the neural network, the number of hidden layers and neurons per layer are chosen among $\{1, 2, 3\}$ and $\{5, 15, 25, 35, 45, 50\}$, respectively. Moreover, the L_1-regularization strength was set to 0.01 and λ was chosen from $\{0.01, 0.1, 1\}$. Equation (7) was minimized using Adam with learning rate given by 0.01. Finally, we evaluate each method on the test set using the best hyperparameters and report the results.

For evaluation, we construct an adjacency matrix of solutions and configured items. For each solution, we randomly choose half of the configured items and mask the corresponding entries. Let $\mathcal{M} = (s, i)$ denote the set of masked items per solution and $n_M := |\mathcal{M}|$ denotes the number of masked items. Further, since we find that the solution data is rather skewed, we perform a log-transformation on the raw-input (i.e., the item counts). We then perform a forward pass through the neural network followed by a multiplication with the item embeddings obtained from the tensor factorization (see Eq. (4)), to obtain a completed matrix. Each row in this matrix corresponds to a solution and the entries in each row are interpreted as scores that determine the likelihood of configuration of the corresponding items in the solution. Based on this interpretation, the items are reordered row-wise, in decreasing order of their scores, resulting in a rank $R_{i,s}$ for each item. Based on these predicted ranks, we compute the following performance metrics:

- Mean rank – Average of the ranks predicted for the items, given by

$$\text{Mean rank} = \frac{1}{n_M} \sum_{(s,i) \in \mathcal{M}} R_{i,s}.$$

- Mean reciprocal rank (MRR) – Average of the multiplicative inverse of the predicted ranks, as given by

$$\text{MRR} = \frac{1}{n_M} \sum_{(s,i) \in \mathcal{M}} \frac{1}{R_{i,s}}.$$

The choice of the MRR is motivated by its stronger robustness to outliers as compared to the Mean rank.
- Hits@k – The proportion of correct entities ranked in the top k, i.e.,

$$\text{Hits@k} = \frac{|R_{i,s} < k|}{n_M}.$$

More specifically, we report the values for k = 1, 3, 5, 10, and 10%.

Furthermore, to tackle the bias introduced by the true triples (as noted in [3]), we report all the above metrics in two settings: raw (where all triples are included in ranking) and filtered (where all true triples, except the test triple in consideration, are excluded from the ranking).

5.3   Results

Table 1 displays the results of the recommendation task for all methods under consideration. As described previously in Sect. 1, matrix factorization, especially non-negative matrix factorization (NMF), has consistently produced good results in recommender systems. So we include results of evaluating NMF in our experimental setting. Recommending items corresponds to proposing new edges of type contains in the knowledge graph (see Fig. 2). Hence, the recommendation task is equivalent to the graph completion task restricted to proposing links between solutions and items. That is the reason for also evaluating TransE [3], a translational model popularly used for link prediction. In addition, we present the results of evaluating RESCOM – a tensor factorization-based recommendation engine developed in the context of engineering solutions (see Sect. 3). The best hyperparamters for $NECTR$ ($NECTR_{cat}$) are determined via the cross-validation setting described in the previous subsection. The reported results correspond to the following hyperparameter values: The number of latent dimensions is 90 (30), the number of hidden layers is equal to 1 (3), the number of hidden neurons are given by 45 (30), $\lambda = 0.1$ (0.01), and the L_1-regularization strength is equal to 0.01 (0.01).

Table 1. Results of all evaluated methods on the test set of the automation solution dataset.

Metric	Mean rank		MRR		Hits@10%		Hits@1		Hits@3		Hits@5		Hits@10	
Eval. setting	Raw	Filt.	Raw	Filt.	Raw	Filt.	Raw	Filt.	Raw	Filt.	Raw	Filt.	Raw	Filt.
TransE	392.01	385.79	0.06	0.07	0.73	0.83	0.02	0.02	0.05	0.07	0.08	0.11	0.14	0.16
NMF	223.2	215.87	0.10	0.25	0.92	0.92	0.016	0.16	0.08	0.27	0.17	0.32	0.31	0.42
RESCOM	160.63	152.66	0.08	0.19	**0.95**	**0.96**	0.003	0.08	0.05	0.2	0.13	0.28	0.28	0.41
$NECTR$	193.04	185.20	0.13	**0.31**	0.94	0.94	0.03	**0.22**	0.11	**0.34**	0.20	**0.40**	**0.37**	**0.50**
$NECTR_{cat}$	**148.82**	**142.17**	**0.16**	0.27	**0.95**	0.95	**0.06**	0.18	**0.16**	0.28	**0.23**	0.35	0.36	0.46

The filtered setting produces lower Mean ranks and higher values of MRR and Hits@k for all the methods, as expected. As described in Sect. 5.2, this setting offers a better evaluation of the real-world performance. $NECTR$ (or $NECTR_{cat}$) outperforms all methods in all of the standard metrics except for Hits@10%. In particular, the performance gains measured by MRR and Hits@k are substantial. Related to our use case, this indicates that $NECTR$ is capable of placing relevant items on top of the list with the highest probability. Furthermore, we find that $NECTR_{cat}$ outperforms all other methods with respect to the Mean Rank by a large margin, while yielding comparable results to $NECTR$ with respect to the other performance measures.

The large improvements that $NECTR$ achieves compared to other methods show the presence of non-negligible, higher order interactions as well as the necessity to consider context information. RESCOM deviates from $NECTR$ in the sense that it employs RESCAL directly to produce recommendations (see Sect. 3). Thus, RESCOM is not able to model non-linear effects among the configured items. Hence, the large performance gains of $NECTR$ can be attributed to this feature. Moreover, $NECTR$ also comprises a model that does not take context information into account. This is achieved by setting λ in Eq. (7) to zero. We found that this model is strictly dominated by a context-aware version of $NECTR$ with respect to all performance measures (result not shown).

5.4   Additional Experiments

In this section, we evaluate and compare $NECTR$ on the standard benchmark dataset Movielens 1M.[2] After preprocessing, it contains around 1 million ratings from 6,038 users on 3,533 movies along with demographic information about users (age, occupation, and gender) and the genres of the movies. Movielens 1M differs from the automation solution dataset in the sense that the items under consideration (movies) are stand-alone homogeneous items. Further, the context information is a lot less rich and less diverse (recall, items in the automation solution use case come with more than 5,000 different attributes). Thus, we do not expect that $NECTR$ can demonstrate its advantages as in the automation solution use case. Following [6], we binarize explicit data by keeping the ratings of four or higher and interpret them as implicit feedback that the user liked the corresponding movies. In order to inject the context information about users into $NECTR$, we consider the implicit feedback movies liked by a user concatenated with the demographic information about the corresponding user as input vector $\hat{x}$ to the neural encoder g. The experimental setting and the evaluation scheme are identical to the previous subsections. The chosen hyperparamters for $NECTR$ are as follows. The number of latent dimensions is 10, the number of hidden layers is equal to 2, the number of hidden neurons are given by 40, $\lambda = 0.1$, and the L_1-regularization strength equals 0.01.

The results are presented in Table 2. As argued above, given the limited complexity of the data, it cannot be expected that $NECTR$ leads to similar performance gains like in Sect. 5.3. Nevertheless, $NECTR$ outperforms all other methods with respect to the Mean rank by a large margin and leads to a comparable performance with respect to the other metrics.

---

[2] https://grouplens.org/datasets/movielens/1m/.

Table 2. Results of all evaluated methods on the MovieLens 1M dataset.

Metric	Mean rank		MRR		Hits@10%		Hits@1		Hits@3		Hits@5		Hits@10	
Eval. setting	Raw	Filt.	Raw	Filt.	Raw	Filt.	Raw	Filt.	Raw	Filt.	Raw	Filt.	Raw	Filt.
TransE	642.90	539.77	0.01	0.02	0.44	0.51	0.001	0.002	0.004	0.008	0.01	0.01	0.02	0.03
NMF	556.43	440.15	0.012	0.06	0.58	0.68	0.0002	0.02	0.002	0.05	0.004	0.08	0.02	0.12
RESCOM	431.18	316.62	0.02	**0.07**	**0.66**	**0.77**	0.002	**0.03**	0.008	**0.07**	0.02	**0.1**	0.04	**0.15**
NECTR	**398.87**	**294.36**	0.03	0.07	0.64	0.74	**0.006**	**0.03**	**0.02**	0.06	**0.03**	0.08	**0.05**	0.14

6   Conclusion

Traditional collaborative filtering methods are not expressive enough in a setting where multiple components form a complex system and technical properties of items play a crucial role. This is the case for industrial engineering solutions where the individual components interact with each other, resulting in higher-order dependencies. Popular methods, such as matrix factorization, are not able to capture such non-linear effects. To address these shortcomings, we have proposed *NECTR* – a novel recommender system, which combines deep representation learning and context information structured in a knowledge graph. While a tensor factorization exploits context information of the available items, an autoencoder models the non-linear dependencies inherent to automation solutions.

We conducted extensive experiments on a real-world dataset for industrial automation solutions. The main findings are:

1. *NECTR* outperforms all baseline methods with respect to most metrics. This shows the presence of non-linear interactions as well as the necessity to include context information.
2. *NECTR* can be trained efficiently end-to-end. Since the recommendation step is performed via a simple forward pass through a neural network, *NECTR* can efficiently work in real-time. This is crucial with regard to its practical applicability.

Finally, we would like to stress that this work evolved from a real-world industrial R&D project. In the following months, we will take further steps towards integrating *NECTR* into one of the major industrial engineering solution configurators at Siemens.

References

1. Bell, R.M., Koren, Y., Volinsky, C.: The Bellkor 2008 solution to the Netflix prize. Statistics Research Department at AT&T Research 1 (2008)
2. Bengio, Y., Courville, A., Vincent, P.: Representation learning: a review and new perspectives. ArXiv e-prints, June 2012
3. Bordes, A., Usunier, N., Garcia-Duran, A., Weston, J., Yakhnenko, O.: Translating embeddings for modeling multi-relational data. In: Advances in Neural Information Processing Systems, pp. 2787–2795 (2013)

4. Burke, R.: Hybrid recommender systems: survey and experiments. User Model. User-Adapt. Interact. **12**(4), 331–370 (2002)
5. Choi, S.M., Han, Y.S.: A content recommendation system based on category correlations. In: 2010 Fifth International Multi-Conference on Computing in the Global Information Technology (ICCGI), pp. 66–70. IEEE (2010)
6. Dong, X., Yu, L., Wu, Z., Sun, Y., Yuan, L., Zhang, F.: A hybrid collaborative filtering model with deep structure for recommender systems. In: AAAI, pp. 1309–1315 (2017)
7. Hildebrandt, M., Sunder, S.S., Mogoreanu, S., Thon, I., Tresp, V., Runkler, T.: Configuration of industrial automation solutions using multi-relational recommender systems. In: Brefeld, U., et al. (eds.) ECML PKDD 2018. LNCS (LNAI), vol. 11053, pp. 271–287. Springer, Cham (2019). https://doi.org/10.1007/978-3-030-10997-4_17
8. Hinton, G., Deng, L., Yu, D., Dahl, G.: Deep neural networks for acoustic modeling in speech recognition. Signal Process. Mag. **29**, 82–97 (2012)
9. Krizhevsky, A.: ImageNet classification with deep convolutional neural networks. In: Advances in Neural Information Processing Systems, vol. 25 (2012)
10. Linden, G., Smith, B., York, J.: Amazon.com recommendations: item-to-item collaborative filtering. IEEE Internet Comput. **7**(1), 76–80 (2003)
11. Lops, P., de Gemmis, M., Semeraro, G.: Content-based recommender systems: state of the art and trends. In: Ricci, F., Rokach, L., Shapira, B., Kantor, P.B. (eds.) Recommender Systems Handbook, pp. 73–105. Springer, Boston (2011). https://doi.org/10.1007/978-0-387-85820-3_3
12. Meng, Q., Catchpoole, D., Skillicorn, D., Kennedy, P.J.: Relational autoencoder for feature extraction. ArXiv e-prints, February 2018
13. Nickel, M., Tresp, V., Kriegel, H.P.: A three-way model for collective learning on multi-relational data. In: ICML, vol. 11, pp. 809–816 (2011)
14. Rifai, S., Vincent, P., Muller, X., Glorot, X., Bengio, Y.: Contracting auto-encoders: explicit invariance during feature extraction. In: Proceedings of the Twenty-Eight International Conference on Machine Learning (ICML 2011) (2011)
15. Strub, F., Gaudel, R., Mary, J.: Hybrid recommender system based on autoencoders. In: Proceedings of the 1st Workshop on Deep Learning for Recommender Systems, pp. 11–16. ACM (2016)
16. Weston, J., Chopra, S., Adams, K.: TagSpace: semantic embeddings from hashtags. In: Empirical Methods in Natural Language Processing (2014)

Learning URI Selection Criteria to Improve the Crawling of Linked Open Data

Hai Huang$^{(\boxtimes)}$(i) and Fabien Gandon(i)

Inria, Université Côte d'Azur, CNRS, I3S, Sophia Antipolis, France
{Hai.Huang,Fabien.Gandon}@inria.fr

Abstract. As the Web of Linked Open Data is growing the problem of crawling that cloud becomes increasingly important. Unlike normal Web crawlers, a Linked Data crawler performs a selection to focus on collecting linked RDF (including RDFa) data on the Web. From the perspectives of throughput and coverage, given a newly discovered and targeted URI, the key issue of Linked Data crawlers is to decide whether this URI is likely to dereference into an RDF data source and therefore it is worth downloading the representation it points to. Current solutions adopt heuristic rules to filter irrelevant URIs. Unfortunately, when the heuristics are too restrictive this hampers the coverage of crawling. In this paper, we propose and compare approaches to learn strategies for crawling Linked Data on the Web by predicting whether a newly discovered URI will lead to an RDF data source or not. We detail the features used in predicting the relevance and the methods we evaluated including a promising adaptation of FTRL-proximal online learning algorithm. We compare several options through extensive experiments including existing crawlers as baseline methods to evaluate their efficacy.

Keywords: Linked Data · Crawling strategy · Machine learning · Online prediction

1 Introduction

Linked Data extends the principles of the World Wide Web from linking documents to that of linking pieces of data to weave a Web of Data. This relies on the well-known linked data principles [1,10] including the use of HTTP URIs that can be dereferenced and the provision of useful and linked description upon access so that we can discover more things.

Recently, a large amount of data are being made available as linked data in various domains such as health, publication, agriculture, music, etc., and the Web of Linked Data is growing exponentially [8]. In order to harvest this enormous data repository, crawling techniques for Linked Data are becoming increasingly important. Different from conventional crawlers, crawling for Linked Data is performed selectively to collect structured data connected by RDF links.

© Springer Nature Switzerland AG 2019
P. Hitzler et al. (Eds.): ESWC 2019, LNCS 11503, pp. 194–208, 2019.
https://doi.org/10.1007/978-3-030-21348-0_13

The target of interest makes it distinct from focused crawlers which select the collection of Web pages to crawl based on their relevance to a specific topic.

The design objective of Linked Data crawlers is to fetch linked RDF data in different formats – RDF/XML, N3, RDFa, JSON-LD, etc. – as much as possible within a reasonable time while minimizing the download of irrelevant URIs – i.e. leading to resources without RDF content. Therefore our challenge is to identify as soon as possible the URIs referencing RDF sources without downloading them. The research question here is: *can we learn efficient URI selection criteria to identify sources of Linked Open Data?*

To solve this problem, in this paper we propose and compare methods on real data to predict whether a newly discovered URI will lead to RDF data source or not. We extract information from the targeting and referring URI and from the context (RDF data graph) where URIs and their links were discovered in order to produce features fed to learning algorithms and in particular to an FTRL-proximal online method employed to build the prediction model. FTRL-proximal is a time efficient and space efficient online learning algorithm, which can handle significantly larger data sets. It is also effective at producing sparse models which is important when the feature space is huge. FTRL-proximal outperforms the other online learning algorithms in terms of accuracy and sparsity.

The contributions of this work include: (1) we identify the features to predict whether a target URI will lead to some RDF data or not; (2) we adapt the FTRL-proximal algorithm to our task and build an online prediction model; and (3) we implement a Linked Data crawler with the online prediction model and evaluate its performance.

The paper is organized as follows. Section 2 introduces related work, followed by preliminary knowledge in Sect. 3. Section 4 describes feature extraction and online prediction model. In Sect. 5 we present the implementation of the proposed crawler. The experimental setup and results are described in Sect. 6. We conclude our work in Sect. 7.

2   Related Work

Semantic Web/Linked Data Crawlers. Semantic web crawlers differ from traditional web crawlers in only two aspects: the format of the source (RDF format) it is traversing, and the means to link RDF across data sources. There exist some work [6,12,13] in the field of Semantic Web/Linked Data crawling. The two main representative crawlers for Linked Data are LDSpider [13] and SWSE crawler [12]. They crawl the Web of Linked Data by traversing RDF links between data sources and follow the Linked Data principles [1,10]. They offer different crawling strategies such as breadth-first and load-balancing traversal.

In order to reduce the amount of HTTP lookups and downloading wasted on URIs referencing non-RDF resources, these previous works apply heuristic rules to identify relevant URIs [12,13]. The URIs with common file extensions (e.g., html/htm, jpg, pdf, etc.) and those without appropriate HTTP Content-Type Header (such as application/rdf+xml) are classified as non-RDF content URIs.

The content of these URIs would not be retrieved by these crawlers. Although this heuristic-based method is efficient, it impairs the recall of the crawling. This method makes the assumption that data publishers have provided correct HTTP Content-Type Header but this is not always the case. It can happen that the server does not provide the desired content type. Moreover, it may happen that the server returns an incorrect content type. For example, Freebase does not provide any content negotiation or HTML resource representation [9], and only text/plain is returned as content type. In [11], it is reported that 17% of RDF/XML documents are returned with a content-type other than application/rdf+xml. As a result, a huge volume of RDF data is missed by these methods.

Focused Crawlers on the Web. Traditional focused crawlers on the Web aim to crawl a subset of Web pages based on their relevance to a specific topic [4,5]. These methods build a relevancy model typically encoded as a classifier to evaluate the web documents for topical relevancy. Our work here is different in the sense that we do not filter on the topics but on the type of content. Meusel et al. [17] proposed a focused crawling approach to fetch microdata embedded in HTML pages. Umbrich et al. [18] built a crawler focused on gathering files of a particular media type and based on heuristics.

Online Prediction. Our problem is also related to the classic online binary prediction in which data becomes available in a sequential order and the learner must make real-time decisions and continuously improve performance with the sequential arrival of data. Some methods have been developed such as Stochastic Gradient Descent (SGD) [3], RDA [20], FOBOS [7] and FTRL-Proximal [15,16]. Among them, FTRL-Proximal which is developed by Google has been proven to work well on the massive online learning problem of predicting ad click-through rates (CTR). We adapt the FTRL-Proximal to our prediction task in this work.

3   Preliminary Knowledge

In this section, we introduce some basic definitions and notations used throughout the paper. The Linked Data crawler targets a kind of structured data represented in RDF format on the Web. The Resource Description Framework (RDF) provides a structured means of publishing information describing entities and their relationships in RDF triples. The main concepts of RDF and Linked Data we need here are:

Definition 1 (RDF Triple). *A triple $t = (s, p, o) \in (U \cup B) \times U \times (U \cup B) \times (U \times B \times L)$ is called an RDF triple where U denotes the set of URI, B the set of blank nodes and L the set of literals. In such a triple, s is called subject, p predicate, and o object.*

Definition 2 (RDF Graph). *An RDF graph $G = (V, E)$ is a set of RDF triples such that V is the node set and E is the edge set of G.*

Definition 3 (*HTTP Dereferencing*). *The act of retrieving a representation of a resource identified by a URI is known as dereferencing that URI. We define HTTP dereferencing as the function* $deref : U \to R$ *which maps a given URI to the representation of a resource returned by performing the HTTP lookup operations upon that URI and following redirections when needed.*

4 Prediction Model for Crawling Criteria

In this section, we present the prediction task, the feature sets extracted for the task of prediction and then describe the prediction model based on FTRL-proximal online learning algorithm.

4.1 Task Description

Since the task of Linked Data crawler is to fetch RDF data on the Web we are interested in a kind of URIs that we call RDF-relevant URIs:

Definition 4 (*RDF-Relevant*). *Given a URI u, we consider that u is RDF-relevant if the representation obtained by dereferencing u contains RDF data. Otherwise, u is called non RDF-relevant. We note* U^R *the set of RDF relevant URIs and* U^I *the set of non RDF-relevant URIs with* $U = U^R \dot\cup U^I$.

For the URIs that have certain file extensions such as *.rdf/owl or HTTP Content Types Headers such as application/rdf+xml, text/turtle, etc., it is trivial to know the RDF-relevance of them. In this work, we focus on a knid of URIs called hard URIs whose RDF-relevance *cannot* be known by these heuristics.

Definition 5 (*Hard URI*). *We call u a hard URI if the RDF relevance of u cannot be known straightforwardly by its file extension or HTTP Content-Type Header.*

For example, URI u with HTTP Content-Type header text/html is a hard URI since RDFa data could be embedded in u. As reported in [9], the URIs with HTTP Content-Type Header text/plain may contain RDF data so they are hard URIs too.

Then, for our prediction task, we consider four types of URIs involved in the prediction we want to make: the target URI, the referring URI, direct property URIs and sibling URIs.

Definition 6 (*Target URI*). *We call target URI and note* u_t *the URI for which we want to predict if the* $deref(u_t)$ *will lead to a representation that contains RDF data i.e. if* u_t *is RDF-Relevant.*

Definition 7 (*Context RDF Graph*). *Given an RDF relevant URI* u_r *containing the RDF graph* G_t^r, *we define* $G_t^r = (V, E)$ *as the context RDF graph of URI* u_t *if* u_t *appears in* G_t^r *as a node, i.e.,* $u_t \in V$.

Definition 8 (Referring URI). *Given a target URI u_t, we call "referring URI" and note u_r the RDF-relevant URI that was dereferenced into a representation $deref(u_r)$ containing the context RDF graph G_t^r in which we discovered the target URI u_t.*

Definition 9 (Sibling Set). *The sibling set of u_t in the context RDF Graph G_t^r denoted by Sib_{u_t} is the set of all other URIs that have common subject-property or property-object pair with u_t in G_t^r. Sib_{u_t} is formally defined as:*

$$Sib_{u_t} = \{s | \exists p, o \in G_t^r, s.t.(u_t, p, o) \in G_t^r \wedge (s, p, o) \in G_t^r\}$$
$$\vee \{o | \exists s, p \in G_t^r, s.t.(s, p, u_t) \in G_t^r \wedge (s, p, o) \in G_t^r\} \tag{1}$$

Definition 10 (Direct property Set). *The direct property set PS_t is the set of properties that connect u_t in the context graph G_t^r:*

$$PS_t = \{p | \exists s, o \in G_t^c, s.t.(u_t, p, o) \in G_t^r \vee (s, p, u_t) \in G_t^r\} \tag{2}$$

Prediction Task. Using these definitions we can now define our prediction task. Suppose that a hard URI u_t is discovered from the context graph G_t^r obtained by dereferencing a referring URI u_r. We want to predict if u_t is RDF-relevant based on some features extracted from u_t, u_r, PS_t and Sib_{u_t}. Our task is to learn the mapping $Relevant : U \to \{0, 1\}$ with $Relevant(u)$ equals 1 if u is RDF-relevant ($Relevant|_{U^R} \mapsto 1$) and equals 0 if u is not RDF-relevant ($Relevant|_{U^I} \mapsto 0$)

4.2   Feature Extraction

We distinguish between two kinds of features that can be exploited for the prediction intrinsic and extrinsic.

Definition 11 (intrinsic URI features). *The intrinsic features of a URI u are features obtained by an extraction $F_{int} : U \to F$ that relies exclusively on the URI identifier itself.*

An example of an intrinsic feature is the protocol used e.g. `http`.

Definition 12 (extrinsic URI features). *The extrinsic features of a URI u are features obtained by performing some network call on the URI $F_{ext} : U \to F$.*

The URI generic syntax consists of a hierarchical sequence of several components[1]. An example of URI is shown in Fig. 1.

The intrinsic features $F_{int}(u)$ consider that the different components of a URI u are informative and contain helpful information for prediction. The components include: scheme, authority, host, path, query, fragment information. We generate the intrinsic features of u based on these components.

For example, the features $F_{int}(u)$ when u equals the URI shown in Fig. 1 are described as follows:

---

[1] RFC 3986, section 3(2005).

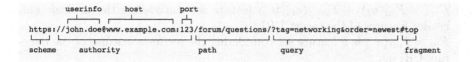

Fig. 1. Example of a URI with component parts.

- feature_u_scheme='https'
- feature_u_authority='john.doe@www.example.com:123'
- feature_u_host='www.example.com'
- feature_u_userinfo='john.doe'
- feature_u_path='forum/questions'
- feature_u_query='?tag=networking&order=newest'
- feature_u_fragment='top'

We further distinguish two kinds of extrinsic features:

Definition 13 (URI header features). *These extrinsic features of a URI u are obtained by an HTTP HEAD call $F_{head} : U \to F$ and do not require to download the representation of the resource identified by u.*

Definition 14 (URI representation features). *These extrinsic features of a URI u are obtained by an HTTP GET call $F_{get} : U \to F$ and characterize the content obtained after a complete download of the representation of the resource identified by u.*

We distinguish F_{head} and F_{get} because they have different costs in terms of network access time. The URI header feature we will consider in this paper is the content type e.g. feature_u_t_contentType='text/html'.

URI representation features come from the content of the referring URI u_r, namely the context graph G_t^r of u_t which include the direct properties and siblings information of u_t.

Definition 15 (URI similarity features). *The similarity between two URIs u_s and u_t denoted by $simValue(u_s, u_t)$ is defined using the Levenshtein distance [14] between the two strings representing these URIs. In order to reduce the feature space, a threshold τ is set for the similarity value and if the similarity value is larger than τ, we discretize the similarity as $simValue(u_t, u_s) = high$ and otherwise $simValue(u_t, u_s) = low$.*

Definition 16 (RDF relevance features). *The boolean characteristic of being RDF-relevant for a URI u is noted $F_{RDFrel}(u)$ and returns true if u is RDF-revelant and false otherwise.*

With the types of features explained above we can now define four atomic feature sets based on the sources the features come from to explore and evaluate when training and predicting the RDF-relevance of a target URI u_t:

- $F_{+t} = F_{int}(u_t) + F_{head}(u_t)$ is a feature set considering the intrinsic and header features of the target URI u_t.
- $F_{+r} = F_{int}(u_r)$ is a feature set considering the intrinsic features of the referring URI u_r.
- $F_{+p} = \bigcup_{p \in PS_t} F_{int}(p)$ is a feature set including the intrinsic features of each direct property of the target URI u_t.
- $F_{+x} = \bigcup_{u_s \in Sib_{u_t}} F_x(u_s)$ is a feature set including feature crosses that combine the intrinsic, header, similarity and relevance features of the sibling URIs of u_t. This supports predictive abilities beyond what those features can provide individually and can be interpreted as using a logical conjunction 'AND' to combine these features $F_x(u_s) = F_{int}(u_s) \times F_{head}(u_s) \times F_{sim}(u_s, u_t) \times F_{RDFrel}(u_s)$

With these definitions we can now consider and evaluate any combination of feature sets. We note F_{+a} the feature set with a being a combination of the atomic feature sets as defined above. For instance an experiment using the feature set F_{+t+r} will only consider as inputs the intrinsic and header features of the target URI u_t and the intrinsic feature of referring URI u_r. In Sect. 6.1, the predictive abilities of different combinations of the feature sets are examined.

4.3 Feature Hashing

During the process of crawling, the crawler will encounter URIs belonging to millions of domains, and the number of properties could be tens of thousands. Obviously, the potential feature space will be huge. Thus, we use feature hashing [19] technique to map high-dimensional features into binary vectors. Feature hashing uses a random sparse projection matrix $A : \mathbb{R}^n \to \mathbb{R}^m$ (where $n \gg m$) in order to reduce the dimension of the data from n to m while approximately preserving the Euclidean norm. In this work, hash function MurmurHash3[2] is adopted to map the feature vectors into binary vectors. By hashing the features we can gain significant advantages in memory usage since we can bound the size of generated binary vectors and we do not need a pre-built dictionary.

4.4 Online Prediction

We now present our prediction method. In this paper we assume that data becomes available in a sequential order during the crawling process. The predictor makes a prediction at each step and can also update itself: it operates in an online style. Compared to batch methods, online methods are more appropriate for the task of crawling since the predictor has to work in a dynamic learning environment. FTRL-Proximal [15, 16] developed by Google has been proven to work well on the massive online learning problems. FTRL-proximal outperforms the other online learning algorithms in terms of accuracy and sparsity, and has

---

[2] https://github.com/aappleby/smhasher/wiki/MurmurHash3.

been widely used in industry, e.g., recommender systems and advertisement systems. We adopt this learning algorithm in our work.

We use $\mathbf{x}_t$ to denote the feature vector of URI u_t and $y_t \in \{0,1\}$ the true class label of u_t. Given a sequence of URIs $u_1, u_2, \cdots, u_r, \cdots, u_t$, the process of online prediction based on FTRL-Proximal algorithm is shown in Algorithm 1. We adapted the original algorithm to make it output binary values by setting a decision threshold τ. If the predicted probability p_t is greater than the decision threshold $\tau \in [0,1]$, it outputs prediction $\hat{y}_t = 1$; otherwise $\hat{y}_t = 0$.

Algorithm 1. Online prediction with the FTRL-Proximal algorithm

---

   Input: URIs $u_1, u_2, \cdots, u_T$
   Result: $\hat{y}_1, \cdots, \hat{y}_T$
1   **for** $t = 1$ *to* T *do* **do**
2   get feature vector $\mathbf{x}_t$ of u_t;
3   probability $p_t = sigmoid(\mathbf{x}_t \cdot \mathbf{w}_t)$;
4   **if** $p_t > \tau$ **then**
5 | output $\hat{y}_t = 1$;
6   **else**
7 | output $\hat{y}_t = 0$;
8   **end**
9   observe real label $y_t \in \{0,1\}$;
10   update $\mathbf{w}_{t+1}$ by equation (3);
11 **end**

At round $t + 1$, the FTRL-Proximal algorithm uses the update formula (3):

$$\mathbf{w}_{t+1} = argmin_\mathbf{w}(\sum_{s=1}^{t} \mathbf{w} \cdot \mathbf{g}_s + \frac{1}{2}\sum_{s=1}^{t}\sigma_s \parallel \mathbf{w} - \mathbf{w}_s \parallel_2^2 + \lambda_1 \parallel \mathbf{w} \parallel_1). \qquad (3)$$

In Eq. (3), $\mathbf{w}_{t+1}$ is the target model parameters to be updated in each round. In the first item of equation (3), $\mathbf{g}_s$ is the gradient of loss function for training instance s. The second item of equation (3) is a smoothing term which aims to speed up convergence and improve accuracy, and σ_s is a non-increasing learning rate defined as $\sum_{s=1}^{t}\sigma_s = \sqrt{t}$. The third item of equation (3) is a convex regularization term, namely L1-norm which is used to prevent over-fitting and induce sparsity.

Subsampling. Not all URIs are considered as training instances since we are interested in hard URIs. We exclude from training URIs with the extensions such as *.rdf/owl. Inversely, URIs with the file extension *.html/htm are included in the training set since they may contain RDFa data.

The true class label y_t is required to update the predictor online. In our scenario, to observe the true class label of a URI we have to download it and check whether it contains RDF data or not. We cannot afford to download all URIs because of the network overhead, and our target is to build a prediction model that avoids downloading unnecessary URIs. There, an appropriate subsampling strategy is needed. We found that the positive URIs are rare (much less than 50%) and relatively more valuable. For each round, if URI u_t is predicted positive namely $\hat{y}_t = 1$, we retrieve the content of u_t and observe the real class label y_t. Then the predictor can be updated by new training instance $(y_t, \mathbf{x_t})$. For those URIs predicted negative, we only select a fraction $\epsilon \in]0,1]$ of them to download and observe their true class label. Here ϵ is a balance between online prediction precision (which requires as many URIs as possible for online training) and downloading overhead (which requires as few non-RDF relevant URIs downloaded as possible). To deal with the bias of this subsampled data, we assign an importance weight $\frac{1}{\epsilon}$ to these examples. In our experiment (Sect. 6.2), we set ϵ as the ratio of the number of positive URIs to the number of negative URIs in the training set.

5   Implementation of Crawler

We now detail the prototype we tested for the Linked Data crawler and explain the Algorithm 2 it implements.

Initialization. As shown in Algorithm 2, the proposed crawler starts from a list of seed URIs and operates an breadth-first crawling since this often leads to a more diverse dataset instead of traversing deep paths within some given sites. The maximum crawl depth d_max is set for crawling. The *Frontier* data structure is initialized by the seed URI list S.

Politeness. At the beginning of each round, a naive crawler obtains a URI from *Frontier* to retrieve. However, it would lead to the problem that the crawler issues too many consecutive HTTP requests to a server and is considered "impolite" by the server. Thus, we group the URIs in *Frontier* into different sets $pld_{0..n}$ based on their Pay Level Domains(PLDs). URIs are polled from PLD sets in a round-robin fashion, which means in a round each set pld_i has one chance to select a URI to retrieve (Line 6). We also set a minimum time delay min_delay for each round. If the minimum crawl time of a round is less than min_delay, the crawler will sleep until the condition of minimum time delay is satisfied (Line 36–Line 39).

Prediction. This is the core of crawling (Line 8–Line 29). Once a URI u_t with feature vector $\mathbf{x_t}$ is polled, the predictor predicts the class label $\hat{y}_t$ of u_t, $\hat{y}_t \in \{0,1\}$. If $\hat{y}_t = 1$, we retrieve the content of u_t and get the real class label y_t, and the predictor can be updated by the new training example $(y_t, \mathbf{x_t})$. If the prediction is correct (u_t is RDF relevant), the RDF graph G_t of u_t is written to local storage and the child URIs in G_t with their feature vector are added to *Frontier* for future rounds (Line 9– Line 17). However, as discussed in Sect. 4.4, naively training on this subsampled data would lead to significantly biased predictions. To deal with this bias (Line 19–Line 28), the crawler downloads a fraction ϵ of URIs that are predicted negative (Line 19–Line 21). For the case of false negative (Line 22–Line 26), the RDF graph is written to local storage and the child URIs with their feature vector are added in *Frontier*. The predictor is updated by the example $(y_t, \mathbf{x_t})$ with importance weight $\frac{1}{\epsilon}$ (Line 27).

Algorithm 2. Crawling on Linked Data

Data: A seed list of URIs S, maximum crawl depth d_max, minimum time
delay min_delay
Result: A collection of RDF triples

1   initialize $Frontier=S$, $pld_{0..n} = \emptyset$;
2   **while** $depth < d\_max$ **do**
3   add URIs in $Frontier$ to $pld_{0..n}$;
4     $startTime$=current_time();
5   **foreach** pld_i **do**
6   get uri u_t from pld_i;
7   **if** $u_t = dref(u_t)$ **then**
8         $\hat{y}_t \in \{0,1\} = predict(\mathbf{x_t}, \mathbf{w})$;
9   **if** $\hat{y}_t = 1$ **then**
10   download the content of u_t;
11   observe class label $y_t \in \{0,1\}$;
12   **if** $y_t = 1$ **then**
13   write RDF graph G_t contained in u_t to the local storage;
14   generate feature vectors for URIs in G_t;
15   add URIs with their feature vectors in Frontier;
16   **end**
17   update the predictor by the new example $(y_t, \mathbf{x_t})$;
18   **else**
19   **if** $random[0,1] < \epsilon$ **then**
20   download the content of u_t;
21   observe class label $y_t \in \{0,1\}$;
22   **if** $y_t = 1$ **then**
23   write RDF graph G_t contained in u_t to the local storage;
24   generate feature vectors for URIs in G_t;
25   add URIs with their feature vectors in Frontier;
26   **end**
27   update the predictor by the new example $(y_t, \mathbf{x_t})$ with important weight $\frac{1}{\epsilon}$;
28   **end**
29   **end**
30   **else**
31   **if** $dref(u_t)$ *is unseen* **then**
32   add uri $dref(u_t)$ in $Frontier$;
33   **end**
34   **end**
35   **end**
36     $timeSpan$=current_time()- $startTime$;
37   **if** $timeSpan < min\_delay$ **then**
38   wait($min\_delay - timeSpan$);
39   **end**
40 **end**

Reducing HTTP Lookup. To generate the feature vector of a URI u_t, the crawler has to send HTTP header requests to get the content type of u_t. There exists a large number of redundant HTTP lookups during crawl. To overcome this issue, we build a bloom filter [2] for each kind of MIME types. Bloom filter is a space-efficient probabilistic data structure which is able to fit a billion of URIs in main memory. Once the content type of a URI is known by HTTP lookup, the URI is added to the corresponding bloom filter. For a newly discovered URI u, we submit u to each bloom filter. If a bloom filter reports positive, it indicates that u has the corresponding content type[3]. If no bloom filter reports positive, we have to get the content type of u by sending HTTP request and then store u in the corresponding bloom filter based on its content type.

6   Evaluation

In this section, we firstly evaluate the predictive ability of different combinations of atomic feature sets introduced in Sect. 4.2 and then compare the performance of the proposed crawler with some baseline methods including offline methods. Lastly, we report on experiments on the processing time to evaluate the efficiency of the proposed method.

6.1   Feature Set Evaluation

In this experiment, we evaluate the predictive ability of different combinations of feature sets introduced in Sect. 4.2 by several offline/batch classifiers. We firstly introduce the dataset, metrics and offline classifiers used in the experiment and then discuss the results of the experiment.

Dataset. The dataset used in the experiment is generated by operating a Breadth-First Search (BFS) crawl. The crawl starts a set of 50 seed URIs which are RDF relevant and randomly selected from 26 hosts. During the crawl, we only keep the hard URIs whose RDF relevance cannot be known straightforwardly. Finally we generate a dataset with 103K URIs. The dataset includes 9,825 different hosts. For each URI, we generate features and the class label. To check RDF relevance for each URI, we use the library *Any23*[4].

Static Classifiers and Metrics. The static classifiers including SVM, KNN and Naive Bayesian are used to examine the performance of different combinations of feature sets. We use accuracy and F-measure as metrics to measure the performance, which are defined as:

$$accuracy = \frac{\#correct\ predictions}{\#predictions}$$

---

[3] Bloom filter may report false positive results (but not false negatives) with a low chance. Thus it is possible that a URI has a wrong content type feature.

[4] https://any23.apache.org/.

$$F - measure = 2 \cdot \frac{precision \cdot recall}{precision + recall}$$

Evaluation of Combinations of Feature Sets. The aim of the experiment is to explore the predictive performance of the combinations of feature sets. As described in Sect. 4.2, the feature sets include F_{+t} derived from the target URI u_t, F_{+r} derived from the referring URI u_r, F_{+p} derived from the direct properties of u_t and F_{+x} derived from the siblings of u_t.

In Table 1 we report the results for the 4-element combination of feature sets ($F_{+t+r+p+x}$), all 3-element combinations and the 2-element combinations (F_{+t+x}, F_{r+p}, F_{+p+x}) which have the best performance in their class.

Table 1. Performance of the combinations of feature sets

Combination of feature sets	KNN		Naive Bayes		SVM	
	F-measure	Accuracy	F-measure	Accuracy	F-measure	Accuracy
$F_{+t+r+p+x}$	0.6951	0.7407	0.7154	0.7462	0.7944	0.7722
F_{+t+p+x}	0.6261	0.6832	0.7094	0.7413	0.7801	0.7643
F_{+t+r+x}	0.6773	0.7121	0.7111	0.7448	0.7829	0.7650
F_{+t+r+p}	0.7592	0.7731	0.7660	0.7701	**0.8216**	**0.7902**
F_{+r+p+x}	0.6015	0.7010	0.6328	0.7075	0.6839	0.7074
F_{+t+x}	0.5582	0.6912	0.6012	0.6172	0.6828	0.6277
F_{r+p}	0.3953	0.5810	0.4874	0.6097	0.6790	0.6424
F_{+p+x}	0.4392	0.5739	0.6086	0.6238	0.6689	0.6269

Generally speaking, from Table 1 we can see the feature sets are helpful to the prediction task. Among all combinations, the 3-element combination F_{+t+r+p} outperforms the other combinations with F-measure 0.8216 and accuracy 0.7902. The 4-element combination $F_{+t+r+p+x}$ as the second best combination scores F-measure 0.7944 and accuracy 0.7722. We found that augmenting sibling features to F_{+t+r+p} is not helpful to improve the performance in the cases of three classifiers. We also found that the performance of F_{+r+p+x} which is derived by excluding feature set F_{+t} from $F_{+t+r+p+x}$ decreases a lot (the worst in all 3-element combinations) compared to the performance of $F_{+t+r+p+x}$. It indicates that the features from target URI u_t are important.

Although the batch classifiers performs well in the experiment, it does not mean they are suited for the task nor that they work well too in an online scenario. We show the performance of crawlers with offline classifiers and the proposed crawler with online classifier in the next section.

6.2   Online Versus Offline

In this experiment, we evaluate the performance of the proposed online prediction method against several baseline methods.

Metrics. The aim of the Linked Data crawler is to maximize the number of RDF-relevant URIs collected while minimizing the number of irrelevant URIs downloaded during the crawl. For our proposed method, the crawler has to download a fraction ϵ of URIs even though they are predicted negative. To better evaluate the performance of our approach, we use a *percentage* measure that equals the ratio of retrieved RDF-relevant URIs to the total number of URIs[5] crawled:

$$percentage = \frac{\#Retrieved\ RDF\ relevant\ URIs}{\#All\ retrieved\ URIs}$$

Methods. We implemented the proposed crawler denoted by **LDCOC** (Linked Data Crawler with Online Classifier). The decision threshold τ in Algorithm 1 is set to 0.5 and the parameter ϵ of **LDCOC** is set to 0.17 according to the ratio of the number of positive URIs to the number of negative URIs in the training set used in Sect. 6.1. As baselines, we also implemented three crawlers with offline classifiers including SVM, KNN and Naive Bayes to select URIs. The classifiers are pre-trained with two training sets (with size 20K and 40K). The BFS crawler is another baseline method to be compared to. As suggested in Sect. 6.1, we use the feature set F_{+t+r+p} for the experiment.

Table 2. Percentage of retrieved RDF relevant URIs by different crawlers

Crawler	Percentage
BFS	0.302
crawler_NB (20K)	0.341
crawler_NB (40K)	0.345
crawler_SVM (20K)	0.402
crawler_SVM (40K)	0.413
crawler_KNN (20K)	0.331
crawler_KNN (40K)	0.324
LDCOC ($\tau = 0.5, \epsilon = 0.17$)	**0.655**

---

[5] We only consider hard URIs.

Results. Table 2 shows the percentage of retrieved RDF relevant URIs by different crawlers after crawling 300K URIs. The results show that the crawlers with offline classifiers perform slightly better than BFS crawler. Considering that the Linked Data Web is a dynamic environment, the crawlers with offline classifiers pre-trained by a small size training set would not improve the performance a lot. This is the reason why we developed the crawler with an online classifier. The results show that our proposed crawler LDCOC outperforms crawlers based on static classifiers.

6.3 Processing Time of Per Selection

The processing time of selecting a URI is important since it affects the throughput of the crawling. The time to select one URIs mainly includes two parts: (1) feature generation; (2) prediction and predictor updating. Table 3 shows the average processing time per selection. LDCOC performs better than the other three crawlers with respect to processing time. Different from LDCOC crawlers with offline classifiers do not have to update during the crawl and only the prediction time is counted. LDCOC is based on FTRL-proximal algorithm which has been proven to work efficiently on the massive online learning problem of predicting ad click-through rates. The online efficiency of LDCOC can be guaranteed.

Table 3. Avg. processing time per selection

Crawler	Avg. processing time
crawler_NB	52.98 ms
crawler_SVM	66.62 ms
crawler_KNN	70.22 ms
LDCOC	**49.78** ms

7   Conclusion

We have presented a solution to learn URI selection criteria in order to improve the crawling of Linked Open Data by predicting their RDF-relevance. The prediction component is able to predict whether a newly discovered URI contains RDF content or not by extracting features from several sources and building a prediction model based on FTRL-proximal online learning algorithm. The experimental results demonstrate that the coverage of the crawl is improved compared to baseline methods. Currently, this work focuses on crawling linked RDF (RDFa) data. Our method can now be generalized to crawl other kinds of Linked Data such as JSON-LD, Microdata, etc. For future work, we are investigating more features such as the subgraphs induced by URIs and additional techniques such as graph embedding to further improve the predictions.

Acknowledgement. This work is supported by the ANSWER project PIA FSN2 N°P159564-2661789/DOS0060094 between Inria and Qwant.

References

1. Berners-Lee, T.: Linked data - design issues (2006). https://www.w3.org/DesignIssues/LinkedData.html
2. Bloom, B.H.: Space/time trade-offs in hash coding with allowable errors. Commun. ACM **13**(7), 422–426 (1970)
3. Burer, S., Monteiro, R.D.C.: A nonlinear programming algorithm for solving semidefinite programs via low-rank factorization. Math. Program. **95**(2), 329–357 (2003)
4. Chakrabarti, S., van den Berg, M., Dom, B.: Focused crawling: a new approach to topic-specific web resource discovery. Comput. Netw. **31**(11–16), 1623–1640 (1999)
5. Diligenti, M., Coetzee, F., Lawrence, S., Giles, C.L., Gori, M.: Focused crawling using context graphs. In: VLDB, pp. 527–534 (2000)
6. Dodds, L.: Slug: A Semantic Web Crawler (2006)
7. Duchi, J.C., Singer, Y.: Efficient learning using forward-backward splitting. In: NIPS, pp. 495–503 (2009)
8. Ermilov, I., Lehmann, J., Martin, M., Auer, S.: LODStats: the data web census dataset. In: Groth, P., et al. (eds.) ISWC 2016. LNCS, vol. 9982, pp. 38–46. Springer, Cham (2016). https://doi.org/10.1007/978-3-319-46547-0_5
9. Färber, M., Bartscherer, F., Menne, C., Rettinger, A.: Linked data quality of dbpedia, freebase, opencyc, wikidata, and YAGO. Seman. Web **9**(1), 77–129 (2018)
10. Heath, T., Bizer, C.: Linked Data: Evolving the Web Into a Global Data Space, vol. 1. Morgan & Claypool Publishers, San Rafael (2011)
11. Hogan, A., Harth, A., Passant, A., Decker, S., Polleres, A.: Weaving the pedantic web. In: LDOW (2010)
12. Hogan, A., Harth, A., Umbrich, J., Kinsella, S., Polleres, A., Decker, S.: Searching and browsing linked data with SWSE: the semantic web search engine. J. Web Sem. **9**(4), 365–401 (2011)
13. Isele, R., Umbrich, J., Bizer, C., Harth, A.: LDspider: an open-source crawling framework for the web of linked data. In: Proceedings of the ISWC 2010 Posters & Demonstrations Track (2010)
14. Levenshtein, V.I.: Binary codes capable of correcting deletions, insertions and reversals. Sov. Phys. Dokl. **6**, 707–710 (1966)
15. McMahan, H.B.: Follow-the-regularized-leader and mirror descent: equivalence theorems and L1 regularization. In: AISTATS, pp. 525–533 (2011)
16. McMahan, H.B., et al.: Ad click prediction: a view from the trenches. In: SIGKDD, pp. 1222–1230 (2013)
17. Meusel, R., Mika, P., Blanco, R.: Focused crawling for structured data. In: CIKM, pp. 1039–1048 (2014)
18. Umbrich, J., Harth, A., Hogan, A., Decker, S.: Four heuristics to guide structured content crawling. In: ICWE, pp. 196–202 (2008)
19. Weinberger, K.Q., Dasgupta, A., Langford, J., Smola, A.J., Attenberg, J.: Feature hashing for large scale multitask learning. In: ICML, pp. 1113–1120 (2009)
20. Xiao, L.: Dual averaging method for regularized stochastic learning and online optimization. In: NIPS, pp. 2116–2124 (2009)

Deontic Reasoning for Legal Ontologies

Cheikh Kacfah Emani and Yannis Haralambous$^{(\boxtimes)}$ (iD)

IMT Atlantique, Lab-STICC, UBL, 29238 Brest, France
{cheikh.kacfah,yannis.haralambous}@imt-atlantique.fr

Abstract. Many standards exist to formalize legal texts and rules. The same is true for legal ontologies. However, there is no proof theory to draw conclusions for these ontologically modeled rules. We address this gap by the proposal of a new modeling of deontic statements, and then we use this modeling to propose reasoning mechanisms to answer deontic questions i.e., questions like "Is it mandatory/permitted/prohibited to...". We also show that using this modeling, it is possible to check the consistency of a deontic rule base. This work stands as a first important step towards a proof theory over a deontic rule base.

1 Introduction

Artificial intelligence for law is a prolific research area. In this area there have been many works on legal texts (e.g., legislation, regulations, contracts, and case law) modeling. This modeling pursues many goals, such as works on rule interchange issues, interoperability of rules' systems which lead to proposal of rules' format [1–4], legal ontologies construction [5,6], design principles [7,8], works on compliance checking problems [9,10] or automatic formalization of rules [11–13], etc. In legal texts which compose corpora for these works, we usually have deontic statements. Some rule representation standards include the modeling of deontic statements [2–4]. But there is no reasoning process using these deontic statements. For example using current standards there is no mechanism that one can use to answer questions like *Is fishing forbidden near the port of Brest?*, or to make inferences like *Since going left is forbidden then I must go straight*, etc. Our goal in this article is to propose mechanisms for answering deontic questions. Our proposal stands as a first attempt for a proof theory for ontologically modeled deontic rules. Our contributions are:

- An ontological modeling of deontic statement suitable for automatic reasoning on deontic rules.
- A first proposal of mechanisms for automatic answering of deontic questions towards a rule base.
- A first proposal of consistency checking process over a deontic rule base.

The rest of the paper starts with a presentation of related work in Sect. 2. Then, in Sect. 3, we introduce our work with a delimitation of the scope of rules we target. Next, in Sect. 4, we detail our modeling of rules. After that, we present

© Springer Nature Switzerland AG 2019
P. Hitzler et al. (Eds.): ESWC 2019, LNCS 11503, pp. 209–224, 2019.
https://doi.org/10.1007/978-3-030-21348-0_14

the mechanisms to answer a deontic question and we discuss consistency checking in Sect. 5 and we illustrate them with detailed examples in Sect. 6. Finally,
we present future work in Sect. 7. A demo is available at https://tinyurl.com/
ydgwznba.

2   Related Work

Rule modeling has been a very active field in the past years and still has a
great interest for researchers. During the last years, many authors have proposed
modeling languages and formalisms to represent rules and/or legal documents.
We present some of their works and we conclude this section with a presentation
of works on a proof theory for defeasible rules for propositional logic.

- Legal Knowledge Interchange Format (LKIF) is a specification that includes
  a legal core ontology and a legal rule language that can be used to deploy
  comprehensive legal knowledge management solutions. LKIF was developed
  in the ESTRELLA project [1,14,15]
- RuleML is a family of languages, whose modular system of schemas for XML
  favors web rule interchange [2,16]. The family's top-level distinction is deliberation rules and reaction rules. Deliberation rules are made of modal and
  derivation rules, which themselves include facts, queries, and Horn rules.
  Reaction rules include Complex Event Processing, Knowledge Representation, Event-Condition-Action rules, as well as Production rules. RuleML rules
  can combine all parts of both derivation and reaction rules. There are many
  engines built for rulebases for subsets of RuleML (OO jDREW[1], Prova[2],
  DR-Device[3], NxBRE[4], PSOATransRun[5], etc.) *but none of them infers on
  deontic rule bases.*
- OWL Judge [17] allows to make deontic inferences on rules modelled in OWL
  DL by using the LKIF modelling. Using a standard OWL reasoner (Pellet in
  their case) authors can classify rule instances as "permitted" or "prohibited".
  This is similar to our goal of deontic QA but we do not work only at instances'
  level and we provide detailed pieces of information (exceptions, related cases,
  etc.) so that a user can really figure out what the legal texts state on its
  question.
- LegalRuleML is a standard (expressed with XML-schema and Relax NG) that
  is able to represent the particularities of the legal normative rules with a rich,
  articulated, and meaningful markup language [3]. LegalRuleML models defeasibility of rules and defeasible logic, deontic operators (e.g., obligations, permissions, prohibitions, rights), temporal management of rules and temporality
  in rules, classification of norms (i.e., constitutive, prescriptive), jurisdiction

---

[1] http://www.jdrew.org/oojdrew/.

[2] https://www.prova.ws/.

[3] http://lpis.csd.auth.gr/systems/dr-device.html.

[4] https://nxbre.soft112.com/.

[5] http://wiki.ruleml.org/index.php/PSOA_RuleML#Implementation.

of norms, isomorphisms between rules and natural language normative provisions, identification of parts of the norms (e.g., bearer, conditions), authorial tracking of rules, etc. Concerning the rules themselves, LegalRuleML models the two main types of rules: (i) *constitutive rules* which define concepts or constitute activities that cannot exist without such rules, and (ii) *prescriptive rules* which regulate actions by making them obligatory, permitted, prohibited, recommended. The general shape of a LegalRuleML rule is body $\implies$ head where, for both constitutive and prescriptive rules, where body is a set of formulas and deontic formulas and head is a formula (more precisely, the head of a constitutive rule is a formula and the one of a prescriptive rule is a set of deontic formulas). In this work, we take advantage of the rich modeling of normative documents within the LegalRuleML ontology and we propose an alternative to the ontological modeling of prescriptive rules. Using this new modeling, we propose mechanisms to answer deontic questions; they stand as a first step for the proposal of a proof theory for ontologically modeled deontic rules.

- To answer deontic questions, we take into account the defeasibility of rules (i.e., rules can be defeated by stronger ones) and the existence of superiority relation between conflicting rules. Antoniou *et al.* [18] present a proof theory for defeasible logic, in the frame for propositional logic. They claim that a conclusion in a defeasible theory D is a tagged literal that can have one of the following forms: $+\Delta q$ if the proposition q is *definitely provable* in D, $+\partial q$ if q is *defeasibly provable* in D, $-\Delta q$ if it is proved that q is *not definitely provable* in D and $-\partial q$ if it is proved that q is *not defeasibly provable* in D. We will see that for a deontic question, we can answer definitely yes/no with or without exceptions or we can answer yes/no for specific cases only, with or without exceptions; there are also some cases where the answer is "unknown," and finally cases for which the reasoner identifies inconsistencies.

3   Scope of the Modeling

As we mentioned in the related work section, our modeling is in line with LegalRuleML ontology (LRO). Our focus is on rule modeling for deontic reasoning. Our concern is the rules themselves and not the ecosystem around rules i.e., temporal data, jurisdiction, authorial tracking of rules, etc., since they are modeled in ontologies like LRO. The questions we intend to answer are:

1. How can we model rules to ease automated legal reasoning on these rules?
2. How can we perform automated reasoning on deontic rules?

In LegalRuleML specifications, the body of rules can have both simple formulas and deontic formulas. Also, the head of rules can be either a simple formula for constitutive rules or a set of deontic formulas for prescriptive rules. Here we consider *prescriptive rules with no deontic formulas in the body part*. A generalization to other types of rules is part of our future work (see Sect. 7).

4 Rule Modeling

We model a rule as a four-dimensional object: We consider that a rule is made of *target(s)*, *condition(s)*, *context(s)* and *requirement(s)*. We provide the definition of these terms and illustrate them using the rule *The captain of any ship, called upon to assist or tow a ship carrying oil or gaseous hydrocarbon residues in French territorial waters, shall immediately inform CROSS.*[6]

- **Target.** The target of a rule is the entity towards which the rule is directed. It is the answer to the question "Who is the rule aimed at?". In our example, the target is *The captain of any ship.*
- **Requirement.** The requirement is what the target should do. In the example, the requirement is *shall immediately inform CROSS.*
- **Context.** To find the context of a rule we answer the question "In which situation should be the target to execute the requirement of the rule?". In our example, the context is that *the captain of the ship being called upon to assist or tow a ship carrying oil or gaseous hydrocarbon residues.*
- **Condition.** Conditions are criteria that must be fulfilled so that the target is able to execute the requirement. In our example, the condition is that *the ship (calling for assistance) facing an emergency is in French territorial waters.*

We use the class `shom:DeonticRule`, the properties `shom:ruleTarget`, `shom:ruleContext`, `shom:ruleRequirement`, `shom:ruleCondition` and `shom:deonticAction` to model a rule. We use these entities to extend LRO as we show in Fig. 1[7].

In addition to the description of rules, LRO is able to describe the superiority relation that can exist between rules. Indeed, in some legal corpora we find conflicting rules and the ability of having a superiority relation avoids inconsistencies. In Sect. 6 we provide detail examples where we can see how LRO models the superiority relation and how this relation impacts inferences. It is crucial to have such priority relation to drive the right conclusion from a rule base.

5 Answering Deontic Questions

In this section, our goal is to draw a conclusion to answer the generic question "Is it `OP` to follow the requirement $\mathcal{R}$ for target $\mathcal{T}$ within the context $\mathcal{C}$ and under the condition $\mathcal{K}$?" where `OP` denotes the correct form of one of the deontic terms *mandatory, permitted, prohibited* or *recommended*. We introduce this section with notation elements and mechanisms to answer a deontic question (Sect. 5.1) and then we detail the concepts introduced to present these mechanisms (Sects. 5.2 and 5.3).

---

[6] Excerpt from Article 10 of arrêté https://tinyurl.com/arrete2002. CROSS is a Regional Operational Centre for Monitoring and Rescue.

[7] The prefixes are the following: `owl`:<http://www.w3.org/2002/07/owl>, `:`<http://example.com/>, `rdf`:<http://www.w3.org/1999/02/22-rdf-syntax-ns>, `rdfs`:<http://www.w3.org/2000/01/rdf-schema>, `shom`:<http://example.com/shom>, `lrmlmm`:<http://docs.oasis-open.org/legalruleml/ns/v1.0/metamodel>,

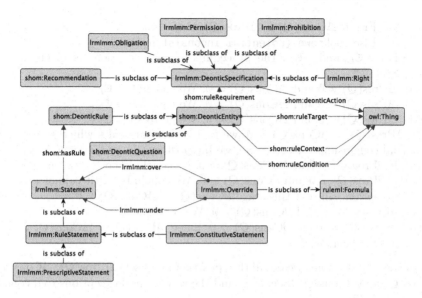

Fig. 1. The Graffoo diagram summarizing the extension of LegalRuleml ontology.

5.1 Drawing a Deontic Conclusion

We use the following notation:

- $\mathcal{Q}_{\mathcal{C},\mathcal{K},\mathcal{T},\text{OP},\mathcal{R}}$ represents the *question*: "Is it OP to follow the requirement $\mathcal{R}$ for target $\mathcal{T}$ within the context $\mathcal{C}$ and under conditions $\mathcal{K}$". We use $\mathcal{Q}$ for the shorten form of $\mathcal{Q}_{\mathcal{C},\mathcal{K},\mathcal{T},\text{OP},\mathcal{R}}$
- $+\mathfrak{C}_{\mathcal{C},\mathcal{K},\mathcal{T},\text{OP},\mathcal{R}}$ denotes the fact that we conclude "yes" to $\mathcal{Q}_{\mathcal{C},\mathcal{K},\mathcal{T},\text{OP},\mathcal{R}}$. $-\mathfrak{C}_{\mathcal{C},\mathcal{K},\mathcal{T},\text{OP},\mathcal{R}}$ stands for the answer "no" to $\mathcal{Q}_{\mathcal{C},\mathcal{K},\mathcal{T},\text{OP},\mathcal{R}}$. Their shortened forms are $+\mathfrak{C}$ and $-\mathfrak{C}$. We write $+\mathfrak{c}$ or $-\mathfrak{c}$ when the "yes" or "no" answer *partially holds*, i.e., only for specific cases (to be determined in practice). $+\mathfrak{C}_E$, $-\mathfrak{C}_E$, $+\mathfrak{c}_E$ and $-\mathfrak{c}_E$ denote the fact that $+\mathfrak{C}$, $-\mathfrak{C}$, $+\mathfrak{c}$ and $-\mathfrak{c}$ are augmented with the list of exceptions.
- $\Delta\text{Pros}(\mathcal{Q})$ is the set of rules that *support a "yes"* to $\mathcal{Q}$, i.e., that support a conclusion $+\mathfrak{C}$. $\Delta\text{Cons}(\mathcal{Q})$ is the set of rules that *support a "no"* to $\mathcal{Q}$, i.e., that elements of $\Delta\text{Cons}(\mathcal{Q})$ support $-\mathfrak{C}$.
- For two sets of rules R_1 and R_2, $R_1 > R_2 \Leftrightarrow \forall r_2 \in R_2, \exists r_1 \in R_1 : r_1 \neq r_2$ *and* $r_1 > r_2$ (i.e. r_1 overrules r_2).
- $\partial\text{Pros}(\mathcal{Q})$ is the set of rules that *partially support a "yes"* to $\mathcal{Q}$, i.e., that support a conclusion $+\mathfrak{c}$. Similarly, $\partial\text{Cons}(\mathcal{Q})$ is the set of rules that *partially support a "no"* to $\mathcal{Q}$, i.e., that support a conclusion $-\mathfrak{c}$.

To answer the question $\mathcal{Q}_{\mathcal{C},\mathcal{K},\mathcal{T},\text{OP},\mathcal{R}}$ (a.k.a. $\mathcal{Q}$), we proceed as follows:

1. We build $\Delta\text{Pros}(\mathcal{Q})$ and $\Delta\text{Cons}(\mathcal{Q})$. Hence, four scenarios can arise:
   (a) $\Delta\text{Pros}(\mathcal{Q}) \neq \emptyset$ and $\Delta\text{Cons}(\mathcal{Q}) \neq \emptyset$.
      - If $\Delta\text{Pros}(\mathcal{Q}) > \Delta\text{Cons}(\mathcal{Q})$ then $+\mathfrak{C}_E$

    – Else if $\Delta\mathrm{Cons}(\mathcal{Q}) > \Delta\mathrm{Pros}(\mathcal{Q})$, then $-\mathfrak{C}_E$

    – Else "unknown (potential inconsistencies)"

    For $+\mathfrak{C}_E$ and $-\mathfrak{C}_E$, the procedure to get exceptions is given in part Sect. 5.3

  (b) $\Delta\mathrm{Pros}(\mathcal{Q}) \neq \emptyset$ and $\Delta\mathrm{Cons}(\mathcal{Q}) = \emptyset$. We conclude $+\mathfrak{C}_E$

  (c) $\Delta\mathrm{Pros}(\mathcal{Q}) = \emptyset$ and $\Delta\mathrm{Cons}(\mathcal{Q}) \neq \emptyset$. We conclude $-\mathfrak{C}_E$

  (d) $\Delta\mathrm{Pros}(\mathcal{Q}) = \emptyset$ and $\Delta\mathrm{Cons}(\mathcal{Q}) = \emptyset$. We go to step (2)

2. If $\Delta\mathrm{Pros}(\mathcal{Q}) = \Delta\mathrm{Cons}(\mathcal{Q}) = \emptyset$, we find if there are rules which support the partial conclusions $+\mathfrak{c}$ or $-\mathfrak{c}$. So, we build $\partial\mathrm{Pros}(\mathcal{Q})$ and $\partial\mathrm{Cons}(\mathcal{Q})$ and:

  (a) If $\partial\mathrm{Pros}(\mathcal{Q}) \neq \emptyset$ and $\partial\mathrm{Cons}(\mathcal{Q}) \neq \emptyset$: we conclude both $+\mathfrak{c}_E$ and $-\mathfrak{c}_E$

  (b) If $\partial\mathrm{Pros}(\mathcal{Q}) \neq \emptyset$ and $\partial\mathrm{Cons}(\mathcal{Q}) = \emptyset$. We conclude $+\mathfrak{c}$ (it cannot have any exception, since at this stage $\partial\mathrm{Cons}(\mathcal{Q}) = \Delta\mathrm{Cons}(\mathcal{Q}) = \emptyset$)

  (c) $\partial\mathrm{Pros}(\mathcal{Q}) = \emptyset$ and $\partial\mathrm{Cons}(\mathcal{Q}) \neq \emptyset$. We conclude $-\mathfrak{c}$

  (d) $\partial\mathrm{Pros}(\mathcal{Q}) = \emptyset$ and $\partial\mathrm{Cons}(\mathcal{Q}) = \emptyset$. Since $\Delta\mathrm{Pros}(\mathcal{Q}) = \Delta\mathrm{Cons}(\mathcal{Q}) = \emptyset$ we answer "unknown"

In the next sections, we detail the construction of sets $\Delta\mathrm{Pros}(\mathcal{Q})$, $\Delta\mathrm{Cons}(\mathcal{Q})$, $\partial\mathrm{Pros}(\mathcal{Q})$ and $\partial\mathrm{Cons}(\mathcal{Q})$ (Sect. 5.2) and the way we find exceptions to a conclusion (Sect. 5.3).

5.2 Building of $\Delta\mathbf{Pros}(\mathcal{Q})$, $\Delta\mathbf{Cons}(\mathcal{Q})$, $\partial\mathbf{Pros}(\mathcal{Q})$ and $\partial\mathbf{Cons}(\mathcal{Q})$

In this section we give the formal expressions of $\Delta\mathrm{Pros}(\mathcal{Q})$, $\Delta\mathrm{Cons}(\mathcal{Q})$, $\partial\mathrm{Pros}(\mathcal{Q})$ and $\partial\mathrm{Cons}(\mathcal{Q})$. These expressions use the following notation:

– A a B represents the assertion "A `rdf:type` B".
– $A \subseteq^+ B$ means one of "A `rdfs:subClassOf` B," "A `owl:sameAs` B," "A a B" is true. In this case we say that A *is included in* B or A *is narrower than* B or B *contains* A or B *is broader than* A. The relation $\subseteq^+$ is *reflexive*
– $A \subseteq^\tau B$ means "$\exists C$ so that $C \subseteq^+ A$ and $C \subseteq^+ B$" is true. A specific case of this relation is when A and B are both superclasses of a third class C. In this case, we say that A *and* B *share a common sub-entity*.
– $A \subseteq^* B$ means one of "$A \subseteq^+ B$" or "$B \subseteq^+ A$" or "$A \subseteq^\tau B$" is true. In this case we say that A *is related to* B.
– $(A_1, \ldots, A_i, \ldots, A_n) \,\mathfrak{R}\, (B_1, \ldots, B_i, \ldots, B_n) \equiv \forall i \in [1, n], A_i \,\mathfrak{R}\, B_i$, where $\mathfrak{R}$ represents the relations $\subseteq^+$ or $\subseteq^*$ or $\subseteq^\tau$.
– We call *parameters of an entity* the quadruple made of its context $\mathcal{C}$, its condition $\mathcal{K}$, its target $\mathcal{T}$ and its requirement $\mathcal{R}$. Here the term "entity" refers to a question $\mathcal{Q}_{\mathcal{C},\mathcal{K},\mathcal{T},\mathrm{OP},\mathcal{R}}$, or to a conclusion $\pm\mathfrak{C}_{\mathcal{C},\mathcal{K},\mathcal{T},\mathrm{OP},\mathcal{R}}$ or to an instance r of `shom:DeonticRule`. We note the parameters of an entity E as $(\mathcal{C}_E, \mathcal{K}_E, \mathcal{T}_E, \mathcal{R}_E)$.
– We define the notion of *conflicting deontic operator*. For each type of deontic operator, Table 1 gives the ones that are in conflict with it.

To understand Table 1 let us take for instance the first deontic operator: $\neg(\mathrm{PER}) = \{\mathrm{PRO}\}$ means that everything that is prohibited (in a given context, conditions, and for a given target), is not permitted (in that same context, under those same conditions and for that same target).

Table 1. Operations on deontic operators. PER: permission, PRO: prohibition, OBL: obligation, REC: recommendation, RIG: right

Deonctic operator (OP)	Conflicting deontic operator ($\neg$(OP))
PER	{PRO}
PRO	{PER, REC, OBL, RIG}
OBL	{PRO}
REC	{PRO}
RIG	{PRO}

Definition 1. *The **sup-rules** of* $(\mathcal{C}, \mathcal{K}, \mathcal{T}, \text{OP}, \mathcal{R})$*, are the* rules *having* a deontic operator equal to OP *and whose parameters* are broader than $(\mathcal{C}, \mathcal{K}, \mathcal{T}, \mathcal{R})$, *i.e.,*

$$sup\text{-}rules(\mathcal{C}, \mathcal{K}, \mathcal{T}, \text{OP}, \mathcal{R}) = \{r, (\mathcal{C}, \mathcal{K}, \mathcal{T}, \mathcal{R}) \subseteq^{+} (\mathcal{C}_r, \mathcal{K}_r, \mathcal{T}_r, \mathcal{R}_r) \wedge \text{OP}_r = \text{OP}\}.$$

Definition 2. *The **neg-sup-rules** of* $(\mathcal{C}, \mathcal{K}, \mathcal{T}, \text{OP}, \mathcal{R})$*, are the* rules *having a deontic operator that* conflicts OP *and whose parameters* are broader than $(\mathcal{C}, \mathcal{K}, \mathcal{T}, \mathcal{R})$, *i.e.,*

$$neg\text{-}sup\text{-}rules(\mathcal{C}, \mathcal{K}, \mathcal{T}, \text{OP}, \mathcal{R}) = \{r, (\mathcal{C}, \mathcal{K}, \mathcal{T}, \mathcal{R}) \subseteq^{+} (\mathcal{C}_r, \mathcal{K}_r, \mathcal{T}_r, \mathcal{R}_r) \wedge \text{OP}_r \in \neg(\text{OP})\}$$

$$= \bigcup_{\text{OP}' \in \neg(\text{OP})} sup\text{-}rules(\mathcal{C}, \mathcal{K}, \mathcal{T}, \text{OP}', \mathcal{R}).$$

The *sup-rules* of $(\mathcal{C}, \mathcal{K}, \mathcal{T}, \text{OP}, \mathcal{R})$ are the rules that (fully) endorse the veracity of the assertion *In context* $\mathcal{C}$, *and under conditions* $\mathcal{K}$, *the target* $\mathcal{T}$ *is* OP *to (do/have/follow)* $\mathcal{R}$. This endorsement relies on the fact that each parameter of a rule of *sup-rules*$(\mathcal{C}, \mathcal{K}, \mathcal{T}, \text{OP}, \mathcal{R})$ is broader than its corresponding parameter in $(\mathcal{C}, \mathcal{K}, \mathcal{T}, \mathcal{R})$ and that the operator of the rule equals OP. On the other hand, *neg-sup-rules* are the rules that counter-attack the aforementioned assertion.

Definition 3. *The **rel-rules** of* $(\mathcal{C}, \mathcal{K}, \mathcal{T}, \text{OP}, \mathcal{R})$ *are the* rules *having* a deontic operator equal to OP *and whose parameters* are related to $(\mathcal{C}, \mathcal{K}, \mathcal{T}, \mathcal{R})$, *i.e.,*

$$rel\text{-}rules(\mathcal{C}, \mathcal{K}, \mathcal{T}, \text{OP}, \mathcal{R}) = \{r, (\mathcal{C}, \mathcal{K}, \mathcal{T}, \mathcal{R}) \subseteq^{*} (\mathcal{C}_r, \mathcal{K}_r, \mathcal{T}_r, \mathcal{R}_r) \wedge \text{OP}_r = \text{OP}\}.$$

Definition 4. *The **neg-rel-rules** of* $(\mathcal{C}, \mathcal{K}, \mathcal{T}, \text{OP}, \mathcal{R})$ *are the* rules *having a deontic operator that* conflicts OP *and whose parameters* are related to $(\mathcal{C}, \mathcal{K}, \mathcal{T}, \mathcal{R})$, *i.e.,*

$$neg\text{-}rel\text{-}rules(\mathcal{C}, \mathcal{K}, \mathcal{T}, \text{OP}, \mathcal{R}) = \{r, (\mathcal{C}, \mathcal{K}, \mathcal{T}, \mathcal{R}) \subseteq^{*} (\mathcal{C}_r, \mathcal{K}_r, \mathcal{T}_r, \mathcal{R}_r) \wedge \text{OP}_r \in \neg(\text{OP})\}$$

$$= \bigcup_{\text{OP}' \in \neg(\text{OP})} rel\text{-}rules(\mathcal{C}, \mathcal{K}, \mathcal{T}, \text{OP}', \mathcal{R}).$$

A rule ρ is an element of *rel-rules*$(\mathcal{C}, \mathcal{K}, \mathcal{T}, \text{OP}, \mathcal{R})$ if each of its parameters $(\mathcal{C}_\rho, \mathcal{K}_\rho, \mathcal{T}_\rho, \mathcal{R}_\rho)$ is related, i.e., is broader or narrower than, or shares a common sub-entity with, the corresponding parameter from $(\mathcal{C}, \mathcal{K}, \mathcal{T}, \mathcal{R})$. So when we put all parameters of ρ together, either: (i) $(\mathcal{C}, \mathcal{K}, \mathcal{T}, \mathcal{R}) \subseteq^+ (\mathcal{C}_\rho, \mathcal{K}_\rho, \mathcal{T}_\rho, \mathcal{R}_\rho)$ or (ii) there is at least a parameter of ρ that is *strictly narrower than*[8] the respective one in $(\mathcal{C}, \mathcal{K}, \mathcal{T}, \mathcal{R})$. Hence, "related" rules in case (i) are also member of *sup-rules*$(\mathcal{C}, \mathcal{K}, \mathcal{T}, \text{OP}, \mathcal{R})$ and those in case (ii) support partially, because of their "strictly narrow" parameters, the assertion behind $(\mathcal{C}, \mathcal{K}, \mathcal{T}, \text{OP}, \mathcal{R})$: we use them to define ∂Pros.

A similar discourse holds for *neg-rel-rules*$(\mathcal{C}, \mathcal{K}, \mathcal{T}, \text{OP}, \mathcal{R})$.

Definition 5. *We say that a rule r **(fully) supports** a "yes" to $\mathcal{Q}$ if* (i) $\text{OP}_r = \text{OP}_\mathcal{Q}$ *and* (ii) $(\mathcal{C}_\mathcal{Q}, \mathcal{K}_\mathcal{Q}, \mathcal{T}_\mathcal{Q}, \mathcal{R}_\mathcal{Q}) \subseteq^+ (\mathcal{C}_r, \mathcal{K}_r, \mathcal{T}_r, \mathcal{R}_r)$. *In other words, if r belongs to* sup-rules$(\mathcal{Q})$. *Hence,*

$$\Delta\text{Pros}(\mathcal{Q}) = \text{sup-rules}(\mathcal{Q}). \tag{1}$$

Definition 6. *We say that a rule r **(fully) supports** a "no" to $\mathcal{Q}$ if* (i) $r \in neg(\mathcal{Q})$ *and* (ii) $(\mathcal{C}_\mathcal{Q}, \mathcal{K}_\mathcal{Q}, \mathcal{T}_\mathcal{Q}, \mathcal{R}_\mathcal{Q}) \subseteq^+ (\mathcal{C}_r, \mathcal{K}_r, \mathcal{T}_r, \mathcal{R}_r)$. *In other words, if r belongs to* neg-sup-rules$(\mathcal{Q})$. *So,*

$$\Delta\text{Cons}(\mathcal{Q}) = \text{neg-sup-rules}(\mathcal{Q}). \tag{2}$$

Definition 7. *We say that a rule r **partially supports** a "yes" to $\mathcal{Q}$ if* (i) $\text{OP}_r = \text{OP}_\mathcal{Q}$, (ii) $(\mathcal{C}_\mathcal{Q}, \mathcal{K}_\mathcal{Q}, \mathcal{T}_\mathcal{Q}, \mathcal{R}_\mathcal{Q}) \subseteq^* (\mathcal{C}_r, \mathcal{K}_r, \mathcal{T}_r, \mathcal{R}_r)$ *and* (iii) $r \notin$ *sup-rule*$(\mathcal{Q})$. *Thus,*

$$\partial\text{Pros}(\mathcal{Q}) = \text{rel-rules}(\mathcal{Q}) \setminus \text{sup-rules}(\mathcal{Q}). \tag{3}$$

Definition 8. *We say that a rule r **partially supports** a "no" to $\mathcal{Q}$ if* (i) $\text{OP}_r \in neg(\mathcal{Q})$, (ii) $(\mathcal{C}_\mathcal{Q}, \mathcal{K}_\mathcal{Q}, \mathcal{T}_\mathcal{Q}, \mathcal{R}_\mathcal{Q}) \subseteq^* (\mathcal{C}_r, \mathcal{K}_r, \mathcal{T}_r, \mathcal{R}_r)$ *and* (iii) $r \notin$ *neg-sup-rule*$(\mathcal{Q})$. *Therefore,*

$$\partial\text{Cons}(\mathcal{Q}) = \text{neg-rel-rules}(\mathcal{Q}) \setminus \text{neg-sup-rules}(\mathcal{Q}). \tag{4}$$

We use the SPARQL query of Listing 1.1 to retrieve elements of *sup-rules*$(\mathcal{Q})$. The WHERE clause of this SPARQL query strictly follows the expression given in Definition 1. In this SPARQL query, Class(OP) represents the class of the deontic operator OP, i.e., a sub-class of lrmlmm:DeonticSpecification as shown in Fig. 1. Definition 6 gives two equivalent expressions of *neg-sup-rules*$(\mathcal{Q})$, where the second reuses *sup-rules*$(\mathcal{Q})$. Therefore we can adapt the SPARQL of Listing 1.1 with the suitable parameters, to build *neg-sup-rules*$(\mathcal{Q})$.

---

[8] I.e., not the same and not broader than (within the meaning of $\subseteq^+$).

Listing 1.1. The SPARQL query to build $sup\text{-}rules(\mathcal{C}_\mathcal{Q}, \mathcal{K}_\mathcal{Q}, \mathcal{T}_\mathcal{Q}, \mathsf{OP}_\mathcal{Q}, \mathcal{R}_\mathcal{Q})$

```
SELECT ?rule WHERE { ?rule a shom:Rule;
 shom:ruleContext ?ctx; shom:ruleCondition ?cdt;
  shom:ruleTarget ?tgt; shom:ruleRequirement ?req.
   {Cǫ rdfs:subClassOf* | a | owl:sameAs ?ctx} .
   {Kǫ rdfs:subClassOf* | a | owl:sameAs ?cdt} .
   {Tǫ rdfs:subClassOf* | a | owl:sameAs ?tgt} .
   {?req a Class(OPǫ); shom:deonticAction ?act .
     {Rǫ  rdfs:subClassOf* | a | owl:sameAs ?act} }
```

We rely on the SPARQL query of Listing 1.2 to build the set $rel\text{-}rules(\mathcal{Q})$. This query follows the expression of $rel\text{-}rules(\mathcal{Q})$ given in Definition 3. Also, following its second expression in Definition 4, we can retrieve elements of $neg\text{-}rel\text{-}rules(\mathcal{Q})$ using the SPARQL query of $rel\text{-}rules(\mathcal{Q})$.

Listing 1.2. The SPARQL query to build $rel\text{-}rules(\mathcal{C}_\mathcal{Q}, \mathcal{K}_\mathcal{Q}, \mathcal{T}_\mathcal{Q}, \mathsf{OP}_\mathcal{Q}, \mathcal{R}_\mathcal{Q})$

```
SELECT ?rule WHERE { ?rule a shom:Rule;
 shom:ruleContext ?ctx; shom:ruleCondition ?cdt;
  shom:ruleTarget ?tgt; shom:ruleRequirement ?req.
   { {Cǫ rdfs:subClassOf* | a | owl:sameAs ?ctx} UNION
     {?ctx rdfs:subClassOf* | a Cǫ} UNION
     {?subCtx rdfs:subClassOf* | a | owl:sameAs Cǫ , ?ctx}} .
   { {Kǫ rdfs:subClassOf* | a | owl:sameAs ?cdt} UNION
     {?cdt rdfs:subClassOf* | a Kǫ} UNION
     {?subCdt rdfs:subClassOf* | a | owl:sameAs Kǫ , ?cdt} } .
   { {Tǫ rdfs:subClassOf* | a | owl:sameAs ?tgt} UNION
     {?tgt rdfs:subClassOf* | a Tǫ} UNION
     {?subTgt rdfs:subClassOf* | a | owl:sameAs Tǫ , ?tgt}} .
   { {?req a Class(OPǫ); shom:deonticAction ?act.
     {Rǫ rdfs:subClassOf* | a | owl:sameAs ?act} UNION
     {?act rdfs:subClassOf* | a Rǫ} UNION
     {?subAct rdfs:subClassOf* | a | owl:sameAs Rǫ , ?act}}} }
```

Having detailed how to obtain $\varDelta\mathrm{Pros}(\mathcal{Q})$, $\varDelta\mathrm{Cons}(\mathcal{Q})$, $\partial\mathrm{Pros}(\mathcal{Q})$ and $\partial\mathrm{Cons}(\mathcal{Q})$, we move to the next section where we present how to obtain exceptions to a conclusion.

5.3   Exceptions to a Conclusion

In some cases there are specific rules that counter-attack the conclusions $+\mathfrak{C}$, $-\mathfrak{C}$, $+\mathfrak{c}$ or $-\mathfrak{c}$. These rules are called "exceptions". In Definition 9 below, $\mathfrak{C}$ represents a conclusion, which can be $+\mathfrak{C}$, $-\mathfrak{C}$, $+\mathfrak{c}$ or $-\mathfrak{c}$.

Definition 9. *An exception to a conclusion $\mathfrak{C}$ is any rule r that (i) is partially in favor of an opposite conclusion $\mathfrak{C}'$ to the one actually made (i.e., $\mathfrak{C}$), and (ii) is not overruled by a rule that fully supports the conclusion $\mathfrak{C}$.*

Since an exception supports an opposite conclusion to the one actually made we must distinguish the case where the current conclusion is $+\mathcal{C}$ or $+\mathfrak{c}$, and the case where it is $-\mathcal{C}$ or $-\mathfrak{c}$. This is necessary because the criteria to be opposed to those two groups of conclusions are not the same:

1. A rule that counter-attacks $+\mathcal{C}$ or $+\mathfrak{c}$ necessarily has a deontic operator that is in conflict with the one of the conclusion. Hence, in this case, a formal transcription of Definition 9 tells us that the set of exceptions equals to:

$$\left\{ r \in \{ \overbrace{\bigcup_{\mathrm{OP}' \in neg(\mathrm{OP}_{\mathfrak{C}})} \partial\mathrm{Pros}(\mathcal{Q}_{\mathcal{C}_{\mathfrak{C}},\mathcal{K}_{\mathfrak{C}},\mathcal{T}_{\mathfrak{C}},\mathrm{OP}',\mathcal{R}_{\mathfrak{C}})\}}^{(i)} \right.$$
$$\left. \wedge \underbrace{\nexists r' \in \varDelta\mathrm{Pros}(\mathcal{Q}_{\mathcal{C}_{\mathfrak{C}},\mathcal{K}_{\mathfrak{C}},\mathcal{T}_{\mathfrak{C}},\mathrm{OP}_{\mathfrak{C}},\mathcal{R}_{\mathfrak{C}}), r' > r}_{(ii)} \right\}. \quad (5)$$

In Eq. 5:
   - Part (i) represents the formal expression of item (i) of Definition 9. There, we mention that a rule that is an exception to a "positive" conclusion (i.e., $+\mathcal{C}$ or $+\mathfrak{c}$) necessarily has a partial support to a "yes" at any question with parameters related to those of the conclusion, *but with a conflicting deontic operator*.
   - Part (ii) represents the fact that the rule must not be overruled by another rule (fully) in favor of the conclusion (hence the use of $\varDelta\mathrm{Pros}$). It corresponds to item (ii) of Definition 9.
2. A rule that counter-attacks $-\mathcal{C}$ or $-\mathfrak{c}$ must have a deontic operator that is the same as the one in the conclusion. Hence, similar to Eq. 5, a formal representation of Definition 9 tells us that, in this case, the set of exceptions equals to:

$$\left\{ r \in \overbrace{\{\partial\mathrm{Pros}(\mathcal{C}_{\mathfrak{C}},\mathcal{K}_{\mathfrak{C}},\mathcal{T}_{\mathfrak{C}},\mathrm{OP}_{\mathfrak{C}},\mathcal{R}_{\mathfrak{C}})\}}^{(i)} \underbrace{\wedge \nexists r' \in \varDelta\mathrm{Cons}(\mathcal{Q}_{\mathcal{C}_{\mathfrak{C}},\mathcal{K}_{\mathfrak{C}},\mathcal{T}_{\mathfrak{C}},\mathrm{OP}_{\mathfrak{C}},\mathcal{R}_{\mathfrak{C}}), r' > r}_{(ii)} \right\}.$$
$$(6)$$

It is important to notice that we must find exceptions to rules *recursively*. In other words, for rules that partially attack a conclusion, we must investigate whether these rules have exceptions in their turn, and so on.

In Fig. 2, we summarize the steps of our deontic reasoning process as it is implemented to answer a deontic question. In this figure:

   - All steps before the dashed line map the process described in Sect. 5.1 where we identify the conclusion to the question.
   - The processes labeled ❶ and ❷ correspond to Eqs. 5 and 6 respectively.

- In the process ❸, we recursively find exceptions, and then in ❹ we build the exceptions dependency graph $\mathcal{G}$. $\mathcal{G}$ is oriented. Vertices of $\mathcal{G}$ are the rules used to answer the question (i.e., ΔPros and ΔCons if non empty or ∂Pros and ∂Cons otherwise), including the exceptions identified during step ❸. Furthermore, (r, ρ) is an edge of $\mathcal{G}$ if ρ is an exception of r. Hence, *a cycle in $\mathcal{G}$ is equivalent to an inconsistency*.
- Step ❺ is a user friendly output of the answer.

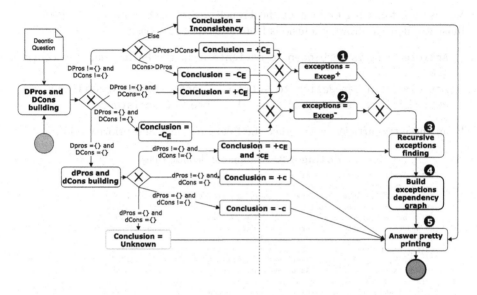

Fig. 2. Pipeline to answer a deontic question. (Color figure online)

Checking the consistency of a deontic rule base By analyzing the structure of the exceptions dependency graph we can now detect inconsistencies. But *this holds only for the subset of rules, including their exceptions, that are used to answer a given deontic question*. Therefore, the challenge is to ask a question $\mathcal{Q}_\Omega$ that embraces all rules of the base, like: *Whatever the context, the condition and the target, is it permitted to do something?*. Formally, all the parameters of $\mathcal{Q}_\Omega$ are equal to owl:Thing, so it is immediate to see that each rule of the base is related (in the meaning of the operator $\subseteq^*$). Consequently, according to Fig. 2, one of the following will always be true:

- We reach the red node so the inconsistency of the base is immediate.
- We reach one of the orange nodes, so there is no exception to a "yes" or "no" to $\mathcal{Q}_\Omega$ and then no inconsistency is possible.
- We reach the yellow node, which means the rule base is empty, since parameters of any rule are necessarily related to those of $\mathcal{Q}_\Omega$, in which case we can conclude that the base is not inconsistent.

– We reach a conclusion which requires to find exceptions (i.e., $+\mathcal{C}_E$, $-\mathcal{C}_E$, $+c_E$ and $-c_E$), and knowing that the parameters of any rule are related to those of $\mathcal{Q}_\Omega$, the recursive search of exceptions will involve every rule of the base; having a cycle in this graph is equivalent to the presence of inconsistent requirements in the base.

6 Detailed Examples

We use the following excerpt of the French *arrêté préfectoral n° 96/2015*[9] to illustrate how we draw conclusions from a deontic rule base:

– **Article 1:** It is forbidden to navigate near the Paluel nuclear center (PNC).
– **Article 2:** In derogation to Article 1, are allowed to sail near the PNC: Military vessels; any vessel in need of assistance.

From these two articles, we extract the following rules and priority relations:

Listing 1.3. Example of deontic rules

```
1    :ps1 a lrmlmm:PrescriptiveStatement; lrmlmm:hasRule :R1.
2    :ps2 a lrmlmm:PrescriptiveStatement; lrmlmm:hasRule :R2, :R3.
3    :R1 a shom:Rule; shom:ruleTarget :Vessel; shom:ruleCondition owl:Thing ;
4       shom:ruleRequirement :ProhibitionNavPaluel ; shom:ruleContext owl:Thing ;
5       rdfs:comment "It is forbidden to navigate near the PNC" . #For any vessel
6    :R2 a shom:Rule; shom:ruleTarget :MilitaryVessel; shom:ruleCondition owl:Thing ;
7       shom:ruleRequirement :PermissionNavPaluel ; shom:ruleContext owl:Thing ;
8       rdfs:comment "Military vessels are authorised to navigate near the PNC" .
9    :R3 a shom:Rule; shom:ruleTarget :Vessel ; shom:ruleCondition owl:Thing ;
10      shom:ruleRequirement :PermissionNavPaluel ; shom:ruleContext :Assistance ;
11      rdfs:comment "Any vessel for assistance purpose is authorised to navigate..." .
12   :ProhibitionNavPaluel a lrmlmm:Prohibition; shom:deonticAction :NavPaluel.
13   :PermissionNavPaluel a lrmlmm:Permission; shom:deonticAction :NavPaluel.
14   :NavPaluel rdfs:subClassOf owl:Thing .
15   :Vessel rdfs:subClassOf owl:Thing .
16   :MilitaryVessel rdfs:subClassOf :Vessel .
17   :Assistance rdfs:subClassOf owl:Thing .
18   :PS2_OVER_PS1 a lrmlmm:Override; lrmlmm:over :ps2; lrmlmm:under :ps1.
```

Hence, for the three rules R1, R2 and R3 above, we have:

– $\mathcal{C}_{R1}$ = owl:Thing   – $\mathcal{C}_{R2}$ = owl:Thing   – $\mathcal{C}_{R3}$ = :Assistance
– $\mathcal{K}_{R1}$ = owl:Thing   – $\mathcal{K}_{R2}$ = owl:Thing   – $\mathcal{K}_{R3}$ = owl:Thing
– $\mathcal{T}_{R1}$ = :Vessel   – $\mathcal{T}_{R2}$ = :MilitaryVessel   – $\mathcal{T}_{R3}$ = :Vessel
– OP_{R1} = PRO   – OP_{R2} = PER   – OP_{R3} = PER
– $\mathcal{R}_{R1}$ = :NavPaluel   – $\mathcal{R}_{R2}$ = :NavPaluel   – $\mathcal{R}_{R3}$ = :NavPaluel

---

[9] The full (French) version of the text is available at https://tinyurl.com/y77x32y3.

The following relations between R1, R2 and R3 hold

$$(\mathcal{C}_{R2}, \mathcal{K}_{R2}, \mathcal{T}_{R2}, \mathcal{R}_{R2}) \subseteq^+ (\mathcal{C}_{R1}, \mathcal{K}_{R1}, \mathcal{T}_{R1}, \mathcal{R}_{R1}) \quad (7) \qquad (\mathcal{C}_{R3}, \mathcal{K}_{R3}, \mathcal{T}_{R3}, \mathcal{R}_{R3}) \subseteq^+ (\mathcal{C}_{R1}, \mathcal{K}_{R1}, \mathcal{T}_{R1}, \mathcal{R}_{R1}) \quad (8)$$

$$(\mathcal{C}_{R2}, \mathcal{K}_{R2}, \mathcal{T}_{R2}, \mathcal{R}_{R2}) \subseteq^* (\mathcal{C}_{R1}, \mathcal{K}_{R1}, \mathcal{T}_{R1}, \mathcal{R}_{R1}) \quad (9) \qquad (\mathcal{C}_{R3}, \mathcal{K}_{R3}, \mathcal{T}_{R3}, \mathcal{R}_{R3}) \subseteq^* (\mathcal{C}_{R1}, \mathcal{K}_{R1}, \mathcal{T}_{R1}, \mathcal{R}_{R1}) \quad (10)$$

Also, we recall that $\subseteq^+$ and $\subseteq^*$ are *reflexive* relations.

6.1 $\mathcal{Q}^a$ Is it Allowed to Navigate Near the PNC for Military Vessels?

We have: $\mathcal{C}_{\mathcal{Q}^a} =$ owl:Thing, $\mathcal{K}_{\mathcal{Q}^a} =$ owl:Thing, $\mathcal{T}_{\mathcal{Q}^a} =$:MilitaryVessel, $OP_{\mathcal{Q}^a} =$ PER, and $\mathcal{R}_{\mathcal{Q}^a} =$:NavPaluel. We note that $\mathcal{Q}^a$ and R2 have the same parameters, and the same deontic parameters, so Eqs. 7 and 9 above hold with $\mathcal{Q}^a$ playing the role of R2. A rule ρ belongs to $\Delta\mathrm{Pros}(\mathcal{Q}^a)$ if and only if $(\mathcal{C}_{\mathcal{Q}^a}, \mathcal{K}_{\mathcal{Q}^a}, \mathcal{T}_{\mathcal{Q}^a}, \mathcal{R}_{\mathcal{Q}^a}) \subseteq^+ (\mathcal{C}_\rho, \mathcal{K}_\rho, \mathcal{T}_\rho, \mathcal{R}_\rho)$ and $OP_{\mathcal{Q}^a} = OP_\rho$. So we have $\Delta\mathrm{Pros}(\mathcal{Q}^a) = \{R2\}$. Also, $\gamma \in \Delta\mathrm{Cons}(\mathcal{Q}^a)$ if and only if $(\mathcal{C}_{\mathcal{Q}^a}, \mathcal{K}_{\mathcal{Q}^a}, \mathcal{T}_{\mathcal{Q}^a}, \mathcal{R}_{\mathcal{Q}^a}) \subseteq^+ (\mathcal{C}_\gamma, \mathcal{K}_\gamma, \mathcal{T}_\gamma, \mathcal{R}_\gamma)$ and $OP_\gamma \in neg(OP_{\mathcal{Q}^a})$. So $\Delta\mathrm{Cons}(\mathcal{Q}^a) = \{R1\}$ (thanks to Eq. 7). Now we must see whether one of $\Delta\mathrm{Pros}(\mathcal{Q}^a)$ or $\Delta\mathrm{Cons}(\mathcal{Q}^a)$ overrules the other. Line 18 of the Listing 1.3 implies $\Delta\mathrm{Pros}(\mathcal{Q}^a) > \Delta\mathrm{Cons}(\mathcal{Q}^a)$. So we conclude that we have $+\mathfrak{C}_E$, i.e., *Yes, it is allowed to do so*. Next, we need to identify potential exceptions. Based on Eq. 5, we say that η is an exception to the above conclusion if $(\mathcal{C}_\eta, \mathcal{K}_\eta, \mathcal{T}_\eta, \mathcal{R}_\eta) \subseteq^* (\mathcal{C}_{\mathcal{Q}^a}, \mathcal{K}_{\mathcal{Q}^a}, \mathcal{T}_{\mathcal{Q}^a}, \mathcal{R}_{\mathcal{Q}^a})$, $(\mathcal{C}_{\mathcal{Q}^a}, \mathcal{K}_{\mathcal{Q}^a}, \mathcal{T}_{\mathcal{Q}^a}, \mathcal{R}_{\mathcal{Q}^a}) \not\subseteq^+ (\mathcal{C}_\eta, \mathcal{K}_\eta, \mathcal{T}_\eta, \mathcal{R}_\eta)$, and $OP_\eta \in neg(OP_{\mathcal{Q}^a})$. No rule in the base meets this criteria, so the answer to $\mathcal{Q}^a$ remains unchanged (no exception added).

6.2 $\mathcal{Q}^b$ Is Any Vessel Allowed to Navigate Near the PNC?

We have: $\mathcal{C}_{\mathcal{Q}^b} =$ owl:Thing, $\mathcal{K}_{\mathcal{Q}^b} =$ owl:Thing, $\mathcal{T}_{\mathcal{Q}^b} =$:Vessel, $OP_{\mathcal{Q}^b} =$ PER, $\mathcal{R}_{\mathcal{Q}^b} =$:NavPaluel. We note that $\mathcal{Q}^b$ and R1 have the same parameters *but have conflicting deontic operators*. $\Delta\mathrm{Pros}(\mathcal{Q}^b) = \emptyset$ and $\Delta\mathrm{Cons}(\mathcal{Q}^b) = \{R1\}$. Hence, we conclude $-\mathfrak{C}_E$ (see item 1c), i.e., *No, it is not allowed*. Let us now find exceptions. In this case, we refer to Eq. 6, so η is an exception to the above conclusion if $(\mathcal{C}_\eta, \mathcal{K}_\eta, \mathcal{T}_\eta, \mathcal{R}_\eta) \subseteq^* (\mathcal{C}_{\mathcal{Q}^b}, \mathcal{K}_{\mathcal{Q}^b}, \mathcal{T}_{\mathcal{Q}^b}, \mathcal{R}_{\mathcal{Q}^b})$, $(\mathcal{C}_{\mathcal{Q}^b}, \mathcal{K}_{\mathcal{Q}^b}, \mathcal{T}_{\mathcal{Q}^b}, \mathcal{R}_{\mathcal{Q}^b}) \not\subseteq^+ (\mathcal{C}_\eta, \mathcal{K}_\eta, \mathcal{T}_\eta, \mathcal{R}_\eta)$, and $OP_\eta = OP_{\mathcal{Q}^b}$. Thanks to Eqs. 7–10 we see that R2 and R3 meet these criteria. To be definitely considered as exceptions, they must not be overruled by any element of $\Delta\mathrm{Cons}(\mathcal{Q}^b)$, i.e., R1. Actually this is the case, so they are exceptions to $-\mathfrak{C}_E$. A (recursive) search of exceptions to them remains unsuccessful. So the final answer to $\mathcal{Q}^b$ is *No, it is not allowed to do so, but there are exceptions: – Military vessels are authorized to do so (Rule R2) – Any vessel in need of assistance does so (Rule R3).*

6.3 $\mathcal{Q}^c$ Is it Prohibited to Any Vessel to Navigate Near the PNC?

We use this question to illustrate partial conclusion. We assume for this case that the rule base contains only R2 and R3. We have: $\mathcal{C}_{\mathcal{Q}^c}$ = owl:Thing, $\mathcal{K}_{\mathcal{Q}^c}$ = owl:Thing, $\mathcal{T}_{\mathcal{Q}^c}$ = :Vessel, OP$_{\mathcal{Q}^c}$ = PRO, $\mathcal{R}_{\mathcal{Q}^c}$ = :NavPaluel. With R1 discarded from the base, we have $\Delta\mathrm{Pros}(\mathcal{Q}^c) = \Delta\mathrm{Cons}(\mathcal{Q}^c) = \emptyset$. Hence, we must find partial support and counter-attack, i.e., $\partial\mathrm{Pros}(\mathcal{Q}^c)$ and $\partial\mathrm{Cons}(\mathcal{Q}^c)$, to the assertion denoted by $\mathcal{Q}^c$. We have $\partial\mathrm{Pros}(\mathcal{Q}^c) = \emptyset$ and $\partial\mathrm{Cons}(\mathcal{Q}^c) = \{\mathrm{R2}, \mathrm{R3}\}$. Hence we conclude that we have $-\mathfrak{c}$, i.e., *No, it is not prohibited to do so, but rules in the base cover only specific parts of this case: – Military vessels are authorized to do so (Rule R2) – Any vessel in need of assistance is authorized to do so (Rule R3).*

7 Future Work

As further developments of this work, we intend to perform the following tasks.

– **Broadening the scope of the rules.** As mentioned in Sect. 3, the scope of rules considered in this work is the one of prescriptive with not deontic formula in their body. We need to cover all types of prescriptive rules, i.e., also the case of constitutive rules. Hence, we must propose a modeling that take into account this extension. An interesting starting point for the modeling of constitutive rules would be the decompositions *The concept X counts as Y* or *The concept X counts as Y in context C* proposed by Searle [19].
– **Towards a proof theory.** We mentioned in the previous point the extension of the scope of rules. This implies updating the mechanisms of answering to deontic questions. Also we intend to propose a proof theory, i.e., how deontic and non deontic assertions are derived in a base made of constitutive and prescriptive rules.
– **Automatic question answering.** Currently we manually identify question parts (i.e., context, condition, target, deontic operator and requirement). It would be very useful to propose an approach to automatically decompose questions into their formal parts and then answer them automatically.

8 Conclusion

In this paper, we address the problem of deontic reasoning for legal ontologies. We tackle this issue in terms of deontic questions answering. First, we propose a new deontic rule modeling paradigm for prescriptive rules and then we use this modeling to present mechanisms for deontic question answering. The possible answers we provide to deontic questions, are as diverse as the ones given by a human, i.e., we are able to answer yes/no for the whole question or only for specific cases, with or without exceptions. We also provide answer unknown when there is no evidence in the rule base allowing to answer the question or unknown (potential inconsistencies) if they are unresolved conflicting rules. This work is a first step towards a proof theory for a deontic rule base.

Acknowledgements. This work is funded by the *Service hydrographique et océanographique de la marine* (Shom) as part of the REIZHMOR project.

References

1. Gordon, T.F.: The legal knowledge interchange format (LKIF). Technical report, ESTRELLA Project http://www.estrellaproject.org/doc/Estrella-D4.1.pdf
2. Boley, H., Tabet, S., Wagner, G.: Design rationale of RuleML: a markup language for semantic web rules. In: 1st International Conference on SW Working, pp. 381–401 (2001)
3. Palmirani, M., Governatori, G., Athan, T., Boley, H., Paschke, A., Wyner, A.: LegalRuleML core specification version 1.0. OASIS Committee Specification Draft 01 / Public Review Draft 01, October 2016
4. OMG: Semantics of Business Vocabulary and Business Rules (SBVR), v1.0. Technical report, Object Management Group (2008). https://www.omg.org/spec/SBVR/1.0/
5. Winkels, R., Boer, A., Hoekstra, R.: CLIME: lessons learned in legal information serving. In: Proceedings of the 15th ECAI, pp. 230–234. IOS Press (2002)
6. Valente, A., Breuker, J.: A functional ontology of law. Artif. Intell. law **7**, 241–361 (1994)
7. Gangemi, A.: Design patterns for legal ontology constructions. LOAIT **2007**, 65–85 (2007)
8. Lame, G.: Using NLP techniques to identify legal ontology components: concepts and relations. In: Benjamins, V.R., Casanovas, P., Breuker, J., Gangemi, A. (eds.) Law and the Semantic Web. LNCS (LNAI), vol. 3369, pp. 169–184. Springer, Heidelberg (2005). https://doi.org/10.1007/978-3-540-32253-5_11
9. Yurchyshyna, A., Zarli, A.: An ontology-based approach for formalisation and semantic organisation of conformance requirements in construction. Autom. Constr. **18**(8), 1084–1098 (2009)
10. Pauwels, P., et al.: A semantic rule checking environment for building performance checking. Autom. Constr. **20**(5), 506–518 (2011)
11. Kacfah Emani, C.: Automatic detection and semantic formalisation of business rules. In: Presutti, V., d'Amato, C., Gandon, F., d'Aquin, M., Staab, S., Tordai, A. (eds.) ESWC 2014. LNCS, vol. 8465, pp. 834–844. Springer, Cham (2014). https://doi.org/10.1007/978-3-319-07443-6_57
12. Hassanpour, S., O'Connor, M.J., Das, A.K.: A framework for the automatic extraction of rules from online text. In: Bassiliades, N., Governatori, G., Paschke, A. (eds.) RuleML 2011. LNCS, vol. 6826, pp. 266–280. Springer, Heidelberg (2011). https://doi.org/10.1007/978-3-642-22546-8_21
13. Kang, S., et al.: Extraction of manufacturing rules from unstructured text using a semantic framework. In: ASME 2015 American Society of Mechanical Engineers (2015)
14. Hoekstra, R., Breuker, J., Di Bello, M., Boer, A., et al.: The LKIF core ontology of basic legal concepts. LOAIT **321**, 43–63 (2007)
15. Gordon, T.F.: Constructing legal arguments with rules in the legal knowledge interchange format (LKIF). In: Casanovas, P., Sartor, G., Casellas, N., Rubino, R. (eds.) Computable Models of the Law. LNCS (LNAI), vol. 4884, pp. 162–184. Springer, Heidelberg (2008). https://doi.org/10.1007/978-3-540-85569-9_11

16. Boley, H., Paschke, A., Shafiq, O.: RuleML 1.0: the overarching specification of web rules. In: Dean, M., Hall, J., Rotolo, A., Tabet, S. (eds.) RuleML 2010. LNCS, vol. 6403, pp. 162–178. Springer, Heidelberg (2010). https://doi.org/10.1007/978-3-642-16289-3_15
17. Van De Ven, S., Hoekstra, R., Breuker, J., Wortel, L., El Ali, A.: Judging amy: automated legal assessment using OWL 2. In: OWLED, vol. 432 (2008)
18. Antoniou, G., Billington, D., Governatori, G., Maher, M.J.: Representation results for defeasible logic. ACM TOCL **2**(2), 255–287 (2001)
19. Searle, J.R.: The Construction of Social Reality. Simon and Schuster, New York (1995)

Incorporating Joint Embeddings into Goal-Oriented Dialogues with Multi-task Learning

Firas Kassawat[1]([✉]), Debanjan Chaudhuri[1,2], and Jens Lehmann[1,2]

[1] Smart Data Analytics Group (SDA), University of Bonn, Bonn, Germany
s6fikass@uni-bonn.de, {chaudhur,jens.lehmann}@cs.uni-bonn.de
[2] Enterprise Information Systems Department, Fraunhofer IAIS, Bonn, Germany
{debanjan.chaudhuri,jens.lehmann}@iais.fraunhofer.de

Abstract. Attention-based encoder-decoder neural network models have recently shown promising results in goal-oriented dialogue systems. However, these models struggle to reason over and incorporate state-full knowledge while preserving their end-to-end text generation functionality. Since such models can greatly benefit from user intent and knowledge graph integration, in this paper we propose an RNN-based end-to-end encoder-decoder architecture which is trained with joint embeddings of the knowledge graph and the corpus as input. The model provides an additional integration of user intent along with text generation, trained with multi-task learning paradigm along with an additional regularization technique to penalize generating the wrong entity as output. The model further incorporates a Knowledge Graph entity lookup during inference to guarantee the generated output is state-full based on the local knowledge graph provided. We finally evaluated the model using the BLEU score, empirical evaluation depicts that our proposed architecture can aid in the betterment of task-oriented dialogue system's performance.

Keywords: Dialogue systems · Knowledge graphs · Joint embeddings · Neural networks

1 Introduction

There is a considerable rise in the need for effective task-oriented dialogue agents that can help the user to achieve specific goals and everyday tasks such as weather forecast assistance, schedule arrangement, and location navigation. Neural network based dialogue models proved to be the most promising architectures so far which can effectively use dialogue corpora in order to build such agents. However, these models struggle to reason over and incorporate state-full knowledge while preserving their end-to-end text generation functionality. They often require additional user supervision or additional data annotation to incorporate some dialogue-state information along with additional knowledge.

© Springer Nature Switzerland AG 2019
P. Hitzler et al. (Eds.): ESWC 2019, LNCS 11503, pp. 225–239, 2019.
https://doi.org/10.1007/978-3-030-21348-0_15

To help the dialogue agents overcome these problems, they have often been built with several pipelined modules such as language understanding, dialog management, question answering components, and natural language generation [16]. However, modeling the dependencies between such modules is complex and may not result in very natural conversations.

The problem becomes much more complicated in multi-domain scenarios, because the text generation in such scenarios hugely depends on the domain the user is talking about, where each domain will have its own vocabulary that differs from other domains. Hence, understanding user intent during the text generation process can be beneficial. Table 1 shows sample user utterances along with its intent. While generating new tokens, the model can benefit from this because separate intents will follow different vocabulary distributions.

Table 1. User query and respective intents

User utterance	Intent
Book a seat for me in any good Chinese restaurant nearby	Restaurant booking
Book a flight ticket for me from Berlin to Paris for tomorrow	Flight booking
Please show me the direction to the main train station	Navigation
Please cancel my appointment with the dentist for tomorrow	Scheduling

In order to tackle the aforementioned problems, we propose a novel neural network architecture trained using a multi-task learning paradigm, which along with generating tokens from the vocabulary also tries to predict the intent of the user utterances. By doing so, the model is able to relate the generated words to the predicted intent and uses this to exclude words unrelated to the current conversation from the next word candidate prediction. Our model utilizes joint text and knowledge graph embeddings as inputs to the model inspired by the works of [18].

Additionally, after projecting the entities and text into the same vector space, we propose an additional training criterion to use as a novel regularization technique called entity loss, which further penalizes the model if the predicted entity is different from the original. The loss is the mean of the vector distance between the predicted and correct entities.

Furthermore, to guarantee a state-full knowledge incorporation we included a knowledge graph (KG) key-value look-up to implement a way of knowledge tracking during the utterances of a dialogue.

A KG in the context of this paper is a directed, multi-relational graph that represents entities as nodes, and their relations as edges, and can be used as an abstraction of the real world. KGs consists of triples of the form $(h, r, t) \in KG$, where h and t denote the head and tail entities, respectively, and r denotes their relation.

Our main contributions in this paper are as follows:

- Utilizing joint text and knowledge graph embeddings into an end-to-end model for improving the performance of task-oriented dialogue systems.
- A multi-task learning of dialogue generation and learning user intent during decoding.
- A novel entity loss based regularization technique which penalizes the model if the predicted entity is further from the true entity in vector space.

2   Related Work

Recently, several works have tried incorporating external knowledge, both structured and unstructured, into dialogue systems. [10,13,27] proposed architectures for incorporating unstructured knowledge into retrieval based dialogue systems targeting the Ubuntu dialogue corpus [14]. More recently, [3] used domain description based unstructured knowledge using an additional recurrent neural network (GRU) architecture added to the word embeddings for domain keywords to further improve the performance of such models. There are also many recent works that incorporated end-to-end models with structured knowledge sources, such as knowledge graphs [5,24,25]. [6] used a key-value retrieval network to augment the vocabulary distribution of the keys of the KG with the attentions of their associated values. We were inspired by this model to add the key-value lookup in the inference stage of the model. Although the work they represented was inspiring, it turns out that using attention over a knowledge graph is inefficient for long sequences. Moreover, they didn't utilize user intent during modeling. In [16], the authors used a memory-to-sequence model that uses multi-hop attention over memories to help in learning correlations between memories which results in faster trained model with a stable performance.

As for using joint learning to support end-to-end dialogue agent the work introduced by [11] showed state-of-the-art results where they used an attention based RNN for the joint learning of intent detection and slot filling. They proposed two methods, an encoder-decoder model with aligned inputs and an attention-Based model. Our intent predictor during decoding is influenced by their architecture. [22] implemented a multi-domain statistical dialogue system toolkit in which they created a topic tracker, which is used to load only the domain-specific instances of each dialogue model. In other words, all the elements in the pipeline (semantic decoder, belief tracker and the language generator) would consist of only domain-specific instances.

Graph embeddings have been used by [4] to predict missing relationships between entities, later on, [26] used knowledge graph embeddings with text descriptions to propose a semantic space projection model that learns from both symbolic triples and their textual description. [1] proposed a model for jointly learning word embeddings using a corpus and a knowledge graph that was used for representing the meaning of words in vector space. They also proposed two methods to dynamically expand a KG. Taking inspirations from these joint embeddings, we incorporate them into our model as inputs for better capturing grounded knowledge.

3 Model Description

In this section, we present our model architecture. Firstly, we discuss the attention based RNN encoder-decoder architecture, and then we explain the intent predictor, joint embedding vector space and additional entity loss based regularization.

3.1 Attention Based Seq-to-Seq Model

Our model is quintessentially based on an RNN-based encoder-decoder architecture taking inspirations from the works proposed by [15,21,23]. Given the input utterances from the user in a dialogue scenario D, the system has to produce an output utterance o_t for each time-step t, i.e. there is a sequence $\{(i_1, o_1), (i_2, o_2), ..., (i_n, o_n)\}$ where n denotes the total number of utterances in a dialogue. We reprocess these utterances and present them as:
$\{(i_1, o_1), ([i_1; o_1; i_2], o_2), ..., ([i_1; o_1; ...; o_{n-1}; i_n], o_n)\}$, where we present an input as the sequence of all previous utterances concatenated with the current input. This is done in order to maintain the context in the dialogue.

Let $x_1, ...x_m$ denote the words in each input utterance (where m is the length of the utterance). We firstly map these words to their embedding vector representations using Φ^{x_t} which can be either a randomly initialized or a pretrained embedding. Then these distributed representations are fed into the RNN-encoder (LSTM [8] in this case) as follows:

$$h_t = LSTM(\Phi^{x_t}, h_{t-1}) \tag{1}$$

$h_t = (h_0, ...h_m)$ represents the hidden states of the encoder.

These encoder inputs are fed into a decoder which is again a recurrent module. It generates a token for every time-stamp t given by the probability

$$p(y_t | y_{t-1}, ..., y_1, x_t) = g(y_{t-1}, s_t, c_t) \tag{2}$$

Where, $g(.)$ is a softmax function, s_t is the hidden state of the decoder at time-step t given by

$$s_t = LSTM(s_{t-1}, y_{t-1}, c_t) \tag{3}$$

Additionally, we use an attention mechanism over the encoder hidden-states as proposed by [2,7]. The attention mechanism is calculated as

$$\alpha_{ij} = \frac{exp(e_{ij})}{\sum_{k=1}^{m} exp(e_{ik})} \tag{4}$$

$$e_{ij} = tanh(W_c[s_{i-1}, h_j]) \tag{5}$$

The final weighted context from the encoder is given by

$$c_i = \sum_m \alpha_{ij} h_j \tag{6}$$

Where, α_{ij} represent the attention weights learned by the model, c_i the context vector, W_c a weight parameter that has to be learned by the model.

3.2   Predicting Intent

The intent predictor module is used to predict the intent from the user utterance. It is computed using the encoder LSTM's hidden representation h_t as computed at every timestamp t. The intent output prediction is given by:

$$i_{out} = W_o(tanh(W_i[h_t; c_t])))$$ (7)

Where, i_{out} is the intent score $\in \mathbf{R}^{i_c}$ for the tth time-step, W_i and W_o are the trainable weight parameters for the intent predictor and i_c is the total number of intent classes. The latter can be the different domains the dialogue system wants to converse upon, for example restaurant booking, flight booking etc.

3.3   Training Joint Text and Knowledge Graph Embeddings

Learning distributed embeddings for words has been widely studied for neural network based natural language understanding. [17] was the first to propose a model to learn such distributed representations. In order to leverage additional information from knowledge graphs in goal-oriented dialogues, we need to first project the embeddings for both texts appearing in the dialogue corpus and knowledge graphs in the same vector space. For learning such word embeddings, we adopted the work done by [18], which proposes a model for training the embeddings from both a corpus and a knowledge graph jointly. The proposed method is described in three steps: firstly training the Global Vectors (GloVe) following [20], secondly incorporating the knowledge graph, and jointly learning the former two using the proposed model with a linear combination of both their objective functions.

Glove Vectors (GloVe). Firstly, we train the embedding vectors by creating a global word co-occurrence matrix X from both the input and target sentences, where each word in these sentences is represented by a row in X containing the co-occurrence of context words in a given contextual window. Finally, the GloVe embedding learning method minimizes the weighted least squares loss presented as:

$$J_C = \frac{1}{2} \sum_{i \in V} \sum_{j \in V} f(X_{ij})(w_i^\top w_j + bi + bj - log(X_{ij}))^2$$ (8)

Where X_{ij} denote the total occurrences of target word w_i and the context word w_j and the weighting function f assigns a lower weight for extremely frequent co-occurrences to prevent their over-emphasis.

Incorporating the Knowledge Graph. The GloVe embeddings themselves do not take the semantic relation between corresponding words into account. Therefore, in order to leverage a knowledge graph while creating the word embeddings, we define an objective J_s that only considers the three-way co-occurrences between a target word w_i and one of its context word w_j along with the semantic relation R that exists between them in the KG. The KG-based objective is defined as follows:

$$J_S = \frac{1}{2} \sum_{i \in V} \sum_{j \in V} R(w_i, w_j)(w_i - w_j)^2 \tag{9}$$

Where $R(w_i, w_j)$ indicates the strength of the relation R between w_i and w_j, which assigns a lower weight for extremely frequent co-occurrences to prevent over-emphasising such co-occurrences and if there is no semantic relation between w_i and w_j then $R(w_i, w_j)$ will be set to zero.

For the final step, to train both the corpus and the KG objectives jointly. We define the combined objective function J as their linearly weighted combination

$$J = J_C + \lambda J_S \tag{10}$$

λ is the regularization coefficient that regulates the influence of the knowledge graph on those learned from the corpus.

3.4 Regularizing Using Additional Entity Loss

After projecting the knowledge graphs and the text in the same vector space, we compute an additional loss which is equal to the vector distances between the predicted entity and correct entity. The intuition behind using this loss is to penalize the model for predicting the wrong entity during decoding, in vector space. We use cosine distance to measure the entity loss as given by:

$$\text{Entity}_l = 1 - \frac{\phi^{e_{corr}} . \phi^{e_{pred}}}{\|\phi^{e_{corr}}\| \|\phi^{e_{pred}}\|} \tag{11}$$

$\phi^{e_{corr}}$ and $\phi^{e_{pred}}$ being the vector embeddings for the correct and predicted entities, respectively.

3.5 Final Objective Function

The final objective function for training the model is the summation of the cross-entropy (CE) loss from the decoder (Vocab_l), the cross-entropy loss from the intent predictor (Intent_l) and the entity loss (Entity_l).

The total loss is given by:

$$L_{tot} = \text{Vocab}_l + \text{Intent}_l + \text{Entity}_l \tag{12}$$

The model is trained with back-propagation using Adam [9] optimizer.

3.6   Key-Value Entity Look-Up

As mentioned before the knowledge graph (KG) can change from one dataset to another or even as in our case from one dialogue to another. This will result in the generation of KG entities that do not belong to the current dialogue. Since we are incorporating global knowledge information using the joint embedding, this additional step would ensure local KG integration aiding in the betterment of the models. To accomplish this, we added an additional lookup step during decoding. While generating a new token during decoding at time-step t, we firstly check if the predicted token is an entity. If it's an entity, we first do a lookup into the local dialogue KG to check its presence. If the entity is not present, then we pick the one with the entity with the highest softmax probability that is present in the local KG using greedy search. The technique is illustrated in Fig. 2. As seen in the figure, for the query *what is the weather like in New York, today?*, during decoding at $t = 2$, the model outputs a softmax distribution with highest probability[1] (0.08) for the token *raining* after predicting *it is*. We keep a copy of all the global KG entities and first check whether the predicted token is an entity in the global KG or not. Since *raining* is indeed an entity, we further do a look up into the local dialogue KG if it exists. For this scenario it doesn't, hence we do a greedy search for the next best-predicted tokens which are present in

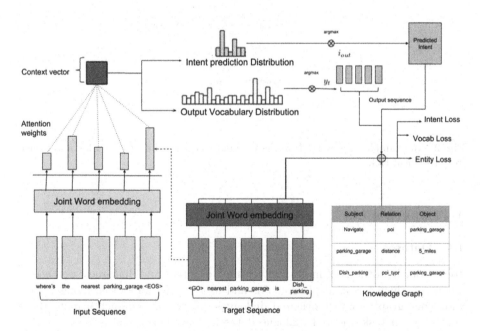

Fig. 1. Sequence-to-Sequence based module with multi-task learning of user intent regularized with additional entity loss

---

[1] This is a fictitious example for explaining the algorithm, the scores are not what is being predicted from the real case scenarios.

the local KG. In this specific case, *sunny* is the next most probable entity that exists in the local KG, We pick this entity for the time-step and feed it into the next. The final output will be *it is sunny today in New York* (Fig. 2).

One such example in a real-case setting is shown in Table 6. The distance for the gas station was generated as *2_miles*, whereas we can observe that in the local KG, the correct distance entity is *5_miles*. Hence by performing the additional entity lookup, we replace *2_miles* with the correct entity during decoding. Empirical evidence suggests that this strategy can gain in performance as depicted in Table 5.

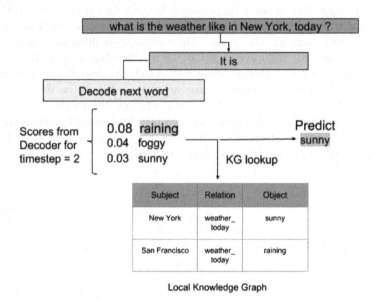

Fig. 2. An example of how KVL works to replace predicted entities with correct ones from the local KG.

4   Experiments

4.1   Dataset

To test our hypothesis of multi-task learning of intent and dialogues, we needed a dataset which has multiple domains and user intents annotated along with a knowledge graph for task-oriented dialogues. [6] introduced such a multi-turn, multi-domain task-oriented dialogue dataset. They performed a Wizard-of-Oz based data collection scheme inspired by [24]. They used the Amazon Mechanical Turk (AMT) platform for data collection. The statics of the datasets are mentioned in Table 2. The dataset is a conversation workflow in an in-car setting where the driver (user) is asking the assistant for scheduling appointments, weather forecasts, and navigation. Both roles are played by AMT turkers (workers). In driver mode, the turker asked a question while the assistant turker responds to the query using the provided knowledge graph. The Knowledge graph statistics are provided in Table 3.

Table 2. Statistics of the in-car multi-turn, multi-domain, goal-oriented dialogue dataset.

Training Dialogues	2,425
Validation Dialogues	302
Test Dialogues	304
Avg. # Utterances Per Dialogue	5.25
Avg. # Tokens Per Utterance	9
Vocabulary Size	1,601

4.2   Pre-processing and Model Hyperparameters

We processed the dataset by creating inputs out of the driver's utterances and the accompanied KG and the model outputs would be the current task intent and the assistants' output. We also processed the entire knowledge graph to identify the entities and convert them into canonicalized forms. We also split entities with multiple objects. For instance, a weather forecast that looks like "frost, low of 20F, high of 30F" can be split into (weather-condition="frost", low-temperature="low of 20F", high-temperature="high of 30F").

For training the Joint Embedding we used a contextual window for the co-occurrence matrix equal to 15 which is $\frac{1}{4}^{th}$ of the mean of input size. We trained the model with $\alpha = 0.01$ and $\lambda = 10000$ and the embedding vectors with dimensions of 300 for 500 epochs with learning rate equals to $1e{-}4$ and a weight-decay of $1e{-}6$. The stats regarding the knowledge graph is provided in Table 3.

As for the sequence-to-sequence model, we trained each of them on a GPU with 3072 CUDA cores and a VRAM of 12 GB. The model is trained for 1000 epoch with a batch size of 128 and a hidden layer size equal to the embedding dimension of 300. We set the learning rate to be $1e{-}4$ for the encoder and $5e{-}4$ for the decoder, we also added a gradient clipping of 50.0 for countering the 'exploding gradient' problem; by doing so we prevent the gradients from growing exponentially and either overflow (undefined values), or overshoot steep cliffs in the cost function. We didn't do any exhaustive hyper-parameter optimization, the values reported here are the ones used for all models. Our codes and preprocessing scripts are available in[2].

---

[2] https://github.com/s6fikass/Chatbot_KVNN.

Table 3. Statistics of the trained Joint Embedding.

Number of entities	291
Number of triples	2,512
Number of triples found in context	1,242
Max triple co-occurrence	750
Unique words co-occurrences	1,30,803

4.3 Results

In this section, we report the results from our model on the mentioned dataset. We evaluate our system using BLEU scores as suggested by [19]. BLEU as defined by [19] analyzes the co-occurrences of n-grams in the reference and the proposed responses. It computes the n-gram precision for the whole dataset, which is then multiplied by a brevity penalty to penalize short translations We are reporting the geometric means of BLEU-1, BLEU-2, BLEU-3, and BLEU-4. In addition to that we evaluated the both our model and the Mem2Seq model proposed by [16] using an Embedding-based metrics such as Greedy Matching, Embedding Average and Vector Extrema as proposed by [12][3]. We are using an Attention based seq-to-seq model as a baseline along with the other state-of-the-art models on this corpora [6] (KV Retrieval Net) and [16] (Mem2Seq H3). We are reporting our best model which is attention based Sequence-to-sequence model (S2S+Intent+JE+EL) with Joint Embeddings (JE) as inputs and trained as a multi-task objective of learning response utterance along with user Intent further, regularized using Entity Loss (EL). This model is further improved with an additional step called Key-Value Entity Look-up (KVL) which is done during inference. The method was explained in Sect. 3.6.

Table 4. Results compared to baseline and State-of-the-art models.

Model	BLEU	Emb. Avg.	Vec. Ext.	Greedy
Attention based Seq-to-Seq	8.4	–	–	–
KV Retrieval Net (no enc attention)	10.8	–	–	–
KV Retrieval Net	13.2	–	–	–
Mem2Seq H3	12.6	0.668	0.742	0.528
S2S+Intent+JE+EL	**14.12**	–	–	–
S2S+Intent+JE+EL+KVL	**18.31**	**0.955**	**0.974**	**0.625**

As seen from the results, our proposed architecture has absolute improvements of 0.92 over KV Retrieval Net and 1.52 over Mem2Seq (H3) on BLEU.

---

[3] We report these metrics for our best model and only for Mem2Seq because their implementation is open-source.

Although, the results are not directly comparable with the latter because we use canonicalized entity forms like [6]. We are reporting BLEU scores because for task-oriented dialogues there's not much variance between the generated answers, unlike open-domain dialogues [12]. We are using the official version (i.e. moses multi-bleu.perl script)[4] for doing all the evaluations. Also, as seen in Table 4, our proposed model performs significantly better than Mem2Seq on embedding-based metrics too.

Table 5. Ablation study.

Model used	BLEU score	BLEU with KVL
S2S+glove	10.42	14.63
S2S+JE	13.35	15.29
S2S+Intent+JE	12.65	17.89
S2S+Intent+glove	13.25	17.27
S2S+Intent+JE+EL	**14.12**	**18.31**

5 Ablation Study

As mentioned in the results, our best model is based on Joint embeddings as inputs, followed by jointly learning user intent and text generation; with entity loss based on further regularization techniques. To analyze which specific part is influencing the performance, we did an ablation study dissecting the different components of the model one by one. The performances are reported in Table 5.

The first model is a sequence-to-sequence (S2S) model with Glove [20] embeddings as input. These embeddings are trained on the training set. It can be seen that with the domain-vocabulary knowledge the model already performs better than vanilla attention sequence-to-sequence model. The next (S2S+JE) is the same model with Joint text and knowledge graph embeddings (also trained on the dialogue corpus and provided knowledge graph). This model has an absolute improvement of 2.93 in BLEU scores. Interestingly, adding the intent along with Joint Embeddings drops the performance by 0.7 but the encounters a little improvement with glove vectors. The model sees a further boost in performances (relative improvement of 3.7) over vanilla models with GloVe. All the models encounter better performances with the proposed key-value lookup (KVL) technique during inferencing.

---

[4] multi-bleu: https://raw.githubusercontent.com/moses-smt/mosesdecoder/master/scripts/generic/multi-bleu.perl.

6 Qualitative Analysis

To qualitatively understand the performance improvements of the model with a different setting as in Table 5 we analyze the outputs from all of them for a given user query. For the user (driver) query *Where is the nearest gas station?*, predicted responses are given in Table 6. The knowledge graph snapshot for this particular dialogue scenario is in Table 7.

Table 6. Example of generated responses on the Navigation domain explaining the improvement process through the model stages.

Driver	Where is the nearest gas station?
S2S	chevron is 5_pm away at <UNK> it is going to snow
S2S+GloVe	chevron is 3_pm at room_215
S2S+JE	chevron is 5_miles at <UNK> high_of_30_f
S2S+Intent+JE	chevron is at 783_arcadia_pl
S2S+Intent+JE+EL	chevron is 2_miles away at 783_arcadia_pl
S2S+Intent+JE+EL+KVL	chevron is 5_miles away at 783_arcadia_pl
Target	chevron is 5_miles away at 783_arcadia_pl

As observed, the sequence-to-sequence (S2S) model is not able to produce knowledge grounded responses since it has no information about the background knowledge graph. Using Joint Embeddings (S2S+JE), although produces more knowledge grounded responses (since chevron is an entity of type gas_station and is at a distance of 5_miles), it outputs entities like high_of_30_f which is not related to navigation intent but the weather. Incorporating intent into the model (S2S+Intent+JE) ensures that it is generating words conditionally dependent on the intent also. Further grammatical improvements in the model response are seen with entity loss (S2S+Intent+JE+EL) which is further made more knowledge grounded with the proposed KVL method as seen in the last response (S2S+Intent+JE+EL+KVL). To further understand the quality of the produced responses, we did a human evaluation of a subset of the predicted responses from the test set. We asked the annotators to judge the response whether it is human-like or not on a scale of 1–5. The average score given by the annotators is 4.51.

Table 7. KG triples for the dialogue in Table 6, for navigation.

Subject	Relation	Object
chevron	distance	5_miles
chevron	traffic_info	moderate_traffic
chevron	poi_type	gas_station
chevron	address	783_arcadia_pl

7   Error Analysis

To further understand the model performance, we did a further analysis of the responses from the test set which gave very low BLEU scores during evaluation. The target and the predicted response are in Table 8.

Table 8. Error analysis.

Predicted sentence	Target sentence
You're welcome	Have a good day
What city do you want the forecast for	What city can i give you this weather for
Setting gps for quickest route now	I picked the route for you drive carefully
It is cloudy with a low of 80f in fresno	There are no clouds in fresno right now

As observed, the model produces fewer word overlaps for generic responses like *have a good day*. But, the responses are grammatically and semantically correct, which cannot be measured using BLEU scores. The other types of errors are factual errors where the model fails because it requires reasoning as in case of the 4th example. The user is asking if the weather is cloudy in this case, in Fresno (Table 9).

Table 9. KG triples and context for the error analysis in Table 8 for weather.

Subject	Relation	Object
fresno	monday	clear_skies
fresno	monday	low_40f

8   Conclusions and Future Work

In this paper, we proposed techniques to improve goal-oriented dialogue systems using joint text and knowledge graph embeddings with learning user query intent as a multi-task learning paradigm. We also further suggested regularization techniques based on entity loss to improve upon the model. Empirical evaluations suggest that our suggested method can gain over existing state-of-the-art systems on BLEU scores for multi-domain, task-oriented dialogue systems. We are not reporting entity-f1 scores since we are treating canonicalized entity forms as vocabulary tokens and BLEU scores will already reflect the presence of the correct entity in the responses.

For future endeavors, we would like to include KVL in the training using memory network modules instead of using it as a separate module during inference. We also observed that our model can benefit from better out-of-vocabulary (OOV) words handling which we would like to keep as a future work. Also, as observed in predicted responses for generic dialogues in first 3 rows in Table 8, it would make sense to incorporate evaluations which also captures semantic similarities between predicted responses, we would like to work on this in future.

Acknowledgements. This work was partly supported by the European Union's Horizon 2020 funded projects WDAqua (grant no. 642795) and Cleopatra (grant no. 812997) as well as the BmBF funded project Simple-ML.

References

1. Alsuhaibani, M., Bollegala, D., Maehara, T., Kawarabayashi, K.: Jointly learning word embeddings using a corpus and a knowledge base. PLoS ONE **13**(3), e0193094 (2018)
2. Bahdanau, D., Cho, K., Bengio, Y.: Neural machine translation by jointly learning to align and translate. arXiv preprint arXiv:1409.0473 (2014)
3. Chaudhuri, D., Kristiadi, A., Lehmann, J., Fischer, A.: Improving response selection in multi-turn dialogue systems by incorporating domain knowledge. In: Proceedings of the 22nd Conference on Computational Natural Language Learning, pp. 497–507 (2018)
4. Dettmers, T., Minervini, P., Stenetorp, P., Riedel, S.: Convolutional 2D knowledge graph embeddings. arXiv arXiv:1707.01476v6 (2018)
5. Dhingra, B., et al.: Towards end-to-end reinforcement learning of dialogue agents for information access. arXiv preprint arXiv:1609.00777 (2016)
6. Eric, M., Manning, C.D.: Key-value retrieval networks for task-oriented dialogue. In: Proceedings of the 18th Annual SIGdial Meeting on Discourse and Dialogue, pp. 37–49. Association for Computational Linguistics, Saarbrucken, August 2017. http://www.aclweb.org/anthology/W17-366
7. Graves, A.: Generating sequences with recurrent neural networks (2015)
8. Hochreiter, S., Schmidhuber, J.: Long short-term memory. Neural Comput. **9**(8), 1735–1780 (1997)
9. Kingma, D.P., Ba, J.: Adam: a method for stochastic optimization. arXiv preprint arXiv:1412.6980 (2014)
10. Kosovan, S., Lehmann, J., Fischer, A.: Dialogue response generation using neural networks with attention and background knowledge. In: Proceedings of the Computer Science Conference for University of Bonn Students (CSCUBS 2017) (2017). http://jens-lehmann.org/files/2017/cscubs_dialogues.pdf
11. Liu, B., Lane, I.: Attention-based recurrent neural network models for joint intent detection and slot filling. arXiv preprint arXiv:1609.01454 (2016)
12. Liu, C.W., Lowe, R., Serban, I.V., Noseworthy, M., Charlin, L., Pineau, J.: How not to evaluate your dialogue system: an empirical study of unsupervised evaluation metrics for dialogue response generation. arXiv preprint arXiv:1603.08023 (2016)
13. Lowe, R., Pow, N., Serban, I., Charlin, L., Pineau, J.: Incorporating unstructured textual knowledge sources into neural dialogue systems. In: Neural Information Processing Systems Workshop on Machine Learning for Spoken Language Understanding (2015)
14. Lowe, R., Pow, N., Serban, I., Pineau, J.: The Ubuntu dialogue corpus: a large dataset for research in unstructured multi-turn dialogue systems. CoRR abs/1506.08909 (2015). http://arxiv.org/abs/1506.08909

15. Luong, M.T., Sutskever, I., Le, Q.V., Vinyals, O., Zaremba, W.: Addressing the rare word problem in neural machine translation. In: Proceeding of Association for Computational Linguistics (2015)
16. Madotto, A., Wu, C.S., Fung, P.: Mem2Seq: effectively incorporating knowledge bases into end-to-end task-oriented dialog systems. In: Proceedings of the 56th Annual Meeting of the Association for Computational Linguistics (Volume 1: Long Papers), pp. 1468–1478. Association for Computational Linguistics (2018). http://aclweb.org/anthology/P18-1136
17. Mikolov, T., Sutskever, I., Chen, K., Corrado, G.S., Dean, J.: Distributed representations of words and phrases and their compositionality. In: Advances in Neural Information Processing Systems, pp. 3111–3119 (2013)
18. Mohammed, A., Danushka, B., Takanori, M., Kenichi, K.: Jointly learning word embeddings using a corpus and a knowledge base. PLoS ONE **13**(3), e0193094 (2018)
19. Papineni, K., Roukos, S., Ward, T., Zhu, W.J.: BLEU: a method for automatic evaluation of machine translation. In: Proceedings of the 40th Annual Meeting on Association for Computational Linguistics, pp. 311–318. Association for Computational Linguistics (2002)
20. Pennington, J., Socher, R., Manning, C.: GloVe: global vectors for word representation. In: Proceedings of the 2014 Conference on Empirical Methods in Natural Language Processing (EMNLP), pp. 1532–1543 (2014)
21. Shang, L., Lu, Z., Li, H.: Neural responding machine for short-text conversation. In: Proceedings of 53rd Annual Meeting of the Association for Computational Linguistics (2015)
22. Ultes, S., et al.: PyDial: a multi-domain statistical dialogue system toolkit. In: Proceedings of ACL 2017, System Demonstrations, pp. 73–78. Association for Computational Linguistics (2017). http://aclweb.org/anthology/P17-4013
23. Vinyals, O., Le, Q.: A neural conversational model. In: International Conference on Machine Learning: Deep Learning Workshop (2015)
24. Wen, T.H., et al.: A network-based end-to-end trainable task-oriented dialogue system. arXiv preprint arXiv:1604.04562 (2016)
25. Williams, J.D., Zweig, G.: End-to-end LSTM-based dialog control optimized with supervised and reinforcement learning (2016)
26. Xiao, H., Huang, M., Meng, L., Xiaoyan, Z.: SSP: semantic space projection for knowledge graph embedding with text descriptions. In: Proceedings of the Thirty-First AAAI Conference on Artificial Intelligence. State Key Lab. of Intelligent Technology and Systems (2017)
27. Xu, Z., Liu, B., Wang, B., Sun, C., Wang, X.: Incorporating loose-structured knowledge into LSTM with recall gate for conversation modeling. arXiv preprint arXiv:1605.05110 (2016)

Link Prediction Using Multi Part Embeddings

Sameh K. Mohamed[1,2,3]([✉]) and Vít Nováček[1,2,3]

[1] Data Science Institute, Galway, Ireland
[2] Insight Centre for Data Analytics, Galway, Ireland
{sameh.kamal,vit.novacek}@insight-centre.org
[3] National University of Ireland Galway, Galway, Ireland

Abstract. Knowledge graph embeddings models are widely used to provide scalable and efficient link prediction for knowledge graphs. They use different techniques to model embeddings interactions, where their tensor factorisation based versions are known to provide state-of-the-art results. In recent works, developments on factorisation based knowledge graph embedding models were mostly limited to enhancing the ComplEx and the DistMult models, as they can efficiently provide predictions within linear time and space complexity. In this work, we aim to extend the works of the ComplEx and the DistMult models by proposing a new factorisation model, TriModel, which uses three part embeddings to model a combination of symmetric and asymmetric interactions between embeddings. We perform an empirical evaluation for the TriModel model compared to other tensor factorisation models on different training configurations (loss functions and regularisation terms), and we show that the TriModel model provides the state-of-the-art results in all configurations. In our experiments, we use standard benchmarking datasets (WN18, WN18RR, FB15k, FB15k-237, YAGO10) along with a new NELL based benchmarking dataset (NELL239) that we have developed.

Keywords: Knowledge graph embedding · Link prediction

1 Introduction

In recent years, knowledge graph embedding (KGE) models have witnessed rapid developments that have allowed them to excel in the task of link prediction for knowledge graphs [22]. They learn embeddings using different techniques like tensor factorisation, latent distance similarity and convolutional filters in order to rank facts in the form of (subject, predicate, object) triples according to their factuality. In this context, their tensor factorisation based versions like the DistMult [23] and the ComplEx [21] models are known to provide state-of-the-art results within linear time and space complexity [22]. The scalable and efficient predictions achieved by these models have encouraged researchers to investigate advancing the DistMult and the ComplEx models by utilising different training objectives and regularisation terms [8,9].

© Springer Nature Switzerland AG 2019
P. Hitzler et al. (Eds.): ESWC 2019, LNCS 11503, pp. 240–254, 2019.
https://doi.org/10.1007/978-3-030-21348-0_16

In this work, our objective is to propose a new factorisation based knowledge graph embedding model that extends the works of the DistMult and the ComplEx models while preserving their linear time and space complexity. We achieve that by modifying two of their main components: the embedding representation, and the embedding interaction function.

While both the DistMult and the ComplEx models use the bilinear product of the subject, the predicate and the object embeddings as an embedding interaction function to encode knowledge facts, they represent their embeddings using different systems. The DistMult model uses real values to represent its embedding vectors, which leads to learning a symmetric representation of all predicates due to the symmetric nature of the product operator on real numbers. On the other hand, the ComplEx model represents embeddings using complex numbers, where each the embeddings of an entity or a relation is represented using two vectors (real and imaginary parts). The ComplEx model also represents entities in the object mode as the complex conjugate of their subject form [21]. This enables the ComplEx model to encode both symmetric and asymmetric predicates.

Since the embeddings of the ComplEx models are represented using two part embeddings (real and imaginary parts), their bilinear product (ComplEx's embedding interaction function) consists of different interaction components unlike the DisMult model with only one bilinear product component. Each of these components is a bilinear product of a combination of real and imaginary vectors of the subject, the predicate and the object embeddings, which gives the ComplEx model its ability to model asymmetric predicates.

In this work, we investigate both the embedding representation and the embedding interaction components of the ComplEx model, where we show that the ComplEx embedding interaction components are sufficient but not necessary to model asymmetric predicates. We also show that our proposed model, TriModel, can efficiently encode both symmetric and asymmetric predicates using simple embedding interaction components that rely on embeddings of three parts. To assess our model compared to the ComplEx model, we carry experiments on both models using different training objectives and regularisation terms, where our results show that our new model, TriModel, provide equivalent or better results than the ComplEx model on all configurations. We also propose a new NELL [12] based benchmarking dataset that contains a small number of training, validation and testing facts that can be used to facilitate fast development of new knowledge graph embedding models.

2   Background and Related Works

Knowledge graph embedding models learn low rank vector representation *i.e.* embeddings for graph entities and relations. In the link prediction task, they learn embeddings in order to rank knowledge graph facts according to their factuality. The process of learning these embeddings consists of different phases.

First, they initialise embeddings using random noise. These embeddings are then used to score a set of true and false facts, where a score of a fact is generated by computing the interaction between the fact's subject, predicate and object embeddings using a model dependent scoring function. Finally, embeddings are updated by a training loss that usually represents a min-max loss, where the objective is to maximise true facts scores and minimise false facts scores.

In this section we discuss scoring functions and training loss functions in state-of-the-art knowledge graph embedding models. We define our notation as follows: for any given knowledge graph, E is the set of all entities, R is the set of all relations *i.e.* predicates, N_e and N_r are the numbers of entities and relations respectively, T is the set of all known true facts, e and w are matrices of sizes $N_e \times K$ and $N_r \times K$ respectively that represent entities and relations embeddings of rank K, ϕ_{spo} is the score of the triple (s, p, o), and $\mathcal{L}$ is the model's training loss.

2.1   Scoring Functions

Knowledge graph embedding models generate scores for facts using model dependent scoring functions that compute interactions between facts' components embeddings. These functions use different approaches to compute embeddings interactions like distance between embeddings [2], embedding factorisation [21] or embeddings convolutional filters [5].

In the following, we present these approaches and specify some examples of knowledge graph embedding models that use them.

• *Distance-based embeddings interactions*: The Translating Embedding model (TransE) [2] is one of the early models that use distance between embeddings to generate triple scores. It interprets triple's embeddings interactions as a linear translation of the subject to the object such that $e_s + w_p = e_o$, and generates a score for a triple as follows:

$$\phi_{spo}^{\text{TransE}} = \|e_s + w_p - e_o\|_{l1/l2}, \qquad (1)$$

where true facts have zero score and false facts have higher scores. This approach provides scalable and efficient embeddings learning as it has linear time and space complexity. However, it fails to provide efficient representation for interactions in one-to-many, many-to-many and many-to-one predicates as its design assumes one object per each subject-predicate combination.

• *Factorisation-based embedding interactions*: Interactions based on embedding factorisation provide better representation for predicates with high cardinality. They have been adopted in models like DistMult [23] and ComplEx [21]. The DistMult model uses the bilinear product of embeddings of the subject, the predicate, and the object as their interaction, and its scoring function is defined as follows:

$$\phi_{spo}^{\text{DistMult}} = \sum_{k=1}^{K} e_{s_k} w_{p_k} e_{o_k} \qquad (2)$$

where e_{s_k} is the k-th component of subject entity s embedding vector e_s. Dist-Mult achieved a significant improvement in accuracy in the task of link prediction over models like TransE. However, the symmetry of embedding scoring functions affects its predictive power on asymmetric predicates as it cannot capture the direction of the predicate. On the other hand, the ComplEx model uses embedding in a complex form to model data with asymmetry. It models embeddings interactions using the product of complex embeddings, and its scores are defined as follows:

$$\phi_{spo}^{\text{ComplEx}} = \text{Re}(\sum_{k=1}^{K} e_{s_k} w_{p_k} \overline{e}_{o_k})$$

$$= \sum_{k=1}^{K} e_{s_k}^r w_{p_k}^r e_{o_k}^r + e_{s_k}^i w_{p_k}^r e_{o_k}^i \tag{3}$$

$$+ e_{s_k}^r w_{p_k}^i e_{o_k}^i - e_{s_k}^i w_{p_k}^i e_{o_k}^r$$

where $Re(x)$ represents the real part of complex number x and all embeddings are in complex form such that $e, w \in \mathbb{C}$, e^r and e^i are respectively the real and imaginary parts of e, and $\overline{e}_o$ is the complex conjugate of the object embeddings e_o such that $\overline{e}_o = e_o^r - ie_o^i$ and this introduces asymmetry to the scoring function. Using this notation, ComplEx can handle data with asymmetric predicates, and to keep scores in the real spaces it only uses the real part of embeddings product outcome. ComplEx preserves both linear time and linear space complexities as in TransE and DistMult, however, it surpasses their accuracies in the task of link prediction due to its ability to model a wider set of predicate types.

• *Convolution-based embeddings interactions*: Following the success of convolutional neural networks image processing tasks, models like R-GCN [17] and ConvE [5] utilized convolutional networks to learn knowledge graph embeddings. The R-GCN model learns entity embeddings using a combination of convolutional filters of its neighbours, where each predicate represent a convolution filter and each neighbour entity represents an input for the corresponding predicate filter. This approach is combined with the DistMult model to perform link prediction. Meanwhile, the ConvE model concatenates subject and predicate embeddings vectors into an image (a matrix form), then it uses a 2D convolutional pipeline to transform this matrix into a vector and computes its interaction with the object entity embeddings to generate a corresponding score as follows:

$$\phi_{spo}^{\text{ConvE}} = f(vec(f([\overline{e_s}; \overline{w_p}] * \omega))W)e_o \tag{4}$$

where $\overline{e_s}$ and $\overline{w_p}$ denotes a 2D reshaping of e_s and w_p, ω is a convolution filter, f denotes a non-linear function, $vec(x)$ is a transformation function that reshape matrix x of size $m \times n$ into a vector of size $mn \times 1$.

2.2 Loss Functions

The task of link prediction can generally be cast as a learning to rank problem where the object is to rank knowledge graph triples according to their factuality. Thus, knowledge graph embedding models traditionally use ranking loss

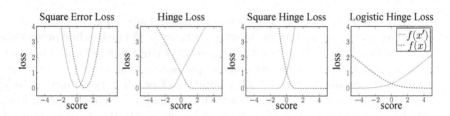

Fig. 1. Plots of different knowledge graph embedding loss functions and their training error slopes. Red lines represent the score/loss slopes of the false triples and blue lines represent the score/loss slopes of the true triples. (Color figure online)

approaches like pairwise and pointwise loss functions as in TransE and ComplEx respectively to model their training loss during the learning process. In these approaches a set of negative facts *i.e.* corruptions, is generated using a uniform random sample of entities to represent false facts, where training loss uses a min-max approach to maximise true facts scores and minimise false facts scores. Meanwhile, recent attempts considered using a multi-class loss to represent training error, where a triple (s, p, o) is divided into an input (s, p) and a corresponding class o and the objective is to assign class o to the (s, p) input.

In the following, we discuss these two approaches with examples from state-of-the-art knowledge graph embedding models.

• *Ranking loss functions*: Knowledge graph embedding models has adopted different pointwise and pairwise ranking losses like hinge loss and logistic loss to model their training loss. Hinge loss can be interpreted as a pointwise loss or a pairwise loss that minimises the scores of negative facts and maximise the scores of positive facts to reach a specific configurable value. This approach is used in HolE [15], and it is defined as:

$$\mathcal{L}_{\text{Hinge}} = \sum_{x \in X} [\lambda - l(x) \cdot f(x)]_+, \tag{5}$$

where $l(x) = 1$ if x is true and -1 otherwise and $[c]_+$ is equal to $\max(c, 0)$. This effectively generates two different loss slopes for positive and negative scores as shown in Fig. 1.

The squared error loss can also be adopted as a pointwise ranking loss function. For example, the RESCAL [16] model uses the squared error to model its training loss with the objective of minimising the difference between model scores and their actual labels:

$$\mathcal{L}_{\text{SE}} = \frac{1}{2} \sum_{i=1}^{n} (f(x_i) - l(x_i))^2. \tag{6}$$

The optimal score for true and false facts is 1 and 0, respectively, as shown in Fig. 1. Also, the squared loss requires less training time since it does not require configurable training parameters, shrinking the search space of hyperparameters compared to other losses (*e.g.*, the margin parameter of the hinge loss).

The ComplEx [21] model uses a logistic loss, which is a smoother version of pointwise hinge loss without the margin requirement (*cf.* Fig. 1). Logistic loss uses a logistic function to minimise negative triples score and maximise positive triples score. This is similar to hinge loss, but uses a smoother linear loss slope defined as:

$$\mathcal{L}_{\text{logistic}_{Pt}} = \sum_{x \in T} \log(1 + \exp(-l(x) \cdot f(x))), \qquad (7)$$

where $l(x)$ is the true label of fact x that is equal to 1 for positive facts and is equal to -1 otherwise.

• *Multi-class loss approach*: ConvE model proposed a new binary cross entropy multi-class loss to model its training error. In this setting, the whole vocabulary of entities is used to train each positive fact that for a triple (s, p, o) all facts (s, p, o') with $o' \in E$ and $o' \neq o$ are considered false. Despite the extra computational cost of this approach, it allowed ConvE to generalise over a larger sample of negative assistances therefore surpassing other approaches in accuracy [5]. In a recent work, Lacroix et al. [9] introduced a softmax regression loss to model the training error of the ComplEx model as a multi-class problem. In this approach, the objective for each triple (s, p, o) is to minimise the following losses:

$$\mathcal{L}_{spo}^{\log-\text{softmax}} = \mathcal{L}_{spo}^{o'} + \mathcal{L}_{spo}^{s'},$$

$$\mathcal{L}_{spo}^{o'} = -\phi_{spo} + \log(\sum_{o'} \exp(\phi_{spo'})) \qquad (8)$$

$$\mathcal{L}_{spo}^{s'} = -\phi_{spo} + \log(\sum_{s'} \exp(\phi_{s'po}))$$

where $s' \in E$, $s' \neq s$, $o' \in E$ and $o' \neq o$. This resembles a log-loss of the softmax value of the positive triple compared to all possible object and subject corruptions where the objective is to maximise positive facts scores and minimise all other scores. This approach achieved a significant improvement to the prediction accuracy of ComplEx model over all benchmark datasets [9].

2.3   Ranking Evaluation Metrics

Learning to rank models are evaluated using different ranking measures including Mean Average Precision (MAP), Normalised Discounted Cumulative Gain (NDCG), and Mean Reciprocal Rank (MRR). In this study, we only focus on the Mean Reciprocal Rank (MRR) since it is the main metric used in previous related works.

Mean Reciprocal Rank (MRR). The Reciprocal Rank (RR) is a statistical measure used to evaluate the response of ranking models depending on the rank of the first correct answer. The MRR is the average of the reciprocal ranks of results for different queries in Q. Formally, MRR is defined as:

$$\text{MRR} = \frac{1}{n} \sum_{i=1}^{n} \frac{1}{\mathcal{R}(\mathbf{x}_i, f)},$$

Table 1. A comparison between the ComplEx model and different variants of its scoring functions on standard benchmarking datasets

Model	Definition	NELL239		WN18RR		FB237	
		MRR	H@10	MRR	H@10	MRR	H@10
ComplEx	$i_1 + i_2 + i_3 - i_4$	0.35	0.51	0.44	0.51	0.22	0.41
ComplEx-V1	$i_1 + i_2 + i_3$	0.34	0.51	0.45	0.52	0.22	0.40
ComplEx-V2	$i_2 + i_3 + i_4$	0.34	0.50	0.44	0.51	0.21	0.38
ComplEx-V3	$i_1 + i_2 - i_4$	0.34	0.51	0.45	0.52	0.22	0.40
ComplEx-V4	$i_1 + i_3 - i_4$	0.33	0.50	0.45	0.50	0.21	0.39

where x_i is the highest ranked relevant item for query q_i. Values of RR and MRR have a maximum of 1 for queries with true items ranked first, and get closer to 0 when the first true item is ranked in lower positions.

3   The TriModel Model

In this section, we motivate for the design decision of TriModel model, and we present its way to model embeddings interaction and training loss.

3.1   Motivation

Currently, models using factorisation-based knowledge graph embedding approaches like DistMult and ComplEx achieve state-of-the-art results across all benchmarking datasets [9]. In the DistMult model, embeddings interactions are modelled using a symmetric function that computes the product of embeddings of the subject, the predicate and the object. This approach was able to surpass other distance-based embedding techniques like TransE [23]. However, it failed to model facts with asymmetric predicate due to its design. The ComplEx model tackle this problem using a embeddings in the complex space where its embeddings interactions use the complex conjugate of object embeddings to break the symmetry of the interactions. This approach provided significant accuracy improvements over DistMult as it successfully models a wider range of predicates.

The ComplEx embeddings interaction function (defined in Sect. 2) can be redefined as a simple set of interactions of two part embeddings as follows:

$$\phi_{spo}^{\text{ComplEx}} = \sum_k i_1 + i_2 + i_3 - i_4 \tag{9}$$

where $\sum_k$ is the sum of all embeddings components of index $k = \{1, ..., K\}$, and interactions i_1, i_2, i_3 and i_4 are defined as follows:

$$i_1 = e_s^1 w_p^1 e_o^1, \quad i_2 = e_s^2 w_p^1 e_o^2, \quad i_3 = e_s^1 w_p^2 e_o^2, \quad i_4 = e_s^2 w_p^2 e_o^1$$

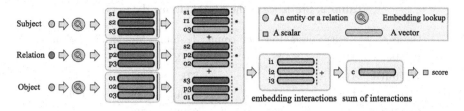

Fig. 2. Visual explanation for the flow of the TriModel model's scoring function, where embedding interactions are represented by $i_1 = e_s^3 w_p^3 e_o^1$, $i_2 = e_s^2 w_p^2 e_o^2$, and $i_3 = e_s^1 w_p^1 e_o^3$.

where e^1 represents embeddings part 1, and e^2 is part 2 ($1 \rightarrow$ real and $2 \rightarrow$ imaginary). Following this notation, we can see that the ComplEx model is a set of two symmetric interaction i_1 and i_2 and two asymmetric interactions i_3 and i_4. Furthermore, this encouraged us to investigate the effect of using other forms of combined symmetric and asymmetric interactions to model embeddings interactions in knowledge graph embeddings. We investigated different combination of interactions i_1, i_2, i_3 and i_4, and we have found that by removing and/or changing the definition of one of these interactions (maintaining that the interactions use all triple components) will preserve similar or insignificantly different prediction accuracy across different benchmarking datasets (See Table 1). This led us to investigate other different forms of interactions that uses a combination of symmetric and asymmetric interactions where we found that using embeddings of three parts can lead to better predictive accuracy than the ComplEx and the DistMult models.

3.2 TriModel Embeddings Interactions

In the TriModel model, we represent each entity and relation using three embedding vectors such that the embedding of entity i is $\{e_i^1, e_i^2, e_i^3\}$ and the embedding of relation j is $\{w_j^1, w_j^2, w_j^3\}$ where e^m denotes the m part of the embeddings and where $m \in 1, 2, 3$ is used to represent the three embeddings parts.

The TriModel model is a tensor factorisation based model, where its embeddings interaction function (scoring function) is defined as follows:

$$\phi_{spo}^{\text{TriPart}} = \sum_{k=1}^{K} e_{sk}^1 w_{pk}^1 e_{ok}^3 + e_{sk}^2 w_{pk}^2 e_{ok}^2 + e_{sk}^3 w_{pk}^3 e_{ok}^1 \tag{10}$$

where k denotes the index of the embedding vector entries. The model uses a set of three interactions: one symmetric interaction: $(e_s^2 w_p^2 e_o^2)$ and two asymmetric interactions: $(e_s^1 w_p^1 e_o^3)$ and $(e_s^3 w_p^3 e_o^1)$ as shown in Fig. 2. This approach models both symmetry and asymmetry in a simple form similar to the DistMult model where the DisMult model can be seen as a special case of the TriModel model if the first and third embeddings part are equivalent ($e^1 = e^3$).

Table 2. Statistics of the benchmarking datasets.

Dataset	Entity count	Relation count	Training	Validation	Testing
WN18	41k	18	141k	5k	5k
WN18RR	41k	11	87k	3k	3k
FB15k	15k	1k	500k	50k	60k
FB15k-237	15k	237	272k	18k	20k
YAGO10	123k	37	1M	5k	5k
NELL239	48k	239	74k	3k	3k

3.3   Training the TriModel Model

Trouillon et al. [20] showed that despite the equivalence of HolE and ComplEx models' scoring functions, they produce different results as they use different loss functions. They concluded that the logistic loss version of ComplEx outperforms its hinge loss version. In addition, we have investigated different other ranking losses with the ComplEx model, and we have found that squared error loss can significantly enhance the performance of ComplEx on multiple benchmarking datasets.

The TriModel model performs its learning process using two different training loss configurations: the traditional ranking loss and the multi-class loss. In the ranking loss configuration, the TriModel model uses the squared error (Eq. 6) and the logistic loss (Eq. 7) to model its training error, where a grid search is performed to choose the optimal loss representation for each dataset. In the multi-class configuration, it uses the negative-log softmax loss (Eq. 8) with the nuclear 3-norm regularisation [9] which is defined as follows:

$$
\begin{aligned}
\mathcal{L}_{spo}^{\text{TriModel}} = &- \phi_{spo} + \log(\sum\nolimits_{o'} \exp(\phi_{spo'})) \\
&- \phi_{spo} + \log(\sum\nolimits_{s'} \exp(\phi_{s'po})) \\
&+ \frac{\lambda}{3} \sum\nolimits_{k=1}^{K} \sum\nolimits_{m=1}^{3} (|e_s^m|^3 + |w_p^m|^3 + |e_o^m|^3)
\end{aligned}
\tag{11}
$$

where m denotes the embedding part index, λ denotes a configurable regularisation weight parameter and $|x|$ is the absolute value of x. This allows the model to answer the link prediction task in both directions: (subject, predicate, ?) and (?, predicate, object). We also consider the use of predicate reciprocals in training as described in Lacroix et al. [9], where inverses of training predicates are added to the training set and trained with their corresponding original facts as shown in the following:

$$\mathcal{L}_{spo}^{\text{TriModel}} = -\phi_{spo} + \log(\sum_{o'} \exp(\phi_{spo'}))$$

$$- \phi_{spo} + \log(\sum_{s'} \exp(\phi_{o(p+N_r)s})) \qquad (12)$$

$$+ \frac{\lambda}{3} \sum_{k=1}^{K} \sum_{m=1}^{3} (|e_s^m|^3 + |w_p^m|^3 + |w_{p+N_r}^m|^3 + |e_o^m|^3)$$

where predicate $p + N_r$ is the inverse of the predicate p where the model learns and evaluates inverse facts using inverses of their original predicates. For all the multi-class configurations, the TriModel model regularises the training facts embeddings using a dropout layer [18] with weighted probability that it learns during the grid search.

4   Experiments

In this section, we discuss the setup of our experiments where we present the evaluation protocol, the benchmarking datasets and our implementation details.

4.1   Data

In our experiments we use six knowledge graph benchmarking datasets:

- WN18 & WN18RR: subsets of the WordNet dataset [11] that contains lexical information of the English language [2,5].
- FB15k & FB15k-237: subsets of the Freebase dataset [1] that contains information about general human knowledge [2,19].
- YAGO10: a subset of the YAGO3 dataset [10] that contains information mostly about people and their citizenship, gender, and professions knowledge [3].
- NELL239: a subset of the NELL dataset [6,12] that we have created to test our model, which contains general knowledge about people, places, sports teams, universities, etc.

Table 2 contains statistics about our experiments' benchmarking datasets[1].

4.2   Implementation

We use TensorFlow framework (GPU) along with Python 3.5 to perform our experiments. All experiments were executed on a Linux machine with processor Intel(R) Core(TM) i70.4790K CPU @ 4.00 GHz, 32 GB RAM, and an nVidia Titan Xp GPU.

---

[1] All the benchmarking datasets can be downloaded using the following url: https://figshare.com/s/88ea0f4b8b139a13224f.

4.3   Experiments Setup

We perform our experiments in two different configurations:

(1) Ranking loss based learning: the models are trained using a ranking based loss function, where our model chooses between squared error loss and logistic loss using grid search.

(2) Multi-class loss based learning: the models is trained using a multi-class based training functions, where our model uses the softmax negative log loss functions described in Eqs. 11 and 12.

In all of our experiments we initialise our embeddings using the Glorot uniform random generator [7] and we optimise the training loss using the Adagrad optimiser, where the learning rate lr $\in \{0.1, 0.3, 0.5\}$, embeddings size $K \in 50, 75, 100, 150, 200$ and batch size $b \in \{1000, 3000, 5000, 8000\}$ except for YAGO10 where we only use $b \in \{1000, 2000\}$. The rest of the grid search hyper parameters are defined as follows: in the ranking loss approach, we use the negative sampling ratio $n \in \{2, 5, 10, 25, 50\}$ and in the multi-class approach we use regularisation weight $\lambda \in \{0.1, 0.3, 0.35, 0.01, 0.03, 0.035\}$ and dropout $d \in \{0.0, 0.1, 0.2, 0.01, 0.02\}$. The number of training epochs is fixed to 1000, where in the ranking loss configuration we do an early check every 50 epochs to stop training when MRR stop improving on the validation set to prevent over-fitting.

In the evaluation process, we only consider filtered MRR and Hits@10 metrics [2]. In addition, in the ranking loss configuration, TriModel model uses a softmax normalisation of the scores of objects and subjects corruptions, that a score of a corrupted object triple (s, p, o_i) is defined as:

$$\phi_{spo_i} = \frac{\exp(\phi_{spo_i})}{\sum_{o' \in E} \exp(\phi_{spo'})},$$

similarly, we apply a softmax normalisation to the scores of all possible subject entities.

5   Results and Discussion

In this section we discuss findings and results of our experiments shown in Tables 3 and 4, where the experiments are divided into two configurations: models with ranking loss functions and models with multi-class based loss functions.

5.1   Results of the Ranking Loss Configuration

In the results of the ranking loss configuration shown in Table 3, the results show that the TriModel model achieves best results in terms of MRR and hits@10 in five out of six benchmarking datasets with a margin of up to 10% as in the YAGO10 dataset. However, on the FB15k-237 ConvKB [14] retains state-of-the-art results in terms of MRR and Hits@10. Results also show that the factorisation

Table 3. Link prediction results on standard benchmarking datasets. ⋆ Results taken from [21] and our own experiments.

	Model	WN18		WN18RR		FB15k		FB15k-237		YAGO10		NELL239	
		MRR	H@10	MRR	H@10	MRR	H@10	MRR	H@10	MRR	H@10	MRR	H@10
Ranking loss	CP	0.08	0.13	-	-	0.33	0.53	-	-	-	-	-	-
	TransE ⋆	0.52	0.94	0.20	0.47	0.52	0.76	.29	0.48	0.27	0.44	0.27	0.43
	ConvKB	-	-	0.25	0.53	-	-	**0.40**	**0.52**	-	-	-	-
	DistMult ⋆	0.82	0.94	0.43	0.49	0.65	0.82	0.24	0.42	0.34	0.54	0.31	0.48
	ComplEx ⋆	0.94	0.95	0.44	0.51	0.70	0.84	0.22	0.41	0.36	0.55	0.35	0.52
	R-GCN	0.81	0.96	-	-	0.70	0.84	0.25	0.42	-	-	-	-
	TriModel	**0.95**	**0.96**	**0.50**	**0.57**	**0.73**	**0.86**	0.25	0.43	**0.46**	**0.62**	**0.37**	**0.53**

based models like the DistMult, ComplEx, R-GCN and TriModel models generally outperform distance based models like the TransE and ConvKB models. However, on the FB15k-237 dataset, both distance based models outperform all other factorisation based models with a margin of up to 15% in the case of the ConvKB and the TriModel model. We intend to perform further analysis on this dataset compared to other datasets to investigate why tensor factorisation models fail to provide state-of-the-art results in future works.

5.2 Results of the Multi-class Loss Configuration

Results of the multi-class based approach show that TriModel model provide state-of-the-art result on all benchmarking datasets, where the ComplEx models provide equivalent results on 3 out 6 datasets. Our reported results of the ComplEx model with multi-class log-loss introduced by Lacroix et al. [9] are slightly different from their reported results as we re-evaluated their models with restricted embeddings size to a maximum of 200. In their work they used an embedding size of 2000, which is impractical for embedding knowledge graphs in real applications. And other previous works using the TransE, DistMult, ComplEx, ConvE, and ConvKB models have limited their experiments to a maximum embedding size of 200. In our experiments, we limited our embedding size to 200 and we have re-evaluated the models of [9] using the same restriction for a fair comparison[2].

5.3 Ranking and Multi-class Approaches

In the link prediction task, the objective of knowledge graph embedding models is to learn embeddings that rank triples according to their faculty. This is achieved by learning to rank original true triples against other negative triple instances, where the negative instances are modelled in different ways in ranking approaches and multi-class loss approaches.

[2] We have used the code provided at: https://github.com/facebookresearch/kbc for the evaluation of the models: CP-N3, CP-N3-R, ComplEx-N3 and ComplEx-N3-R.

Table 4. Link prediction results on standard benchmarking datasets. † Results taken from [9] with embedding size (K) limited to 200.

	Model	WN18		WN18RR		FB15k		FB15k-237		YAGO10		NELL239	
		MRR	H@10	MRR	H@10	MRR	H@10	MRR	H@10	MRR	H@10	MRR	H@10
Multi-class loss	ConvE	0.94	0.95	0.46	0.48	0.75	0.87	0.32	0.49	0.52	0.66	0.37	0.45
	CP-N3 †	0.12	0.18	0.08	0.14	0.35	0.56	0.22	0.42	0.40	0.64	-	-
	ComplEx-N3 †	0.92	0.95	0.44	0.52	0.58	0.79	0.30	0.51	0.46	0.67	-	-
	CP-N3-R †	0.93	0.94	0.41	0.45	0.62	0.78	0.30	0.47	0.55	0.69	-	-
	ComplEx-N3-R †	**0.95**	**0.96**	**0.47**	**0.54**	0.79	0.88	**0.35**	**0.54**	**0.57**	0.70	-	-
	TriModel - N3	**0.95**	**0.96**	**0.47**	**0.54**	**0.84**	**0.91**	**0.35**	**0.54**	**0.57**	**0.71**	**0.41**	0.57
	TriModel -N3-R	**0.95**	**0.96**	**0.47**	**0.54**	0.81	**0.91**	**0.35**	**0.54**	**0.57**	0.70	**0.41**	**0.58**

In learning to rank approach, models use a ranking loss *e.g.* pointwise or pairwise loss to rank a set of true and negative instances [4], where negative instances are generated by corrupting true training facts with a ratio of negative to positive instances [2]. This corruption happens by changing either the subject or object of the true triple instance. In this configuration, the ratio of negative to positive instances is traditionally learnt using a grid search, where models compromise between the accuracy achieved by increasing the ratio and the runtime required for training.

On the other hand, multi-class based models train to rank positive triples against all their possible corruptions as a multi-class problem where the range of classes is the set of all entities. For example, training on a triple (s, p, o) is achieved by learning the right classes "s" and "o" for the pairs (?, p, o) and (s, p, ?) respectively, where the set of possible class is E of size N_e. Despite the enhancements of the predictions accuracy achieved by such approaches [5,9], they can have scalability issues in real-world large sized knowledge graphs with large numbers of entities due to the fact that they use the full entities' vocabulary as negative instances [13].

In summary, our model provides significantly better results than other SOTA models in the ranking setting, which is scalable and thus better-suited to real-world applications. In addition to that, our model has equivalent or slightly better performance than SOTA models on the multi-class approach.

6 Conclusions and Future Work

In this work, we have presented the TriModel model, a new tensor factorisation based knowledge graph embedding model that represents knowledge entities an relation using three parts embeddings, where its embedding interaction function can model both symmetric and asymmetric predicates. We have shown by experiments that the TriModel model outperforms other tensor factorisation based models like the ComplEx and the DistMult on different training objectives and across all standard benchmarking datasets. We have also introduced a new challenging small size benchmarking datasets, NELL239, that can be used to facilitate fast development of new knowledge graph embedding models.

In our future works, we intend to investigate new possible approaches to model embedding interactions of tensor factorisation models, and we intend to analyse the effects of properties of knowledge graph datasets like FB15k-237 on the efficiency of tensor factorisation based models.

Acknowledgements. This work has been supported by the TOMOE project funded by Fujitsu Laboratories Ltd., Japan and Insight Centre for Data Analytics at National University of Ireland Galway, Ireland (supported by the Science Foundation Ireland grant 12/RC/2289). The GPU card used in our experiments is granted to us by the Nvidia GPU Grant Program.

References

1. Bollacker, K.D., Evans, C., Paritosh, P., Sturge, T., Taylor, J.: Freebase: a collaboratively created graph database for structuring human knowledge. In: SIGMOD Conference, pp. 1247–1250. ACM (2008)
2. Bordes, A., Usunier, N., García-Durán, A., Weston, J., Yakhnenko, O.: Translating embeddings for modeling multi-relational data. In: NIPS, pp. 2787–2795 (2013)
3. Bouchard, G., Singh, S., Trouillon, T.: On approximate reasoning capabilities of low-rank vector spaces. In: AAAI Spring Symposium on Knowledge Representation and Reasoning (KRR): Integrating Symbolic and Neural Approaches. AAAI Press (2015)
4. Chen, W., Liu, T., Lan, Y., Ma, Z., Li, H.: Ranking measures and loss functions in learning to rank. In: NIPS, pp. 315–323. Curran Associates, Inc. (2009)
5. Dettmers, T., Minervini, P., Stenetorp, P., Riedel, S.: Convolutional 2D knowledge graph embeddings. In: AAAI. AAAI Press (2018)
6. Gardner, M., Mitchell, T.M.: Efficient and expressive knowledge base completion using subgraph feature extraction. In: EMNLP, pp. 1488–1498. The Association for Computational Linguistics (2015)
7. Glorot, X., Bengio, Y.: Understanding the difficulty of training deep feedforward neural networks. In: AISTATS. JMLR Proceedings, vol. 9, pp. 249–256. JMLR.org (2010)
8. Kadlec, R., Bajgar, O., Kleindienst, J.: Knowledge base completion: baselines strike back. In: Rep4NLP@ACL, pp. 69–74. Association for Computational Linguistics (2017)
9. Lacroix, T., Usunier, N., Obozinski, G.: Canonical tensor decomposition for knowledge base completion. In: ICML. JMLR Workshop and Conference Proceedings, vol. 80, pp. 2869–2878. JMLR.org (2018)
10. Mahdisoltani, F., Biega, J., Suchanek, F.M.: YAGO3: a knowledge base from multilingual Wikipedias. In: CIDR (2015). www.cidrdb.org
11. Miller, G.A.: WordNet: a lexical database for English. Commun. ACM **38**(11), 39–41 (1995)
12. Mitchell, T.M., et al.: Never-ending learning. Commun. ACM **61**(5), 103–115 (2018)
13. Mnih, A., Kavukcuoglu, K.: Learning word embeddings efficiently with noise-contrastive estimation. In: NIPS, pp. 2265–2273 (2013)

14. Nguyen, D.Q., Nguyen, T.D., Nguyen, D.Q., Phung, D.Q.: A novel embedding model for knowledge base completion based on convolutional neural network. In: NAACL-HLT (2), pp. 327–333. Association for Computational Linguistics (2018)
15. Nickel, M., Rosasco, L., Poggio, T.A.: Holographic embeddings of knowledge graphs. In: AAAI, pp. 1955–1961. AAAI Press (2016)
16. Nickel, M., Tresp, V., Kriegel, H.: A three-way model for collective learning on multi-relational data. In: ICML, pp. 809–816. Omnipress (2011)
17. Schlichtkrull, M., Kipf, T.N., Bloem, P., van den Berg, R., Titov, I., Welling, M.: Modeling relational data with graph convolutional networks. In: Gangemi, A., et al. (eds.) ESWC 2018. LNCS, vol. 10843, pp. 593–607. Springer, Cham (2018). https://doi.org/10.1007/978-3-319-93417-4_38
18. Srivastava, N., Hinton, G., Krizhevsky, A., Sutskever, I., Salakhutdinov, R.: Dropout: a simple way to prevent neural networks from overfitting. J. Mach. Learn. Res. **15**, 1929–1958 (2014)
19. Toutanova, K., Chen, D., Pantel, P., Poon, H., Choudhury, P., Gamon, M.: Representing text for joint embedding of text and knowledge bases. In: EMNLP, pp. 1499–1509. The Association for Computational Linguistics (2015)
20. Trouillon, T., Nickel, M.: Complex and holographic embeddings of knowledge graphs: a comparison. In: StarAI, vol. abs/1707.01475 (2017)
21. Trouillon, T., Welbl, J., Riedel, S., Gaussier, É., Bouchard, G.: Complex embeddings for simple link prediction. In: ICML. JMLR Workshop and Conference Proceedings, vol. 48, pp. 2071–2080. JMLR.org (2016)
22. Wang, Q., Mao, Z., Wang, B., Guo, L.: Knowledge graph embedding: a survey of approaches and applications. IEEE Trans. Knowl. Data Eng. **29**(12), 2724–2743 (2017)
23. Yang, B., Yih, W., He, X., Gao, J., Deng, L.: Learning multi-relational semantics using neural-embedding models. In: ICLR (2015)

Modelling the Compatibility of Licenses

Benjamin Moreau[1,2(✉)], Patricia Serrano-Alvarado[1], Matthieu Perrin[1],
and Emmanuel Desmontils[1]

[1] Nantes University, LS2N, CNRS, UMR6004, 44000 Nantes, France
{Benjamin.Moreau,Patricia.Serrano-Alvarado,Matthieu.Perrin,
Emmanuel.Desmontils}@univ-nantes.fr
[2] OpenDataSoft, Paris, France
Benjamin.Moreau@opendatasoft.com

Abstract. Web applications facilitate combining resources (linked data, web services, source code, documents, etc.) to create new ones. For a resource producer, choosing the appropriate license for a combined resource is not easy. It involves choosing a license compliant with all the licenses of combined resources and analysing the reusability of the resulting resource through the compatibility of its license. The risk is either, to choose a license too restrictive making the resource difficult to reuse, or to choose a not enough restrictive license that will not sufficiently protect the resource. Finding the right trade-off between compliance and compatibility is a difficult process. An automatic ordering over licenses would facilitate this task. Our research question is: *given a license l_i, how to automatically position l_i over a set of licenses in terms of compatibility and compliance?* We propose CaLi, a model that partially orders licenses. Our approach uses restrictiveness relations among licenses to define compatibility and compliance. We validate experimentally CaLi with a quadratic algorithm and show its usability through a prototype of a license-based search engine. Our work is a step towards facilitating and encouraging the publication and reuse of licensed resources in the Web of Data.

1   Introduction

Web applications facilitate combining resources (linked data, web services, source code, documents, etc.) to create new ones. To facilitate reuse, resource producers should systematically associate licenses with resources before sharing or publishing them [1]. Licenses specify precisely the conditions of reuse of resources, i.e., what actions are *permitted*, *obliged* and *prohibited* when using the resource.

For a resource producer, choosing the appropriate license for a combined resource or choosing the appropriate licensed resources for a combination is a difficult process. It involves choosing a license compliant with all the licenses of combined resources as well as analysing the reusability of the resulting resource through the compatibility of its license. The risk is either, to choose a license too restrictive making the resource difficult to reuse, or to choose a not enough restrictive license that will not sufficiently protect the resource.

© Springer Nature Switzerland AG 2019
P. Hitzler et al. (Eds.): ESWC 2019, LNCS 11503, pp. 255–269, 2019.
https://doi.org/10.1007/978-3-030-21348-0_17

Relations of compatibility, compliance and restrictiveness on licenses could be very useful in a wide range of applications. Imagine license-based search engines for services such as GitHub[1], APISearch[2], LODAtlas[3], DataHub[4], Google Dataset Search[5] or OpenDataSoft[6] that could find resources licensed under licenses compatible or compliant with a specific license. Answers could be partially ordered from the least to the most restrictive license. We argue that a model for license orderings would allow the development of such applications.

We consider simplified definitions of compliance and compatibility inspired by works like [2–5]: *a license l_j is compliant with a license l_i if a resource licensed under l_i can be licensed under l_j without violating l_i*. If a license l_j is compliant with l_i then we consider that l_i is compatible with l_j and that resources licensed under l_i are reusable with resources licensed under l_j. In general, if l_i is compatible with l_j then l_j is more (or equally) restrictive than l_i. We also consider that *a license l_j is more (or equally) restrictive than a license l_i if l_j allows at most the same permissions and has at least the same prohibitions/obligations than l_i.*

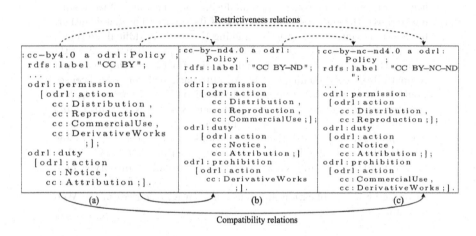

Fig. 1. Three Creative Commons licenses described in RDF.

Usually but not always, when l_i is less restrictive than l_j then l_i is compatible with l_j. For instance, see Fig. 1 that shows an excerpt of three Creative Commons (CC)[7] licenses described in RDF and using the ODRL vocabulary[8].

---

[1] https://github.com/.

[2] http://apis.io/.

[3] http://lodatlas.lri.fr/.

[4] https://datahub.io/.

[5] https://toolbox.google.com/datasetsearch.

[6] https://data.opendatasoft.com/.

[7] https://creativecommons.org/.

[8] The term *duty* is used for obligations https://www.w3.org/TR/odrl-model/.

Notice that there exists a restrictiveness order among these licenses, (a) is less restrictive than (b) and (b) is less restrictive than (c). By transitivity (a) is less restrictive than (c). Notice also that (a) is compatible with (b) and (c), but (b) is not compatible with (c). This is due to the semantics of the prohibited action *DerivativeWorks* that forbids the distribution of a derivation (remix, transform or build upon) of the protected resource under a different license. Thus, depending on the semantics of their actions, a restrictiveness relation between two licenses does not imply a compatibility relation.

Our research question is: *given a license l_i, how to automatically position l_i over a set of licenses in terms of compatibility and compliance?* The challenge we face is how to generalise the automatic definition of the ordering relations among licenses while taking into account the influence of the semantics of actions.

Inspired by lattice-based access control models [6, 7], we propose CaLi (ClAssification of LIcenses), a model for license orderings that uses restrictiveness relations and constraints among licenses to define compatibility and compliance. We validate experimentally CaLi with a quadratic algorithm and show its usability through a prototype of a license-based search engine. Our work is a step towards facilitating and encouraging the publication and reuse of licensed resources in the Web of Data. However, it is not intended to provide legal advice.

This paper is organised as follows. Section 2 discusses related works, Sect. 3 introduces the CaLi model, Sect. 4 illustrates the usability of our model, Sect. 5 shows experiments of the implemented algorithm as well as the prototype of a license-based search engine, and Sect. 6 concludes.

2   Related Work

Automatic license classification requires machine-readable licenses. License expression languages such as CC REL[9], ODRL, or L4LOD[10] enable fine-grained RDF description of licenses. Works like [8] and [9] use natural language processing to automatically generate RDF licenses from licenses described in natural language. Other works such as [10–12] propose a set of well-known licenses in RDF described in CC REL and ODRL. Thereby, in this work, we suppose that there exist consistent licenses described in RDF.

There exist some tools to facilitate the creation of license compliant resources. TLDRLegal[11], CC Choose[12] and ChooseALicense[13] help users to choose actions to form a license for their resources. CC search[14] allows users to find images licensed under Creative Commons licenses that can be commercialized, modified, adapted, or built upon. Web2rights proposes a tool to check compatibility

---

[9] https://creativecommons.org/ns.
[10] https://ns.inria.fr/l4lod/.
[11] https://tldrlegal.com/.
[12] https://creativecommons.org/choose/.
[13] https://choosealicense.com/.
[14] https://ccsearch.creativecommons.org/.

among Creative Commons licenses[15]. DALICC [12] allows to compose arbitrary licenses and provides information about equivalence, similarity and compatibility of licenses. Finally, Licentia[16], based on deontic logic to reason over the licenses, proposes a web service to find licenses compatible with a set of permissions, obligations and prohibitions chosen by the user. From these tools, only Licentia and DALICC use machine-readable licenses[17,18] in RDF. But unfortunately, these works do not order licenses in terms of compatibility or compliance.

The easiest way to choose a license for a combined resource is to create a new one by combining all resource licenses to combine. Several works address the problem of license compatibility and license combination. In web services, [2] proposes a framework that analyses compatibility of licenses to verify if two services are compatible and then generates the composite service license. [13] addresses the problem of license preservation during the combination of digital resources (music, data, picture, etc.) in a collaborative environment. Licenses of combined resources are combined into a new one. In the Web of Data, [3] proposes a framework to check compatibility among CC REL licenses. If licenses are compatible, a new license compliant with combined ones is generated. [4] formally defines the combination of licenses using deontic logic. [14] proposes PrODUCE, an approach to combine usage policies taking into account the usage context. These works focus on combining operators for automatic license combination but do not propose to position a license over a set of licenses.

Concerning the problem of license classification to facilitate the selection of a license, [15] uses Formal Concept Analysis (FCA) to generate a lattice of actions. Once pruned and annotated, this lattice can be used to classify licenses in terms of features. This classification reduces the selection of a license to an average of three to five questions. However, this work does not address the problem of license compatibility. Moreover, FCA is not suitable to generate compatibility or restrictiveness relations among licenses. FCA defines a derivation operator on objects that returns a set of attributes shared by the objects. We consider that the set of actions in common of two licenses is not enough to infer these relations. If applied to our introductory example, FCA can only work with permissions but not with obligations and prohibitions. That is because l_i is less restrictive than l_j if permissions of l_i are a superset of permissions of l_j, but regarding obligations and prohibitions, l_i is less restrictive than l_j if they are a subset of those of l_j. In the context of Free Open Source Software (FOSS), [5] proposes an approach, based on a directed acyclic graph, to detect license violations in existing software packages. It considers that license l_i is compatible with l_j if the graph contains a path from l_i to l_j. However, as such a graph is build from a manual interpretation of each license, its generalisation and automation is not possible.

In the domain of access control, [6] proposes a lattice model of secure information flow. This model classifies security classes with associated resources. Like

---

[15] http://www.web2rights.com/creativecommons/.
[16] http://licentia.inria.fr/.
[17] http://rdflicense.appspot.com/rdflicense.
[18] https://www.dalicc.net/license-library.

in the compatibility graph of [5], security class sc_i is compatible with sc_j if the lattice contains a path from sc_i to sc_j. Thus, this path represents the authorized flow of resources (e.g., resource r_i protected with sc_i can flow to a resource protected by sc_j without violating sc_i.). The lattice can be generated automatically through a pairwise combination of all security classes if sc_i combined with sc_k gives sc_j where sc_i and sc_k are both compatible with sc_j. [7] describes several models based on this approach but none focuses on classifying licenses.

None of these works answers our research question. They do not allow to automatically position a license over a set of licenses in terms of compatibility or compliance. In our work we propose a lattice-based model inspired by [6]. This model is independent of any license description language, application context and licensed resource so that it can be used in a wide variety of domains.

3 CaLi: A Lattice-Based License Model

The approach we propose to partially order licenses in terms of compatibility and compliance passes through a restrictiveness relation. In a license, actions can be distributed in what we call *status*, e.g., permissions, obligations and prohibitions. To decide if a license l_i is less restrictive than l_j, it is necessary to know if an action in a status is considered as less restrictive than the same action in another status. In the introductory example (Fig. 1), we consider that permissions are less restrictive than obligations, which are less restrictive than prohibitions, i.e., $Permission \leqslant Duty \leqslant Prohibition$. This relation can be seen in Fig. 2b.

We remark that if two licenses have a restrictiveness relation then it is possible that they have a compatibility relation too. The restrictiveness relation between the licenses can be automatically obtained according to the status of actions without taking into account the semantics of the actions. Thus, based on lattice-ordered sets [16], we define a restrictiveness relation among licenses.

To identify the compatibility among licenses, we refine the restrictiveness relation with constraints. The goal is to take into account the semantics of actions. Constraints also distinguish valid licenses from non-valid ones. We consider a license l_i as non-valid if a resource can not be licensed under l_i, e.g., a license that simultaneously permits the *Derive* action[19] and prohibits *DerivativeWorks*[20].

This approach is based on:

1. a set of *actions* (e.g., *read, modify, distribute*, etc.);
2. a *restrictiveness lattice of status* that defines (i) all possible status of an action in a license (i.e., permission, obligation, prohibition, recommendation, undefined, etc.) and (ii) the restrictiveness relation among status; a *restrictiveness lattice of licenses* is obtained from a combination of 1 and 2;
3. a set of *compatibility constraints* to identify if a restrictiveness relation between two licenses is also a compatibility relation; and

---

[19] https://www.w3.org/TR/odrl-vocab/#term-derive.
[20] https://www.w3.org/TR/odrl-vocab/#term-DerivativeWorks.

4. a set of *license constraints* to identify non-valid licenses.

Next section introduces formally the CaLi model and Sect. 3.2 introduces a simple example of a CaLi ordering.

3.1 Formal Model Description

We first define a *restrictiveness lattice of status*. We use a lattice structure because it is necessary, for every pair of status, to know which status is less (or more) restrictive than both.

Definition 1 (Restrictiveness lattice of status $\mathcal{LS}$). *A restrictiveness lattice of status is a lattice* $\mathcal{LS} = (S, \leqslant_S)$ *that defines all possible status S for a license and the relation $\leqslant_S$ as the* restrictiveness relation *over S. For two status s_i, s_j, if $s_i \leqslant_S s_j$ then s_i is less restrictive than s_j.*

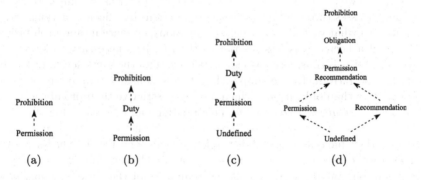

Fig. 2. Examples of restrictiveness lattices of status ($\mathcal{LS}$). Dashed arrows represent restrictiveness, e.g., in (a) Permission is less restrictive than Prohibition.

Different $\mathcal{LS}$s can be defined according to the application domain. Figure 2a shows the diagram of a $\mathcal{LS}$ inspired by file systems where actions can be either prohibited or permitted. With this lattice, prohibiting to read a file is more restrictive than permitting to read it. Figure 2b illustrates a $\mathcal{LS}$ for CC licenses where actions are either permitted, required (Duty) or prohibited. Figure 2c shows a $\mathcal{LS}$ inspired by the ODRL vocabulary. In ODRL, actions can be either permitted, obliged, prohibited or not specified (i.e., undefined). In this lattice, the undefined status is the least restrictive and the prohibited one the most restrictive. Figure 2d shows a $\mathcal{LS}$ where a recommended or permitted action is less restrictive than the same action when it is permitted and recommended.

Now we formally define a license based on the status of its actions.

Definition 2 (License). *Let $\mathcal{A}$ be a set of actions and $\mathcal{LS} = (S, \leqslant_S)$ be a restrictiveness lattice of status. A license is a function $l : \mathcal{A} \to S$. We denote by $\mathcal{L}_{\mathcal{A},\mathcal{LS}}$ the set of all licenses.*

For example, consider $\mathcal{A} = \{read, modify, distribute\}$, $\mathcal{LS}$ the lattice of Fig. 2c and two licenses: l_i which permits *read* and *distribute* but where *modify* is undefined and l_j where *modify* is also undefined but which permits *read* and prohibits *distribute*. We define l_i and l_j as follows:

$\forall a \in \mathcal{A}$:

$$l_i(a) = \begin{cases} \text{Undefined} & \text{if } a \in \{modify\}; \\ \text{Permission} & \text{if } a \in \{read, distribute\}. \end{cases}$$

$$l_j(a) = \begin{cases} \text{Undefined} & \text{if } a \in \{modify\}; \\ \text{Permission} & \text{if } a \in \{read\}; \\ \text{Prohibition} & \text{if } a \in \{distribute\}. \end{cases}$$

A restrictiveness lattice of status and a set of licenses make possible to partially order licenses in a restrictiveness lattice of licenses.

Definition 3 (Restrictiveness relation over licenses). *Let A be a set of actions and $\mathcal{LS} = (S, \leqslant_S)$ be a restrictiveness lattice of status associated to the join and meet operators $\vee_S$ and $\wedge_S$, and $l_i, l_j \in \mathcal{L}_{A,\mathcal{LS}}$ be two licenses. We say that l_i is less restrictive than l_j, denoted $l_i \leqslant_{\mathcal{R}} l_j$, if for all actions $a \in \mathcal{A}$, the status of a in l_i is less restrictive than the status of a in l_j. That is, $l_i \leqslant_{\mathcal{R}} l_j$ if $\forall a \in \mathcal{A}, l_i(a) \leqslant_S l_j(a)$.*

Moreover, we define the two operators $\vee$ and $\wedge$ as follows. For all actions $a \in \mathcal{A}$, the status of a in $l_i \vee l_j$ (resp. $l_i \wedge l_j$) is the join (resp. meet) of the status of a in l_i and the status of a in l_j. That is, $(l_i \vee l_j)(a) = l_i(a) \vee_S l_j(a)$ and $(l_i \wedge l_j)(a) = l_i(a) \wedge_S l_j(a)$.

For example, consider $\mathcal{LS}$ the lattice of Fig. 2c, and licenses l_i and l_j defined previously; $l_i \leqslant_{\mathcal{R}} l_j$ because $l_i(read) \leqslant_S l_j(read), l_i(modify) \leqslant_S l_j(modify)$ and $l_i(distribute) \leqslant_S l_j(distribute)$. In this example, $l_i \vee l_j = l_j$ because $\forall a \in \mathcal{A}$, $(l_i \vee l_j)(a) = l_j(a)$, e.g., $(l_i \vee l_j)(distribute) = l_j(distribute) = Prohibition$. If for an action, it is not possible to say which license is the most restrictive then the compared licenses are not comparable by the restrictiveness relation.

Remark 1. *The pair $(\mathcal{L}_{A,\mathcal{LS}}, \leqslant_{\mathcal{R}})$ is a restrictiveness lattice of licenses, whose $\vee$ and $\wedge$ are respectively the join and meet operators.*

In other words, for two licenses l_i and l_j, $l_i \vee l_j$ (resp. $l_i \wedge l_j$) is the least (resp. most) restrictive license that is more (resp. less) restrictive than both l_i and l_j.

Remark 2. *For an action $a \in \mathcal{A}$, we call $(\mathcal{L}_{\{a\},\mathcal{LS}}, \leqslant_{\mathcal{R}})$ the action lattice of a. Remark that $(\mathcal{L}_{A,\mathcal{LS}}, \leqslant_{\mathcal{R}})$ and $\prod_{a \in \mathcal{A}}(\mathcal{L}_{\{a\},\mathcal{LS}}, \leqslant_{\mathcal{R}})$ are isomorphic. That is, a restrictiveness lattice of licenses can be generated through the coordinatewise product [16] of all its action lattices. The total number of licenses in this lattice is $|\mathcal{LS}|^{|A|}$.*

For example, consider $\mathcal{A} = \{read, modify\}$, $\mathcal{LS}$ the lattice of Fig. 2a, $(\mathcal{L}_{A,\mathcal{LS}}, \leqslant_{\mathcal{R}})$ is isomorphic to $(\mathcal{L}_{\{read\},\mathcal{LS}}, \leqslant_{\mathcal{R}}) \times (\mathcal{L}_{\{modify\},\mathcal{LS}}, \leqslant_{\mathcal{R}})$. Figure 3a, b, c illustrates the product of these action lattices and the produced restrictiveness lattice of licenses.

To identify the compatibility relation among licenses and to distinguish valid licenses from non-valid ones it is necessary to take into account the semantics of actions. Thus, we apply two types of constraints to the restrictiveness lattice of licenses: license constraints and compatibility constraints.

Definition 4 (License constraint). *Let $\mathcal{L}_{A,\mathcal{LS}}$ be a set of licenses. A license constraint is a function $\omega_{\mathcal{L}} : \mathcal{L}_{A,\mathcal{LS}} \rightarrow Boolean$ which identifies if a license is valid or not.*

For example, the license constraint $\omega_{\mathcal{L}_1}$ considers a license $l_i \in \mathcal{L}_{A,\mathcal{LS}}$ non-valid if *read* is prohibited but modification is permitted (i.e., a *modify* action implies a *read* action):

$$\omega_{\mathcal{L}_1}(l_i) = \begin{cases} False \text{ if } l_i(read) = \text{Prohibition and } l_i(modify) = \text{Permission}; \\ True \text{ otherwise.} \end{cases}$$

Definition 5 (Compatibility constraint). *Let $(\mathcal{L}_{A,\mathcal{LS}}, \leqslant_{\mathcal{R}})$ be a restrictiveness lattice of licenses. A compatibility constraint is a function $\omega_{\rightarrow} : \mathcal{L}_{A,\mathcal{LS}} \times \mathcal{L}_{A,\mathcal{LS}} \rightarrow Boolean$ which constraints the restrictiveness relation $\leqslant_{\mathcal{R}}$ to identify compatibility relations among licenses.*

For example, consider that a license prohibits the action *modify*. In the spirit of *Derivative Work*, we consider that the distribution of the modified resource under a different license is prohibited. Thus, the compatibility constraint $\omega_{\rightarrow_1}$, considers that a restrictiveness relation $l_i \leqslant_{\mathcal{R}} l_j$ can be also a compatibility relation if l_i does not prohibit *modify*. This constraint is described as: For $l_i, l_j \in \mathcal{L}_{A,\mathcal{LS}}$,

$$\omega_{\rightarrow_1}(l_i, l_j) = \begin{cases} False \text{ if } l_i(modify) = \text{Prohibition}; \\ True \text{ otherwise.} \end{cases}$$

Now we are able to define a CaLi ordering from a restrictiveness lattice of licenses and constraints defined before.

Definition 6 (CaLi ordering). *A CaLi ordering is a tuple $\langle A, \mathcal{LS}, C_{\mathcal{L}}, C_{\rightarrow} \rangle$ such that A and $\mathcal{LS}$ form a restrictiveness lattice of licenses $(\mathcal{L}_{A,\mathcal{LS}}, \leqslant_{\mathcal{R}})$, $C_{\mathcal{L}}$ is a set of license constraints and $C_{\rightarrow}$ is a set of compatibility constraints. For two licenses $l_i \leqslant_{\mathcal{R}} l_j \in \mathcal{L}_{A,\mathcal{LS}}$, we say that l_i is compatible with l_j, denoted by $l_i \rightarrow l_j$, if $\forall \omega_{\mathcal{L}} \in C_{\mathcal{L}}, \omega_{\mathcal{L}}(l_i) = \omega_{\mathcal{L}}(l_j) = True$ and $\forall \omega_{\rightarrow} \in C_{\rightarrow}, \omega_{\rightarrow}(l_i, l_j) = True$.*

Remark 3. *We define the* compliance *relation as the opposite of the* compatibility *relation. For two licenses l_i, l_j, if $l_i \rightarrow l_j$ then l_j is compliant with l_i.*

A CaLi ordering is able to answer our research question, *given a license l_i, how to automatically position l_i over a set of licenses in terms of compatibility and compliance?* It allows to evaluate the potential reuse of a resource depending on its license. Knowing the compatibility of a license allows to know to which extent the protected resource is reusable. On the other hand, knowing the compliance of a license allows to know to which extent other licensed resources can be reused. Next section shows an example of CaLi ordering.

3.2   Example 1

Consider a CaLi ordering $\langle \mathcal{A}, \mathcal{LS}, \{\omega_{\mathcal{L}_1}\}, \{\omega_{\rightarrow_1}\} \rangle$ such that:

- $\mathcal{A}$ is the set of actions {*read, modify*},
- $\mathcal{LS}$ is a restrictiveness lattice of status where an action can be either permitted or prohibited, and *Permission* $\leqslant_S$ *Prohibition* (cf Fig. 2a),
- $\omega_{\mathcal{L}_1}$ is the license constraint introduced in the example of Definition 4, and
- $\omega_{\rightarrow_1}$ is the compatibility constraint introduced in the example of Definition 5.

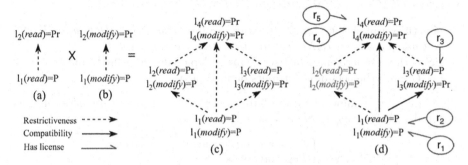

Fig. 3. (a) and (b) are the action latices $(\mathcal{L}_{\{read\}, \mathcal{LS}}, \leqslant_{\mathcal{R}})$ and $(\mathcal{L}_{\{modify\}, \mathcal{LS}}, \leqslant_{\mathcal{R}})$, where $\mathcal{A} = \{read, modify\}$ and $\mathcal{LS}$ is the lattice of Fig. 2a (Pr=Prohibition and P=Permission). The product of these action lattices gives the restrictiveness lattice of licenses (c) $(\mathcal{L}_{\mathcal{A}, \mathcal{LS}}, \leqslant_{\mathcal{R}})$ (reflexive relations are not represented). (d) is the CaLi ordering $\langle \mathcal{A}, \mathcal{LS}, \{\omega_{\mathcal{L}_1}\}, \{\omega_{\rightarrow_1}\} \rangle$.

Figure 3d shows a visual representation of this CaLi ordering. Licenses in grey are identified as non-valid by $\omega_{\mathcal{L}_1}$. They are part of the ordering but cannot protect resources. Dashed arrows represent restrictiveness relations $\leqslant_{\mathcal{R}}$. Black arrows represent restrictiveness relations that are also compatibility relations.

Consider a set of resources $R = \{r_1, r_2, r_3, r_4, r_5\}$. $\rightharpoonup$ is the *has license* relation such that $\{r_1, r_2\} \rightharpoonup l_1; r_3 \rightharpoonup l_3; \{r_4, r_5\} \rightharpoonup l_4$. Thanks to our CaLi ordering, next questions can be answered.

- *Which licensed resources can be reused in a resource that has as license l_3?* Those resource whose licenses are compatible with l_3: r_1 and r_2 that have license l_1 which precedes l_3, as well as r_3 that has the license l_3 itself.
- *Which licensed resources can reuse a resource that has as license l_1?* Those resource whose licenses are compliant with l_1: r_3, r_4 and r_5 that have licenses l_3 and l_4 which follow l_1, as well as r_1 and r_2 that have the license l_3 itself.

Resulting licenses can be returned ordered in a graph of compatibility.

We illustrated CaLi with a simple restrictiveness lattice of status, next section introduces a more realistic CaLi ordering inspired by licenses of Creative Commons.

4 A CaLi Ordering for Creative Commons

Creative Commons proposes 7 licenses that are legally verified, free of charge, easy-to-understand and widely used when publishing resources on the Web. These licenses use 7 actions that can be permitted, required or prohibited. In this CaLi example, we search to model a complete compatibility ordering of all possible valid licenses using these 7 actions.

4.1 Description of a CC Ordering Based on CaLi

Consider CC_CaLi, a CaLi ordering $\langle \mathcal{A}, \mathcal{LS}, C_{\mathcal{L}}, C_{\rightarrow} \rangle$ such that:

- $\mathcal{A}$ is the set of actions {cc:Distribution, cc:Reproduction, cc:DerivativeWorks, cc:CommercialUse, cc:Notice, cc:Attribution, cc:ShareAlike},
- $\mathcal{LS}$ is the restrictiveness lattice of status depicted in Fig. 2b[21], and
- $C_{\mathcal{L}}, C_{\rightarrow}$ are the sets of constraints defined next.

$C_{\mathcal{L}} = \{\omega_{\mathcal{L}_2}, \omega_{\mathcal{L}_3}\}$ allows to invalidate a license (1) when cc:CommercialUse is required and (2) when cc:ShareAlike is prohibited:

$$\omega_{\mathcal{L}_2}(l_i) = \begin{cases} False \text{ if } l_i(cc{:}CommercialUse) = \text{Duty;} \\ True \text{ otherwise.} \end{cases}$$

$$\omega_{\mathcal{L}_3}(l_i) = \begin{cases} False \text{ if } l_i(cc{:}ShareAlike) = \text{Prohibition;} \\ True \text{ otherwise.} \end{cases}$$

$C_{\rightarrow} = \{\omega_{\rightarrow_2}, \omega_{\rightarrow_3}\}$ allows to identify (1) when cc:ShareAlike is required and (2) when cc:DerivativeWorks is prohibited. That is because cc:ShareAlike requires that the distribution of derivative works be under the same license only, and cc:DerivativeWorks, when prohibited, does not allow the distribution of a derivative resource, regardless of the license.

$$\omega_{\rightarrow_2}(l_i, l_j) = \begin{cases} False \text{ if } l_i(cc{:}ShareAlike) = \text{Duty;} \\ True \text{ otherwise.} \end{cases}$$

$$\omega_{\rightarrow_3}(l_i, l_j) = \begin{cases} False \text{ if } l_i(cc{:}DerivativeWorks) = \text{Prohibition;} \\ True \text{ otherwise.} \end{cases}$$

Other constraints could be defined to be closer to the CC schema[22] but for the purposes of this compatibility ordering these constraints are enough.

4.2 Analysis of CC_CaLi

The size of the restrictiveness lattice of licenses is 3^7 but the number of valid licenses of CC_CaLi is 972 due to $C_{\mathcal{L}}$. That is, 5 actions in whatever status and 2 actions (cc:CommercialUse and cc:ShareAlike) in only 2 status: $3^5 * 2^2$.

---

[21] To simplify, we consider that a requirement is a duty.
[22] https://creativecommons.org/ns.

The following CC_CaLi licenses are like the official CC licenses.

$$CCBY(a) = \begin{cases} \text{Permission if } a \in \{cc\text{:}Distribution,\ cc\text{:}Reproduction \\ \qquad\qquad\qquad cc\text{:}Derivative Works,\ cc\text{:}CommercialUse \\ \qquad\qquad\qquad cc\text{:}ShareAlike\}; \\ \text{Duty} \qquad\quad \text{if } a \in \{cc\text{:}Notice,\ cc\text{:}Attribution\}. \end{cases}$$

$$CCBYNC(a) = \begin{cases} \text{Permission if } a \in \{cc\text{:}Distribution,\ cc\text{:}Reproduction \\ \qquad\qquad\qquad cc\text{:}Derivative Works,\ cc\text{:}ShareAlike\}; \\ \text{Duty} \qquad\quad \text{if } a \in \{cc\text{:}Notice,\ cc\text{:}Attribution\}; \\ \text{Prohibition if } a \in \{cc\text{:}CommercialUse\}. \end{cases}$$

The following CC_CaLi licenses are not part of the official CC licenses. License $CC\ l_1$ is like CC BY-NC but without the obligation to give credit to the copyright holder/author of the resource. $CC\ l_2$ is like CC BY but with the prohibition of making multiple copies of the resource. License $CC\ l_3$ allows only exact copies of the original resource to be distributed. $CC\ l_4$ is like $CC\ l_3$ with the prohibition of commercial use.

$$CC\ l_1(a) = \begin{cases} \text{Permission if } a \in \{cc\text{:}Distribution,\ cc\text{:}Reproduction, \\ \qquad\qquad\qquad cc\text{:}Derivative Works,\ cc\text{:}ShareAlike, \\ \qquad\qquad\qquad cc\text{:}Notice,\ cc\text{:}Attribution\}; \\ \text{Prohibition if } a \in \{cc\text{:}CommercialUse\}. \end{cases}$$

$$CC\ l_2(a) = \begin{cases} \text{Permission if } a \in \{cc\text{:}Distribution,\ cc\text{:}Derivative Works, \\ \qquad\qquad\qquad cc\text{:}CommercialUse,\ cc\text{:}ShareAlike\}; \\ \text{Duty} \qquad\quad \text{if } a \in \{cc\text{:}Notice,\ cc\text{:}Attribution\}; \\ \text{Prohibition if } a \in \{cc\text{:}Reproduction\}. \end{cases}$$

$$CC\ l_3(a) = \begin{cases} \text{Permission if } a \in \{cc\text{:}Distribution,\ cc\text{:}ShareAlike,\ cc\text{:}CommercialUse\}; \\ \text{Duty} \qquad\quad \text{if } a \in \{cc\text{:}Notice,\ cc\text{:}Attribution,\ cc\text{:}Reproduction\}; \\ \text{Prohibition if } a \in \{cc\text{:}Derivative Works\}. \end{cases}$$

$$CC\ l_4(a) = \begin{cases} \text{Permission if } a \in \{cc\text{:}Distribution,\ cc\text{:}ShareAlike\}; \\ \text{Duty} \qquad\quad \text{if } a \in \{cc\text{:}Notice,\ cc\text{:}Attribution,\ cc\text{:}Reproduction\}; \\ \text{Prohibition if } a \in \{cc\text{:}Derivative Works,\ cc\text{:}CommercialUse\}. \end{cases}$$

In CC_CaLi, the minimum is the license where all actions are permitted (i.e., CC Zero) and the maximum is the license where all actions are prohibited.

Figure 4 shows two subgraphs of CC_CaLi with only the compatibility relations. Figure 4a shows only the 7 official CC licenses and Fig. 4b includes also $CC\ l_1$ to $CC\ l_4$. These graphs can be generated using the CaLi implementation (cf Sect. 5). Thanks to $\omega_{\rightarrow_2}$, the restrictiveness relation between CC BY-SA and CC BY-NC-SA is not identified as a compatibility relation and thanks to $\omega_{\rightarrow_3}$, the restrictiveness relation between CC BY-ND and CC BY-NC-ND is not identified as a compatibility relation. We recall that a license that prohibits $cc\text{:}Derivative Works$ is not compatible even with itself.

The compatibility relations of Fig. 4a are conform to the ones obtained from the Web2rights tool. This example shows the usability of CaLi with a real set of licenses.

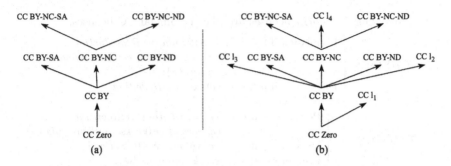

Fig. 4. Compatibility subgraphs of CC_CaLi: (a) contains the 7 official CC licenses and (b) contains $CC\ l_1$ to $CC\ l_4$ in addition to the 7 official CC licenses.

5   Implementation of CaLi Orderings

The goal of this section is twofold, to analyse the algorithm we implemented to produce CaLi orderings and to illustrate the usability of CaLi through a prototype of a license-based search engine.

5.1   Experimental Validation

The size growth of CaLi orderings is exponential, i.e., $|\mathcal{LS}|^{|\mathcal{A}|}$. Nevertheless, it is not necessary to explicitly build a CaLi ordering to use it. Sorting algorithms like insertion sort can be used to produce subgraphs of a CaLi ordering.

We implemented an algorithm that can sort any set of licenses using the $\mathcal{LS}$ of Fig. 2c in $\sum_{i=0}^{n-1} i = \frac{n(n-1)}{2}$ comparisons of restrictiveness (approx. $n^2/2$), n being the number of licenses to sort, i.e., $O(n^2)$. The goal is to be able to insert a license in a graph in linear time $O(n)$ without sorting again the graph.

We use a heuristic, based on the restrictiveness of the new license, to chose between two strategies, *(1)* to insert a license traversing the graph from the minimum or *(2)* from the maximum. To do this, our algorithm calculates the relative position of the new license (node) from the number of actions that it obliges and prohibits. The median depth (number of levels) of the existing graph is calculated from the median of the number of prohibited and obliged actions of existing licenses. Depending on these numbers, a strategy is chosen to find the place of the new license in the graph.

Results shown in Fig. 5 demonstrate that our algorithm sorts a set of licenses with at most $n^2/2$ comparisons. We used 20 subsets of licenses of different sizes from the CC_CaLi ordering. Size of subsets was incremented by 100 up to 2187 licenses. Each subset was created and sorted 3 times randomly. The curve was produced with the average of the number of comparisons to sort each subset.

A comparison of restrictiveness takes on average $6\,\mathrm{ms}$[23], thus to insert a license in a 2000 licenses graph takes an average of $12\,\mathrm{s}$. Building a whole graph

---

[23] With a 160xIntel(R) Xeon(R) CPU E7-8870 v4 2.10 GHz 1,5 Tb RAM.

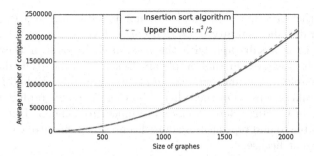

Fig. 5. Performance of the implemented insertion sort algorithm in number of comparisons of restrictiveness with incremental size of subsets of licenses.

is time consuming (a 2000 licenses graph takes on average 8 h to sort) but this time can be reduced with further optimisations of the process to compare the restrictiveness of two licenses. The implementation in Python of our algorithm and details of our experiments are available on GitHub[24].

5.2   A Search Engine Based on an ODRL CaLi Ordering

We implemented a prototype of a search engine that allows to find linked data[25] and source code repositories[26] based on the compatibility or the compliance of their licenses. We use licenses described with the ODRL vocabulary. ODRL proposes properties to define semantic dependencies among actions[27] that we translate as CaLi constraints. *Included In* is defined as "An Action transitively asserts that another Action encompasses its operational semantics". *Implies* is defined as "An Action asserts that another Action is not prohibited to enable its operational semantics". Thereby we consider that if an action a_i is included in another action a_j then a_i implies a_j. For example, *CommercialUse* is included in *use*, therefore we consider that *CommercialUse* implies *use*. That means that if *CommercialUse* is permitted then *use* should be permitted too. To preserve this dependency we implemented the constraint $\omega_{\mathcal{L}_4}$.

$$\omega_{\mathcal{L}_4}(l_i) = \begin{cases} \textit{False} \text{ if } a_i \text{ odrl:includedIn } a_j \\ \qquad \text{AND } (l_i(a_i) = \text{Permitted OR } l_i(a_i) = \text{Obliged}) \\ \qquad \text{AND } l_i(a_j) = \text{Prohibited}; \\ \textit{True} \text{ otherwise.} \end{cases}$$

We use $ODRL\_CaLi$, a CaLi ordering $\langle \mathcal{A}, \mathcal{LS}, C_{\mathcal{L}}, C_{\rightarrow} \rangle$ such that:

- $\mathcal{A}$ is the set of 72 actions of ODRL,
- $\mathcal{LS}$ is the restrictiveness lattice of status of Fig. 2c,
- $C_{\mathcal{L}} = \{\omega_{\mathcal{L}_2}, \omega_{\mathcal{L}_3}, \omega_{\mathcal{L}_4}\}$, and
- $C_{\rightarrow} = \{\omega_{\rightarrow_2}, \omega_{\rightarrow_3}\}$.

---

[24] https://github.com/benjimor/CaLi-Search-Engine.
[25] http://cali.priloo.univ-nantes.fr/ld/.
[26] http://cali.priloo.univ-nantes.fr/rep/.
[27] https://www.w3.org/TR/odrl-vocab/#actionConcepts.

The size of this ordering is 4^{72} and it is not possible to build it. This search engine illustrates the usability of *ODRL_CaLi* through two subgraphs. On the one side, there is a subgraph with the most used licenses in DataHub[28] and OpenDataSoft. Licenses in this graph are linked to some RDF datasets such that it is possible to find datasets whose licenses are compatible (or compliant) with a particular license. On the other side, there is a subgraph with the most used licenses in GitHub. Here, licenses are linked to some GitHub repositories and it is possible to find repositories whose licenses are compatible (or compliant) with a particular license.

Discussion. The model we propose uses restrictiveness as the basis to define compatibility and compliance among licenses. This strategy works most of the time, as we have shown in this paper, but it has certain limitations. In particular, CaLi is not designed to define the compatibility of two licences if it is not coherent with their restrictiveness relation. As an example consider two versions of MPL licenses. Version 2.0 relaxes some obligations compared to version 1.1. Thus, MPL-2.0 is less restrictive than MPL-1.1. With CaLi constraints, it can only be possible to say that MPL-2.0 is compatible with MPL-1.1. But in the legal texts it is said the opposite, i.e., MPL-1.1 is compatible with MPL-2.0.

Thereby, particularities in the usage of compatibility of licenses, the granularity of the semantisation of licenses and the understanding of some actions (like *ShareAlike*) are the main reasons of the difference between CaLi orderings and other classifications. This is the case, for instance, of our compatibility graph devoted to licenses of GitHub and the graph presented in [5].

6 Conclusions and Perspectives

We proposed a lattice-based model to define compatibility and compliance relations among licenses. Our approach is based on a restrictiveness relation that is refined with constraints to take into account the semantics of actions existing in licenses. We have shown the feasibility of our approach through two CaLi orderings, one using the Creative Commons vocabulary and the second using ODRL. We experimented the production of CaLi orderings with the implementation of an insertion sort algorithm whose cost is $n^2/2$. We implemented a prototype of a license-based search engine that highlights the feasibility and usefulness of our approach. Our compatibility model does not intent to provide a legal advice but it allows to exclude those licenses that would contravene a particular license.

A perspective of this work is to take into account other aspects of licenses related to usage contexts like jurisdiction, dates of reuse, etc. Another perspective is to analyse how two compatibility orderings can be compared. That is, given two CaLi orderings, if there is an alignment between their vocabularies and their restrictiveness lattices of status are homomorphic then find a function to pass from a CaLi ordering to another.

---

[28] https://old.datahub.io/.

Acknowledgments. Authors thank Margo Bernelin and Sonia Desmoulin-Canselier (laboratory of *Droit et Changement Social* - UMR CNRS 6297) for our helpful discussions on this work.

References

1. Seneviratne, O., Kagal, L., Berners-Lee, T.: Policy-aware content reuse on the web. In: Bernstein, A., et al. (eds.) ISWC 2009. LNCS, vol. 5823, pp. 553–568. Springer, Heidelberg (2009). https://doi.org/10.1007/978-3-642-04930-9_35
2. Gangadharan, G.R., Weiss, M., D'Andrea, V., Iannella, R.: Service license composition and compatibility analysis. In: Krämer, B.J., Lin, K.-J., Narasimhan, P. (eds.) ICSOC 2007. LNCS, vol. 4749, pp. 257–269. Springer, Heidelberg (2007). https://doi.org/10.1007/978-3-540-74974-5_21
3. Villata, S., Gandon, F.: Licenses compatibility and composition in the web of data. In: Workshop Consuming Linked Data (COLD) Collocated with ISWC (2012)
4. Governatori, G., Rotolo, A., Villata, S., Gandon, F.: One license to compose them all. In: Alani, H., et al. (eds.) ISWC 2013. LNCS, vol. 8218, pp. 151–166. Springer, Heidelberg (2013). https://doi.org/10.1007/978-3-642-41335-3_10
5. Kapitsaki, G.M., Kramer, F., Tselikas, N.D.: Automating the license compatibility process in open source software with SPDX. J. Syst. Softw. **131**, 386–401 (2017)
6. Denning, D.E.: A lattice model of secure information flow. Commun. ACM **19**(5), 236–243 (1976)
7. Sandhu, R.S.: Lattice-based access control models. Computer **26**(11), 9–19 (1993)
8. Sadeh, N., Acquisti, A., Breaux, T.D., Cranor, L.F., et al.: Towards usable privacy policies: semi-automatically extracting data practices from websites' privacy policies. In: Symposium on Usable Privacy and Security (SOUPS) Poster (2014)
9. Cabrio, E., Palmero Aprosio, A., Villata, S.: These are your rights. In: Presutti, V., d'Amato, C., Gandon, F., d'Aquin, M., Staab, S., Tordai, A. (eds.) ESWC 2014. LNCS, vol. 8465, pp. 255–269. Springer, Cham (2014). https://doi.org/10.1007/978-3-319-07443-6_18
10. Rodríguez Doncel, V., Gómez-Pérez, A., Villata, S.: A dataset of RDF licenses. In: Legal Knowledge and Information Systems Conference (ICLKIS) (2014)
11. Creative Commons licenses in RDF. https://github.com/creativecommons/cc.licenserdf. Accessed 26 Nov 2018
12. Havur, G., et al.: DALICC: a framework for publishing and consuming data assets legally. In: International Conference on Semantic Systems (SEMANTICS), Poster & Demo (2018)
13. Mesiti, M., Perlasca, P., Valtolina, S.: On the composition of digital licenses in collaborative environments. In: Decker, H., Lhotská, L., Link, S., Basl, J., Tjoa, A.M. (eds.) DEXA 2013. LNCS, vol. 8055, pp. 428–442. Springer, Heidelberg (2013). https://doi.org/10.1007/978-3-642-40285-2_37
14. Soto-Mendoza, V., Serrano-Alvarado, P., Desmontils, E., Garcia-Macias, J.A.: Policies composition based on data usage context. In: Workshop Consuming Linked Data (COLD) Collocated with ISWC (2015)
15. Daga, E., dAquin, M., Motta, E., Gangemi, A.: A bottom-up approach for licences classification and selection. In: Gandon, F., Guéret, C., Villata, S., Breslin, J., Faron-Zucker, C., Zimmermann, A. (eds.) ESWC 2015. LNCS, vol. 9341, pp. 257–267. Springer, Cham (2015). https://doi.org/10.1007/978-3-319-25639-9_41
16. Davey, B.A., Priestley, H.A.: Introduction to Lattices and Order. Cambridge university press, Cambridge (2002)

GConsent - A Consent Ontology Based on the GDPR

Harshvardhan J. Pandit[✉], Christophe Debruyne, Declan O'Sullivan,
and Dave Lewis

ADAPT Centre, Trinity College Dublin, Dublin, Ireland
{pandith,debruync,declan.osullivan,dave.lewis}@tcd.ie

Abstract. Consent is an important legal basis for the processing of personal data under the General Data Protection Regulation (GDPR), which is the current European data protection law. GPDR provides constraints and obligations on the validity of consent, and provides data subjects with the right to withdraw their consent at any time. Determining and demonstrating compliance to these obligations require information on how the consent was obtained, used, and changed over time. Existing work demonstrates feasibility of semantic web technologies in modelling information and determining compliance for GDPR. Although these address consent, they currently do not model all the information associated with it. In this paper, we address this by first presenting our analysis of information associated with consent under the GDPR. We then present GConsent, an OWL2-DL ontology for representation of consent and its associated information such as provenance. The paper presents the methodology used in the creation and validation of the ontology as well as an example use-case demonstrating its applicability. The ontology and this paper can be accessed online at https://w3id.org/GConsent.

Keywords: Consent · GDPR · Regulatory compliance · OWL2-DL ontology

1 Introduction

The General Data Protection Regulation (GDPR) [19] is the current European data protection law, which affects any service or organisation that uses personal data, and uses large fines to deter non-compliance. Consent is one of the legal basis for processing of personal data under the GDPR (Rec.40, Art.6)[1], and is considered valid only when it is freely given, specific, informed, and unambiguous (Rec.32, Art.2-11); and in the case of minors should be given by their legal guardian (Art.8). GDPR also provides rights regarding changing and withdrawing consent at any time (Art.7-3). To demonstrate compliance with these conditions and obligations of the GDPR, Data Controllers, which are the organisations responsible for deciding how personal data is collected and processed and therefore the ones responsible

---

[1] This is a form of legal notation to denote Recitals (Rec) or Articles (Art) in legal text. These are hyperlinked to where they occur in GDPR using GDPRtEXT [14].

© Springer Nature Switzerland AG 2019
P. Hitzler et al. (Eds.): ESWC 2019, LNCS 11503, pp. 270–282, 2019.
https://doi.org/10.1007/978-3-030-21348-0_18

for obtaining consent when needed, should maintain a demonstrable proof of the given consent [20] by collecting and storing information on how consent was collected, used, and any changes made to it [11] over time.

The information regarding consent and compliance needs to be maintained and shared by multiple parties - data subject, controller, processor, and authorities - which requires its representation to be interoperable between them. Additionally, querying of information is required to comply with requests by data subjects and authorities. Semantic Web technologies are ideal for representing this information because of the flexibility provided for expressing concepts and relationships in an open, interoperable and queryable manner based on standards. Existing work [1,5,8,13–16] has demonstrated the feasibility of using semantic web technologies for representing and querying metadata for assisting with the GDPR compliance process.

The focus of existing work in terms of consent is mostly on the 'given' aspect of consent i.e. consent provided by the data subject. There is a lack of work regarding representing other aspects, or states, of consent such as 'not given' or 'refused' or 'withdrawn' which cannot be modelled in the same manner as 'given consent'. There is also a lack of modelling representations for events such as delegation or associations with third parties regarding consent which have an effect on its validity regarding compliance.

In this paper, we present our analysis of information associated with consent under the GDPR. We present this through a methodology that creates possible use-cases and scenarios to determine information required for representing consent with a view towards GDPR compliance. We then present the resulting modelling of an ontology in the form of GConsent - an OWL2-DL ontology for representing information associated with consent. The ontology, along with its documentation, is available online at https://w3id.org/GConsent under the CC-by-4.0 license.

The rest of the paper is structured as follows: Sect. 2 presents an overview of the related work regarding representation of consent using semantic web, Sect. 3 presents the methodology used to create GConsent, Sect. 4 presents an overview of the GConsent ontology with an example use-case and discusses limitations, with Sect. 5 concluding the paper by discussing potential future work.

2   Related Work

This section provides an overview of the existing related work in the context of representing information pertaining to consent using semantic web ontologies. Other relevant work can be found through the W3C Community Group for Data Protection Vocabularies and Controls (DPVCG).

A precursor to GConsent was the consent ontology part of the Consent and Data Management Model (CDMM) [5], created before requirements were documented regarding consent and GDPR. GConsent reuses modelling choices such as consent attributes for medium, location, and delegation, and improves upon the overall ontology by adding additional concepts such as consent status and states, processing, and additional relationships for context, provision of consent, and relationship between instances of consent. GConsent is also linked to the GDPR and is based on guidance and clarifications provided by authorities and legal-domain organisations regarding consent.

The SPECIAL Usage Policy Language (SPL) [8] defines an usage policy as a set consisting of five items - personal data, purpose, processing, storage, and recipients - which represents authorisation provided by the consent. SPL combines several such (basic) policies into a general usage policy, which is used to enforce and verify compliance by ensuring the requirements of executed processes are within the subset of those permitted by the (consent) usage policy. The core attributes describing consent are similar between GConsent and the SPL, which provides some form of compatibility. SPL provides rigid modelling of storage and data recipient while GConsent leaves it open to the adopter. There are also differences in how provenance is modelled, with SPL focusing on maintaining a log of events for the controller, while GConsent is focused on capturing information about all entities and activities as provenance.

Consent Receipt [10] by the Kantara Initiative provides a way to represent the consent granted by the data subject to a controller using JSON. It provides a specification which controllers can implement to provide a receipt of the given consent to the data subject. There is a large semantic overlap between the information modelled by Consent Receipt and GConsent, such as the modelling of data subject, personal data, and purposes. It is currently not compatible with GConsent due to the differences in terminology as the Consent Receipt was created well before the GDPR. For example, Consent Receipt uses the term "PII" (personally identifiable information) whereas GDPR uses "personal data". A key difference is that the Consent Receipt is a record of consent between two parties that is provided to the data subject, whereas GConsent is used to specify the role of various parties and activities in the context of consent. Both feature information that can be useful towards documenting compliance. By aligning the concepts between the two, GConsent can be used to create an updated semantic GDPR-version of the Consent Receipt, which is part of the planned future work.

3   Ontology Creation

3.1   Methodology

The foremost methodology we used in the creation of GConsent was the seminal guide "Ontology Development 101" by Noy and McGuiness [12], which included using Protégé in maintaining the correctness (e.g. unwanted inferences) of the ontology using the HermiT reasoner. The creation of the ontology followed an iterative model. Each iteration of the ontology was tested for suitability and expressiveness by modelling the collected use-cases and scenarios, then evaluating using competency questions. The methodology can be summarised with the following steps:

1. Gather information about consent from GDPR, articles, academic papers, communications from various supervisory bodies and regulatory authorities

2. Create use-cases and competency questions based on collected information
3. Create ontology to express information about use-cases
4. Evaluate suitability to express information using competency questions

3.2   Information Collection and Analysis

This section describes the information collection process and its analysis used to model the information associated with consent. The primary source of information were the articles and recitals pertaining to consent within the GDPR [19]. Additionally, Article 29 Working Party, which was the official advisory body providing expert opinions regarding data protection, has provided guidelines on consent [17] that assisted in the interpretation of the GDPR. Apart from these, various guidelines and reports published by the Data Protection Offices and legal firms, Handbook on European Data Protection Law, and relevant court laws[2] were also used to understand and formulate technical requirements regarding consent.

For the scope of our work, we only considered consent as defined within Art.4-11 of the GDPR. Other special cases of consent (Art.9) such scientific research (Rec.33) and children's personal data (Art.8, Rec.38) were not included due to additional requirements and complexity, as well as lack of legal guidance on their compliance requirements. The use of consent as a legal basis (Art.6, Rec.40) includes conditions for consent to be considered valid (Art.7, Rec.42, Rec.43). The burden of proof and requirements for consent is specified to be on the Data Controller (Rec.42), which requires demonstrable proof that the data subject provided the consent and that it was valid as per the obligations specified in the GDPR.

For consent to be informed, it is necessary to provide certain information to the data subject, such as the specific purposes the personal data will be used for. GDPR also provides data subjects with the right to modify or withdraw consent (Art.7-3). In cases where the consent is withdrawn, processing done prior to the withdrawal is considered valid under the valid consent applicable at that time. This information along with other guidelines provided by the collected resources was used to iterate on a model of consent that could represent the required information.

The information regarding consent can be summarised as follow. Consent has associated attributes regarding the data subject the consent is about, their personal data, the purposes and processing operations associated with personal data, and who the consent is provided to. This is similar to the existing model used by SPL for given consent [8].

In addition to these, there are additional attributes such as - entity that provided consent, status, context (location, medium, instant of creation), and expiry that are useful in determining whether the specific instance of consent satisfies the obligations of the GDPR. It is also necessary to include the provenance

---

[2] The recent decision by CNIL (Décision n°MED-2018-042 du 30 octobre 2018) regarding validity of consent was particularly influential.

of consent to determine its validity, particularly for qualitative requirements which cannot be machine-evaluated. The provenance aspect shows some overlap with GDPRov [15] which models provenance of consent based on GDPR. This is resolved by clarifying the scope of GConsent to be limited to modelling consent as an entity, and using GDPRov along with PROV-O [9] to define the provenance.

3.3   Use-Cases and Scenarios

This section describes the use-cases and scenarios that were used in the creation of GConsent. The use-cases reflect the requirements gathered from the legal documents as well as various real-world scenarios. They were used to identify the information required regarding consent, and how it should be modelled in the form of an ontology. They were also useful to test the expression of consent using GConsent in different contexts. The complete list of use-cases and scenarios can be found in the documentation.

The use-cases are categorised based on the specific information they relate to. There are a total of 15 categories for use-cases based on the provenance of consent, involved persons and organisations, use of delegation, and third-parties. An example use-case for obtaining consent contains scenarios where consent is given via different mediums such as a web-form or a signed document, as well as when it is given implicitly or via delegation. Similarly, use-cases focusing on the agent that provided consent contain scenarios involving a legal representative of the data subject such as parent or guardian for a minor. Use-cases about the provenance identify the agents and activities involved. Similarly, there are use-cases regarding expiry, medium, modification, and revocation of consent.

3.4   Evaluation

The ontology was evaluated regarding its capability to express information about consent using a set of competency questions. The competency questions, listed in Table 1, were based on the collected use-cases and scenarios, and reflect the queries that can arise regarding compliance of consent under the GDPR. The questions were used as SPARQL queries over the information modelled using GConsent.

The validation of GConsent was done by exploring the suitability of using the ontology to define the information required by each competency question. This was an iterative process where the ontology was tested and modified to accommodate the requirements of the competency questions. Changes were made to the ontology where information was found to be missing or incorrectly modelled. The complete list of these questions along with the specific classes and properties involved in answering them can be found in the documentation. The use of competency questions as compliance queries was based on prior work that demonstrated the use of SPARQL in evaluating GDPR compliance [16].

The questions are grouped into four broad categories based on their context. The first category of questions relates to consent itself, and inquires about things such as personal data or purpose associated with consent. The second category of questions relates to the activity responsible for creation or invalidation of consent. It inquires whether consent was given by delegation, the role played by the person in delegation, and the activity responsible for delegation. The third category of questions inquire about the context of consent, such as location, medium, expiry, or timestamp of instantiation. The fourth and final category of questions inquire about involvement and role of third parties in any purpose or processing.

Table 1. Competency Questions used to evaluate and validate the ontology

ID	Question
Questions about consent	
C1	Who is the consent about?
C2	What type of Personal Data are associated with the Consent?
C3	What type of Purposes are associated with the Consent?
C4	What type of Processing are associated with the Consent?
C5	What is the Status of Consent?
C6	Is the current status valid for processing?
C7	Who is the consent given to?
Questions about how the consent was created/given/changed/invalidated	
P1	Who created/gave/acquired/invalidated the consent?
P2	If consent was created/given/acquired/invalidated through Delegation, who acted as the Delegate?
P3	If consent was created/gave/acquired/invalidated through Delegation, what was the role played by Delegate?
P4	If consent was created/gave/acquired/invalidated through Delegation, how was the delegation executed?
Questions about the context of how consent was created/given/invalidated	
T1	What is the location of associated with consent?
T2	What is the medium associated with consent?
T3	What is the timestamp associated with the consent?
T4	What is the expiry of the consent?
T5	How was the consent acquired/changed/created/invalidated?
T6	What artefacts were shown when consent was acquired/changed/created/invalidated?
Questions related to Third Party associated with the consent	
D1	Is the purpose or processing associated with a third party?
D2	What is the role played by the third party in the purpose or processing?

4 GConsent Ontology

Based on the methodology described in Sect. 3, we identified requirements in terms of information required to model the use-cases and scenarios identified in Sect. 4. These were then used to develop GConsent - an OWL2-DL ontology to express information associated with consent for GDPR. We chose OWL2-DL for its expressibility of relationship and constraints while maintaining reasoning capabilities. GConsent aims to model the context, state, and provenance of consent. Its scope is limited to consent as defined in the GDPR, and is meant to assist in the modelling of information associated with compliance but not determining the compliance itself. GConsent does not model consent as a policy or contract, and therefore is not useful for expressing information such as conditions or clauses that affect consent.

GConsent reuses existing vocabularies such as PROV-O [9] and its GDPR-specific extension GDPRov [15] to model provenance and Time Ontology in OWL [3] for temporal values. It has a preferred namespace of gc as used in this paper. Terms within GConsent are linked to their respective definitions in the GDPR using GDPRtEXT [14].

GConsent follows best practices and guidelines advocated by the community for self-documenting ontologies [2,6,7,18] and uses a persistent identifier (w3id) for its IRIs. The ontology and its documentation are available online at https://w3id.org/GConsent under the CC-by-4.0 license. The online documentation presents a comprehensive overview of the ontology along with describing the methodology used in its creation, including an analysis of the GDPR. The documentation also presents examples of how the ontology can be used using use-cases and scenarios, with one presented in Sect. 4.2. All figures follow the Graffoo specification [4] and were created using yEd tool.

4.1 Ontology Overview

The core concepts within GConsent, as presented in Fig. 1 are *Consent, Data Subject, Personal Data, Purpose, Processing,* and *Status*. These form the essential information that constitute consent as a legal basis under the GDPR. This is similar to other approaches [8] in the state of the art. The status of consent refers to its state or suitability with respect to use as a valid legal basis under the GDPR.

To facilitate its usage, GConsent distinguishes between valid and invalid states for consent, and provides instances to define states such as implicitly or explicitly given, given via delegation, withdrawn, not given, refused, expired, invalidated, and unknown. The property *invalidates* defines the relation between two iterations of consent - such as when a data subject withdraws given consent where only the latest iteration is considered valid.

Context of consent refers to the information associated with how the consent was created, or obtained, or 'given'. GConsent provides classes and properties, as depicted in Fig. 2, to represent location (using *prov:Location*), medium, and instance of creation (using *time:Instant*). Expiry of consent is defined as the duration or instant after which the consent is no longer considered valid. It is modelled using *time:TemporalEntity* which makes it possible to define it either as a duration (e.g. 6 months) or as an instant in time. To represent the entity that provided consent, GConsent provides the *isProvidedBy* property, whose range is

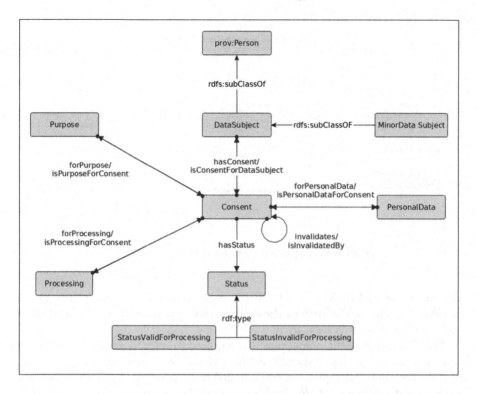

Fig. 1. Overview of the GConsent core ontology

defined as the union of *prov:Person*, *Data Subject*, and *Delegation*, since it is not necessary that the person that provided consent (by delegation) must be a data subject as well. To define other aspects of context, GConsent defines generic properties *hasContext* and its inverse *isContextForConset* that act as the parent properties for all context relationships.

4.2   Example Use-Case

The example use-case described in Fig. 3 shows implied consent[3] in an emergency ward where a nurse provides consent on behalf of the patient. The status of consent in this case is set as implicitly given[4] even though consent was provided by a delegation where the nurse is the agent that provided consent. The example

---

[3] Although the legal basis for obtaining this data under the GDPR could be interpreted as legitimate interest or benefit of data subject, it highlights the recording of information associated with such consent. The example also highlights the potential applicability of GConsent to scenarios other than GDPR such medical consent where additional laws and guidelines apply regarding consent.

[4] The nurse is the agent that assumes and collects the given consent of the patient, making it an implicit consent given by delegation.

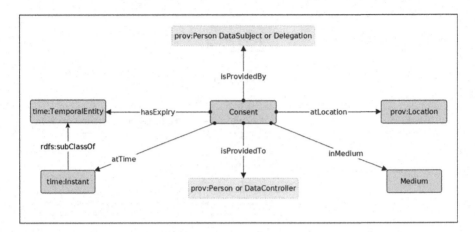

Fig. 2. Concepts representing context of consent

also shows use of PROV-O and GDPRov vocabularies in capturing provenance aspects of given consent such as the activity that generated consent and entities such as patient records used by it.

When giving consent, sometimes it is required to refer to an abstraction such as a category rather than a specific instance for personal data, processing, or purpose. In the above example, consent is linked using property *gc:forPersonalData* to the broader category of '*Health Data*' rather than some specific instance such as blood group. Such use of punning[5] allows using a class rather as an instance with a property. As this makes *gc:PersonalData* a meta-class for *ex:HealthData*, further specialisation can be done by defining it as a subclass of an arbitrary class such as *ex:PersonalDataCategory*. Creating examples and guidelines regarding the semantics of such modelling to accurately reflect the use of such abstractions in the real-world[6] are part of the future work.

4.3   Limitations

GConsent as an ontology has some limitations due to the novelty of consent under the GDPR and the challenges in creating a common ontology for all possible use-cases. In particular, GConsent does not provide a fixed vocabulary for representing temporal and location associated with processing operations such as data sharing or storage. This is due to the perceived ambiguity over whether such attributes only apply to a particular (sub-)set of personal data or processing, or to the consent as a whole. Additionally, the validity of conditions such as "as long as required" for data storage makes modelling these values difficult.

---

[5] Punning allows reuse of types. See https://www.w3.org/TR/owl2-new-features/#F12:_Punning.

[6] Example: privacy policies which mention consent for data categories such as "Account Information" rather than specific instances.

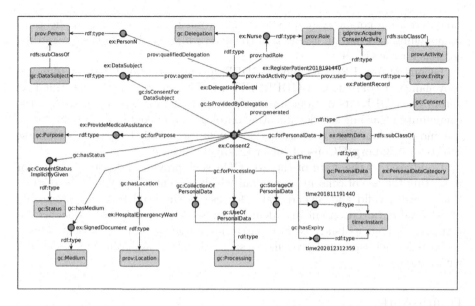

Fig. 3. Example use-case showing delegation of consent and use of punning

This is expected to be clarified with time as authorities and court cases provide declarative information on their validity. Until then, one can use Time ontology in OWL [3] to model timestamps and durations. Using this pattern in GConsent itself can break future versions where non-specific time values, such as those above, are found to be valid in relation to consent. Similarly, the granularity of location is an issue for modelling as it can refer to exact location (GPS), a city, country or a region such as the EU. Additionally, there can be multiple locations that store the same data, and be under different jurisdictions. Therefore, we plan to provide separate design patterns for time and location in the documentation, and use them to extend the ontology in future.

GConsent does not provide any information or modelling of compliance regarding the various obligations of the GDPR. For example, it does not require the specification of legal justification (also termed as legal basis) with the purpose or processing. Planned future work is the creation of a property to specify the legal justification for processing of personal data using GDPRtEXT [14] to indicate the possible legal basis.

5 Conclusion and Future Work

This paper presented GConsent, an OWL2-DL ontology for representing information associated with consent for the GDPR. The paper described the methodology used to create the ontology, which used an analysis of compliance requirements gathered from official publications and related resources. This was used to iteratively develop the ontology using a set of use-cases and scenarios which were validated using competency questions. The resulting ontology has applications in modelling information essential in the determination of compliance regarding consent for the GDPR.

GConsent uses PROV-O and its GDPR-specific extension GDPRov to model provenance of consent, and GDPRtEXT to link concepts to the relevant text within the GDPR. Its documentation followed best practices advocated by the community regarding self-documenting ontologies, and contains examples for its use and adoption. The ontology, its documentation, and this paper is available at https://w3id.org/GConsent under CC-by-4.0 license.

Compared to the state of the art, GConsent provides additional states for indicating the use of consent other than 'given consent'. It provides the distinction between valid and invalid states for use as the legal basis for processing of personal data. GConsent also demonstrates the modelling of provenance for activities and agents (such as third parties) and their role in the consent. This is useful to model aspects of provenance such as delegation and agents associated with consent.

Future Work

GConsent provides a generic way to model consent under the GDPR. While the aim of the ontology is to encompass as many use-cases and scenarios as possible, there needs to be a clear and demonstrable application of the work in specific use-cases to drive adoption in the wider community. We plan to develop design patterns that demonstrate the modelling information related to consent and its associated compliance in a variety of contexts. GConsent will play a vital role in such approaches for evaluating compliance based on using consent as a legal basis for processing of data.

One specific example we are working towards takes an existing RDBMS that stores (given) consent information and uses R2RML to produce mappings for generating RDF metadata using GConsent. The resulting data can then be explored and evaluated for compliance using SPARQL queries. The work also aims to address the practice of storing partial information regarding the given consent and combining this information with a common model of the system using GDPRov to generate documentation of consent using GConsent. The approach is expected to demonstrate the feasibility of using a common model versus storing all the information for each instance of consent. This would also facilitate using data validation of information regarding consent.

Acknowledgements. This paper is supported by the ADAPT Centre for Digital Content Technology, which is funded under the SFI Research Centres Programme (Grant 13/RC/2106) and is co-funded under the European Regional Development Fund.

The authors wish to thank the members of Data Protection Vocabularies and Controls Community Group (DPVCG) for their inputs in the discussion of consent and its related research. The authors also wish to thank Pat McBennett for their help in this work.

References

1. Bartolini, C., Muthuri, R.: Reconciling data protection rights and obligations: an ontology of the forthcoming EU regulation. In: Workshop on Language and Semantic Technology for Legal Domain, p. 8 (2015)
2. Berrueta, D., Phipps, J., Miles, A., Baker, T., Swick, R.: Best practice recipes for publishing RDF vocabularies. Working draft, W3C (2008)
3. Cox, S., Little, C.: Time ontology in OWL. World Wide Web Consortium (2017). https://www.w3.org/TR/owl-time
4. Falco, R., Gangemi, A., Peroni, S., Shotton, D., Vitali, F.: Modelling OWL ontologies with Graffoo. In: Presutti, V., Blomqvist, E., Troncy, R., Sack, H., Papadakis, I., Tordai, A. (eds.) ESWC 2014. LNCS, vol. 8798, pp. 320–325. Springer, Cham (2014). https://doi.org/10.1007/978-3-319-11955-7_42
5. Fatema, K., Hadziselimovic, E., Pandit, H.J., Debruyne, C., Lewis, D., O'Sullivan, D.: Compliance through informed consent: Semantic based consent permission and data management model. In: Proceedings of the 5th Workshop on Society, Privacy and the Semantic Web - Policy and Technology (PrivOn2017) (PrivOn) (2017). http://ceur-ws.org/Vol-1951/#paper-05
6. Garijo, D.: WIDOCO: a wizard for documenting ontologies. In: d'Amato, C., et al. (eds.) ISWC 2017. LNCS, vol. 10588, pp. 94–102. Springer, Cham (2017). https://doi.org/10.1007/978-3-319-68204-4_9
7. Gurk, S.M., Abela, C., Debattista, J.: Towards ontology quality assessment. In: Joint Proceedings of the MEPDaW, p. 12 (2017)
8. Kirrane, S., et al.: A scalable consent, transparency and compliance architecture. In: Gangemi, A., et al. (eds.) ESWC 2018. LNCS, vol. 11155, pp. 131–136. Springer, Cham (2018). https://doi.org/10.1007/978-3-319-98192-5_25
9. Lebo, T., et al.: PROV-O: the PROV ontology (2013)
10. Lizar, M., Turner, D.: Consent receipt specification (2017). https://docs.kantarainitiative.org/cis/consent-receipt-specification-v1-1-0.pdf
11. Mittal, S., Sharma, P.P.: The role of consent in legitimising the processing of personal data under the current EU data protection framework. Asian J. Comput. Sci. Inf. Technol. **7**, 76–78 (2017). https://papers.ssrn.com/abstract=2975277
12. Noy, N.F., McGuinness, D.L., et al.: Ontology development 101: a guide to creating your first ontology. Stanford Knowledge Systems Laboratory Technical report KSL-01-05 and ... (2001)
13. Palmirani, M., Martoni, M., Rossi, A., Bartolini, C., Robaldo, L.: PrOnto: privacy ontology for legal reasoning. In: Kő, A., Francesconi, E. (eds.) EGOVIS 2018. LNCS, vol. 11032, pp. 139–152. Springer, Cham (2018). https://doi.org/10.1007/978-3-319-98349-3_11
14. Pandit, H.J., Fatema, K., O'Sullivan, D., Lewis, D.: GDPRtEXT - GDPR as a linked data resource. In: Gangemi, A., et al. (eds.) ESWC 2018. LNCS, vol. 10843, pp. 481–495. Springer, Cham (2018). https://doi.org/10.1007/978-3-319-93417-4_31. https://doi.org/10/c3n4
15. Pandit, H.J., Lewis, D.: Modelling provenance for GDPR compliance using linked open data vocabularies. In: Proceedings of the 5th Workshop on Society, Privacy and the Semantic Web - Policy and Technology (PrivOn2017) (PrivOn) (2017). http://ceur-ws.org/Vol-1951/#paper-06
16. Pandit, H.J., O'Sullivan, D., Lewis, D.: Queryable provenance metadata for GDPR compliance. Procedia Comput. Sci. **137**, 262–268 (2018). https://doi.org/10/gfdc6r10/gfdc6r. Proceedings of the 14th International Conference on Semantic Systems 10th - 13th of September 2018 Vienna, Austria

17. Party, A.W.: Guidelines on consent under regulation 2016/679 (wp259rev.01) (2018). https://ec.europa.eu/newsroom/article29/item-detail.cfm?item_id=623051
18. Poveda-Villalón, M., Suárez-Figueroa, M.C., Gómez-Pérez, A.: Validating ontologies with OOPS! In: ten Teije, A., et al. (eds.) EKAW 2012. LNCS (LNAI), vol. 7603, pp. 267–281. Springer, Heidelberg (2012). https://doi.org/10.1007/978-3-642-33876-2_24. https://doi.org/10/gfkzwf
19. Regulation (EU) 2016/679 of the European parliament and of the council of 27 April 2016 on the protection of natural persons with regard to the processing of personal data and on the free movement of such data, and repealing directive 95/46/EC (general data protection regulation) (2016). http://eur-lex.europa.eu/legal-content/EN/TXT/?uri=OJ:L:2016:119:TOC
20. Tikkinen-Piri, C., Rohunen, A., Markkula, J.: EU general data protection regulation: changes and implications for personal data collecting companies. Comput. Law Secur. Rev. **34**(1), 134–153 (2018). https://doi.org/10/gc484m

Latent Relational Model
for Relation Extraction

Gaetano Rossiello[1(✉)], Alfio Gliozzo[2], Nicolas Fauceglia[2],
and Giovanni Semeraro[1]

[1] Department of Computer Science, University of Bari, Bari, Italy
gaetano.rossiello@uniba.it
[2] IBM Research AI, Yorktown Heights, NY, USA

Abstract. Analogy is a fundamental component of the way we think and process thought. Solving a word analogy problem, such as *mason* is to *stone* as *carpenter* is to *wood*, requires capabilities in recognizing the implicit relations between the two word pairs. In this paper, we describe the analogy problem from a computational linguistics point of view and explore its use to address relation extraction tasks. We extend a relational model that has been shown to be effective in solving word analogies and adapt it to the relation extraction problem. Our experiments show that this approach outperforms the state-of-the-art methods on a relation extraction dataset, opening up a new research direction in discovering implicit relations in text through analogical reasoning.

Keywords: Information extraction · Distributional semantics

1 Introduction

Relation Extraction (RE) is a very important capability of Natural Language Processing (NLP) systems. It identifies semantic relations between pre-identified entities in text. RE is particularly useful for Knowledge Base Population (KBP), which is the task of populating Knowledge Bases (KBs) whose schemata have been previously defined by a set of types and relations exploiting information from a text corpus, as well as for building KBs from scratch. For instance, if the target relation is presidentOf, a RE system should be able to detect an occurrence of this relation between the entities DONALD TRUMP and UNITED STATES in the sentence *"Trump issued a presidential memorandum for the US"*.

Several methodologies have been proposed to face the RE problem [1,10–12,18,20,21,26,27]. Recently, [6,15,32] propose neural-based models in an end-to-end fashion through increasingly complex architectures.

Although the neural-based RE approaches show good performance, we contend that they present two limitations. First, they do not fit well for limited domains, where only few seed examples are available. Complex architectures have many parameters, therefore they require a considerable amount of training data in order to learn good representations. It is not surprising, because these

© Springer Nature Switzerland AG 2019
P. Hitzler et al. (Eds.): ESWC 2019, LNCS 11503, pp. 283–297, 2019.
https://doi.org/10.1007/978-3-030-21348-0_19

approaches completely rely on the power of deep neural networks that consist of a blind feature learning without considering the linguistic and cognitive insights that this problem requires. Furthermore, the generalization capability of these approaches is limited to the relation types seen during the training phase, thus they are not applicable to discover relations in new domains or in building a new relational data source from scratch.

We approach the RE task from a different angle by addressing it as an analogy problem. Solving analogies, such as ITALY:ROME=FRANCE:PARIS, consists of identifying the implicit relations between two pairs of entities. The research hypothesis that we will be exploring throughout this work is that a method used to recognizing analogies can be useful to discover relations in text. In other words, relation extraction and word analogy are "two sides of the same coin".

These concerns lead to the following research questions: [**RQ1**] *How to address relation extraction as an analogy problem?* [**RQ2**] *Can a relational model be compared with the state-of-the-art RE methods?* In order to answer these questions, we propose an Analogy-based Relation Extraction System (ARES) by exploiting a relational model [28] which still holds the best scores in solving word analogies. Our method projects entity pairs in a relational vector space built by embedding the implicit properties which are observed in the text about how two entities are related.

In this paper, we formalize relation extraction as an analogy problem through its geometric interpretation in the relational vector space. We show that following this idea it is possible to face the RE in different scenarios (unsupervised, semi-supervised, supervised) through the same relational representations. Then, we measure the performance of our approach on a popular dataset designed for distantly supervised RE. The evaluation shows that ARES, with a simple linear classifier, outperforms the previously known approaches. This achievement opens up new promising research directions for relation extraction by exploiting analogical reasoning.

The paper is structured as follows: Section 2.1 describes the state-of-the-art and the recent progress in RE. In Sect. 2.2 we introduce the word analogy problem and the relative approaches. In Sect. 3 we describe ARES and we provide an evaluation of it in contrast with the most popular distant supervised RE approaches in Sect. 4. Section 5 concludes the paper, highlighting the possible new directions for RE.

2 Related Work

2.1 Relation Extraction

Given two entities e_1 and $_2$ that occur in a sentence S, Relation Extraction (RE) is the process to understand the meaning of S and extract a triple $r(e_1, e_2)$, where r represents the semantic relation between the two entities. In the literature several paradigms have been proposed to address the RE problem which differ in terms of input, output and technique adopted, such as pattern-based [10], bootstrapping [1], supervised [12,21,26] or OpenIE [18].

A promising idea, called *distant supervision* [20], consists in using existing KBs, like Freebase [2], as source of supervision without any human intervention. The pairs of entities that belong to a certain relation in the KB are linked with their surface forms in the textual corpus given as input. For each pair, all sentences in the corpus in which the two entities occur together are collected. However, the wrong labeling caused by the automatic matching between the entity pairs in the KB and in the textual content as well as the overlapping relations due to the intrinsic multi-graph structure of the KBs, require more complex training and prediction phases. This paradigm is commonly addressed as a multi-instance [23] and multi-label [11,27] classification task.

The deep neural network models proposed in [6,15,32] attempt to solve the multi-label and/or multi-instance setting in an end-to-end fashion through neural-based architectures with the aim to avoid the error propagation that could be raised by the use of lexical and syntactic tools for feature extraction.

Another method, so-called universal schema [24,30], faces RE by combining the OpenIE and KB relations. This method is related to our, in the sense that a pair-relation matrix is built, but it differs from the idea. Indeed, the goal of the universal schema is to address RE using a collaborative filtering approach typically adopted in recommender systems.

2.2 Word Analogy

The word analogy task, namely the proportional analogy between two word pairs such as $a : b = c : d$, has been popularized by [19] with the aim to show the capability of their neural-based model, so-called word2vec, in discovering the "linguistic regularities" just using vector offsets ($king - man + woman = queen$ is the most cited example). Several studies [14,16] have been proposed to deeply analyze the use of word embeddings and vector operations in attempting to achieve better performance on the same Google analogy dataset. The works in [5,31] explore the use of word vectors to model the semantic relations.

However, the word analogy task has been originally addressed by [29] who investigate several similarity measures on Scholastic Aptitude Test (SAT) dataset, composed of 374 multiple-choice analogy questions. Given *mason : stone*, this task consists of selecting the right analogy among 5 possible choices (*carpenter : wood* in this case). The authors provide an interesting argumentation regarding the different types of similarities, *attributional* and *relational*, and their use in facing the word analogy problem. The lesson learned is that the attributional similarity, typical of the word space models [13,22,25], is useful for synonyms detection, word sense disambiguation and so on. Instead, the relational similarity fits better in understanding word analogies. This intuition is confirmed by [3] who shows that word2vec is less effective on the SAT dataset. Conversely, the relational model proposed in [28] achieves a performance (56.1%) close to the human level (57.0%) on the same benchmark. Therefore, in this work we extend and adapt this relational model in order to address the relation extraction problem.

3   Methodology

In this section we present ARES and we explore its use to face the RE problem through analogical reasoning. First, we describe the Latent Relational Model (LRM), the foundation of our method. Then, we show that an extensional representation of the relations can be provided through the geometric interpretation of analogy between entity pairs. Finally, we explore the application of ARES to different RE scenarios.

3.1   Latent Relational Model

LRM provides an intensional representation of relations by embedding the implicit properties observed in the text about how two entities are related. This idea relies on the *distributional hypothesis* [9] which finds its roots in psychology, linguistics and statistical semantics: *"linguistic items with similar distributions have similar meanings"*.

Given a textual corpus T, the aim is to build a vocabulary V, composed of the unique entity pairs extracted from T, and a lookup table $M^{n,k}$, with $n = |V|$, consisting of k-dimensional latent relational vectors associated to each element of V. The idea to build a relational vector space model was originally proposed in [28,29] to solve a word analogy task. We extend and adapt it to address the RE problem. The main differences concern the use of an entity-entity vocabulary, instead of a word-word one, and a different way to extract the contexts around a pair as explained in the following paragraphs.

Entity Pair Vocabulary. Given a textual corpus T, the first step is to build a vocabulary $V = \{(X_1, Y_1), \ldots, (X_n, Y_n)\}$, where (X_i, Y_i) are the distinct entity pairs that occur together at least in one sentence. The question is how to identify the atomic lexical units in T that are considered as entities (X_i, Y_i). This can be done in different ways based on the specific RE scenario. For instance, in an unsupervised RE a Named Entity Recognizer (NER) or, more generally, a noun phrase chunker can be adopted. It depends from the types of relations to be extracted. In a distant supervised RE, V can be built using entities coming from the KB linked in the text.

Entity Pair Contexts. Once the vocabulary V is built, the next step is to extract the contexts around each entity pair when they occur together into the same sentences across the corpus T. A careful choice of the contexts is fundamental because they are the properties that define the intensional representation of a relation. Differently from [28,29], we adopt a richer set of lexical and syntactical features extracted from each sentence as proposed in [20].

Given an entity pair, from each sentence in which the pair occurs we extract:

1. The entity types provided by the NER;
2. The sequence of words between the two entities;

3. The part-of-speech tags of these words;
4. A flag indicating which entity came first;
5. An n-gram to the left of the first entity;
6. An n-gram to the right of the second entity;
7. A dependency path between the two entities.

If an entity pair occur in more than one sentence, we collect the features extracted from each sentence into a single bag. It should be noted that this may involve the wrong labeling issue using a distant supervised approach, which requires a multi-instance setting to be addressed [23]. Instead, in our model the context aggregation helps to provide a more accurate intensional representation of the relations between an entity pair.

Relational Vector Space Model. In this step a sparse matrix $X^{n,m}$ is built by mapping the n entity pairs in V to the rows and the m distinct features/contexts extracted in the previous step to the columns. Each element $X_{i,j}$ represents the weight of the j-th context in relation to the i-th entity pair. This weight might be computed using different well-known weighing schemes in information retrieval [4] and distributional semantic models [13], such as binary, tf-idf, entropy and so on. Indeed, our *pair-context* matrix is the relational version of the classic *document-term* or *term-term* vector space models.

There is not a theoretical motivation about which weighing schema is better: the choice is empirical, and depends on the specific purpose and on the distribution of the information in the textual corpus. In our experiments we found that when applied to the RE task, tf-idf weights tend to produce more precise results, while the binary schema achieves a recall-oriented performance.

Matrix Factorization. Since $X^{n,m}$ is a highly sparse matrix, this representation is not able to catch the implicit meaning across the textual contexts which express the same semantics. For instance, the phrases *"A is the author of B"* and *"C wrote D"* have the same meaning w.r.t. the relation `authorOf`, but the patterns *"is the author of"* and *"wrote"* are represented as separate features in X. As consequence, the vectors related to the pairs (A,B) and (C,D) in X are orthogonal even if they convey the same concept. In line with [4,13,28], we address this issue by applying Singular Value Decomposition (SVD) to the sparse matrix X.

SVD decomposes a matrix X into a product of three matrices $U\Sigma V^T$, where $U^T U = I = V^T V$ and Σ is a diagonal matrix of sorted singular values having the same rank r of X. Let Σ_k, with $k \ll r$, be the truncated version of Σ by considering only the first k singular values, the SVD finds the best matrix $X_k = U_k \Sigma_k V_k^T$ by minimizing the cost function $||X - X_k||_F$. We adopt the fast and scalable algorithm proposed in [8].

Thus, the SVD applied to X produces a low-rank approximation of X:

$$X \approx X_k = U_k \Sigma_k V_k^T \tag{1}$$

where k is a hyper-parameter. For our purpose, we are mainly interested in the matrices $(U_k \Sigma_k)^{n,k}$ and $V^{k,m}$. Indeed, the lookup table $M^{n,k}$ that we are looking for is obtained by:

$$M^{n,k} = (U_k \Sigma_k)^{n,k} \tag{2}$$

Each i-th row in M is a k-dimensional latent relational vector associated to each entity pair in V. SVD allows to take into account the global distribution of the pair contexts in the corpus and to *understand* the implicit relationships among them. This latent information is embedded into the k-dimensional dense vectors.

On the other hand, $V^{k,m}$ contains the latent vectors of each m feature/context. Thus, the SVD has the big advantage of projecting the pairs and the contexts into the same vector space. The role of $V^{k,m}$ is crucial for two reasons. Firstly, in a supervised RE the k-dimensional vectors of new entity pairs in the test set are obtained by $M^{n,k} = X V_k^T$ without retraining the SVD. However, the most interesting aspect regards *transfer learning* domain adaptation: the SVD can be applied to a pair-context matrix X^{Web} build on a large web scale corpus, so V_k^{Web} condenses a rich prior knowledge that can be infused into a new domain just using a matrix multiplication [7].

Finally, many other techniques can be applied to solve the sparsity issue, such as Non-negative Matrix Factorization (NMF) or deep neural network, like Auto-Encoders (AE) that learn latent representation through a non-linear dimensionality reduction. A comprehensive comparison of all these methods as well as the application of transfer learning for domain adaptation are out of the scope of this work, but, surely, they represent a very promising directions for future investigations.

3.2 Geometric Interpretation of Analogy

Through LRM, each entity pair occurring in the corpus is projected into a relational vector space, therefore it is possible to exploit its geometric interpretation to measure similarities between entity pairs. Thus, we can assert that there is an *analogy* between two pairs of entities (A, B) and (C, D) iff their latent vectors are close in the relational vector space. For instance, we can measure this proximity with the angle between the relational vectors using the cosine similarity.

Formally, given $r_{(A,B)}$ and $r_{(C,D)}$ the relational vectors in M related to the entity pairs (A, B) and (C, D):

$$A : B = C : D \Leftrightarrow cosine(r_{(A,B)}, r_{(C,D)}) > t \tag{3}$$

where

$$cosine(r_{(A,B)}, r_{(C,D)}) = \frac{r_{(A,B)} \bullet r_{(C,D)}}{||r_{(A,B)}|| \cdot ||r_{(C,D)}||} \tag{4}$$

and t is a threshold that establishes the breadth of the analogy between the two pairs.

This intensional representation of the relations well models the fuzzy meaning of *relation* between two entities. In fact, let us first consider the boundary cases with the cosine similarity equal to 1 and 0. If 1 it means that (A, B) and (C, D)

share exactly the same properties observed in the text, therefore the pairs are strictly analogous. Instead, the value 0 means that their vectors are orthogonal, so we can state that the pairs are not analogous at all[1]. However, since the range of the cosine is $[-1, 1]$, infinite degrees of analogy might be defined between two entity pairs, and this aspect depends on the value of the threshold t in Eq. (3).

This is useful to define the granularity of the type of a relation: higher values of t mean fine-grained relations, otherwise lower values mean relations that are more inclusive and coarse-grained. For instance, given the following sentences: (1) ROME *is the capital of* ITALY; (2) *The capital of* FRANCE *is* PARIS; (3) BROOKLYN *is a borough of* NEW YORK. Into a hypothetical vector space, the latent vectors $r_{(Italy,Rome)}$ and $r_{(France,Paris)}$ are close because they share the same context *"capital of"*. On the other hand, $r_{(NewYork,Brooklyn)}$ is farther to the other two vectors, but it is not orthogonal because the concept of *"borough of"* is semantically related, in some way, to *"capital of"*. Indeed, both patterns *"borough of"* and *"capital of"* express the meaning of inclusion between two locations. Therefore, we can say that ITALY:ROME=FRANCE:PARIS. But what about ITALY:ROME=NEW YORK:BROOKLYN? This depends on the granularity of the relation that we are taking into account. If we want to model the relation `capital`, then we can say that (ITALY, ROME) and (NEW YORK, BROOKLYN) are not analogous. Instead, the result changes if we imagine a coarse-grained relation like `contains`. The different scopes of `capital` and `contains` depend on the value of the threshold t.

3.3   Relation Extraction as Analogy Problem

Our aim is to use the geometric interpretation of analogy in attempting to emulate the task in identifying tuples in texts that share the same relations. Formally, given as input a textual corpus T and a semantic relation R, the problem of RE is to extract all pairs of entities that have the relation R in the corpus. Therefore, the output of RE is an extensional representation of the relation R by listing all entity pairs in the corpus that belong to R. The question is: how is R defined in T? Let us consider M_T as the LRM built on the corpus T. Based on the geometric interpretation of analogy described in Sect. 3.2, we can define the relation R in an extensional way through the intensional vector representations in M_T as follow:

Definition 1. *A semantic relation R is a region in a relational vector space M_T that outlines the boundaries among those entity-pair vectors that are analogous to each other.*

Since computing the analogy, hence the similarity, of all possible combination of the entity pair vectors is infeasible, RE is reduced to an optimization problem in finding the boundaries of that *region* in M_T. In the next paragraphs we show the use of ARES to address the different RE scenarios.

---

[1] Based on the world described in the textual corpus.

Unsupervised Relation Extraction. In absence of training examples, a clustering algorithm can be applied on M_T in order to find $C_1 \dots C_n$ centroids. For instance, the k-means or DBSCAN algorithms can be used depending on if we want to fix or not the number of the centroids. A centroid C_i represents the relational vector that condenses the *meaning* of a relation R_i. Thus, given the relational vectors of the entity pairs in M_T, the relation R_i in the corpus T is defined as follow:

$$R_i = \{(A, B) \mid cosine(r_{(A,B)}, C_i) > t\} \tag{5}$$

The value of t is user-defined parameter that determines the scope of the region around the centroid vector and so the granularity of the relation R_i.

Semi-supervised Relation Extraction. ARES can be adopted also when a small set of few seed pairs that express a relation R is provided as input. Let $R_I = \{(X_1, Y_1), \dots, (X_n, Y_n)\}$ a set of seed pairs with n small, then the centroid vector is obtained by averaging the relational vectors in M_T related to each input pair as follow:

$$C_{R_I} = \frac{1}{n} \sum_{i=1}^{n} r_{(X_i, Y_i)} \tag{6}$$

In this few-shot setting, ARES can be applied in an information retrieval style by finding the nearest neighbors of the centroid C_{R_I} used as a query. Thus, the pairs of entities in the corpus T that have the relation R are extracted as follow:

$$R_O = \{(A, B) \mid cosine(r_{(A,B)}, C_{R_I}) > t\} \tag{7}$$

The entity pairs are ranked based on the similarity with the centroid/query C_{R_I} and a user can fix the value of t in order to cut the pairs that have a similarity below that threshold.

Supervised Relation Extraction. In a supervised RE setting a bigger training set of seed entity pairs is available. In particular, the distant supervision ensures a large amount of training data by exploiting existing relational data sources, like Freebase, without any human intervention. Since an entity pair can belong to more relations at the same time, the distant supervised RE is commonly addressed as a multi-label classification task where each relation is a class.

In this setting, ARES exploits the training set in order to find that *region* where the entity-pair vectors are analogous to each other, as stated in Definition (1). For instance, a Support Vector Machine (SVM) classifier trained on the relational vectors of the entity pairs in the training set finds a hyperplane into the hyperspace defined by M_T. In fact, the hyperplane splits the region into the vector space M_T by grouping the analogous entity pair vectors for a specific relation. During the test phase, a new entity pair is projected into M_T and the classifier predict at which region the new instance belong.

4   Experiment

This section describes our evaluation by providing a comparison with the state-of-the-art methods and a further analysis in order to show the flexibility of our approach.

4.1   Experimental Setting

We evaluate ARES on the real-world dataset NYT10 [23], that is commonly used by the community to evaluate the distant supervised RE methods. This dataset was created by aligning Freebase tuples with the New York Times (NYT) corpus from the years 2005–2007.

We adopt the original held-out setting that consists of 51 relations/classes. The training set has 4700 positive and 63596 negative relation instances. While the test set has 1950 positive and 94917 negative examples. We build our LRM using only the sentences in the training set. For LRM we adopt the binary weights and we fix to 2000 the dimension of the relational vectors. The pair contexts are extracted as explained in Sect. 3.1.

We train a set of linear SVM on LRM in a *one-vs-rest* multi-label setting with a penalty equal to 10, chosen with a 3-fold stratified cross validation on the training set. In the prediction phase, we first project the unseen entity pairs into the latent space using LRM as described in Sect. 3.1, then we predict the scores for each relations/classes based on the decision functions of the SVMs.

We evaluate the performance using Precision-Recall curve and P@n metrics. However, during our experiments we tried also other non-linear functions, such as polynomial and rbf kernels, and a Multi-Layer Perceptron (MLP) with a sigmoid function as last layer to avoid the *one-vs-rest* strategy. These classifiers show more stable performance across the classes compared with a linear SVM when learned on our LRM. However, using a simple classifier, without many (hyper)parameters, allow us to evaluate more easily the quality of our relational representations, that is the *research question* of this study.

4.2   Results and Discussion

We compare ARES with the popular feature-based and neural-based distant supervised RE approaches. **MINTZ++** [20] is the first distant supervised method for open domain KB that uses a logistic regression classifier. We adopt the multi-label version. **MIML-RE** [27] is a multi-instance multi-label approach using a probabilistic graphical model to address the wrong labeling issue. **PCNN+ONE** [32] uses a convolutional neural network for sentence representations with the *at-least-one* strategy for multi-instance. **PCNN+ATT** [15] improves the previous deep architecture by adding a sentence-level attention to face the multi-instance learning.

Figure 1 shows the precision-recall curves of each model. The curves proof clearly that our approach outperforms consistently all the state-of-the-art methods with a particular emphasis on the boosted precision at the first part of the

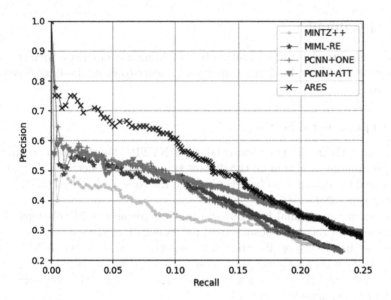

Fig. 1. Precision-Recall curves comparison on NYT10 dataset.

Table 1. Precision values for the top extracted entity pairs.

	P@10	P@100	P@1000	AvgPr
MINTZ++	0.55	0.46	0.32	0.08
MIML-RE	0.64	0.55	0.34	0.10
PCNN+ONE	0.64	0.55	0.33	0.10
PCNN+ATT	0.64	0.55	**0.37**	0.12
ARES (only syntactical)	0.38	0.55	0.29	0.10
ARES (only lexical)	**0.82**	0.66	0.33	0.13
ARES	0.70	**0.68**	0.36	**0.14**

curve. Table 1 shows this aspect with more detail. In fact, ARES achieves a P@100 equal to 0.68, while the other multi-instance methods obtain 0.55.

However, this improvement remains constant along the curve as showed by the average precision in Table 1. ARES achieves these performances just using a simple linear classifier against more complex deep learning architectures. Therefore, our latent relational vectors promote the generalization capability of a classifier. We performed an ablation test over the lexical and syntactical features groups and their combination. As showed in Table 1, the SVM classifier trained only on the lexical group has an average precision very close to that obtained by training the classifier on the full set of features. This result suggests that our approach can be applied also on web-scale corpora since the extraction of the lexical features can be done efficiently.

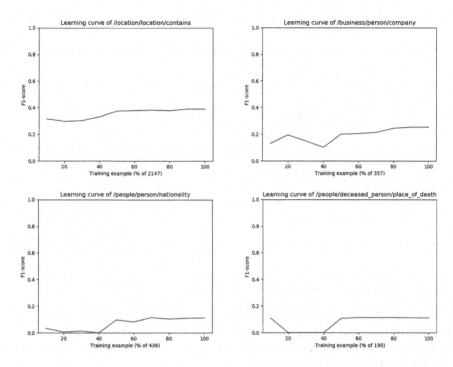

Fig. 2. Learning curves by training the SVMs on different size on the training set.

Moreover, this dataset is highly unbalanced, therefore an end-to-end model trained on this setting tends to overfit on the most frequent relations, like `contains`, and provides a poor representation for the others. Our model alleviates the overfitting because LRM learns the entity pairs vectors in a unsupervised way by taking in account the global distribution of the contexts across the entire corpus. That means better representations also for those relations with few examples, therefore better generalization capability for the classifier.

To confirm this aspect, Fig. 2 shows the learning curves obtained by training the SVMs on different size of training set. We performed this analysis on four frequent relations of the NTY10 dataset by randomly choosing the different buckets of the training instances for each relation. For relations, such as `contains` and `company`, our model reaches almost the best F1-scores just using about the 20% of training examples.

However, it is worth to note that the attention mechanism of PCNN+ATT shows a robust behavior when the recall increases. This suggests that a combination of our LRM with deep neural networks represents an interesting direction for future investigations.

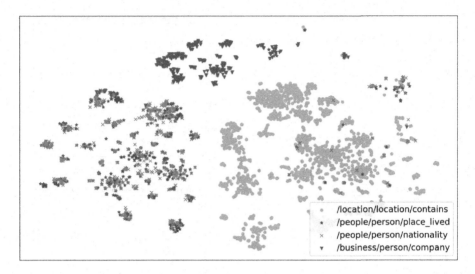

Fig. 3. 2D visualization, using t-SNE [17], of entity pair embeddings learned on the textual corpus of the NYT10 [23] dataset. Each point represents an entity pair vector learned from text through LRM. The entity pairs are aligned with the relation types in Freebase. Each marker represents a different relation type. The distribution of the entity pair embeddings in the vector space approximates the relational structure of the knowledge graph. (Color figure online)

4.3 Unsupervised Relational Analysis

Since LRM is an unsupervised model we can exploit the relational vectors to understand the distribution of the relations in a given textual corpus. Figure 3 shows the 2D projection of the relational representations using t-SNE [17] a techniques used to visualize high-dimensional embeddings. We built a LRM on the whole NYT10 corpus (train+test) and each point in the space is a entity pair vector. For instance, a (red) point marker in Fig. 3 refers to an instance of the relation `location/location/contains`, such as (NEW YORK, BROOKLYN).

Since the entity pairs are aligned with those in Freebase, we can label them with their relations used as ground truth. As we can see from the figure, the distribution of the entity pair clusters is very close to the ground truth. For instance, the cluster consisting of the (purple) triangle markers represents a group of entity pair vectors with well-defined boundaries and with a strong overlap with the instances of the relation `business/person/company`. Similar behavior occurs for the (red) point markers and the instances of the relation `location/location/contains`. This shows that the LRM is able to produce latent vectors for each entity pair, learned from a corpus, which approximate the relational structure of a knowledge graph like Freebase.

However, there is a strong overlap for certain relations, such as people/person/nationality and people/person/place_lived. In fact, they are strongly related, but this does not necessary mean that LRM provides poor representations. Instead, we can conclude that the properties in the text are not enough to discriminate the semantics of these relations, hence those in overlap can be removed or merged. In summary, this study shows that LRM is a flexible tool, e.g., also to analyze a corpus and to establish if it is proper or not in application to distant supervision paradigm.

5   Conclusion and Future Work

In this work we explored the use of analogical reasoning to address the problem of extracting relations from textual corpora. We extended a model proposed to solve word analogies in order to provide relational representations that have been proven to be effective for a relation extraction system. Indeed, our approach, using a simple linear classifier, achieves promising results when compared with state-of-the-art deep neural-based models. In our research agenda, we plan to learn non-linear relational representations from text using unsupervised deep neural networks, such as auto-encoders, as well as to explore the use of analogy in transfer learning in order to address more challenging problems, such as domain adaption and automatic ontology construction.

Acknowledgement. This work was conducted during an internship at the IBM Thomas J. Watson Research Center in Yorktown Heights, NY, USA. We thank Anastas Stoyanovsky, Steven Pritko and Gabe Hart, software engineers at the IBM Watson Groups in Pittsburgh and Denver, USA, for helping and inspiring us during the "Fast Domain Adaptation in IBM Watson Discovery" project.

References

1. Agichtein, E., Gravano, L.: Snowball: extracting relations from large plain-text collections. In: ACM DL, pp. 85–94 (2000)
2. Bollacker, K.D., Evans, C., Paritosh, P., Sturge, T., Taylor, J.: Freebase: a collaboratively created graph database for structuring human knowledge. In: SIGMOD Conference, pp. 1247–1250. ACM (2008)
3. Church, K.W.: Word2vec. Nat. Lang. Eng. **23**(1), 155–162 (2017)
4. Deerwester, S.C., Dumais, S.T., Landauer, T.K., Furnas, G.W., Harshman, R.A.: Indexing by latent semantic analysis. JASIS **41**(6), 391–407 (1990)
5. Gladkova, A., Drozd, A., Matsuoka, S.: Analogy-based detection of morphological and semantic relations with word embeddings: what works and what doesn't. In: SRW@HLT-NAACL, pp. 8–15. The Association for Computational Linguistics (2016)
6. Glass, M., Gliozzo, A., Hassanzadeh, O., Mihindukulasooriya, N., Rossiello, G.: Inducing implicit relations from text using distantly supervised deep nets. In: Vrandečić, D., et al. (eds.) ISWC 2018. LNCS, vol. 11136, pp. 38–55. Springer, Cham (2018). https://doi.org/10.1007/978-3-030-00671-6_3

7. Gliozzo, A.M., Strapparava, C.: Semantic Domains in Computational Linguistics. Springer, Heidelberg (2009). https://doi.org/10.1007/978-3-540-68158-8
8. Halko, N., Martinsson, P., Tropp, J.A.: Finding structure with randomness: probabilistic algorithms for constructing approximate matrix decompositions. SIAM Review **53**(2), 217–288 (2011)
9. Harris, Z.: Distributional structure. Word **10**(23), 146–162 (1954)
10. Hearst, M.A.: Automatic acquisition of hyponyms from large text corpora. In: COLING, pp. 539–545 (1992)
11. Hoffmann, R., Zhang, C., Ling, X., Zettlemoyer, L.S., Weld, D.S.: Knowledge-based weak supervision for information extraction of overlapping relations. In: ACL, pp. 541–550. The Association for Computer Linguistics (2011)
12. Jiang, J., Zhai, C.: A systematic exploration of the feature space for relation extraction. In: HLT-NAACL, pp. 113–120. The Association for Computational Linguistics (2007)
13. Landauer, T.K., Foltz, P.W., Laham, D.: An introduction to latent semantic analysis. Discourse Processes **25**(2–3), 259–284 (1998)
14. Levy, O., Goldberg, Y.: Linguistic regularities in sparse and explicit word representations. In: CoNLL, pp. 171–180. ACL (2014)
15. Lin, Y., Shen, S., Liu, Z., Luan, H., Sun, M.: Neural relation extraction with selective attention over instances. In: ACL. The Association for Computer Linguistics (2016)
16. Linzen, T.: Issues in evaluating semantic spaces using word analogies. In: RepEval@ACL, pp. 13–18. Association for Computational Linguistics (2016)
17. Maaten, L., Hinton, G.: Visualizing data using t-SNE. J. Mach. Learn. Res. **9**(Nov), 2579–2605 (2008)
18. Mausam, Schmitz, M., Soderland, S., Bart, R., Etzioni, O.: Open language learning for information extraction. In: EMNLP-CoNLL, pp. 523–534. ACL (2012)
19. Mikolov, T., Sutskever, I., Chen, K., Corrado, G.S., Dean, J.: Distributed representations of words and phrases and their compositionality. In: NIPS, pp. 3111–3119 (2013)
20. Mintz, M., Bills, S., Snow, R., Jurafsky, D.: Distant supervision for relation extraction without labeled data. In: ACL/IJCNLP, pp. 1003–1011. The Association for Computer Linguistics (2009)
21. Nguyen, T.H., Grishman, R.: Relation extraction: perspective from convolutional neural networks. In: VS@HLT-NAACL, pp. 39–48. The Association for Computational Linguistics (2015)
22. Pennington, J., Socher, R., Manning, C.D.: Glove: global vectors for word representation. In: EMNLP, pp. 1532–1543. ACL (2014)
23. Riedel, S., Yao, L., McCallum, A.: Modeling relations and their mentions without labeled text. In: Balcázar, J.L., Bonchi, F., Gionis, A., Sebag, M. (eds.) ECML PKDD 2010. LNCS (LNAI), vol. 6323, pp. 148–163. Springer, Heidelberg (2010). https://doi.org/10.1007/978-3-642-15939-8_10
24. Riedel, S., Yao, L., McCallum, A., Marlin, B.M.: Relation extraction with matrix factorization and universal schemas. In: HLT-NAACL, pp. 74–84. The Association for Computational Linguistics (2013)
25. Sahlgren, M.: An introduction to random indexing (2005)
26. Sun, L., Han, X.: A feature-enriched tree kernel for relation extraction. In: ACL, vol. 2, pp. 61–67. The Association for Computer Linguistics (2014)
27. Surdeanu, M., Tibshirani, J., Nallapati, R., Manning, C.D.: Multi-instance multi-label learning for relation extraction. In: EMNLP-CoNLL, pp. 455–465. ACL (2012)

28. Turney, P.D.: Similarity of semantic relations. Comput. Linguist. **32**(3), 379–416 (2006)
29. Turney, P.D., Littman, M.L.: Corpus-based learning of analogies and semantic relations. Mach. Learn. **60**(1–3), 251–278 (2005)
30. Verga, P., McCallum, A.: Row-less universal schema. In: AKBC@NAACL-HLT, pp. 63–68. The Association for Computer Linguistics (2016)
31. Vylomova, E., Rimell, L., Cohn, T., Baldwin, T.: Take and took, gaggle and goose, book and read: evaluating the utility of vector differences for lexical relation learning. In: ACL. The Association for Computer Linguistics (2016)
32. Zeng, D., Liu, K., Chen, Y., Zhao, J.: Distant supervision for relation extraction via piecewise convolutional neural networks. In: EMNLP, pp. 1753–1762. The Association for Computational Linguistics (2015)

Mini-ME Swift: The First Mobile OWL Reasoner for iOS

Michele Ruta[✉], Floriano Scioscia, Filippo Gramegna, Ivano Bilenchi,
and Eugenio Di Sciascio

Polytechnic University of Bari, via E. Orabona 4, 70125 Bari, Italy
{michele.ruta,floriano.scioscia,filippo.gramegna,
ivano.bilenchi,eugenio.disciascio}@poliba.it

Abstract. Mobile reasoners play a pivotal role in the so-called Semantic Web of Things. While several tools exist for the Android platform, iOS has been neglected so far. This is due to architectural differences and unavailability of OWL manipulation libraries, which make porting existing engines harder. This paper presents Mini-ME Swift, the first Description Logics reasoner for iOS. It implements standard (Subsumption, Satisfiability, Classification, Consistency) and non-standard (Abduction, Contraction, Covering, Difference) inferences in an OWL 2 fragment. Peculiarities are discussed and performance results are presented, comparing Mini-ME Swift with other state-of-the-art OWL reasoners.

1 Introduction and Motivation

Semantic Web technologies have been increasingly adopted in resource-constrained volatile environments through the *Semantic Web of Things* (SWoT) [8,25], whose goal is embedding intelligence in pervasive contexts. Semantic Web languages underlie knowledge representation and interoperability in the SWoT, particularly the Resource Description Framework (RDF)[1] and the Web Ontology Language (OWL)[2]. Anyway, although mobile devices are even more powerful, porting existing Semantic Web inference engines to mobile operating systems is not a straightforward task and it may result in suboptimal performance. Among the challenges for the next decade of the Semantic Web, Bernstein *et al.* [3] outlined *"languages and architectures that will provide [. . .] knowledge to the increasingly mobile and application-based Web"*. More specifically, Yus and Pappachan [37] pointed out the *"lack of semantic reasoners for certain mobile operating systems (such as iOS)"* among the problems of developing semantic mobile apps. Several solutions are currently available for Android [4], due to its support for the Java language, allowing to port popular OWL manipulation

---

[1] RDF 1.1 Concepts and Abstract Syntax, W3C Recommendation 25 February 2014, https://www.w3.org/TR/rdf11-concepts/.

[2] OWL 2 Web Ontology Language Document Overview (Second Edition), W3C Recommendation 11 December 2012, https://www.w3.org/TR/owl2-overview/.

© Springer Nature Switzerland AG 2019
P. Hitzler et al. (Eds.): ESWC 2019, LNCS 11503, pp. 298–313, 2019.
https://doi.org/10.1007/978-3-030-21348-0_20

libraries. Conversely, the Apple iOS mobile platform has been neglected so far, due to differences in architecture and development tools.

Hence, this paper introduces *Mini-ME Swift*, the first Description Logics reasoner and matchmaker for iOS. It has been developed in Swift 4 language aiming to the Application Programming Interface (API) parity with the Java-based *Mini Matchmaking Engine* [26], though it has been designed and implemented from scratch to achieve significantly better performance. Logic expressiveness is limited to an OWL fragment corresponding to the $\mathcal{ALN}$ (Attributive Language with unqualified Number restrictions) Description Logic (DL) on acyclic Terminological boxes (TBoxes). It efficiently implements standard (Subsumption, Satisfiability, Classification, Consistency) and non-standard (Abduction, Contraction, Covering, Difference) inferences. A case study on semantic-enhanced Point of Interest (POI) discovery in Mobile Augmented Reality (MAR) has allowed validating the effectiveness and ease of integration of the proposed matchmaker in iOS apps. Architectural and optimization solutions have been assessed in an experimental campaign, comparing Mini-ME Swift with the Java-based Mini-ME as well as with four popular Semantic Web reasoners. Inference time and memory usage are reported on a conventional desktop testbed, and required computational resources have been evaluated on current mobile devices.

The remainder of the paper is as follows. Section 2 recalls essential background information and relevant related work. Mini-ME Swift design and optimization strategies are discussed in Sect. 3. Section 4 presents the case study, while performance assessment is in Sect. 5, before conclusions.

2   Background

Related Work. Due to architectural constraints and computational complexity of Description Logics reasoning, the majority of early mobile inference engines provided only rule processing for entailment materialization in a Knowledge Base (KB); proposals include *3APL-M* [11], *COROR* [31], *MiRE4OWL* [10], *Delta-Reasoner* [17] and the system in [27]. The μOR reasoner [1] adopts a resolution algorithm on the *OWL-Lite⁻* language, while *LOnt* [12] works on *DL Lite*, a subset of OWL-Lite. The mobile OWL2 RL engine in [36] exploits an optimization of the classic *RETE* algorithm for rule systems. More expressive DLs were supported by exploiting tableau algorithms: *Pocket KRHyper* [28] adopted the $\mathcal{ALCHIR}+$ DL, but memory limitations curbed the size and complexity of manageable KBs. Tableaux optimization was exploited in *mTableaux* [30] to reduce memory consumption. Fuzzy $\mathcal{ALN}(D)$ was supported in [21] via structural algorithms. Android is currently the most widespread mobile platform and Java is its primary application development language. The majority of state-of-the-art OWL reasoners runs on Java Standard Edition (SE) [14], mature Semantic Web language manipulation libraries are available such as *Jena* [15] and the *OWL API* [7]. Anyway, porting existing systems requires significant effort, due to architectural differences and incomplete support of Java SE class libraries under Android. Bobed *et al.* [4] met such barriers when porting *Hermit* [6],

JFact (a Java variant of *Fact++* [34]) and three other OWL reasoners to Android. Jena was ported by *AndroJena*[3], albeit with deep re-design and feature limitations. The *ELK* reasoner has an Android port [9] as well. To the best of our knowledge, no previous reasoner has supported iOS, preventing a relevant segment of users and application developers from exploiting semantic technologies effectively. In fact, a few semantic-based iOS apps and prototypes do exist, but they either exploit remote servers for reasoning [19,23,35] or precompute inferences on a conventional computer, storing results on the mobile device [20]. The iOS port of a subset of the OWL API [22] has enabled the development of Mini-ME Swift. From a performance optimization standpoint, *TrOWL* [33], *Konclude* [29] and other recent inference engines implement multiple different techniques and then select the best one according to the logical expressiveness of the particular KB and/or the required inference task. Konclude can also exploit parallel execution on multi-core processors and it has been the top performer in latest OWL DL reasoner competitions [18]. Nevertheless, SWoT application surveys [5,13] evidence inherently unpredictable contexts requiring mobile agents endowed with quick decision support, query answering and stream reasoning capabilities. Specific non-standard inference services may be more suitable than standard ones in those cases [26].

Inference Services. The proposed reasoner leverages polynomial-complexity structural algorithms exploiting KB preprocessing stages for concept *unfolding* and *Conjunctive Normal Form* (CNF) normalization through recursive procedures. In $\mathcal{ALN}$ CNF, every concept expression is either $\bot$ (*Bottom* a.k.a. *Nothing*) or the conjunction ($\sqcap$) of: (possibly negated) atomic concepts; greater-than ($\geq$) and less-than ($\leq$) number restrictions, no more than one per type per role; universal restrictions ($\forall$), no more than one per role, with filler recursively in CNF. As said, Mini-ME Swift supplies *standard Subsumption* and *Satisfiability*. In advanced scenarios they are not enough, as they provide only a Boolean answer. Therefore, *non-standard Concept Abduction* (CA) and *Concept Contraction* (CC) allow extending, respectively, (missed) subsumption and (un)satisfiability, in the Open World Assumption [26]. Based on CNF norm, they also provide a *penalty* metric evidencing a semantic distance ranking of KB instances (a.k.a. resources in matchmaking settings) w.r.t. a target individual (a.k.a. request). Mini-ME Swift further includes *Concept Difference* (CD) [32] to subtract information in a concept description from another one. While CA, CC and CD are useful in one-to-one discovery, matchmaking and negotiation scenarios, Mini-ME also includes the *Concept Covering Problem* (CCoP) non-standard inference for many-to-one composition of a set of elementary instances to answer complex requests [26]. Mini-ME Swift can be also exploited in more general knowledge-based applications, as it provides *Coherence* and *Classification* services over ontologies: Coherence is close to *Ontology Satisfiability*, but it does not process individuals [16]; Ontology Classification computes the overall concept taxonomy induced by the subsumption relation, from $\top$ (*Top* a.k.a. *Thing*) to $\bot$.

---

[3] AndroJena project page: https://github.com/lencinhaus/androjena.

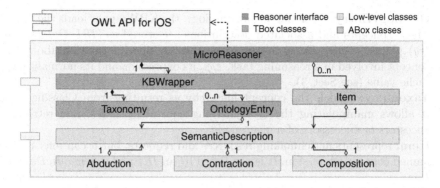

Fig. 1. Reasoner architecture

3 Description Logics Reasoning for iOS Devices

Reasoner Architecture. The proposed tool is written in Swift 4. It can be compiled as *iOS Framework*, *i.e.*, as dynamic linking library. It targets all iOS devices running system version 8 or later, and it also runs unmodified on macOS 10.11 and later. By leveraging the expressive power of the Swift language – particularly its functional features, such as *optionals*, *optional binding* and *higher order functions*[4] – the codebase is still compact, with a good readability. The reasoner architecture, in Fig. 1, has been kept purposefully simple to avoid unnecessary layers of abstraction and the associated overhead. Main components are described hereafter. Particularly, the **KBWrapper** and **SemanticDescription** classes implement most of the available reasoning tasks on ontologies and concept descriptions, respectively. The **MicroReasoner** class acts as a facade hiding the interactions between lower-level components. In detail:

- **OWL API for iOS:** is the port [22] of the OWL API to the iOS platform, providing support for parsing and manipulating OWL2 KBs in $\mathcal{ALEN}$ (Attributive Language with unqualified Existential and Number restrictions) DL with RDF/XML syntax.
- **MicroReasoner:** is the library entry point, exposing KB operations such as parsing the target ontology and loading/fetching instances to be used for matchmaking. It also exposes standard and non-standard inferences.
- **KBWrapper:** allows KB management, *i.e.*, creation of internal data structures and concept unfolding as well as Classification and Coherence check on ontologies.
  Storage, preprocessing and inference procedures on concept expressions are implemented by methods of different high-level data structures owned by the *KBWrapper*:

---

[4] Swift documentation: https://developer.apple.com/library/content/documentation/ Swift/Conceptual/Swift_Programming_Language.

- **OntologyEntry:** when parsing an ontology, the KBWrapper loads the TBox, whose concepts and associated descriptions are stored as (*IRI, OntologyEntry*) pairs. *OntologyEntry* instances encapsulate the information about any concept involved in a reasoning task, *e.g.*, its expression and its normalization cache value (see Sect. 3).
- **Taxonomy:** models the concept hierarchy as resulting from Classification. It allows manipulating the tree, merging equivalent nodes, and retrieving ancestors or successors of a given node.
- **Item:** represents matchmaking resources and requests, but it can refer to any named concept expression. It is composed by an *IRI* and a *SemanticDescription*.

  TBox and Assertion Box (ABox) manipulation and reasoning are supported by the following low-level data structure layer:
- **SemanticDescription:** models an $\mathcal{ALN}$ concept expression in CNF as conjunction of C_{CN}, $C_{\geq}$, $C_{\leq}$, $C_{\forall}$ components, stored in collections of *AtomicConcept*, *GreaterThanRole*, *LessThanRole* and *UniversalRole* Swift class instances, respectively.
- **Abduction, Contraction, Composition:** model the results of CA, CC and CCoP, respectively. *Abduction* and *Contraction* include a penalty score [26].

Optimization Strategies. Some of the lower-level optimizations in Mini-ME Swift have been achieved thanks to specific characteristics and implementation details of the programming language. The implicit use of *Copy on Write* (CoW) for Swift collections –transparent to the developer– has enabled a straightforward performance improvement in algorithms heavily relying on conditionally mutating collections (concept unfolding and normalization). Further benefits stem from the adoption of *structs* instead of classes for some of the lower-level data structures, since they are often allocated on the stack rather than on the heap. However, *Automatic Reference Counting* (ARC)[5] –the memory management strategy employed by the Swift compiler– sometimes would have led to performance degradation in critical code sections. As an example, one of the recursive tree traversal algorithms implemented in Mini-ME Swift originally spent about 80% of its total CPU time in *retain* and *release* function calls on the nodes of the tree. This has been addressed by leveraging *unmanaged references*[6] wherever needed. High-level optimization has also been carried out in order to improve both inference turnaround time and memory usage. Enhancements concern:

- **Ontology loading and preprocessing:** once Mini-ME Swift is instantiated, the target ontology is loaded into the internal data structures and preprocessed. At this stage, terminological equivalences are transitively unfolded and merged in single entries (*e.g.*, if $C \equiv D$ and $D \equiv E$, then $C \equiv D \equiv$

---

[5] Automatic reference counting documentation: https://developer.apple.com/library/content/documentation/Swift/Conceptual/Swift_Programming_Language/AutomaticReferenceCounting.html.

[6] Unmanaged references documentation: https://developer.apple.com/documentation/swift/unmanaged.

$E \equiv C \sqcap D \sqcap E$), saving memory and processing time. Furthermore, *told subsumption cycles* [34] are identified and marked in order to be efficiently solved while classifying. These are the only possible cyclic references supported by Mini-ME Swift. Finally, concept and role names are translated to internal numerical identifiers, allowing for more efficient storage and processing. In particular, memory addresses are exploited as IDs, leveraging the uniqueness of IRI in-memory instances obtained from the OWL API iOS port [22].

– **Concept unfolding and normalization:** the *unfolding* and *CNF normalization* algorithms were initially optimized by caching completely unfolded and normalized concepts. However, it soon became evident that caching could be extended to *intermediate unfolded concepts* as well: given an acyclic concept B, every other concept C recursively unfolded as part of the unfolding of B is also completely unfolded, making it suitable for caching. However, C is not yet in normal form, therefore the concept cache must keep track of whether stored concepts have been only unfolded or both unfolded and normalized. This strategy has two benefits: (i) it enables the reuse of the unfolded description of C as part of the normalization of further concepts; (ii) it minimizes computation when C needs to be normalized, since the unfolding step is executed just once.

– **Classification:** Mini-ME Swift adopts a variant of the *enhanced traversal* algorithm in [2], which also accounts for subsumption cycles detected while preprocessing the ontology. Subsumption check results are *cached*, as customary for OWL reasoners, though significant effort went in ensuring checks are avoided whenever possible: classification is performed according to the concept *definition order* [2], which allows skipping the *bottom search* step for primitive concepts having acyclic descriptions. The exploitation of *told disjoints* [34] and *told subsumers* has been implemented. Moreover, *synonym merging* (*e.g.*, if it is inferred that $B \equiv C$, then the taxonomy nodes for B and C are merged) reduces memory usage and search time by making the tree smaller.

– **Ontology Coherence:** a naive approach involves performing CNF normalization for every concept in the TBox [26]. However, earlier experimental results showed this process is time consuming (particularly for larger TBoxes). This could be smoothed by adopting forceful caching policies for unfolded concepts, albeit paying additional occupancy of memory. Mini-ME Swift sidesteps this problem by computing the Coherence check through a modified version of the Classification algorithm, which stops as soon as an unsatisfiable concept is detected. Since normalization is *lazy* –*i.e.*, it is computed only when needed for an inference task– and Classification explicitly avoids subsumptions as much as possible, the overall number of performed normalizations is also reduced. This results in significantly improved time and memory efficiency w.r.t. the naive approach. Furthermore, the Coherence check of a TBox $\mathcal{T}$ can be skipped in the following cases: (i) $\mathcal{T}$ is *trivially incoherent* if $\exists$ a concept expression C in $\mathcal{T} \mid C \sqsubseteq \bot$; (ii) $\mathcal{T}$ is *trivially coherent* if $\mathcal{T}$ contains no *disjoint concept* axioms and *number restrictions* are either absent or all of the same type (*i.e.*, either minimum or maximum cardinality).

Both conditions can be verified inexpensively while loading the KB, since this only entails checking whether given constructors are in the TBox.

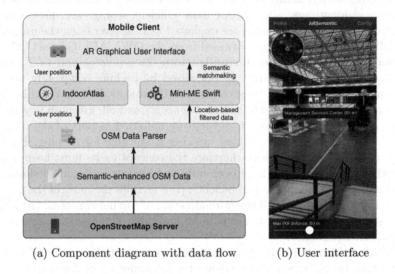

(a) Component diagram with data flow   (b) User interface

Fig. 2. MAR POI semantic discovery prototype

4   Case-Study: Semantic-Based POI Discovery in Augmented Reality

In order to validate the effectiveness and the ease of use of Mini-ME Swift in ubiquitous computing applications, the existing Android framework in [24] has been rewritten in Swift as a prototypical iOS app. The tool leverages crowd-sourced OpenStreetMap[7] (OSM) cartography, annotated exploiting Semantic Web technologies to provide POIs with rich structured descriptions. Figure 2a illustrates application components. The mobile client communicates with an OSM server, providing map elements enriched with formal machine-understandable metadata. The app uses Mini-ME Swift to execute semantic matchmaking [26] between an annotated user profile and POIs in the area surrounding user's location. Position is obtained from embedded smartphone devices, including accelerometer, compass and Wi-Fi trilateration. *IndoorAtlas*[8] toolkit, relying on the device magnetometer, provides accurate localization in indoor contexts. As shown in Fig. 2b, semantic matchmaking outcomes are displayed as color-coded markers in a MAR graphical UI leveraging *ARKit*[9] iOS library. Colors from green to red

---

[7] OpenStreetMap: https://www.openstreetmap.org/.

[8] IndoorAtlas: https://www.indooratlas.com/.

[9] Apple ARKit 2: https://developer.apple.com/arkit/.

represent semantic distance, from full to partial matches. The user can touch a marker to access result explanation, in terms of missing and/or conflicting characteristics between her profile and the POI. Due to lack of space, the reader is referred to [24] for details on the map annotation method and POI discovery algorithm. By following iOS developer guidelines, the integration of Mini-ME Swift, IndoorAtlas and ARKit has been straightforward.

Table 1. Dataset-wide times and min/max memory peak for Classification

		Fastest in # tests	Parsing Time (s)	Classification time (s)	Min Mem. Peak (MB)	Max Mem. Peak (MB)
Reasoners running on Mac Pro	Fact++	0	1507.92	430.61	81.00	3330.00
	HermiT	0	614.57	682.95	62.49	8547.68
	Konclude	351	132.04	89.60	14.10	3797.46
	TrOWL	0	621.35	401.79	54.74	4427.46
	Mini-ME Java	2	629.96	9841.24	58.15	11854.69
	Mini-ME Swift	948	209.10	60.28	5.92	1546.07
Mini-ME Swift on mobile devices	iPhone 7		180.15	83.78	15.11	1198.80
	iPad Mini 4		411.42	191.38	12.88	1182.57
	iPhone 5s		539.17	292.84	9.56	449.08

5   Experiments

An experimental evaluation of the proposed system has been carried out on desktop and mobile devices, for standard and non-standard inference services, by means of a bespoke test framework[10]. Desktop tests have been performed on a 2009 Mac Pro[11], while mobile experiments on an iPhone 7[12], an iPad Mini 4[13] and an iPhone 5s[14]. Correctness and completeness of inference services have been checked by comparing obtained results with other state-of-the-art reasoners, used as test oracles. Outcomes returned by Mini-ME Swift have been considered correct in case of unanimous match with all the oracles and incorrect

---

[10] Code and instructions available under the Eclipse Public License 1.0 at https://github.com/sisinflab-swot/owl-reasoner-test-framework.

[11] Dual Intel Xeon 5500 quad-core CPUs at 2.26 GHz clock frequency, 32 GB DDR3 RAM at 1066 MHz, 640 GB 7200 RPM HDD, OS X 10.11.6 El Capitan.

[12] Apple A10 CPU (2 high-performance cores at 2.34 GHz and 2 low-energy cores), 2 GB LPDDR4 RAM, 32 GB flash storage, iOS 10.1.1.

[13] Dual-core 1.5 GHz Apple A8 CPU, 2 GB LPDDR3 RAM, 16 GB flash storage, iOS 9.3.3.

[14] Dual-core 1.3 GHz Apple A7 CPU, 1 GB LPDDR3 RAM, 16 GB flash storage, iOS 10.3.2.

in case of no match; manual investigation has been performed for partial matches. Performance evaluation has been focused on turnaround time and peak memory usage for each inference task: results are the average of five repeated runs, with a timeout of 30 min for each run. Reported memory peak values represent the maximum resident set size (*MRSS*) for the process, extracted via *BSD time* on Mac, and equivalently through the *getrusage* POSIX call on mobile. The reader can refer to the Mini-ME Swift Web page[15] for getting the reasoner and in-depth documentation on how to reproduce the benchmarks reported hereafter.

5.1 Standard Inference Services

Ontology Classification and **Coherence** have been evaluated on a set of 1364 KBs, obtained from the 2014 *OWL Reasoner Evaluation Workshop* competition reference dataset[16] considering all the KBs supported by Mini-ME Swift (*e.g.*, having at most $\mathcal{ALN}$ as indicated expressiveness, without general concept inclusions and other unsupported logic constructors). The following reasoners have been used as test oracles of correctness and completeness, as well as references for performance comparison: Fact++ (version 1.6.5) [34], HermiT (1.3.8) [6], Konclude (0.6.2-544) [29], TrOWL (1.5) [33] and Mini-ME Java (2.0) [26]. Before presenting the results of the experimental campaign, it is important to point out that:

- Since Konclude can only parse ontologies in OWL functional syntax and Mini-ME Swift currently only supports the RDF/XML serialization, RDF/XML parsing has been restricted to Mini-ME Swift only, and every other reasoner has been configured to use the functional syntax. This is a worst-case scenario w.r.t. turnaround time, since in general the functional representation is shorter and easier to parse than the equivalent RDF/XML. This is evident in Fig. 3 particularly for the smallest and the largest ontologies, where data points for Mini-ME Swift appear shifted to the right.
- Mini-ME does not process the ABox when computing standard inferences, therefore Ontology Coherence has been informally compared to Consistency as supported by other reasoners, and mismatches have been manually analyzed in order to evaluate the correctness of the reasoner output.
- Since the coherence check is based on a modified version of the Classification algorithm (as stated in Sect. 3), the Ontology Coherence performance results are similar to Classification, hence they have not been reported here.

Correctness. Mini-ME Swift has classified all the 1364 ontologies correctly. The Coherence test has returned matching results for 1353 ontologies (99.2% of the dataset). The remaining 11 ontologies contain unsatisfiable classes with no instances, resulting in being considered incoherent by Mini-ME but consistent by other reasoners.

---

[15] http://sisinflab.poliba.it/swottools/minime-swift.
[16] http://dl.kr.org/ore2014.

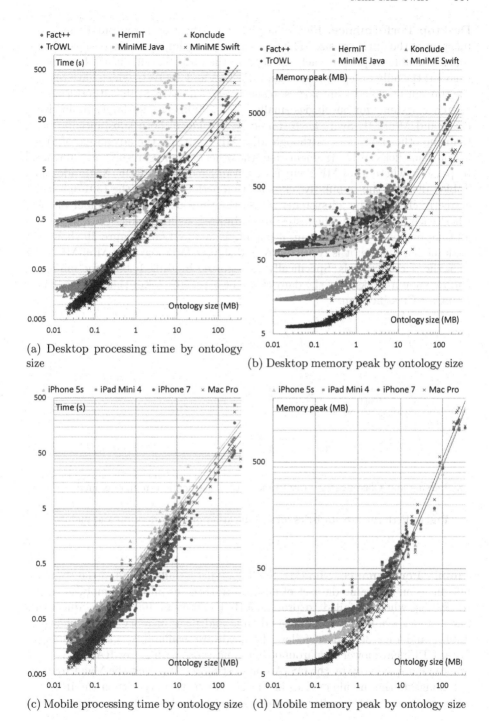

(a) Desktop processing time by ontology size

(b) Desktop memory peak by ontology size

(c) Mobile processing time by ontology size

(d) Mobile memory peak by ontology size

Fig. 3. Performance results for the classification task on desktop and mobile devices

Desktop Performance. Figure 3a plots Classification turnaround times as a function of the ontology size. The time axis scale is limited to 600 s since all reasoners are able to process each ontology in the dataset well within the imposed timeout; the only exceptions are Mini-ME Java and TrOWL, which have reached the timeout on 8 and 1 ontologies, respectively. Mini-ME Swift outperformed all reference systems for ontologies smaller than 200 kB ca.; for larger input, Konclude and Mini-ME Swift have similar performance, both substantially faster than the other reasoners. Although Mini-ME Swift has the advantage of focusing on a smaller OWL2 fragment than the other reasoners, results are influenced by parsing, where Mini-ME Swift is disadvantaged due to RDF/XML adoption. Table 1 displays the cumulative classification performance on the 1301 ontologies correctly classified by all systems within the timeout, and the number of cases where each reasoner was the fastest one; Mini-ME Swift exhibits the lowest overall time by a significant margin, if parsing is factored out. Figure 3b shows the peak memory usage: it is consistently and significantly lower for Mini-ME Swift than the reference tools. Specifically, as reported in Table 1, both the minimum and maximum peaks over the dataset are at least 50% lower than the next-best result for Classification.

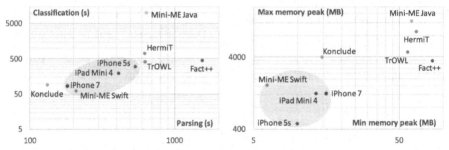

(a) Parsing and Classification: total time   (b) Classification: min/max memory peak

Fig. 4. Performance statistics for classification on both desktop and mobiles

Mobile Performance. Mini-ME Swift has successfully executed the standard inferences on the same dataset of desktop testbed for all tested mobiles except iPhone 5s, where it failed to process KBs larger than 100 MB ca. due to its low memory availability. Turnaround time and peak memory results shown in Table 1 and Figs. 3c and 3d follow the hardware availability, *i.e.*, devices with faster CPUs have lower turnaround times and those with larger RAM have been granted more memory by the OS. An interesting result is that the Mac Pro, plotted alongside the mobile devices in Fig. 3c, has been quicker than the iPhone 7 when reasoning over smaller ontologies, but it has been clearly outperformed starting from medium-sized ones. This is likely due to the implemented algorithms being single-threaded, not exploiting the higher level of parallelism in the desktop CPU w.r.t. mobile ones. Furthermore, Fig. 3d shows lower memory peaks for small ontologies on the Mac Pro: since all iOS applications must have a graphical user interface, mobile tests are affected by a systematic memory overhead w.r.t. tests executed through command line interface on the Mac[17]. In order to provide further insight, Fig. 4 compares all reasoners (on workstation and mobile) on the whole set of KBs which have been correctly processed by all tools. The area with blue background encloses Mini-ME Swift instances running on desktop and mobile devices. In Fig. 4a inference tasks are split in ontology parsing and actual reasoning; the overall time spent in each step is displayed on the axes. Figure 4b shows on both the axes the lowest and highest memory peak values across the whole dataset. Although iPhone 5s maximum peak value is biased by failed tests, the overall results highlight Mini-ME Swift has a comparatively low memory footprint.

Table 2. Features of KBs used for non-standard tests and memory peak (MB)

		Toy	Agriculture	Building	MatchAndDate
Ontology features	Size (kB)	30.43	128.35	142.08	590.54
	#concepts	48	134	180	157
	#roles	8	17	27	11
	#instances	7	16	29	100
	#matchmaking	28	48	493	10000
Memory peak (MB)	Mac Pro (Java)	53.48	68.72	75.46	130.40
	Mac Pro (Swift)	6.26	6.78	6.98	8.55
	iPhone 7	15.76	16.09	18.09	19.22
	iPad Mini 4	14.72	14.22	14.36	16.16
	iPhone 5s	9.60	9.97	10.05	12.37

5.2 Non-standard Inference Services

Non-standard inference services have been evaluated on four $\mathcal{ALN}$ KBs. Their features are summarized in the upper section of Table 2: size, number of concepts, roles, instances and number of matchmaking tasks to be performed in the tests, where each task has been executed on a ⟨*request, resource*⟩ pair involving the following steps: (i) resource and request are checked for compatibility; (ii) if they are compatible, CA is performed; otherwise CC is executed, followed by CA on the compatible part of the request [26]. Mini-ME Java has been used as

---

[17] Mobile tests could have been run from command line interface by *jailbreaking* iOS devices. This has been avoided, in order to assess performance in the standard iOS configuration.

test oracle and reference for performance comparison, because other reasoners evaluated in Sect. 5.1 do not provide Concept Abduction and Contraction.

Correctness. Mini-ME Swift has correctly performed the CA and CC tests for all the pairs of individuals in the test set.

Performance. As shown in Fig. 5 (average time per matchmaking task) and the lower section of Table 2 (memory peak), Mini-ME Swift significantly outperforms its Java counterpart on the desktop. Memory usage is an order of magnitude lower, also due to the overhead induced by the Java Virtual Machine.

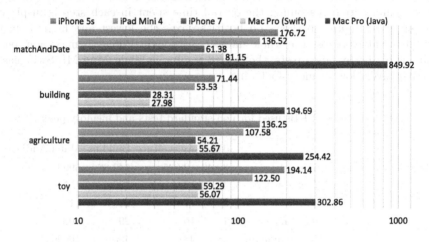

Fig. 5. Average time per matchmaking task (μs)

6   Conclusion and Future Work

The paper introduced Mini-ME Swift, the first OWL reasoner for iOS. It runs natively on iOS for SWoT scenarios, as well as on macOS for classical Semantic Web use cases, providing standard and non-standard inference services. Several optimization techniques have allowed for satisfactory time and memory performance, as evidenced in a comparative assessment with popular Semantic Web reasoners on desktop and mobile testbeds.

Future work concerns the extension of the supported logic language with concrete domains and $\mathcal{EL}$ (Existential Languages) family. Furthermore, implementing an OWL functional syntax parser will enable performance improvements. Concerning the prototype in Sect. 4, early investigations are ongoing on the integration of semantic-enhanced navigation by embedding inferences within the *GraphHopper* routing engine for iOS[18].

---

[18] GraphHopper iOS port: https://github.com/graphhopper/graphhopper-ios.

References

1. Ali, S., Kiefer, S.: μOR – a micro OWL DL reasoner for ambient intelligent devices. In: Abdennadher, N., Petcu, D. (eds.) GPC 2009. LNCS, vol. 5529, pp. 305–316. Springer, Heidelberg (2009). https://doi.org/10.1007/978-3-642-01671-4_28

2. Baader, F., Hollunder, B., Nebel, B., Profitlich, H.J., Franconi, E.: Am empirical analysis of optimization techniques for terminological representation systems. Appl. Intell. **4**(2), 109–132 (1994)

3. Bernstein, A., Hendler, J., Noy, N.: A new look at the Semantic Web. Commun. ACM **59**(9), 35–37 (2016)

4. Bobed, C., Yus, R., Bobillo, F., Mena, E.: Semantic reasoning on mobile devices: do Androids dream of efficient reasoners? J. Web Semant. **35**, 167–183 (2015)

5. Ermilov, T., Khalili, A., Auer, S.: Ubiquitous semantic applications: a systematic literature review. Int. J. Semant. Web Inf. Syst. **10**(1), 66–99 (2014)

6. Glimm, B., Horrocks, I., Motik, B., Stoilos, G., Wang, Z.: HermiT: an OWL 2 reasoner. J. Autom. Reasoning **53**(3), 245–269 (2014)

7. Horridge, M., Bechhofer, S.: The OWL API: a java API for OWL ontologies. Semant. Web **2**(1), 11–21 (2011)

8. Jara, A.J., Olivieri, A.C., Bocchi, Y., Jung, M., Kastner, W., Skarmeta, A.F.: Semantic Web of Things: an analysis of the application semantics for the IoT moving towards the IoT convergence. Int. J. Web Grid Serv. **10**(2–3), 244–272 (2014)

9. Kazakov, Y., Klinov, P.: Experimenting with ELK reasoner on android. In: OWL Reasoner Evaluation Workshop (ORE). CEUR Workshop Proceedings, vol. 1015, pp. 68–74. CEUR-WS, Aachen (2013)

10. Kim, T., Park, I., Hyun, S.J., Lee, D.: MiRE4OWL: mobile rule engine for OWL. In: Proceedings of the 2010 IEEE 34th Annual Computer Software and Applications Conference Workshops, pp. 317–322. IEEE Computer Society, Piscataway (2010)

11. Koch, F., Meyer, J.-J.C., Dignum, F., Rahwan, I.: Programming deliberative agents for mobile services: the 3APL-M platform. In: Bordini, R.H., Dastani, M.M., Dix, J., El Fallah Seghrouchni, A. (eds.) ProMAS 2005. LNCS (LNAI), vol. 3862, pp. 222–235. Springer, Heidelberg (2006). https://doi.org/10.1007/11678823_14

12. Koziuk, M., Domaszewicz, J., Schoeneich, R.O., Jablonowski, M., Boetzel, P.: Mobile context-addressable messaging with DL-lite domain model. In: Roggen, D., Lombriser, C., Tröster, G., Kortuem, G., Havinga, P. (eds.) EuroSSC 2008. LNCS, vol. 5279, pp. 168–181. Springer, Heidelberg (2008). https://doi.org/10.1007/978-3-540-88793-5_13

13. Li, Y.F., Pan, J.Z., Hauswirth, M., Nguyen, H.: The ubiquitous Semantic Web: promises, progress and challenges. In: Web-Based Services: Concepts, Methodologies, Tools, and Applications, pp. 272–289. IGI Global, Hershey (2016)

14. Matentzoglu, N., Leo, J., Hudhra, V., Sattler, U., Parsia, B.: A survey of current, stand-alone OWL reasoners. In: 4th OWL Reasoner Evaluation Workshop (ORE). CEUR Workshop Proceedings, vol. 1387, pp. 68–79. CEUR-WS, Aachen (2015)

15. McBride, B.: Jena: a Semantic Web toolkit. IEEE Internet Comput. **6**(6), 55–59 (2002)

16. Moguillansky, M.O., Wassermann, R., Falappa, M.A.: An argumentation machinery to reason over inconsistent ontologies. In: Kuri-Morales, A., Simari, G.R. (eds.) IBERAMIA 2010. LNCS (LNAI), vol. 6433, pp. 100–109. Springer, Heidelberg (2010). https://doi.org/10.1007/978-3-642-16952-6_11

17. Motik, B., Horrocks, I., Kim, S.M.: Delta-reasoner: a Semantic Web reasoner for an intelligent mobile platform. In: Proceedings of the 21st International Conference on World Wide Web, pp. 63–72. ACM, New York (2012)
18. Parsia, B., Matentzoglu, N., Gonçalves, R.S., Glimm, B., Steigmiller, A.: The OWL reasoner evaluation (ORE) 2015 competition report. J. Autom. Reasoning **59**(4), 455–482 (2017)
19. Patton, E.W., McGuinness, D.L.: The mobile wine agent: pairing wine with the social Semantic Web. In: 2nd Social Data on the Web Workshop - 8th International Semantic Web Conference. CEUR Workshop Proceedings, vol. 520. CEUR-WS, Aachen (2009)
20. Pizzocaro, D., Preece, A., Chen, F., La Porta, T., Bar-Noy, A.: A distributed architecture for heterogeneous multi sensor-task allocation. In: 2011 International Conference on Distributed Computing in Sensor Systems (DCOSS), pp. 1–8. IEEE, Piscataway (2011)
21. Ruta, M., Scioscia, F., Di Sciascio, E.: Mobile semantic-based matchmaking: a fuzzy DL approach. In: Aroyo, L., et al. (eds.) ESWC 2010. LNCS, vol. 6088, pp. 16–30. Springer, Heidelberg (2010). https://doi.org/10.1007/978-3-642-13486-9_2
22. Ruta, M., Scioscia, F., Di Sciascio, E., Bilenchi, I.: OWL API for iOS: early implementation and results. In: Dragoni, M., Poveda-Villalón, M., Jimenez-Ruiz, E. (eds.) OWLED/ORE -2016. LNCS, vol. 10161, pp. 141–152. Springer, Cham (2017). https://doi.org/10.1007/978-3-319-54627-8_11
23. Ruta, M., Scioscia, F., Gramegna, F., Di Sciascio, E.: A mobile knowledge-based system for on-board diagnostics and car driving assistance. In: 4th International Conference on Mobile Ubiquitous Computing, Systems, Services and Technologies (UBICOMM), pp. 91–96. ThinkMind, Wilmington (2010)
24. Ruta, M., Scioscia, F., Ieva, S., De Filippis, D., Di Sciascio, E.: Indoor/outdoor mobile navigation via knowledge-based POI discovery in augmented reality. In: Web Intelligence and Intelligent Agent Technology (WI-IAT), vol. 3, pp. 26–30. IEEE, Piscataway (2015)
25. Scioscia, F., Ruta, M.: Building a Semantic Web of Things: issues and perspectives in information compression. In: Proceedings of the 3rd IEEE International Conference on Semantic Computing, pp. 589–594. IEEE Computer Society, Piscataway (2009)
26. Scioscia, F., Ruta, M., Loseto, G., Gramegna, F., Ieva, S., Pinto, A., Di Sciascio, E.: Mini-ME matchmaker and reasoner for the Semantic Web of Things. In: Innovations, Developments, and Applications of Semantic Web and Information Systems, pp. 262–294. IGI Global, Hershey (2018)
27. Seitz, C., Schönfelder, R.: Rule-based OWL reasoning for specific embedded devices. In: Aroyo, L., Welty, C., Alani, H., Taylor, J., Bernstein, A., Kagal, L., Noy, N., Blomqvist, E. (eds.) ISWC 2011. LNCS, vol. 7032, pp. 237–252. Springer, Heidelberg (2011). https://doi.org/10.1007/978-3-642-25093-4_16
28. Sinner, A., Kleemann, T.: KRHyper – in your pocket. In: Nieuwenhuis, R. (ed.) CADE 2005. LNCS (LNAI), vol. 3632, pp. 452–457. Springer, Heidelberg (2005). https://doi.org/10.1007/11532231_33
29. Steigmiller, A., Liebig, T., Glimm, B.: Konclude: system description. J. Web Semant. **27**, 78–85 (2014)
30. Steller, L., Krishnaswamy, S.: Pervasive service discovery: mTableaux mobile reasoning. In: International Conference on Semantic Systems (I-Semantics), pp. 93–101. TU Graz, Graz (2008)
31. Tai, W., Keeney, J., O'Sullivan, D.: Resource-constrained reasoning using a reasoner composition approach. Semant. Web **6**(1), 35–59 (2015)

32. Teege, G.: Making the difference: a subtraction operation for description logics. In: Proceedings of the Fourth International Conference on the Principles of Knowledge Representation and Reasoning (KR 1994), pp. 540–550. ACM, New York (1994)

33. Thomas, E., Pan, J.Z., Ren, Y.: TrOWL: tractable OWL 2 reasoning infrastructure. In: Aroyo, L., Antoniou, G., Hyvönen, E., ten Teije, A., Stuckenschmidt, H., Cabral, L., Tudorache, T. (eds.) ESWC 2010. LNCS, vol. 6089, pp. 431–435. Springer, Heidelberg (2010). https://doi.org/10.1007/978-3-642-13489-0_38

34. Tsarkov, D., Horrocks, I.: FaCT++ description logic reasoner: system description. In: Furbach, U., Shankar, N. (eds.) IJCAR 2006. LNCS (LNAI), vol. 4130, pp. 292–297. Springer, Heidelberg (2006). https://doi.org/10.1007/11814771_26

35. van Aart, C., Wielinga, B., van Hage, W.R.: Mobile cultural heritage guide: location-aware semantic search. In: Cimiano, P., Pinto, H.S. (eds.) EKAW 2010. LNCS (LNAI), vol. 6317, pp. 257–271. Springer, Heidelberg (2010). https://doi.org/10.1007/978-3-642-16438-5_18

36. Van Woensel, W., Abidi, S.S.R.: Optimizing semantic reasoning on memory-constrained platforms using the RETE algorithm. In: Gangemi, A., Navigli, R., Vidal, M.-E., Hitzler, P., Troncy, R., Hollink, L., Tordai, A., Alam, M. (eds.) ESWC 2018. LNCS, vol. 10843, pp. 682–696. Springer, Cham (2018). https://doi.org/10.1007/978-3-319-93417-4_44

37. Yus, R., Pappachan, P.: Are apps going semantic? a systematic review of semantic mobile applications. In: 1st International Workshop on Mobile Deployment of Semantic Technologies (MoDeST). CEUR Workshop Proceedings, vol. 1506, pp. 2–13. CEUR-WS, Aachen (2015)

Validation of SHACL Constraints over KGs with OWL 2 QL Ontologies via Rewriting

Ognjen Savković[1]($\boxtimes$), Evgeny Kharlamov[2,3], and Steffen Lamparter[4]

[1] Free University of Bozen-Bolzano, Bolzano, Italy
ognjen.savkovic@unibz.it
[2] University of Oslo, Oslo, Norway
[3] Bosch Centre for Artificial Intelligence, Robert Bosch GmbH, Renningen, Germany
[4] Siemens CT, Siemens AG, Munich, Germany

Abstract. Constraints have traditionally been used to ensure data quality. Recently, several constraint languages such as SHACL, as well as mechanisms for constraint validation, have been proposed for Knowledge Graphs (KGs). KGs are often enhanced with ontologies that define relevant background knowledge in a formal language such as OWL 2 QL. However, existing systems for constraint validation either ignore these ontologies, or compile ontologies and constraints into rules that should be executed by some rule engine. In the latter case, one has to rely on different systems when validating constrains over KGs and over ontology-enhanced KGs. In this work, we address this problem by defining rewriting techniques that allow to compile an OWL 2 QL ontology and a set of SHACL constraints into another set of SHACL constraints. We show that in the general case the rewriting may not exists, but it always exists for the positive fragment of SHACL. Our rewriting techniques allow to validate constraints over KGs with and without ontologies using the same SHACL validation engines.

1 Introduction

Constraints have traditionally been used to ensure quality of data in relational [5] and semi-structured DBs [4]. Recently constraints have attracted considerable attention in the context of graph data [16,17], and in particular for *Knowledge Graphs* (KGs) (e.g, [35,36,42]), i.e., large collections of interconnected entities that are annotated with data values and types [7]. KGs have become powerful assets for enhancing search and data integration and they are now widely used in both academia and industry [1,2,6,19,22–25,28,40,41]. Prominent examples of constraint languages for KGs include SHACL [31], ShEx[1]; and of constraint validation systems Stardog[2] and TopBraid[3].

---

[1] https://www.w3.org/2001/sw/wiki/ShEx.
[2] https://www.stardog.com/.
[3] https://www.topquadrant.com/technology/shacl/.

© Springer Nature Switzerland AG 2019
P. Hitzler et al. (Eds.): ESWC 2019, LNCS 11503, pp. 314–329, 2019.
https://doi.org/10.1007/978-3-030-21348-0_21

KGs are often enhanced with *ontologies*, expressed in, e.g., the OWL 2 ontology language [3]. Ontologies capture the relevant background knowledge with axioms over the terms from the KG's vocabulary e.g., by assigning attributes to classes, by defining relationships between classes, composed classes, and class hierarchies. We refer to ontology enhanced KGs as *Knowledge Bases (KBs)*.

Ontologies significantly impact constraint validation over KGs. Indeed, constraints over KGs have Closed-World semantics, or Assumption (CWA) in the sense that their validation over a KG boils down to checking whether sub structures of the KG comply with the patterns encoded in the constraints [8,12,15]. On the other hand, KBs have open-world semantics (OWA) in the sense that ontologies allow to derive information from a KG that is not explicitly there.

As a result, constraint validation over KGs in the presence of ontologies requires to bridge the CWA of constraints and OWA of ontologies [20,21,35,42]. A promising semantics that offers the bridge was proposed in [35]: given a set of constraints $\mathcal{C}$, ontology $\mathcal{O}$, and KG $\mathcal{G}$, validating the KB $\langle \mathcal{O}, \mathcal{G} \rangle$ against $\mathcal{C}$ requires to validate all first-order logic models of $\mathcal{O}$ and $\mathcal{G}$ that are set-inclusion minimal against $\mathcal{C}$. This can be done via a rewriting mechanism: in order to validate $\langle \mathcal{O}, \mathcal{G} \rangle$ against $\mathcal{C}$, one can compile $\mathcal{O}$ and $\mathcal{C}$ into a (possibly disjunctive) logic program and then evaluate the program over $\mathcal{G}$ [20,35]. A disadvantage of this approach is that constraint validation in the presence of ontologies requires a different evaluation engine than in their absence: it requires an engine for disjunctive logic programs, rather than an engine for validating graph constraints. However, from practical point of view it is desirable to have a mechanism that allows to evaluate constraints over KBs using the same engine as over KGs.

In this work we address this issue. We first formalise the problem of constraints rewriting over ontologies: we require that the result of rewriting is again a set of constraints $\mathcal{C}'$ in the same formalism as the original $\mathcal{C}$. We then study the existence of such a rewriting function for the constraint language SHACL and the ontology language OWL 2 QL which is commonly used profile of OWL 2. Our results show that rewriting may not exist in the general case unless CO-NP = NP, since constraint validation in presence of ontologies is CO-NP-complete, while in absence it is NP-complete. We next consider the restriction of SHACL to positive constraints, that we call SHACL$^+$, and show that in this case the rewriting always exists and provide an algorithm for such rewriting.

2   Preliminaries and Running Example

In this section we recall required definitions. We assume a signature Σ of three infinite countable sets of *constants*, that correspond to entities, *classes* of unary predicates, that correspond to types, and *properties* or binary predicates, that correspond to object properties or a special predicate "a" that labels entities with classes. Note that do not consider datatypes and data properties, and leave them for the future study. We assume an infinite countable *domain* Δ of entities.

2.1 Knowledge Graph

A Knowledge Graph (KG) $\mathcal{G}$ is a possibly infinite directed labeled graph that consists of triples of the form (s, p, o) over Σ, where s is a constant, p – property, and o – constant or class (in this case p is the special predicate "a").

Example 1. Consider the following fragment of the Siemens KG $\mathcal{G}_{SIEM}$ from [23], which describes Siemens industrial assets including two turbines with the identifiers :t177 and :t852 and one power plant (PPlant) with the identifier :p063, as well as information about equipment (turbine) categories (hasTuCat, hasCat), their deployment sites (deplAt), and enumeration of turbines at plants (hasTurb):

> $\{$(:p063, a, :PPlant), (:p063, :hasTurb, :t852), (:t852, a, :Turbine),
>
> (:t852, :deplAt, :p063), (:t852, :hasCat, :SGT-800),
>
> (:t177, :deplAt, :p063), (:t177, :hasTuCat, :SGT-800)$\}$.   □

2.2 SHACL Syntax

We next briefly recall relevant notions of SHACL using a compact syntax of [12] which is equivalent to SHACL's "Core Constraint Components" [12]. SHACL stands for *Shapes Constraint Language*. Each SHACL constraint in a set of constraints $\mathcal{C}$, usually referred to as *shape*, is defined as a triple: $\langle s, \tau_s, \phi_s \rangle$, where

- s is the *name*,
- τ_s is the *target definition*, a SPARQL query with one output variable whose purpose is to retrieve *target entities* of s from $\mathcal{G}$, i.e., entities (nodes) occurring in $\mathcal{G}$ for which the following constraint of the shape should be verified,
- and ϕ_s is the *constraint*, an expression defined according to the following grammar:

$$\phi ::= \top \mid s' \mid c \mid \phi_1 \wedge \phi_2 \mid \phi_1 \vee \phi_2 \mid \neg\phi \mid \geq_n R.\phi \mid \leq_n R.\phi \mid EQ(r_1, r_2), \quad (1)$$

where $\top$ stands for the Boolean truth values, s' is a shape name occurring in $\mathcal{C}$, c is a constant, R is a property, and $n \in \mathbb{N}$; moreover, $\wedge$ denotes the conjunction, $\neg$ – negation, "$\geq_n R.\phi$" – "must have at least n-successors in $\mathcal{G}$ verifying ϕ", r_1 and r_2 are SPARQL property paths and "$EQ(r_1, r_2)$" means that "r_1 and r_2 successors of a node must coincide".

With a slight abuse of notation we identify the shape with its name. We note that the syntax for constraints allows for shapes to reference each other. A set of constraints is *recursive* if it contains a shape that reference itself, either directly or via a reference cycle.

Example 2. Consider $\mathcal{C}_{SIEM} = \{\langle s_i, \tau_{s_i}, \phi_{s_i}\rangle \mid i = 1, 4\}$, where:

$$\tau_{s_1} = \exists y(\text{:deplAt}(x, y)), \qquad \phi_{s_1} = (\geq_1 \text{:hasCat.}\top),$$
$$\tau_{s_2} = \exists y(\text{:hasTuCat}(x, y)), \qquad \phi_{s_2} = (\geq_1 \text{ a.:Turbine}),$$
$$\tau_{s_3} = \text{:PPlant}(?x), \qquad \phi_{s_3} = (\geq_1 \text{:hasTurb.}s_4),$$
$$\tau_{s_4} = \text{:Turbine}(?x), \qquad \phi_{s_4} = (\geq_1 \text{:deplAt.}s_3).$$

Here s_1 essentially says that any deployed artifact should have a category, and s_2 says that only turbines can have a turbine category. The last two shapes s_3 and s_4 are mutually recursive, and they respectively say that each power plant should have at least one turbine and each turbine should be deployed in at least one location. □

2.3 SHACL Semantics

Given a shape s, a KG $\mathcal{G}$, and an entity e occurring $\mathcal{G}$, we say that e *verifies* s in $\mathcal{G}$ if the constraint ϕ_s applied to e is valid in $\mathcal{G}$. Finally, $\mathcal{G}$ is *valid* against $\mathcal{C}$ if for each $s \in \mathcal{C}$, each target entity retrieved by τ_s from $\mathcal{G}$ verifies s in $\mathcal{G}$. Since a constraint ϕ_s may refer to a shape s', the definition of validity for KGs is non-trivial. Indeed, the SHACL specification leaves the difficult case of recursion up to the concrete implementation[4] and a formal semantics via so-called *shape assignments* has only recently been proposed [12]. Intuitively, $\mathcal{G}$ is valid against $\mathcal{C}$ if one can label its entities with shape names, while respecting targets and constraints. A shape assignment σ is a function mapping each entity of $\mathcal{G}$ to a set of shape names in $\mathcal{C}$. We call an assignment *target-compliant* if it assigns (at least) each shape to each of its targets, *constraint-compliant* if it complies with the constraints, and *valid* if it complies with both targets and constraints. Then, $\mathcal{G}$ is valid against $\mathcal{C}$ if there exists a valid assignment for $\mathcal{G}$ and $\mathcal{C}$.

Example 3. Observe that $\mathcal{G}_{SIEM}$ is not valid against $\mathcal{C}_{SIEM}$. Shape s_1 has targets :t852 and :t177, since both are deployed. :t852 satisfies the constraint for s_1, since it has a category, but :t177 violates it. Shape s_2 has the target :t177 only, which violates it, since it is not declared to be a turbine. Shape s_3 has no target in $\mathcal{G}_{SIEM}$. The case of shape s_4 is more involved. It has only :t852 as the target, and one may assign s_4 to :t852 and s_3 to :p063, in order to satisfy the recursive constraint. But since :t177 violates s_1 and s_2, there is no "global" valid shape assignment for $\mathcal{G}$ and $\mathcal{S}$, i.e. which would satisfy all targets and constraints simultaneously. □

2.4 OWL 2 QL

We now recall the syntax and semantics of OWL 2 QL relying on the the Description Logics *DL-Lite$_R$* [9] that is behind this profile. (Complex) classes and properties in OWL 2 QL are recursively defined as follows:

$$B:: = A \mid \exists R, \; C:: = B \mid \neg B, \; R:: = P \mid P^-, \text{ and } E:: = R \mid \neg R,$$

---

[4] https://www.w3.org/TR/shacl/.

where A is a class from Σ, P a property from Σ, and P^- the inverse of P. Expression A we call also an *atomic* class or concepts and B a *basic* class or concepts. A *DL-Lite$_R$* ontology is a finite set of axioms of the form $B \sqsubseteq C$ or $R \sqsubseteq E$. A *Knowledge Base* (KB) is a pair $\langle \mathcal{O}, \mathcal{G} \rangle$ of an ontology and a KG. The formal semantics of *DL-Lite$_R$* is given in terms of first-order logic interpretations $\mathcal{I} = (\Delta, \cdot^{\mathcal{I}})$ over Δ in the standard way.

Example 4. Consider the following OWL 2 QL ontology $\mathcal{O}_{SIEM}$:

$$\{ \texttt{:hasTuCat} \sqsubseteq \texttt{:hasCat}, \ \exists \texttt{:hasTuCat}.\top \sqsubseteq \texttt{:Turbine} \},$$

that says that if x has y as a turbine category, then x has y as a category, and also x can be inferred to be a turbine.   □

A useful property of *DL-Lite$_R$* exploited in Sect. 4, is the existence, for any satisfiable KB $\langle \mathcal{O}, \mathcal{G} \rangle$, of a so-called *canonical model*, which can be homomorphically mapped to any model of $\langle \mathcal{O}, \mathcal{G} \rangle$.

2.5   Constraint Validation over KGs Enhanced with Ontologies

Consider the semantics of [35], that naturally extends constraint validation from KGs to ontology-enhanced KGs and has been adopted in, e.g., [20]. Given a KG $\mathcal{G}$, ontology $\mathcal{O}$, and a set of constraints $\mathcal{C}$, the idea of this semantics is to validate $\mathcal{C}$ over all set inclusion minimal models of $\mathcal{G}$ and $\mathcal{O}$. Formally, $\mathcal{G}$ enhanced with $\mathcal{O}$ is *valid* against $\mathcal{C}$ if for each minimal model $\mathcal{M}$ of $\mathcal{G}$ with $\mathcal{O}$, the KG $skol(\mathcal{M})$ is valid against $\mathcal{C}$, where $skol(\mathcal{M})$ is the Skolemization of models.

Example 5. Observe that $\langle \mathcal{O}, \mathcal{G}, \rangle$ is valid against $\mathcal{C}_{SIEM}$. Indeed, shape s_1 is still satisfied by :t852, since no new information can be entailed about :t852 from $\langle \mathcal{O}_{SIEM}, \mathcal{G}_{SIEM} \rangle$. Moreover, s_1 is now not violated by :t177: $\langle \mathcal{O}_{SIEM}, \mathcal{G}_{SIEM} \rangle$ entails that :t177 has a category. Similarly, s_2 is now not violated by :t177: one can can infer that it is a turbine. The shape s_4 now has an additional target (:t177), and it is verified by both its targets, thanks to the following assignment: $\{ s_1 \mapsto \{ \texttt{:t852}, \texttt{:t177} \}, s_2 \mapsto \{ \texttt{:t177} \}, s_3 \mapsto \{ \texttt{:p063} \}, s_4 \mapsto \{ \texttt{:t852}, \texttt{:t177} \} \}$.   □

3   The Problem of Constraint Rewriting

We now formalise and discuss the problem of constraint rewriting over ontologies.

3.1   SHACL-Rewriting

In order to define SHACL rewriting we adapt the notion of rewriting (or reformulation) of queries over ontologies from [9,18].

Definition 1. *Let $\mathcal{C}$ be a set of constraints and $\mathcal{O}$ an ontology. A set of constraints $\mathcal{C}'$ is a* constraint-rewriting *of $\mathcal{C}$ over $\mathcal{O}$ if for any KG $\mathcal{G}$ it holds that:*

$$\langle \mathcal{O}, \mathcal{G} \rangle \text{ is valid against } \mathcal{C} \text{ iff } \mathcal{G} \text{ is valid against } \mathcal{C}'.$$

We now illustrate this notion on the following example.

Example 6. Consider a set of SHACL constraints and an OWL 2 QL ontology:

$$\mathcal{C} = \{\langle s, \tau_s, \phi_s \rangle\}, \text{ where } \tau_s = \text{:MechDevice}(x) \text{ and } \phi_s = (\geq_1 \text{:hasCat}.\top),$$
$$\mathcal{O} = \{\text{:Turbine} \sqsubseteq \text{:MechDevice}, \exists\text{:hasTuCat} \sqsubseteq \exists\text{:hasCat}\}.$$

One can show that a rewiring of $\mathcal{C}$ over $\mathcal{O}$ is $\mathcal{S}' = \{\langle s, \tau_s', \phi_s' \rangle\}$, where

$$\tau_s' = \text{:MechDevice}(x) \vee \text{:Turbine}(x) \text{ and}$$
$$\phi_s' = (\geq_1 \text{:hasCat}.\top) \vee (\geq_1 \text{:hasTuCat}.\top). \qquad \square$$

Observe that in the example both the target definition τ_s and the constraint definition ϕ_s were rewritten over $\mathcal{O}$ in order to guarantee that the ontology $\mathcal{O}$ can be safely ignored. In particular, the rewriting of τ_s guarantees that in any graph $\mathcal{G}$, each instance of :Turbine should also be verified against s, whereas the rewriting of ϕ_s guarantees that any entity in $\mathcal{G}$ with a :hasTuCat-successor validates s, even if it has no :hasCat-successor.

Thus, despite the similarity of query and constraint rewriting overt ontologies there are significant differences[5]. The first difference as illustrated above is that a shape contains a target definition and a constraint that in the general case should be rewritten independently. But more importantly, as opposed to queries, SHACL constraints can be recursive which makes the rewriting significantly more involved (see Sect. 4 for details).

We now show that rewritings may not exist.

3.2 Non-existence of SHACL-Rewritings

We start with the hardness of SHACL validation that can be shown by reduction from the 3-coloring co-problem.

Theorem 1. *There exists a DL-Lite$_R$ ontology, a set of SHACL constraints $\mathcal{C}$, and a KG $\mathcal{G}$ such that deciding whether $\langle \mathcal{O}, \mathcal{G} \rangle$ is valid against $\mathcal{C}$ is* CO-NP-*hard in the size of $\mathcal{G}$.*

Proof. [Sketch] The proof is based on an encoding of the 3-coloring co-problem into the validity problem. For a given undirected graph $\mathcal{F} = \langle V, E \rangle$, where V is a set of vertices and E of edges, we construct the following KG $G_{\mathcal{F}}$:

$$\{(v_i, \text{ a, } V) \mid v_i \in V\} \cup \{(v_i, \text{ E, } v_j) \mid (v_i, \ v_j) \in E\}$$
$$\cup \{(v', \text{ U, } v_i) \mid v_i \in V\} \cup \{(v', \text{ a, } T)\},$$

where v', U and T are needed for technical reasons as will be explained below.

---

[5] Recall that for query rewriting the input is a query q and ontology $\mathcal{O}$ and the output is another query q' such that for any database D so-called certain answers of q over $\langle \mathcal{O}, \mathcal{D} \rangle$ coincide with the answers of q' over $\mathcal{D}$ alone [9].

Then, we define $\mathcal{O} = \{V \sqsubseteq \exists R.C, C_{red} \sqsubseteq C, C_{blue} \sqsubseteq C, C_{red} \sqsubseteq \neg C_{blue}\}$, where the axiom $V \sqsubseteq \exists R.C$ enforces that in each minimal model $\mathcal{M}$ of $\langle \mathcal{O}, \mathcal{G_F} \rangle$, each vertex v_i has an R-successor a_i, which intuitively stands for the color of vertex v_i in $\mathcal{F}^6$. The two other axioms intuitively enforce that either $(a_i, \mathsf{a}, C_{red}) \in \mathcal{M}$ or $(a_i, \mathsf{a}, C_{blue}) \in \mathcal{M}$, or none of the two. Intuitively, v_i is either red, or blue or none of the two (i.e. green).

Now we introduce a singleton set of constraints $\mathcal{C} = \{\langle s, \tau_s, \phi_s \rangle\}$ that requires that at least one pair of adjacent vertices has the same color:

$$\tau_s = T(x), \text{ and } \phi_s = (\geq_1 U.(\phi_1 \vee \phi_2 \vee \phi_3)), \text{ where}$$

$\phi_1 = (\geq_1 R. \geq_1 \mathsf{a}.C_{red}) \wedge (\geq_1 E. \geq_1 R. \geq_1 \mathsf{a}.C_{red})$
$\phi_2 = (\geq_1 R. \geq_1 \mathsf{a}.C_{blue}) \wedge (\geq_1 E. \geq_1 R. \geq_1 \mathsf{a}.C_{blue})$
$\phi_3 = (\geq_1 R. \geq_1 \mathsf{a}.(\neg C_{red} \wedge \neg C_{blue})) \wedge (\geq_1 E. \geq_1 R. \geq_1 \mathsf{a}.(\neg C_{red} \wedge \neg C_{blue})).$

Intuitively, the formula ϕ_1 evaluates to true at the node v_i if v_i is colored as red and has a red neighbour. The formulas ϕ_2 and ϕ_3 evaluate similarly, but for blue and green. Finally, the shape s has the node v' as the unique target, and v has every other node in $G_\mathcal{F}$ as a U-successor, ensuring that $G_\mathcal{F}$ is valid against $\mathcal{C}$ iff there is no 3-colouring for $\mathcal{F}$.   □

In [13] it has been shown that validation of SHACL constraints over KGs without ontologies is NP-complete in the size of the graph. Thus, we can immediately conclude the following negative result that holds under the assumption that CO-NP $\not\subseteq$ NP.

Corollary 1. *There exists an DL-Lite$_R$ ontology and a set of SHACL constraints for which no SHACL-rewriting over this ontology exists.*

In order to overcome the non-existence problem we found a restriction on SHACL as will be presented in the following section.

4   Rewriting of SHACL$^+$ Constraints over OWL 2 QL

As discussed above, a rewriting may not exist for an arbitrary set of SHACL shapes and a *DL-Lite$_R$* ontology. Thus, in order to gain rewritability one can restrict the expressivity of SHACL. In the following we do so by restricting SHACL to positive SHACL shapes. For this setting we develop Algorithm 1 that allows to compute constraint rewritings. A SHACL shape is in SHACL$^+$ if it does not contain negation and cardinality restriction of kind "$\leq_n R.\phi$".

---

[6] The axiom of the kind $V \sqsubseteq \exists R.C$ in syntactically not in *DL-Lite$_R$* but it can be expressed using a "fresh" role R_1 and three axioms: $V \sqsubseteq \exists R_1$, $R_1 \sqsubseteq R$ and $\exists R_1^- \sqsubseteq C$.

The rest of this section we organize in four parts. *(i)* First we show why it is sufficient to consider only satisfiable KGs; *(ii)* Then we show that over such satisfiable KGs it sufficient to focus only on their canonical models *(iii)* then we show how to rewrite shape targets given an ontology, and *(iv)* finally we show how to rewrite ontologies.

4.1   Satisfiable Knowledge Graphs

We observe that in general KGs may contain disjointness and thus they may be unsatisfiable (that is, they have no model). First we introduce an axillary property that shows that for constraint validation it is sufficient to consider only satisfiable KGs.

Lemma 1. *Let $\mathcal{O}$ be a DL-Lite$_R$ ontology and $\mathcal{G}$ a graph. If $\langle \mathcal{O}, \mathcal{G} \rangle$ is unsatisfiable then for any shape s and any node in v in $\mathcal{G}$ there is exists no satisfying shape assignment over $\mathcal{G}$ and the set of shapes $\mathcal{C}_{\mathcal{O}}$ that validates $s(v)$.*

Proof. Assume that $\langle \mathcal{O}, \mathcal{G} \rangle$ is unsatisfiable. Wlog we assume that the cause of being unsatisfiable is the following: $\langle \mathcal{O}, \mathcal{G} \rangle \models C(a) \wedge D(a)$ holds for some node a in $\mathcal{G}$ and some basic concepts C and D, and at same time $\mathcal{O} \models C \sqsubseteq \neg D$ holds (similarly it can be shown for role disjointness).

From $\langle \mathcal{O}, \mathcal{G} \rangle \models C(a) \wedge D(a)$ we conclude (using the properties on PERFREF in [9]) that $\mathcal{G} \models \text{PERFREF}(C(a) \wedge D(a), \mathcal{O})$. Then, since we have $\tau_{s_{C \sqsubseteq \neg D}} = \text{PERFREF}(C(x) \wedge D(x), \mathcal{O})$ it follows that a is the target of the shape $s_{C \sqsubseteq \neg D}$. On the other hand $\phi_{s_{C \sqsubseteq \neg D}} = \bot$, thus for every shape assignment σ it must be $\sigma(s_{C \sqsubseteq \neg D}) = \bot$, i.e., there exists no satisfying assignment for $s_{C \sqsubseteq \neg D}$. Hence, there exist no satisfying assignment over $\mathcal{G}$ and $\mathcal{C}_{\mathcal{O}}$ that also validates $s(v)$.   □

4.2   Validity over Canonical Models

In this part we show that in order to check the validity over all minimal models it is sufficient to check the validity over the canonical model for the given KG. In [9], the authors defined a canonical model of a KB as a model that can be homomorphically mapped to any other model of that KB. Now we extend this notion to shapes: Given two graphs $\mathcal{G}_1$ and $\mathcal{G}_2$ with set of constants Δ_1 and Δ_2 respectively, and the set of shapes $\mathcal{C}$, a *SHACL-homomorphism* μ from $\mathcal{G}$ to $\mathcal{G}'$ is a mapping $\mu : \Delta_1 \rightarrow \Delta_2$ such that, for each shape $s \in \mathcal{C}$ and each constant $v \in \Delta_1$, if $\langle \mathcal{G}_1, \mathcal{C} \rangle \models \phi_s(v)$ then $\langle \mathcal{G}_2, \mathcal{C} \rangle \models \phi_s(\mu(v))$.

Lemma 2 (canonical homomorphism for positive shapes). *Let $\mathcal{O}$ be a DL-Lite$_R$ ontology, $\mathcal{G}$ a graph, and let $\mathcal{M}$ be a minimal model of $\langle \mathcal{O}, \mathcal{G} \rangle$. Let $\mathcal{C}$ be a set of SHACL$^+$ shapes. Then, there is a SHACL-homomorphism from $can(\mathcal{O}, \mathcal{G})$ to $\mathcal{M}$ given $\mathcal{C}$. In particular, there exists a SHACL-homomorphism that maps every node from $\mathcal{G}$ to itself.*

Proof. From [9], we have that there exists a homomorphism μ from $can(\mathcal{O}, \mathcal{G})$ to $\mathcal{M}$ such that for a basic concept C and node v it holds if $C(v) \in can(\mathcal{O}, \mathcal{G})$ (resp. $R(v_1, v_2) \in can(\mathcal{O}, \mathcal{G})$) then $C(\mu(v)) \in \mathcal{M}$ (resp. $R(\mu(v_1), \mu(v_2)) \in \mathcal{M}$. In particular, it is possible to select μ such that $\mu(v) = v$ for $v \in \mathcal{G}$. We also notice that μ has to be surjective; otherwise the μ-image of $can(\mathcal{O}, \mathcal{G})$ would be a minimal model "smaller" than $\mathcal{M}$ which is a contradiction.

Assume now that $\langle can(\mathcal{O}, \mathcal{G}), \mathcal{C} \rangle \models \phi_s(v)$ for some shape s from $\mathcal{C}$ and node v in $can(\mathcal{O}, \mathcal{G})$. Let σ be a satisfying assignment for $can(\mathcal{O}, \mathcal{G}), \mathcal{C}$ such that $\llbracket \phi_s \rrbracket^{can(\mathcal{O}, \mathcal{G}), \sigma, v} = true$. We define an assignment σ' over $\mathcal{M}, \mathcal{C}$ in the following way: for a shape s_1 and node v_1 in $\mathcal{M}$ we set $s_1 \in (v_1, \sigma')$ iff exists a node v_2 in $can(\mathcal{O}, \mathcal{G})$ such that $\mu(v_2) = v_1$ and $s_1 \in (v_2, \sigma)$. Now analyzing different cases for s: $\phi_s = \top$, $\phi_s = I$, $\phi_s = {\geq_k} R.s_1$, $\phi_s = s_1 \wedge s_2$, $\phi_s = s_1 \vee s_2$ and $\phi_s = EQ(r_1, r_2)$, it is not hard to show that if $\llbracket \phi_s \rrbracket^{can(\mathcal{O}, \mathcal{G}), \sigma, v} = true$ then $\llbracket \phi_s \rrbracket^{\mathcal{M}, \sigma', \mu(v)} = true$.   □

Using the lemmas above we show the following property of canonical models.

Lemma 3 (canonical model characterization). *For a DL-Lite$_R$ ontology $\mathcal{O}$, basic concept C, graph G, node v in $\mathcal{G}$, set $\mathcal{C}$ of SHACL$^+$ shapes and shape s defined in $\mathcal{C}$ we have that:* $\langle \mathcal{O}, \mathcal{G}, \mathcal{C} \rangle \models \phi_s(v)$ *iff* $\langle can(\mathcal{O}, \mathcal{G}), \mathcal{C} \rangle \models \phi_s(v)$.

Proof. ($\Leftarrow$) The entailment $\langle \mathcal{O}, \mathcal{G}, \mathcal{C} \rangle \models \phi_{s(v)}$ holds if $\langle \mathcal{M}, \mathcal{C} \rangle \models \phi_{s(v)}{}^7$ in each minimal model $\mathcal{M}$, including $can(\mathcal{O}, \mathcal{G})$.
($\Rightarrow$) Let $\mathcal{M}$ be a minimal model of $\langle \mathcal{O}, \mathcal{G} \rangle$. Lemma 2 implies the existence of a homomorphism μ from $can(\mathcal{O}, \mathcal{G})$ to $\mathcal{M}$ s.t. $\mathcal{M}, \mathcal{C} \models \phi_s(\mu(v))$ for $\mu(v) = v$.   □

4.3   Rewriting of Shape Targets

In the absence of an ontology, the targets of shapes s are retrieved by evaluating the target definitions τ_s over the graph $\mathcal{G}$, written $\llbracket \tau_s \rrbracket^{\mathcal{G}}$. In SHACL, a target definition is a monadic query with a single atom that corresponds to a basic concept in an ontology. In the presence of an ontology, we follow the semantics described in Sect. 2.5, and retrieve targets over all minimal models, or equivalently over the canonical model, written as $\llbracket \tau \rrbracket^{\langle \mathcal{O}, \mathcal{G} \rangle}$. To achieve this, since τ_s is a unary conjunctive query, one can apply PERFREF.

Lemma 4. *For any shape s from SHACL, DL-Lite$_R$ ontology $\mathcal{O}$, and graph $\mathcal{G}$ it holds that* $\llbracket \tau_s \rrbracket^{\langle \mathcal{O}, \mathcal{G} \rangle} = \llbracket \text{PERFREF}(\tau_s, \mathcal{O}) \rrbracket^{\mathcal{G}}$.

Proof. The authors in [9] established the correspondence between certain answers of conjunctive queries over knowledge graphs and perfect reformulation (Lemma 35): For a KG $\langle \mathcal{O}, \mathcal{G} \rangle$ and conjunctive query q we have that the certain answers of q over the KG correspond to perfect reformulation in the sense that $cert(q, \langle \mathcal{O}, \mathcal{G} \rangle) = \llbracket \text{PERFREF}(\tau_s, \mathcal{O}) \rrbracket^{\mathcal{G}}$, where, $a \in cert(q, \langle \mathcal{O}, \mathcal{G} \rangle)$ iff for every minimal model $\mathcal{M}$ of $\langle \mathcal{O}, \mathcal{G} \rangle$ it holds that $a \in q^{\mathcal{M}}$. At the same time

---

^{7} In this entailment we consider $\mathcal{M}$ as an infinite conjunction of atoms.

Algorithm 1. CONSTRAINT REWRITING

Input: ontology $\mathcal{O}$ possible with existential rules, set of positive shapes $\mathcal{C}$
1: $\mathcal{C}_\mathcal{O} \leftarrow$ SHAPET$(\mathcal{O})$
2: $\mathcal{C}_\mathcal{O}^v \leftarrow$ SHAPEVIRTUAL$(\mathcal{O})$
3: $\mathcal{C}_\mathcal{O}^s \leftarrow$ SUCCESSORT$(\mathcal{O})$
4: $\mathcal{C}'' \leftarrow \{\langle \text{PERFREF}(\tau_s, \mathcal{O}), \text{REWRITECOMPL}(\phi_s, \mathcal{O})\rangle \mid s \in \mathcal{C}\}$
5: **return** $\mathcal{C}_\mathcal{O} \cup \mathcal{C}_\mathcal{O}^v \cup \mathcal{C}_{\mathcal{O},\mathcal{C}}^s \cup \mathcal{C}''$

---

the formula $[\![\tau_s]\!]^{\langle\mathcal{O},\mathcal{G}\rangle}$ defines a special set of target nodes over the graph and ontology: $[\![\tau_s]\!]^{\langle\mathcal{O},\mathcal{G}\rangle}$ returns a node v iff it does so for every minimal model M of $\langle\mathcal{O},\mathcal{G}\rangle$. □

In other words, the targets of s according to the KB $\langle\mathcal{O},\mathcal{G}\rangle$ can be retrieved by evaluating the query $\text{PERFREF}(\tau_s, \mathcal{O})$ over $\mathcal{G}$ alone.

4.4 Rewriting of the Ontology

In this part, we present our rewriting algorithm. In order to make notations more concise, we write $\mathcal{G}, \mathcal{C} \models \phi(v)$ to denote that the node v satisfies the constraint ϕ in the graph $\mathcal{G}$ given a set $\mathcal{C}$ of shapes. Similarly, we use $\langle\mathcal{O},\mathcal{G}\rangle, \mathcal{C} \models \phi(v)$ to denote that v satisfies ϕ in the graph that corresponds to the canonical model of $\langle\mathcal{O},\mathcal{G}\rangle$ given $\mathcal{C}$. Then, we assume that the shape constraints in $\mathcal{C}$ are normalised, i.e. contain at most one operator. Note that this can always be obtained by introducing nested shape names.

Our rewriting procedure is presented in Algorithm 1 and we now guide the reader through it. Our algorithm relies on auxiliary shapes of three kinds:

- $\mathcal{C}_\mathcal{O}$ that contains for each concept C in $\mathcal{O}$ the corresponding shape s_C in $\mathcal{C}_\mathcal{O}$; this ensures that for every node v the fact $C(v)$ is in the canonical model iff v is valid in the shape s_C.
- "virtual" shapes $\mathcal{C}_\mathcal{O}^v$ and $\mathcal{C}_\mathcal{O}^s$ that are used to capture the part of the canonical model generated by existential quantification.

The shapes $\mathcal{C}_\mathcal{O}$, $\mathcal{C}_\mathcal{O}^v$ and $\mathcal{C}_\mathcal{O}^s$ will help us to establish rewriting over $\mathcal{O}$ of the original shapes from $\mathcal{C}$ into $\mathcal{C}''$. We now define $\mathcal{C}_\mathcal{O}$, $\mathcal{C}_\mathcal{O}^v$ and $\mathcal{C}_\mathcal{O}^s$ explain how they are used in Algorithm 1 and show correctness of the algorithm.

Rewriting SHAPET for Active Nodes: $\mathcal{C}_\mathcal{O}$. For every concept of the form A (resp. $\exists R$) in $\mathcal{O}$, we introduce a shape s_A (resp. $s_{\exists R}$), with targets $\tau_{s_A} = A$ (resp. $\tau_{s_{\exists R}} = \exists R$) and with constraint where R, R' may be inverse roles:

$$\phi_{s_A} = (\geq_1 a.A) \vee \bigvee_{\mathcal{O} \models C \sqsubseteq A} s_C, \qquad \phi_{s_{\exists R}} = (\geq_1 R.\top) \vee \bigvee_{\mathcal{O} \models C \sqsubseteq \exists R} s_C \vee \bigvee_{\mathcal{O} \models R' \sqsubseteq R} s_{\exists R'}.$$

Next, we introduce shapes that encode negative assertions. For each GCI of the form $(C \sqsubseteq \neg D)$ in $\mathcal{O}$, we introduce one shape $s_{C \sqsubseteq \neg D}$, where targets are all instances of C and D in $\mathcal{G}$, where the constraint is always violated. To this end, we exploit results based on PERFREF [9]: $\tau_{s_{C \sqsubseteq \neg D}} = \text{PERFREF}(C(x) \wedge D(x), \mathcal{O})$, and $\phi_{s_{C \sqsubseteq \neg D}} = \bot$. Similarly, for negative role inclusions, we use $s_{R_1 \sqsubseteq \neg R_2}$, with $\tau_{s_{R_1 \sqsubseteq \neg R_2}} = \text{PERFREF}(\exists y R1(x,y) \wedge R_2(x,y), \mathcal{O})$, and $\phi_{s_{R_1 \sqsubseteq \neg R_2}} = \bot$.

We denote the set of shapes produced above with $\mathcal{C}_{\mathcal{O}}$, and the corresponding translation function as SHAPET in Algorithm 1, i.e., $\text{SHAPET}(\mathcal{O}) = \mathcal{C}_{\mathcal{O}}$.

With $cl(\mathcal{O}, \mathcal{G})$ we denote the maximal subset of $can(\mathcal{O}, \mathcal{G})$ without fresh nodes. If there were no fresh nodes, i.e., when $can(\mathcal{O}, \mathcal{G}) = cl(\mathcal{O}, \mathcal{G})$, we observe that shapes in $\mathcal{C} \cup \text{SHAPET}(\mathcal{O})$ would be sufficient to validate the facts in $can(\mathcal{O}, \mathcal{G})$. Intuitively, this is because dependencies among shapes in SHAPET$(\mathcal{O})$ corresponds to the construction of the "closure" $cl(\mathcal{O}, \mathcal{G})$.

Fresh Nodes in Canonical Models. Observe that for DL-Lite$_R$ ontologies $\mathcal{O}$ the canonical model $can(\mathcal{O}, \mathcal{G})$ can be arbitrary large (even infinite) in which case it will contain "fresh" nodes that are not occurring in $\mathcal{G}$. Thus, one should be able to check constraints also on this fresh nodes, as shown next.

Example 7. Consider the ontology $\mathcal{O} = \{A \sqsubseteq \exists U, \exists U^- \sqsubseteq \exists P\}$ and graph $\mathcal{G} = \{(v, \mathsf{a}, A)\}$. Then $can(\mathcal{O}, \mathcal{G}) = \{(v, \mathsf{a}, A), (v, U, a_1), (a_1, P, a_2)\}$ where a_1 and a_2 are fresh nodes. Now consider shapes $\langle s_1, A(x), (\geq_1 U.s_2) \rangle$ and $\langle s_2, \bot(x), (\geq_1 P.\top) \rangle$. It is not hard to see that $\mathcal{C}$ is valid over $(\mathcal{O}, \mathcal{G})$. □

These properties of $can(\mathcal{O}, \mathcal{G})$ make rewriting technically involved since SHACL constraints cannot express fresh values. We address this with auxiliary shapes $\mathcal{C}_{\mathcal{O}}^v$ and $\mathcal{C}_{\mathcal{O}}^s$ that mimic the construction of the canonical model and validate facts in $\mathcal{G}' = can(\mathcal{O}, \mathcal{G}) \setminus cl(\mathcal{O}, \mathcal{G})$. The graph $\mathcal{G}'$ is a forest (by construction of $can(\mathcal{O}, \mathcal{G})$) where each tree has the root in some assertion of $cl(\mathcal{O}, \mathcal{G})$. We call this root the *witness* of the tree. In example above, (v, a, A) is the only witness.

Rewriting SHAPEVIRTUAL for Fresh Nodes: $\mathcal{C}_{\mathcal{O}}^v$. For each concept C appearing in a GCI in $\mathcal{O}$, we introduce a shape $s_C^{virtual}$, such that, for a node v in $\mathcal{G}$, verifies $s_C^{virtual}(v)$ iff there is a node v' in $\mathcal{G}'$ with v as witness such that $\mathcal{G}' \models C(v')$. For instance, in Example 8, we introduce shape $s_{\exists R}^{virtual}$ which is verified by the witness v. Note that v' is not necessarily an immediate successor of v in $\mathcal{G}'$.

More formally, for concept C, the virtual shape $s_C^{virtual} = \langle \text{PERFREF}(C), \phi_{s_C^{virtual}} \rangle$ is created. Then a function similar to REWRITESIM is applied to each $\phi_{s_C^{virtual}}$, in order to ensure the above property. In our running example, this yields $\phi_{s_A^{virtual}} = s_A$, i.e. $\phi_{s_A^{virtual}}$ remains unchanged, but $\phi_{s_{\exists U}^{virtual}} = s_{\exists U} \vee s_A^{virtual} \vee s_{\exists U^-}^{virtual}$. Here, sub-formula $s_A^{virtual}$ is added because of the GCI $A \sqsubseteq U$, and $s_{\exists U^-}$ is added because if $\exists U$ holds at some node a_1 in the tree of $\mathcal{G}'$ rooted in v, then $\exists U^-$ must hold at some U-successor a_2 of a_1. Let SHAPEVIRTUAL be the function which produces (and rewrites) these "virtual" shapes.

Rewriting SUCCESSORT for Fresh Nodes: $\mathcal{C}_{\mathcal{O}}^s$. The second kind of shapes is needed in order to check if two roles are concatenated in the same tree in $\mathcal{G}'$. For each pair of roles R_1 and R_2 in $\mathcal{O}$, we introduce the shape s_{R_1, R_2}^{succ} such that a node $v \in \mathcal{G}$ verifies $\phi_{s_{R_1, R_2}^{succ}}$ iff (a_1, R_1, a_2) and (a_2, R_2, a_3) are on the subtree with the witness v, for some a_1, a_2, a_3 in $\mathcal{G}'$. In our running example, v verifies $\phi_{s^{succ}_{R,P}}$, but not $\phi_{s^{succ}_{P,R}}$. Formally, for every two roles R_1 and R_2 in $\mathcal{O}$, $\tau_{s^{succ}_{R_1,R_2}} = \bot(x)$, and if $\mathcal{O} \models \exists R_1^- \sqsubseteq \exists R_2$, then $\phi_{s^{succ}_{R_1,R_2}} = s_{\exists R_1}$, otherwise $\phi_{s^{succ}_{\exists R_1, \exists R_2}} = \bot$. The special case $R_2 = R_1^-$, is also covered by the definition $\phi_{s^{succ}_{R_1,R_1^-}} = s_{\exists R_1}$. Let SUCCESSORT denote the function creating these fresh shapes.

Rewriting REWRITECOMPLT for Shapes. Finally, we need to rewrite the shapes in $\mathcal{C}$. To this end, we extend the procedure REWRITESIM in the following way. For each shape s in $\mathcal{C}$, we set $s' = \text{REWRITECOMPL}(s) \vee s^{virtual}$ where REWRITECOMPL is identical to REWRITESIM for operators $\wedge$, $\vee$ and constant I but it changes for $\phi_s = (\geq_k R.s_1)$ as follows:

$$\phi'_s = (\geq_k R.s'_1) \vee s^{virtual} \quad \text{where} \quad \phi_{s^{virtual}} = s^{virtual}_{\exists R} \wedge s_1^{virtual} \wedge s_{\exists R, s_1}.$$

In other words, the witness v verifies $s^{virtual}$ if it verifies both $s^{virtual}_{\exists R}$ and $s_1^{virtual}$ (that is, both are verified by some anonymous node with v as the witness), and the range of R can be validated against s_1, expressed with the new shape $s_{\exists R, s_1}$. Then $\phi_{s_{\exists R, s_1}} = s_{\exists R, s_2} \wedge s_{\exists R, s_3}$ if $\phi_{s_1} = s_2 \wedge s_3$ (and similarly for $\vee$). If $\phi_{s_1} = (\geq_k P.s_2)$, then $\phi_{\exists R, s_1} = s^{succ}_{R,P}$, that is P has to be the successor of R in $\mathcal{G}'$. Let REWRITECOMPLT denote the corresponding rewriting of $\mathcal{C}$.

Correctness of Rewriting. We now proceed to the correctness of our rewriting procedure and start with the property of possibly infinite canonical models.

Lemma 5 (Infinite canonical model). *Let $\mathcal{O}$ be a DL-Lite$_R$ ontology, C a concept in $\mathcal{O}$, R and P properties in $\mathcal{O}$, $\mathcal{G}$ a graph, v a node in $\mathcal{G}$, and shapes $\mathcal{C}_\mathcal{O}$, $\mathcal{C}_\mathcal{O}^v$ and $\mathcal{C}_\mathcal{O}^s$ as specified in Algorithm 1. Then, the following holds:*

- *$\mathcal{G}, \mathcal{C}_\mathcal{O} \cup \mathcal{C}_\mathcal{O}^v \cup \mathcal{C}_\mathcal{O}^s \models \phi_{s_C^{virtual}}(v)$ iff there is a node a_1 in $can(\mathcal{O}, \mathcal{G})$ with the witness v such that $can(\mathcal{O}, \mathcal{G}) \models C(a_1)$.*
- *$\mathcal{G}, \mathcal{C}_\mathcal{O} \cup \mathcal{C}_\mathcal{O}^v \cup \mathcal{C}_\mathcal{O}^s \models \phi_{s^{succ}_{R,P}(v)}$ iff there are nodes a_1, a_2, a_3 in $can(\mathcal{O}, \mathcal{G})$ with the witness v such that $can(\mathcal{O}, \mathcal{G}) \models R(a_1, a_2)$ and $can(\mathcal{O}, \mathcal{G}) \models P(a_2, a_3)$.*

Example 8. We illustrate the rewriting of the running example. Shapes that are not relevant for the reasoning are omitted. The presented shapes are ordered in the way one would reason with them, starting bottom-up (which is possible if $\mathcal{C}$ is not recursive). To illustrate the reasoning, we underline in each formula the disjuncts for which one can construct a satisfying shape assignment.

$$\phi_{s_A^{virtual}} = \underline{s_A}, \quad \phi_{s_{\exists U}^{virtual}} = s_{\exists U} \vee \underline{s_A^{virtual}} \vee \underline{s_{\exists U^-}^{virtual}},$$

$$\phi_{s_{\exists U}} = (\geq_1 U.\top) \vee \underline{s_{\exists U}^{virtual}}, \quad \phi_{s^{succ}_{U,P}} = \underline{s_{\exists U}}, \quad \phi_{s_{\exists U, s_2}} = s^{succ}_{U,P},$$

$$\phi_{s_1^{virtual}} = \underline{s_{\exists U}^{virtual}} \wedge \underline{s_2^{virtual}} \wedge \underline{s_{\exists U, s_2}}, \quad \phi_{s'_1} = \geq_1 U.s'_2 \vee \underline{s_1^{virtual}},$$

$$\phi_{s_2^{virtual}} = \underline{s_{\exists P}^{virtual}}, \quad \phi_{s_{\exists P}^{virtual}} = s_{\exists P} \vee \underline{s_{\exists U^-}^{virtual}} \vee \underline{s_{\exists P^-}^{virtual}}, \quad \phi_{s_{\exists U^-}^{virtual}} = \underline{s_{\exists U}^{virtual}}.$$

The only target of s is v, and v verifies ϕ_s w.r.t the rewritten set of shapes. $\square$

We are ready to present the main result of this section.

Theorem 2. *Let $\mathcal{O}$ be a DL-Lite$_R$ ontology, $\mathcal{C}$ a set of SHACL$^+$ shapes, $s \in \mathcal{C}$, $\mathcal{C}'$ the shapes returned by Algorithm 1, and s' the rewriting of s in $\mathcal{C}'$. Then, for any graph $\mathcal{G}$ and node v in $\mathcal{G}$ it holds that: $\langle \mathcal{O}, \mathcal{G} \rangle, \mathcal{C} \models \phi_s(v)$ iff $\mathcal{G}, \mathcal{C}' \models \phi'_s(v)$.*

Note the size of the returned rewriting is polynomial in the size of $\mathcal{O}$ and $\mathcal{C}$.

5   Related Work

As discussed in Sect. 1, constraint validation in the presence of ontologies was studied in [20,35,42]. While these approaches allow for very expressive ontologies (e.g., $\mathcal{SHOIN}$) they require an engine for disjunctive logic programs, which we believe makes these approaches less practically interesting.

Rewriting of conjunctive queries over OWL 2 QL ontologies of [9] cannot be applied to SHACL shapes since they may be recursive or contain negation.

From a more general prospective our rewriting can be seen a special case of the *backward-chaining algorithm* [32] over $\forall\exists$-rules (where the body and the head are conjunctions of atoms, and only the variables that occur in the head can be existentially quantified). However, in such cases the existence of a rewriting is undecidable in general for arbitrary rules, and even for some decidable fragments, differently from our approach, such algorithms may not terminate.

Naturally, one may think of relating SHACL to Datalog programs [14] since they poses recursion and negation. However, Datalog programs can at most have one unique minimal model, and SHACL constraints should be checked for all possible assignments [12] (including also non-minimal ones). If we consider more expressive version of Datalog like Datalog with negation under the stable model semantics (SMS) [14], then relating it to SHACL is more promising, while the actual relation is not obvious as SMS is also based on minimal models. Nevertheless, our preliminary results show that this is not straightforward.

6   Conclusion

We have studied the rewriting of constraints over ontologies for constrain validation. We focused on a prominent language for graph constraints SHACL and on ontologies from the widely used OWL 2 QL ontology language. We defined semantics for constraint rewriting, showed the non-existence of such rewritings in the general case, and identified restrictions on SHACL to positive (but recursive) fragment SHACL$^+$ for which they always exist. For SHACL$^+$ we showed how to rewrite ontologies and SHACL$^+$ constraints into the unique set of SHACL$^+$ constraints. Moreover, SHACL$^+$ validation over OWL 2 QL is tractable.

We see this work as an important step towards practical constraint rewriting algorithms and systems. Next, we plan to analyse optimisation techniques in order to obtain more efficient rewritings. For instance, we plan to consider datatypes. They can be used to optimize eliminate unnecessary rewritings, but this need to be done in a controlled way to ensure tractability (e.g., [38]).

Then, we plan to extend this work to account for OWL 2 EL. Moreover, we plan to implement our approach and evaluate it in various industrial settings [11,24–27,33,34,37,39]. An important research direction is also to understand how to repair data that fails to satisfy SHACL constraints and we see the work on ontology evolution as a good source of inspiration [10,29,30,43].

Acknowledgments. This work was partially funded by the SIRIUS Centre, Norwegian Research Council project number 237898; by the Free University of Bozen-Bolzano projects QUEST, ROBAST and ADVANCED4KG.

References

1. Freebase: an open, shared database of the world's knowledge. freebase.com/
2. Google KG. google.co.uk/insidesearch/features/search/knowledge.html
3. W3C: OWL 2 Web Ontology Language. www.w3.org/TR/owl2-overview/
4. Abiteboul, S., Buneman, P., Suciu, D.: Data on the Web: From Relations to Semistructured Data and XML. Morgan Kaufmann, Burlington (1999)
5. Abiteboul, S., Hull, R., Vianu, V.: Foundations of Databases. Addison-Wesley, Boston (1995)
6. Arenas, M., Grau, B.C., Kharlamov, E., Marciuska, S., Zheleznyakov, D.: Faceted search over RDF-based knowledge graphs. J. Web Semant. **37–38**, 55–74 (2016)
7. Arenas, M., Gutiérrez, C., Pérez, J.: Foundations of RDF databases. In: Tessaris, S., et al. (eds.) Reasoning Web 2009. LNCS, vol. 5689, pp. 158–204. Springer, Heidelberg (2009). https://doi.org/10.1007/978-3-642-03754-2_4
8. Boneva, I., Labra Gayo, J.E., Prud'hommeaux, E.G.: Semantics and validation of shapes schemas for RDF. In: d'Amato, C., et al. (eds.) ISWC 2017. LNCS, vol. 10587, pp. 104–120. Springer, Cham (2017). https://doi.org/10.1007/978-3-319-68288-4_7
9. Calvanese, D., De Giacomo, G., Lembo, D., Lenzerini, M., Rosati, R.: Tractable reasoning and efficient query answering in description logics: the DL-Lite family. JAR **39**, 385–429 (2007)
10. Calvanese, D., Kharlamov, E., Nutt, W., Zheleznyakov, D.: Evolution of *DL – Lite* knowledge bases. In: Patel-Schneider, P.F., et al. (eds.) ISWC 2010. LNCS, vol. 6496, pp. 112–128. Springer, Heidelberg (2010). https://doi.org/10.1007/978-3-642-17746-0_8
11. Cheng, G., Kharlamov, E.: Towards a semantic keyword search over industrial knowledge graphs (extended abstract). In: IEEE Big Data, pp. 1698–1700 (2017)
12. Corman, J., Reutter, J.L., Savković, O.: Semantics and validation of recursive SHACL. In: Vrandečić, D., et al. (eds.) ISWC 2018. LNCS, vol. 11136, pp. 318–336. Springer, Cham (2018). https://doi.org/10.1007/978-3-030-00671-6_19
13. Corman, J., Reutter, J.L., Savkovic, O.: Semantics and validation of recursive SHACL (extended version). Technical report KRDB18-1, KRDB Research Center, Free University of Bozen-Bolzano (2018). https://www.inf.unibz.it/krdb/pub/tech-rep.php
14. Dantsin, E., Eiter, T., Gottlob, G., Voronkov, A.: Complexity and expressive power of logic programming. ACM Comput. Surv. **33**(3), 374–425 (2001)
15. Ekaputra, F.J., Lin, X.: SHACL4p: SHACL constraints validation within Protégé ontology editor. In: ICoDSE (2016)

16. Fan, W., Fan, Z., Tian, C., Dong, X.L.: Keys for graphs. PVLDB **8**(12), 1590–1601 (2015)
17. Fan, W., Wu, Y., Xu, J.: Functional dependencies for graphs. In: SIGMOD, pp. 1843–1857 (2016)
18. Hansen, P., Lutz, C., Seylan, I., Wolter, F.: Efficient query rewriting in the description logic EL and beyond. In: IJCAI, pp. 3034–3040 (2015)
19. Horrocks, I., Giese, M., Kharlamov, E., Waaler, A.: Using semantic technology to tame the data variety challenge. IEEE Internet Comput. **20**(6), 62–66 (2016)
20. Kharlamov, E., et al.: Capturing industrial information models with ontologies and constraints. In: Groth, P., et al. (eds.) ISWC 2016. LNCS, vol. 9982, pp. 325–343. Springer, Cham (2016). https://doi.org/10.1007/978-3-319-46547-0_30
21. Kharlamov, E., et al.: SOMM: industry oriented ontology management tool. In: ISWC Posters & Demos (2016)
22. Kharlamov, E., et al.: Ontology based data access in Statoil. J. Web Semant. **44**, 3–36 (2017)
23. Kharlamov, E., et al.: Semantic access to streaming and static data at Siemens. J. Web Semant. **44**, 54–74 (2017)
24. Kharlamov, E., Martín-Recuerda, F., Perry, B., Cameron, D., Fjellheim, R., Waaler, A.: Towards semantically enhanced digital twins. In: IEEE Big Data, pp. 4189–4193 (2018)
25. Kharlamov, E., et al.: Towards simplification of analytical workflows with semantics at Siemens (extended abstract). In: IEEE Big Data, pp. 1951–1954 (2018)
26. Kharlamov, E., et al.: Diagnostics of trains with semantic diagnostics rules. In: Riguzzi, F., Bellodi, E., Zese, R. (eds.) ILP 2018. LNCS (LNAI), vol. 11105, pp. 54–71. Springer, Cham (2018). https://doi.org/10.1007/978-3-319-99960-9_4
27. Kharlamov, E., et al.: Semantic rules for machine diagnostics: execution and management. In: CIKM, pp. 2131–2134 (2017)
28. Kharlamov, E., et al.: Finding data should be easier than finding oil. In: IEEE Big Data, pp. 1747–1756 (2018)
29. Kharlamov, E., Zheleznyakov, D.: Capturing instance level ontology evolution for DL-Lite. In: Aroyo, L., et al. (eds.) ISWC 2011. LNCS, vol. 7031, pp. 321–337. Springer, Heidelberg (2011). https://doi.org/10.1007/978-3-642-25073-6_21
30. Kharlamov, E., Zheleznyakov, D., Calvanese, D.: Capturing model-based ontology evolution at the instance level: the case of DL-Lite. J. Comput. Syst. Sci. **79**(6), 835–872 (2013)
31. Knublauch, H., Ryman, A.: Shapes constraint language (SHACL). W3C Recommendation, vol. 11, no. 8 (2017)
32. König, M., Leclère, M., Mugnier, M., Thomazo, M.: Sound, complete and minimal UCQ-rewriting for existential rules. Semant. Web **6**(5), 451–475 (2015)
33. Mehdi, G., et al.: Semantic rule-based equipment diagnostics. In: d'Amato, C., et al. (eds.) ISWC 2017. LNCS, vol. 10588, pp. 314–333. Springer, Cham (2017). https://doi.org/10.1007/978-3-319-68204-4_29
34. Mehdi, G., et al.: SemDia: semantic rule-based equipment diagnostics tool. In: CIKM, pp. 2507–2510 (2017)
35. Motik, B., Horrocks, I., Sattler, U.: Bridging the gap between OWL and relational databases. Web Semant. Sci. Serv. Agents World Wide Web **7**(2), 74–89 (2009)
36. Patel-Schneider, P.F.: Using description logics for RDF constraint checking and closed-world recognition. In: AAAI (2015)
37. Ringsquandl, M., et al.: On event-driven knowledge graph completion in digital factories. In: IEEE Big Data, pp. 1676–1681 (2017)

38. Savkovic, O., Calvanese, D.: Introducing datatypes in DL-Lite. In: ECAI, pp. 720–725 (2012)
39. Savković, O., et al.: Semantic diagnostics of smart factories. In: Ichise, R., Lecue, F., Kawamura, T., Zhao, D., Muggleton, S., Kozaki, K. (eds.) JIST 2018. LNCS, vol. 11341, pp. 277–294. Springer, Cham (2018). https://doi.org/10.1007/978-3-030-04284-4_19
40. Soylu, A., et al.: OptiqueVQS: a visual query system over ontologies for industry. Semant. Web **9**(5), 627–660 (2018)
41. Suchanek, F.M., Kasneci, G., Weikum, G.: YAGO: a core of semantic knowledge. In: Proceedings of WWW, pp. 697–706 (2007)
42. Tao, J., Sirin, E., Bao, J., McGuinness, D.L.: Integrity constraints in OWL. In: AAAI (2010)
43. Zheleznyakov, D., Kharlamov, E., Horrocks, I.: Trust-sensitive evolution of DL-Lite knowledge bases. In: AAAI, pp. 1266–1273 (2017)

An Ontology-Based Interactive System for Understanding User Queries

Giorgos Stoilos$^{(\boxtimes)}$, Szymon Wartak, Damir Juric, Jonathan Moore, and Mohammad Khodadadi

Babylon Health, London SW3 3DD, UK
{giorgos.stoilos,szymon.wartak,damir.juric,jonathan.moore,
mohammad.khodadadi}@babylonhealth.com

Abstract. The use of ontologies in applications like dialogue systems, question-answering or decision-support is gradually gaining attention. In such applications, keyword-based user queries are mapped to ontology entities and then the respective application logic is activated. This task is not trivial as user queries may often be vague and imprecise or simply don't match the entities recognised by the application. This is for example the case in symptom-checking dialogue systems where users can enter text like "I am not feeling well", "I sleep terribly", and more, which cannot be directly matched to entities found in formal medical ontologies. In the current paper we present a framework for automatically building a small dialogue for the purposes of bridging the gap between user queries and a set of pre-defined (target) ontology concepts. We show how we can use the ontology and statistical techniques to select an initial small set of candidate concepts from the target ones and how these can then be grouped into categories using their properties in the ontology. Using these groups we can ask the user questions in order to try and reduce the set of candidates to a single concept that captures the initial user intention. The effectiveness of this approach is hindered by well-known underspecification of ontologies which we address by a concept enrichment pre-processing step based on information extraction techniques. We have instantiated our framework and performed a preliminary evaluation largely motivated by a real-world symptom-checking application obtaining encouraging results.

1 Introduction

Knowledge Bases (KBs) have started to play a key role in many academic and industrial-strength applications like recommendation systems [8], dialogue-systems [19], and more. In such applications users form their requests using short queries, e.g., "I want to book a flight", "I am looking for Italian Restaurants", "I have a fever", and so forth, and these should be used to activate the proper KB entities which are used to encode or control the background application logic. In particular, symptom-checking dialogue-systems (SCDSs) have attracted considerable attention due to their promise of low-cost and continuous availability and many academic [5,6,12,18] and industrial systems are also starting to emerge (see also [13] for an overview).

© Springer Nature Switzerland AG 2019
P. Hitzler et al. (Eds.): ESWC 2019, LNCS 11503, pp. 330–345, 2019.
https://doi.org/10.1007/978-3-030-21348-0_22

All previous approaches assume that users express their requests in a precise and clear way like "I have a stomach ache", "I want to book a flight", "I want a loan", "I am looking for a thriller movie", from which the relevant terms ("stomach ache", "book flight", etc.) can be extracted using Machine Learning or rule-based slot-filling techniques. However, this assumption fails in applications where users need to convey complex meaning to the service. For example, in a symptom-checking scenario [13] user input may often be highly vague like "I have a pain" in which case several entities in the KB may be relevant like "Abdominal Pain", "Low Back Pain", and more, or be highly colloquial like "I feel my head will explode". In all these cases it is impossible to match user input to the right entities in the inference model. In addition, there is usually a gap between the formal medical language encountered in medical KBs and the terms used by users. For example, a symptom-checker may contain nodes that represent the medical entities "Periumbilical pain" and "sputum in throat", however, users will never use such formal language to report their symptoms.

The above issue is partially solved by using information retrieval techniques like full-text search or sentence embeddings which can retrieve the top-k most "similar" KB entities and then ask the user to select from them, an approach that is actually followed by many free as well as commercial SCDSs. Unfortunately, this approach suffers from several drawbacks. First, it is clearly not user friendly and, second, especially in the symptom-checking scenario users may still find it difficult to browse through the list and understand the differences of the (possibly similar in many cases) symptoms. Third, there is clearly a limit to the number of candidate entities that users can browse, which drops even more if we consider speech-based dialogue systems where the list needs to be read to them.

To address the above issues we designed a framework and algorithm that can be used to "guide" users into associating to their initial query an entity from a pre-defined set of target entities, that most closely matches their intention. First, an initial "small" subset of the target entities is extracted using the hierarchy of the KB together with statistical techniques like embeddings. Second, the properties of these candidates in the KB are used to group them into categories. These categories are then used to ask the user specific questions. For instance, in our running example the system could ask the user "Where is your problem located?" with potential answers "In eye", "On Leg", etc. The effectiveness of the grouping algorithm crucially depends on the number of properties that the target entities share and given the well-known underspecification of KBs [9] this step is not expected to behave well in practice. For this reason we propose an entity enrichment step that uses information extraction techniques and a custom scoring model to prioritise the verification of the newly extracted properties.

Our approach combines in a non-trivial way techniques from guided navigation [10,17] and dialogue systems and also extends previous works to mapping keywords to KBs [16] in an attempt to set a framework for understanding vague and imprecise user queries in a user-friendly and interactive way. Moreover, at a technical level it combines various technologies like ontologies (their hierarchical structure and domain/range constraints), statistical techniques (sentence embeddings and triple scoring), and information extraction (text annotation and some simple triple extraction).

Differently to typical approaches to dialogue-systems our approach does not assume a fixed set of frames with a pre-defined set of slots that need to be filled [19]. In contrast, the target set of entities may contain highly diverse elements and the user query may match any subset of them. Hence, the algorithm is highly dynamic and modular and is able to handle highly diverse and broad domains like symptom-checking, the complexity of which has been noted in the past [15]. Moreover, our approach is largely unsupervised as does not depend on any pre-existing corpora of sample dialogues [15,20] or user queries from logs where a mapping from user text to KB entities can be learned.

Compared to guided navigation and faceted search, our approach is implemented as a short dialogue that presents one question at a time and has to prioritise which question to ask first. In contrast, faceted navigation is prevalently click-based and all facets with result counts and current candidates are presented to the user. Moreover, in our case the set of property-values over which the grouping is applied is not completely available a priori but has to be obtained by our enrichment process.

Our work was motivated by a real-world industrial strength use case in Babylon Health[1]. Babylon Health is a digital healthcare provider and one of its services is an SCDS that is implemented via a Probabilistic Graph Model (PGM) [12]. Users of chatbot enter text like "My stomach hurts" and subsequently the relevant nodes (symptoms) in the PGM need to be activated in order to proceed with symptom-checking. These nodes are encoded using concepts from a medical KB [14] and can either be simple like Fever or also complex like AnteriorKneeTenderness. Babylon's SCDS is experiencing a drop-off when users enter text that is vague or simply does not match complex symptoms. We used our framework to build a prototype system with the aim of reducing Babylon's drop-off. We applied our entity enrichment step on the PGM entities, associated actual questions to each of our concept categories and conducted a preliminary evaluation obtaining encouraging results.

2   Preliminaries

For a set of tuples $\mathsf{tup} = \{\langle k_1, v_1 \rangle, \langle k_2, v_2 \rangle, ..., \langle k_n, v_n \rangle\}$, the *projection* of tup on the first argument is defined as $\pi_1 \mathsf{tup} = \{k_1, k_2, ..., k_n\}$; dually we have $\pi_2 \mathsf{tup} = \{v_1, v_2, ..., v_n\}$. A map is a collection of *key/value* pairs. We allow for *semi-structured* maps, that is, maps where the values of different keys may be of a different type. For M a map and k some key we use the notation $\mathsf{M}.k$ to denote the value associated with k. If no key k exists, then $\mathsf{M}.k := v$ means that a new key k is added to the map and its value is set to v.

---

[1] https://www.babylonhealth.com/.

2.1   Knowledge Bases

Let $\mathbf{C}$ and $\mathbf{R}$ be countably disjoint sets of *concepts* and *properties*. A Knowledge Base (KB) is a tuple $\langle \mathcal{K}, \mathbb{T}, \mu, \rho, \delta \rangle$, where $\mathcal{K}$ is a set of *subject, property, object* triples of the form $\langle s\ p\ o \rangle$ like in the RDF standard[2], $\mathbb{T}$ is a subset of concepts from $\mathcal{K}$ called *semantic types* (stys), μ is a mapping from every concept in $\mathcal{K}$ to a non-empty subset of $\mathbb{T}$ and both ρ and δ are mappings from each $R \in \mathbf{R}$ to a possibly empty subset of $\mathbf{C}$. In addition, we assume that every concept C is associated with a preferred label and a user-friendly label both of which are unique. We use the notation $C.\ell$ and $C.\text{lay}$ to refer to these two labels and we also use the notation $C.p$ to refer to the set $\{C' \mid \langle C\ p\ C' \rangle \in \mathcal{K}\}$. Finally, for a concept C we also use the function $\mu^+(C)$ to denote the set $\mu(C) \cup \bigcup_{C' \in C.p} \mu(C')$.

Intuitively, stys denote general/abstract categories of interest in the KB and are used to group other concepts while ρ and δ define the range and domains of properties. For example, in a medical KB we can have stys like Disease, Drug, BodyPart and the like, and then we can have that Malaria has sty Disease. This information can also be encoded within $\mathcal{K}$ using triples of the form $\langle$Disease is_sty *true*$\rangle$ and $\langle$Malaria has_sty Disease$\rangle$. Moreover, for concept MyocardialInfarction we can have MyocardialInfarction.ℓ = "Myocardial infarction" and MyocardialInfarction.lay = "Heart attack". A key property that we use from the RDF standard is subClassOf ($\sqsubseteq$ for short) that can be used to specify that the subject of a triple implies the object, e.g., $\langle$VivaxMalaria subClassOf Malaria$\rangle$.

We say that C is *subsumed by* D w.r.t. a KB $\mathcal{K}$ if $\mathcal{K} \models \langle C$ subClassOf $D \rangle$ where $\models$ is entailment under the standard FO-semantics. For simplicity and without loss of generality we assume that μ is closed under subClassOf, that is, if $C \in \mu(A)$ and C' is some sty s.t. $\mathcal{K} \models \langle C$ subClassOf $C' \rangle$, then $C' \in \mu(A)$.

For efficient storage and querying we assume that the KB is loaded to a triple-store employed with (at least) RDFS forward-chaining reasoning. Forward-chaining implies that inferences under the RDFS-semantics are materialised during loading. Hence, if $\mathcal{K} \models \langle C$ subClassOf $D \rangle$ under the RDFS-semantics then $\langle C$ subClassOf $D \rangle \in \mathcal{K}$.

2.2   Problem Statement

The problem we study is the following: given a subset of concepts TargetCons defined in a KB $\mathcal{K}$ (target concepts or concepts of interest) and a text query Q, provide mechanisms to "guide" the user to a *single* $C \in$ TargetCons that expresses best the intention of Q. This problem is important especially in cases that TargetCons contains concepts representing complex real-world entities like AmenorrheaAfterMenopause, AcuteDyspnoea, AnteriorKneeTenderness, which are unlikely that a user can express with Q. Restricting the problem to single concepts is motivated by the fact that systems like virtual assistants and task-oriented dialogue systems usually require a single entity (frame) to be activated in order to proceed with their application logic.

---

[2] https://www.w3.org/RDF/.

3   An Interactive Search Approach

Most previous works to task-oriented dialogue systems and virtual assistants are focused on fairly precise tasks and domains like flight booking, bank transfer, home automation, and more. However, as we move towards more complex problems and domains the developed systems would need to be able to deal with vague or imprecise user text.

Example 1. Consider a user that intends to use a symptom-checking dialogue system (SCDS). In such a scenario a user can enter text like $Q =$ "i have a rash". Such a statement is quite vague and an SCDS is likely to contain more specific symptoms like CircularRash, RashInAbdomen, RashInArm, and BumpyRash, all of which are relevant to the user text. Even when people visit clinics, doctors usually need to ask a series of questions about the nature of the reported symptom, like its location, its onset, severity, and more, in order to understand the patient conditions better.   ◇

A first challenge in the above scenario is to determine an initial and highly relevant set of concepts from the set of concepts that the dialogue system "understands" (TargetCons). Several different alternatives can be considered for this step. A popular approach which is actually used in some SCDS is by using sentence embeddings [1]. Sentence embeddings can be used to map text to a vector space with the property that (semantically) similar text is clustered closely in the space. In our scenario, all labels of the entities in TargetCons as well as a given user query can be embedded in the vector space and then the top-k closest (w.r.t. cosine similarity) vectors of entities in TargetCons can be returned. For the above two operations we assume two functions vectorize and sim. The former takes as input some text ℓ and returns a vector in some vector space while the latter is the similarity between two vectors. Alternatively, one could use text annotation [4] in combination with some form of KB-based reasoning.

Example 2. Consider Example 1, the input sentence Q and the concepts of the SCDS mentioned. Assume also some text annotator that annotates text with entities from some medical KB $\mathcal{K}$ like SNOMED CT. When applied to Q the annotator will return concept $C :=$ Rash. It is expected that in SNOMED CT, concept C is somehow semantically related to the symptoms and conditions of SCDS that are potentially relevant to the patient condition, e.g., that RashInAbdomen is a sub-concept of C.

Relevance between two concepts can be defined in a strong way as "all those $D \in$ TargetCons such that $\mathcal{K} \models D \sqsubseteq C$" or maybe also in a more loose way as, "all $D \in$ TargetCons s.t. some path of triples from D to C exists in $\mathcal{K}$".   ◇

The above let us to the development of method GENERATECANDIDATES that is depicted in Algorithm 1. The method takes as input some text, a set of concepts of interest, a positive integer k that controls the number of candidates to be considered by the embedding approach, and a set of stys that can be used for additional filtering. The algorithm internally uses a text annotator and a

---

Algorithm 1. GenerateCandidates$_\mathcal{K}$ (txt, TargetCons, k, styList)

1: txtAnn := AnnotateText$_\mathcal{K}$ (txt)
2: CandCons := $\{C \mid \langle C \sqsubseteq A \rangle \in \mathcal{K}, A \in$ txtAnn$, C \in$ TargetCons$\}$
3: **if** CandCons == $\emptyset$ **then**
4:     ConsWithWeight := $\{\langle C, \text{sim}(\text{vectorize}(C.\ell), \text{vectorize}(\text{txt})) \rangle \mid C \in$ TargetCons$\}$
5:     $S_1 := \bigcup_{A \in \text{txtAnn}} \mu(A)$
6:     ConsWithWeight := $\{\langle C, n \rangle \in$ ConsWithWeight $\mid S_1 \cap \mu^+(C) \neq \emptyset\}$
7:     CandCons := $\pi_1$top$(k,$ ConsWithWeight$)$
8: **end if**
9: CandCons := $\{C \in$ CandCons $\mid \mu^+(C) \cap$ styList $\neq \emptyset\}$
10: **return** CandCons

Knowledge Base ($\mathcal{K}$) which the annotator uses to link text phrases to concepts. In order to abstract from implementation details of different annotators we define the following function.

Definition 1. *Function* AnnotateText$_\mathcal{K}$ *takes as input a text* txt *and returns a set of concepts* $\{C_1, ..., C_n\}$ *from* $\mathcal{K}$ *such that for every* C_i *some substring str of* txt *exists such that* str-sim$(str, C_i.\ell) \geq$ thr *where* str-sim *is some similarity function and* thr *some threshold.*

The algorithm first uses the semantic approach described in Example 2 since this is expected to be more selective and with higher precision (fewer false positives). If no candidates can be computed, then the more "relaxed" embedding approach is employed. Finally, candidates computed by either method can be further filtered according to a set of stys of interest (line 9). In the evaluation section we analyse the effectiveness of various combinations of these methods.

After computing an initial list of candidates the most relevant one of those needs to be selected and passed to the dialogue-system. In a naive approach the user can be presented with the full list of candidates and asked to choose, an approach that is actually followed in many free on-line as well as commercial SCDSs. Unfortunately, this approach is not user-friendly and still users may find it hard to pick the correct entities if their differences are not clear to them or more than one seem relevant. Even worse, this approach cannot be implemented in spoken dialogue-systems where a potentially long list of candidates needs to be read to the user. Ideally we need a way to group the candidates according to some set of properties and ask the user which value of that properties are most closely related to the condition they report.

Example 3. Consider again Example 1. As can be seen many of the potentially relevant concepts are about some kind of "Rash" which is further specialised with either the body location where it manifests ("Abdomen", "Arm", etc.) or its appearance ("Circular", "Bumpy"). We can assume that these differences are also explicated in a medical KB using appropriate triples like the following ones:

$\langle$RashInAbdomen location Abdomen$\rangle$ $\langle$RashInArm location Arm$\rangle$
$\langle$CircularRash shape Circular$\rangle$ $\langle$BumpyRash shape Bumpy$\rangle$

Algorithm 2. CandidateSearch$_\mathcal{K}$(CandCons, styList, n)

Input: A set of concepts and stys styList from the KB and a positive integer.

1: **while** $|$CandCons$| \geq n$ **do**
2:      Create a map styToCands such that for every $sty \in$ styList we have
              styToCands.$sty := \{\langle C, C' \rangle \mid C \in$ CandCons, $C' \in C.p, sty \in \mu(C')\}$
3:      Let sty_m be some key in styToCands with the most values.
4:      **if** $|$styToCands.$sty_m| < n$ **then** break
5:      ansCons := askUser(styToCands.sty_m, sty_m)
6:      **if** ansCons $== \emptyset$ **then**
7:          **then** CandCons := CandCons $\setminus \pi_1$styToCands.sty_m
8:      **else**
9:          CandCons := ansCons
10:     **end if**
11: **end while**
12: **if** $|$CandCons$| > 1$ **then**
13:     CandCons := askUser($\{\langle C, \bot \rangle \mid C \in$ CandCons$\}$, null)
14: **end if**
15: **return** CandCons

The semantic types of the objects in these triples (e.g., BodyPart for Abdomen and Arm and Shape for Circular and Bumby) provide the categories over which grouping can be performed and questions asked. For example, for the above candidates the questions that arise are "Where is your Rash?" and "How does its shape look like?". The potential answers for the first question are "Abdomen", "Arm", or "None of the above", and the last answer includes candidates CircularRash and BumpyRash that are not connected in the KB with any body part.   ◇

Based on the above intuition we designed Algorithm 2. The algorithm takes as input a set of candidate concepts (possibly computed using Algorithm 1), a set of stys styList over which grouping is done and a positive integer which is used to control the grouping process. The algorithm enters a loop where it groups the current set of candidates according to the semantic types of concepts to which candidates are connected in the KB and builds pairs of the form $\langle C, C' \rangle$ where $C \in$ CandCons and C' is a concept that C points to. A pair of this form is built because the label of C' will be used as an answer value for the question that would be generated. Subsequently, the algorithm selects the group that contains the most candidates and asks a question related to the type of that group. Our strategy of selecting the group with the most members is similar to selecting facets with the largest specificity [17], however, different strategies or more complex models can also be used [11].

Generating the question to be asked for the selected group as well as the potential answer values is done using function askUser which is discussed in Sect. 4. The possible values of the answers also include a "None of the above" answer in which case this function returns the empty set. If this is the answer of the user then all candidates in the group are removed (line 7). The algorithm stops the grouping process and exits the while loop when the set of candidates has

---

Algorithm 3. askUser(ConceptPairs, sty)

Input: A set of pairs of concepts and a semantic type (sty)

1: **if** sty == null **then**
2:     println "Which of the following?"
3:     **for** $\langle C, \_ \rangle \in$ ConceptPairs **do**
4:         println "\t " + C.lay
5:     **end for**
6:     print "\t None"
7:     $ans :=$ **read** answer from console
8:     **return** $\{C \mid C.\text{lay} = ans\}$
9: **else**
10:     println fetchQuery(sty)
11:     **for** $\langle C, C' \rangle \in$ ConceptPairs such that C'.lay hasn't been printed before **do**
12:         println "\t " + C'.lay
13:     **end for**
14:     println "\t None"
15:     $ans :=$ **read** answer from console
16:     **return** $\{C \mid \langle C, C' \rangle \in$ ConceptPairs with C'.lay $= ans\}$
17: **end if**

---

dropped below a threshold n. In this case the set is considered to be sufficiently small that the remaining candidates can be presented to the user to select the most relevant one.

For the concepts of Example 3 the algorithm would create the following two groups:

styToCands.BodyPart   := $\{\langle$RashInAbdomen, Abdomen$\rangle, \langle$RashInArm, Arm$\rangle\}$
styToCands.Shape   := $\{\langle$CircularRash, Circular$\rangle, \langle$BumpyRash, Bumpy$\rangle\}$

4   Question Generation

Algorithm 2 generates two types of questions, one that asks users to clarify the value of a specific property of the candidates (line 5) and one that simply prints all candidates and asks users to choose one of them (line 13). The generation of fluent and natural questions is a non-trivial problem and simple but effective template-based shallow generation approaches are usually preferred in real-world applications [6], which we also follow as an initial approach.

Our two types of questions are generated by Algorithm 3 which takes as input a pair of concepts and an sty. If the sty is null then the algorithm proceeds with printing a question of the form "Which of the following?" and then the user-friendly label of each candidate (line 4). Note that since the set of candidates does not contain duplicates and by the assumption of uniqueness of user-friendly labels in the KB these labels are unique.

In case the semantic type is not null a specific query that depends on the semantic type needs to be printed. A question has been assigned to each semantic

Table 1. Questions associated to Semantic Types and potential answer values

Semantic type	Question	Answer values
BodyPart	"Is your problem located in:"	abdomen, leg, finger, . . .
NeurologicalFinding	"Do you feel/experience:"	pain, irritation, . . .
Severity	"How severe is your problem?"	severe, moderate, mild, . . .
BiologicalSubstance	"Do you see:"	urine, mucus, blood, . . .
Appearance		bruised, scared, clear, . . .
Colour	"Does it look:"	red, black, yellow, . . .
Shape		circular, bent, curved, . . .
SpatialQualifier	"Is it:"	left, right, top, bottom, . . .

type at design time. An excerpt of questions for a symptom-checking scenario as well as some potential answer values are depicted in Table 1. Regarding answer values the user-friendly label of the possible property value concepts are used. In this case duplicates may exist. Consider for example, that the candidate selection step has returned concepts C_1 = HeadInjury and C_2 = HeadPain which we have grouped according to body structure generating pairs $\langle C_1, \text{Head} \rangle$ and $\langle C_2, \text{Head} \rangle$. In that case the answer value for the question "Where is your problem located?" is the same for both concepts (i.e., "Head"). The algorithm takes care to print "Head" only once and if the user selects this as an answer then both concepts C_1 and C_2 would need to be returned by the algorithm.

5 Knowledge Base Enrichment

Algorithm 2 is using the properties of concepts in the KB in order to group the candidate concepts. It is clear that the more properties these concepts have and the more they share them with each other, the more effective these groupings would be. In a different case, groups will mostly contain a single concept and all the other would be in the "None of the above" answer. Unfortunately, several authors have noted the "incompleteness" and "underspecification" of medical KBs [9]. For example, in SNOMED CT concept RecentInjury is not associated with concepts Recent and Injury and SevereAbdominalPain is not linked with concept Severe. The same issue can easily be observed in other KBs like DBpedia [2] where the category ItalianRenaissancePainters is not connected to concepts Painter or ItalianRenaissance.

In order to improve the effectiveness of the grouping strategy all concepts in TargetCons need to be enriched with as many triples as possible. This task can be manual but it would be beneficial if automatic ways could also be employed to assist it. It has been noted that labels of concepts in (biomedical) ontologies are a good source of additional information [3]. For instance, in Example 1 we can immediately see that the label of concept RashInHead implies a link between Rash and Head.

Algorithm 4. conceptEnrichment$_\mathcal{K}$(TargetCons, styList, thr)

Input: A set of concepts and stys from some KB $\mathcal{K}$ and a real number thr

1: Inspect := $\emptyset$
2: **for all** $C \in$ TargetCons **do**
3:      **for all** $C' \in$ AnnotateText$_\mathcal{K}(C.\ell)$ such that $\mu(C') \cap$ styList $\neq \emptyset$ **do**
4:          **if** score$_{\mathsf{model}}(\langle C\ C' \rangle) \geq thr$ **then**
5:              Add $\langle C\ p\ C' \rangle$ to $\mathcal{K}$ for some p with domain in $\mu(C)$ and range in $\mu(C')$
6:          **else**
7:              Inspect := Inspect $\cup \{\langle C\ p\ C' \rangle\}$
8:          **end if**
9:      **end for**
10: **end for**

Building on this idea we designed a semi-automatic pipeline depicted in Algorithm 4 that can be used to extract such information from concept labels. The algorithm takes as input a set of concepts and uses their label to extract triples of the form $\langle C\ p\ C' \rangle$ which is again achieved using text annotation. To control the number of new triples extracted some list of stys of interest (styList) is also passed as a parameter.

Clearly, triples extracted from such an automated pipeline can be erroneous. To assist in the manual verification, techniques to score them and focus validation on the low-scored pairs would be beneficial. Several different methods can be used like KB embedding models [7], training a custom deep NN classifier using label embeddings, or training a traditional classifier using features like n-grams or the dependency-parse tree of concept labels. We have experimented with a custom deep neural classifier which we detail in the evaluation section.

6   Evaluation

We have used our methodology and framework in order to build an interactive system that can be used to help understand vague user text in Babylon Health's SCDS. The current version of Babylon Health's SCDS contains about 2261 symptoms which correspond to a small subset of a much larger medical Knowledge Base [14]. This KB is built by aligning and integrating ontologies like SNOMED CT, NCI, and more [14] and currently contains 1,5m concepts, 173 properties, 1,8 million subsumption axioms, 2,2m labels, 93 semantic types and 34 domain/range axioms. It is stored and queried using RDF4J[3] and saturated using RDFS inference rules.

We collected 265 user text queries from the Babylon SCDS and asked medical doctors to map each of them to the most relevant concept in PGM; we call these concepts the *user intended concepts*. We also prepared another variation on the input text queries where we tried to 'degenerate' them by removing some of the parts of the text in an attempt to make them more vague. For example, if the user text is "I feel pain around my heart" we try to construct text "I feel pain".

---

[3] http://rdf4j.org/.

Table 2. Counts of PGM concepts with the given semantic types (stys) shown before and after concept enrichment.

sty	Before	After	sty	Before	After
BodyPart	1585	2566	ClinicalFinding	1049	1567
ObservableEntity	728	1102	AbnormalBodyPart	452	712
QualifierValue	31	652	AnatomyQualifier	42	218
Substance	17	139	SpatialQualifier	3	119
Organism	3	16	ClinicalQualifier	2	11

To do so we used sentence embeddings between original input text and labels of PGM concepts that appear in the object position of triples. For example, we can use the triple ⟨Pain findingSite Heart⟩ and the label Heart.ℓ = "Heart" to remove the respective text from the above sentence.

6.1   Concept Enrichment

First, we run the enrichment pipeline presented in Sect. 5 in order to extract additional triples for all PGM concepts. To control the process we fixed a list of 10 stys of interest (parameter styList in Algorithm 4). All extracted triples were scored using two different models and evaluated using 240 labelled data. The first method used the RESCAL [7] approach for KB embeddings and this model yielded an AUC of 0.52 on the testing data. The second approach was a three layer Neural Network developed using Keras[4] with two hidden layers of sizes 3 and 5. The input was the concatenation of the sentence embeddings of the PGM node text and the extracted triple. Both embeddings were of size 512, yielding a combined input layer of size 1024. The training and test sets were of sizes 192 and 48, respectively, with the network trained using a binary cross-entropy loss function. Resulting accuracy was 0.84 while AUC was 0.73. Our result is interesting in the sense that even simple custom approaches work better than off-the-shelf involved KB embedding approaches.

The enrichment process increased the triples of the 2261 symptoms from 3920 to 7102. The breakdown of these triples per sty before and after enrichment is depicted in Table 2. From those numbers we can conclude that, in spite of the enrichment, some stys will most likely not be very effective in grouping candidates as they do not appear often in the PGM nodes (e.g., all below a count of 100). In Sect. 6.4, we will investigate further which of those stys were actually the most frequently used ones when we run the main algorithm on input user text.

---

[4] https://keras.io/.

6.2   Evaluating the Effect of k in Selecting the Top-k Candidates

A crucial property of the candidate selection algorithm is the number of top-k candidates that we need to compute in order for this set to always include the user intended concept. To evaluate the sensitivity of the embedding approach on the selection of k we varied the value of k starting with $k = 5$ and using increment of 5 we established in how many cases (out of the 265) the intended user concept was in the top-k candidates. The results are presented in Table 3. As can be seen for $k = 30$ the embedder was able to include the user intended concept in 257 (97%) and 169 (64%) cases in the two different test query sets in contrast to 245 (92%) and 117 (44%) for $k = 10$ which is the usual one. As can be seen for vague (degenerated) queries going above the fairly standard top-10 is highly beneficial.

Table 3. Number of correct concepts distributed in various ranks according to k; e.g., (5,10] denotes how many intended concepts appear between the top-5 and top-10.

k value	[1, 5]	(5, 10]	(10, 15]	(15, 20]	(20, 25]	(25, 30]	[1, 30]	(30, 256]
Degenerated	91	26	20	14	10	8	169	96 (36%)
Full Queries	229	16	5	4	1	2	257	8 (3%)

6.3   Evaluating Candidate Selection and Depth of Correct Answer

We evaluated two variations of the candidate selection algorithm (Algorithm 1). The first implements Algorithm 1 as presented, that is, first uses subClassOf traversal on the KB (line 2 of Algorithm 1) and if this step returns an empty set then it falls back to embeddings, while the second only uses the embedding approach. In both cases k was set to 30 for the embedder.

Table 4 shows the number of times that the correct answer was included in the candidate set computed by the two algorithms in the two different sets of queries. We further broke down the first approach and measured in how many cases the KB descendant approach returned a non-empty set of candidates and in how many of them the intended concept was within the candidates. As can be seen there are quite a few cases where the KB approach returns an empty set (68 in the first and 18 in the second set of queries) and the fall-back needs to be employed. Moreover, even if a non-empty set is returned, in quite a few cases this set does not contain the intended user query. This is because the current implementation of checking descendants in the KB is semantically "very strict" compared to the flexible way in which a query can be formed in text. For example, the behaviour of this approach is considerably different if the input text is "Blood in stool" or "Bleeding". In this case the annotator associates KB concepts of even different sty. In contrast the embedder works considerably better due to the fact of loosely capturing the semantics and similarities between concepts.

Table 4. Frequency where correct answer was included in the candidate set by each approach (correct cases/cases that approach was employed).

Input text	KB+Embedder		Embedder (only)
	KB	Embedder	
Degenerated	90/197	38/68	169/265
Full queries	181/247	15/18	257/265

Table 5. Number of cases and questions required to reach the intended concept.

Input text	KB+Embedder		Embedder (only)
	KB	Embedder	
Degenerate	48(1), 31(2), 8(3), 3(4)	10(1), 25(2), 3(3)	68(1), 67(2), 32(3), 2(4)
Full queries	115(1), 53(2), 12(3), 1(4)	3(1), 10(2), 2(3)	50(1), 127(2), 71(3), 9(4)

After candidate selection we want to evaluate how many questions would be required before Algorithm 2 returned the user intended concept. This is similar to the number of *clicks* (scan effort) in faceted search evaluation. We only consider the cases that the candidate selection approaches did manage to return the user intended concept in the set of candidates. The results are depicted in Table 4; the format X (Y) means that in X number of cases the intended user concept is reachable after Y questions. As can be seen most concepts are reachable after one or two questions and all concepts are reachable at most after four (Table 5).

6.4 Further Evaluation of Grouping Algorithm

Table 6 (left) shows which stys were used to group the set of candidates in any of the user queries of our test sets. Results were very similar in all variations we ran. In 51% of tests, the final question of the algorithm did not have an sty to distinguish the correct answer from the others (although previous question would have), so the answers were collapsed to a generic question.

Ideally the groups created by the algorithm should neither be very small (which leads to too many questions) nor too large (which leads to few question with too many answers). We provide summary statistics for these results in Table 6 (right). As expected degenerated text queries result in larger answer sets since they are more vague. Another aspect to note is the smaller answer sets produced with the annotation filter compared to the embedding filter. This comes as a trade off against the lower recall of the annotation filter, which we can interpret as a more homogeneous set of candidates being returned by the stricter filter.

Table 6. Left: stys that appeared in evaluation (% of total tests); Right: Number of answers per question (median; mean)

Anatomical structure	75%
Qualifier value	36%
Observable entity	11%
Morphologically altered Str.	6.3%

	KB+Embedder		Embedder
Input Text	KB	Embedder	
Degenerated	4; 26.2	15; 12.3	13; 11.8
Full Queries	4; 4.3	13; 11.0	6; 9.8

7 Conclusions

In the current paper we studied the problem of interpreting and understanding (possibly vague and imprecise) user queries over KBs. This problem is highly relevant in applications like ontology-based dialogue systems and virtual assistants where user requests need to be mapped to KB entities that activate some background service. First, users may not have prior knowledge of the content and entities that the service supports, second, they may not know how to accurately express their request and, third, in applications like symptom-checking the language they use may be substantially different compared to the formal medical language used to construct the service by doctors. Hence, we may either be unable to match a user query to any entity in the KB (technically involved domains) or more than one entities may be relevant (vague input queries). To be able to associate the "intended" entity to the user query we developed a framework which can construct on the fly a small dialogue that asks the user few "clarification" questions in an attempt to "activate" the proper entity. Semantic and ML-based techniques were proposed for selecting an initial (small) set of candidates and then an algorithm for grouping those candidates according to their properties in the KB was designed. The "most relevant" group is then selected according to some cost model and the question associated to the group is printed. To improve the effectiveness of the approach and overcome underspecification issues of KBs an information extraction-based enrichment pipeline is proposed and various scoring models were used to assess the soundness of the extracted information. This process should be complemented with manual curation in order to build questions that are more user friendly and fluent.

We implemented our framework and evaluated it using real world data obtained from the symptom-checking service provided by Babylon Health. We evaluated the two different approaches for obtaining candidates, the sensitivity of the approach with respect to top-k retrieval, and the number of questions and size of answer values constructed in the small dialogues. Although largely motivated by symptom-checking, we envision that our work is relevant and useful in any domain and can greatly contribute towards building more user-friendly ontology-based intelligent systems. It can be used to form the basis for providing a bridge between initial vague, imprecise, or noisy user text and the services implemented by an ontology-based dialogue system or for accessing large KBs.

References

1. Arora, S., Liang, Y., Ma, T.: A simple but tough-to-beat baseline for sentence embeddings. In: Proceedings of the 5th International Conference on Learning Representations (ICLR), pp. 1–14 (2017)
2. Auer, S., Bizer, C., Kobilarov, G., Lehmann, J., Cyganiak, R., Ives, Z.: DBpedia: a nucleus for a web of open data. In: Aberer, K., et al. (eds.) ASWC/ISWC -2007. LNCS, vol. 4825, pp. 722–735. Springer, Heidelberg (2007). https://doi.org/10.1007/978-3-540-76298-0_52
3. Fernandez-Breis, J.T., Iannone, L., Palmisano, I., Rector, A.L., Stevens, R.: Enriching the gene ontology via the dissection of labels using the ontology pre-processor language. In: Cimiano, P., Pinto, H.S. (eds.) EKAW 2010. LNCS (LNAI), vol. 6317, pp. 59–73. Springer, Heidelberg (2010). https://doi.org/10.1007/978-3-642-16438-5_5
4. Hachey, B., Radford, W., Nothman, J., Honnibal, M., Curran, J.R.: Evaluating entity linking with wikipedia. Artif. Intell. **194**, 130–150 (2013)
5. Kao, H., Tang, K., Chang, E.Y.: Context-aware symptom checking for disease diagnosis using hierarchical reinforcement learning. In: Proceedings of the Thirty-Second AAAI Conference on Artificial Intelligence (AAAI) (2018)
6. Milward, D., Beveridge, M.: Ontology-based dialogue systems. In: 3rd Workshop on Knowledge and Reasoning in Practical Dialogue Systems (2003)
7. Nickel, M., Murphy, K., Tresp, V., Gabrilovich, E.: A review of relational machine learning for knowledge graphs. Proc. IEEE **104**(1), 11–33 (2016)
8. Oramas, S., Ostuni, V.C., Noia, T.D., Serra, X., Sciascio, E.D.: Sound and music recommendation with knowledge graphs. ACM Trans. Intell. Syst. Technol. **8**(2), 21:1–21:21 (2016)
9. Pacheco, E.J., Stenzhorn, H., Nohama, P., Paetzold, J., Schulz, S.: Detecting underspecification in SNOMED CT concept definitions through natural language processing. In: Proceedings of the American Medical Informatics Association Annual Symposium (2009)
10. Papadakos, P., Armenatzoglou, N., Kopidaki, S., Tzitzikas, Y.: On exploiting static and dynamically mined metadata for exploratory web searching. Knowl. Inf. Syst. **30**(3), 493–525 (2012)
11. Qarabaqi, B., Riedewald, M.: User-driven refinement of imprecise queries. In: IEEE 30th International Conference on Data Engineering ICDE, pp. 916–927 (2014)
12. Razzaki, S., et al.: A comparative study of artificial intelligence and human doctors for the purpose of triage and diagnosis. CoRR abs/1806.10698 (2018)
13. Semigran, H.L., Linder, J.A., Gidengil, C., Mehrotra, A.: Evaluation of symptom checkers for self diagnosis and triage: audit study. BMJ **351**, h3480 (2015)
14. Stoilos, G., Geleta, D., Shamdasani, J., Khodadadi, M.: A novel approach and practical algorithms for ontology integration. In: Vrandečić, D., et al. (eds.) ISWC 2018. LNCS, vol. 11136, pp. 458–476. Springer, Cham (2018). https://doi.org/10.1007/978-3-030-00671-6_27
15. Tang, K., Kao, H., Chou, J., Chang, E.: Inquire and diagnose: neural symptom checking ensemble using deep reinforcement learning. In: 3rd Deep Reinforcement Learning Workshop (2016)
16. Tran, T., Cimiano, P., Rudolph, S., Studer, R.: Ontology-based interpretation of keywords for semantic search. In: Aberer, k, et al. (eds.) ASWC/ISWC -2007. LNCS, vol. 4825, pp. 523–536. Springer, Heidelberg (2007). https://doi.org/10.1007/978-3-540-76298-0_38

17. Vandic, D., Aanen, S., Frasincar, F., Kaymak, U.: Dynamic facet ordering for faceted product search engines. IEEE Trans. Knowl. Data Eng. **29**(5), 1004–1016 (2017)
18. Wei, Z., et al.: Task-oriented dialogue system for automatic diagnosis. In: Proceedings of the 56th Annual Meeting of the Association for Computational Linguistics, pp. 201–207. ACL (2018)
19. Wessel, M., Acharya, G., Carpenter, J., Yin, M.: OntoVPA - an ontology-based dialogue management system for virtual personal assistants. In: 8th International Workshop on Spoken Dialog Systems, IWSDS, pp. 219–233 (2017)
20. Yan, Z., Duan, N., Chen, P., Zhou, M., Zhou, J., Li, Z.: Building task-oriented dialogue systems for online shopping. In: Proceedings of the Thirty-First AAAI Conference on Artificial Intelligence (AAAI), pp. 4618–4626 (2017)

Knowledge-Based Short Text Categorization Using Entity and Category Embedding

Rima Türker[1,2(✉)], Lei Zhang[1], Maria Koutraki[1,2,3], and Harald Sack[1,2]

[1] FIZ Karlsruhe – Leibniz Institute for Information Infrastructure,
Karlsruhe, Germany
{rima.tuerker,lei.zhang,maria.koutraki,harald.sack}@fiz-karlsruhe.de
[2] Karlsruhe Institute of Technology, Institute AIFB, Karlsruhe, Germany
{rima.tuerker,maria.koutraki,harald.sack}@kit.edu
[3] L3S Research Center, Leibniz University of Hannover, Hannover, Germany
koutraki@l3s.de

Abstract. Short text categorization is an important task due to the rapid growth of online available short texts in various domains such as web search snippets, etc. Most of the traditional methods suffer from sparsity and shortness of the text. Moreover, supervised learning methods require a significant amount of training data and manually labeling such data can be very time-consuming and costly. In this study, we propose a novel probabilistic model for Knowledge-Based Short Text Categorization (KBSTC), which does not require any labeled training data to classify a short text. This is achieved by leveraging entities and categories from large knowledge bases, which are further embedded into a common vector space, for which we propose a new entity and category embedding model. Given a short text, its category (e.g. *Business*, *Sports*, etc.) can then be derived based on the entities mentioned in the text by exploiting semantic similarity between entities and categories. To validate the effectiveness of the proposed method, we conducted experiments on two real-world datasets, i.e., AG News and Google Snippets. The experimental results show that our approach significantly outperforms the classification approaches which do not require any labeled data, while it comes close to the results of the supervised approaches.

Keywords: Short text classification · Dataless text classification · Network embeddings

1 Introduction

Short text categorization is gaining more and more attention due to the availability of a huge number of text data, which includes search snippets, short messages as well as text data generated in social forums [1, 17, 18]. Although, traditional text classification methods perform well on long text such as news article, yet, by considering short text, most of them suffer from issues such as data sparsity and insufficient text length, which is no longer than 200 characters [13]. In other words, simple text classification approaches based on bag of words (BOW) cannot properly

© Springer Nature Switzerland AG 2019
P. Hitzler et al. (Eds.): ESWC 2019, LNCS 11503, pp. 346–362, 2019.
https://doi.org/10.1007/978-3-030-21348-0_23

represent short text as the semantic similarity between single words is not taken into account [21]. Also, approaches that utilize word embeddings for classification perform better when dealing with longer text, where ambiguities can be resolved based on the provided context information within the given text. In the case of short text, where the available context is rather limited and each word obtains significant importance, such approaches often lead to inaccurate results.

Another characteristic of existing approaches is that they all require a significant amount of labeled training data and a sophisticated parameter tuning process [24]. Manual labeling of such data can be a rather time-consuming and costly task. Especially, if the text to be labeled is of a specific scientific or technical domain, crowd-sourcing based labeling approaches do not work successfully and only expensive domain experts are able to fulfill the manual labeling task. Alternatively, semi-supervised text classification approaches [8,22] have been proposed to reduce the labeling effort. Yet, due to the diversity of the documents in many applications, generating small training set for semi-supervised approaches still remains an expensive process [4].

To overcome the requirement for labeled data, a number of *dataless text classification* methods have been proposed [2,14]. These methods do not require any labeled data as a prerequisite. Instead, they rely on the semantic similarity between a given document and a set of predefined categories to determine which category the given document belongs to. More specifically, documents and categories are represented in a common semantic space based on the words contained in the documents and category labels, which allows to calculate a meaningful semantic similarity between documents and categories. The classification process depends on this semantic similarity. However, the most prominent and successful dataless classification approaches are designed for long documents.

Motivated by the already mentioned challenges, we propose a novel probabilistic model for Knowledge-Based Short Text Categorization (KBSTC), which does not require any labeled training data. It is able to capture the semantic relations between the entities represented in a short text and the predefined categories by embedding them into a common vector space using the proposed network embedding technique. Finally, the category of the given text can be derived based on the semantic similarity between entities present in the given text and the set of predefined categories. The similarity is computed based on the vector representation of entities and categories. Overall, the main contributions of the paper are as follows:

- a new paradigm for short text categorization, based on a knowledge base;
- a probabilistic model for short text categorization;
- a new method of entity and category embedding;
- an evaluation using standard datasets for short text categorization.

The rest of this paper is structured as follows: Sect. 2 discusses related work. In Sect. 3, the proposed approach for short text categorization is explained. Section 4 presents the joint entity and category embeddings used in this paper, while Sect. 5 describes the experimental setup for the evaluation as well as the applied baselines. It further illustrates and discusses the achieved results. Last, Sect. 6, concludes the paper with a discussion of open issues and future work.

2   Related Work

The aim of this work is to categorize (e.g. *Business, Sports*, etc.) a given short text by utilizing entity and category embeddings without requiring any labeled data for training. Thus, our work is mainly related to three prior studies: Short Text Classification, Dataless Text Classification as well as Entity and Category Embedding.

Short Text Classification. In order to overcome the data sparsity problem of short text, recent works [20,21] proposed deep learning based approaches for short text classification. The results of these approaches have been compared with traditional supervised classification methods, such as SVM, multinomial logistic regression, etc., where the authors showed that in most of the cases their approach achieved superior results. While performing well in practice, the aforementioned approaches are slow both in the training and in the test phase. In addition, their performance highly depends on the size of training data, its distribution, and the chosen hyper parameters. In difference, our approach does not require any training data nor any parameter tuning.

Dataless Text Classification. In order to address the problem of missing labeled data, [2] introduced a dataless text classification method by representing documents and category labels in a common semantic space. As source, the online encyclopedia, Wikipedia was utilized supported with Explicit Semantic Analysis (ESA) [3] to quantify semantic relatedness between the labels to be assigned and the documents. As a result, it was shown that ESA is able to achieve better classification results than the traditional BOW representations. Further, [14] proposed a dataless hierarchical text classification by dividing the dataless classification task into two steps. In the semantic similarity step, both labels and documents were represented in a common semantic space, which allows to calculate semantic relatedness between documents and labels. In the bootstrapping step, the approach made use of a machine learning based classification procedure with the aim of iteratively improving classification accuracy.

In contrast to these approaches, our proposed approach differs in two main aspects. First, all the mentioned studies were designed for the classification of documents of arbitrary length. However the main purpose of this work is to categorize short text documents without the necessity of labeled training data. Second, none of the mentioned approaches did make use of the entities present in a short text document. To represent a document, all the mentioned approaches consider the words contained in the document.

Entity and Category Embeddings. To generate entity and category embeddings, different embedding models can be employed. For instance, RDF2Vec [11] and DeepWalk [9] adopt a language modeling approach to learn the representation of vertices in a large network. Further, DeepWalk is designed for homogeneous networks, while RDF2Vec aims to deal with RDF graphs, however, it treats each type of vertices and edges equally. HCE [5], as the state-of-the-art entity and category embedding model, integrates the category hierarchy structure into the embedding space. This model has been applied to the dateless

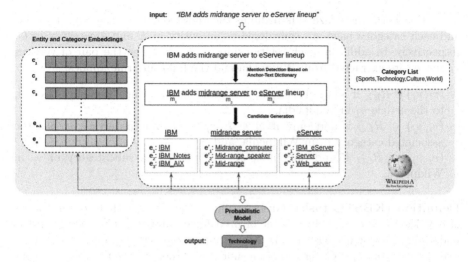

Fig. 1. The work flow of the proposed KBSTC approach (best viewed in color) (Color figure online)

classification task and it has outperformed the baselines. Recently, [15] proposed a *Predictive Text Embedding* (PTE) model, which uses labeled data and word co-occurrence information to build a heterogeneous text network, where multiple types of vertices exist, and then applies the proposed algorithm to learn the embedding of text. Inspired by PTE, our proposed entity and category embedding model firstly constructs a weighted network of entities and categories, and then jointly learns their embeddings from the network.

3   Knowledge-Based Short Text Categorization (KBSTC)

This section provides a formal definition of the Knowledge-Based Short Text Categorization (KBSTC) task, followed by the description of the proposed probabilistic approach for KBSTC.

Preliminaries. Given a knowledge base KB containing a set of entities $E = \{e_1, e_2, .., e_n\}$ and a set of hierarchically related categories $C = \{c_1, c_2, .., c_m\}$, we model KB as a graph $G_{KB} = (V, R)$ with $V = E \cup C$ as the set of vertices and $R = R_{EE} \cup R_{EC} \cup R_{CC}$ as the set of edges of the form (v_i, v_j) reflecting various relationships between the vertices v_i and v_j, where each edge in R_{EE} with $v_i, v_j \in E$ represents an entity-entity relation, each edge in R_{EC} with $v_i \in E$ and $v_j \in C$ represents an entity-category association, and each edge in R_{CC} with $v_i, v_j \in C$ reflects the category hierarchy.

In this work, we utilize Wikipedia as the knowledge base, where each article and each category page are considered as an entity in E and a category in C, respectively. In addition, each relationship (v_i, v_j) between the pair of vertices v_i and v_j are extracted from Wikipedia and the following rule applies:

- $(v_i, v_j) \in R_{EE}$ if and only if $v_i, v_j \in E$ and there is a link from the article v_i to the article v_j in Wikipedia,
- $(v_i, v_j) \in R_{EC}$ if and only if $v_i \in E, v_j \in C$ and the article v_i has the associated category v_j in Wikipedia, and
- $(v_i, v_j) \in R_{CC}$ if and only if $v_i, v_j \in C$ and v_i is subcategory of v_j in Wikipedia.

Definition (KBSTC task). Given an input short text t that contains a set of entities $E_t \subseteq E$ as well as a set of predefined categories $C' \subseteq C$ (from the underlying knowledge base KB), the output of the KBSTC task is the most relevant category $c_i \in C'$ for the given short text t, i.e., we compute the category function $f_{cat}(t) = c_i$, where $c_i \in C'$.

KBSTC Overview. The general workflow of KBSTC is shown in Fig. 1. In the first step, each entity mention present in a given short text t is detected. Next, for each mention, a set of candidate entities are generated based on a prefabricated Anchor-Text Dictionary, which contains all mentions and their corresponding Wikipedia entities. In order to detect entity mentions, first all n-grams from the input text are gathered and then the extracted n-grams matching surface forms of entities (based on the Anchor-Text dictionary) are selected as entity mentions. To construct the Anchor-Text Dictionary, all the anchor texts of hyperlinks in Wikipedia pointing to any Wikipedia articles are extracted, whereby the anchor texts serve as mentions and the links refer to the corresponding entities. Given the short text t as *"IBM adds midrange server to eServer lineup"*, the detected mentions are *"IBM"*, *"midrange server"* and *"eServer"*. Likewise the predefined categories, $C' = \{Sports, Technology, Culture, World\}$, are mapped to Wikipedia categories. Finally, applying the proposed probabilistic model (see Sect. 3) by utilizing the entity and category embeddings that have been pre-computed from Wikipedia (see Sect. 4), the output of the KBSTC task is the semantically most relevant category for the entities present in t. Thereby, in the given example the category *Technology* should be determined.

Note that in this work we have utilized Wikipedia as a KB. However, KBSTC is applicable to any arbitrary domain as long as there exists a KB providing domain-specific entities and categories.

3.1 Probabilistic Approach

The KBSTC task is formalized as estimating the probability of $P(c|t)$ of each predefined category c and an input short text t. The result of this probability estimation can be considered as a score for each category. Therefore, the most relevant category c for a given text t should maximize the probability $P(c|t)$. Based on Bayes' theorem, the probability $P(c|t)$ can be rewritten as follows:

$$P(c|t) = \frac{P(c,t)}{P(t)} \propto P(c,t) \,, \tag{1}$$

where the denominator $P(t)$ can be ignored as it has no impact on the ranking of the categories.

To facilitate the following discussion, we first introduce the concepts of *mention* and *context*. For an input text t, a *mention* is a term in t that can refer to an entity e and the *context* of e is the set of all other mentions in t except the one for e. For each candidate entity e contained in t, the input text t can be decomposed into the mention and context of e, denoted by m_e and C_e, respectively. For example, given the entity e as IBM, the input text *"IBM adds midrange server to eServer lineup."* can be decomposed into a mention m_e as *"IBM"* and a context C_e as { *"midrange server"*, *"eServer"* }, where *"midrange server"* and *"eServer"* can refer to the context entities Midrange_computer and IBM_eServer, respectively.

Based on the above introduced concepts, the joint probability $P(c,t)$ is given as follows:

$$\begin{aligned} P(c,t) &= \sum_{e \in E_t} P(e,c,t) = \sum_{e \in E_t} P(e,c,m_e,C_e) \\ &= \sum_{e \in E_t} P(e)P(c|e)P(m_e|e,c)P(C_e|e,c) \tag{2} \\ &= \sum_{e \in E_t} P(e)P(c|e)P(m_e|e)P(C_e|e) \,, \tag{3} \end{aligned}$$

where E_t represents the set of all possible entities contained in the input text t. We assume that in Eq. (2) m_e and C_e are conditionally independent given e, in Eq. (3) m_e and C_e are conditionally independent of c given e. The intuition behind these assumptions is that a mention m_e and a context C_e only rely on the entity e which refers to and co-occurs with, such that once the entity e is fixed, m_e and C_e can be considered as conditionally independent. The main problem is then to estimate each probability in Eq. (3), which will be discussed in the next section.

3.2 Parameter Estimation

Our probabilistic model has four main components, i.e., $P(e)$, $P(c|e)$, $P(m_e|e)$ and $P(C_e|e)$. This section provides the estimation of each component in detail.

Entity Popularity. The probability $P(e)$ captures the popularity of the entity e. Here, we simply apply a uniform distribution to calculate $P(e)$ as follows: $P(e) = \frac{1}{N}$, where N is the total number of entities in the KB.

Entity-Category Relatedness. The probability $P(c|e)$ models the relatedness between an entity e and a category c. With the pre-built entity and category embeddings (see Sect. 4), there are two cases to consider for estimating $P(c|e)$. Firstly, when the entity e is directly associated with the category, denoted by c_{a_e}, in KB, i.e., e appears in some Wikipedia articles that have associated category c_{a_e}, the probability $P(c_{a_e}|e)$ can be approximated based on similarity as

$$P(c_{a_e}|e) = \frac{sim(c_{a_e}, e)}{\sum\limits_{c'_{a_e} \in C_{a_e}} sim(c'_{a_e}, e)}, \tag{4}$$

where C_{a_e} is the set of categories that are directly associated with e, and $sim(c_{a_e}, e)$ denotes the cosine similarity between the vectors of the category c_{a_e} and the entity e in the embedding space. Secondly, in case where the entity e is not directly associated with the category c, the hierarchical structure of categories in KB is considered. More specifically, the categories in C_{a_e} are incorporated into the estimation of the probability $P(c|e)$ as follows:

$$P(c|e) = \sum_{c_{a_e} \in C_{a_e}} P(c_{a_e}, c|e) = \sum_{c_{a_e} \in C_{a_e}} P(c_{a_e}|e)P(c|c_{a_e}, e) = \sum_{c_{a_e} \in C_{a_e}} P(c_{a_e}|e)P(c|c_{a_e}), \tag{5}$$

where we consider that e is related to c only through its directly associated category c_{a_e}, such that once c_{a_e} is given, e and c are conditionally independent.

In Eq. (5), the probability $P(c_{a_e}|e)$ then can be simply calculated based on Eq. (4) and the probability $P(c|c_{a_e})$ that captures the hierarchical category structure, is estimated as follows:

$$P(c|c_{a_e}) = \begin{cases} \frac{1}{|A_{c_{a_e}}|} & \text{if } c \text{ is an ancestor of } c_{a_e}, \\ 0 & \text{otherwise,} \end{cases} \tag{6}$$

where $A_{c_{a_e}}$ is the set of ancestor categories of c_{a_e}, which can be obtained by using the category hierarchy in KB.

Mention-Entity Association. The probability $P(m_e|e)$ of observing a mention m_e given the entity e is calculated based on the *Anchor-Text Dictionary* as follows:

$$P(m_e|e) = \frac{count(m_e, e)}{\sum\limits_{m'_e \in M_e} count(m'_e, e)}, \tag{7}$$

where $count(m_e, e)$ denotes the number of links using m_e as anchor text pointing to e as the destination, and M_e is the set of all mentions that can refer to e.

Entity-Context Relatedness. The probability $P(C_e|e)$ models the relatedness between the entity e and its context C_e that consists of all the other mentions in the input text t except m_e. Each mention in C_e refers to a context entity e_c from the given KB. The probability $P(C_e|e)$ can be calculated as follows:

$$P(C_e|e) = \sum_{e_c \in E_{C_e}} P(e_c, C_e|e) = \sum_{e_c \in E_{C_e}} P(e_c|e)P(C_e|e_c, e)$$

$$= \sum_{e_c \in E_{C_e}} P(e_c|e)P(C_e|e_c) \tag{8}$$

$$= \sum_{e_c \in E_{C_e}} P(e_c|e)P(m_{e_c}|e_c), \tag{9}$$

where E_{C_e} denotes the set of entities that can be referred to by the mentions in C_e. In Eq. (8), the context C_e is conditionally independent of e given the context entity e_c, and in Eq. (9) e_c is assumed to be only related to its corresponding mention $m_{e_c} \in C_e$ such that the other mentions in C_e can be ignored.

Similar to $P(c_{a_e}|e)$ (cf Eq. (4)), the probability $P(e_c|e)$ in Eq. (9) can also be estimated based on the pre-built entity and category embeddings. Let $sim(e_c, e)$ be the cosine similarity between the entity vectors of e_c and e. Then the probability $P(e_c|e)$ can be calculated as follows:

$$P(e_c|e) = \frac{sim(e_c, e)}{\sum_{e' \in E} sim(e', e)}, \tag{10}$$

where E is the set of all entities in KB. In addition, the probability $P(m_{e_c}|e_c)$ in Eq. (9) can be calculated based on Eq. (7).

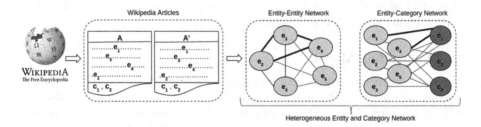

Fig. 2. Entity category network construction (best viewed in color) (Color figure online)

4 Entity and Category Embedding

This section provides a description of the proposed embedding model that embeds entities and categories into a common vector space by integrating knowledge from a knowledge base. We firstly present the entity-entity and entity-category network construction in Sect. 4.1, and subsequently, the joint entity and category embedding model is presented in Sect. 4.2.

4.1 Network Construction

To calculate the meaningful semantic relatedness between entities and categories, the proper semantic representation of them in a common vector space is essential for KBSTC. For this reason, two types of networks, i.e., entity-entity and entity-category, are firstly constructed, which are later utilized to generate the entity and category embeddings.

Figure 2 depicts the process of the entity-entity and entity-category network construction, where the *heterogeneous network* consists of both entity vertices and category vertices, and accordingly two types of edges, i.e., edges between two entity vertices and edges between an entity vertex and a category vertex. The weights of the edges between different vertices are crucial due to their significant impact on the embedding model (see Sect. 4.2). By leveraging the hyperlink structure in Wikipedia, we propose a method to calculate the edge weights for both entity-entity and entity-category networks.

Weights for Entity-Entity Edges. In order to explain the weight calculation, firstly the concept of *linked entity* has to be defined. The hyperlinks that are present in an arbitrary Wikipedia article and refer to another Wikipedia article are called linked entities. The weight of an edge between an entity-entity pair is the number of Wikipedia articles where both entities appear as a linked entity.

Weights for Entity-Category Edges. The weight of an edge between an entity-category pair is the number of Wikipedia articles where the entity appears as a linked entity and simultaneously the corresponding article containing the linked entity belongs to the category in Wikipedia.

As shown in Fig. 2, the linked entities and the associated categories for each Wikipedia article are used to generate the entity-entity and the entity-category edges. The edges of (e_1, e_2), (e_1, e_4), (e_2, e_4), (e_1, c_1) and (e_4, c_1) are thicker due to their higher co-occurrence frequency.

4.2 Embedding Model

As introduced before, the overall heterogeneous network consists of two homogeneous networks, i.e., the entity-entity and entity-category networks. Similar to PTE [15], to embed each of these networks, our proposed embedding model aims to capture the second-order proximity [16]. More specifically, the second-order proximity is calculated between two vertices in a network by considering their common (shared) vertices. Therefore, vertices that share many same neighbors should be placed closely in the vector space.

To model the second-order proximity of a homogeneous network, for each edge (v_i, v_j), the conditional probability $p(v_j|v_i)$ is defined as follows [16]:

$$p(v_j|v_i) = \frac{exp(-\boldsymbol{u}_j^T \cdot \boldsymbol{u}_i)}{\sum\limits_{v_k \in V} exp(-\boldsymbol{u}_k^T \cdot \boldsymbol{u}_i)}, \tag{11}$$

where V is the set of vertices connected with v_i in the network, $\boldsymbol{u}_i$, $\boldsymbol{u}_j$ and $\boldsymbol{u}_k$ are the vectors of vertices v_i, v_j and v_k, respectively. The empirical probability of $p(v_j|v_i)$ can be defined as $\hat{p}(v_j|v_i) = \frac{w_{ij}}{d_i}$, where d_i is the out-degree of v_i and w_{ij} is the weight of the edge (v_i, v_j).

In order to preserve the second-order proximity, the conditional distribution $p(v_j|v_i)$ is made close to $\hat{p}(v_j|v_i)$ based on the KL-divergence over the entire set of vertices in the network, such that the model minimizes the following objective function:

$$O_{homo} = - \sum_{(v_i,v_j)\in E} w_{ij}\log\left(p(v_j|v_i)\right), \qquad (12)$$

The embedding of the individual entity-entity and entity-category networks can be learned by utilizing the second-order proximity between vertices. However, our goal is to simultaneously learn the embedding of the constructed heterogeneous network by minimizing the following objective function:

$$O_{heter} = O_{ee} + O_{ec}, \qquad (13)$$

where O_{ee} and O_{ec} are the objective functions defined in Eq. (12) for the homogeneous entity-entity and entity-category networks, respectively. To optimize the objective function in Eq. (13), we adopt a similar approach as described in [15], where all the edges are firstly collected from these two homogeneous networks as two sets, one for entity-entity edges and the other for entity-category edges, and then in each training iteration, edges are sampled from both sets to update the model. Readers can refer to [15,16], for the detailed optimization process.

5 Experimental Results

This section provides a detailed description of the datasets and the baselines for evaluating the proposed approach, followed by the experimental results as well as a comparison to the existing state-of-the-art approaches in the related areas.

Table 1. Data distribution of the AG News dataset

Category	#Train	#Test
Business	30,000	1,900
Sports	30,000	1,900
World	30,000	1,900
Sci/Tech	30,000	1,900
Total	120,000	7,600

Table 2. Data distribution of the Google Snippets dataset

Category	#Train	#Test
Business	1200	300
Computers	1200	300
Cult-arts-entertainment	1880	330
Education-Science	2360	300
Engineering	220	150
Health	880	300
Politics-Society	1200	300
Sports	1120	300
Total	10,060	2,280

5.1 Datasets

AG News (AG)[1]: This dataset is adopted from [23], which contains both titles and short descriptions (usually one sentence) of news articles. The data distribution of the training and test datasets is shown in Table 1. In our experiments, the dataset has two versions, where one contains only titles and the other contains both titles and descriptions. The total number of entities and the average number of entities and words per text in the test datasets are shown in Table 3.

Google Snippets (Snippets)[2]: This is a well-known dataset for short text classification, which was introduced in [10] and contains short snippets from Google search results. The data distribution of the dataset is shown in Table 2. As shown in Table 3, the test dataset has in total 20,284 entities, an average of 8.9 entities and an average of 17.97 words in each snippet.

Table 3. Statistical analysis of the test datasets

Dataset	#Entities	Avg. #Ent	Avg. #Word
AG News (Title)	24,416	3.21	7.14
AG News (Title+Description)	89,933	11.83	38.65
Google Snippets	20,284	8.90	17.97

As the focus of this work is the KBSTC task, where the goal is to derive the most relevant category from the knowledge base for a given short text, we need to adapt these datasets by aligning the labels/categories with the categories in the used knowledge base. More specifically, each label/category in these datasets is manually mapped to its corresponding Wikipedia category, e.g., the category *Sports* from the AG dataset is mapped to the Wikipedia category *Sports*[3]. Furthermore, as KBSTC does not depend on any training/labeled data, the training

Table 4. The classification accuracy of KBSTC against baselines (%)

Model	AG (title)	AG (title+description)	Snippets
Dataless ESA [14]	53.5	64.1	48.5
Dataless Word2Vec [14]	49.5	52.7	52.4
NB+TF-IDF	86.6	90.2	64.4
SVM+TF-IDF	**87.6**	**91.9**	69.1
LR+TF-IDF	87.1	91.7	63.6
KBSTC+Our Embedding	67.9	80.5	**72.0**

[1] http://goo.gl/JyCnZq.
[2] http://jwebpro.sourceforge.net/data-web-snippets.tar.gz.
[3] https://en.wikipedia.org/wiki/Category:Sports.

datasets of AG and Snippets are only used for the training of the supervised baseline methods. Lastly, to measure the performance of KBSTC, the classification accuracy (the ratio of correctly classified data over all the test data) was used.

5.2   Baselines

Dataless ESA and Dataless Word2Vec: As described in Sect. 2, the dataless approaches do not require any labeled data or training phase, therefore, they can be considered as the most similar approaches to KBSTC. Two variants of the state-of-the-art dataless approach [14] are considered as baselines, which are based on ESA [3] and Word2Vec [7], respectively.

NB, SVM, LR: Additional baselines include the traditional supervised classifiers, i.e., Naive Bayes (NB), Support Vector Machine (SVM) and Logistic Regression (LR), with the features calculated based on the term frequency and the inverse document frequency (TF-IDF).

5.3   Evaluation of KBSTC

Table 4 shows that the accuracy of the proposed probabilistic KBSTC approach (see Sect. 3) based on our entity and category embedding model (see Sect. 4) in comparison to the baselines on the AG and Snippets datasets.

It is observed that the KBSTC approach considerably outperforms the dataless classification approaches. While Dataless ESA and Dataless Word2Vec have been assessed with longer news articles and achieved promising results in [14], they cannot perform well with short text due to the data sparsity problem.

Remarkably, KBSTC outperforms all the baselines on the Snippets dataset, however, all supervised approaches outperform KBSTC on the AG dataset. The reason here can be attributed to the different characteristics of the two datasets. AG is a larger dataset with more training samples (see Table 1) in comparison to Snippets (see Table 2). Moreover, the AG dataset provides only 4 different categories in comparison to 8 categories of the Snippets dataset. Those differences might be the reason of the significant decrease in accuracy for the supervised approaches on the Snippets dataset in comparison to the AG dataset. This could be an indicator that the size of the training data and the number of classes make a real impact on the classification accuracy for the supervised approaches. Since KBSTC does not require or use any labeled data, the number of the available training samples has no impact on its accuracy.

Regarding the results of KBSTC, the AG (title+description) dataset yields better accuracy than the Snippets dataset, which in turn, results in better accuracy than the AG (title) dataset. The reason might be found in the nature of the datasets. As shown in Table 3, the average number of entities per text in AG (title+description) is greater than Snippets, followed by AG (title). Often a richer context with more entities can make the categorization more accurate.

Overall, the results in Table 4 have demonstrated that for short text categorization, KBSTC achieves a high accuracy without requiring any labeled data, a time-consuming training phase, or a cumbersome parameter tuning step.

Table 5. The classification accuracy of KBSTC with different embedding models (%)

Model	AG (title)	AG (title+description)	Snippets
KBSTC+HCE	67.0	79.6	**72.3**
KBSTC+DeepWalk	57.1	74.2	64.3
KBSTC+RDF2Vec	62.7	77.5	68.2
KBSTC+Our Embedding	**67.9**	**80.5**	72.0

5.4 Evaluation of Entity and Category Embedding

To assess the quality of the proposed entity and category embedding model (see Sect. 4), we compared it with HCE [5], DeepWalk [9] and RDF2Vec [11] in the context of the KBSTC task.

While the Wikipedia entity and category embeddings generated by HCE can be directly used, DeepWalk has been applied on the network constructed using Wikipedia and RDF2Vec has been applied on the RDF graph of DBpedia to obtain the needed embeddings. Then, these embeddings are integrated into KBSTC to compute the entity-category and entity-context relatedness (see Eqs. (4) and (10)). The results of KBSTC with different embedding models are shown in Table 5. The proposed entity and category embedding model outperforms all other embedding models for the KBSTC task on the AG dataset, while HCE performs slightly better than our model on the Snippets dataset.

As HCE is a more specific embedding model that has been designed to learn the representation of entities and their associated categories from Wikipedia, it is not flexible to be adapted to other networks. In contrast, our model can deal with more general networks. For example, with words and word-category relations as an additional type of vertices and edges in the heterogeneous network described in Sect. 4.1, it is straightforward to adapt our embedding model by involving a new object function O_{wc} into Eq. (13), which is considered as our future work.

Although DeepWalk and RDF2Vec aim to learn the representation of vertices in general networks and RDF graphs, respectively, they have been either designed for homogeneous networks or treated each type of vertices and edges in a RDF graph equally. The results also indicate that our embedding model enables to capture better semantic representation of vertices by taking into account different types of networks, i.e., the entity-entity and entity-category networks.

5.5 Evaluation of Entity Linking

As discussed in Sect. 3, the first step of KBSTC is to detect entity mentions in a given short text and then for each mention to generate a candidate list of entities based on the anchor text dictionary, which are employed to determine the most relevant category for the input text based on the proposed probabilistic approach. An alternative way could be to firstly use an existing entity linking (EL) system to obtain the referent entity for each mention and then based on

Table 6. Statistics of the entity linking datasets

Dataset	#Doc	Avg. #Ent	Avg. #Word
Spotlight	58	5.69	32
RSS-500	500	1.18	34

Table 7. Micro F1 results for the entity linking task

Methods	Spotlight	RSS-500
AIDA	0.25	0.45
AGDISTS	0.27	**0.66**
Babelfly	0.52	0.44
DBpedia Spotlight	**0.71**	0.20
Our EL Method	0.69	0.64

that derive the category of the input short text. The reason we did not adopt the latter solution is that most of the existing EL systems rely on the rich context of the input text for the collective inference to boost the overall EL performance. However, due to the lack of such context in short text, existing EL systems might not perform well in our case, i.e., the correct entities in the input short text cannot be found, which play a vital role in our KBSTC approach.

Instead of directly using an existing EL system, our probabilistic approach actually involves an internal step of EL for the input short text t, where the main difference is that we consider a list of candidate entities for each mention. The output is a set of possible entities E_t present in t with the confidence score of each entity $e \in E_t$ as $P(e)P(m_e|e)P(C_e|e)$ (see Eq. (3)), where $P(e)$ captures the popularity of e, $P(m_e|e)$ and $P(C_e|e)$ reflect the likelihood of observing the mention m_e and the context C_e given e. By incorporating the confidence score of each $e \in E_t$ and its relatedness to each predefined category c, represented by $P(c|e)$, we can compute the final joint probability $P(c,t)$ to determine the most relevant category for t (see Eq. (3)).

To evaluate the effectiveness of the EL step in our approach, the experiments have been conducted on two datasets from the general entity linking benchmark GERBIL [19], i.e., DBpedia Spotlight released in [6] and N^3 RSS-500 as one of the N^3 datasets [12]. We have chosen these two datasets for the EL evaluation, because they contain only short text, similar to our test datasets (see Table 6). To make our EL method be comparable with existing EL systems, in the experiments we also generate one single entity for each mention, which maximizes the confidence score, computed by $P(e)P(m_e|e)P(C_e|e)$. The results of Micro F1 for various EL systems and our method are shown in Table 7. It is observed that our EL method achieves promising results for both datasets, which are very close to the best results yielded by the state-of-the-art EL systems. More importantly, because of insufficient context of short text required by the collective inference for EL, it is difficult to provide the correct referent entity for each mention in many cases, such that our EL method used in KBSTC takes into account a list of candidate entities with their confidence scores for each mention.

5.6 Using Wikipedia as a Training Set

To further demonstrate the effectiveness of the proposed KBSTC approach, an additional experiment has been conducted. The results in Table 4 indicates that supervised methods can perform well in case of existence of sufficient amount of training data. However, the labeled data might not be available and this is the case most of the time. An alternative solution to the expensive manual process of compiling a labeled training dataset would be to automatically extract the training data from existing publicly available sources such as Wikipedia.

Table 8. The classification accuracy of KBSTC against a traditional classifier (%)

Method	AG (title+description)	Google Snippets
SVM+TF-IDF	59.9	53.9
KBSTC	**80.5**	**72.0**

To generate the training data, for each category from the two datasets (AG and Snippets), training samples have to be assembled. For this purpose, Wikipedia articles associated with the corresponding categories (or their subcategories) are firstly collected, where 10,000 Wikipedia articles are then randomly selected as training data per category, which constitute the training datasets for AG and Snippets. Since SVM achieved the best results among the supervised approaches (see Table 4), two SVM classifiers are trained with the generated training data for AG and Snippets, respectively. In the experiments, we used the original test datasets from AG and Snippets for evaluating the trained SVM classifiers.

The results are shown in Table 8, which indicate that the KBSTC approach achieved higher accuracy in comparison to the SVM classifiers. More interesting, the same approach (SVM+TF-IDF) trained with the AG and Snippets datasets achieved the accuracy scores of 91.9% and 69.1% (see Table 4), while it only achieved the accuracy scores of 59.9% and 53.9% when trained with the collected Wikipedia articles. This provides us some insights that it might not be suitable to directly use Wikipedia as the training datasets for supervised approaches and also serves as the motivation of the KBTSC approach proposed in this work.

6 Conclusion and Future Work

We have proposed KBSTC, a new paradigm for short text categorization based on KB. KBSTC does not require any labeled training data, instead it considers entities present in the input text and their semantic relatedness to the predefined categories to categorize short text. The experimental results have proven that it is possible to categorize short text in an unsupervised way with a high accuracy. As for future work, we aim to include words along with entities for the KBSTC task, which requires also the extension of the proposed embedding model towards the additional inclusion of word embeddings into the common entity and category vector space. Further, the performance of KBSTC will also be evaluated on social media text such as tweets.

References

1. Burel, G., Saif, H., Alani, H.: Semantic wide and deep learning for detecting crisis-information categories on social media. In: d'Amato, C., et al. (eds.) ISWC 2017. LNCS, vol. 10587, pp. 138–155. Springer, Cham (2017). https://doi.org/10.1007/978-3-319-68288-4_9
2. Chang, M.W., Ratinov, L.A., Roth, D., Srikumar, V.: Importance of semantic representation: dataless classification. In: AAAI (2008)
3. Gabrilovich, E., Markovitch, S.: Computing semantic relatedness using wikipedia-based explicit semantic analysis. In: IJCAI (2007)
4. Li, C., Xing, J., Sun, A., Ma, Z.: Effective document labeling with very few seed words: a topic model approach. In: CIKM (2016)
5. Li, Y., Zheng, R., Tian, T., Hu, Z., Iyer, R., Sycara, K.P.: Joint embedding of hierarchical categories and entities for concept categorization and dataless classification. In: COLING (2016)
6. Mendes, P.N., Jakob, M., García-Silva, A., Bizer, C.: Dbpedia spotlight: shedding light on the web of documents. In: I-SEMANTICS (2011)
7. Mikolov, T., Sutskever, I., Chen, K., Corrado, G.S., Dean, J.: Distributed representations of words and phrases and their compositionality. In: NIPS (2013)
8. Nigam, K., McCallum, A., Thrun, S., Mitchell, T.M.: Text classification from labeled and unlabeled documents using EM. Mach. Learn. **39**, 103–134 (2000)
9. Perozzi, B., Al-Rfou, R., Skiena, S.: Deepwalk: online learning of social representations. In: KDD (2014)
10. Phan, X.H., Nguyen, L.M., Horiguchi, S.: Learning to classify short and sparse text & web with hidden topics from large-scale data collections. In: WWW (2008)
11. Ristoski, P., Paulheim, H.: RDF2Vec: RDF graph embeddings for data mining. In: Groth, P., et al. (eds.) ISWC 2016. LNCS, vol. 9981, pp. 498–514. Springer, Cham (2016). https://doi.org/10.1007/978-3-319-46523-4_30
12. Röder, M., Usbeck, R., Hellmann, S., Gerber, D., Both, A.: N^3 - a collection of datasets for named entity recognition and disambiguation in the NLP interchange format. In: LREC (2014)
13. Song, G., Ye, Y., Du, X., Huang, X., Bie, S.: Short text classification: a survey. J. Multimedia **9**(5), 635–644 (2014)
14. Song, Y., Roth, D.: On dataless hierarchical text classification. In: AAAI (2014)
15. Tang, J., Qu, M., Mei, Q.: PTE: predictive text embedding through large-scale heterogeneous text networks. In: KDD (2015)
16. Tang, J., Qu, M., Wang, M., Zhang, M., Yan, J., Mei, Q.: LINE: large-scale information network embedding. In: WWW (2015)
17. Türker, R., Zhang, L., Koutraki, M., Sack, H.: TECNE: knowledge based text classification using network embeddings. In: EKAW (2018)
18. Türker, R., Zhang, L., Koutraki, M., Sack, H.: "The less is more" for text classification. In: SEMANTiCS (2018)
19. Usbeck, R., et al.: GERBIL: general entity annotator benchmarking framework. In: WWW (2015)

20. Wang, J., Wang, Z., Zhang, D., Yan, J.: Combining knowledge with deep convolutional neural networks for short text classification. In: IJCAI (2017)
21. Wang, P., Xu, B., Xu, J., Tian, G., Liu, C.L., Hao, H.: Semantic expansion using word embedding clustering and convolutional neural network for improving short text classification. Neurocomputing **174**, 806–814 (2016)
22. Xuan, J., Jiang, H., Ren, Z., Yan, J., Luo, Z.: Automatic bug triage using semi-supervised text classification. In: SEKE (2010)
23. Zhang, X., LeCun, Y.: Text understanding from scratch. CoRR (2015)
24. Zhang, X., Wu, B.: Short text classification based on feature extension using the n-gram model. In: FSKD. IEEE (2015)

A Hybrid Approach for Aspect-Based Sentiment Analysis Using a Lexicalized Domain Ontology and Attentional Neural Models

Olaf Wallaart and Flavius Frasincar[✉] ⓘ

Erasmus University Rotterdam,
P.O. Box 1738, 3000 DR Rotterdam, The Netherlands
olafwallaart@student.eur.nl, frasincar@ese.eur.nl

Abstract. This work focuses on sentence-level aspect-based sentiment analysis for restaurant reviews. A two-stage sentiment analysis algorithm is proposed. In this method, first a lexicalized domain ontology is used to predict the sentiment and as a back-up algorithm a neural network with a rotatory attention mechanism (LCR-Rot) is utilized. Furthermore, two features are added to the backup algorithm. The first extension changes the order in which the rotatory attention mechanism operates (LCR-Rot-inv). The second extension runs over the rotatory attention mechanism for multiple iterations (LCR-Rot-hop). Using the SemEval-2015 and SemEval-2016 data, we conclude that the two-stage method outperforms the baseline methods, albeit with a small percentage. Moreover, we find that the method where we iterate multiple times over a rotatory attention mechanism has the best performance.

1 Introduction

Since the enormous increase of unstructured review data on the Web, the interest in sentiment analysis [8] has risen as well. The main goal of sentiment analysis is to extract the sentiment and opinions of content creators and combine this information into useful results for companies, researchers, and users. Where for small companies it might be manually possible to obtain their costumers' opinion, this task becomes labor-intensive and time-expensive for large companies. Hence, sentiment analysis can be a useful tool. A subtask of sentiment analysis is aspect-based sentiment analysis [15]. Here, instead of computing a sentiment score (usually positive or negative) for the entire review or sentence, the task is to identify different aspects or characteristics in the review and compute the sentiment of the reviewer towards these specific aspects.

The main task at hand is to create a method that accurately and efficiently predicts the sentiment about a given aspect. Methods can generally be classified as knowledge-based or as machine learning approaches [15]. Both methods have their strong and weak points and recent research shows that the two types of

© Springer Nature Switzerland AG 2019
P. Hitzler et al. (Eds.): ESWC 2019, LNCS 11503, pp. 363–378, 2019.
https://doi.org/10.1007/978-3-030-21348-0_24

methods are complementary to each other [16]. It is shown that a hybrid method, using both statistical learning and a knowledge-based approach, outperforms many of the existing methods that use one type of method [16].

The problem still at hand is what combination of these types of methods will yield the best performance, both in terms of accuracy and efficiency. This work will extend and try to improve the results obtained in [16] by implementing state-of-the-art machine learning methods. Precisely we will make use of a combination between available domain knowledge, in the form of an ontology as described in [16] and a neural rotatory attention model as introduced in [21]. In addition, we investigate two extensions of the used neural network: changing the order in the rotary attention mechanism and iterating several times over the rotary attention mechanism.

The paper is organized as follows. In Sect. 2 we provide and discuss the relevant literature that is available with respect to sentiment analysis using an ontology and neural models. Section 3 gives an overview and explanation of the data used in this work. Next, a description of the proposed framework is given in Sect. 4 and results of the proposed methods are evaluated in Sect. 5. Finally, in Sect. 6 conclusions are made and suggestions for future research are provided. The source code used to implement our methods is written in Python and can be found at https://github.com/ofwallaart/HAABSA.

2   Related Work

In [15] an overview of aspect-based sentiment analysis is given. The goal of aspect-based sentiment analysis is to find the sentiment of a group of people with regard to a certain topic. A sentiment or aspect can be mentioned explicitly but also remain implicit. For instance the sentence 'You can't go wrong here' has an implicit aspect and an explicit sentiment, since the aspect is not literally in the text but a positive sentiment can be derived from the sentence directly. In this work, we will ignore implicitly mentioned aspects since the methods proposed rely on the presence of predefined aspects. Implicitly mentioned sentiments are taken into consideration since they pose no problem for the proposed methods. There are three different categories of algorithms for aspect-based sentiment analysis [15]: knowledge-based approaches, machine learning approaches, and hybrid approaches.

Knowledge-based algorithms often use a sentiment dictionary that finds a sentiment score for a specific word. Subsequently, these sentiment scores are combined by a method to determine the sentiment of all the relevant words with respect to an aspect [15]. Using the SenticNet knowledge base, in [5] a polarity detection method is developed by means of sentic patterns. Sentic patterns are linguistic patterns which allow sentiments to flow from concept to concept based on the dependency relation of the input sentence. First, each sentence is processed to find the expressed concepts. The discovered concepts are then linked to the SenticNet knowledge base by using sentic patterns to make an inference of the sentiment value linked to the sentence.

In [16], a common domain knowledge in the form of an ontology is used to construct a knowledge-based method. Sentiment-indicating words are split into three types. The first type contains expressions that, regardless of the aspect, always indicate the same sentiment. The second type of sentiment expressions only belong to one specific aspect category, whereas the third type of words are words of which the expressed sentiment depends on their context. The ontology approach used in this work will be similar to this procedure, due to the high performance of this solution [16].

The general increase in interest of machine learning methods such as neural networks has also caused an increase of their usage for the purpose of sentiment analysis. Especially the usage of neural attention models has been a field of high interest lately [6,20]. [9] uses a neural attention model with an attention mechanism that can enforce a model to pay more attention to the important parts of a sentence. The mechanism is able to focus on a certain region with 'high attention' while perceiving the surrounding with 'low attention' and adjusting the focal point over time [20].

The model introduced in [9], is a so-called Content Attention Based Aspect-based Sentiment Classification (CABASC) model. It uses a weighted memory module by introducing a context attention mechanism in the model that is responsible for simultaneously taking the order of the words and their correlations into account. When considering the SemEval-2014 data [14], it is shown that CABASC outperforms widely-known methods, such as a support vector machine (SVM) and a Long Short-Term Memory model (LSTM). CABASC even outperforms RAN, which is a state-of-the-art model that uses a multi-hop attention mechanism, a deep bidirectional LSTM, and a position attention mechanism to provide tailor-made memories for different aspects in a sentence [6].

In [21] an approach called a Left-Center-Right separated neural network with Rotatory attention (LCR-Rot) is proposed. This model is able to better represent the sentiment aspect, especially when the aspect contains multiple words, and improve the interaction between aspect and left/right contexts to capture the most important words in the aspect and context. The model consists of three separated LSTMs with 300 hidden units each, corresponding to the three parts of a review (left context, target phrase, and right context). Furthermore, it uses a rotatory attention mechanism which models the relation between aspect and left/right contexts. This is done by letting the left/right context and target phrase both use information of the other part to capture indicative sentiment words. Obtained results again show an improved performance over an SVM and an LSTM model. Furthermore, results indicate that LCR-Rot also outperforms CABASC. However, a direct comparison between the two models has not yet been made and would give a more profound conclusion on which model performs better. This paper aims to also answer this question by directly comparing these two methods.

The proposed idea of using a hybrid method, combining a knowledge-driven approach and a statistical method has been marked as the most promising way to improve the effectiveness of affective computing, which includes sentiment analysis [4]. [16] propose two hybrid methods for aspect-based sentiment analysis where their previously mentioned ontology-based approach is used as a knowledge-based method. As a machine learning approach, a bag-of-words model combined with an SVM classifier is used. The first approach proposed by [16] uses this bag-of-words model with the addition of two binary features that indicate the sentiment prediction from the ontology method. The second approach uses a two-step procedure where first the ontology method is used to predict a sentiment and if this method is not able to make a prediction, the bag-of-words model is used as a backup method. The latter model performs the best and has a state-of-the-art performance of 85.7% on the SemEval-2016 [13] data. This two-step approach is superior to the global vector approach as proposed by [17], which also combines ontology and non-ontology-based features.

3   Specification of Data and Tasks

SemEval (Semantic Evaluation) is a widely used evaluation method for computational semantic analysis systems [9,16,21]. In this paper we use the SemEval-2015 Task 12 [12] and SemEval-2016 Task 5 Subtask 1 [13] datasets to train and evaluate our models. By using these datasets we are able to compare our outcomes with that of other methods using the same datasets and thus making it a convenient choice.

The datasets consist of restaurant reviews with one or multiple sentences. These sentences contain one or multiple opinions about a certain aspect category. Such an opinion consists of the aspect category where an opinion is given about and the actual aspect. In the dataset this aspect is marked as `target` and refers to the word or words in the sentence that is/are opinionated with respect to an aspect category. In addition, for each opinion a polarity is given that expresses whether the reviewer is positive, negative, or neutral towards a specific aspect. In Fig. 1 a sentence from the SemEval-2016 dataset in the XML markup language is shown as an example. The dataset consists of training data, that will be used

```
<sentence id="430342:0">
    <text>delicious simple food in nice outdoor atmosphere.</text>
    <Opinions>
        <Opinion from="17" to="21" polarity="positive" category="FOOD#
            QUALITY" target="food"/>
        <Opinion from="17" to="21" polarity="positive" category="FOOD#
            STYLE_OPTIONS" target="food"/>
        <Opinion from="30" to="48" polarity="positive" category="AMBIENCE#
            GENERAL" target="outdoor atmosphere"/>
    </Opinions>
</sentence>
```

Fig. 1. A sentence from the SemEval-2016 data set.

Table 1. Polarity frequencies in the data set.

	Negative		Neutral		Positive		Total	
	Freq.	%	Freq.	%	Freq.	%	Freq.	%
SemEval-2016 train data	488	26.0	72	3.8	1319	70.2	1879	100
SemEval-2016 test data	135	20.8	32	4.9	483	74.3	650	100

to train our proposed machine learning methods, and test data that is used to evaluate our methods.

The obtained XML data is preprocessed so that it can be used efficiently by our algorithms. To make our results as verifiable and as comparable as possible we will use similar procedures as in [20] and [21]. First of all, all opinions where the aspect is implicit are removed from the dataset. The remaining sentences are then processed using the NLTK platform [3]. The data is tokenized and all words are lemmatized using the WordNet lexical database [10].

The word embedding vectors used in this paper will have a dimension (vector size) of 300. In theory higher dimensions can store more information and perform better. In practice however, the benefit from vectors with a dimensionality higher than 300 is small [11]. We use a pre-trained word vector vocabulary from the GloVe framework [11], with a vocabulary size of 1.9 million words. We choose GloVe because it is superior to CBOW and skip-gram methods [11]. Words that do not appear in the GloVe vocabulary are randomly initialized by a normal distribution $N(0, 0.05^2)$ as in [21].

Since the SemEval-2015 data is contained in the SemEval-2016 data, it has similar properties and therefore we will not discuss it separately and only provide insights for the SemEval-2016 data. Table 1 shows how the opinions are distributed after preprocessing, considering the opinion polarities. The majority of the opinions, around 70% have a 'positive' polarity. From the relative frequencies it can be observed that, with respect to polarity frequencies, the test and training datasets are similar.

4 Method

In this section we present the used methods in this research. First, in Sect. 4.1 we describe the ontology-based approach. Then, in Sect. 4.2 we depict the employed neural attention model. Last, in Sects. 4.3, 4.4, and 4.5 we give our proposed models that build on the previous ones.

4.1 Ontology-Based Approach

By employing an ontology approach for aspect-based sentiment analysis we are able to predict sentiment by using predefined classes, relations between these classes, and axioms that entail either a positive or negative opinion in a sentence. The approach used in this paper is similar to the ontology reasoning proposed

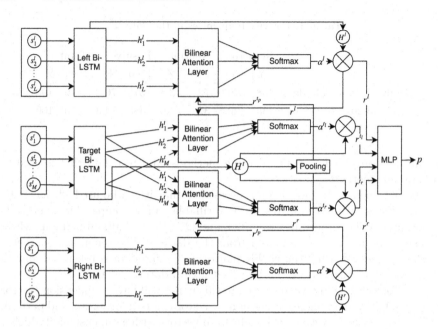

Fig. 2. Visual representation of the LCR-Rot models architecture.

by [16]. Note that the ontology does not contain any classes or relations for the neutral sentiment. Hence, the only possible outcomes are either positive or negative.

The ontology consists of three main classes: *SentimentValue, AspectMention,* and *SentimentMention. SentimentValue* contains the subclasses `Positive` and `Negative` and simply assigns these classes to, respectively, positive and negative expressions. The *AspectMention* class describes the mentions of aspects by linking the lexical representation of a word to the corresponding concept in the ontology. For example, the word 'atmosphere' is linked to the concept `Ambience` by the following axiom: `Ambience` $\equiv$ $\exists$ *lex.*{'atmosphere'}.

The *SentimentMention* class models the expressions of sentiment and is divided into three types of subclasses. A type-1 *SentimentMention* contains concepts that express the same sentiment for every aspect. For instance, the word 'good' always implies a positive expression and does not depend on the given aspect. Type-2 concepts contain expressions that always have the same sentiment but only belong to a unique set of aspects. The word 'delicious' is a good example since it always expresses a positive sentiment towards the aspect categories `FOOD#QUALITY` and `DRINKS#QUALITY`, but does not apply towards other categories and is therefore ignored towards these other aspects. The final, type-3 *SentimentMention* class contains expressions that do not belong to any of the above mentioned types because the sentiment of the expression depends on the context around the aspect. For instance the expression 'cheap' is positive when combined with the word 'price' but is negative with regard to 'atmosphere'.

4.2   Left-Center-Right Separated Neural Network with Rotatory Attention

The LCR-Rot base model used in this paper is described by [21], and we propose two extensions and compare these extensions with the base model. The architecture of the LCR-Rot model is illustrated in Fig. 2.

We define $S = [s_1, s_2, \ldots, s_N]$ as a sentence that contains N words. We first split this sentence into three parts, namely: left context $[s_1^l, s_2^l, \ldots, s_L^l]$, target phrase $[s_1^t, s_2^t, \ldots, s_M^t]$ (the relevant aspect), and right context $[s_1^r, s_2^r, \ldots, s_R^r]$. L, M, R are the lengths of the three parts, respectively.

Next, we build the model by adding three bi-directional long-short-term-memory (Bi-LSTM) modules with 300 hidden units each. Namely, a left-, center-, and right-Bi-LSTM that respectively model left context, target phrase, and right context in the sentence. LSTMs are specialized in remembering information for a long period of time. Moreover, the bidirectional property keeps the contextual information in both directions. The input of each Bi-LSTM is a word embedding representation of the words for that specific part. We use the GloVe vocabulary where all the words are represented in a matrix $K \in \mathbb{R}^{d \times |V|}$, where d is the dimension of the word embedding and $|V|$ is the total vocabulary size. After using the initial word embeddings as an input, the Bi-LSTMs give back hidden states $[h_1^l, h_2^l, \ldots, h_L^l]$ for left context, $[h_1^t, h_2^t, \ldots, h_t^t]$ for target phrase, and $[h_1^r, h_2^r, \ldots, h_R^r]$ for right context as initial representations.

Next we apply a rotatory attention mechanism to the hidden state outputs of the Bi-LSTMs to capture the most indicative words in the left/right context and the target phrase. The mechanism is divided into two steps, where the first step will try to capture the most indicative words in the left/right context. In the second step the left/right representations from the previous step are used to capture the most indicative words in the target phrase. These four representations together form the final sentence representation.

Step 1: Target2Context Attention Mechanism. To obtain a better representation of the left and right contexts we use an average representation of the target phrase. To achieve this average target representation we use an average pooling layer, which works well in this context [1]:

$$r^{t_p} = \text{pooling}([\ \underset{2d \times 1}{h_1^t}\ ,\ \underset{2d \times 1}{h_2^t}\ , \ldots, \underset{2d \times 1}{h_M^t}]). \tag{1}$$

with r^{t_p} being $2d \times 1$.

We then define an attention function f to obtain a representation of the left and rights contexts. This is done by using the average target pooling r^{t_p} and the hidden states of each word in the context. For example, when considering the left context, the hidden states are h_i^l, for $i = 1, \ldots, L$, and f is defined as:

$$\underset{1 \times 1}{f(h_i^l, r^{t_p})} = \tanh(\ \underset{1 \times 2d}{h_i^{l'}}\ \times\ \underset{2d \times 2d}{W_c^l}\ \times\ \underset{2d \times 1}{r^{t_p}}\ +\ \underset{1 \times 1}{b_c^l}\ ), \tag{2}$$

where W_c^l is a weight matrix and b_c^l is a bias. The obtained context attention scores f are then fed into a softmax function that scales the scores on an interval between 0 and 1. Taking again the left context as an example, normalized attention scores α_i^l are computed by:

$$\alpha_i^l = \frac{\exp(f(h_i^l, r^{t_p}))}{\sum_{j=1}^{L} \exp(f(h_j^l, r^{t_p}))}. \tag{3}$$

At last we retrieve a left context representation by taking a weighted combination of the word hidden states:

$$\underset{2d\times1}{r^l} = \sum_{i=1}^{L} \underset{1\times1}{\alpha_i^l} \times \underset{2d\times1}{h_i^l}. \tag{4}$$

By following Eqs. (2)–(4) in a similar way we can obtain r^r for right context.

Step 2: Context2Target Attention Mechanism. The left and right context representations obtained in step 1 are now used to construct an improved representation of the target phrase. Again, we first define an attention function f by using the context representations r^l/r^r of the left and right contexts and the hidden states of each word in the target h_i^t, for $i = 1, \ldots, M$. If we take the left context as an example:

$$\underset{1\times1}{f(h_i^t, r^l)} = \tanh(\underset{1\times2d}{h_i^{t\prime}} \times \underset{2d\times2d}{W_t^l} \times \underset{2d\times1}{r^l} + \underset{1\times1}{b_t^l}), \tag{5}$$

where W_t^l is a weight matrix and b_t^l is a bias. The obtained target attention scores f are then fed into a softmax function that scales the scores on an interval between 0 and 1. Normalized attention scores α_i^r are computed by:

$$\alpha_i^{t_l} = \frac{\exp(f(h_i^t, r^l))}{\sum_{j=1}^{M} \exp(f(h_j^t, r^l))}. \tag{6}$$

At last we retrieve a target phrase representation by taking a weighted combination of the word hidden states:

$$\underset{2d\times1}{r^{t_l}} = \sum_{i=1}^{M} \underset{1\times1}{\alpha_i^{t_l}} \times \underset{2d\times1}{h_i^t}, \tag{7}$$

which we call left-aware target representation, since it denotes the amount that words in the target phrase are influenced by the left context. By following Eqs. (5)–(7) in a similar way we can obtain the right-aware target representation, r^{t_r}.

Sentiment Prediction. The final representation for a sentence is acquired by concatenating the left-context representation r^l, right-context representation r^r, and both the two side-target representations, r^{t_l} and r^{t_r}:

$$\underset{8d\times1}{v} = [\underset{2d\times1}{r^l} ; \underset{2d\times1}{r^{t_l}} ; \underset{2d\times1}{r^{t_r}} ; \underset{2d\times1}{r^r}]. \tag{8}$$

The sentence representation vector is converted by a linear layer to compute the sentiment prediction vector p of length $|C|$, where C is the number of different sentiment categories. The vector is then fed into a softmax layer to predict the sentiment polarity of the target phrase:

$$\underset{|C|\times 1}{p} = \text{softmax}(\ \underset{|C|\times 8d}{W_c} \times\ \underset{8d\times 1}{v}\ +\ \underset{|C|\times 1}{b_c}\ ), \tag{9}$$

where p is a conditional probability distribution, W_c is a weight matrix, and b_c is a bias.

Model Training. The model is trained in a supervised manner by minimizing a cross-entropy loss function. The loss function is defined as:

$$\underset{1\times 1}{L} = -\sum_j \underset{|C|\times 1}{y_j} \times \log(\underset{|C|\times 1}{\hat{p}_j}) + \lambda\|\Theta\|^2, \tag{10}$$

where y_j is a vector that contains the true sentiment value for the j-th training opinion, $\hat{p}_j$ is a vector containing the predicted sentiment for the j-th training opinion, λ is the weight of the L_2-regularization term, and Θ is the parameter set which contains $\{W_c^l, b_c^l, W_c^r, b_c^r, W_t^l, b_t^l, W_t^r, b_t^r, W_c, b_c\}$ and the LSTM parameters.

For loss minimization we use backward propagation where we initialize the weight matrices by a uniform distribution $U(-0.1, 0.1)$ and all bias are set to zero, as is done by [21]. To update the weights and biases we use stochastic gradient descent with momentum. Furthermore, the dropout technique is applied to all hidden layers to avoid overfitting [19]. The dropout technique randomly drops units from the neural network during training to prevent units from co-adapting too much on the training data.

Before training, the required hyperparameters of the proposed models are tuned. Parameters that are tuned include the learning rate, the L_2-norm regularization term (λ in Eq. 10), the dropout rate, and the momentum term. 80% of the training data is used for tuning and the other 20% is used for validation to test hyperparameter configurations. For a fast convergence speed we use a tree-structured Parzen estimators (TPE) algorithm [2] for tuning. TPE allows to learn from the training history and hence is able to give better estimations for the next set of parameters.

4.3   Two-Step Approach

The algorithm proposed in this paper will combine the ontology-based approach and LCR-Rot method into a hybrid method. The algorithm will iterate over all the opinions in the test dataset and predict the sentiment towards the aspects mentioned. The algorithm framework is explained in detail in [16] and hence we refer to this work for further details. In short, the algorithm will first use the previously described ontology to predict a positive or negative sentiment. If the ontology is not able to give a conclusive result, the algorithm will use a machine learning method (in our case the LCR-Rot algorithm) as a backup method.

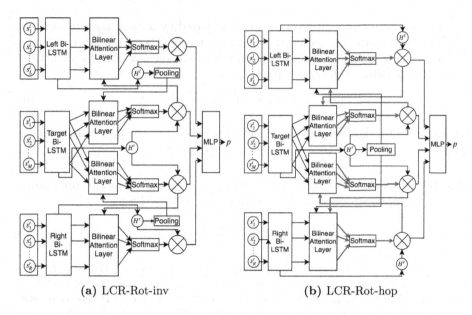

(a) LCR-Rot-inv   (b) LCR-Rot-hop

Fig. 3. Visual representations of the LCR-Rot-inv and LCR-Rot-hop architectures.

4.4   Inversed LCR-Rot

A possible alteration of the LCR-Rot algorithm as described in Sect. 4.2 is to inverse the rotatory attention mechanism. We will call this method LCR-Rot-inv. Instead of first applying a target2context attention algorithm and subsequently applying a context2target attention algorithm, it is also possible to first perform the context2target algorithm and then use the target2context algorithm. Instead of only one target pooling layer (for the target sentence), now two context pooling layers (for the left and right context) are used. By altering the order of the rotatory attention mechanism, the algorithm might be able to give important words more weight and/or catch semantic relations better. An illustration of this altered model is provided in Fig. 3a.

4.5   Multi-hop LCR-Rot

Another possible alteration of the LCR-Rot method is to repeat the rotatory attention mechanism for x times. This method is called LCR-Rot-hop since multiple hops are performed over the attention weights. By increasing the number of rotatory attention iterations, the model might be able to better represent aspects and contexts by improving the interaction between aspects and contexts. Furthermore, the iterative nature of the method might let the attention weights converge to their optimal values and achieve a higher accuracy. Figure 3b gives an illustration of the architecture of this method. The attention mechanism, that is iterated over for a certain amount of times, is marked with bold, red arrows. The main difference from the LCR-Rot method is that after step 2 the representation outputs are fed back into the rotatory attention mechanism.

5   Evaluation

To evaluate the performance of the models proposed in this paper against the baseline methods, training is performed on the training data and testing is done on the official test data. The evaluation metric is classification accuracy. Our models are compared to the following baseline methods:

Ont [16]: Uses a domain knowledge, as encoded in an ontology, to determine aspect sentiment.

BoW [16]: Bag-of-words model combined with an SVM classifier to determine sentiment. Hyperparameters C and *gamma* for the SVM are tuned in a similar way as described in Sect. 4.2 using a TPE algorithm.

CABASC [9]: Neural network that contains a context attention-based memory module for aspect-based sentiment analysis.

Ont+BoW [16]: Two step approach where an ontology method is first used and a backup bag-of-words method is used.

Ont+CABASC: Two step approach where first an ontology method is used [16] and as a backup method the CABASC model [9] is used.

In order to guarantee a fair comparison, we opt to program the baseline models instead of copying results reported in other papers. Since our code is written in Python, the Stanford CoreNLP package [18] that is used in [16] to find a sentence sentiment score for the BoW model is not available. Hence, we use the VADER sentiment score [7] as an alternative.

Accuracy results for the SemEval-2015 and SemEval-2016 dataset are given in Table 2. For each dataset, the first two columns show out-of-sample and in-sample results, respectively, of a single run. For this, the in-sample accuracy uses the complete training dataset and the out-of-sample accuracy uses the test dataset. The last two columns of each dataset present the average results of a 10-fold cross-validation procedure using the training data. For the LCR-Rot-hop model, preliminary results on the training data show that when the number of iterations x is set to three attention rotations, the highest accuracy is achieved.

We conclude that the ontology method by itself does not perform well. This is not surprising since it is only able to make a prediction in around 60% of all sentiment opinions. In the other 40%, the majority class is predicted, which is not a very good predictor. Furthermore, we can conclude that, in the case of restaurant reviews, LCR-Rot indeed outperforms CABASC by 1.8%–2.3%. LCR-Rot-inv also outperforms CABASC but by a smaller percentage of 0.5%–1.9%. Remarkably for the SemEval-2016 dataset the LCR-Rot-hop method performs around 0.8% better then the LCR-Rot method. This improved performance is however not apparent in the 2015 dataset, here the two methods perform equally well. Hence, LCR-Rot-hop is the best performing machine learning method for this specific task. By inversing the rotatory attention mechanism, we cannot

Table 2. Comparison of the models using out-of-sample, in-sample, and 10-fold cross-validation accuracy

	SemEval-2015				SemEval-2016			
	Out-of-sample	In-sample	Cross-validation		Out-of-sample	In-sample	Cross-validation	
	Acc.	Acc.	Acc.	St. dev.	Acc.	Acc.	Acc.	St. dev.
Ont	65.8%	79.7%	79.7%	0.0183	78.3%	75.3%	75.3%	0.0152
BoW	76.2%	91.0%	87.9%	0.0311	83.2%	89.3%	84.5%	0.0254
CABASC	76.6%	85.8%	87.1%	0.0138	84.6%	79.2%	84.0%	0.0218
LCR-Rot	**78.4%**	86.2%	88.0%	0.0144	86.9%	92.9%	85.8%	0.0214
LCR-Rot-inv	77.1%	85.2%	88.1%	0.0146	86.5%	93.9	85.5%	0.0161
LCR-Rot-hop	**78.4%**	88.6%	87.6%	0.0181	**87.7%**	86.3	85.6%	0.0169
Ont+BoW	79.5%	86.9%	83.5%	0.0308	85.6%	86.7%	85.7%	0.0329
Ont+CABASC	79.6%	84.3%	83.2%	0.0138	85.9%	82.3%	85.5%	0.0298
Ont+LCR-Rot	**80.6%**	84.5%	83.7%	0.0144	87.0%	88.3%	86.3%	0.0323
Ont+LCR-Rot-inv	79.9%	89.0%	83.7%	0.0146	86.6%	88.7%	86.2%	0.0296
Ont+LCR-Rot-hop	**80.6%**	85.7%	83.5%	0.0298	**88.0%**	86.7%	86.2%	0.0308

derive more information about relevant words. However, when iterating over the rotatory attention mechanism for three times, the model is able to improve the attention and interaction between aspect and context.

When analyzing the two-stage approaches we can observe an improved performance with respect to the base ontology approach. For each case, the ontology is able to provide additional information that the backup methods do not capture. Again, we observe that the hybrid method that uses LCR-Rot-hop performs the best and this is also the only hybrid method that outperforms the individual LCR-Rot-hop method, albeit with a very small percentage of 0.3%.

In order to find an explanation why LCR-Rot-hop and LCR-Rot perform better then CABASC, and why LCR-Rot-hop performs better then LCR-Rot, we will analyze the differences between the attention weights. Figure 4 gives a visualization of a sentence where LCR-Rot and LCR-Rot-hop make a correct prediction and CABASC makes an incorrect prediction. The analyzed sentence

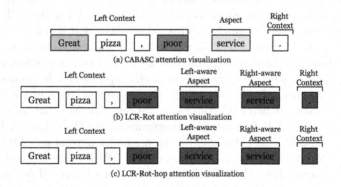

Fig. 4. Attention visualizations of the LCR-Rot, LCR-Rot-hop, and CABASC models for the phrase 'Great pizza, poor service'.

is 'Great pizza, poor service.' The red color denotes words to which the model pays attention. The darker the color, the higher the attention weight and the more important a word is for the representation.

The LCR-Rot model (Fig. 4b) and LCR-Rot-hop model (Fig. 4c) are both able to capture the most indicative sentiment word with respect to the aspect, i.e., 'poor'. The CABASC (Fig. 4a) model is also able to capture the words in the sentence that indicate a sentiment. However, it pays attention to both the words 'great' and 'poor', where the former word belongs to the aspect 'pizza' and only the latter is relevant for the aspect 'service'. In this simple case, where two different sentiments are expressed with respect to two aspects, CABASC finds it difficult to address which sentiment indicating words belong to which aspect. This might be due the fact that the sentences are short and both the aspects and sentiment indicating words are close to each other. On the contrary, both rotatory attention models are able to make this distinction, by better capturing the relevant sentiment words that belong to a specific aspect.

Figure 5 graphically shows attention weights for the sentence 'The food in here is incredible, though the quality is inconsistent during lunch'. Again, two sentiments are expressed, positive and negative, respectively related to two aspects, 'food' and 'lunch'. However, regarding sentiment, the sentence has a more difficult structure, since both aspects are closely related to each other. Similar as in Fig. 4a CABASC (Fig. 5a) is not able to detect which sentiment indicating words belong to which aspect and hence pays equal attention to both the words 'incredible' and 'inconsistent'. This also holds for the LCR-Rot method

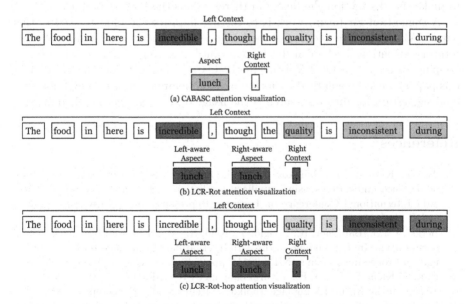

Fig. 5. Attention visualizations of the LCR-Rot, LCR-Rot-hop, and CABASC models for the phrase 'The food in here is incredible, though the quality is inconsistent during lunch'.

(Fig. 5b), it is not able to notice the irrelevance of the word 'incredible'. However, it is able to detect the relation between the word 'inconsistent' and the aspect, by paying attention to the preposition 'during'.

LCR-Rot-hop (Fig. 5c) is the only method that fully focuses attention to the relevant sentiment word 'inconsistent' and capture the connecting preposition 'during'. For these reasons it makes a correct prediction. When the sentiment expressed in a sentence is constructed in a more complex manner, repeating the rotatory attention mechanism helps to separate irrelevant sentiment words from relevant sentiment words.

6   Conclusion

This paper focuses on aspect-based sentiment analysis of restaurant reviews on a sentence level. We employ an ontology-driven hybrid approach, following the main idea of [16] and using the LCR-Rot method [21] as a backup algorithm. The two-stage algorithms outperform one-stage baseline models, albeit with a small percentage. Our best performing method (Ont+LCR-Rot-hop) outperforms the Ont+BoW model proposed by [16] by 2% point when considering the SemEval-2016 dataset.

We conclude that all the machine learning methods are able to effectively find words that carry sentiment. However, the models differ in how much they are able to focus on sentiment words that are only relevant for the given aspect. By repeating the rotatory attention mechanism, the LCR-Rot-hop method is able to make this distinction the best and therefore has the highest performance.

A suggestion for future work is to further improve the models used in this paper. With regard to the neural models, one can experiment further with the rotatory attention mechanism by looping until a convergence is reached or by hopping through the LCR-Rot-inv method. Considering the ontology used in this paper, it can be enlarged by including more lemmas, classes, and axioms. A final suggestion for future research is the usage of different word embeddings.

References

1. Adi, Y., Kermany, E., Belinkov, Y., Lavi, O., Goldberg, Y.: Fine-grained analysis of sentence embeddings using auxiliary prediction tasks. In: Proceedings of the 2017 International Conference on Learning Representations (ICLR 2017) (2017). CoRR abs/1608.04207
2. Bergstra, J.S., Bardenet, R., Bengio, Y., Kégl, B.: Algorithms for hyper-parameter optimization. In: Proceedings of the 24th International Conference on Neural Information Processing Systems (NIPS 2011), pp. 2546–2554. Curran Associates (2011)
3. Bird, S., Klein, E., Loper, E.: Natural Language Processing with Python: Analyzing Text with the Natural Language Toolkit. O'Reilly Media, Sebastopol (2009)
4. Cambria, E.: Affective computing and sentiment analysis. IEEE Intell. Syst. 31(2), 102–107 (2016). https://doi.org/10.1109/mis.2016.31

5. Cambria, E., Hussain, A.: Sentic Computing: A Common-Sense-Based Framework for Concept-Level Sentiment Analysis. SC, vol. 1. Springer, Cham (2015). https://doi.org/10.1007/978-3-319-23654-4
6. Chen, P., Sun, Z., Bing, L., Yang, W.: Recurrent attention network on memory for aspect sentiment analysis. In: Proceedings of the 2017 Conference on Empirical Methods in Natural Language Processing (EMNLP 2017), pp. 452–461. Association for Computational Linguistics (2017)
7. Hutto, C.J., Gilbert, E.: VADER: a parsimonious rule-based model for sentiment analysis of social media text. In: Proceedings of the 8th International Conference on Weblogs and Social Media (ICWSM 2014). AAAI Press (2014)
8. Liu, B.: Sentiment Analysis: Mining Opinions, Sentiments, and Emotions. Cambridge University Press, New York (2015)
9. Liu, Q., Zhang, H., Zeng, Y., Huang, Z., Wu, Z.: Content attention model for aspect based sentiment analysis. In: Proceedings of the 27th International World Wide Web Conference (WWW 2018), pp. 1023–1032. ACM Press (2018). https://doi.org/10.1145/3178876.3186001
10. Miller, G.A.: WordNet: a lexical database for English. Commun. ACM **38**(11), 39–41 (1995). https://doi.org/10.1145/219717.219748
11. Pennington, J., Socher, R., Manning, C.D.: GloVe: global vectors for word representation. In: Proceedings of The 2014 Conference on Empirical Methods in Natural Language Processing (EMNLP 2014), pp. 1532–1543. Association for Computational Linguistics (2014)
12. Pontiki, M., Galanis, D., Papageorgiou, H., Manandhar, S., Androutsopoulos, I.: Semeval-2015 task 12: aspect based sentiment analysis. In: Proceedings of the 9th International Workshop on Semantic Evaluation (SemEval 2015), pp. 486–495. Association for Computational Linguistics (2015)
13. Pontiki, M., Galanis, D., Papageorgiou, H., Manandhar, S., Androutsopoulos, I.: Semeval-2016 task 5: aspect based sentiment analysis. In: Proceedings of the 10th International Workshop on Semantic Evaluation (SemEval 2016), pp. 19–30. Association for Computational Linguistics (2016)
14. Pontiki, M., Galanis, D., Pavlopoulos, J., Papageorgiou, H., Androutsopoulos, I., Manandhar, S.: Semeval-2014 task 4: aspect based sentiment analysis. In: Proceedings of the 8th International Workshop on Semantic Evaluation (SemEval 2014), pp. 27–35. Association for Computational Linguistics and Dublin City University, August 2014
15. Schouten, K., Frasincar, F.: Survey on aspect-level sentiment analysis. IEEE Trans. Knowl. Data Eng. (TKDE) **28**(3), 813–830 (2016)
16. Schouten, K., Frasincar, F.: Ontology-driven sentiment analysis of product and service aspects. In: Gangemi, A., et al. (eds.) ESWC 2018. LNCS, vol. 10843, pp. 608–623. Springer, Cham (2018). https://doi.org/10.1007/978-3-319-93417-4_39
17. Schouten, K., Frasincar, F., de Jong, F.: Ontology-enhanced aspect-based sentiment analysis. In: Cabot, J., De Virgilio, R., Torlone, R. (eds.) ICWE 2017. LNCS, vol. 10360, pp. 302–320. Springer, Cham (2017). https://doi.org/10.1007/978-3-319-60131-1_17
18. Socher, R., et al.: Recursive deep models for semantic compositionality over a sentiment treebank. In: Proceedings of the 2013 Conference on Empirical Methods on Natural Language Processing (EMNLP, 2013), vol. 1631, pp. 1631–1642. ACL, January 2013
19. Srivastava, N., Hinton, G., Krizhevsky, A., Sutskever, I., Salakhutdinov, R.: Dropout: a simple way to prevent neural networks from overfitting. J. Mach. Learn. Res. **15**, 1929–1958 (2014)

20. Wang, Y., Huang, M., Zhu, X., Zhao, L.: Attention-based LSTM for aspect-level sentiment classification. In: Proceedings of the 2016 Conference on Empirical Methods on Natural Language Processing (EMNLP 2016), pp. 606–615. Association for Computational Linguistics (2016). https://doi.org/10.18653/v1/d16-1058
21. Zheng, S., Xia, R.: Left-center-right separated neural network for aspect-based sentiment analysis with rotatory attention (2018). arXiv preprint arXiv:1802.00892

Predicting Entity Mentions in Scientific Literature

Yalung Zheng[1], Jon Ezeiza[2], Mehdi Farzanehpour[2], and Jacopo Urbani[1(✉)]

[1] Vrije Universiteit Amsterdam, Amsterdam, The Netherlands
jacopo@cs.vu.nl
[2] SCITODATE B.V., Amsterdam, The Netherlands

Abstract. Predicting which entities are likely to be mentioned in scientific articles is a task with significant academic and commercial value.
For instance, it can lead to monetary savings if the articles are behind
paywalls, or be used to recommend articles that are not yet available.
Despite extensive prior work on entity prediction in Web documents, the
peculiarities of scientific literature make it a unique scenario for this task.
In this paper, we present an approach that uses a neural network to predict whether the (unseen) body of an article contains entities defined in
domain-specific knowledge bases (KBs). The network uses features from
the abstracts and the KB, and it is trained using open-access articles and
authors' prior works. Our experiments on biomedical literature show that
our method is able to predict subsets of entities with high accuracy. As
far as we know, our method is the first of its kind and is currently used
in several commercial settings.

1 Introduction

Retrieving relevant scientific literature is crucial to advance the state-of-the-art
in many disciplines. Unfortunately, a considerable subset of scientific articles is
unavailable to the general public. For instance, recent estimates suggest that so
far only 28% of publications are released as Open Access [22], and this excludes
publications which are not yet available (e.g., preprints). In this case, third
parties can only use public metadata to search for relevant literature, but this
might be only a subset of all information contained in the article.

Typically, the search of scientific articles is driven by some entities of interest. For instance, one user might be interested in retrieving all papers that
mention "cardiovascular disorders" or "phosphorene". These entities are often
domain-specific (e.g., drugs, or experimental procedures) and are contained in
high-quality knowledge bases (e.g., BioPortal [20]). Unfortunately, if the full article is missing then this process can only return articles which explicitly mention
these entities in their abstracts or other metadata.

To overcome this limitation, one would need to be able to predict whether
a paper might contain a given entity. This task, which we call entity prediction
(EP), but is also known as entity suggestion [31], recommendation [5], or set

© Springer Nature Switzerland AG 2019
P. Hitzler et al. (Eds.): ESWC 2019, LNCS 11503, pp. 379–393, 2019.
https://doi.org/10.1007/978-3-030-21348-0_25

expansion [29], can be used to rank unseen articles and can lead to significant monetary savings if the articles are behind paywalls. Moreover, EP can also be used for other tasks like to augment existing knowledge bases, or might contribute for capturing the results of certain experiments in a more formal way (e.g., see the movement around nanopublications [10]).

In the literature, entity prediction has been previously applied to improve Web search results [3,12] or for knowledge base expansion [23]. In these cases, the prediction models use the entities contained in the queries as a seed to predict related entities mentioned in larger collections of documents (e.g., Web pages). Our context, however, is more challenging. First, scientific articles contain more technical nomenclature than regular Web pages and fewer entities are relevant. Second, it is harder for us to acquire large amounts of training data due the extreme coverage of topics, and because a significant number of articles is either behind paywalls or available in obsolete formats.

In this paper, we address this challenge by proposing a novel method for entity prediction on scientific literature. Our strategy is to construct a statistical model to predict which entities are likely to be mentioned in an article given its abstract and other metadata. We rely on knowledge bases to detect domain-specific entities of interest and use scientific articles released with Open Access to construct a training dataset of entity co-occurrences. After some initial failed attempts where we tried different types of models, which range from standard binary classifiers to neural networks with dense embeddings, linguistic, and other semantic features extracted from the KB, we finally obtained satisfactory results by restricting our focus to specific target entities. In this case, our model consists of a multi-layer neural network that is trained to predict whether the body of an article is likely to mention one entity of interest (or a class of entities). As input, the network receives a Bag-Of-Word (BOW) feature vector constructed using the entities in the abstract, and, optionally, also the entities mentioned in prior works of the authors. As output, it returns the probability that one or more target entities are mentioned.

We empirically evaluated our method considering scientific literature in the biomedical field. In this context, our results are encouraging: The average accuracy on predicting eight example entities from the NCIT ontology [24] in about 2K scientific articles from PubMed was 0.865 (0.804 AUC). As far as we know, we are not aware of other techniques for predicting entities in unseen articles, and our results indicate that this is a valuable asset to improve semantic search of scientific literature. In a more commercial setting, these predictions can also be used to connect suppliers of scientific equipment (e.g., special machines or chemical compounds) to potential customers (i.e., research labs) by looking at the customers' published papers. This last use case is precisely the one that motivated our research and is currently explored in a number of industrial scenarios.

2   Related Work

Semantic Search. Our work falls into the broad research topic of semantic search which largely focuses on searching related entities in knowledge bases using structured and unstructured inputs. In this context, it is important to discover related entities, and this is a process that usually starts with a small entity subset of the target, namely the seed entities. In [9], the authors propose a Bayesian model to determine if an entity belongs to a cluster or concept, and use it to expand the set with more entities belonging to the same cluster as the seeds. In [23], it is proposed to crawl the Web to get coordinated words which are conjuncted by "and", "or" and commas, then define similarity on top of them. Moreover, the authors of [29] propose to learn wrappers of the seeds from the semi-structured documents, e.g., HTML, then use learned wrappers to find new entities in a bootstrap manner. Finally, [12] proposes GQBE, a system that takes entity tuples as examples to find similar combinations from knowledge graph. Our setting differs from these works since we assume that a large part of the related entities are not available and we focus on the retrieval of domain-specific entities which appear with lower frequencies.

In the context of query answering, the works at [14,30] propose to use language models to estimate the probability of an entity given query term and category. Furthermore, [28] proposes to use lexical similarity to constrain the entity results with categories while [3] introduces a probabilistic framework to model the query focusing on category information. More recently, [5] proposes to take the neighbor nodes of the initial entities in a knowledge graph and rank them with a learn-to-rank framework using co-occurrence, popularity and graph attributes as features. This work takes only the entity from user query and outperforms [7] which requires long descriptive text that contains concepts. Also, the authors of [31] have proposed a technique to conceptualize the input entities and build two probabilistic models between entities and concepts, thus they give not only the related entities but also the concept that explains the relationship. While these works are related in terms of objective, they are applied to domains which are significantly different. To the best of our knowledge, we are not aware of any previous works that apply EP to scientific literature using abstracts as seeds.

Co-occurrence Analysis. We use co-occurrence as a measure of relatedness. Co-occurrence is widely studied, especially in the biomedical field, in order to discover new connections between entities of interest. The most related field is *literature-based discovery* where the co-occurrence in academic publications is used as the evidence of links between concepts [25]. Moreover, many researchers have used co-occurrence for domain-specific tasks: For instance, the authors of [13] use co-occurrence as a source of information to retrieve the biological relationships between genes while [8] use co-occurrence information to form indirect links and discover the hidden connections between drugs, genes, and diseases. The work at [15] also uses co-occurrence in scientific articles to predict implicit relations between biomedical entities. While these works also make use of explicit mentions to draw conclusions, they focus on specific problems and do not consider the co-occurrence relations between abstracts (which are highly dense summaries) and the full document. Another emerging form of co-occurrence is encoded in a latent space in the form of dense numerical vectors. The seminal work *word2vec* [17] is perhaps the most popular example of this kind applied to English words. In our work, we did use a *"word2vec"*-like approach to encode the co-occurrence of entities but we did not obtain good results.

Bag of Words (BOW). Finally, our approach uses a bag-of-words vector to represent the entities. Typically BOW models treat all the words in the same piece of text equally, but there is a significant research to enhance the performance by adding a weighting scheme [26]. In our work, we choose standard intra-document term frequency as a weighting scheme. The application of more sophisticated weighting scheme should be seen as future work.

3   Entity Prediction in Scientific Literature

Our goal is to predict whether the unseen body of the article contains some entities of interest given in input some author information and abstract. To this end, our proposal is to train a model that learns correlations between entity mentions in the abstract and in the full body and use these to make the predictions. More formally, let E and A be two predefined sets of entities and authors. Given two sequences $\langle e_1, \ldots, e_n \rangle$ and $\langle a_1, \ldots a_m \rangle$, which represent respectively the list of entities that appear in the abstract and list of authors, we want to build a model to predict with high confidence whether some entities $t_1, \ldots, t_n \in E$ appear in the body (which we assume is not accessible).

We make a few assumptions: First, we assume that we have available a significant number of full articles which we can use for training our model. This assumption is met in practice by considering articles published using the open-access model. Second, we assume that entities are available in knowledge bases which allow us to exploit semantic relations to improve the prediction. In practice, useful knowledge bases can be large domain-specific ontologies such as Unified Medical Language System (UMLS) [16], National Cancer Institute Thesaurus (NCIT) [24], Headings and Systematized Nomenclature of Medicine-Clinical Terms (SNOMED-CT) [6], or other encyclopedic ones like DBpedia [2]. For the purpose of this work, we view a knowledge base as a graph G where E is a set of vertices (i.e., the entities in our case) while the edges encode semantic relations between them. For instance, $\langle Odontogenesis, IsA, Organogenesis \rangle$ is an example of such relation taken from the NCIT ontology.

We distinguish two operations: *training*, that is when our objective is to construct a suitable model, and *prediction*, that is when we use the model to make the predictions. In both cases, the first operation consists of applying a state-of-the-art entity recognition (NER) tool and disambiguate the entity mentions to entities in the knowledge base. In this work, we used NobleTools [27] for the recognition and the disambiguation to the KB. For each extracted entity we extract from the knowledge base its semantic type and neighbors. Moreover, we store also the position of the entity in the original text. Then, we "embed" each entity mention into a sequence of numerical features so that it can be used by the statistical model. During the training phase, the embeddings of entities in both metadata and body are used to train a statistical model. During the prediction, the model is used to predict new entity mentions.

In the following, we first describe two early attempts at implementing the model using two well-known techniques: A standard binary classifier and a Recurrent Neural Network (RNN) [11] used in combination with word embeddings. Neither of these methods returned adequate performance. In Sect. 4, we describe how we overcame the limitations of these two methods with a more performant approach.

3.1 Failed Attempts

As a first step in our research, we decided to investigate how a well-known technique such as a binary classifier would perform in our context. To this end, we followed the standard practice of representing entities with feature vectors and trained a classifier (we used a Support Vector Machine (SVM) [4]) to predict to what extent a given entity in the abstract correlates with the appearance of another entity in the article's body.

We proceeded as follows. First, we created a feature vector for each entity appearing in the abstract or body of the paper. Then, we concatenated the feature vectors of one entity in the abstract, one entity in the body, and some additional shared features together. The resulting vector was used as positive example while pairs or non-existing random pairs of entities were used as negative examples.

The entity feature vectors are composed of 13 features:

1. Two structural features: the distance from the start of the text and spread of an entity, namely distance between the first and the last mention of one entity. These features are introduced because typically important entities are mentioned first in the text;
2. Seven standard statistical features: TF, IDF, TF*IDF on both abstract and body entities, and respective co-occurrence frequencies;
3. Four features extracted from the considered ontologies: Jaccard, Dice, Milne-Witten [18], and Adamic-Adar [1] distances between the entities in the repository. These features aim at capturing how close the two entities are in the semantic domain which is represented by the ontology.

We calculated the Pearson coefficient of each feature against the true label and did a feature ablation study by removing the feature with the worst coefficient one by another to find the best feature subset. Unfortunately, none of these operations returned satisfactory performance. Using a training set of 3K articles and a test set of 3K Pubmed articles, our best results were 0.309 as precision and 0.394 as F1 score.

A limitation of the previous approach is that it does not take the sequence of entities into account. To include this aspect in our prediction, we considered the usage of Recurrent Neural Networks (RNN) and build a language model using the appearance sequence of entities in the abstracts and bodies as input.

To create suitable embeddings for the entities, we tried both a state-of-the-art word2vec-variant called *Entity2Vec* [19] (using sequences of entities in the paper as the "sentences") and another technique called *DeepWalk* [21] which performs random walks on the knowledge graph. During the training of the language model, we only considered the body of open access articles as training data since because the articles' bodies contain many more entities and about 85% of the entities which are mentioned in the abstract are also mentioned in the body. During the testing phase, we fed the RNN with the sequence of entities in an abstract (in the order they appear) and then computed the cosine distance between the output of the network and the embeddings of all the entities in our repository. The ones with the smallest values were selected as the output of the prediction.

Unfortunately, also this method did not return satisfactory results with the best precision, recall and F1 score averaging under 0.1. First, we observed that taking the whole body as one single sequence of entities dilutes the semantic relations between the tokens and adds noises to the model. A better approach would be to segment the text into smaller sequences depending on domain knowledge. Second, the quality of the entity embedding is not perfect and errors in this space affect the downstream application. To evaluate this problem, we took the embedding of one entity in the knowledge graph and calculated the cosine similarity against all other entities in E, rank them according to this measure, and extract the position of the synonyms. We repeated this process for 100 known synonyms pairs but the average position was below the top 10% with either method. This indicates that the quality of the entity embeddings is not high. Our third method, described in the next section, overcomes this problem by adopting a sparse representation of the entities instead.

4   Using a Neural Network with BOW

We now describe our third attempt which uses a neural network with bag-of-words (BOW) embeddings to perform the prediction. First, we map the list of entities in E into a BOW vector $\mathbf{e}$ of length $|E|$. We use different weighting scheme for the entities in the abstract and body. For the firsts, we use term frequency as the feature value. For the seconds, we use a binary value depending on the entity's appearance.

Then, we train a neural network that takes in input the vector with the frequency of entities in the abstract, which we call $\mathbf{e}_{abs}$, and in output another vector with the entities found in the body, which we call $\mathbf{e}_{bdy}$. More formally, let abs and bdy be the multisets of entities that appear in the paper's abstract and body respectively and let bdy_n the set of entities that appear only in bdy. Then,

$$\mathbf{e}_{abs} = \langle TF(e_1, abs), TF(e_2, abs), ..., TF(e_{|E|}, abs)\rangle \tag{1}$$

$$\mathbf{e}_{bdy} = \langle \chi(e_1, bdy_n), \chi(e_2, bdy_n), ..., \chi(e_{|E|}, bdy_n)\rangle \tag{2}$$

where $TF(e, t)$ denotes the number of mentions of entity e in t while $\chi(e, t)$ is a function that returns 1 if e appears in t or 0 otherwise.

We add a number of hidden layers to bridge through the high-level latent semantic correlations and add non-linearity to the model. Considering that the dimension of the input is high (i.e., $|E|$), we set the size of hidden layers much smaller than $|E|$ to densify the representation. Finally, the model is trained by minimizing the cross-entropy as usual.

After the training is finished, the network is ready to make the prediction. Let $\mathbf{e}_{\widehat{bdy}} = \langle \widehat{e}_1, \ldots, \widehat{e_{|E|}} \rangle$ be the output of the network for a given abstract. The likelihood $P(e_i)$ that entity e_i appears in the body of the article is computed as:

$$P(e_i) = \frac{\widehat{e}_i}{\|\mathbf{e}_{\widehat{bdy}}\|_2} \tag{3}$$

Since the network outputs a likelihood score for all entities, Eq. 3 can be used to make a prediction for either *all* entities in E or for a subset of them. If we restrict our focus to one or a few specific entities, then we can substantially reduce the size of the BOW vectors to only the entities which are related to our focus. To this end, let us assume that we are interested only on predicting whether the paper mentions one entity of interest e^*. In this case, we can identify all entities which are close to e^* in the knowledge base and reduce the size of the BOW vector to only those entities. We use the length of the paths between entities in the knowledge graph as distance value. More formally, let the set $N(e) = \{e\} \cup \{e_j \in V(G) | \langle e_j, e \rangle \in E(G) \vee \langle e, e_j \rangle \in E(G)\}$ be the neighbour set of the entity e in the graph G. Then we define $N^0(e) = N(e)$ and $N^{i+1}(e) = N^i(e) \cup \bigcup_{e_j \in N^i(e)} N(e_j)$ for all $i \geq 0$. In some of our experiments, we considered entities in $N^i(e^*)$ where $1 \leq i \leq 2$. This reduces the size of the embeddings from $|E|$ to $|N^i(e*)|$ and this consequently improves significantly training time. In Sect. 5, we report the performance of the model for predicting either all entities, multiple or a single class of entities, or a single one.

4.1   Including Author's Co-authorship

So far, only the entities in the abstract were considered for the prediction. However, researchers tend to specialize on specific topics, and co-authorships indicate shared interests. Therefore, the list of authors is also a valuable asset for our goal.

We propose one extension to our previous method to exploit this information. The main idea consists of using the authors as proxies to collect more relevant entities. More specifically, our approach is to first collect up to n previous publications from each of the m authors of an article, and then construct the BOW vectors for the abstract and body of a given article as follows.

$$\mathbf{e}'_{abs} = (1 - \alpha)\mathbf{e}_{abs} + \alpha\frac{1}{mn}\sum_{j=1}^{m}\sum_{i=1}^{n}\mathbf{e}_{abs_{ij}}, \tag{4}$$

$$\mathbf{e}'_{\widehat{bdy}} = (1 - \beta)\mathbf{e}_{\widehat{bdy}} + \beta\frac{1}{mn}\sum_{j=1}^{m}\sum_{i=1}^{n}\mathbf{e}_{bdy_{ij}}, \tag{5}$$

where $\mathbf{e}_{abs}$ and $\mathbf{e}_{\widehat{bdy}}$ are the BOW vectors of the abstract and the body of the given article constructed with Eqs. 1 and 2, $\mathbf{e}_{abs_{11}}, \ldots, \mathbf{e}_{abs_{mn}}$ and $\mathbf{e}_{bdy_{11}}, \ldots, \mathbf{e}_{bdy_{mn}}$ are the vectors of the abstracts and bodies of the previous n papers of m authors, and α and β are two hyperparameters used to control the weights given to the modeled histories.

Initially, we gave an equal weight to all authors. However, since they can contribute non-equivalently to the article, we decided to first determine the importance of each author by comparing the frequencies of the entities in the authors' abstracts with the content of the paper and then consider only the author with the highest overlap. In this way, we can exclude authors which have also published in many other domains and therefore might introduce noise.

5   Evaluation

We report an empirical evaluation of the approach described in Sect. 4 on biomedical scientific literature. We chose this field since it contains high quality knowledge bases and many scientific papers. The goal of our experiments was to evaluate the accuracy in predicting either a single or all entities (Sect. 5.1), the effect of hyperparameters like the network structure or training size (Sect. 5.2), and what is the impact of adding also author information in the prediction (Sect. 5.3). All code, models, and data is available at https://github.com/NiMaZi/BioPre.

Input.   As input, we considered the scientific publications which are archived in PubMed, the largest repository of biomedical articles. This collection contains about 27M articles, of which about 17M (65.5%) of them contain only the abstract, while 8M (32.3%) contain both abstract and full body. About 93.3% of the papers in the second subset contain also author information. The content of these papers is available and stored in raw text on Elasticsearch[1], which we use to query and retrieve the content of the papers.

Preprocessing.   We extracted the entities in the articles with NobleTools [27], which is a popular entity annotator for biomedical text. This tool can be configured to use ontologies as the entity thesaurus. In our experiments, we used the NCIT ontology since it is a well-known ontology that covers concepts that range from disease to clinical care and is compatible with NobleTools. This ontology can be seen as a knowledge graph with 133K entities and 1.6M relations. Noble-Tools uses a number of heuristics to select potential entity candidates for each mention. Then, it selects one candidate among them by preferring first candidates with most synonyms, rejecting candidates that resemble abbreviations but lack a case-sensitive match, and preferring at last candidates that are unstemmed. Using NCIT, we extracted on average 59 entity mentions per abstract and 496 entity mentions in each body. Finally, we used an adapted version of *Beard*[2] for author disambiguation.

---

[1] https://elastic.co.
[2] https://github.com/inspirehep/beard.

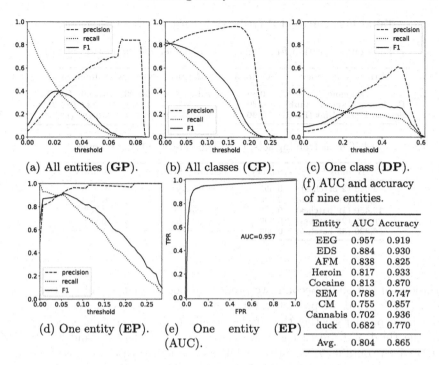

(a) All entities (**GP**).   (b) All classes (**CP**).   (c) One class (**DP**).

(d) One entity (**EP**).   (e) One entity (**EP**) (AUC).

(f) AUC and accuracy of nine entities.

Entity	AUC	Accuracy
EEG	0.957	0.919
EDS	0.884	0.930
AFM	0.838	0.825
Heroin	0.817	0.933
Cocaine	0.813	0.870
SEM	0.788	0.747
CM	0.755	0.857
Cannabis	0.702	0.936
duck	0.682	0.770
Avg.	0.804	0.865

Fig. 1. Precision, recall, and F1 for four types of predictions. (e) reports also the area under the curve (AUC) for the **EP** prediction.

Testbed. We used Keras[3] to implement the various models and Tensorflow[4] as backend. All the models are constructed with fully connected layers, and have batch-wise L1 normalization and 0.5 dropout rate associated with each layer. Unless otherwise specified, the models were trained with binary cross-entropy as loss function and the weight matrix was updated with Nesterov-accelerated Adaptive Moment Estimation (Nadam). We used mini-batch strategy for updating the model, where each batch contains 1024 articles. All the models were trained using a machine with a dual 8-core 2.4 GHz (Intel Haswell E5-2630-v3) CPU, 64 GB RAM, and two NVIDIA TITAN X graphic cards with Pascal architecture and one NVIDIA GTX 980 graphic card. Training a batch of articles took about 6.5 min and we did not observe improvements after 5–10 epochs of training.

5.1   Entity Prediction Using Abstract Entities

We trained a number of models to perform four types of predictions: First, we perform a general prediction (**GP**), which means that try to predict all entity

---

[3] https://github.com/keras-team/keras.

[4] https://www.tensorflow.org/.

Table 1. Accuracy (**EP** prediction) changing several parameters.

(a) Different activation functions.   (b) Different number of entities.

Activation Function	Accuracy		Entities	Accuracy	Input Size
Sigmoid	0.894		All entities	**0.903**	133,609 (100%)
Hyperbolic Tangent (tanh)	0.800		N^2	0.878	**33,934 (25.4%)**
Rectified Linear Unit (ReLU)	**0.903**		Leaf Nodes	0.663	110,184 (82.5%)

(c) Different training sets.   (d) Different weighting scheme.

Training Set	Accuracy	Weighting Scheme	Accuracy
2,048 (2 batches)	0.693	binary	0.877
10,240 (10 batches)	0.840	tf	**0.903**
19,456 (19 batches)	0.873	$log(tf)$	0.887
28,672 (28 batches)	0.890	$tf \cdot idf$	0.881
56,320 (55 batches)	0.903		

mentions in the body. Second, we predict all possible *classes* of entities in the body (**CP**). Third, we predict whether the article mentions one class of entities. Fourth, we predict whether the article contains the mention of one specific entity. For the third and fourth cases, we chose the class "Disease and Syndromes" (**DP**) which contains 5227 entities while for the fourth case we chose the entity "electroencephalography (EEG)" (**EP**). This arbitrary choice was selected due to a real-world business case.

We created a neural network with one hidden layer of 512 units and the Rectified Linear Unit (ReLU) as a global activation function. Then, we selected a random subset of 147K articles as training data and 3K articles as test data for the first three types of predictions. For the fourth type of prediction, we selected 56K and 2K random articles as training and test data respectively. In this case, the test dataset contains about 1K positive examples and 1K negative ones.

We performed various experiments changing the output threshold value and calculated the precision and recall (for **EP** we also computed the area under the curve of ROC). The results are shown in Fig. 1. As we can observe from the graphs, the F1 score for the **GP** predictions is significantly lower than for the prediction of a single entity (**EP**). The F1 for **CP** is high as well, but this is misleading because here we are predicting all classes and the articles almost always contain the same classes of entities. For them, the model learns to always return true (and indeed the best results are obtained by setting the threshold closed to zero). In contrast, the F1 for predicting EEGs (**EP**) is high, but in this case the threshold is not zero which means that the network has learned to discriminate. From these results, we conclude that our model has indeed learned to predict the occurrence of one entity of interest with high accuracy.

It is important to mention that Figs. 1d and e report the results for one specific entity, namely EEGs. In order to verify whether similar results can also be obtained with other entities, we selected eight different entities and repeat the same experiment. Instead of picking random entities, we made an effort to select a representative sample that contains entities which both are specific and generic, and which belong to different classes. More specifically, we picked "Energy Dispersive Spectroscopy (EDS)" from the category of spectroscopy, "Atomic Force Microscope (AFM)", "Scanning Electron Microscope (SEM)" and "Confocal Microscope (CM)" from the category of microscope, "Heroin", "Cocaine" and "Cannabis" from the category of drugs, and "duck" from the category of birds. Figure 1f reports the Area Under the ROC Curve (AUC) and accuracy for each entity (note that the table reports also the same AUC of EEG shown in Fig. 1(e). As we can see from the table, the models are able to return fairly high scores also for other entities, which means that it can handle other types of entities as well.

5.2   Entity Prediction with Different Hyperparameters

We have also performed a series of experiments changing some hyperparameters or configurations of the network to see to what extent the performance of the single entity prediction (EEG) is affected by these changes. More in particular, we tested different activation functions (Table 1a), different subsets of entities, i.e., all entities, only the neighbours in $N^2(x)$ where x is the target entity, and only the "leaf" entities in KB (Table 1b), different training set sizes (Table 1c), and different weighting schemes (Table 1d). All these models, except the study on different training set size, are trained on 56K articles and share the same network settings as the previous experiments.

We can draw some conclusions from these results. First, we observe from Table 1a that ReLU delivers the best results. Second, the study reported in Table 1b shows that while the best results are obtained by considering all entities, if we consider only the neighbors of the entity (N^2), then we still get a fairly high accuracy, but with the additional advantage that we reduced the size of the input vectors to 25% of the original size. This loss in terms of accuracy might be acceptable if the domain contains a very large number of entities. Table 1c shows that while the accuracy gradually saturates with more than ten batches of training articles, we still need to use the entire training set to get the best results. Finally, we learn from Table 1d that the term frequency (tf) is the best weighting scheme for the BOW vector.

5.3   Entity Prediction Including Co-Authorship

We now provide some preliminary results on including authors' information in the prediction as described in Sect. 4.1. First, we selected three representative authors whose history vectors have different variances (anonymized details are reported in Fig. 2a). For each author, we randomly picked 200 articles to create the history of abstracts. Then, we used these vectors to predict all entities in the body of other 100 random articles. We measure the F1 score by changing the complement parameter α from 0.0 to 1.0 (if α is zero then the approach is not considering any prior work while if it is 1 it only considers prior works). The results, shown in Fig. 2b, show that including the information of authors with lower variance does improve the F1 but this is true as long as the author

(a) Statistics of three sampled authors.

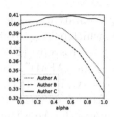

Author	Articles	Variance
Author A	6,742	0.63
Author B	1,384	0.48
Author C	1,312	0.32

(b) F1 with author embeddings.

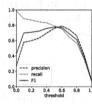 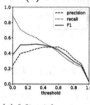

(c) DD without authors.   (d) DD with authors.   (e) Mi without authors.   (f) Mi with authors.

Fig. 2. a–b: Statistics and performance including author embeddings. c–f: Performance on entities "Drug Dependencies (DD)" and "Microscope (Mi)" with and without author embeddings.

publishes in the same domain (i.e., with low variance) because otherwise noise is introduced (as shown for authors A and B in Fig. 2b). This motivates our choice of selecting only the author with the highest overlap with the content of the paper.

We then evaluate the change of performance if we restrict our focus to the prediction of small groups of entities that are in the same category. We picked the class "microscopes" (that contains entities like "Scanning Electron Microscope", "Transmission Electron Microscope", "Scanning Tunneling Microscope", "Confocal Microscope", etc.) and "drug dependences" (with entities like "Alcohol Dependence", "Cannabis Dependence", "Cocaine Dependence", etc.) as our target groups (we selected these two classes of entities since they are the ones whether the authors have published). The results, shown in Figs. 2c–f, show a moderate increase of the F1 when we include prior abstracts of the selected author. In the first case, the increase of the F1 was about 0.8% while in the second case it was about 2.5%[5]. These results confirm that indeed the authors constitute a valuable asset to improve the performance of the prediction.

5.4   Limitations

Table 2 reports, as anecdotal evidence, the top 10 relevant entities identified for EEG. The relevance scores in this table were computed by simply creating a fake abstract where only EEG was mentioned and ranking the entities with the highest output values. While these results do not reflect completely the output

---

[5] These experiments are repeated multiple time (≥ 5).

Table 2. Top 10 relevant entities of EEG.

Entity	Relevance score	Entity	Relevance score
Pharmacodynamic Study	13.98	NIPBL wt Allele	12.68
Obstructive Sleep Apnea	13.91	Audit	12.39
Proband	13.23	Central Nervous System Involvement	12.38
Lactic Acidosis	13.12	Cornelia De Lange Syndrome	12.35
Sweden	13.00	Reye Syndrome	12.19

of the network (since typically more entities are added in the input), they give us an indication on which are the most relevant entities according to our model. As we can see from the table, the model recognizes some relevant entities (like diseases which require the use of EEG), but also returns some generic entities (like Sweden).

We investigated the causes of errors using the optimal configuration to gain some insights into the limitations of our method. If we consider once again the prediction of EEG, then we obtained 244 errors in our test set, of which 118 were false positives and 126 false negatives. After analyzing the false positives, we divided the errors into three major problems:

1. The prediction might become too much biased towards entities with high intra-document frequency.
2. A similar bias is given for common entities which appear frequently in a wide variety of topics.
3. The method is not able to distinguish secondary content in the abstract that will not be discussed in detail in the corresponding body.

The first two problems make up 96% of all the false positives while the third problem makes up for 4% of the cases. We believe that the first two problems can be addressed by introducing more sophisticated weighting schemes to balance different intra-frequencies and by giving smaller weights to abstract concepts. Addressing the third cause of error requires a deeper understanding of the organization of a scientific article. Intuitively, the important content is mentioned in the front of the abstract, thus the position of each entity in the abstract could be used as a naive measurement of importance. A deeper investigation on these issues should be seen as future work.

6   Conclusion

We proposed a machine-learning-based technique to predict entities mentioned in scientific articles using the articles' metadata. This task is useful to improve the retrieval of relevant publications when the full content is not available either because of a paywall or due to other reasons (e.g., preprints). Our technique can be used to search for classes of entities or be targeted to specific entities (e.g., some special equipment, as it was for one of our business cases). Moreover, it can be also useful for performing knowledge base completion, or more generally to discover related entities based on co-occurrences.

Our best-performing approach uses a neural network and a sparse representation such as BOW vectors using the entities in the abstract. We also show that the performance can be further improved if we also consider prior works by the authors. The results on the biomedical field are encouraging, especially if we restrict the focus to subsets of entities. To the best of our knowledge, ours is the first technique of its kind and several directions for future research come to mind. First, we plan to address the limitations outlined in Sect. 5.4. Second, it is interesting to research more sophisticated mechanisms to include author information to further improve the performance. It is also interesting to improve the predictions in order to distinguish principal and secondary entities, or to determine also the position of the entity in the paper (e.g., either in the evaluation or in the related work section). Finally, we plan to extend the application of this work also to other fields such as physics or chemistry.

References

1. Adamic, L.A., Adar, E.: Friends and neighbors on the web. Soc. Netw. **25**(3), 211–230 (2003)
2. Auer, S., Bizer, C., Kobilarov, G., Lehmann, J., Cyganiak, R., Ives, Z.: DBpedia: a nucleus for a web of open data. In: Aberer, K., et al. (eds.) ASWC/ISWC - 2007. LNCS, vol. 4825, pp. 722–735. Springer, Heidelberg (2007). https://doi.org/10.1007/978-3-540-76298-0_52
3. Balog, K., Bron, M., De Rijke, M.: Query modeling for entity search based on terms, categories, and examples. ACM Trans. Inf. Syst. (TOIS) **29**(4), 22 (2011)
4. Bishop, C.: Pattern Recognition and Machine Learning. Springer, New York (2006)
5. Blanco, R., Cambazoglu, B.B., Mika, P., Torzec, N.: Entity recommendations in web search. In: Alani, H., et al. (eds.) ISWC 2013. LNCS, vol. 8219, pp. 33–48. Springer, Heidelberg (2013). https://doi.org/10.1007/978-3-642-41338-4_3
6. Côté, R.A., College of American Pathologists, et al.: Systematized nomenclature of medicine. College of American Pathologists (1977)
7. Damljanovic, D., Stankovic, M., Laublet, P.: Linked data-based concept recommendation: comparison of different methods in open innovation scenario. In: Simperl, E., Cimiano, P., Polleres, A., Corcho, O., Presutti, V. (eds.) ESWC 2012. LNCS, vol. 7295, pp. 24–38. Springer, Heidelberg (2012). https://doi.org/10.1007/978-3-642-30284-8_9
8. Frijters, R., Van Vugt, M., Smeets, R., Van Schaik, R., De Vlieg, J., Alkema, W.: Literature mining for the discovery of hidden connections between drugs, genes and diseases. PLoS Comput. Biol. **6**(9), e1000943 (2010)
9. Ghahramani, Z., Heller, K.A.: Bayesian sets. In: Proceedings of NIPS, pp. 435–442 (2005)
10. Groth, P., Gibson, A., Velterop, J.: The anatomy of a nanopublication. Inf. Serv. Use **30**(1–2), 51–56 (2010)
11. Hopfield, J.J.: Neural networks and physical systems with emergent collective computational abilities. Proc. Nat. Acad. Sci. **79**(8), 2554–2558 (1982)
12. Jayaram, N., Gupta, M., Khan, A., Li, C., Yan, X., Elmasri, R.: GQBE: querying knowledge graphs by example entity tuples. In: Proceedings of ICDE, pp. 1250–1253 (2014)

13. Jelier, R., Jenster, G., Dorssers, L.C., van der Eijk, C.C., van Mulligen, E.M., Mons, B., Kors, J.A.: Co-occurrence based meta-analysis of scientific texts: retrieving biological relationships between genes. Bioinformatics **21**(9), 2049–2058 (2005)
14. Jiang, J., Lu, W., Rong, X., Gao, Y.: Adapting language modeling methods for expert search to rank Wikipedia entities. In: Geva, S., Kamps, J., Trotman, A. (eds.) INEX 2008. LNCS, vol. 5631, pp. 264–272. Springer, Heidelberg (2009). https://doi.org/10.1007/978-3-642-03761-0_27
15. Kastrin, A., Rindflesch, T.C., Hristovski, D.: Link prediction on a network of co-occurring MeSH terms: towards literature-based discovery. Methods Inf. Med. **55**(04), 340–346 (2016)
16. Lindberg, D.A., Humphreys, B.L., McCray, A.T.: The unified medical language system. Methods Inf. Med. **32**(04), 281–291 (1993)
17. Mikolov, T., Sutskever, I., Chen, K., Corrado, G.S., Dean, J.: Distributed representations of words and phrases and their compositionality. In: Proceedings of NIPS, pp. 3111–3119 (2013)
18. Milne, D., Witten, I.H.: Learning to link with Wikipedia. In: Proceedings of CIKM, pp. 509–518 (2008)
19. Ni, Y., Xu, Q.K., Cao, F., Mass, Y., Sheinwald, D., Zhu, H.J., Cao, S.S.: Semantic documents relatedness using concept graph representation. In: Proceedings of WSDM, pp. 635–644 (2016)
20. Noy, N.E., et al.: BioPortal: ontologies and integrated data resources at the click of a mouse. Nucleic Acids Res. **37**, W170–W173 (2009)
21. Perozzi, B., Al-Rfou, R., Skiena, S.: DeepWalk: online learning of social representations. In: Proceedings of KDD, pp. 701–710 (2014)
22. Piwowar, H., et al.: The state of OA: a large-scale analysis of the prevalence and impact of open access articles. PeerJ **6**, e4375 (2018)
23. Sarmento, L., Jijkuon, V., de Rijke, M., Oliveira, E.: More like these: growing entity classes from seeds. In: Proceedings of CIKM, pp. 959–962 (2007)
24. Sioutos, N., de Coronado, S., Haber, M.W., Hartel, F.W., Shaiu, W.L., Wright, L.W.: NCI Thesaurus: a semantic model integrating cancer-related clinical and molecular information. J. Biomed. Inform. **40**(1), 30–43 (2007)
25. Swanson, D.R.: Fish oil, Raynaud's syndrome, and undiscovered public knowledge. Perspect. Biol. Med. **30**(1), 7–18 (1986)
26. Tirilly, P., Claveau, V., Gros, P.: A review of weighting schemes for bag of visual words image retrieval. Technical report (2009)
27. Tseytlin, E., Mitchell, K., Legowski, E., Corrigan, J., Chavan, G., Jacobson, R.S.: NOBLE-Flexible concept recognition for large-scale biomedical natural language processing. BMC Bioinformatics **17**(1), 32 (2016)
28. Vercoustre, A.-M., Pehcevski, J., Thom, J.A.: Using Wikipedia categories and links in entity ranking. In: Fuhr, N., Kamps, J., Lalmas, M., Trotman, A. (eds.) INEX 2007. LNCS, vol. 4862, pp. 321–335. Springer, Heidelberg (2008). https://doi.org/10.1007/978-3-540-85902-4_28
29. Wang, R.C., Cohen, W.W.: Iterative set expansion of named entities using the web. In: Proceedings of ICDM, pp. 1091–1096 (2008)
30. Weerkamp, W., Balog, K., Meij, E.: A generative language modeling approach for ranking entities. In: Geva, S., Kamps, J., Trotman, A. (eds.) INEX 2008. LNCS, vol. 5631, pp. 292–299. Springer, Heidelberg (2009). https://doi.org/10.1007/978-3-642-03761-0_30
31. Zhang, Y., Xiao, Y., Hwang, S.w., Wang, H., Wang, X.S., Wang, W.: Entity suggestion with conceptual explanation. In: Proceedings of IJCAI, pp. 4244–4250 (2017)

Resources Track

AYNEC: All You Need for Evaluating Completion Techniques in Knowledge Graphs

Daniel Ayala[1]([✉]), Agustín Borrego[1], Inma Hernández[1], Carlos R. Rivero[2], and David Ruiz[1]

[1] University of Seville, Seville, Spain
{dayala1,borrego,inmahernandez,druiz}@us.es
[2] Rochester Institute of Technology, Rochester, NY, USA
crr@cs.rit.edu

Abstract. The popularity of knowledge graphs has led to the development of techniques to refine them and increase their quality. One of the main refinement tasks is completion (also known as link prediction for knowledge graphs), which seeks to add missing triples to the graph, usually by classifying potential ones as true or false. While there is a wide variety of graph completion techniques, there is no standard evaluation setup, so each proposal is evaluated using different datasets and metrics. In this paper we present AYNEC, a suite for the evaluation of knowledge graph completion techniques that covers the entire evaluation workflow. It includes a customisable tool for the generation of datasets with multiple variation points related to the preprocessing of graphs, the splitting into training and testing examples, and the generation of negative examples. AYNEC also provides a visual summary of the graph and the optional exportation of the datasets in an open format for their visualisation. We use AYNEC to generate a library of datasets ready to use for evaluation purposes based on several popular knowledge graphs. Finally, it includes a tool that computes relevant metrics and uses significance tests to compare each pair of techniques. These open source tools, along with the datasets, are freely available to the research community and will be maintained.

Keywords: Knowledge graph · Graph refinement · Evaluation · Datasets

1 Introduction

The recent years have seen an increase in popularity of the representation of large databases as graphs with nodes that represent entities and edges that represent relations between them. The advent of Linked Open Data [4], and the development of connected sources of structured data [1,5,13–15,19,22,23] have

© Springer Nature Switzerland AG 2019
P. Hitzler et al. (Eds.): ESWC 2019, LNCS 11503, pp. 397–411, 2019.
https://doi.org/10.1007/978-3-030-21348-0_26

drawn attention towards the use of knowledge graphs to represent knowledge, as well as the development of techniques that work on graph data [2,10].

These graphs are not perfect and may be incomplete or contain errors [16]. The techniques that attempt to improve the quality of knowledge graphs are known in general as graph refinement proposals [16], a category that includes two types of proposals: those that detect incorrect information on graphs, and those that complete the graphs with missing information. We focus on the latter, also known as knowledge graph completion proposals, or link prediction for knowledge graphs. Adding missing knowledge to a graph might be seen as a binary classification problem in which the input is a triple $<s, r, t>$ (source entity, relation, target entity, also known as subject, predicate, object) that represents an edge in the graph, and the output is a binary value denoting whether or not that triple should be included in the graph.

There is a wide variety of graph completion proposals based on different approaches like embeddings [9,21] or path-based features [8,11]. Deep learning techniques have seen popularity in the recent years [18]. However, their evaluation is not homogeneous, that is, each proposal is evaluated on different knowledge graphs, using different methodologies and metrics to analyse results. There are well-known knowledge graphs that are commonly used for evaluation purposes, such as Freebase [8,9,11,21] or WordNet [9,11,21]. However, when used for the specific task of evaluating graph completion proposals, these graphs are usually pre-processed by the different authors, who apply different criteria to obtain smaller and cleaner versions of the datasets, such as FB13 [21] or WN18 [6]. This makes it difficult to compare different proposals side by side, especially considering that evaluating graph refinement proposals is not trivial with many considerations and variants [16].

There is a clear need for a standard suite that defines both datasets and metrics to be used in the evaluation of graph completion proposals. To fulfill that need, in this paper we present AYNEC (**A**ll **Y**ou **N**eed for **E**valuating **C**ompletion), a resource for the evaluation of knowledge graph completion proposals that covers the entire evaluation workflow: preprocessing, training/testing splitting, generation of negative examples (which we refer to as negatives generation for the sake of brevity), and statistical analysis. The main contributions of AYNEC are: AYNEC-DataGen, a tool for the generation of evaluation datasets, which includes options for exporting the datasets in open formats for their easy visualisation, and offers several variation points in the preprocessing, splitting, and negatives generation steps; AYNEC-ResTest, a tool for computing metrics and significance tests from the results of several techniques in the statistical analysis step; and an initial collection of evaluation datasets generated from high quality subgraphs of popular knowledge graphs: WN11, WN18, FB13, FB15K, and NELL. If the specific datasets that we offer are not suited for a certain task, or if new requirements arise in the future, AYNEC-DataGen allows to easily extend the collection with new datasets.

Our datasets can be freely downloaded from Zenodo[1], under the CC BY 4.0 license. Our tools are open source and available as a public repository in GitHub[2] under the GPLv3 license. The source code of the tools is documented, describing each configurable parameter and function.

The rest of this paper is structured as follows: Sect. 2 describes each step in the evaluation workflow that we have identified, Sect. 3 shows what evaluation setups were used in several completion proposals in terms of the aforementioned workflow, Sect. 4 describes how AYNEC-DataGen implements the dataset creation steps, Sect. 5 describes AYNEC-ResTest, our metrics evaluation tool, Sect. 6 describes the specific datasets we propose for homogeneous evaluation, and Sect. 7 summarises our work and concludes the paper.

2   Workflow

We have identified the necessary steps to evaluate graph completion proposals, and we have defined an abstract workflow that can be used to describe or compare different evaluation setups in the same terms.

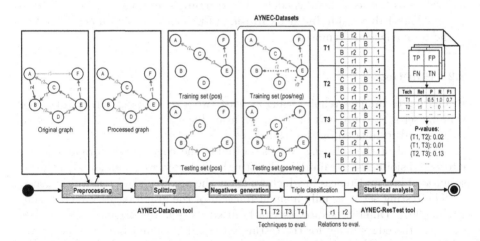

Fig. 1. Knowledge graph completion evaluation workflow.

Figure 1 depicts the evaluation workflow we have identified, which is composed of five steps. The external inputs are the original knowledge graph to use for evaluation, the techniques that are evaluated, and the relations on which the techniques will be evaluated. The final output is the comparison of the techniques according to a number of metrics and significance tests. For example, Gardner and Mitchell [8] take Freebase and NELL as original graphs, and evaluate two techniques on a total of 34 relations according to the metrics MAP and MRR.

---

[1] http://doi.org/10.5281/zenodo.1744988.

[2] https://github.com/tdg-seville/AYNEC.

The shadowed steps in Fig. 1 (preprocessing, splitting, negatives generation, and metrics analysis) are the ones covered by our suite, while triple classification is the main task to be performed by each completion proposal.

Next, we discuss every step, its inputs and outputs, and we provide examples based on Fig. 1.

2.1   Preprocessing

The goal of this step is to load and preprocess the original knowledge graph (which may have undergone previous preprocessing) in any way that is considered convenient. This can include, for example, the removal of relations with frequency below a threshold, the transformation of entity or relation names, or the insertion of new relations to enrich the graph.

Regarding the input, in some knowledge graphs, entities have literals attached that represent simple values related to the entity (e.g. data properties in DBpedia [1]). In other graphs, this kind of data is represented with additional nodes (e.g., a node that represents the year 2008, as happens in NELL [14]).

The **input** to this step is a knowledge graph that represents entities as nodes, and relations between them as edges. The **output** is an updated version of the original knowledge graph. In the **example** of Fig. 1, relations with less than 20% of the total edges are removed.

2.2   Splitting

Evaluating techniques require using at least two sets: training and testing. The training set is the only part of the graph available when training a model, which is afterwards evaluated on the testing set.

The goal of the splitting step is to divide the edges in the original graph into two disjoint sets (training and testing). This way, we simulate a controlled scenario of incompleteness in which we know the missing edges (the testing set).

The testing set is usually a small fraction of the graph edges, ranging from 10% to 30%. Different strategies can be used to split the original dataset. For example, the edges taken for the testing set could be completely random, or we could take a fixed fraction of each relation for testing.

The **input** to this step is the preprocessed knowledge graph. The **outputs** are two disjoint sets of edges from the input graph, corresponding to the training and testing sets. In the **example** of Fig. 1, 50% of the edges of each relation are taken for the testing set.

2.3   Negatives Generation

The goal of this step is to generate negative triples, usually by creating new ones that are not found in the original knowledge graph.

The negative examples in the training set help learn a model. Their inclusion is optional, since the techniques themselves may be able to generate them.

The negative examples in the testing set are used to compute metrics like precision or recall. If negatives are not explicitly included in the testing set, any triple that is not found in the training or testing sets would be a negative when computing metrics. This would be the case, for example, if we want to test a technique that, instead of giving a score to input triples, outputs a set of triples as the positives, and assumes every other triple is negative.

The negative examples, when generated, should pose a challenge for the classification model [21]. For instance, it is trivial to classify <John-S., cousin-of, Republic-of-Guatemala> as false by checking that "Republic-of-Guatemala" is outside the range of relation "cousin-of". A more compelling example would be <John-S, cousin-of, Mary-S.>, in which the former sanity check is not enough.

The first point of variability when generating negative examples is how many of them should be generated. Usually, a fixed numbers of negative examples are generated per each positive example.

The second point of variability is the generation strategy. The idea is to take a positive example and change its source, target, or both, by choosing a replacement among a set of candidates. Some proposals [9,11,21] select as candidates the entities that are known to appear in the same position of the same relation, keeping the domain (if it is the source) or range (if it is the target) to avoid trivial cases like the <John-S., cousin-of, Republic-of-Guatemala> example. Others follow more elaborate approaches, such as giving a higher probability to nodes that are close to the original ones [8].

One of the problems when generating negative examples is that knowledge graphs are usually ruled by the open world assumption, which means that the absence of a triple in the graph does not necessarily mean that the triple is not true, just unknown. However, since knowledge graphs tend to be sparse, the probability of a true missing edge being chosen as a negative example should be negligible, which is why related datasets in practice follow a closed world assumption [8,9,11,21].

The **inputs** to this step are the testing set and, optionally, the training set. The **outputs** are the sets with added negative edges. In the **example** of Fig. 1 one negative example is generated for each positive one by changing the target entity while keeping the range of the relation.

2.4 Triple Classification

The result of this step is a set of classifications per technique and triple, which may be a binary result (usually 1 or -1), or a probabilistic score. Some techniques do not explicitly classify triples, but output a set of new triples after learning from the training set, or output a source/target node for a query such as <John-S, father-of, ?>. In these cases, there is also a latent classification: the former classifies any triple that is not part of the output as negative, while the later classifies the triples in a group obtained by the query (e.g., all triples with John-S as source and father-of as relation).

Since a knowledge graph may contain thousands of relations, the evaluation of techniques is usually limited to the few ones that are considered specially frequent or relevant [8,11,21].

The **inputs** of this step are the training and testing sets, the set of techniques to be compared, and the set of relations to test. The **output** is the set of results from applying each technique to each edge of the input relations in the testing set. In the **example** of Fig. 1 four techniques are compared, and only two of the three existing relations are evaluated.

2.5   Statistical Analysis

The goal of this step is to generate a report that summarises the results obtained in the classification step with metrics used to evaluate each technique.

The results of the classification can be used to generate a confusion matrix for each evaluated relation, obtaining metrics like precision or recall. The metrics are usually focused on precision [8,11], since the added knowledge, even if it is a small amount, should be reliable. A proposal with high recall but poor precision results in a high number of false positives that have to be manually checked and removed, defeating the purpose of automated graph refinement.

The difference between techniques regarding each metric is assessed with significance tests, usually paired ones (the observations of a sample can be paired with those of another sample) computed from the metrics of each relation [8,11].

The **input** of this step is the set of classification results from each technique. The output is a report with metrics and a comparison of the techniques. In the **example** of Fig. 1 precision, recall, and F_1 are measured for each relation, and a significance test is used to compare the differences between techniques.

3   Related Datasets

Our study of the literature reveals that there is no consensus when it comes to evaluating graph completion proposals. Next, we describe several evaluation datasets in a non-exhaustive study to show that there is variability and what the popular choices are in the workflow. Table 1 summarises our findings.

Table 1. Summary of related datasets.

Proposal	Original graphs	Preprocessing	Splitting	Negatives generation	Triple Classification	Statistical analysis
Socher et al. (2013)	Freebase and WordNet.	Freebase: 13 relations. Wordnet 11 relations.	~10% for testing. Filtering of "trivial triplets".	1 per positive. Only in Freebase the range is kept.	7 Freebase relations and all WordNet ones are tested.	Accuracy per relation. Averaged in techniques comparison. No sign. tests.
Gardner and Mitchell (2015)	Freebase and NELL.	NELL: some handpicked relations were removed.	25% for testing.	Several per positive. PPR used for selection of new source/target.	24 Freebase and 10 NELL relations are tested.	MAP, MRR, average precision. A paired permutation test measures significance.
Ji et al. (2015)	FB13, WN11, and FB15K	None	FB13, WN11: same as Socher et al. FB15K: 20% for testing.	Generated in the same way as Socher et al.	FB13 and WN11: same as Socher et al. FB15K: all relations are tested.	Accuracy per relation. No sign. tests (only report on their proposal).
Mazumder and Liu (2017)	FB15K, WN18, and ConceptNet	FB15K: 1000 triples from 25 relations. ConceptNet relations >1000	20% for testing.	4 per positive. 2 change the source, 2 change the target. Keeping the domain/range.	All relations are tested.	MAP and averaged F1. A paired t-test measures significance.

Socher et al. [21] evaluate their proposal using Freebase [5] and WordNet [13] as their original graphs. Preprocessing removes all but 13 relations from the People domain in Freebase, and all but 11 in WordNet. During splitting, they take around 10% of the edges for testing, and remove what they call "trivial test tuples", described as tuples from the testing set in which either or both of their two entities also appear in the training set in a different relation or order. They generate one negative per positive in the testing set by switching the target entity of the positive. Regarding Freebase, they keep the domain/range of the relation, but since in WordNet all entities share the same type (word), all entities are actual potential candidates. During triple classification, they only test 7 relations from Freebase and all relations from WordNet. They measure the accuracy per relation of their proposal, and the average across relations when comparing several proposals, without using significance tests.

Gardner and Mitchell [8] use Freebase and NELL as their original knowledge graphs. During preprocessing they remove some Freebase relations considered too specific or unhelpful. During splitting, they take 25% of the edges for testing. They do not mention how many negatives are generated, but the datasets they provide show a variable number, usually more than 5 negatives per positive in both training and testing sets. They generate them by changing the source and target in each positive, keeping the domain and range, and weighting candidates by personalised page rank to favour nearby entities. Testing is limited to 25 relations from Freebase (random ones with a number of instances between 1000 and 10000, excluding those with Freebase's mediators [3]), and 10 relations from NELL (the ones with highest frequency and reasonable precision). They measure mean average precision (MAP) and mean reciprocal rank (MRR), using an undisclosed paired permutation test to measure significance.

Ji et al. [9] use Socher et al. [21]'s datasets (FB13 and WN11) as the original graphs, adding Freebase 15K (FB15K) [7]. There is no additional preprocessing. Splitting is the same as the original datasets, which in the case of FB15K is 20% for testing. Since FB15K does not include negative examples in the testing set, they are generated in the same way as Socher et al. The relations used for testing are the same as Socher et al. [21], and all relations for FB15K. They measure the accuracy per relation, without using significance tests, since they only report on the results of their proposal.

Mazumder and Liu [11] use a subset of WordNet with only 18 relations (WN18) [6], FB15K, and ConceptNet [22] as original graphs. During preprocessing, they keep from FB15K 1000 triples from each of 25 randomly selected relations with more than 1000 instances, all triples from WN18, and all triples from relations with more than 1000 instances from ConceptNet (18 in total). During splitting, they take 20% of the edges for testing. They generate four negatives per positive in both training and testing sets. Two are generated by changing the source, and other two by changing the target, both keeping the domain/range of the relation. Testing includes all relations. They measure MAP and averaged F_1 across relations, using a paired t-test to measure significance.

4   AYNEC-DataGen

AYNEC-DataGen, our datasets generation tool, implements the first three steps of the workflow in Fig. 1 with several variation points.

Next we describe how our tool implements the aforementioned steps of the workflow, presenting the variation points (VP) that can be configured.

4.1   Preprocessing

AYNEC-DataGen takes as input a file with the input graph. Note that the most popular graphs we have identified (Freebase, WordNet, NELL) do not include literals, but use the additional nodes we mentioned in Sect. 1.

VP1. Fraction of the graph: The original knowledge graph can be read entirely or only a fraction of it. Each triple has a configurable probability of being ignored, which can be useful to generate reduced versions of large knowledge graphs.

VP2. Relation frequency threshold: Relations with a frequency below a given threshold can be removed. This is useful to remove very specific relations that may be problematic.

VP3. Relation accumulated fraction threshold: A fraction can be set so that only the most frequent relations that cover that fraction of the edges are retained, removing the rest. This is useful to remove large amounts of relations with low frequency while keeping most of the graph intact.

VP4. Inverse removal: Relations r_1 and r_2 are inverses of each other if for each instance of r_1, there is an instance of r_2 with swapped source and target, and vice versa. If this option is toggled, one of the relations in each pair of inverses is removed. This reduces the size of the datasets without removing actual information, and avoids situations where triples are trivially classified as true merely by checking that the inverse relation exists between the entities, which may happen with some datasets [8,24].

4.2   Splitting

The triples resulting from preprocessing are split into the training and testing sets.

VP5. Testing fraction: The graph can be split using a fraction that is applied to every relation, so that said fraction is taken from the triples of each relation for testing.

VP6. Testing fraction per relation: The graph can be split using a fraction for each existing relation, so that, for each relation, the specified fraction is taken from its triples for testing. This enables full control of the representation of each relation in the testing set.

4.3   Negatives Generation

Once the graph is split into two sets of positive examples, we generate negative examples for each positive one.

VP7. Training negatives: Negatives can be generated or not for the training set, depending on whether or not techniques are expected to generate their own negatives.

VP8. Negatives per positive: the number of negatives to generate per positive can be a real number. The decimals represent the probability of generating an extra negative example. For example, 2.4 negatives per positive implies that, for each positive, 2 negatives will be generated, with a probability of 0.4 of generating a third one.

VP9. Generation strategy: the generation of negatives is modular, so that several strategies can be chosen and new ones can be easily created. We have implemented the following strategies:

- Changing the source and/or the target of the triple with all entities as candidates [9,21].
- Changing the source and/or target of the triple with candidates that keep the domain/range of the relation [9,11,21].
- Changing the source and target with candidates that keep the domain/range of the relation while weighting by PPR [8].

4.4   Output

The main output of AYNEC-DataGen are two files, "train.txt" and "test.txt", each of which contains a triple per line, and a label which can be "1" or "−1" depending on whether it is a positive or a negative example. Additionally, we generate the following items:

1. Files listing the relations and entities in the graph. Relations are sorted by their frequency, included in the file. Entities are sorted by their total degree in the original graph, included along with the outward and inward degrees.
2. An interactive visual summary with the aforementioned frequencies and degrees, as depicted in Fig. 2 which shows the tables and plots in the file.
3. A file with each identified pair of inverse relations.
4. A file in gexf format with the entire dataset, including the negatives and positives of both training and testing sets. This open format enables to import the dataset in visualisation tools such as Gephi[3]. This is important when developing a completion technique, since it allows the visual study of the topology of the graph and its relations. For example Fig. 3 shows a visual representation of positives in WN11-A (one of our generated datasets) where the training and testing sets have a similar topology.

---

[3] https://gephi.org/.

AYNEC summary - FB15K

Relations

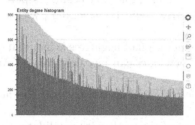

Entities

Generated with AYNEC 1.0 at 2018-11-22 15:46:09.203628. For issues or suggerences send a mail to dayala1@us.es

Fig. 2. Visual summary example.

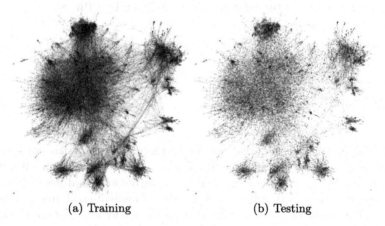

(a) Training   (b) Testing

Fig. 3. Visual representation of positives in WN11-A with Gephi.

5   AYNEC-ResTest

AYNEC-ResTest takes the results of several techniques, and computes metrics for each technique and pairwise comparisons using significance tests.

The input of AYNEC-ResTest is a file with the classification results of each technique when applied to every triple. The result of a technique can be binary or a probabilistic score.

AYNEC-ResTest computes, for each technique and relation, the confusion matrix. These matrices are used to compute metrics per technique and relation: precision, recall, and F_1. We consider these metrics to be the most adequate ones, especially precision. We also compute ranking-based metrics: MAP and MRR, which are also popular [8,11], but are only adequate when the input of the techniques is a query, and the output a ranking of potential results sorted by score [12].

In addition to the per-relation metrics, our tool computes the macro-average and micro-average of each metric. The macro-average of a metric is computed by averaging the metric of each relation, while the micro-average is computed from the sum of the confusion matrices of each relation. The macro-average is less influenced than the micro-average by unbalanced relation frequencies.

Finally, since the output of a technique can be a probabilistic score, AYNEC-ResTest offers the possibility of computing all the former metrics for different values of the score threshold. The results are, consequently, computed for each relation, for each threshold, and for each technique, allowing the user to compute other metrics related to the precision-recall curve.

Regarding significance, our tool computes the paired, non-parametric Wilcoxon signed rank test [25] to test distribution equivalence, by checking whether or not we can reject the null hypothesis that the difference between each pair of observations (each observation being the value of a metric for a relation) follows a symmetrical distribution around 0. Sometimes, however, due to the behaviour of a technique, some metric values may be missing (for example, it is impossible to compute precision if there are no true or false positives for a relation), which makes it impossible to apply paired tests. To cover this situation, our tool also computes the non-paired Kolmogorov-Smirnov test [25], which is sensitive not only to differences in the median of the distributions, but also to any difference in shape. These tests are computed for each threshold, each metric, and each pair of techniques.

6   AYNEC-Datasets

We have used AYNEC-DataGen to generate specific datasets as a standard evaluation set that we intend to maintain in the future if we identify convenient new configurations or graphs. Regarding the original knowledge graphs they are generated from, we have reused existing high quality resources, some of them from the related datasets we described in Sect. 3. We have generated our datasets from the following knowledge graphs:

1. **WN18** [6]: a subset of the WordNet dataset with 18 relations, after filtering the entities that appear in less than 15 triples.
2. **WN11** [21]: a subset of the WordNet dataset with 11 relations. We only take the positive examples.
3. **FB13** [21]: a subset of the Freebase dataset with 13 relations from the People domain. We only take the positive examples.

4. **FB15K** [7]: a subset of the Freebase dataset with almost 15000 entities, after filtering those that are not present in the Wikilinks database [20] and appear in less than 100 triples. Some inverse relations are also removed.
5. **NELL** [14]: a knowledge graph crawled from the Web. It is a particularly noisy graph [17].

Table 2. AYNEC-datasets.

Original graph	Preprocessing				Splitting		Negatives generation			# of relations	# of entities	# of triples (+/-)	AYNEC-ID
	VP1	VP2	VP3	VP4	VP5	VP6	VP7	VP8	VP9				
WN18									Replace target (random)	18	40943	292884	WN18-A
WN11										11	38195	220724	WN11-A
FB13			All	Keep inverses	20% for test	N/A	Training and testing	1		13	74998	570403	FB13-A
FB15K	100%	Freq > 1							Replace target (keep range)	1219	14951	1075216	FB15K-AF
NELL										515	53934	403734	NELL-AF
FB15K			Accumulate 95%	Remove inverses						341	14951	1022541	FB15K-AR
NELL										148	53934	217296	NELL-AR

After feeding them to our tool, we generated a total of 7 evaluation datasets as depicted in Table 2, which shows the choices regarding every variation point in AYNEC-DataGen. The rationale behind each choice is as follows:

VP1. Fraction of the graph: There is no random filtering of the triples in the datasets, since their size is manageable.

VP2. Relation frequency threshold: We removed relations with one instance, since we cannot include them in both training and testing sets.

VP3. Relation accumulated fraction threshold: Since FB15K and NELL have a large amount of low frequency relations (long tail), we created, apart from datasets with the full set of relations (FB15K-AF and NELL-AF), reduced datasets that only keep 95% of the triples (FB15K-AR and NELL-AR), greatly reducing the number of relations in both cases.

VP4. Inverse removal: We removed inverses in FB15K-AR and NELL-AR.

VP5. Testing fraction: We took 20% of the triples for testing, in line with the related datasets.

VP6. Testing fraction per relation: We took the same fraction from every relation, since we do not focus on some relations in particular that need greater representation.

VP7. Training negatives: We generated negatives for both the training and the testing sets, in order to ease the training of techniques.

VP8. Negatives per positive: We generated one negative per positive, which is the most frequent amount in the related datasets.

VP9. Generation strategy: We generated negatives by changing the target of each positive example, since graphs are completed by applying the classifier of a relation to every possible target of one source entity, and this generation strategy creates the most similar scenario. In most datasets, we kept the range of each relation by using as candidates entities that appear as target in another triple of the same relation. However, since all entities in WordNet share the same nature (they are all words), all entities are candidates for all relations. The strategy by Gardner and Mitchell [8] is more complex, but it has not been assessed or discussed whether or not it makes the evaluation better.

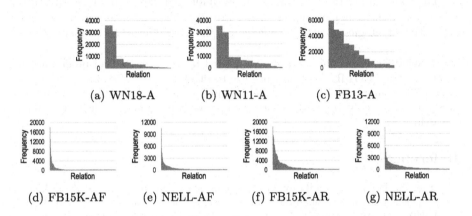

Fig. 4. Relation frequency histogram, with relations sorted by frequency.

Figure 4 shows several plots with the frequencies of the relations in each dataset. FB15K-AR and NELL-AR reduce the long tail by trimming the less frequent relations. The minimum relation frequency in FB15K-AF is 2, while in FB15K-AR it is 153. Similarly, the minimum relation frequency in NELL-AF is 3, while in NELL-AR it is 120.

Compared to the related datasets [8,9,11,21], ours include more knowledge graphs, they solve some existing problems like the presence of inverses or low frequency relations, they follow similar strategies when it comes to parameters like the testing fraction or negatives generation strategy, they contain meta-information about relations and entities, and they are presented in a format that makes it easy to import them into graph visualisation tools.

7 Conclusions

In this paper, we have presented a new suite for the evaluation of knowledge graph completion techniques. In the literature, each proposal is evaluated with a different setup and using different metrics and significance tests, which motivated the creation of an unified suite that streamlines evaluation.

The tools and datasets of our suite are customisable so that they adapt to a variety of scenarios, in case a different configuration is needed beyond the original ones. The source code of the tools is documented, and uses popular input/output formats in order to ease its adoption by researchers.

The generated datasets follow what we consider to be the most interesting strategies for homogeneous out-of-the-box evaluation, reusing popular subgraphs with useful preprocessing. The metrics and significance tests best suited for the datasets are implemented in AYNEC-ResTest, which takes care of the comparative analysis of techniques from a set of results.

The tools and datasets are publicly available online. We intend to maintain and expand them if new requirements are identified, such as novel negatives generation strategies or new knowledge graphs with interesting properties.

Acknowledgements. Our work was supported the Spanish R&D&I programme by grant TIN2016-75394-R. We would also like to thank Prof. Dr. José Luis Ruiz-Reina, head of the Computer Science and Artificial Intelligence Department at the University of Seville, who kindly provided us with the invaluable resources that helped us in our research.

References

1. Auer, S., Bizer, C., Kobilarov, G., Lehmann, J., Cyganiak, R., Ives, Z.: DBpedia: a nucleus for a web of open data. In: Aberer, K., et al. (eds.) ASWC/ISWC 2007. LNCS, vol. 4825, pp. 722–735. Springer, Heidelberg (2007). https://doi.org/10.1007/978-3-540-76298-0_52
2. Ayala, D., Hernández, I., Ruiz, D., Toro, M.: TAPON: a two-phase machine learning approach for semantic labelling. Knowl.-Based Syst. **163**, 931–943 (2019)
3. Bast, H., Bäurle, F., Buchhold, B., Haußmann, E.: Easy access to the freebase dataset. In: Proceedings of the 23rd International Conference on World Wide Web, pp. 95–98. ACM (2014)
4. Bizer, C., Heath, T., Berners-Lee, T.: Linked data - the story so far. Int. J. Semant. Web Inf. Syst. **5**(3), 1–22 (2009). https://doi.org/10.4018/jswis.2009081901
5. Bollacker, K.D., Cook, R.P., Tufts, P.: Freebase: a shared database of structured general human knowledge. In: AAAI, vol. 22, pp. 1962–1963 (2007)
6. Bordes, A., Glorot, X., Weston, J., Bengio, Y.: A semantic matching energy function for learning with multi-relational data - application to word-sense disambiguation. Mach. Learn. **94**(2), 233–259 (2014). https://doi.org/10.1007/s10994-013-5363-6
7. Bordes, A., Usunier, N., García-Durán, A., Weston, J., Yakhnenko, O.: Translating embeddings for modeling multi-relational data. In: Advances in Neural Information Processing Systems, pp. 2787–2795 (2013)
8. Gardner, M., Mitchell, T.M.: Efficient and expressive knowledge base completion using subgraph feature extraction. In: Proceedings of the 2015 Conference on Empirical Methods in Natural Language Processing, pp. 1488–1498 (2015)
9. Ji, G., He, S., Xu, L., Liu, K., Zhao, J.: Knowledge graph embedding via dynamic mapping matrix. In: Proceedings of the 53rd Annual Meeting of the Association for Computational Linguistics, pp. 687–696 (2015). https://doi.org/10.3115/v1/P15-1067
10. Junghanns, M., Kießling, M., Teichmann, N., Gómez, K., Petermann, A., Rahm, E.: Declarative and distributed graph analytics with GRADOOP. PVLDB **11**(12), 2006–2009 (2018)

11. Mazumder, S., Liu, B.: Context-aware path ranking for knowledge base completion. In: Proceedings of the 26th International Joint Conference on Artificial Intelligence, pp. 1195–1201 (2017). https://doi.org/10.24963/ijcai.2017/166
12. McFee, B., Lanckriet, G.R.: Metric learning to rank. In: Proceedings of the 27th International Conference on Machine Learning, pp. 775–782 (2010)
13. Miller, G.A.: WordNet: a lexical database for English. Commun. ACM **38**(11), 39–41 (1995). https://doi.org/10.1145/219717.219748
14. Mitchell, T.M., et al.: Never-ending learning. Commun. ACM **61**(5), 103–115 (2018). https://doi.org/10.1145/3191513
15. Pasca, M., Lin, D., Bigham, J., Lifchits, A., Jain, A.: Organizing and searching the world wide web of facts - step one: the one-million fact extraction challenge. In: AAAI, pp. 1400–1405 (2006)
16. Paulheim, H.: Knowledge graph refinement: a survey of approaches and evaluation methods. Semant. Web **8**(3), 489–508 (2017)
17. Paulheim, H., Bizer, C.: Improving the quality of linked data using statistical distributions. Int. J. Semant. Web Inf. Syst. **10**(2), 63–86 (2014). https://doi.org/10.4018/ijswis.2014040104
18. Schlichtkrull, M., Kipf, T.N., Bloem, P., van den Berg, R., Titov, I., Welling, M.: Modeling relational data with graph convolutional networks. In: Gangemi, A., et al. (eds.) ESWC 2018. LNCS, vol. 10843, pp. 593–607. Springer, Cham (2018). https://doi.org/10.1007/978-3-319-93417-4_38
19. Shao, B., Wang, H., Li, Y.: The trinity graph engine. Microsoft Research 54 (2012)
20. Singh, S., Subramanya, A., Pereira, F., McCallum, A.: Wikilinks: a large-scale cross-document coreference corpus labeled via links to Wikipedia. University of Massachusetts, Amherst, Technical report UM-CS-2012 15 (2012)
21. Socher, R., Chen, D., Manning, C.D., Ng, A.Y.: Reasoning with neural tensor networks for knowledge base completion. In: Advances in Neural Information Processing Systems, pp. 926–934 (2013)
22. Speer, R., Havasi, C.: Representing general relational knowledge in ConceptNet 5. In: LREC, pp. 3679–3686 (2012)
23. Suchanek, F.M., Kasneci, G., Weikum, G.: YAGO: a core of semantic knowledge. In: WWW 2007, pp. 697–706 (2007). https://doi.org/10.1145/1242572.1242667
24. Toutanova, K., Chen, D.: Observed versus latent features for knowledge base and text inference. In: Workshop on Continuous Vector Space Models and their Compositionality, pp. 57–66 (2015)
25. Woolson, R.: Wilcoxon Signed-Rank Test. Wiley Encyclopedia of Clinical Trials, pp. 1–3 (2007)

RVO - The Research Variable Ontology

Madhushi Bandara$^{(\boxtimes)}$ (iD), Ali Behnaz, and Fethi A. Rabhi

University of New South Wales, Sydney, Australia
{k.bandara,a.behnaz,f.rabhi}@unsw.edu.au

Abstract. Enterprises today are presented with a plethora of data, tools and analytics techniques, but lack systems which help analysts to navigate these resources and identify best fitting solutions for their analytics problems. To support enterprise-level data analytics research, this paper presents Research Variable Ontology (RVO), an ontology designed to catalogue and explore essential data analytics design elements such as variables, analytics models and available data sources. RVO is specialised to support researchers with exploratory and predictive analytics problems, popularly practiced in economics and social science domains. We present the RVO design process, its schema, how it links and extends existing ontologies to provide a holistic view of analytics related knowledge and how data analysts at the enterprise level can use it. Capabilities of RVO are illustrated through a case study on House Price Prediction.

Keywords: Data analytics · Semantic modeling · Research variables

1 Introduction

Motivation: Designing correct analytics solutions which meet the respective business objectives is challenging [15]. It involves different decision making such as selecting suitable tools, algorithms, datasets and deciding how to generate results and report them accurately. A data analytics researcher in an organisation spends lots of his/her time understanding the domain, analytics problem at hand and the existing related knowledge. Many new analytics research projects start with a literature survey to investigate and find a suitable approach, explore available data, and run numerous trial-and-error experiments. The iterative process includes cleaning and pre-processing data, identifying suitable variables to input into the right model, and evaluating the output of the model. Yet the outcome of the project is limited to an analytics model, usually in the form of a spreadsheet or a software code, and all the experience and knowledge accumulated by the researchers are not recorded or made available for future use. As no data analytics solution fits all problems [11], a solution cannot constantly perform well over a long period without accommodating changes in data and business goals. In order to maintain the expected performance, designed analytics solutions require frequent interventions and modifications from researchers.

While there are numerous papers on designing data analytics models, surprisingly only limited number of work is focused on providing adequate analytics

© Springer Nature Switzerland AG 2019
P. Hitzler et al. (Eds.): ESWC 2019, LNCS 11503, pp. 412–426, 2019.
https://doi.org/10.1007/978-3-030-21348-0_27

infrastructures such as knowledge repositories or design engines to assist data analytics solution design and management [5]. Existing platforms that use meta-learning [4] or SOA and workflow-based platforms (e.g. WINGS [8], ADAGE [6]) to deliver analytics services, lack a sound information model that can capture the semantics of the analytics models [5]. Hence, they have limited ability to accumulate expert knowledge and reuse it for efficient solution design. Benefits of an enterprise-wide knowledge repository that can accumulate and link analytics related expert knowledge and resources together are multifold. It can store and link domain knowledge, analytics related facts and findings and available resources (i.e. data providers, execution services etc.) together. Data analysts can interrogate the knowledge repository to learn and get recommendations from accumulated knowledge. This reduces the time and resource spent on initial experiments and literature surveys.

As ontologies provide flexibility and extensibility to knowledge as well as the ability to integrate existing linked data, we believe capturing this knowledge through semantic models will significantly help researchers.

Limitations of Existing Resources: To identify how semantic technology is used to aid data analytics researchers, we conducted a systematic literature survey [2]. Based on the survey, we concluded that researchers could benefit from four spheres of knowledge related to an analytics problem: domain, analytics, service and intent. A majority of identified studies only used ontologies to support isolated activities such as data integration or model selection. We observed that the literature was able to cover data mining and knowledge discovery process to a certain extent (e.g., OntoDM by Panov et al. [14]). Yet there was no semantic model that can capture multiple aspects of the solution design, from variables, data, analytics models and data sources, with the ability to answer questions raised by analysts, particularly when conducting empirical analytics that try to prove a hypothesis expressed through variables via building a model [16].

RVO and Advances to State of the Art: RVO proposes a schema that can be used to record empirical data analytics research details. It can also serve as a knowledge-base to support the knowledge exploration phase in a new analytics project with the purpose of learning and recommending the choice of variables. Therefore, RVO is designed around the research variables, which form the basis of the hypothesis that analysts test through building a model [16]. Main tasks of such empirical analytics process [16] are shown in Fig. 1.

Fig. 1. Steps of building an empirical analytics model [16].

RVO can help answer an array of questions (a few examples are listed in Table 1) raised by data analysts when conducting a study. It can also provide recommendations and alternatives to assist in analysts decision making. All facts or expert knowledge recorded in RVO are traceable to its origin (i.e. a person, publication, validated model). RVO follows best practices in ontology design and integrates with existing data models and vocabularies (such as DBpedia[1], RDF Data Cube vocabulary[2], FaBIO[3]) to facilitate efficient reuse in real-world applications by using semantic technologies and open standards (RDF, OWL, SPARQL). The main strength of RVO is its linking with other analytics-related and domain-specific ontologies.

The objectives of RVO are to:

– Assist data analytics process stages such as variable selection, data source selection, dataset selection and evaluation.
– Capture established (even if contradictory) complex analytics knowledge in a particular domain and its origin. The knowledge may include known relationships between different variables, how a variable is linked to a particular model, what the relationships are between variables and datasets, and what are the relationships between variables and analytics models.
– Establish a common terminology for the organisations to represent classes and properties in the empirical analytics domain, relating to existing taxonomies, ontologies and data standards.
– Integrate existing ontologies to enrich the knowledge base in an organisation when conducting analytics. These ontologies can be domain-specific ontologies, ontologies representing analytical models, people, standards, etc.

Comparison to Other Existing Resources: Through our survey [2] we observed that domain ontologies such as DBpedia, SSN or Gene Ontology are used to express domain knowledge used for analytics. There are also ontologies to capture metadata about datasets or describe data such as RDF Data Cube vocabulary, OntoDT[4], and many researchers use domain ontologies to annotate datasets or streams to support data integration.

Besides, semantic models such as OntoDM [14] and OntoKDD [6] are designed to capture particular aspects of data analytics. For example, OntoDM has a suite of ontologies to capture the CRISP-DM process for data mining (OntoDM-KDD) and data mining entities (OntoDM-core) such as data mining tasks and algorithms. Its main limitation is in supporting empirical analytics approaches which start from hypothesis and explore variables and measures. MAMO [10], the MAthematical Modelling Ontology, provides a classification of the different types of mathematical models and their variables. However, it has limited ability to capture relationships between models, variables and expert knowledge. Ontologies such as FOAF[5] or FaBIO are useful to capture traceability or origin of the knowledge, which are both critical for researchers.

---

[1] https://wiki.dbpedia.org.
[2] http://www.w3.org/TR/vocab-data-cube/.
[3] http://purl.org/spar/fabio.
[4] http://www.ontodm.com/doku.php?id=ontodt.
[5] http://xmlns.com/foaf/spec/.

All these ontologies represent some aspects of data analysis research; however, literature considers them in isolation. RVO is aimed to integrate these different knowledge spheres that represent domain concepts, data definitions, variables, analytic models, and their origins together to align with the thinking pattern of analytics researchers. It makes querying and exploring the knowledge intuitive and user-friendly. RVO provides a generic schema, not limited for a particular application domain or an analytics platform.

2 Relevance

Relevance to the Semantic Web community and Society: Researchers in organisations of any scale who conduct data analytics research or those who are attempting to design analytics systems, can significantly benefit from RVO. RVO can be used to accumulate and organise knowledge and learn from analytics experiments and systems. It supports linked open data practices, and resulting data can be published, shared with the wider analytics community and reused to gain insights into a problem at hand.

Relevance to Data Analytics Researchers: RVO is a schema which can be used by data analysts to record or explore knowledge related to research variables. An enterprise can adapt RVO and build analytics supporting systems around that as proposed by Bandara et al. [1]. Then researchers can easily reuse knowledge published as linked data by other data analysts using RVO or create their knowledge repository by conducting literature surveys or hiring data analytics professionals. Once the knowledge repository is in place, a minimal cost will incur for any background study in future data analytics projects. Enterprises can maintain the knowledge repository and update it when new knowledge (i.e. new models, data sources, facts) becomes available.

Impact in Supporting the Adoption of Semantic Web Technologies: RVO follows best practices in ontology design and publishing. Firstly it relies on W3C standards to make the data reusable for a variety of real-world applications. Open world assumption allows the analytics knowledge to be flexible and malleable to different organisational contexts. Moreover, it supports smooth integration with existing ontologies and the ability to be extended.

3 RVO - The Research Variable Ontology

3.1 Ontology Development Process

The ontology development process we followed aggregates ontology design principles from the NeOn methodology [17] and the methods proposed by Grüninger and Fox [9] and Ushold and King [18]. Also, we followed the FAIR principles[6] and the guidelines and best practices proposed by Noy and McGuinness [12].

---

[6] https://www.force11.org/group/fairgroup/fairprinciples.

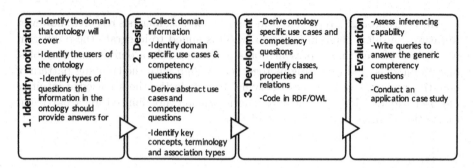

Fig. 2. Steps of the RVO development process.

The ontology development process includes four steps as illustrated in Fig. 2. We designed two domain-specific data analytics use cases in digital marketing [19] and commodity trading domains [3], to identify specific relations and terms which are required to model the domain. Use cases were designed based on data analytics literature in digital marketing and commodity trading domains as well as the authors' expertise and involvement in related projects. The use cases capture the thought process of analysts attempting an analytics problem and questions they seek answers for when designing a solution. Based on the use cases, we derived two sets of domain-specific competency questions in natural language. They formed a basis for a set of abstract competency questions that can satisfy requirement for studying and supporting data analytics solution design in general.

At the stage of identifying key concepts and association types, several meetings were held with analysts from economics and social science backgrounds to clarify and verify terminology and to identify gaps. We identified Variable, Measure, Model and Concept as four key elements for RVO. Around them, ontology specific use cases and competency questions were developed, and the classes, properties and relations were identified. A selected set of competency questions are shown in Table 1. Finally, the ontology was designed using the Protégé tool.

Ontology development was an iterative process where each version was evaluated over the generic and domain-specific competency questions and iteratively improved by evaluating its ability to answer the competency questions. After designing the ontology, we created two instance repositories for digital marketing and commodity trading and were able to answer all the generic and domain-specific competency questions via SPARQL queries. Finally, the RVO's ability to represent analytics research knowledge and support data analytics researchers in a large-scale project are illustrated through a case study, as discussed in Sect. 4.

3.2   Ontology

The components of the ontology are shown in Fig. 3. Main classes of the ontology are Variable, Measure, Model and LinkedVariables. LinkedVariables class captures a link between any two variables. Details of the classes are given in Table 2.

Table 1. Ontology specific competency questions for RVO.

Competency questions about variables
What are the variables linked to the variable of interest (V1)?
What type of relationship exists between two variables of interest (V1 & V2)?
What are the variables which have a causal impact on V1?
What variables are assumed to be linked (hypothetically) with V1?
What variables can be used to proxy V1?
What is the origin/proof of relationship exists between V1 & V2?
Given there is a causal link between V1 & V2, which research publications established that?
Given there is a causal link between V1 & V2, which expert established that?
Given there is a causal link between V1 & V2, which model was used to establish that?
Which model has V1 as a dependent variable?
Competency questions about measures
What are the measures for V1?
Which dataset contains measures for V1?
Competency questions about domain concept
What domain concept is represented by V1?
What are the properties of a domain concept related to V1?
Competency questions about model
What variables are involved in a model of interest (M1)?
What dataset is used to train the model?
What type of model is M1?

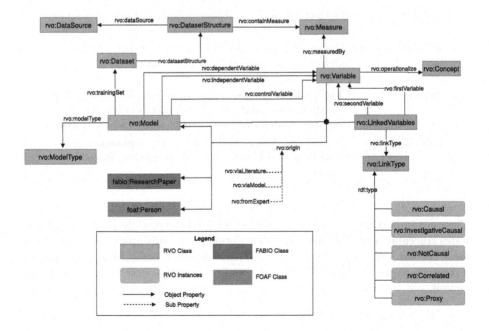

Fig. 3. Main classes and properties of RVO.

Table 2. Definitions of the classes in RVO.

Class	Definition
Concept	Concept is used to identify any domain concept that links a variable to a real-world entity. This is used to link domain ontologies to RVO and provide context to the variable
Variable	Variables exist as metrics to quantify concepts associated with a value and whose associated value may be changed
Measure	Measures are the metrics for observed values for a variable
LinkedVariables	LinkedVariables class describes a connection between two variables, the nature of this connection and its origin
LinkType	LinkType describes the type of link that exists between two or more variables. Identified LinkTypes are:- Causal: a variable causes another variable, Investigative Causal: there is a hypothesis that one variable cause another and the hypothesis needs to be tested, NonCausal: Proven not to have a causal relationship between two variables, Correlated: Two variables are dependence or associated, Proxy: One variable can be used in place of the other
DataSource	Datasource refers to a data generator or provider
Dataset	Dataset refers to a collection of observations for a set of measures, usually stored in a data file
DatasetStructure	DatasetStructure refers to the metadata for understanding a dataset such as what measures are captured, unit of measure
Model	The model is composed of a set of variables and a set of equations that establish relationships between the variables to describe particular phenomena or a system
ModelType	ModelType class is used to define types of model, (e.g.:- statistical model such as logistic regression, Bayesian model)

The most important association in RVO is defined by rvo:origin property. It facilitates traceability of the knowledge and contains three sub-properties. The origin for a certain Variable, Model or LinkedVariable could come from an expert or a research paper. Additionally, the origin of a LinkedVariable could be a Model as well.

3.3   Integrating Existing Ontologies

Domain Concepts: To fulfil the researchers' need to explore and understand the context of research, RVO facilitates linking existing domain ontologies to variables via rvo: operationalise property. For example, researches can define a variable for Gross Domestic Production and link it to DBpedia definition of GDP[7], enabling all the meta-data about GDP accessible via RVO.

Connecting to Origin: Related to rvo:origin property, we identified experts and published literature as two main types of origins. Hence we integrated two well-developed public ontologies: FOAF and FaBIO, that can represent knowledge about people and research papers respectively. Coloured rectangles in Fig. 3 illustrates the link between RVO and the concepts from FOAF and FaBIO.

Representing Data: RVO facilitates integration and reuse of existing ontologies that represent datasets and their structures. This capability is illustrated by integrating RVO with two prominent ontologies as shown in Table 3. This table shows that the RDF Data Cube vocabulary (presented by the prefix "qb") can be used to represent datasets and link rvo:Measure concept with RDF-Cube qb:MeasureProperty. This way our ontology can be easily integrated into existing linked datasets defined in RDF-Cube structure. OntoDT is a comprehensive ontology designed to capture knowledge about data types. rvo:DatasetStructure can be aligned with the aggregate datatype class that represents metadata about datasets.

Table 3. Aligning RVO with existing ontologies.

RVO concept	Aligning concept	Aligning ontology URI	Related by property
rvo:Dataset	qb:Dataset	http://purl.org/linked-data/cube	owl:sameAs
rvo:Dataset Structure	qb:DataStructure Definition	http://purl.org/linked-data/cube	owl:subClassOf
rvo:Dataset Structure	ontodt:OntoDT_378476 (aggregate datatype)	http://www.ontodm.com/OntoDT/	owl:subClassOf
rvo:Measure	qb:MeasureProperty	http://purl.org/linked-data/cube	owl:subClassOf
rvo:Model	ontodm:OntoDM_000228 (predictive model specification)	http://www.ontodm.com/OntoDM-core/	owl:subClassOf
rvo:Model	mamo:MAMO_0000037 (model)	http://identifiers.org/mamo/	owl:sameAs

Representing Models: There are many taxonomies and ontologies published by analysts and data mining experts. RVO encourages to reuse them to extend the knowledge about analytics models. RVO presents rvo:Model class as an anchor to link existing ontologies. For example, Table 3 illustrates how concepts from two prominent ontologies: OntoDM-Core and MAMO can be integrated to RVO so that data published through those can be integrated and queried through RVO.

---

[7] http://dbpedia.org/resource/Gdp.

3.4 How RVO Can Assist in the Analytics Process

Figure 4 presents different tasks associated with an example predictive analytics process instance to highlight how RVO can be used in multiple stages of analytics research to assist in domain understanding, planning and decision making. The classes and associations in RVO can help researchers to filter and select suitable variables, measures, compatible models and datasets from the instance repository at each stage of the analytics process. This can be done directly by answering questions as SPARQL queries or by building applications with dialogue-based front ends to support specific process flows with a SPARQL query engine in the back end. Bandara et al. [1] discuss further on how RVO can be used to express analytics requirements and use it for analytics process planning.

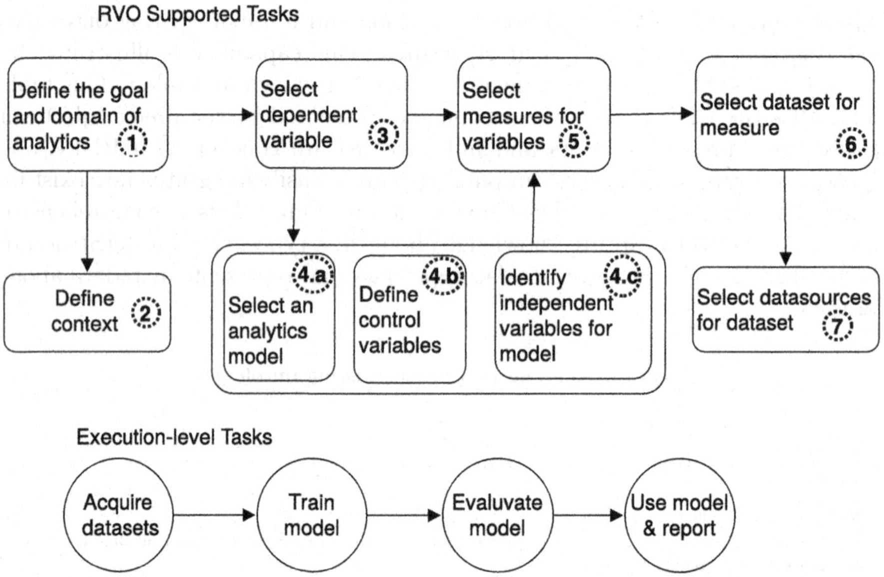

Fig. 4. Different tasks associated with an example predictive analytics process instance.

Please note that Fig. 4 is only an example process instance, and there can be other different processes with similar tasks arranged in a variety of combinations. For example, an analyst may select data first and identify model and variables aligning with that. Supporting the execution-level tasks is out of RVO's scope.

3.5 Reusability of RVO

To facilitate researcher communities to access and reuse RVO efficiently we provide the latest version of the RVO ontology to be download in RDF/XML format and turtle format. We also publish a SPARQL query interface and a REST API[8] to

---

[8] http://adage2.cse.unsw.edu.au/rvo/sparqlEnd.html.

explore the ontology and datasets associated with that related to a case study, so that users can navigate and understand how to use RVO to capture their analytics related knowledge. The home page of RVO website provides comprehensive documentation of the resource including schema diagram and example queries. RVO is modelled in RDF and is highly extensible. Interlinking with existing ontologies is important in reuse. We demonstrated in Sect. 3.3 how to link RVO with other ontologies. Users can replicate such integrations with other similar ontologies.

RVO follows best practices in ontology design. It uses RDF W3C standard to model and interlink the concepts. RVO adopts the open source and open data approach to make it available to a wide audience and facilitates ontology and data reuse. RVO provides differentiable URIs and implements a persistent strategy to maintain its URIs, ensuring that the same URIs are consistently reused for the same real-world objects. RVO follows FAIR principles[9] to make it findable, accessible, interoperable and reusable. The RVO description is available in human and machine readable formats at the RVO homepage and BioPortal. RVO reuses and extends into established ontologies to describe analytics and variables related information. It includes, and reuses existing vocabularies (e.g. FOAF, FaBIO).

It was a design decision to publish RVO with a small number of classes, making it more flexible and adaptable. A large taxonomy may overwhelm the users as we have observed in many existing ontologies. Further, it provides the ability to integrate existing taxonomies of models, variables etc. without any conflicts.

At the moment, RVO is used to capture variables related to a house price prediction research project, and we believe due to its unique nature of capturing and linking analytics variables, it would be used by third parties such as analytics researchers or system designers as discussed in Sect. 2. Details on how to use RVO to support data analysts can be found in our recent work [1,3].

3.6   Availability

RVO uses open standards and is publicly available under a persistent URI[10] under the MIT license[11]. The RVO homepage[12] is also published under a persistent URI, and provides information on how to use the resource. We have published software scripts to transform analytics knowledge in tabular format into RVO as open source software on GitHub[13] under the MIT License. RVO is also available in BioPortal[14] for the public to search and access.

The sustainability of RVO is ensured through three building blocks: (1) Publishing ontology as an open source resource, so that community can reuse the

---

[9] https://www.force11.org/group/fairgroup/fairprinciples.
[10] http://w3id.org/rv-ontology.
[11] https://opensource.org/licenses/MIT.
[12] http://w3id.org/rv-ontology/info.
[13] https://github.com/madhushib/RVO.
[14] http://bioportal.bioontology.org/ontologies/RVO/.

ontology to extract and represent new datasets or extend the ontology to include more classes and properties. (2) Integration of existing publicly available ontologies: the reference ontologies that are integrated with RVO are publicly available, and many of them are maintained by the community so that it is possible to maintain a fresh version of the ontology, in particular, to include new analytics knowledge. (3) Maintenance of RVO: the authors plan to perform regular RVO updates. The URIs of RVO resources will be maintained and remain stable across versions.

4   Case Study

4.1   Introduction

We conducted an application case study for RVO as a part of an ongoing data analytics solution design project, conducted by a team of researchers from the University of New South Wales, the University of Technology Sydney and the University of Wollongong in Australia. The research team comes from different backgrounds including urban planning, real estate, econometrics, statistics and software engineering. The research aim is to develop a framework that provides an accurate, long-term (20 years) forecast of real estate prices in Sydney residential property market [13]. The project outcome will contribute to the decision making of New South Wales state government, regarding complex urban transformation projects across Sydney. Based on the knowledge gathered by the research team via a literature survey and experimentations, we created an instance repository of RVO and a navigation and visualisation tool that can support analysts to explore and gain insights.

We used RVO to create an instance repository of concepts identified in the literature survey related to house price prediction, investigating more than 90 research papers. It contains knowledge about 188 variables linked to respective DBpedia concepts, 267 measures, 14 dataset types from 9 data sources, 11 house price prediction models of 9 model types and 49 research papers. Users can access and explore this knowledge through our publicly available query interface and REST API[15].

Figure 5 represents a snapshot of knowledge extracted from the work by Esteban and Altuzarra [7], represented in RVO and aligned with the analytics process presented in Fig. 4. The numbers are used to match the steps in the process with the concepts defined in the instance repository. Furthermore, each concept type according to the RVO is indicated in italic. This case study illustrates the unique capabilities of RVO as none of the related work identified through the literature survey [2] would be able to capture the links between variables, analytics models, measures and domain concepts.

---

[15] http://adage2.cse.unsw.edu.au/rvo/sparqlEnd.html.

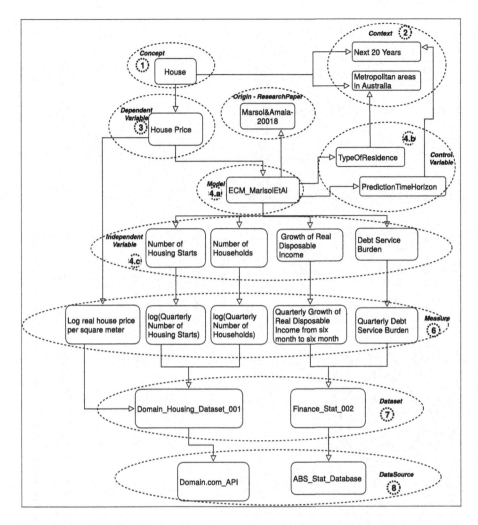

Fig. 5. Snapshot of information captured through RVO related to the house price prediction study.

4.2 Visualizing RVO

This section illustrates a tool for visualising RVO instances implemented as a web-based front end[16]. It is a navigation and visualisation tool linked to the RVO query processor. The current knowledge map demonstrates the ontological concepts and instances of RVO captured through the case study.

Figure 6 illustrates a screen-shot of the implementation for the navigation and visualisation tool. In this figure, the variables linked to "House Price" concept are shown. The top drop-down menu allows the user to select variables based

---

[16] http://adage2.cse.unsw.edu.au:3000/model-builder.

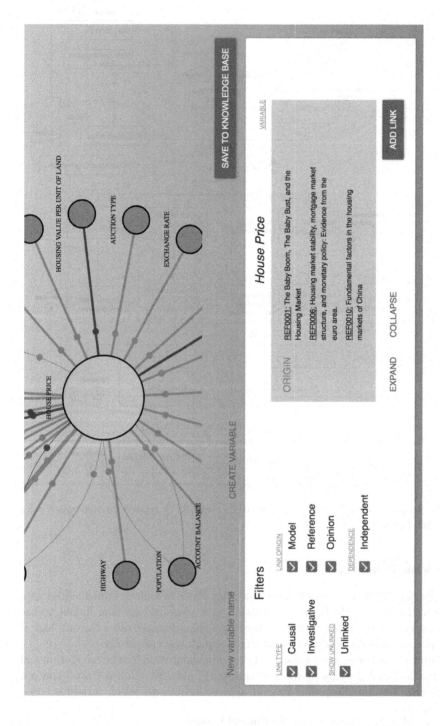

Fig. 6. Snapshot of RVO visualization & navigation tool.

on their categories. The bubble size is proportional to the number of variables connected to each variable. The directed links illustrate the connection from independent variables to dependent variables. The knowledge map interface creates an ecosystem where expert users can collaborate and contribute to forming of the knowledge base. Furthermore, the knowledge base can be applied to answer complex queries. This application can be used by research teams to explore variables, and identify those worth investigating further given their impact on house price. It saves significant time from researchers by abstracting and modelling the knowledge presented in those research papers.

5   Conclusion

This paper presents RVO- the Research Variable Ontology, designed to capture knowledge around empirical data analytics process and support researchers in different stages of the analytics process by providing recommendations and resources accessible via queries. We followed a formal process and best practices in designing the ontology and provided quality documentation and resources to reuse RVO. Further, guidelines are provided to integrate existing ontologies, and the case study demonstrates how this ontology can be used in data analytics projects.

In future, we plan to publish on how to integrate RVO with existing analytics related ontologies identified through the survey [2]. Furthermore, we plan to create more datasets around RVO, and extend its capability in capturing different knowledge spheres related to analytics. Based on that, authors plan to improve and publish new versions of RVO, and share new datasets for the use of the analytics and semantic web community.

Acknowledgment. We are grateful to Capsifi, especially Dr. Terry Roach, for sponsoring the research which led to this paper and Gilles Sainte-Marie for developing RVO web page.

References

1. Bandara, M., Behnaz, A., Rabhi, F.A., Demirors, O.: From requirements to data analytics process: an ontology-based approach. In: Daniel, F., Sheng, Q.Z., Motahari, H. (eds.) BPM 2018. LNBIP, vol. 342, pp. 543–552. Springer, Cham (2019). https://doi.org/10.1007/978-3-030-11641-5_43
2. Bandara, M., Rabhi, F.A.: Semantic modeling for engineering data analytic solutions. Semant. Web J. (2019, in press)
3. Behnaz, A., Natarajan, A., Rabhi, F.A., Peat, M.: A semantic-based analytics architecture and its application to commodity pricing. In: Feuerriegel, S., Neumann, D. (eds.) FinanceCom 2016. LNBIP, vol. 276, pp. 17–31. Springer, Cham (2017). https://doi.org/10.1007/978-3-319-52764-2_2
4. Brazdil, P., Carrier, C.G., Soares, C., Vilalta, R.: Metalearning: Applications to Data Mining. Springer, Heidelberg (2008). https://doi.org/10.1007/978-3-540-73263-1

5. Crankshaw, D., Gonzalez, J., Bailis, P.: Research for practice: prediction-serving systems. Commun. ACM **61**(8), 45–49 (2018). https://doi.org/10.1145/3190574
6. Diamantini, C., Potena, D., Storti, E.: KDDONTO: an ontology for discovery and composition of KDD algorithms. In: Third Generation Data Mining: Towards Service-Oriented Knowledge Discovery (SoKD 2009), pp. 13–24 (2009)
7. Esteban, M., Altuzarra, A.: A model of the spanish housing market. J. Post Keynes. Econ. **30**(3), 353–373 (2008)
8. Gil, Y., Kim, J., Ratnakar, V., Deelman, E.: Wings for Pegasus: a semantic approach to creating very large scientific workflows. In: OWLED (2006)
9. Grüninger, M., Fox, M.S.: Methodology for the design and evaluation of ontologies (1995)
10. Imbert, S.: Mathematical Modelling Ontology (2017). http://bioportal. bioontology.org/ontologies/MAMO. Accessed 30 Nov 2018
11. Magdon-Ismail, M.: No free lunch for noise prediction. Neural Comput. **12**(3), 547–564 (2000). https://doi.org/10.1162/089976600300015709
12. Noy, N.F., McGuinness, D.L., et al.: Ontology development 101: a guide to creating your first ontology (2001)
13. UrbanGrowth NSW: Funding cities community of practice. Review and development of a predictive housing price model for the Sydney housing market (2017)
14. Panov, P., Džeroski, S., Soldatova, L.: OntoDM: an ontology of data mining. In: IEEE International Conference on Data Mining Workshops, ICDMW 2008, pp. 752–760 (2008)
15. Rabhi, F., Bandara, M., Namvar, A., Demirors, O.: Big data analytics has little to do with analytics. In: Beheshti, A., Hashmi, M., Dong, H., Zhang, W.E. (eds.) ASSRI 2015/2017. LNBIP, vol. 234, pp. 3–17. Springer, Cham (2018). https://doi. org/10.1007/978-3-319-76587-7_1
16. Shmueli, G., Koppius, O.R.: Predictive analytics in information systems research. Mis Q. **35**, 553–572 (2011)
17. Suárez-Figueroa, M.C.: NeOn Methodology for building ontology networks: specification, scheduling and reuse. Ph.D. thesis, Informatica (2010)
18. Uschold, M., King, M.: Towards a methodology for building ontologies. Citeseer (1995)
19. Yang, S., Lin, S., Carlson, J.R., Ross Jr., W.T.: Brand engagement on social media: will firms' social media efforts influence search engine advertising effectiveness? J. Mark. Manag. **32**(5–6), 526–557 (2016)

EVENTSKG: A 5-Star Dataset of Top-Ranked Events in Eight Computer Science Communities

Said Fathalla[1,2]([✉])[iD], Christoph Lange[1,3][iD], and Sören Auer[4][iD]

[1] Smart Data Analytics (SDA), University of Bonn, Bonn, Germany
{fathalla,langec}@cs.uni-bonn.de
[2] Faculty of Science, University of Alexandria, Alexandria, Egypt
[3] Fraunhofer IAIS, Sankt Augustin, Germany
[4] TIB Leibniz Information Centre for Science and Technology, L3S Research Center,
University of Hannover, Hannover, Germany
soeren.auer@tib.eu

Abstract. Metadata of scientific events has become increasingly available on the Web, albeit often as raw data in various formats, disregarding its semantics and interlinking relations. This leads to restricting the usability of this data for, e.g., subsequent analyses and reasoning. Therefore, there is a pressing need to represent this data in a semantic representation, i.e., Linked Data. We present the new release of the EVENTSKG dataset, comprising comprehensive semantic descriptions of scientific events of eight computer science communities. Currently, EVENTSKG is a 5-star dataset containing metadata of 73 top-ranked event series (almost 2,000 events) established over the last five decades. The new release is a Linked Open Dataset adhering to an updated version of the Scientific Events Ontology, a reference ontology for event metadata representation, leading to richer and cleaner data. To facilitate the maintenance of EVENTSKG and to ensure its sustainability, EVENTSKG is coupled with a Java API that enables users to add/update events metadata without going into the details of the representation of the dataset. We shed light on events characteristics by analyzing EVENTSKG data, which provides a flexible means for customization in order to better understand the characteristics of renowned CS events.

Keywords: Scientific Events Ontology · Scholarly data ·
Linked open data · EVENTSKG · Metadata Analysis · 5-star dataset

1 Introduction

Recently, large collections of events metadata have become publicly available on the Web. However, this data is not well-organized, distributed over digital libraries and event websites, and not integrated. The existence of such data freely available online has motivated us to create a comprehensive dataset for renowned

© Springer Nature Switzerland AG 2019
P. Hitzler et al. (Eds.): ESWC 2019, LNCS 11503, pp. 427–442, 2019.
https://doi.org/10.1007/978-3-030-21348-0_28

computer science events. A good practice in the Semantic Web community is to publish datasets as Linked Data. Therefore, this paper introduces the second release of the EVENTSKG dataset, which is the new release of the EVENTSKG dataset [5], as Linked Data. Currently, EVENTSKG contains 73 event series (i.e., 75% series in addition to the first release) from eight CS communities[1]: Artificial Intelligence (AI), Software and its engineering (SE), World Wide Web (WEB), Security and Privacy (SEC), Information Systems (IS), Computer Systems Organization (CSO), Human-Centered Computing (HCC) and Theory of Computation (TOC). The latter two communities are new in the current release. Further new features of the new release include the use of the latest version of the Scientific Events Ontology (SEO)[2] (more details in Sect. 3), a Java API that has been developed for maintaining and updating the dataset, and a public Virtuoso SPARQL endpoint that has been established for querying the new release. EVENTSKG is a 5-star dataset [3], i.e., following a set of design principles for sharing machine-readable interlinked data on the Web, which enable data publishers to link their data to linked open data sources to provide context. Therefore, more *related* data can be discovered, enabling data consumers to directly learn about the data, thus increasing the value of the data and sharing the benefits from data already defined by others, i.e., enabling incremental work rather than working from scratch. In EVENTSKG, we map research fields and both countries and cities to SEO and DBpedia respectively. Events are linked by research fields, hosting country, and publishers. A key overarching research question that motivates our work is: *What is the effect of digitization on scholarly communication in computer science events?* In particular, we address specific questions such as the following:

– *What is the trend of submissions and publications of renowned CS events?*
– *Which CS communities have attracted increasing attention in the last decade?*
– *Have top-ranked events changed their publishers?*
– *Which continent hosts most events of a given CS community?*

A key benefit of this work is the availability of the dataset as LOD, as well as a collection of open source tools for maintaining and updating the dataset, with the goal to ensure the sustainability and usability of the dataset and to support the analysis of scholarly events metadata. EVENTSKG can answer the following competency questions:

– *What is the average acceptance rate of renowned Software Engineering events?*
– *To what venues can I submit my work to be published by Springer?*
– *Which CS communities have a growing popularity over the last decade?*

The analysis results presented in this work give some insights to answer these questions. The dataset documentation page (cf. Table 2) describes the dataset

---

[1] These communities have been identified using the ACM Computing Classification System: https://dl.acm.org/ccs/ccs.cfm.
[2] https://w3id.org/seo#.

structure and its releases. It also contains a description of each release and a chart comparing statistics of each release. The URI of each resource, i.e., of an individual events or an event series, is formed of the dataset URL (http:// w3id.org/EVENTSKG-Dataset/ekg) followed by the event's acronym and the year, e.g., http://w3id.org/EVENTSKG-Dataset/ekg#ESWC2018 is the URI of the 2018 ESWC conference. EVENTSKG stores data relevant to these events in RDF, and each event's metadata is described appropriately by means of the data and object properties in the Scientific Events Ontology (SEO). All data within EVENTSKG is available as dumps in the JSON-LD, Turtle, and RDF/XML serializations, and via our SPARQL endpoint. Previous versions of EVENTSKG are archived in data dumps in both CSV and RDF formats. CSV data is available in ZIP archives, with one CSV file per event series. Updating resources and adding new ones to a Linked Dataset is a time consuming and error-prone task. EVENTSKG is coupled with a Java API for this purpose (more details in Sect. 5). To illustrate the potential use of EVENTSKG for tracking the evolution of scholarly communication practices, we analyzed the key characteristics of scholarly events over the last five decades, including their geographic distribution, time distribution over the year, submissions, publications, ranking in several ranking services, publisher, and progress ratio (cf. Sect. 2). An exploratory data analysis is performed aiming at inferring facts and figures about CS scholarly events over the last five decades. We believe that EVENTSKG will bridge the gap between stakeholders involved in the scholarly events life cycle, starting from event establishment through paper submission till proceedings publishing, including events organizers, potential authors, publishers, and sponsors. This is, therefore, an area of particular interest for: (1) *event organizers* to measure the impact of their events in comparison with other events in their community or events in other communities by identifying success factors, (2) *potential authors* to assess the characteristics of high-impact events for deciding to what events to submit their work, (3) *scientometrics researchers* to identify metrics to consider when ranking scholarly events, and (4) *proceedings publishers* to study the impact of their events, or of other events they would be interested to publish.

The remainder of the article is structured as follows: Sect. 2 presents a brief review of the related work. Section 3 outlines the SEO ontology. Section 4 presents the main characteristics of EVENTSKG. Section 5 explains its curation process. Section 6 presents some examples of queries that EVENTSKG can answer. Section 7 discusses the results of analyzing the EVENTSKG data. Section 8 concludes and outlines possible future work.

2   Related Work

The past decade has witnessed increased attention to providing a comprehensive semantic description of scholarly events and their related entities [2,4,6,11,13]. Recently, publishing scholarly events metadata as Linked Data has become of prime interest to several publishers, such as Springer and Elsevier. Few researchers have addressed the problem of identifying the characteristics of renowned events in CS overall or within a particular CS communities. However, none of them provides services to ease the process of gaining an overview of a field, which is the contribution of this work. Overall, we found that the characteristics of these events have not been dealt with in depth. We have divided the literature on this topic into two areas: datasets, and analysis of scholarly events metadata.

Datasets. The Semantic Web Dog Food (SWDF) dataset is one of the pioneers of datasets of comprehensive scholarly communication metadata [13]. The first attempt to create a dataset containing metadata of top-ranked computer science events categorized by five communities is represented by our own EVENTS dataset [4]. EVENTS contains metadata of 25 event series in terms of 15 attributes, such as the geographical distribution (by hosting country) and the time distribution over the year. The main shortcoming of this dataset is that it is published as individual RDF dumps, which are not linked using well-formed URIs in a linked data style. This results in losing the links between dataset elements, such as events addressing topics in the same field or being hosted in the same country. Vasilescu et al. [15] presented a dataset of just eleven renowned software engineering conference series, such as ICSE and ASE, containing accepted papers along with their authors, programme committee members and the number of submissions each year. Luo and Lyons [12] presented a dataset with the metadata, including authors' names, the number of papers, and the number of workshops of every edition of the annual conference of the IBM Centre for Advanced Studies (CAS) in the period 1993–2017.

Metadata Analysis. Osborne et al. [14] developed the Rexplore tool for exploring and making sense of scholarly data through integrating visual and statistical analytics. Hiemstra et al. [11] analyzed the trends in information retrieval research community through co-authorship analysis of ACM SIGIR conference proceedings. Barbosa et al. [2] studied the evolution of Human-computer interaction research field in Brazil through analyzing the metadata of full papers of 14 editions of the Brazilian HCI conference (IHC). Agarwal et al. [1] analyzed the bibliometric metadata of seven ACM conferences in information retrieval, data mining, and digital libraries. Fathalla et al. [6,7] analyzed the evolution of key characteristics of CS events over a period of 30 years using descriptive data analysis, including continuity, geographic and time distribution, and submission and acceptance numbers

Despite these continuous efforts, most of the previous work has only focused on analyzing metadata of events of one series. What additionally distinguishes our work from the related work mentioned above, including our own previous version, is the creation of a Linked Dataset, with dereferenceable IRIs, under a persistent URL following W3C standards and best practices. In addition, EVENTSKG can be queried through a SPARQL endpoint.

3   Scientific Events Ontology

The Scientific Events Ontology (SEO) [8] is our ontology of choice to describe scientific events because it integrates the state-of-the-art ontologies for events in addition to its own vocabularies. SEO is the ontology of the OpenResearch[3] platform for curating scholarly communication metadata. It does not only represent what happened, i.e., the scholarly event and its date and location, but also the roles that each agent played, and the time at which a particular role was held by an agent at an event. Best practices within the Semantic Web community (cf., e.g., [9]) have been considered when designing and publishing the ontology. SEO reuses several well-designed ontologies, such as the Conference Ontology[4], FOAF, SIOC, Dublin Core and SWRC (Semantic Web for Research Communities), and defines some of its own vocabularies. All namespace prefixes are used according to prefix.cc[5]. The OR-SEO concepts used to represent events metadata in EVENTSKG are: `OrganisedEvent` (and its subclasses), `Site`, `EventSeries` (and its subclasses), `ResearchField` and `Agent`. Furthermore, several properties have been used, including data properties and object properties (Table 1).

Table 1. Events properties

Property	Type	Source	Description
`acronym`	datatype	conf-onto	The acronym of an event
`endDate`	datatype	conf-onto	The date of the last day of an event
`startDate`	datatype	conf-onto	The date of the first day of an event
`field`	datatype	seo	The research field which the event belongs to
`country`	datatype	DBpedia	The country hosting the event
`state`	datatype	seo	The state hosting the event (if applicable)
`city`	datatype	seo	The city hosting the event
`submittedPapers`	datatype	seo	The number of papers submitted to an event
`acceptedPapers`	datatype	seo	The number of papers accepted at an event
`acceptanceRate`	datatype	seo	The acceptance rate of an event
`eventWebsite`	datatype	seo	The website of an event
`belongsToSeries`	object	seo	The series which an event belongs to
`colocatedWith`	object	seo	Links an event to another, co-located one
`hasTrack`	object	seo	Specifies the different tracks associated to an event

---

[3] http://openresearch.org/.
[4] http://www.scholarlydata.org/ontology/doc/.
[5] A namespace look-up tool for RDF developers: http://prefix.cc/.

4   EVENTSKG Characteristics

Currently, EVENTSKG covers three types of computer science events since 1969[6]: conferences, workshops, and symposia. EVENTSKG contains metadata of 73 events series, representing 1951 events with 17 attributes each. The total number of triples is 29,255, i.e., counting all available attributes of all events. EVENTSKG is a 5-star dataset [3]. Each resource is denoted by a URI and links to other datasets on the Web, such as DBpedia (to represent countries) and SEO entities (to represent terms such as "Symposium"), to provide context. The locations of the further EVENTSKG-related resources mentioned below are given in Table 2. *Availability and Best Practices*: EVENTSKG is available as a Linked Dataset, with dereferenceable IRIs, under the persistent URL (http://w3id.org/EVENTSKG-Dataset/ekg), and as structured CSV tables. In addition, we established a SPARQL endpoint (using Virtuoso) to enable users to query the dataset. EVENTSKG is licensed under the terms of Creative Commons Attribution 4.0 Unported (CC-BY-4.0). *Extensibility:* There are three dimensions to extend EVENTSKG to meet future requirements: (a) add more events in each community, (b) cover more CS communities and (c) add event properties, such as deadlines, registration fees, and chairs. *Documentation*: The documentation of the dataset is available online[7] and has been checked using the W3C Markup Validation Service[8]. *Sustainability*: To ensure the sustainability of EVENTSKG, we developed an API for updating and maintaining the dataset. The dataset is replicated on its GitHub repository and our servers. *Announcement*: we announced EVENTSKG on several mailing lists, such as the W3C LOD list[9], the discussion list of the open science community[10], and discussion forums, such as those of the Open Knowledge Foundation. We got valuable feedback, addressing issues such as inconsistencies in the data (in values, not in the semantics), from several parties, including researchers in our community and also librarians, e.g., from the German national library. *Quality assurance*: the Vapour Linked Data validator is used to check whether EVENTSKG is correctly published according to the Linked Data principles and related best practices [9].

5   Data Curation

The lack of clear guidelines for data generation and maintenance has motivated us to propose a workflow for the curation process of EVENTSKG to serve as a guideline for linked datasets generation and maintenance. EVENTSKG is generated from metadata collected from several data sources (e.g., DBLP, WikiCFP, and digital libraries). Therefore, a data curation process is crucial.The curation

---

[6] the date of the oldest events in the dataset.

[7] http://kddste.sda.tech/EVENTSKG-Dataset/.

[8] https://validator.w3.org/.

[9] public-lod@w3.org.

[10] open-science@lists.okfn.org.

Table 2. EVENTSKG-related resources

Resource	URL
Turtle file	http://kddste.sda.tech/EVENTSKG-Dataset/EVENTSKG_R2.ttl
RDF/XML file	http://kddste.sda.tech/EVENTSKG-Dataset/EVENTSKG_R2.rdf
JSON-LD file	http://kddste.sda.tech/EVENTSKG-Dataset/EVENTSKG_R2.json
SEO Ontology	https://w3id.org/seo#
Issue Tracker	https://github.com/saidfathalla/EVENTSKG-Dataset/issues/
API	https://github.com/saidfathalla/EVENTSKG_API
GitHub repository	https://github.com/saidfathalla/EVENTS-Dataset
SPARQL endpoint	http://kddste.sda.tech/sparql
DataHub	https://datahub.ckan.io/dataset/eventskg
VoID	http://kddste.sda.tech/EVENTSKG-Dataset/VoID.nt
Documentation	http://kddste.sda.tech/EVENTSKG-Dataset/

of EVENTSKG dataset is an incremental process starting from the identification of top-ranked events in each CS community until the maintenance phase, which is performed continuously. It has been carried out comprising eight steps as shown in Fig. 1. During the curation process, several problems have been encountered, such as (1) identification of top-ranked events in each CS community, (2) data collection problems, such as data duplication, inconsistencies, and erroneous data, (3) data integration problems, such as integrating data about the same event collected from various data sources and unifying event names, (4) data transformation problems, such as converting unstructured to structured data, i.e., from text to CSV and consequently to RDF, and (5) LD generation, interlinking and validation. In the following subsections, we report only the major problems we faced, and how we solved these problems; mainly, they were data preprocessing problems.

Events Identification: At the very beginning, we should identify the top-ranked events in each CS community. To identify a subset of these events to be added to EVENTSKG, we used the following metrics, which are used widely by CS communities to identify top-ranked events in various CS communities. CORE[11]: Computing Research and Education Association of Australasia uses community-defined criteria for ranking journals and events in the computing disciplines. The rankings have periodic rounds, usually every year, of updates for adding or re-ranking conferences. Based on these metrics an event can be ranked into eight classes – in decreasing order: A*, A, B, C, Australian, National, Regional, and un-ranked. *QUALIS:* It uses the h-index as a performance measure for conferences. Based on the h-index percentiles, the conferences are ranked into

---

[11] http://www.core.edu.au/.

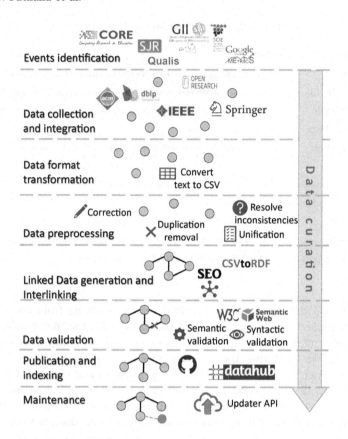

Fig. 1. Data curation of EVENTSKG.

seven classes – in decreasing order: A1, A2, B1, ..., and B5. ERA^{12}: Excellence in Research for Australia ranking is created by the Australian Research Council. The classes, in decreasing order, are: A , B, and C. GGS^{13}: The ratings are generated by an automatic algorithm based on existing international classifications. The classes are, in decreasing order: A++, A+, A, A−, B, B−, and C. While identifying top-ranked events in each community, we observed a heterogeneity of the ranking of them in the aforementioned services, e.g., FOGA is ranked A* in CORE, i.e., ranked 1st, while ranked B3 in QUALIS, i.e., ranked 5th. In addition, the rank of FSE in CORE is B, while its rank in GGS is A+ and in ERA it is A. Therefore, we propose the Scientific Events Ranking (SER) (available at http://kddste.sda.tech/SER-Service/), in which we unified the ranking of each event in the dataset using the sum of weight method. SER is represented by the function $SER: C \times Q \times E \times G \to S$, where C is the set of CORE classes, Q is the set of QUALIS classes, E is the set of ERA classes, G is the set of GGS classes,

[12] https://www.arc.gov.au/excellence-research-australia/era-2018.
[13] http://gii-grin-scie-rating.scie.es/ratingSearch.jsf.

and S is the set of SER classes. The range of $SER(x)$ is defined in Eq. 1, where x is the sum of weights of each class in CORE, QUALIS, ERA, and GGS for each event series. We only choose the top-5 events according to SER.

$$SER(x) = \begin{cases} A+ \text{ if } 100 < x \leq 75 \\ A \text{ if } 75 < x \leq 50 \\ B+ \text{ if } 50 < x \leq 25 \\ B \text{ if } 25 < x \leq 0 \end{cases} \tag{1}$$

Data Collection and Integration: Still, metadata collection is considered a time-consuming task because of the diversity of data sources available on the Web. Actually, data collection for EVENTSKG is a semi-automated process in which the OpenResearch.org data crawlers are executed monthly to collect metadata of scientific events. In addition, we collected data from different unstructured and semi-structured data sources, such as IEEE Xplore, ACM DL, DBLP, and web pages. Therefore, this data should be integrated and cleaned to be exposed as Linked Data. Then, we initiate a data integration process, which involves integrating collected data from disparate sources into a unified view.

Data Preprocessing: The goal of the data preprocessing phase is to prepare the collected data for performing the analysis by integrating data from several data sources, eliminating irrelevant data and resolving inconsistencies. Three preprocessing tasks have been carried out: *data cleansing and completion, data structure transformation* and *event name unification.*

- *Data cleansing and completion:* involves removing duplicates, and identifying and correcting unsound data. Where we found incomplete information for some events, we complemented it as available. For instance, we double checked this information against the events' official websites or proceedings published in digital libraries, where they are trusted information sources. In addition, we periodically explore online digital libraries for the missing information.
- *Data structure transformation:* involves transforming cleaned data into a structured format, i.e., CSV.
- *Event name unification:* for the analysis purpose, we unified the names of all editions of an event series to the most recent name. For example, the unified name of The Web conference is *TheWeb*, formerly the World Wide Web conference (WWW).

Linked Data Generation and Interlinking: The adoption of the Linked Data best practices has led to the enrichment of data published on the Web by linking data from diverse domains, such as scholarly communication, digital libraries, and medical data [10]. The objective of this phase is to generate linked data from the less reusable, intermediate CSV representation. Using an ad-hoc transformation tool[14], we transformed the CSV data to a RDF graph, after mapping several events attributes given in the CSV file to the corresponding OR-SEO properties.

---

[14] http://levelup.networkedplanet.com/.

Using a comprehensive ontology as a dataset's schema gives the ability to obtain insights from the data by applying inference engines. Interlinking is required to achieve the 5th star of the 5-star deployment scheme proposed by Berners-Lee [3].

Data Validation: The next step is to semantically and syntactically validate the RDF graph to ensure the quality of the data produced. The validation has been carried out using the W3C RDF online validation service[15] to ensure conformance with the W3C RDF standards. The Hermit Reasoner is used to detect inconsistencies. Detecting inconsistencies is important because they result in a false semantic understanding of the knowledge. We resolve detected inconsistencies and periodically run the reasoner to ensure that no other inconsistencies arise after the interlinking process.

Data Publication: The objective of data publication is to enable humans and machines to share structured data on the Web. Therefore, EVENTSKG is published according to the Linked Data best practices [10] and it is registered in a GitHub repository (cf. Table 2). The commonly used way to let make a dataset easier to find, share and download is to index it in a public data portal, e.g., DataHub (cf. Table 2). A complete resource of the AAAI 2017 conference in the RDF/XML serialization can be found on the EVENTSKG documentation page.

Maintenance: To maintain EVENTSKG and to keep it sustainable, there are several challenges to be considered; here is how we address them: (1) A Java API for updating and maintaining the dataset has been developed, source code is available on GitHub (cf. Table 2). It facilitates the modification of EVENTSKG resources without going into the details of how this data is represented in the dataset since it has a natural language interface, in which casual users use only text fields, calendars and lists for modifying data, and it also facilitates the addition of new events to the dataset. For instance, metadata for each individual event, e.g., TheWeb, can be easily updated or added using a friendly user interface, and (2) GitHub Issue tracker: EVENTSKG has an issue tracker on GitHub, enabling the community to report bugs or to request features.

6   Use Case

This section presents some competency queries ($Q_1 - Q_4$) that EVENTSKG can answer. A concrete use case for querying EVENTSKG is to disclose the hidden characteristics of top-ranked events and also to help researchers in taking decisions on what event to submit their work to, or whether to accept invitations for being a chair or PC member. Event chairs will be able to assess their selection process, e.g., to keep the acceptance rate stable even when the submissions increase, to make sure the event is held around the same time each year, and to compare it against other competing events. For instance, "Q_1: *What is the Average Acceptance Rate for a particular conference series, e.g., ESWC, in the last*

---

[15] https://www.w3.org/RDF/Validator/.

decade?" In addition, the productivity and the popularity of a CS community over time can be analyzed by studying the number of accepted and submitted papers respectively. For instance, "Q_2: *Compare the popularity of the CS communities in the past decade*" (Listing 1). Regarding country-level analysis, the popularity of a CS community in a particular country can be determined by such a query: "Q_3: What are the top-5 countries hosting most of the events belonging to *Security and Privacy* in the past decade?" Listing 2 shows such a query. In fact, EVENTSKG is not only able to answer quantitative questions, but it also provides qualitative information, such as countries hosted most events related to a paricular community.

Listing 1. SPARQL query for comparing the popularity of the CS communities.

```
SELECT ?field (SUM(?sub) AS ?numOfSubmissions)
WHERE{
?e seo:field ?field.
?e conference-ontology:startDate ?d.
FILTER (?d >="2009-01-01T00:00:00.0000000+00:00"^^xsd:dateTime)
?e seo:submittedPapers ?sub.
}
ORDER BY DESC(?numOfSubmissions)
```

Listing 2. SPARQL query for finding top-5 countries host most of the events belonging to *Security and Privacy* in the past decade.

```
SELECT ?country (count(?country) as ?numOfEvents)
WHERE{
?e seo:heldInCountry ?country.
?e seo:field <https://w3id.org/seo#SecurityAndPrivacy>.
?e conference-ontology:startDate ?sd.
FILTER(?sd >="2009-01-01T00:00:00.0000000+00:00"^^xsd:dateTime)
}
GROUP BY(?country)
ORDER BY DESC(?numOfEvents)
LIMIT 5
```

7   Metadata Analysis

In this section, we present a part of the exploratory data analysis we performed on EVENTSKG. Further details can be found in [4,5,7]. The objective here is to emphasize the usefulness of EVENTSKG in exploring new features and unknown relationships in the data to provide recommendations. Furthermore, we summarize the main characteristics of top-ranked CS events using visual methods. We report the results of analyzing metadata of events, including the proceedings publishers, time distribution, geographical distribution (with two different granularities) and events progress ratio. These results provide some insights towards answering the research questions mentioned in Sect. 1.

Time distribution (TD): refers to the month of each year in which an event takes place. We computed the frequency of occurrence, in terms of the month of the year, of top-5 events (identified using the SER ranking) for each event since its establishment. Figure 2 shows the most frequent month in which events take place along with the number of editions of each event. We observed that most of the renowned events usually took place around the same month each year. For instance, CVPR has been held 28 times (out of 31) in June and PLDI has been held 33 times (out of 36) in June. This helps potential authors to expect when the event will take place next year, which helps with the submission schedule organization.

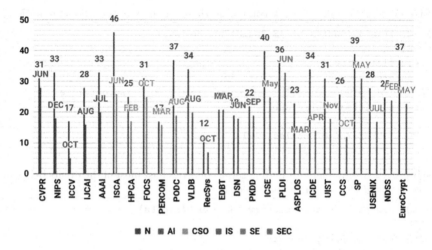

Fig. 2. TD of all events in terms of the most months where the event was held.

Geographical distribution (GD): refers to the distribution of events among countries (country-level GD) and continent (continent-level GD) each year since the beginning. We recorded, for each distinct location (either a country or continent), the number of times the event took place there. Events in EVENTSKG were distributed among 69 countries, with the USA having hosted the largest number (of 1042) events, then Canada comes with 124 events, then Italy, France, and Germany with 67, 67 and 64 events respectively. *Continent-level GD* refers to the frequency of occurrence of events among continents each year since the beginning. We computed the frequency of occurrence f_{ij} of all events belonging to community i in continent j. Then, we normalized these values to q_{ij} to ensure that the frequencies of occurrence of events in each community (C) sum up to one (Eq. 2).

$$f_{ij} = \sum_{k \in C} E_{ijk} \quad , \quad q_{ij} = \frac{f_{ij}}{\sum_{k=1}^{n} f_{kj}} \tag{2}$$

Here, E_{ijk} is the number of events of an event series k in a community i taking place in continent j, and m is the number of event series in each community. As shown in Table 3, Europe hosted IS events the most, followed by SEC events. North America has almost the same ratio for all communities. The remarkable observation emerging here is that Africa and South America host a significantly low number of events in all communities. For instance, South America hosted only four AI events and three IS events, while Africa hosted only one IS and one SE event. On the other hand, North America hosted the largest number of events (f_{ij}) in to all communities. *Country-level GD* refers to the change of the location of each event from year to year and denoted by ΔL_n (Eq. 3), where l_n is the location of an event in a year and l_{n+1} is the location of the same event in the next year.

$$\Delta L_n = \begin{cases} 1 \text{ if } l_n \neq l_{n-1} \\ 0 \text{ otherwise} \end{cases} \tag{3}$$

We computed the mean of these changes ($\bar{x} = (\sum_{i=0}^{n-2} (l_i - l_{i-1}))/n$) to measure the rate of the distribution of each event since the beginning. The higher this value is for an event, the more frequently the host country of an event changed. For instance, ICCV and ISMAR have $\bar{x} = 1$, which means that they moved to a different country every year, while SP and DCC have $\bar{x} = 0$, which means that they remained in the same country every year.

Table 3. Normalized frequency of occurrence (q_{ij}) of events by continent.

q_{ij}	Europe	N. America	Asia	Africa	S. America	Australia
AI	0.06	0.13	0.11	0.00	0.44	0.18
CSO	0.08	0.14	0.11	0.00	0.00	0.12
HCC	0.08	0.15	0.11	0.00	0.00	0.06
IS	0.22	0.11	0.15	0.50	0.33	0.24
SE	0.13	0.15	0.22	0.50	0.11	0.18
SEC	0.16	0.13	0.05	0.00	0.00	0.00
TOC	0.13	0.13	0.08	0.00	0.00	0.06
WWW	0.13	0.05	0.18	0.00	0.11	0.18

Progress ratio (PR): refers to the progress of an event in a given year within a fixed period of time. We define the PR of an event by the ratio of the number of publications of that event in a given year to the total number of publications in a given period of time. The progress ratio for an event e in a year y is defined in Eq. 4, where $P_y(e)$ is the number of publications of e in y and n is the number of years in the time span of the study. We computed the PR of the top-ranked events in each CS community in the period 1997–2017. As shown in Fig. 3, the PR of all events had a slight rise in the period 1997–2005; then, they all rose noticeably in the last decade. Overall, events of all CS communities have shown a drastic increase in PR since the beginning. We consider this to be an

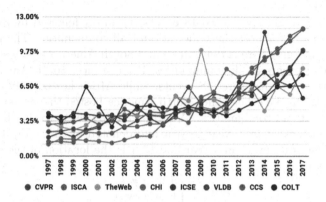

Fig. 3. PR of the top event in each CS sub-community in the last two decades.

effect of digitization, which has made event organization and paper submission considerably easier, thanks to conference management systems.

Publishers: It is observed that several events series organizers publish the proceedings of their events in their own digital library, e.g., AAAI, VLDB, or NIPS. On the other hand, ACM publishes the proceedings of 42% of the events in EVENTSKG, and IEEE comes next with 26%.

$$PR_y(e) = \frac{P_y(e)}{\sum\limits_{i=1}^{n} P_i(e)} \tag{4}$$

8   Conclusions and Future Work

This paper presents a new release of the EVENTSKG dataset, a 5-star Linked Dataset, with dereferenceable IRIs, of all events of the 73 most renowned event series in computer science. The SEO ontology is used as the reference model for creating the dataset. We proposed a workflow of the curation process of EVENTSKG, starting from events identification until the publication and maintenance of the dataset. In addition, we present a new event ranking service (SER), which combines the rankings of CS events from four well-known ranking services. To the best of our knowledge, this is the first time a knowledge graph of metadata of top-ranked events in eight CS communities has been published as a linked open dataset. The dataset is coupled with an API for updating and maintaining the dataset, without going into the details of how this data is represented. We analyze EVENTSKG content over the last 50 years but found, during data acquisition, that there is not much information about events prior to 1990, in particular on the number of submissions and accepted papers. The most striking findings from the analysis of EVENTSKG's data are:

- The progress ratio of all events kept growing over the last two decades, most likely thanks to the digitization of scholarly communication,

- The USA have hosted most editions of events in all communities, followed by Canada, Italy, France, and Germany,
- The most of the events have a high distribution among countries to attract potential authors around the world,
- ACM publishes most of the proceedings of the events, and IEEE comes next,
- Europe hosted IS events the most, followed by SEC events, North America has almost the same ratio for all communities, and
- Africa and South America hosted a significantly low number of CS events.

These findings highlight the usefulness of EVENTSKG for events organizers, researchers interested in data publishing, as well as librarians. Finally, we believe that EVENTSKG can closes an important gap in analyzing the productivity and popularity of CS communities, i.e., publications and submissions, and it is of primary interest to steering committees, proceedings publishers and prospective authors.

To further our research, we are working in automating its subtasks; i.e., Data cleansing and completion, Data structure transformation and Event name unification. We are also planning to add more events from other fields of science, such as Physics, Mathematics, and Engineering, in addition to events from other CS communities such as Networks, Hardware and Applied computing. Furthermore, extending the OR-SEO ontology to cover authors, affiliations, titles and keywords in addition to adding a set of features to each event series that could be used to efficiently compare events in the same community, such as acceptance rate, h-index, and organizers' reputation, defined, e.g., in terms of their h-index and i10-index. Finally, we are planning to adopt a disambiguation mechanism for different events that have the same acronym, and to perform more complex semantic data analysis by querying EVENTSKG and automatically generating charts and figures from the obtained results.

Acknowledgments. This work has been supported by the European Union through the H2020 ERC ScienceGRAPH project (GA no. 819536). First author would like to thank the Ministry of Higher Education of Egypt for the financial support to conduct this work.

References

1. Agarwal, S., Mittal, N., Sureka, A.: A glance at seven ACM SIGWEB series of conferences. SIGWEB Newsl. (Summer), 5:1–5:10 (2016)
2. Barbosa, S.D.J., Silveira, M.S., Gasparini, I.: What publications metadata tell us about the evolution of a scientific community: the case of the Brazilian human-computer interaction conference series. Scientometrics **110**(1), 275–300 (2017)
3. Berners-Lee, T.: Is your linked open data 5 star. In: Berners-Lee, T. (ed.) Linked Data. Cambridge: W3C (2010)
4. Fathalla, S., Lange, C.: EVENTS: a dataset on the history of top-prestigious events in five computer science communities. In: González-Beltrán, A., Osborne, F., Peroni, S., Vahdati, S. (eds.) SAVE-SD 2017-2018. LNCS, vol. 10959, pp. 110–120. Springer, Cham (2018). https://doi.org/10.1007/978-3-030-01379-0_8

5. Fathalla, S., Lange, C.: EVENTSKG: a knowledge graph representation for top-prestigious computer science events metadata. In: Nguyen, N.T., Pimenidis, E., Khan, Z., Trawiński, B. (eds.) ICCCI 2018. LNCS (LNAI), vol. 11055, pp. 53–63. Springer, Cham (2018). https://doi.org/10.1007/978-3-319-98443-8_6

6. Fathalla, S., Vahdati, S., Lange, C., Auer, S.: Analysing scholarly communication metadata of computer science events. In: Kamps, J., Tsakonas, G., Manolopoulos, Y., Iliadis, L., Karydis, I. (eds.) TPDL 2017. LNCS, vol. 10450, pp. 342–354. Springer, Cham (2017). https://doi.org/10.1007/978-3-319-67008-9_27

7. Fathalla, S., Vahdati, S., Auer, S., Lange, C.: Metadata analysis of scholarly events of computer science, physics, engineering, and mathematics. In: Méndez, E., Crestani, F., Ribeiro, C., David, G., Lopes, J.C. (eds.) TPDL 2018. LNCS, vol. 11057, pp. 116–128. Springer, Cham (2018). https://doi.org/10.1007/978-3-030-00066-0_10

8. Fathalla, S., Vahdati, S., Auer, S., Lange, C.: The scientific events ontology of the openresearch.org curation platform. In: Proceedings of the 34th ACM/SIGAPP Symposium on Applied Computing, pp. 2311–2313. ACM (2019)

9. Gyrard, A., Serrano, M., Atemezing, G.A.: Semantic web methodologies, best practices and ontology engineering applied to Internet of Things. In: 2015 IEEE 2nd World Forum on Internet of Things (WF-IoT). IEEE (2015)

10. Heath, T., Bizer, C.: Linked data: evolving the web into a global data space. Synth. Lect. Semant. Web: Theory Technol. 1(1), 1–136 (2011)

11. Hiemstra, D., Hauff, C., De Jong, F., Kraaij, W.: SIGIR's 30th anniversary: an analysis of trends in IR research and the topology of its community. In: ACM SIGIR Forum, vol. 41(2). ACM (2007)

12. Luo, D., Lyons, K.: CASCONet: A Conference dataset. arXiv (2017)

13. Möller, K., Heath, T., Handschuh, S., Domingue, J.: Recipes for semantic web dog food — the ESWC and ISWC metadata projects. In: Aberer, K., et al. (eds.) ASWC/ISWC -2007. LNCS, vol. 4825, pp. 802–815. Springer, Heidelberg (2007). https://doi.org/10.1007/978-3-540-76298-0_58

14. Osborne, F., Motta, E., Mulholland, P.: Exploring scholarly data with rexplore. In: Alani, H., et al. (eds.) ISWC 2013. LNCS, vol. 8218, pp. 460–477. Springer, Heidelberg (2013). https://doi.org/10.1007/978-3-642-41335-3_29

15. Vasilescu, B., Serebrenik, A., Mens, T.: A historical dataset of software engineering conferences. In: 10th Working Conference on Mining Software Repositories. IEEE Press (2013)

CORAL: A Corpus of Ontological Requirements Annotated with Lexico-Syntactic Patterns

Alba Fernández-Izquierdo(✉), María Poveda-Villalón(✉),
and Raúl García-Castro

Ontology Engineering Group, Universidad Politécnica de Madrid, Madrid, Spain
{albafernandez,mpoveda,rgarcia}@fi.upm.es

Abstract. Ontological requirements play a key role in ontology development as they determine the knowledge that needs to be modelled. In addition, the analysis of such requirements can be used (a) to improve ontology testing by easing the automation of requirements into tests; (b) to improve the requirements specification activity; or (c) to ease ontology reuse by facilitating the identification of patterns. However, there is a lack of openly available ontological requirements published together with their associated ontologies, which hinders such analysis. Therefore, in this work we present CORAL (Corpus of Ontological Requirements Annotated with Lexico-syntactic patterns), an openly available corpus of 834 ontological requirements annotated and 29 lexico-syntactic patterns, from which 12 are proposed in this work. CORAL is openly available in three different open formats, namely, HTML, CSV and RDF under "Creative Commons Attribution 4.0 International" license.

Keywords: Corpus · Linked data · Ontological requirements · Lexico-syntactic patterns

Resource type: Dataset
DOI: https://doi.org/10.5281/zenodo.1967306
URL: http://coralcorpus.linkeddata.es

1 Introduction

In recent years, the definition of functional ontological requirements [3,17,18], which represent the needs that the ontology to be built should cover, and their automatic formalization into axioms or tests (e.g., [5,13,19]) have been studied.

This work is partially supported by the H2020 project VICINITY: Open virtual neighbourhood network to connect intelligent buildings and smart objects (H2020-688467), by ETSI Specialist Task Force 534, and by a Predoctoral grant from the I+D+i program of the Universidad Politécnica de Madrid. The authors want to thank Agnieszka Ławrynowicz and her team for helping in the collection of ontological requirements.

© Springer Nature Switzerland AG 2019
P. Hitzler et al. (Eds.): ESWC 2019, LNCS 11503, pp. 443–458, 2019.
https://doi.org/10.1007/978-3-030-21348-0_29

The aim of these studies is to reduce the time consumed by ontology developers during the ontology verification activity, in which the ontology is compared against the ontological requirements, thus ensuring that the ontology is built correctly [16]. Functional ontological requirements can be written in the form of competency questions, which are natural language questions that the ontology to be modelled should be able to answer, or as statements, which are sentences that determine what should be built in the ontology.

However, to accurately define ontological requirements is not a trivial task and, therefore, neither is their automatic translation into a formal language. Due to the fact that some requirements are ambiguous [9] or vague, their transformation into axioms or tests is not usually direct and, consequently, it is very difficult to automate such translation. The analysis of these functional ontological requirements can be used in several domains, e.g., to improve ontology testing by easing the automation of requirements into tests, to improve the requirements specification activity by identifying problems in the definition of the requirements that should be avoided, or to ease ontology reuse by facilitating the identification of patterns to implement such requirements. However, there is a lack of openly available ontological requirements published together with their associated ontologies, which hinders such analysis.

In order to solve this limitation of data, the work presented here presents CORAL (Corpus of Ontological Requirements Annotated with Lexico-syntactic patterns), a corpus of 834 functional ontological requirements collected from different projects, websites and papers with the aim of providing a resource that could help the formalization of ontological requirements in an ontology. Additionally, this work provides a dictionary of lexico-syntactic patterns (LSPs) which includes LSPs collected from the state of the art and also defines new ones. This dictionary of LSPs have been used to annotate the set of ontological requirements. The aim of these annotations is to provide a mechanism for analyzing how these requirements are defined and, consequently, identifying whether there is ambiguity in their specification, with the ultimate goal of generating tests automatically.

The paper is organized as follows. Section 2 presents the process we followed to generate and annotate the corpus of ontological requirements. Section 3 describes the structure of the corpus, and how it can be maintained. Section 4 presents a set of statistics related to the corpus and Sect. 5 describes possible applications and usages. Section 6 describes the related work. Finally, Sect. 7 presents the conclusions we obtained and gives an overview on future work.

2   Building the Corpus

The corpus of annotated ontological requirements was generated through a set of five steps. This section summarizes them and also describes how this corpus is going to be extended and maintained.

2.1   Steps for Generating the Corpus

The steps carried out to generate the corpus, which are summarized in Fig. 1, were the following:

1. *To search for ontological requirements.* A set of 834 functional requirements, which have their corresponding ontology implementation available, was collected. These requirements were written as competency questions and as statements, and collected from several projects, as well as from papers and from resources available on the Web. These 834 functional requirements were associated to 14 different ontologies, whose names and requirements provenance are summarized in Table 1. These ontologies are built by different authors, and cover different topics and sizes.

2. *To search for existing LSPs.* In order to annotate the corpus of ontological requirements, a dictionary of LSPs was created. LSPs are understood as "formalized linguistic schemas or constructions derived from regular expressions

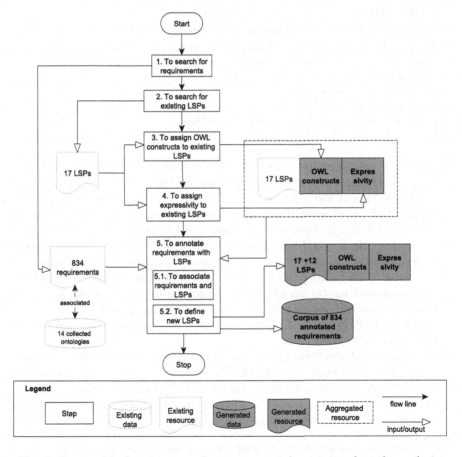

Fig. 1. Steps, with their inputs and outputs, carried out to conduct the analysis.

Table 1. Collected ontologies with their requirements

Ontology name	Provenance	Number of requirements
SAREF4ENVI	ETSI Technical Report [14]	58
OneM2M	ETSI Technical Report [14]	58
SAREF	ETSI Technical Report [14]	71
SAREF4BLDG	ETSI Technical Report [14]	98
BTN100	Github repository[a]	77
OntoDT	Paper [10]	14
Video Game	Paper [11]	66
Software Ontology	Paper [8]	90
Dem@care Ontology	Project deliverable[b]	107
ODRL	Website[c]	15
WoT mappings	Website[d]	15
Building Topology Ontology	Website[e]	18
WoT VICINITY	Website (See Footnote d)	24
VICINITY Core	Website (See Footnote d)	127

[a]https://github.com/oeg-upm/ontology-BTN100/tree/master/requirements.
[b]http://www.demcare.eu/downloads/D5.1SemanticKnowledgeStructures_and
Representation.pdf.
[c]http://w3c.github.io/poe/ucr/.
[d]http://vicinity.iot.linkeddata.es.
[e]https://w3c-lbd-cg.github.io/bot/#Requirements.

in natural language that consist of certain linguistic and paralinguistic elements, following a specific syntactic order, and that permit to extract some conclusions about the meaning they express" [1]. Daga et al. [4] proposed a corpus of 17 LSPs[1], each of which has associated one or more ontology design patterns (ODPs) [6] that indicates how the LSP could be implemented in an ontology. It is possible that one LSP is associated with several disjoint ODPs, resulting in several possible ontology implementations. These LSPs are going to be called polysemous LSPs. Besides these ODPs, each LSP is also associated to: (a) an identifier, (b) formalization according to a BNF extension[2] and (c) examples of sentences in natural language which match with such LSP. It is worth noting that there can be more than one possible formalization for each LSP.

3. *To assign OWL constructs to existing LSPs.* Based on the ODPs associated to each LSP, we identify the set of OWL constructs needed to implement each LSP. The information related to how each ODP should be implemented was extracted from Suarez et al. [15], which defines a repository for ODPs along with their formal representation in an ontology. It was decided to consider

---

[1] http://ontologydesignpatterns.org/wiki/Submissions:LexicoSyntacticODPs.
[2] https://www.w3.org/Notation.html.

every OWL construct except for the annotation or versioning constructs, due to the fact that they do not add expressivity to the ontology and as they are used as metadata. Considering that in some cases the LSPs can be associated with several disjoint ODPs and, therefore, implemented in alternative models, each LSP has OWL constructs for each alternative model.

4. *To assign expressivity to existing LSPs.* According to the previously identified OWL constructs, the DL expressivity [2] of each LSP was determined. Because of the fact that some LSPs can be implemented into several models involving different OWL constructs, different expressivity has been associated to each model.

5. *To annotate ontological requirements with LSPs.* The annotation of ontological requirements is divided into two sub-steps:

   5.1 *To associate requirements and LSPs.* The association between ontological requirements and LSP was manually made based on the syntax of each requirement and on its mapping with the formalization of each LSP.

   5.2 *To define new LSPs.* For those ontological requirements which do not match with any of the state of the art LSPs, new patters were provided to support them. These new patterns include the same information as the state of the art LSPs, such as the formalization, ODPs associated (if exists) and examples of use. Altogether, a set of 12 new LSPs were added to the dictionary of patterns. If there are no ODPs associated to the LSP, then the OWL constructs were determined based on how each type of requirement is usually implemented in ontologies, e.g., a requirement related to a union between two concepts will be related with the OWL construct related to union, i.e., *owl:unionOf.*

2.2 Availability, Extensibility and Maintenance of the Annotated Corpus

The dictionary of patterns and the annotated corpus are openly available in HTML,[3] CSV and RDF format as Zenodo resources. They have a canonical citation using the DOI https://doi.org/10.5281/zenodo.1967306 and are published under Creative Commons Attribution 4.0 International license (CC BY 4.0).[4] Additionally, the corpus is also available in DataHub[5] and from Google Dataset search.

Maintenance of the corpus will be facilitated through the continuous process of gathering requirements from projects where ontologies are involved, as well as from periodic searches for gathering new openly available requirements on the Web and on papers. If new LSPs need to be defined to support these new ontological requirements, they will also be added to the dictionary of LSPs. For the time being the addition of new requirements and LSPs is manual. However, if CORAL is adopted by the community, it will be considered to provide an automatic service to allow users to add their requirements to the corpus.

---

[3] http://coralcorpus.linkeddata.es/.

[4] https://creativecommons.org/licenses/by/4.0.

[5] https://datahub.io/albaizq13/coralcorpus.

3   Corpus Description

The corpus presented here is divided into two resources, i.e., the dictionary of LSPs and the corpus of annotated requirements, which is annotated using the dictionary of LSPs. Each of these resources has a different structure, which is described below. Additionally, this section includes the description of the vocabulary used to publish the corpus as Linked Data and an example of use.

3.1   Dictionary of Lexico-Syntactic Patterns

For each LSP we have stored the following items:

- **Identifier of the LSP**. It contains an acronym composed of LSP (Lexico-Syntactic Pattern), plus the acronym of the relation captured by the ODP, plus the ISO-639[6] code for representing the name of the language for which the LSP is valid.
- **Description of the LSP**. It contains a brief description of the LSPs and the associated ODPs (if exist).
- **NeOn ODP identifier**. It determines the identifier used in the NeOn ODP repository [15] of the ODPs that can be used to implement the LSP. If the ODP was not contained in that repository, an acronym is created following the same rules. Identifiers are composed by the component type (e.g., LP standing for Logical Pattern), component (e.g., SC standing for SubClassOf), and number of the pattern (e.g., 01). If the LSP does not match with any ODP, then this information
- **Formalization**. The LSPs have been formalized according to the BNF notation.
- **Examples**. Sentences in natural language that exemplify the corresponding LSPs.
- **OWL constructs** associated to the LSP. These OWL constructs have been extracted from the ODPs, which indicates how it should be implemented in the ontology. As mentioned before, if there is no associated ODP then the OWL constructs are determined based on how that type of LSP is usually implemented in ontologies.
- **DL Expressivity**. It is related to the OWL constructs that are associated to each LSP.

3.2   Annotated Corpus of Ontological Requirements

Each ontological requirement includes the following information:

- **Identifier of the requirement**. This identifier can be used to differentiate each requirement.
- **Competency question or statement**. It represents the need the ontology is expected to cover.

---

[6] https://iso639-3.sil.org/code_tables/639/data.

– **Answer to the competency question.** If the requirement is written as a competency question, it needs an answer. As an example, the sentence *"There are two types of devices, sensor and actuator"* could be the answer to the previous competency question.
– **Provenance.** This information indicates the URI of the ontology for which the requirement was defined.
– **Corresponding LSP.** It indicates the LSP extracted from the proposed dictionary of LSPs (see Sect. 3.1) which matches the ontological requirement.

Due to the fact that for each LSP we have stored the OWL constructs and expressivity, it is possible to obtain the OWL constructs and expressivity of each requirement. However, because there are several polysemous LSPs, some of the requirements can be implemented in alternative models and, consequently, they have OWL constructs for each model.

3.3 Example of Use

Along this subsection an example of annotated requirement and LSP is presented in order to ease the understanding of how the corpus was built as well as how the corpus can be used to annotate ontological requirements.

In this example, a user needs to annotate a requirement with an appropriate LSP. The requirement is a competency question that states "There are different types of devices: sensor and actuator". To achieve this goal, the user has to manually look for the LSP in the corpus that best matches with such requirement. After this analysis, the user obtains that the requirement can be represented with the BNF formalization *"There are QUAN CN-CATV NP<superclass> PARA [(NP<subclass>,)* and] NP<subclass>"*, which is the formalization associate to the LSP with identifier "LSP-SC-EN". Therefore, such requirement is annotated with the LSP "LSP-SC-EN", which has the following characteristics:

– **Identifier:** "LSP-SC-EN".
– **BNF formalization:** "There are QUAN CN-CATV NP<superclass> PARA [(NP<subclass>,)* and] NP<subclass>".
– **Description:** "The definition of a subsumption relation in an ontology".
– **Identifier of the associated ODP:** "LP-SC-01", which represent the ODP related to subclassOf relations.
– **Example:** "There are several kinds of memory: fast, expensive, short term memory and long-term memory".
– **OWL constructs:** "subclassOf, Class (Thing, Nothing)".
– **DL Expressivity:** "AL".

From this annotation it can also be deduced that the annotated requirement should be implemented following the ODP "LP-SC-01", which represent the ODP related to subclassOf relations. This ODP indicates that the two classes involved in the requirement need to be defined in the ontology together with the relation subclassOf between them.

3.4   Publishing the Corpus as Linked Data

The vocabulary used for publishing the corpus as linked data, depicted in Fig. 2, models the ontological requirements and their relations with the associated ontologies and LSPs. The proposed vocabulary can be extended with more information related to ontological requirements. Figure 3 shows an example of an ontological requirement following this vocabulary.

There are four main concepts in this proposed vocabulary[7], i.e., *ontological requirement, ontology, lexico-syntactic pattern* and *lexico-syntactic pattern implementation.*

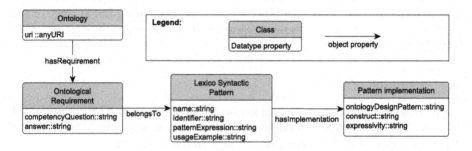

Fig. 2. Overview of the vocabulary for ontological requirements.

An *ontological requirement* is associated with two main types of elements: (1) *ontology*, which determines the provenance of the requirement, and (2) the correspondent *lexico-syntactic pattern*. The *ontological requirement* concept also includes as properties the competency question and its answer (if exists). Each *lexico-syntactic pattern*, in turn, is associated with the *lexico-syntactic pattern implementation*. It also includes as properties the name of the LSP, the identifier, the LSPs formalization and the usage example. The *lexico-syntactic pattern implementation* concept has as properties the ODPs, the constructs associated to the ODPs, and the expressivity of the implementation. Finally, the *ontology* concept, which represents the ontology from which the requirement is extracted, has as property its associated URI.

4   Corpus Statistics

This section introduces a set of statistics on the LSPs and ontological requirements present in the corpus.

Table 2 shows the total number of the collected ontological requirements and identified LSPs. Additionally, it shows the average and median ontological requirements and LSPs per ontology. According to Table 2, the analysed ontologies have an average of 56.15 ontological requirements in their specification, but these specifications are only related to an average of 7.07 LSPs.

---

[7] http://w3id.org/def/ontoreq.

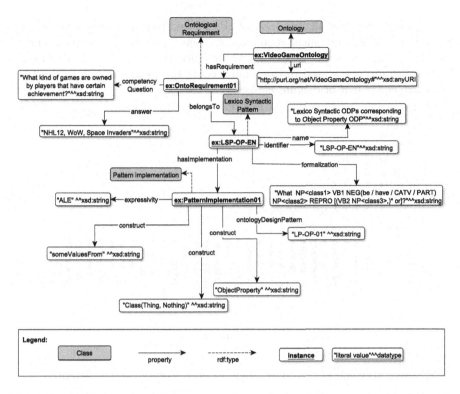

Fig. 3. Example of ontological requirement using the vocabulary proposed in this work.

The distribution of the LSPs according to their possible implementations, i.e., 1 LSP to 1 implementation in case that there is only one implementation for the LSP, and 1 LSP to N implementations in case that a LSP is related to several implementations, was also analysed. We observed that the majority of the LSPs, more precisely 88%, have a direct translation into a set of OWL constructs in an ontology. However, 12% of the ontological requirements are polysemous, that means, they can be implemented in several ontology models.

Table 2. Average and median of requirements per ontology and average of lexico-syntactic patterns per ontology

	Ontological requirements	Lexico-syntactic patterns
Average per ontology	56.15	7.07
Median per ontology	58	6
Total	834	29

Figures 4 and 5 show the number of ontologies in whose requirements specification each LSPs and each OWL constructs are used, respectively. According to the results depicted in Fig. 4, the LSPs related to object properties are the most used in the ontological requirements, being present in the requirements specification of almost all the analyzed ontologies. However, there is also a set of LSPs which are never used in the requirements specification, such as the LSPs related to equivalent or disjoint classes.

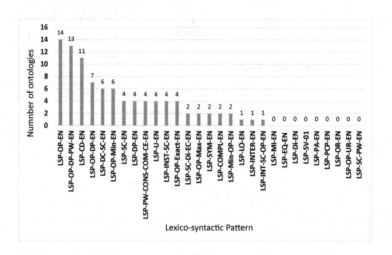

Fig. 4. Number of ontologies that use each lexico-syntactic pattern.

We can observe from Fig. 4 that polysemous LSPs, i.e., those LSPs that have more than one possible implementation in the ontology, are very common in the specification of the ontologies. Examples of this type of LSPs are LSP-OP-DP-PW-EN or LSP-OP-DP-EN, associated to "Object Property or Datatype Property or Simple Part-Whole relation ODPs" and "Object Property or Datatype Property ODPs", respectively. Therefore, even though there are few polysemous LSPs (only 12% of the set of LSPs), they have an important impact in the specification of ontological requirements.

The results shown in Fig. 5 indicate that all the requirement specifications includes the definition of classes, properties, domain and range. Additionally, the figure also depicts that there is a set of OWL constructs that are never associated to the requirements, such as those related to functional or transitive properties. Specifically, 19,23% of OWL constructs are present in all the ontologies requirements, 38,46% of OWL constructs are not present in any of the ontologies, and 61,54% of OWL constructs are present in at least one of the ontologies requirement specification.

Figure 6 shows the number of ontological requirements that are associated to each LSP. This figure only includes those LSPs with at least one requirement associated. We observed that the most common LSP in the requirement specifications is LSP-OP-EN, which is related to object properties. Other popular LSPs are LSP-OP-DP-EN and LSP-OP-DP-PW-EN, are polysemous LSPs and,

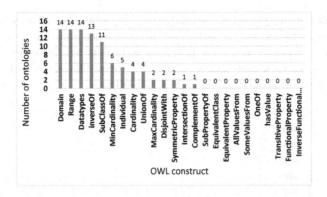

Fig. 5. Number of ontologies that uses each OWL construct.

therefore, they do not have direct translation to axioms or tests. It should be taken into account that there are several requirements that, due to they are long and include several sentences, they are associated to several LSPs. Therefore, the sum of the values in columns in Fig. 6 is higher than 834.

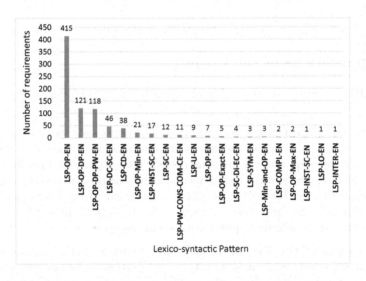

Fig. 6. Number of requirements per Lexico-Syntactic Pattern.

Finally, Fig. 7 illustrates the number of requirements associated to each DL expressivity. From this table it can be deduced that the majority of the requirements are related only to attributive language, which allows allows atomic negation, concept intersection, universal restrictions, and limited existential quantification, and to existential restriction, i.e., ALE. Only few requirements include more complex logic related, for example, with cardinality or with inverse relationships, i.e., ALU or ALI. It should be taken into account that if an ontological requirement is associated with a polysemous LSP it will have several possible implementations, each one with a particular expressivity. Therefore, the sum of the values in columns in Fig. 7 is higher than 834.

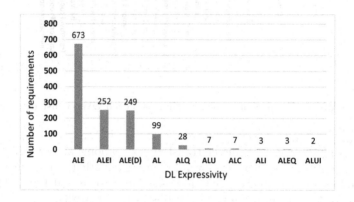

Fig. 7. Number of ontological requirements per DL expressivity.

5 Applications of the Corpus

The CORAL corpus can be used in several scenarios, including:

Automation of Ontology Testing. In order to automate as much as possible the translation of ontological requirements into axioms or tests it is needed to analyze how the requirements are constructed. The corpus presented in this work helps to identify LSPs in the requirements, as well as the set of OWL constructs associated to them. The OWL constructs associated to the LSPs can be used to automatically generate tests cases in order to verify whether the ontology satisfies the corresponding requirements, easing the testing process.

Improvement of the Requirements Specification Activity. The ontology requirements should be defined with the collaboration of domain experts, which are the responsible of identifying the needs the ontologies need to cover. However, there are considerable differences between what is defined in the requirements and what is implemented in the ontologies. For example, there are OWL constructs that are not associated to any ontological requirement, but are common in ontology implementations, such as axioms related to transitive or functional properties. In addition, due to the ambiguity of the requirements, some of them are associated to more than one possible implementation in the ontology. It should be necessary to improve the ontology elicitation activity in order to produce more precise requirements. This corpus can be used for a deeper analysis on how requirements are specified, as well as for identifying ambiguous expressions that should be removed from the requirements definition in order to ease their formalization into axioms.

Ontology Reuse. The eXtreme Design methodology [12] is a collaborative, incremental and iterative method for pattern-based ontology design. This methodology is based on the application, exploitation, and definition of ODPs for solving ontology development issues. It uses competency questions in order to manually select the appropriate ODP to implement them in the ontologies. The dictionary of LSPs proposed here, can be used for the automatic suggestion of LSPs that can be associated to each competency question. Consequently, using this association between LSP and competency question, it can be proposed the ODPs needed to implement each competency question.

6   Related Work

After analyzing the literature, we conclude that in the state of the art there are no works which deal with the same motivation as the one presented here. However, there are similar initiatives. On the one hand, there are several works related to the analysis of lexico-syntactic patterns (LSPs) from ontological requirements. On the other hand, there are works which deal with ontology testing and which use small corpora of requirements in order to support their transformation between natural language and SPARQL queries.

Regarding the analysis of patterns, Daga et al. [4] provide a set of LSPs extracted from ontological requirements which have a direct correspondence with one or more ontology design patterns (ODPs). These LSPs are also described in Montiel-Ponsoda [9]. They help users in the development of ontologies by using a system that permits an automatic detection of the ontological relations expressed as requirements. However, the analysis on LSPs carried out by the authors is not exhaustive, and even though they support sentences written in natural language, they do not support ontological requirements written as competency questions, which are very common in the specification of requirements. CORAL corpus extends the LSPs presented by Daga et al. [4].

Concerning the use of corpora about ontological requirements in order to propose testing approaches, Ren et al. [13] introduce a work in which they use natural language processing to analyze competency questions written in controlled natural language. From this controlled natural language they create competency question patterns that could be automatically tested in the ontology. However, these competency questions are extracted from only one project and from a tutorial. Because of the limitation of data, this work can only support a small set of patterns related to ontological requirements. Additionally, another example of work which tries to translate natural language sentences into a formal language is the one presented by Lopez et al. [7]. In this work, the authors show a subset of the sentences used to automatically generate SPARQL queries. However, the set of sentences is not published and, therefore, cannot be reused. Finally, the dataset presented by Wisniewski et al.[8] provides a corpus of 234 competency questions related to 5 different ontologies[9]. This dataset includes competency questions and their formalization into manually extracted SPARQL-OWL queries. Nevertheless, the dataset provided by Wisniewski et al. does not include any annotation or information related to the lexico-syntactic analysis needed to translate the competency questions into SPARQL queries and only the list of competency questions is available in a reusable format, namely, CSV.

The corpus presented is this work aims to solve these limitations of data by providing a openly available and reusable corpus of ontological requirements written in the form of competency questions and sentences. This corpus includes ontological requirements extracted from different ontologies and written by different authors, avoiding bias in writing the requirements. Additionally, it provides a dictionary of LSPs which is used to annotate these requirements and determine how each ontological requirement could be implemented.

7   Conclusions

The work presented here provides (1) a dictionary of 29 LSPs, from which 12 are new ones and 17 are LSPs already defined in the state of the art, and (2) an corpus of 834 ontological requirements annotated with these LSPs. This annotation determines the associated OWL constructs needed to implement each requirement in an ontology based, in most cases, on ODPs. Both the dictionary of patterns and the annotated corpus are provided in the machine-readable format RDF, in CSV and in HTML as Zenodo and Datahub resources. Additionally, CORAL is accessible from Google Dataset Search.

From the dictionary of LSPs, it was confirmed that there are several polysemous expressions that could result in different ontology structures. Therefore, the requirements associated with these polysemous patterns could also result in different ontology models. This result illustrates the need of improvement of the specification of requirements, which should aim to avoid ambiguities and to be more precise in order to identify the appropriate needs to model the ontologies. With this, it should be possible to reduce errors during the modelling of ontologies and also ease the automation from requirements into tests.

During the process of collecting requirements, significant difficulties to find available real-world functional requirements were found. We consider that publishing this kind of data is helpful not only of reusability, but also for ontology testing to verify completeness and conformance between ontologies.

We believe that the proposed corpus can promote research in several problems, such as ontology testing and ontology requirements specification, while it can also facilitate research in other topics such as in natural language processing. Future work will be directed to a further evaluation of how CORAL requirements are annotated and to automate the requirements annotation.

---

[8] https://github.com/CQ2SPARQLOWL/.

[9] Please note that we consider 4 of the 5 ontologies analyzed by them. The only ontology left was not considered due to the fact that their requirements were published recently (November 26, 2018). It will be included in future releases (see Sect. 2.2).

References

1. Aguado de Cea, G., Gómez-Pérez, A., Montiel-Ponsoda, E., Suárez-Figueroa, M.C.: Natural language-based approach for helping in the reuse of ontology design patterns. In: Gangemi, A., Euzenat, J. (eds.) EKAW 2008. LNCS (LNAI), vol. 5268, pp. 32–47. Springer, Heidelberg (2008). https://doi.org/10.1007/978-3-540-87696-0_6

2. Baader, F., Horrocks, I., Sattler, U.: Description logics. Found. Artif. Intell. **3**, 135–179 (2008)

3. Bezerra, C., Freitas, F., Santana, F.: Evaluating ontologies with competency questions. In: 2013 IEEE/WIC/ACM International Joint Conferences on Web Intelligence (WI) and Intelligent Agent Technologies (IAT), vol. 3, pp. 284–285. IEEE (2013)

4. Daga, E., et al.: NeOn D2. 5.2 Pattern Based Ontology Design: Methodology and Software Support (2010)

5. Dennis, M., van Deemter, K., Dell'Aglio, D., Pan, J.Z.: Computing authoring tests from competency questions: experimental validation. In: d'Amato, C., et al. (eds.) ISWC 2017. LNCS, vol. 10587, pp. 243–259. Springer, Cham (2017). https://doi.org/10.1007/978-3-319-68288-4_15

6. Gangemi, A., Presutti, V.: Ontology design patterns. In: Staab, S., Studer, R. (eds.) Handbook on Ontologies. IHIS, pp. 221–243. Springer, Heidelberg (2009). https://doi.org/10.1007/978-3-540-92673-3_10

7. Lopez, V., Pasin, M., Motta, E.: AquaLog: an ontology-portable question answering system for the semantic web. In: Gómez-Pérez, A., Euzenat, J. (eds.) ESWC 2005. LNCS, vol. 3532, pp. 546–562. Springer, Heidelberg (2005). https://doi.org/10.1007/11431053_37

8. Malone, J., Brown, A., Lister, A.L., Ison, J., Hull, D., Parkinson, H., Stevens, R.: The software ontology (SWO): a resource for reproducibility in biomedical data analysis, curation and digital preservation. J. Biomed. Semant. **5**(1), 25 (2014)

9. Montiel-Ponsoda, E.: Multilingualism in Ontologies - Building Patterns and Representation Models. LAP Lambert Academic Publishing, Germany (2011)

10. Panov, P., Soldatova, L.N., Džeroski, S.: Generic ontology of datatypes. Inf. Sci. **329**, 900–920 (2016)

11. Parkkila, J., Radulovic, F., Garijo, D., Poveda-Villalón, M., Ikonen, J., Porras, J., Gómez-Pérez, A.: An ontology for videogame interoperability. Multimedia Tools Appl. **76**(4), 4981–5000 (2017)

12. Presutti, V., Daga, E., Gangemi, A., Blomqvist, E.: eXtreme design with content ontology design patterns. In: Proceedings of Workshop on Ontology Patterns (2009)

13. Ren, Y., Parvizi, A., Mellish, C., Pan, J.Z., van Deemter, K., Stevens, R.: Towards competency question-driven ontology authoring. In: Presutti, V., d'Amato, C., Gandon, F., d'Aquin, M., Staab, S., Tordai, A. (eds.) ESWC 2014. LNCS, vol. 8465, pp. 752–767. Springer, Cham (2014). https://doi.org/10.1007/978-3-319-07443-6_50

14. SmartM2M: SAREF extension investigation Technical report (TR 103 411)

15. Suárez-Figueroa, M.C., et al.: NeOn D5.1.1 NeOn Modelling Components (2007)

16. Suárez-Figueroa, M.C., Gómez-Pérez, A.: First attempt towards a standard glossary of ontology engineering terminology. In: Proceedings of 8th International Conference on Terminology and Knowledge Engineering (TKE 2008), p. 1 (2008)

17. Suárez-Figueroa, M.C., Gómez-Pérez, A., Fernandez-Lopez, M.: The NeOn methodology framework: a scenario-based methodology for ontology development. Appl. Ontol. **10**(2), 107–145 (2015)

18. Suárez-Figueroa, M.C., Gómez-Pérez, A., Villazón-Terrazas, B.: How to write and use the ontology requirements specification document. In: Meersman, R., Dillon, T., Herrero, P. (eds.) OTM 2009. LNCS, vol. 5871, pp. 966–982. Springer, Heidelberg (2009). https://doi.org/10.1007/978-3-642-05151-7_16
19. Zemmouchi-Ghomari, L., Ghomari, A.R.: Translating natural language competency questions into SPARQLQueries: a case study. In: The First International Conference on Building and Exploring Web Based Environments, pp. 81–86 (2013)

MMKG: Multi-modal Knowledge Graphs

Ye Liu[1(✉)], Hui Li[2], Alberto Garcia-Duran[3], Mathias Niepert[4],
Daniel Onoro-Rubio[4], and David S. Rosenblum[1]

[1] National University of Singapore, Singapore, Singapore
{liuye,david}comp.nus.edu.sg
[2] Xiamen University, Xiamen, China
huili.xmu@gmail.com
[3] EPFL, Lausanne, Switzerland
alberto.duran@epfl.ch
[4] NEC Labs Europe, Heidelberg, Germany
{mathias.niepert,daniel.onoro}@neclab.eu

Abstract. We present MMKG, a collection of three knowledge graphs
that contain both numerical features and (links to) images for all entities
as well as entity alignments between pairs of KGs. Therefore, multi-
relational link prediction and entity matching communities can benefit
from this resource. We believe this data set has the potential to facilitate
the development of novel multi-modal learning approaches for knowledge
graphs. We validate the utility of MMKG in the sameAs link prediction
task with an extensive set of experiments. These experiments show that
the task at hand benefits from learning of multiple feature types.

Github Repository: https://github.com/nle-ml/mmkb
Permanent URL: https://zenodo.org/record/1245698

1 Introduction

A large volume of human knowledge can be represented with a multi-relational
graph. Binary relationships encode *facts* that can be represented in the form of
RDF [11] type triples (head, predicate, tail), where head and tail are entities and predicate is the relation type. The combination of all triples form a
multi-relational graph, where nodes represent entities and directed edges represent relationships. The resulting multi-relational graph is often referred to as a
Knowledge Graph.

Knowledge Graphs (KGs) provide ways to efficiently organize, manage and
retrieve this type of information, being increasingly used as external source
of knowledge for a number of problems. While ranging from general purpose
(DBPEDIA [2] or FREEBASE [3]) to domain-specific (IMDB or UNIPROTKB),
KGs are often highly incomplete and, therefore, research has focused heavily on

---

Y. Liu, H. Li and A. Garcia-Duran—Contributed equally. Work done while at NEC
Labs Europe.

P. Hitzler et al. (Eds.): ESWC 2019, LNCS 11503, pp. 459–474, 2019.
https://doi.org/10.1007/978-3-030-21348-0_30

the problem of knowledge graph completion [15]. Link prediction [15], relationship extraction [18] and ontology matching [20] are some of the different ways to tackle the incompleteness problem.

Novel data sets for benchmarking knowledge graph completion approaches, therefore, are important contributions to the community. This is especially true since one method performing well on one data set might perform poorly on others [23]. With this paper we introduce MMKG (Multi-Modal Knowledge Graphs), a collection of three knowledge graphs for link prediction and entity matching research. Contrary to existing data sets, these knowledge graphs contain both numerical features and images for all entities as well as entity alignments between pairs of KGs. There is a fundamental difference between MMKG (Fig. 1) and other visual-relational resources (e.g. [12,24]). While MMKG is intended to perform relational reasoning across different entities and images, previous resources are intended to perform visual reasoning within the same image.

We use FREEBASE15K [4] as the blue print for the multi-modal knowledge graphs we constructed. FREEBASE15K is the major benchmark data set in the recent link prediction literature. In a first step, we aligned most FB15k entities to entities from DBPEDIA and YAGO through the sameAs links contained in DBPEDIA and YAGO dumps. Since the degree of a node relates to the probability of an entity to appear in a subsampled version of a KG, we use this measure to populate our versions of DBpedia and YAGO with more entities. For each knowledge graph, we include entities that are highly connected to the aligned entities so that the number of entities in each KG is similar to that of FB15K. Lastly, we have populated the three knowledge graphs with numeric literals and images for (almost) all of their entities. We name the two new data sets DBPE-DIA15K and YAGO15K. Although all three data sets contain a similar number of entities, this does not prevent potential users of MMKG from filtering out entities to benchmark approaches in scenarios where KGs largely differ with respect to the number of entities that they contain.

The contributions of the present paper are the following:

- The creation of two knowledge graphs DBPEDIA15K and YAGO15K, that are the DBPEDIA and YAGO [21] counterparts, respectively, of FREEBASE15K. Furthermore, all three KGs are enriched with numeric literals and image information, as well as sameAs predicates linking entities from pairs of knowledge graphs. sameAs predicates, numerical literals and (links to) images for entities so as the relational graph structure are released in separate files.
- We validate our hypothesis that knowledge graph completion related problems can benefit from multi-modal data:
  - We elaborate on a previous learning framework [9] and extend it by also incorporating image information. We perform completion in queries such as (head?, sameAs, tail) and (head, sameAs, tail?), where head and tail are entities, each one from a different KG. This task can be deemed something in-between link prediction and entity matching.
  - We analyze the performance of the different modalities in isolation for different percentages of known aligned entities between KGs, as well as for different combinations of feature types.

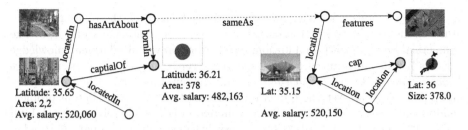

Fig. 1. Illustration of MMKG.

2   Relevance

There are a number of problems related to knowledge graph completion. *Named-entity linking* (NEL) [6] is the task of linking a named-entity mention from a text to an entity in a knowledge graph. Usually a NEL algorithm is followed by a second procedure, namely *relationship extraction* [18], which aims at linking relation mentions from text to a canonical relation type in a knowledge graph. Hence, relation extraction methods are often used in conjunction with NEL algorithms to perform KG completion from natural language content.

Link prediction and entity matching are two other popular tasks for knowledge graph completion. MMKG has been mainly created targeting these two tasks.

Link Prediction. It aims at answering completion queries of the form (`head?`, `predicate, tail`) or (`head, predicate, tail?`), where the answer is supposed to be always within the KG.

Entity Matching. Given two KGs, the goal is to find pairs of records, one from each KG, that refer to the same entity. For instance, `DBpedia:NYC` ≡ `FB:NewYork`.

2.1   Relevance for Multi-relational Link Prediction Research

The core of most of multi-relational link prediction approaches is a scoring function. The scoring function is a (differentiable) function whose parameters are learned such that it assigns high scores to true triples and low scores to triples assumed to be false. The majority of recent work fall into one of the following two categories:

1. Relational approaches [10,14] wherein features are given as logical formulas which are evaluated in the KG to determine the feature's value. For instance, the formula $\exists x$ (`A, bornIn`, x) $\wedge$ (x, `capitalOf, B`) corresponds to a binary feature which is 1 if there exists a path of that type from entity `A` to entity `B`, and 0 otherwise.
2. Latent approaches [15] learn fixed-size vector representations (embeddings) for all entities and relationships in the KG.

While previous work has almost exclusively focused on the relational structure of the graph, recent approaches have considered other feature types like numerical literals [9,17]. In addition, recent work on visual-relational knowledge graphs [16] has introduced novel visual query types such as "*How are these two unseen images related to each other?*" and has proposed novel machine learning methods to answer these queries. Different to the link prediction problem addressed in this work, the methods evaluated in [16] solely rely on visual data.

MMKG provides three data sets for evaluating multi-relational link prediction approaches where, in addition to the multi-relational links between entities, all entities have been associated with numerical and visual data. An interesting property of MMKG is that the three knowledge graphs are very heterogeneous (w.r.t. the number of relation types, their sparsity, and so on) as we show in Sect. 3. It is known that the performance of multi-relational link prediction methods depends on the characteristics of the specific knowledge graphs [23]. Therefore, MMKG is an important benchmark data set for measuring the robustness of the approaches.

2.2 Relevance for Entity Matching Research

There are numerous approaches to find sameAs links between entities of two different knowledge graphs. Though there are works [8] that solely incorporate the relational graph structure, there is an extensive literature on methods that perform the matching by combining relational structural information with literals of entities, where literals are used to compute prior confidence scores [13,20].

A large number of approaches of the entity matching literature have been evaluated as part of the Ontology Alignment Evaluation Initiative (OAEI) [1] using data sets such as YAGO, FREEBASE, and IMDB[13,20]. Contrary to the proposed multi-modal knowledge graph data sets, however, the OAEI does not focus on tasks with visual and numerical data. The main advantages of MMKG over existing benchmark data sets for entity matching are: (1) MMKG's entities are associated with visual and numerical data, and (2) the availability of ground truth entity alignments for a high percentage of the KG entities. The former encourages research in entity matching methods that incorporate visual and numerical data. The latter allows one to measure the robustness in performance of entity matching approaches with respect to the number of given alignments between two KGs. The benchmark KGs can also be used to evaluate different active learning strategies. Traditional active learning approaches ask a user for a small set of alignments that minimize the uncertainty and, therefore, maximize the quality of the final alignments.

3   MMKG: Dataset Generation

We chose FREEBASE-15K (FB15K), a data set that has been widely used in the knowledge graph completion literature, as a starting point to create the multi-modal knowledge graphs. Facts of this KG are in N-Triples format, a line-based plain text format for encoding an RDF graph. For example, the triple

Table 1. Files from which we extract the different subcomponents of MMKG.

DB15K	
sameAs	http://downloads.dbpedia.org/2016-10/core-i18n/en/freebase_links_en.ttl.bz2
Relational Graph	http://downloads.dbpedia.org/2016-10/core-i18n/en/mappingbased_objects_en.ttl.bz2
	http://downloads.dbpedia.org/2016-10/core-i18n/en/instance_types_en.ttl.bz2
Numeric Literals	http://downloads.dbpedia.org/2016-10/core-i18n/en/geo_coordinates_en.tql.bz2
	http://downloads.dbpedia.org/2016-10/core-i18n/en/mappingbased_literals_en.tql.bz2
	http://downloads.dbpedia.org/2016-10/core-i18n/en/persondata_en.tql.bz2
YAGO15K	
sameAs	http://resources.mpi-inf.mpg.de/yago-naga/yago3.1/yagoDBpediaInstances.ttl.7z
Relational Graph	http://resources.mpi-inf.mpg.de/yago-naga/yago3.1/yagoFacts.ttl.7z
Numeric Literals	http://resources.mpi-inf.mpg.de/yago-naga/yago3.1/yagoDateFacts.ttl.7z
	http://resources.mpi-inf.mpg.de/yago-naga/yago3.1/yagoGeonamesOnlyData.ttl.7z

Table 2. Statistics of the MMKG knowledge graphs.

KG	#Entities	#Relationships	Number of triples			
			Relational Graph	Numeric Literals	Images	sameAs
FB15k	14,951	1,345	592,213	29,395	13,444	-
DB15k	14,777	279	99,028	46,121	12,841	12,846
Yago15k	15,283	32	122,886	48,405	11,194	11,199

</ns/g.112ygbz6> </ns/type.object.type> </ns/film.film>.

indicates that the entity with identifier </ns/g.112ygbz6> is connected to the entity with identifier </ns/film.film> via the relationship </ns/type.object.type>.

We create versions of DBPEDIA and YAGO, called DBPEDIA-15K (DB15K) and YAGO15K, by aligning entities in FB15K with entities in these other knowledge graphs. More concretely, for DB15K we performed the following steps.

1. **sameAs.** We extract alignments between entities of FB15K and DBPEDIA in order to create DB15K. These alignments link one entity from FB15K to one from DBPEDIA via a sameAs relation.
2. **Relational Graph.** A high percentage of entities from FB15K can be aligned with entities in DBPEDIA. However, to make the two knowledge graphs have roughly the same number of entities and to also have entities that cannot be aligned across the knowledge graphs, we include additional entities in DB15K. We chose entities with the highest connectivity to the already aligned entities to complete DB15K. We then collect all the triples where both head and tail entities belong to the set of entities of DB15K. This collection of triples forms the relational graph structure of DB15K.
3. **Numeric Literals.** We collect all triples that associate entities in DB15K with numerical literals. For example, the relations /location/geocode/ latitude links entities to their latitude. We refer to these relation types as numerical relations. Figure 2 shows the most common numerical

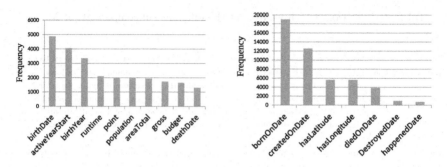

Fig. 2. Most common numerical relationships in DB15K (left) and YAGO15K (right).

relationships in the knowledge graphs. In previous work [9] we have extracted numeric literals for FB15K only.

4. **Images.** We obtain images related to each of the entities of FB15K. To do so we implemented a web crawler that is able to parse query results for the image search engines Google Images, Bing Images, and Yahoo Image Search. To minimize the amount of noise due to polysemous entity labels (for example, there are two FREEBASE entities with the text label "Paris") we extracted, for each entity in FB15K, all Wikipedia URIs from the 1.9 billion triple FREEBASE RDF dump[1]. For instance, for Paris, we obtained URIs such as `Paris(ile-de-France,France)` and `Paris(City_of_New_Orleans, Louisiana)`. These URIs were processed and used as search queries for disambiguation purposes. We crawled web images also following other type of search queries, and not only the Wikipedia URIs. For example, we used (i) the entity name, and (ii) the entity name followed by the entity's notable type as query strings, among others. After visual inspection of polysemous entities (as they are the most problematic entities), we observed that using Wikipedia URIs as query strings was the strategy that alleviated most the polysemy problem. We used the crawler to download a number of images per entity. For each entity we stored the 20 top ranked images retrieved by each browser. We filtered out images with a side smaller than 224 pixels, and images with a side 2.5 bigger than the other. We also removed corrupted, low quality, and duplicate images (pairs of images with a pixel-wise distance below a certain threshold). After all these steps, we kept 55.8 images per entity on average. We also scaled the images to have a maximum height or width of 500 pixels while maintaining their aspect ratio. Finally, for each entity we distribute a distinct image to FB15K and DB15K.

We repeat the same sequence of steps for the creation of YAGO15K with one difference. `sameAs` predicates from the YAGO dump align entities from that knowledge graph to DBPEDIA entities. We used them along with the previously extracted alignments between DB15K and FB15K to eventually create the alignment between YAGO and FB15K entities. Table 1 depicts the hyperlinks from where we extracted the different component for the generation of DB15K and YAGO15K.

---

[1] https://developers.google.com/freebase/.

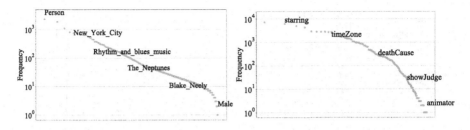

Fig. 3. Entity (left) and relation type (right) frequencies in YAGO15K.

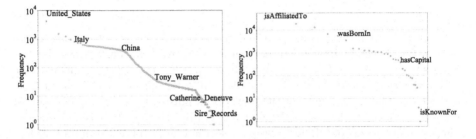

Fig. 4. Entity (left) and relation type (right) frequencies in DB15K.

Statistics of FB15K, DB15K and YAGO15K are depicted in Table 2. The frequency of entities and relationships in YAGO15K and DB15K are depicted in Figs. 3 and 4, respectively. Entities and relationships are sorted according to their frequency. They show in logarithmic scale the number of times that each entity and relationship occurs in YAGO15K and DB15K. Relationships like `starring` or `timeZone` occur quite frequently in YAGO15K, while others like `animator` are rare. Contrary to FB15K, the entity `Male` is unusual in YAGO15K, which illustrates, to a limited extent, the heterogeneity of the KGs.

3.1 Availability and Sustainability

MMKG can be found in the Github repository https://github.com/nle-ml. We will actively use Github issues to track feature requests and bug reports. The documentation of the framework has been published on the repository's Wiki as well. To guarantee the future availability of the resource, it has also been published on Zenodo. MMKG is released under the BSD-3-Clause License.

The repository contains a number of files, all of them formatted following the N-Triples guidelines (https://www.w3.org/TR/n-triples/). These files contain information regarding the relational graph structure, numeric literals and visual information. Numerical information is formatted as RDF literals, entities and relationships point to their corresponding RDF URIs[2]. We also provide separates files that link both DB15K and YAGO15K entities to FB15K ones via `sameAs` predicates, also formatted as N-Triples.

---

[2] Unfortunately, Freebase has deprecated RDF URIs.

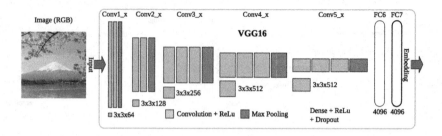

Fig. 5. Low-dimensional embeddings learned for images through VGG16.

To avoid copyright infringement and guarantee the access to the visual information (i.e. URLs to images are not permanent), we learn embeddings for the images through the VGG16 model introduced in [19]. The VGG16 model used for this work was previously trained on the ILSVRC 2012 data set derived from IMA-GENET [5]. The architecture of this network is illustrated in Fig. 5. We remove the softmax layer of the trained VGG16 and obtain the 4096-dimensional embeddings for all images of MMKG. We provide these embeddings in hdf5 [22] format. The Github repository contains documentation on how to access these embeddings. Alternatively, one can use the crawler (also available in the Github repository) to download the images from the different search engines.

4   Technical Quality of MMKG

We provide empirical evidence that knowledge graph completion related tasks can benefit from the multi-modal data of MMKG. Our hypothesis is that different data modalities contain complementary information beneficial for both multi-relational link prediction and entity matching. For instance, in the entity matching problem if two images are visually similar they are likely to be associated with the same entity and if two entities in two different KGs have similar numerical feature values, they are more likely to be identical. Similarly, we hypothesize that multi-relational link prediction can benefit from the different data modalities. For example, learning that the mean difference of birth years is 0.4 for the Freebase relation /people/marriage/spouse, can provide helpful evidence for the linking task.

In recent years, numerous methods for merging feature types have been proposed. The most common strategy is the concatenation of either the input features or some intermediate learned representation. We compare these strategies to the recently proposed learning framework [9], which we have found to be superior to the concatenation and an ensemble type of approach.

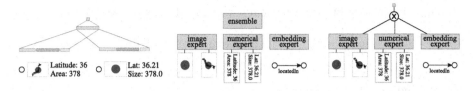

Fig. 6. Illustration of the methods we evaluated to combine various data modalities.

4.1   Task: SAMEAS Link Prediction

We validate the hypothesis that different modalities are complementary for the `sameAs` link prediction task. Different to the standard link prediction problem, here the goal is to answer queries such as (`head?,sameAs,tail`) or (`head,sameAs,tail?`) where `head` and `tail` are entities from different KGs. We do not make the one-to-one alignment assumption, that is, the assumption that one entity in one KG is identical to exactly (at most) one in the other. A second difference is that in the evaluation of the SAMEAS prediction task, and in general in the link prediction literature, *only* one argument of a triple is assumed to be missing at a time. That partial knowledge of the ground truth is not given in the entity matching literature.

4.2   Model: Products of Experts

We elaborate on previous work [9] and extend it by incorporating visual information. Such learning framework can be stated as a Product of Experts (PoE).

In general, a PoE's probability distribution is

$$p(\mathbf{d} \mid \theta_1, ..., \theta_n) = \frac{\prod_i f_i(\mathbf{d} \mid \theta_i)}{\sum_{\mathbf{c}} \prod_i f_i(\mathbf{c} \mid \theta_i)},$$

where $\mathbf{d}$ is a data vector in a discrete space, θ_i are the parameters of individual model f_i, $f_i(\mathbf{d} \mid \phi_i)$ is the value of d under model f_i, and the $\mathbf{c}$'s index all possible vectors in the data space. The PoE model is now trained to assign high probability to observed data vectors.

In the KG context, the data vector $\mathbf{d}$ is always a triple $\mathbf{d} = (\mathbf{h}, \mathbf{r}, \mathbf{t})$ and the objective is to learn a PoE that assigns high probability to true triples and low probabilities to triples assumed to be false. For instance, the triple (`Paris,locatedIn,France`) should be assigned a high probability and the triple (`Paris,locatedIn,Germany`) a low probability. If $(\mathbf{h}, \mathbf{r}, \mathbf{t})$ holds in the KG, the pair's vector representations are used as positive training examples. Let $\mathbf{d} = (\mathbf{h}, \mathbf{r}, \mathbf{t})$. We can now define one individual expert $f_{(\mathbf{r},\mathbf{F})}(\mathbf{d} \mid \phi_{(\mathbf{r},\mathbf{F})})$ for each (relation type $\mathbf{r}$, feature type $\mathbf{F}$) pair

$$f_{(\mathbf{r},\mathbf{L})}(\mathbf{d} \mid \theta_{(\mathbf{r},\mathbf{L})}) : \text{the embedding expert for relation type } \mathbf{r}$$
$$f_{(\mathbf{r},\mathbf{R})}(\mathbf{d} \mid \theta_{(\mathbf{r},\mathbf{R})}) : \text{the relational expert for relation type } \mathbf{r}$$
$$f_{(\mathbf{r},\mathbf{N})}(\mathbf{d} \mid \theta_{(\mathbf{r},\mathbf{N})}) : \text{the numerical expert for relation type } \mathbf{r}$$
$$f_{(\mathbf{sameAs},\mathbf{I})}(\mathbf{d} \mid \theta_{(\mathbf{r},\mathbf{I})}) : \text{the visual expert for relation type } \mathbf{sameAs}$$

The joint probability for a triple $d = (h, r, t)$ of the PoE model is now

$$p(d \mid \theta_1, ..., \theta_n) = \frac{\prod_{F \in \{R,L,N,I\}} f_{(r,F)}(d \mid \theta_{(r,F)})}{\sum_c \prod_{F \in \{R,L,N,I\}} f_{(r,F)}(c \mid \theta_{(r,F)}))},$$

where c indexes all possible triples.

For information regarding the latent, relational and numerical experts, we refer the reader to [9]. Although entity names are not used to infer sameAs links in this work, one may also define an expert for such feature.

Visual Experts. The visual expert is only learned for the sameAs relation type. The scores for the image experts is computed by the cosine similarity between two 4096-dimensional feature vectors from the two images.

Let $d = (h, r, t)$ be a triple. The visual expert for relation type r is defined as

$$f_{(r,I)}(d \mid \theta_{(r,I)}) = \exp(i_h \cdot i_t) \text{ and}$$
$$f_{(r',I)}(d \mid \theta_{(r',I)}) = 1 \text{ for all } r' \neq r,$$

where $\cdot$ is the dot product and i_h and i_t are embeddings of the images for the head and tail entities.

Learning. The logarithmic loss for the given training triples $\mathbf{T}$ is defined as

$$\mathcal{L} = -\sum_{t \in \mathbf{T}} \log p(t \mid \theta_1, ..., \theta_n).$$

To fit the PoE to the training triples, we follow the derivative of the log likelihood of each observed triple $d \in \mathbf{T}$ under the PoE

$$\frac{\partial \log p(d \mid \theta_1, ..., \theta_n)}{\partial \theta_m} = \frac{\partial \log f_i(d \mid \theta_i)}{\partial \theta_m} - \frac{\partial \log \sum_c \prod_i f_i(c \mid \theta_i)}{\partial \theta_m}$$

We follow [9] and we generate for each triple $d = (h, r, t)$ a set $\mathbf{E}$ consisting of N triples (h, r, t') by sampling exactly N entities t' uniformly at random from the set of all entities. In doing so, the right term is then approximated by

$$\frac{\partial \log \sum_{c \in \mathbf{E}} \prod_i f_i(c \mid \theta_i)}{\partial \theta_m}.$$

This is often referred to as negative sampling.

4.3   Additional Baseline Approaches

Apart from the product of experts, we also evaluate other approaches to combine various data modalities. All the evaluated approaches are illustrated in Fig. 6.

Concatenation. Given pairs of aligned entities, each pair is characterized by a single vector wherein all modality features of both entities are concatenated. For each pair of aligned entities we create a number of negative alignments, each of which is also characterized by a concatenation of all modality features of both entities. A logistic regression is trained taking these vectors as input, and their corresponding class label ($+1$ and -1 for positive and negative alignments, respectively). The output of the logistic regression indicates the posterior probability of two entities being the same. In Sect. 5 we refer to this approach as CONCAT.

Ensemble. The ensemble approach combines the various expert models into an ensemble classifier. Instead of training the experts jointly and end-to-end, here each of the expert models is first trained independently. At test time, the scores of the expert models are added and used to rank the entities. We refer to this approach as ENSEMBLE.

5   Experiments

We conducted experiments on two pairs of knowledge graphs of MMKG, namely, (FB15K *vs.* DB15K and YAGO15K *vs.* FB15K). We evaluate a number of different instances of the product of experts (PoE) model, as well as the other baseline methods, in the sameAs prediction task. Because of its similarity with link prediction, we use metrics commonly used for this task. The main objective of the experiments is to demonstrate that MMKG is suitable for the task at hand, and specifically that the related problems can benefit from learning of multiple feature types.

5.1   Evaluation

MMKG allows to experiment with different percentages of aligned entities between KGs. These alignments are given by the sameAs predicates that we previously found. We evaluate the impact of the different modalities in scenarios wherein the number of given alignments P [%] between two KGs is low, medium and high. We reckon that such scenarios would correspond to 20%, 50% and 80% out of all sameAs predicates, respectively. We use these alignments along with the two KGs as part of our observed triples **T**, and split equally the remaining sameAs triples into validation and test.

We use AMIE+ [7] to mine relational features for the relational experts. We used the standard settings of AMIE+ with the exception that the minimum absolute support was set to 2 and the maximum number of entities involved in the rule to four. The latter is important to guarantee that AMIE+ retrieves rules like $(x, \mathbf{r_1}, w), (w, \mathsf{SameAs}, z), (z, \mathbf{r_2}, y) \Rightarrow (x, \mathsf{SameAs}, y)$, wherein $\mathbf{r_1}$ is a relationship that belongs to the one KG, and $\mathbf{r_2}$ to the other KG. One example of retrieved rule by AMIE+ is:

$$(x, \mathtt{father\_of}_{\mathsf{DB15k}}, w), (w, \mathsf{SameAs}, z), (z, \mathtt{children\_of}_{\mathsf{FB15k}}, y) \Rightarrow (x, \mathsf{SameAs}, y)$$

Table 3. sameAs queries for which numerical experts led to good performance. Left and right column correspond to FB15K and DB15K, respectively.

/m/015dcj		Marc_Christian	
date_of_birth	1925.11	birthDate	1925.11
date_of_death	1985.10	deathDate	1985.10
height_meters	1.93	height	1.9558
/m/07zhjj		How_i_met_your_mother	
number_of_seasons	9.0	numberOfSeasons	9.0
air_date_of_final_episode	2014.03	completionDate	2014.03
number_of_episodes	208.0	numberOfEpisodes	208.0

Fig. 7. sameAs queries for which visual experts led to good performance. Left and right images within each pair correspond to FB15K and DB15K, respectively.

In this case both father_of$_{DB15k}$ and children_of$_{FB15k}$ are (almost) functional relationships. A relationship r is said to be functional if an entity can only be mapped exactly to one single entity via r. The relational expert will learn that the body of this rule leads to a sameAs relationship between entities x and y and with a very high likelihood.

We used ADAM for parameter learning in a mini-batch setting with a learning rate of 0.001, the categorical cross-entropy as loss function and the number of epochs was set to 100. We validated every 5 epochs and stopped learning whenever the MRR (Mean Reciprocal Rank) values on the validation set decreased. The batch size was set to 512 and the number N of negative samples to 500 for all experiments.

We follow the same evaluation procedure as previous works of the link prediction literature. Therefore, we measure the ability to answer completion queries of the form (h, SameAs, t?) and (h?, SameAs, t). For queries of the form (h, SameAs, t?), wherein h is an entity of the first KG, we replaced the tail by each of the second KB's entities in turn, sorted the triples based on the scores or probabilities, and computed the rank of the correct entity. We repeated the

Table 4. sameAs prediction on FB15K-DB15K for different percentages of P.

P [%]	20%			50%			80%		
	MRR	Hits@1	Hits@10	MRR	Hits@1	Hits@10	MRR	Hits@1	Hits@10
PoE-n	12.8	10.1	18.6	23.0	16.8	34.1	28.2	21.8	37.4
PoE-r	12.9	10.7	16.5	26.3	22.9	31.7	35.9	33.6	38.6
PoE-l	12.2	7.9	20.3	42.8	34.9	58.2	63.1	55.6	76.6
PoE-i	1.6	0.8	2.7	2.3	1.3	3.8	3.3	1.7	5.9
PoE-lni	16.7	12.0	25.6	48.1	40.9	62.1	68.5	62.0	79.3
PoE-rni	**28.3**	**23.2**	**39.0**	44.2	38.0	55.7	55.8	50.2	64.1
PoE-lri	12.5	8.8	19.1	40.4	33.4	53.9	67.0	60.3	78.3
PoE-lrn	16.0	11.5	24.1	47.9	41.2	60.3	67.1	60.6	79.1
PoE-$lrni$	17.0	12.6	25.1	**53.3**	**46.4**	**65.8**	**72.1**	**66.6**	**82.0**

Table 5. sameAs prediction on FB15K-YAGO15K for different percentages of P.

P [%]	20%			50%			80%		
	MRR	Hits@1	Hits@10	MRR	Hits@1	Hits@10	MRR	Hits@1	Hits@10
PoE-n	22.2	15.4	33.7	38.9	29.7	56.1	35.8	27.1	53.5
PoE-r	9.9	8.4	12.3	20.0	18.0	23.1	29.9	28.1	31.9
PoE-l	10.1	6.4	16.9	32.0	25.8	44.1	50.5	43.7	63.6
PoE-i	1.4	2.4	0.7	2.0	1.1	3.2	3.2	1.7	5.5
PoE-lni	15.4	10.9	24.1	39.8	32.8	52.6	59.0	52.5	70.5
PoE-rni	**33.4**	**25.0**	**49.5**	**49.8**	**41.1**	**66.9**	57.2	49.2	70.5
PoE-lri	11.3	7.7	18.1	34.0	28.1	44.7	55.5	49.3	66.7
PoE-lrn	13.9	10.2	20.9	37.3	31.6	47.4	57.7	51.3	68.9
PoE-$lrni$	15.4	11.3	22.9	41.4	34.7	53.6	**63.5**	**57.3**	**74.6**

same process for the queries of type (h?, SameAs, t), wherein t in this case corresponds to an entity of the second KG and we iterate over the entities of the first KG to compute the scores. The mean of all computed ranks is the Mean Rank (lower is better) and the fraction of correct entities ranked in the top n is called hits@n (higher is better). We also computer the Mean Reciprocal Rank (higher is better) which is an evaluation metric that is less susceptible to outliers. Note that the filtered setting described in [4] does not make sense in this problem, since an entity can be linked to an entity via a SameAs relationship only once.

We report the performance of the PoE in its full scope in Tables 4 and 5. We also show feature ablation experiments, each of which corresponds to removing one modality from the full set. The performance of each modality in isolation is also depicted. We use the abbreviations PoE-*suffix* to refer to the different

Table 6. Performance comparison for $P = 80\%$.

		MRR	HITS@1	HITS@10
	CONCAT	2.1	1.7	2.7
FB-DB	ENSEMBLE	40.1	34.3	50.2
	PoE-*lrni*	**72.1**	**66.6**	**82.0**
	CONCAT	0.18	0.18	0.04
FB-YAGO	ENSEMBLE	47.6	42.3	57.5
	PoE-*lrni*	**63.5**	**57.3**	**74.6**

instances of PoE. *suffix* is a combination of the letters L (Latent), R (Relational), N (Numerical) and I (Image) to indicate the inclusion of each of the four feature types. Generalizations are complicated to make, given that performance of PoE's instances differ across percentages of aligned entities and pairs of knowledge graphs. Nevertheless, there are two instances of our PoE approach, PoE-*lrni* and PoE-*rni*, that tend to outperform all others for low and high percentages of aligned entities, respectively. Results seem to indicate that the embedding expert response dominates over others, and hence its addition to PoE harms the performance when such expert is not the best-performing one. Table 3 and Fig. 7 provides examples of queries where numerical and visual information led to good performance, respectively. It is hard to find one specific reason that explains when adding numerical and visual information is beneficial for the task at hand. For example, there are entities with a more canonical visual representation than others. This relates to the difficulty of learning from visual data in the sameAs link prediction problem, as visual similarity largely varies across entities. Similarly, the availability of numerical attributes largely varies even for entities of the same type within a KG. However, Tables 4 and 5 provide empirical evidence of the benefit from including additional modalities.

Table 6 depicts results for the best-performing instance of PoE and baselines discussed in Sect. 4. The best performing instance of PoE significantly outperforms the approaches CONCAT and ENSEMBLE. This validates the choice of the PoE approach, which can incorporate data modalities to the link prediction problem in a principled manner.

6   Conclusion

We present MMKG, a collection of three knowledge graphs that contain multimodal data, to benchmark link prediction and entity matching approaches. An extensive set of experiments validate the utility of the data set in the sameAs link prediction task.

References

1. Achichi, M., et al.: Results of the ontology alignment evaluation initiative 2016. In: OM: Ontology Matching, pp. 73–129 (2016). No commercial editor
2. Auer, S., Bizer, C., Kobilarov, G., Lehmann, J., Cyganiak, R., Ives, Z.: DBpedia: a nucleus for a web of open data. In: Aberer, K., et al. (eds.) ASWC/ISWC -2007. LNCS, vol. 4825, pp. 722–735. Springer, Heidelberg (2007). https://doi.org/10.1007/978-3-540-76298-0_52
3. Bollacker, K.D., Evans, C., Paritosh, P., Sturge, T., Taylor, J.: Freebase: a collaboratively created graph database for structuring human knowledge. In: SIGMOD Conference, pp. 1247–1250 (2008)
4. Bordes, A., Usunier, N., García-Durán, A., Weston, J., Yakhnenko, O.: Translating embeddings for modeling multi-relational data. In: NIPS, pp. 2787–2795 (2013)
5. Deng, J., Dong, W., Socher, R., Li, L.J., Li, K., Fei-Fei, L.: ImageNet: a large-scale hierarchical image database. In: 2009 IEEE Conference on Computer Vision and Pattern Recognition, CVPR 2009, pp. 248–255. IEEE (2009)
6. Dredze, M., McNamee, P., Rao, D., Gerber, A., Finin, T.: Entity disambiguation for knowledge base population. In: Proceedings of the 23rd International Conference on Computational Linguistics, pp. 277–285. Association for Computational Linguistics (2010)
7. Galárraga, L., Teflioudi, C., Hose, K., Suchanek, F.M.: Fast rule mining in ontological knowledge bases with AMIE+. VLDB J. **24**(6), 707–730 (2015)
8. Galárraga, L.A., Preda, N., Suchanek, F.M.: Mining rules to align knowledge bases. In: Proceedings of the 2013 Workshop on Automated Knowledge Base Construction, pp. 43–48. ACM (2013)
9. Garcia-Duran, A., Niepert, M.: KBLRN: end-to-end learning of knowledge base representations with latent, relational, and numerical features. In: Uncertainty in Artificial Intelligence Proceedings of the 34th Conference (2018)
10. Gardner, M., Mitchell, T.M.: Efficient and expressive knowledge base completion using subgraph feature extraction. In: EMNLP, pp. 1488–1498 (2015)
11. Klyne, G., Carroll, J.J., McBride, B.: Resource description framework (RDF): concepts and abstract syntax. W3C Recommendation, February 2004
12. Krishna, R., et al.: Visual genome: connecting language and vision using crowdsourced dense image annotations (2016). https://arxiv.org/abs/1602.07332
13. Lacoste-Julien, S., Palla, K., Davies, A., Kasneci, G., Graepel, T., Ghahramani, Z.: SiGMa: simple greedy matching for aligning large knowledge bases. In: Proceedings of the 19th ACM SIGKDD International Conference on Knowledge Discovery and Data Mining, pp. 572–580. ACM (2013)
14. Lao, N., Mitchell, T., Cohen, W.W.: Random walk inference and learning in a large scale knowledge base. In: EMNLP, pp. 529–539 (2011)
15. Nickel, M., Murphy, K., Tresp, V., Gabrilovich, E.: A review of relational machine learning for knowledge graphs. Proc. IEEE **104**(1), 11–33 (2016)
16. Oñoro-Rubio, D., Niepert, M., García-Durán, A., González-Sánchez, R., López-Sastre, R.J.: Representation learning for visual-relational knowledge graphs. arXiv preprint arXiv:1709.02314 (2017)
17. Pezeshkpour, P., Chen, L., Singh, S.: Embedding multimodal relational data for knowledge base completion. In: EMNLP (2018)
18. Riedel, S., Yao, L., McCallum, A., Marlin, B.M.: Relation extraction with matrix factorization and universal schemas. In: Proceedings of the 2013 Conference of the North American Chapter of the Association for Computational Linguistics: Human Language Technologies, pp. 74–84 (2013)

19. Simonyan, K., Zisserman, A.: Very deep convolutional networks for large-scale image recognition. arXiv preprint arXiv:1409.1556 (2014)
20. Suchanek, F.M., Abiteboul, S., Senellart, P.: PARIS: probabilistic alignment of relations, instances, and schema. Proc. VLDB Endow. **5**(3), 157–168 (2011)
21. Suchanek, F.M., Kasneci, G., Weikum, G.: YAGO: a core of semantic knowledge. In: Proceedings of the 16th International Conference on World Wide Web, pp. 697–706. ACM (2007)
22. The HDF Group: Hierarchical Data Format, version 5 (1997-NNNN). http://www.hdfgroup.org/HDF5/
23. Toutanova, K., Chen, D.: Observed versus latent features for knowledge base and text inference. In: Proceedings of the 3rd Workshop on Continuous Vector Space Models and their Compositionality, pp. 57–66 (2015)
24. Wu, Q., Wang, P., Shen, C., Dick, A., van den Hengel, A.: Ask me anything: free-form visual question answering based on knowledge from external sources. In: Proceedings of the IEEE Conference on Computer Vision and Pattern Recognition, pp. 4622–4630 (2016)

BeSEPPI: Semantic-Based Benchmarking of Property Path Implementations

Adrian Skubella[1(✉)], Daniel Janke[1], and Steffen Staab[1,2]

[1] Institute for Web Science and Technologies, Universität Koblenz-Landau,
Koblenz, Germany
{skubella,danijank,staab}@uni-koblenz.de
[2] Web and Internet Science Group, University of Southampton, Southampton, UK
s.r.staab@soton.ac.uk
http://west.uni-koblenz.de/, http://wais.ecs.soton.ac.uk/

Abstract. In 2013 property paths were introduced with the release of
SPARQL 1.1. These property paths allow for describing complex queries
in a more concise and comprehensive way. The W3C introduced a formal
specification of the semantics of property paths, to which implementations
should adhere. Most commonly used RDF stores claim to support property paths. In order to give insight into how well current implementations
of property paths work we have developed BeSEPPI, a benchmark for the
semantic-based evaluation of property path implementations. BeSEPPI
checks whether RDF stores follow the W3Cs semantics by testing the correctness and completeness of query result sets. The results of our benchmark show that only one out of 5 benchmarked RDF stores returns complete and correct result sets for all benchmark queries.

1 Introduction

The SPARQL Protocol and RDF Query Language (SPARQL) is the standard
query language for RDF stores. In 2013 property paths were introduced with
SPARQL 1.1. Property paths allow for describing paths of arbitrary length
in graphs, which cannot be described with a single SPARQL 1.0 query. For
instance, all friends of a friend of a friend etc. from a social network cannot be
retrieved with a single SPARQL 1.0 query. With property paths the construct
foaf:knows* could be used to obtain all desired results with a single query.
Furthermore, property paths provide a more concise way to formulate queries.
A query that should return all friends of a friend in a social network could use
the construct foaf:knows/foaf:knows.

In [13] it is shown that more and more queries containing property paths
are run against the Wikipedia Knowledge Graph. For instance, of all queries
scheduled in January 2018, over 20% contained property paths. In order to ensure
that queries containing property paths return the same result sets independently
of the used RDF store, the W3C released the official semantics of property
paths in [9].

© Springer Nature Switzerland AG 2019
P. Hitzler et al. (Eds.): ESWC 2019, LNCS 11503, pp. 475–490, 2019.
https://doi.org/10.1007/978-3-030-21348-0_31

The comparison of query execution times is only meaningful, if the result sets are complete and correct. Therefore, we have developed a benchmark for semantic-based evaluation of property path implementations (*BeSEPPI*). BeSEPPI does not only measure the execution times of property path queries, but also provides unit tests to check if the result sets are complete and correct based on the W3Cs semantics (see Sect. 3). Our benchmark comes with 236 queries and respective reference result sets, testing various semantic aspects of property paths. Thus, BeSEPPI may also be used by RDF store developers as a unit test to analyze their own implementation of property paths.

We used BeSEPPI to evaluate Blazegraph, AllegroGraph, Virtuoso, RDF4J and Apache Jena Fuseki (see Sect. 4). Due to space limitations we omit the evaluation of the execution times in this paper. The interested reader may refer to the technical report [17]. Our evaluation of correctness and completeness of result sets indicates that most RDF stores do not adhere to the W3Cs semantics completely. The original contributions of this paper[1] are:

1. BeSEPPI: A benchmark testing the execution times as well as the result set correctness and completeness of property path queries (see Sect. 3).
2. An extensive evaluation of 5 common RDF stores (see Sect. 4).

2   Preliminaries

In the following, common definitions for RDF, SPARQL and property paths based on [1,6] and [12] are given in order to define the terminology used in this work.

2.1   Graph

The Resource Description Framework (RDF) [16] is a general-purpose language for representing information in the web. It uses triples to represent the information as directed, labeled graphs. A graphical representation of an RDF dataset is shown in Fig. 1. For better legibility prefixes can be used to abbreviate IRIs. An example for such a prefix is given by PREFIX ppb: <http://ppbenchmark.com/>. This prefix defines that for instance ppb:B1 means <http://www.ppbenchmark.com/B1>.

Definition 1 (RDF triple)
A triple $(s, p, o) \in (I \cup B) \times I \times (I \cup B \cup L)$ *is called* RDF triple *where* I, L *and* B *are disjoint sets of IRIs, literals and blank nodes, respectively. Furthermore,* s *is called the* subject, p *the* predicate *and* o *the* object *of the triple* [1].

---

[1] We have presented some preliminary results in a non-archival workshop contribution in [11]. For this paper, we have improved the benchmark by creating a larger variety of queries as well as their correct results sets. These queries are a unit test to check whether property paths implementations adhere to the W3C's semantics.

Definition 2 (RDF graph)
An RDF graph G is a finite set of RDF triples. Furthermore, the subjects and objects occurring in G are vertices and occurring predicates are edges in G. $\mathcal{V}_G$ is the set of all vertex labels *in G and $\mathcal{E}_G$ is the* set of all edge labels *in G.*

Definition 3 (RDF term)
An RDF term t is an element of $I \cup L \cup B$. The set of all RDF terms *in a graph G is denoted by T_G.*

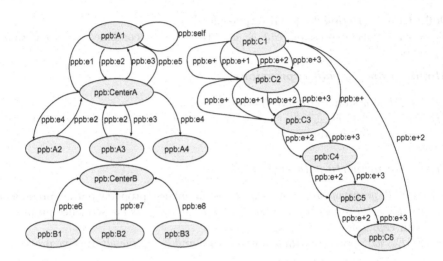

Fig. 1. RDF graphs that are part of BeSEPPI.

Definition 4 (Path and Cycle)
A path $P = \ll v_0, e_1, v_1, e_2, v_2, ..., e_n, v_n \gg$ in an RDF graph G connects two vertices v_0 and v_n with each other. In a path v_i are vertices, e_i are edges, $\forall i, j \in [0, n-1] : i \neq j \Rightarrow v_i \neq v_j$ and $\forall i \in [1, n-1] : v_i \neq v_n$. A path is called cycle *if $v_0 = v_n$. Furthermore, the* path length *is defined by the number of edges between v_0 and v_n.*[2]

Example 1. An example for a path between the vertices ppb:A1 and ppb:A3 in Fig. 1 is: $P = \ll$ppb:A1, ppb:e1, ppb:CenterA, ppb:e3, ppb:A3$\gg$. The length of this path is 2. Moreover, a *self loop* is a cycle of length one. In case of Fig. 1 the path $P = \ll$ppb:A1, ppb:eSelf, ppb:A1$\gg$ is a self loop.

---

[2] With our definition of paths, we do not allow cycles to appear within a path. We use this definition since the auxiliary function ALP which is used by the transitive and transitive reflexive property path expression in the W3Cs semantics of property paths [9] uses the same definition of paths.

2.2 SPARQL 1.1 Property Paths

The *SPARQL Protocol and RDF Query Language (SPARQL)* 1.1 is used to query RDF graphs. In the following section the syntax and semantics of the subset of SPARQL 1.1 that is needed for this paper is introduced. The syntax and semantics of property paths are defined following the semantic specification of the W3C in [9].[3]

Syntax

Definition 5 (Property path expression)
A property path expression *can be an* atomic *or a* combined *property path expression.*

Atomic property path expressions:

(1) iri $\in I$ is a simple property path expression.
(2) !$(iri_1|...|iri_n| \hat{\ }iri_{n+1}|...| \hat{\ }iri_m)$ *with* $iri_1,...iri_m \in I$ *is the* negated and inverse negated property set.

Combined property path expressions:

(3) $\hat{\ }E$ with property path expression E, is the inverse property path expression.
(4) E_1/E_2, with property path expressions E_1 and E_2, is the sequence property path *expression.*
(5) $E_1|E_2$, with property path expressions E_1 and E_2, is the alternative property path expression.
(6) E? with property path expression E is the existential property path expression.
(7) $E*$, with property path expression E, is the transitive reflexive closure property path expression.
(8) $E+$, with property path expression E, is the transitive closure property path *expression.*
(9) (E), groups the expression E.

Example 2 An example for an existential property path expression with the IRI `ppb:e1` is `ppb:e1?`.

Definition 6 (Property path)
A property path P is defined as sEo where $s \in V \cup I \cup L \cup B$, $o \in V \cup I \cup L \cup B$ and E is a property path expression.

Example 3. An example for a property path with an existential property path expression and the variable *?o* is *ppb:notExisting ppb:e1? ?o.*

---

[3] The notation of property path semantics presented in this section, is based on the definitions of property paths in [12].

Definition 7 (Property path Query)
If P is a property path and V' is a set of variables, then **SELECT** V' **WHERE** $\{P\}$
and **SELECT * WHERE** $\{P\}$ *are* SELECT *queries.*
If P is a property path, then **ASK WHERE** $\{P\}$ *is an* ASK *query [15].*

Example 4. An example of a SELECT property path query with one variable is
shown in Listing 1.1.

```
PREFIX ppb:   <http://www.ppbenchmark.com/>
SELECT ?o WHERE {ppb:notExisting ppb:e1? ?o.}
```

Listing 1.1. Example of a SELECT property path query.

Semantics

Definition 8 (Evaluation of property path expressions)[4]
Γ *denotes a set of vertex labels with* $\Gamma \supseteq \mathcal{V}_G$ *and* $p, iri_1..iri_m \in I$. *The evaluation*
$[[E]]_G$ *of a property path expression E over an RDF graph G is a subset of*
$(I \cup L \cup B)^2$ *defined as follows:*

$$(1)[[p]]_G^\Gamma := \{(s,o)|(s,p,o) \in G\}$$

$$(2a)[[!(iri_1|...|iri_n)]]_G^\Gamma := \{(s,o)|(s,p,o) \in G \wedge p \notin \{iri_1,...,iri_n\}\}$$

$$(2b)[[!(\,\hat{}\,iri_1|...|\,\hat{}\,iri_n)]]_G^\Gamma := [[\,\hat{}\,!(iri_1|...|iri_n)]]_G^\Gamma$$

$$(2c)[[!(iri_1|...|iri_n|\,\hat{}\,iri_{n+1}|...|\,\hat{}\,iri_m)]]_G^\Gamma := [[!(iri_1|...|iri_n)]]_G^\Gamma \cup [[(\,\hat{}\,iri_{n+1}|...|\,\hat{}\,iri_m)]]_G^\Gamma$$

$$(3)[[\,\hat{}\,E]]_G^\Gamma := \{(s,o)|(o,s) \in [[E]]_G^\Gamma\}$$

$$(4)[[E_1/E_2]]_G^\Gamma := \{(s,o)|\exists r : (s,r) \in [[E_1]]_G^\Gamma \wedge (r,o) \in [[E_2]]_G^\Gamma\}$$

$$(5)[[E_1|E_2]]_G^\Gamma := [[E_1]]_G^\Gamma \cup [[E_2]]_G^\Gamma$$

$$(6)[[E?]]_G^\Gamma := [[E]]_G^\Gamma \cup \{(a,a)|a \in \Gamma\}$$

$$(7)[[E+]]_G^\Gamma := \bigcup_{i=1}^\infty \underbrace{[[E/E/.../E]]_G^\Gamma}_{i \text{ times}}$$

$$(8)[[E*]]_G^\Gamma := [[E+]]_G^\Gamma \cup [[E?]]_G^\Gamma$$

$$(9)[[(E)]]_G^\Gamma := [[E]]_G^\Gamma$$

Example 5. Assume the existential property path expression *ppb:e1?*, the RDF
graph G depicted in Fig. 1 and $\Gamma = \{ppb:notExisting\} \cup \mathcal{V}_G$. The evaluation R
of the property path expression is: $R = [[ppb:e1?]]_G^\Gamma = [[ppb:e1]]_G^\Gamma \cup \{(a,a)|a \in \Gamma\} = \{(ppb:A1, ppb:centerA)\} \cup \{(ppb:A1, ppb:A1), (ppb:A2, ppb:A2),...\} \cup \{(ppb:notExisting, ppb:notExisting)\}$. The first set of the union is the evaluation
of $[[ppb:e1]]_G^\Gamma$. The second set denotes all tuples of vertex labels in G and the third
part denotes the tuple of the element that was included in Γ additionally to $\mathcal{V}_G$.

---

[4] In [12] the evaluation of the existential property path expression and the transitive
reflexive closure property path expression are defined slightly differently from the
definition of the W3C in [9]. We have contacted members of the SPARQL working
group in order to resolve these differences [4,5].

In order to obtain information from an RDF store, elements of Γ are bound to variables. These bindings are called *variable bindings*.

Definition 9 (Variable bindings)
The partial function $\mu : V \rightarrow T$ with variables V and RDF terms T, is called a variable binding. The domain $dom(\mu)$ of a variable binding μ is the set of variables on which μ is defined.

Definition 10 (Evaluation of property paths)
For constants $s \in I \cup B \cup L$, $o \in I \cup B \cup L$ and variables $v, v_1, v_2 \in V$ the evaluation of property paths is defined as:

(1) $[[sEo]]_G$ $\qquad := \begin{cases} \{\{\}\}, if(s,o) \in [[E]]_G^\Gamma \text{ where } \Gamma = \mathcal{V}_G \cup \{s,o\} \\ \{\}, else \end{cases}$

(2) $[[sEv]]_G$ $\qquad := \{\mu | (s, \mu(v)) \in [[E]]_G^\Gamma \wedge dom(\mu) = \{v\} \text{ where } \Gamma = \mathcal{V}_G \cup \{s\}\}$

(3) $[[vEo]]_G$ $\qquad := \{\mu | (\mu(v), o) \in [[E]]_G^\Gamma \wedge dom(\mu) = \{v\} \text{ where } \Gamma = \mathcal{V}_G \cup \{o\}\}$

(4) $[[v_1 E v_2]]_G$ $\qquad := \{\mu | (\mu(v_1), \mu(v_2)) \in [[E]]_G^\Gamma \wedge dom(\mu) = \{v_1, v_2\} \text{ where } \Gamma = \mathcal{V}_G\}$

Example 6. Assume the property path *ppb:notExisting   ppb:e1? ?o* where *ppb:notExisting* $\notin \mathcal{V}_G$. Furthermore, assume R from Example 5 as the result of the evaluation of the property path expression *ppb:e1?*. According to Definition 10 the evaluation of the property path is: $[[ppb:notExisting\ ppb:e1?\ ?o]]_G = \{\mu_1\}$ with $\mu_1 = \{(?o,\ ppb:notExisting)\}$.

Definition 11 (Semantics of SELECT query)
The evaluation $[[Q]]_G$ of a query Q of the form **SELECT** W **WHERE** $\{P\}$ *is the set of all projections $\mu|_W$ of bindings μ from $[[P]]_G$ to W, where the projection of $\mu|_W$ is the binding that coincides with μ on W and is undefined elsewhere.*
The evaluation of **SELECT** $*$ **WHERE** $\{P\}$ *is equal to the evaluation of* **SELECT** W **WHERE** $\{P\}$ *where $W = var(P)$ and $var(P)$ denotes the set of all variables in P.*

Definition 12 (Semantics of ASK query) [3]
The evaluation $[[Q]]_G$ of a query Q of the form **ASK WHERE** $\{P\}$ *over an RDF graph G is defined as:*

$$[[Q]]_G = \begin{cases} false & if \quad [[P]]_G^\Gamma = \{\} \\ true & otherwise \end{cases}$$

3   Property Path Benchmark BeSEPPI

In order to benchmark the performance of RDF stores with regard to property path queries we introduce our novel benchmark for semantic-based evaluation of property path implementations (BeSEPPI)[5]. BeSEPPI measures the execution times of 236 property path queries. These queries are executed on a small dataset that was created for evaluating various aspects of property paths. Furthermore, BeSEPPI comes with reference result sets for each query, which allow for evaluating correctness and completeness of result sets.

---

[5] Available as open source under https://github.com/Institute-Web-Science-and-Technologies/BeSEPPI.

3.1   Dataset

The benchmark dataset is a graph consisting of 28 triples. It allows for testing various semantic aspects of each property path expression. The dataset is kept small so that humans can easily create reference result sets for property path queries and evaluate the correctness and completeness of query result sets. The graph is depicted in Fig. 1.

3.2   Queries

The query set of BeSEPPI consists of 236 queries of which 73 are ASK queries and 163 are SELECT queries. In our benchmark we want to evaluate the performance of each property path expression individually with regard to various semantic aspects. Therefore, we test each expression separately and omit combinations of property path expressions. The queries are organized according to the following 3 dimensions.

Dimension 1: The property path expression
The first dimension is the property path expression that is tested.

Dimension 2: The number and positions of variables and terms
According to Definition 10 there are 4 possibilities for the number and positions of variables and terms in a query containing a single property path: sEo, sEv, vEo and v_1Ev_2 where s and o are terms v, v_1 and v_2 are variables and E is a property path expression. Queries of the form sEo test for the existence of the path in the dataset and do not return any variable bindings. During our evaluation we have observed that some stores do not support queries with * after the SELECT statement, which do not contain any variables, even though these queries are syntactically correct. Due to the fact that such a query simply returns an empty set if the path in the query does not exist and otherwise an empty variable binding, we have transformed such queries to ASK queries which return **false** or **true**. We expect ASK queries to be supported in all cases whereas SELECT queries with * and without variables have shown to be not supported in some cases.

Dimension 3: Semantic aspects
Semantic aspects are certain characteristics a query fulfills. Semantic aspects are for instance, that a query returns an empty result set or that the traversed path in the graph has a length of at least 4. Each property path expression has different semantics and therefore, not all semantic aspects can be considered for all property path expressions. Due to the high number of queries in BeSEPPI, describing all queries and the respective semantic aspects is beyond the scope of this paper. In order to still give insight into the query structure we give an overview of queries for each expression and variable-constant combination in Table 1. Additionally, we explain two benchmark queries for the existential property path expression in the following section.

Table 1. Overview of number of queries for each property path expression.

Expression	sEo	sEv	vEo	v_1Ev_2	Total
Inverse	6	5	5	4	20
Sequence	7	6	6	5	24
Alternative	6	6	6	5	23
Existential	9	6	6	3	24
Transitive Closure	12	9	9	8	38
Transitive Reflexive Closure	11	8	8	7	34
Negated Property Set	6	5	5	5	21
Inverse Negated Property Set	6	5	5	5	21
Negated and Inverse Negated Property Set	10	7	7	7	31
Total	**73**	**57**	**57**	**49**	**236**

Existential Property Path Expression Queries

In order to evaluate the performance of RDF stores for property path queries with the existential property path expression, we use 24 queries. Two exemplary queries and their semantic aspects are presented below. For all queries reference result sets were created to evaluate the correctness and completeness of the result sets returned by the RDF stores.

```
PREFIX ppb:   <http://www.ppbenchmark.com/>
ASK WHERE {
    ppb:notExisting1  ppb:notExisting2?  ppb:notExisting1 .}
```

Listing 1.2. Existential property path query where vertices and edge are not existing in the dataset.

In the query shown in Listing 1.2 none of the stated IRIs exist in the graph. According to Definition 8 *(ppb:notExisting1, ppb:notExisting1)* $\in$ $[[ppb:notExisting2?]]_G^\Gamma$. Due to Definition 10 the evaluation of the property path in the query is $[[ppb:notExisting1\ \ ppb:notExisting2?\ \ ppb:notExisting1]]_G^\Gamma = \{\{\}\}$. Less formally speaking, this query returns **true** because *ppb:notExisting1* is connected to itself by a path of length zero.

```
PREFIX ppb:   <http://www.ppbenchmark.com/>
SELECT * WHERE{
    ppb:A1 ppb:e1? ?o.}
```

Listing 1.3. Existential property path query with existing predicate and one variable.

The query shown in Listing 1.3 is of the form sEv. This means that there is one variable in the property path. According to Definition 8 (6) the evaluation of the property path expression is: $[[ppb{:}e1\,?]]_G^{\Gamma} = \{(ppb{:}A1,\ ppb{:}CenterA)\} \cup \{(a,a)|a \in \Gamma\}$. Following Definition 10 the evaluation of the property path is $[[ppb{:}A1 \quad ppb{:}e1? \quad ?o]]_G^{\Gamma} = \{\{?o,\ ppb{:}centerA\}, \{?o,\ ppb{:}A1\}\}$. Less formally speaking $ppb{:}centerA$ is returned because the triple *(ppb:A1, ppb:e1, ppb:centerA)* exists in the dataset and *ppb:A1* is returned because a path of length 0 exists between *ppb:A1*.

3.3 Metrics

In order to allow for comparing benchmark results of different stores with each other and to make the results comprehensible, meaningful metrics need to be used. For BeSEPPI we focus on the following metrics.

1. *Query correctness*
   The percentage of correct query results that are returned for each query. For SELECT queries: If R_q is the set of all correct results for a query q and $R_q^{\mathcal{S}}$ is the set of returned results of query q executed on RDF store $\mathcal{S}$, then the query correctness is defined as:

   $$corr(q) := \begin{cases} 1, & if\ |R_q^{\mathcal{S}}| = 0 \\ \dfrac{|R_q \cap R_q^{\mathcal{S}}|}{|R_q^{\mathcal{S}}|}, & otherwise \end{cases}$$

   For ASK queries: If r_q is the correct boolean result for the ASK query and $r_q^{\mathcal{S}}$ is the returned boolean result for an RDF store $\mathcal{S}$, then the correctness is defined as: $corr(q) = \begin{cases} 1, & if\ r_q = r_q^{\mathcal{S}} \\ 0 & otherwise \end{cases}$

2. *Query completeness*
   The percentage of all possible query results of the query.
   For SELECT queries: If R_q is the set of all correct results for a query q and $R_q^{\mathcal{S}}$ is the set of returned results of query q executed on RDF store $\mathcal{S}$, then the query completeness is defined as:

   $$comp(q) := \begin{cases} 1, & if\ |R_q| = 0 \\ \dfrac{|R_q \cap R_q^{\mathcal{S}}|}{|R_q|}, & otherwise \end{cases}$$

   For ASK queries: If r_q is the correct boolean result for the ASK query and $r_q^{\mathcal{S}}$ is the returned boolean result for an RDF store $\mathcal{S}$, then the completeness is defined as: $comp(q) = \begin{cases} 1 & if\ r_q = r_q^{\mathcal{S}} \\ 0 & otherwise \end{cases}$

3. *Average execution time per query*
   The arithmetic mean $avexec(q)$ of the execution time $t(q)$ of each query q is defined as: $avexec(q) = \dfrac{\sum_{i=1}^{n} t_i(q)}{n}$ where n is the number of times a query was executed.

3.4   Execution Strategy

In the first step of the benchmark execution, the complete dataset is loaded into the RDF store that should be benchmarked. Afterwards, all 236 queries are executed once without measuring any metrics in order to warm up the store. After that the 236 queries are executed 10 times and the metrics are measured. The queries are executed one after another and not in parallel. To prevent outliers the highest and lowest execution times are deleted. Finally, the average execution time, the correctness and the completeness are stored in a human readable CSV file.

4   Benchmark Results

In order to evaluate the performance of RDF stores in regard to queries containing property paths we use the property path benchmark BeSEPPI described in Sect. 3. Due to space limitations we omit the evaluation of the execution times in this paper. The evaluation of execution times can be found in the technical report [17].

4.1   Experimental Setting

We benchmarked the property path implementations of 5 common RDF stores, namely Blazegraph 2.1.4[6], AllegroGraph 6.4.1 free edition[7], Virtuoso 7.2 open source edition[8], RDF4J 2.2.4[9] and Apache Jena Fuseki 3.8.0[10]. The RDF stores were benchmarked on an Ubuntu 16.04 machine with 8 GB memory, 500 GB disk space and 4 1.7 Ghz processor cores. The Java version on the machine was 1.8.0.171.

4.2   Completeness and Correctness

In this section the correctness $corr(q)$ and completeness $comp(q)$ of result sets for each store are presented and it is discussed how the difference between the returned results and the reference result sets might be caused.

In Table 2 an overview of the numbers of queries, which returned only incomplete, only incorrect or incomplete and incorrect result sets, or caused an error during the execution of the query is given. Furthermore, the rightmost column shows the total number of queries for the respective property path expression.

One observation is that all stores return complete, correct and error-free result sets for the inverse, sequence and alternative expressions. A reason for this might be the clarity of their semantics, since their definition is the same in

---

[6] https://www.blazegraph.com/.

[7] https://franz.com/agraph/downloads.lhtml.

[8] http://vos.openlinksw.com/owiki/wiki/VOS.

[9] http://rdf4j.org/.

[10] https://jena.apache.org/documentation/fuseki2/.

Table 2. Number of queries that returned incomplete, incorrect, or incomplete and incorrect result sets, or threw an error during the execution.

Expression \ Store	Blaze-graph				Allegro-Graph				Virtuoso				RDF4J				Jena Fuseki				Total Number of Queries
	Incompl. & Correct	Complete & Incor.	Incompl. & Incor.	Error	Incompl. & Correct	Complete & Incor.	Incompl. & Incor.	Error	Incompl. & Correct	Complete & Incor.	Incompl. & Incor.	Error	Incompl. & Correct	Complete & Incor.	Incompl. & Incor.	Error	Incompl. & Correct	Complete & Incor.	Incompl. & Incor.	Error	
Inverse	0	0	0	0	0	0	0	0	0	0	0	0	0	0	0	0	0	0	0	0	20
Sequence	0	0	0	0	0	0	0	0	0	0	0	0	0	0	0	0	0	0	0	0	24
Alternative	0	0	0	0	0	0	0	0	0	0	0	0	0	0	0	0	0	0	0	0	23
Existential	3	0	1	0	6	0	2	0	0	0	0	3	0	0	3	0	0	0	0	0	24
Transitive Closure	0	0	1	0	0	0	0	0	6	0	4	8	0	0	4	0	0	0	0	0	34
Transitive Reflexive Closure	7	0	1	0	5	0	0	0	0	0	0	7	0	0	0	0	0	0	0	0	38
Negated Property Set	0	0	0	0	3	0	0	0	0	0	0	0	0	0	0	11	0	0	0	0	21
Inverse Negated Property Set	0	0	0	0	4	0	6	0	0	0	0	11	0	0	0	11	0	0	0	0	21
Negated and Inverse Negated Property Set	0	0	0	0	6	2	8	0	0	0	0	0	0	0	0	17	0	0	0	0	31
Total	10	0	3	0	24	2	16	0	6	0	4	29	0	0	7	39	0	0	0	0	236

different sources, such as the official SPARQL 1.1 definition, [9] and [12]. Furthermore, the transformation of these property path expressions into SPARQL 1.0 queries is straightforward, such that already implemented SPARQL1.0 query operators could be reused.

In the rest of this section the cases in which queries did not return correct, complete and error-free result sets for each store are discussed.

Blazegraph: Blazegraph returns complete and correct result sets for most queries, but there are 13 result sets which are not complete or correct. The first three queries that did not return complete and correct result sets are ASK queries. These three queries incorrectly returned **true** and have in common that the combination of subject and predicate can be found in the graph whereas the object does not occur. For queries in which also the object occurred in the graph, **true** was correctly returned.

All other queries with incomplete result sets return correct results. The tested property paths of these queries are of the form variable, property path expression, variable. Furthermore, they all involve either the existential or the transitive reflexive closure expression. After examining the missing results, we noticed that only results produced by the term $\{(a,a)|a \in \Gamma\}$ from Definition 8 (6) are missing.

AllegroGraph: Our evaluation indicates that the semantics used by Allegro-Graph deviates from the W3Cs semantics in case of existential $E?$ and transitive reflexive closure property path expressions $E*$. If $[[E]]_G^{\mathcal{V}_G} \neq \{\}$, AllegroGraph uses the W3Cs semantics. But in cases of $[[E]]_G^{\mathcal{V}_G} = \{\}$, AllegroGraph always returns $\{\}$. Furthermore, if the object and subject are equal in ASK queries the query returns `false` even though `true` would be correct.

AllegroGraph also returns empty result sets, if the negated property set contains at least one non-existing property. Furthermore, if the property path contains two variables, AllegroGraph interprets the inverse negated property set as negated property set, leading to result sets in which the assignments of the two variables to terms are swapped. The same applies to the inverse part of the negated and inverse negated property set.

Virtuoso: Virtuoso does not execute queries with two variables combined with the existential, the transitive closure or the transitive reflexive closure property path expression. For such queries the store returns an error, which says "Transitive start not given". This behavior seems to be a deliberate choice in the design of the RDF store and might have to do with the fact that Virtuoso is built on relational databases. In relational databases very large joins might be necessary in order to answer these queries and therefore, this feature may have not been implemented.

For queries with one or no variable and the existential or transitive reflexive closure property path expression Virtuoso returns complete and correct result sets. For the transitive closure property path expression there are 10 queries, which do not return complete result sets for Virtuoso. These queries all have a cycle like $\ll v_1, e, v_2, ..., v_n, e, v_1 \gg$ as tested semantic aspect and the missing result is always the start vertex v_1 of the cycle. This indicates that the transitive closure property path expression might be implemented in such a way that $[[P*]]_G^{\Gamma}$ is evaluated and the reflexive start is removed from the result set. In such a case, queries with cycles would return correct results except for the starting and the end vertex respectively.

For the negated property set Virtuoso returns correct and complete result sets for each query. For 11 queries with the inverse negated property set Virtuoso returns errors. The queries that return errors are distributed over all query forms and semantic aspects such that we could not identify the underlying cause. Finally, the combination of the negated and inverse negated property set returns complete and correct result sets.

RDF4J: RDF4J returns `false` for three ASK queries with the existential property path expression where the correct result is `true`. In each of the three queries, the subject and object are equal. This indicates, that RDF4J ignores the results included in $\{(a,a) \in \Gamma\}$ in ASK queries with the existential property path expression. Furthermore, RDF4J incorrectly returns `false` as result for ASK queries with a transitive closure property path expression, if they have a cycle as tested aspect.

For queries with the negated property set, the inverse negated property set and the combination of both sets RDF4J does not execute queries of the form subject property path expression object or variable property path object. This means every time such a query is executed the store returns an error.

Apache Jena Fuseki: Fuseki was the only store that executed every benchmark query without errors and returned complete and correct result sets. It seems that the store follows the W3Cs definition of property path semantics.

4.3 Summary of Results

In summary, all stores returned complete and correct result sets for queries with an inverse, sequence or alternative property path expression. For queries containing an existential property path expression in it, Blazegraph, AllegroGraph and RDF4J all handle the term $\{(a, a)|a \in \Gamma\}$ differently and are not following the W3Cs semantics. In case of transitive closure property path expressions, Virtuoso and RDF4J ignore results from cyclic paths. AllegroGraph returns empty result sets for queries with the negated property set, if one of the IRIs in the negated property set does not exist in the dataset. Furthermore, AllegroGraph seems to interpret the inverse negated property set as negated property set in queries with two variables. Virtuoso throws errors for ample queries with the inverse negated property set and RDF4J does not execute queries with the negated property set, inverse negated property set or the combination of both sets, where the object of the property path is an RDF term.

Furthermore, Virtuoso does not allow queries with variable path length without a fixed starting or ending point. This means whenever a query with 2 variables containing an existential, a transitive closure or a transitive reflexive closure property path expression is executed, Virtuoso returns an error. From the tested 5 RDF stores only Apache Jena Fuseki could return complete and correct result sets for all queries.

5 Related Work

Common benchmarks for RDF stores like the Lehigh University Benchmark [8], the DBPedia SPARQL Benchmark [14] or the Berlin SPARQL Benchmark [2] are designed to test the performance of RDF stores in different application scenarios. Since they were created before the release of SPARQL 1.1 they do not test property paths. Furthermore, the Lehigh University Benchmark is the only benchmark that also evaluates completeness and correctness of result sets.

In [7] Gubichev et al. propose an indexing approach called FERRARI to efficiently evaluate property paths. In order to show the efficiency of their approach they also propose a small benchmark with 6 queries over the YAGO2 [10] RDF dataset. Although this approach tests queries with property paths, it only measures execution times and does not evaluate correctness or completeness of result sets.

In spite of the fact that the benchmark proposed in [19] is not a benchmark for property paths in particular rather than a benchmark primarily designed for streaming RDF/SPARQL engines it tests property paths among various other SPARQL 1.1 features. Even though the completeness and correctness of result sets is not calculated, the results of the benchmark show that most of the benchmarked stream processing systems do not support property path queries.

In [18] a system is presented that generates small datasets based on given queries, their query features (e.g., the OPTIONAL or FILTER construct) and a data set. Additionally to the small datasets, the system returns the reference result sets for the given queries. They allow for checking the completeness and correctness of the query result sets returned from the evaluated RDF stores. This system is not a benchmark in particular but could be used to create datasets for benchmarks, which evaluate the completeness and correctness of result sets.

In [11] a benchmark for the evaluation of property path support is introduced. This benchmark can use an arbitrary RDF dataset as benchmark dataset and creates queries based on 8 query templates. Due to the small number of queries and the fact, that these queries do not test all property path expressions, this benchmark cannot be used for the semantic evaluation of property path implementations. Nevertheless the results of this benchmark indicate that ample RDF stores return incomplete or incorrect result sets for property path queries.

To the best of our knowledge no RDF benchmark exists that tests if the result sets of property path queries are complete and correct based on the W3Cs semantics.

6 Conclusion

Property paths were introduced with SPARQL 1.1 in 2013. They allow for describing complex queries in a more concise and comprehensive way. In order to evaluate the performances of property path query executions of RDF stores, we have developed a benchmark for semantic-based evaluation of property path implementations called BeSEPPI. BeSEPPI comes with a small RDF dataset especially created for the evaluation of property path queries and 236 queries, which test each property path expression. By calculating the completeness and correctness of result sets, our benchmark checks whether property path implementations adhere to the W3Cs semantics of property paths. Furthermore, our benchmark can also be used to measure execution times. The evaluation of execution times of the benchmarked stores can be found in the technical report [17].

With BeSEPPI we have benchmarked 5 common stores, namely Blazegraph, AllegroGraph, Virtuoso, RDF4J and Apache Jena Fuseki. The results of BeSEPPI show that only Apache Jena Fuseki could return complete and correct result sets for all 236 queries. Each of the other 4 stores returned incomplete or incorrect result sets for some queries and Virtuoso and RDF4J do not support all types of queries.

With our evaluation we could observe that ample RDF stores do not completely adhere to the W3Cs semantics of property paths. Therefore, BeSEPPI seems to be useful for RDF store developers to evaluate or improve their property path implementations.

The results in [11] have shown, that the correctness and completeness of property path query result sets may depend on the size of the loaded dataset. Therefore, we will perform a semantic evaluation of property path implementations on a large dataset in the future. Furthermore, we will evaluate the correct associativity (i.e. $[[E_1/E_2/E_3]]_G^\Gamma = [[(E_1/E_2)/E_3]]_G^\Gamma = [[E_1/(E_2/E_3)]]_G^\Gamma$) and the correct precedence (i.e. $[[E_1|E_2*]]_G^\Gamma = [[E_1/(E_2*)]]_G^\Gamma$) of several combined property path expressions in the future.

References

1. Arenas, M., Pérez, J.: Federation and navigation in SPARQL 1.1. In: Eiter, T., Krennwallner, T. (eds.) Reasoning Web 2012. LNCS, vol. 7487, pp. 78–111. Springer, Heidelberg (2012). https://doi.org/10.1007/978-3-642-33158-9_3

2. Bizer, C., Schultz, A.: The Berlin SPARQL benchmark. Int. J. Semant. Web Inf. Syst. **5**, 1–24 (2009)

3. https://www.w3.org/2001/sw/DataAccess/rq23/sparql-defns.html#defn_ASK

4. https://lists.w3.org/Archives/Public/public-sparql-dev/2017OctDec/0009.html

5. https://lists.w3.org/Archives/Public/public-sparql-dev/2018JanMar/0004.html

6. DuCharme, B.: Learning SPARQL. O'Reilly Media Inc., Sebastopol (2011). Chap. 2, pp 19–44; Chap. 3. pp 45–100

7. Gubichev, A., Bedathur, S., Seufert, S.: Sparqling kleene: fast property paths in RDF-3X, June 2013

8. Guo, Y., Pan, Z., Heflin, J.: LUBM: A benchmark for OWL knowledge base systems. Web Semant. **3**(2–3), 158–182 (2005). https://doi.org/10.1016/j.websem.2005.06.005

9. Harris, S., Seaborne, A.: SPARQL 1.1 query language. https://www.w3.org/TR/sparql11-query/

10. Hoffart, J., Suchanek, F.M., Berberich, K., Weikum, G.: YAGO2: a spatially and temporally enhanced knowledge base from Wikipedia. Artif. Intell. **194**, 28–61 (2013). https://doi.org/10.1016/j.artint.2012.06.001. http://www.sciencedirect.com/science/article/pii/S0004370212000719. artificial Intelligence, Wikipedia and Semi-Structured Resources

11. Janke, D., Skubella, A., Staab, S.: Evaluating SPARQL 1.1 property path support. In: BLINK/NLIWoD3@ISWC (2017)

12. Kostylev, E.V., Reutter, J.L., Romero, M., Vrgoč, D.: SPARQL with property paths. In: Arenas, M., Corcho, O., Simperl, E., Strohmaier, M., d'Aquin, M., Srinivas, K., Groth, P., Dumontier, M., Heflin, J., Thirunarayan, K., Staab, S. (eds.) ISWC 2015. LNCS, vol. 9366, pp. 3–18. Springer, Cham (2015). https://doi.org/10.1007/978-3-319-25007-6_1

13. Malyshev, S., Krötzsch, M., González, L., Gonsior, J., Bielefeldt, A.: Getting the most out of Wikidata: semantic technology usage in Wikipedia's knowledge graph. In: Vrandečić, D., Bontcheva, K., Suárez-Figueroa, M.C., Presutti, V., Celino, I., Sabou, M., Kaffee, L.-A., Simperl, E. (eds.) ISWC 2018. LNCS, vol. 11137, pp. 376–394. Springer, Cham (2018). https://doi.org/10.1007/978-3-030-00668-6_23

14. Morsey, M., Lehmann, J., Auer, S., Ngonga Ngomo, A.-C.: DBpedia SPARQL benchmark – performance assessment with real queries on real data. In: Aroyo, L., Welty, C., Alani, H., Taylor, J., Bernstein, A., Kagal, L., Noy, N., Blomqvist, E. (eds.) ISWC 2011. LNCS, vol. 7031, pp. 454–469. Springer, Heidelberg (2011). https://doi.org/10.1007/978-3-642-25073-6_29. http://dl.acm.org/citation.cfm?id=2063016.2063046
15. Prud'hommeaux, E., Seaborne, A.: SPARQL query language for RDF W3C recommendation (2008). https://www.w3.org/TR/rdf-sparql-query/#ask
16. Cyganiak, R., Wood, D.,Lanthaler, M.: RDf 1.1 concepts and abstract syntax. Technical report, W3C Recommendation (2014)
17. Skubella, A., Janke, D., Staab, S.: BeSEPPI: semantic-based benchmarking of property path implementations technical report. Technical report, Institute for Web Science and Technologies (2019)
18. Thost, V., Dolby, J.: QED: out-of-the-box datasets for SPARQL query evaluation. In: Proceedings of the ISWC 2018 Posters & Demonstrations, Industry and Blue Sky Ideas Tracks co-located with 17th International Semantic Web Conference (ISWC 2018), Monterey, USA, 8th–12th October 2018. (2018). http://ceur-ws.org/Vol-2180/paper-69.pdf
19. Zhang, Y., Duc, P.M., Corcho, O., Calbimonte, J.-P.: SRBench: a streaming RDF/SPARQL benchmark. In: Cudré-Mauroux, P., Heflin, J., Sirin, E., Tudorache, T., Euzenat, J., Hauswirth, M., Parreira, J.X., Hendler, J., Schreiber, G., Bernstein, A., Blomqvist, E. (eds.) ISWC 2012. LNCS, vol. 7649, pp. 641–657. Springer, Heidelberg (2012). https://doi.org/10.1007/978-3-642-35176-1_40

QED: Out-of-the-Box Datasets for SPARQL Query Evaluation

Veronika Thost[1](✉) ⓘ and Julian Dolby[2]

[1] MIT-IBM-Watson AI Lab, IBM Research, Cambridge, MA, USA
veronika.thost@ibm.com
[2] IBM Research, Yorktown Heights, NY, USA
dolby@us.ibm.com

Abstract. In this paper, we present SPARQL QED, a system generating out-of-the-box datasets for SPARQL queries over linked data. QED distinguishes the queries according to the different SPARQL features and creates, for each query, a small but exhaustive dataset comprising linked data and the query answers over this data. These datasets can support the development of applications based on SPARQL query answering in various ways. For instance, they may serve as SPARQL compliance tests or can be used for learning in query-by-example systems. We ensure that the created datasets are diverse and cover various practical use cases and, of course, that the sets of answers included are the correct ones. Example tests generated based on queries and data from DBpedia have shown bugs in Jena and Virtuoso.

Keywords: SPARQL datasets · Compliance tests · Benchmark

1 Introduction

The SPARQL query language is widely used and probably the most popular technology when it comes to querying linked data. Most triple stores and graph databases support the user-friendly declarative query language [7,22,23]. There are several benchmarks targeting the performance of SPARQL query answering, amongst others [3,14,18,19]. But, to the best of our knowledge, for SPARQL compliance testing, the W3C compliance tests[1] are the only test suite publicly available and commonly applied [2,16]. They have been proposed originally in 2001 for SPARQL 1.0 and were extended in 2009 regarding the new features of SPARQL 1.1. Correctness tests differ from benchmarks targeting scalability: the queries cover the various SPARQL features, the data is rather small – so that SPARQL engine developers can easily trace bugs and analyze the processing –, and the correct answers to the queries are included.

However, the W3C tests mostly contain synthetic queries over similarly artificial example data and, especially, comprise only few more complex queries

---

[1] https://www.w3.org/2009/sparql/docs/tests/.

© Springer Nature Switzerland AG 2019
P. Hitzler et al. (Eds.): ESWC 2019, LNCS 11503, pp. 491–506, 2019.
https://doi.org/10.1007/978-3-030-21348-0_32

nesting different SPARQL features, which model real user queries more faith-
fully. A simple text search reveals, for example, that the UNION keyword only
occurs in nine[2] rather simple SELECT queries, such as the following query Q.[3]

```
SELECT * WHERE {
  ?city a <http://dbpedia.org/ontology/Place>; rdfs:label 'Gomeciego'@en.
  ?airport a <http://dbpedia.org/ontology/Airport>.
  {?airport <http://dbpedia.org/ontology/city> ?city} UNION
  {?airport <http://dbpedia.org/ontology/location> ?city} UNION
  {?airport <http://dbpedia.org/property/cityServed> ?city.} UNION
  {?airport <http://dbpedia.org/ontology/city> ?city. }
  OPTIONAL { ?airport foaf:homepage ?airport_home. }
  OPTIONAL { ?airport rdfs:label ?name. }
  FILTER ( !bound(?name) || langMatches( lang(?name), 'de') ) }
```

Fig. 1. A SPARQL query from DBpedia.

```
SELECT DISTINCT * WHERE { { ?s :p ?o } UNION { ?s :q ?o } }
```

For a given dataset, this query retrieves all those tuples (s, o) for which the data
contains either the triple s :p o, or s :q o, or both s :p o and s :q o. We
assume the reader to be familiar with SPARQL. The concept of matching query
patterns and triples for obtaining answers, which are *solution mappings* (also
solutions) of the query variables to terms, is defined formally in the SPARQL
specification[4]. In the W3C tests, UNION occurs only together with the GRAPH
or OPTIONAL key and once with FILTER, but with none other. Naturally, hand-
crafted tests cannot cover all possible combinations of features. But an example
from the DBpedia query log depicted in Fig. 1 shows that real queries often
contain various nested features in combination.[5] We thus have a considerable
gap between the queries in the tests and those in reality. And this is similar with
the data. While the test data for Q consists of the below three triples, the latest
DBpedia dump contains more than 13 billion triples[6]. These triples usually cover
various *situations* modeled in queries (i.e., distinct and sometimes only partial
instantiations of the query patterns).

```
:x1 :p "abc". :x1 :q "abc". :x2 :p "abc".
```

Here, we only have triples on the single literal "abc", but not the situation that
the pattern ?s :q ?o is satisfied alone.

---

[2] The 2009 tests actually contain some more such queries, but these consider an empty
dataset and hence are rather unrealistic.

[3] For readability, we generally drop prefix declarations.

[4] https://www.w3.org/TR/sparql11-query/.

[5] We obtained the query from LSQ: http://aksw.github.io/LSQ/.

[6] http://wiki.dbpedia.org/develop/datasets/dbpedia-version-2016-10.

As a consequence of this mismatch, it is likely that many endpoints that pass the W3C compliance tests exhibit non-standard behavior in practice. In fact, later in the paper, we show that this is the case even for endpoints like Jena and Virtuoso, which are heavily used in practice. More realistic compliance tests could also serve as evaluation datasets for developing add-ons for auto-completion or query suggestion based on examples (i.e., answer samples), and hence enhance the support for users; observe that standard benchmarks do not fit these tasks. In short, we are missing test datasets which – in contrast to the existing performance benchmarks – contain real-world queries, diverse and comprehensive samples of data (i.e., triples), and the answers to the queries.

In this paper, we present the SPARQL Query Evaluation Dataset generator (QED), which closes the aforementioned gap by generating out-of-the-box datasets for SPARQL queries over linked data (note that the approach similarly works for local RDF data). QED distinguishes queries given by the user according to the different SPARQL features, selects some of them, and creates a test case for each query, a dataset[7] comprising linked data and the query answers over this data. Thereby, it is ensured that the created datasets are small, but diverse, and cover various practical use cases and, of course, that the sets of answers included are the correct ones. QED is available at https://github.com/vthost/qed.

The paper is structured as follows. Section 2, describes applications for our datasets and corresponding requirements. In Sect. 3, QED is presented in detail, and Sect. 4 describes example datasets generated based on DBpedia and Wikidata, including a test that revealed a bug in both Jena and Virtuoso.

2   Motivation

In this section, we outline use cases for QED and specify the corresponding requirements for (or features of) the system. While some of the existing benchmarks targeting performance already rely on real-world queries [14,18], the W3C test suite does not do so. By integrating not only real queries, but also linked data and the corresponding query answers over this data, we hence augment – or rather complement – the two kinds of existing benchmarks. In particular, we open the door for various applications. First of all, the generated tests may serve as SPARQL compliance tests. But they can also support the development and optimization of other systems, for instance: query-by-example approaches [6,8,12,15], where queries are to be learnt from a small set of tuples of URIs that are or, especially, are not among the queries' answers; and auto-completion add-ons [11]. These approaches need test data that is *relevant* for the corresponding queries; that is, data containing positive and negative examples (i.e., answers and approximate answers) instead of arbitrary triples. Our goal was

---

[7] The term "datasets" usually denotes the sets of data included in the test cases. However, we may also use it for the entire test cases consisting of a query, data, and answers (e.g., in the acronym QED); this is to emphasize that they can be applied for multiple purposes, besides correctness testing, and should be clear from context.

therefore to keep QED modular, parameterizable, and extensible, in order to allow for as many applications as possible. Specifically, we derived the following requirements.

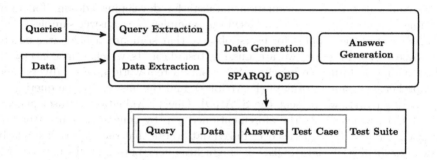

Fig. 2. The architecture of SPARQL QED. The input consists of a query set and the data, or the address of an endpoint providing it. The application first extracts queries from the set based on their features. Then, a test case is created for each of them by creating a dataset comprising both data from the input and generated, synthetic data, and by computing the answers over this data. This test suite is the output.

R1 Originality. QED should fill the gaps in existing benchmarks and produce datasets comprising diverse query and data samples from real applications, and corresponding sets of answers. The queries should cover different SPARQL features: the solution modifiers, keywords associated to algebra operators, and the aggregation operators. The data should be relevant for the corresponding query, cover various situations, and be of reasonable size.

R2 Reusability. QED should be applicable to arbitrary SPARQL queries and corresponding data, and hence be kept as general as possible. It should also be modular and open for and adaptable to various use cases. Next to that, the system should be easy to handle.

R3 Quality. The QED approach is based on existing query logs and linked data and hence integrates existing resources. The system design should further follow common practices (e.g., use Semantic Web data formats). Beyond that, the correctness of the produced datasets should be formally verified.

These aspects capture the scope of QED we envision. Regarding **R1**, note that the quality and variety of the generated datasets (e.g., the coverage of SPARQL features) strongly depends on the input, especially on the queries. However, we will propose means to filter the queries and generate data to augment the one given, and further discuss the topic later, in Sect. 3.

3   SPARQL QED

SPARQL QED is a framework for generating datasets for SPARQL query evaluation as outlined in Fig. 2. The input consists of an endpoint providing the data, and queries over that data (e.g., from a log). QED distinguishes the given queries according to different SPARQL features, selects some of them, and creates, for each query, a dataset comprising comprehensive samples of the linked data (i.e., triples) and the query answers over this data. Thereby, it is ensured that the created datasets are small, but diverse, that they cover various practical use cases and, of course, that the sets of answers included are the correct ones.

1. Query Extraction. The queries are assumed to be given in the LSQ RDF format [17], which contains the SPARQL queries themselves, but also captures specific characteristics, such as number of triples, features contained in them (e.g., the OPTIONAL or FILTER), and number of answers. This allows query extraction to be configurable accordingly. For instance, the configuration $(2, 1, \{\{\texttt{OPTIONAL}, \texttt{FILTER}\}, \{\texttt{UNION}\}\}, 10)$ makes QED construct a test suite containing 10 test cases with queries that contain both OPTIONAL and FILTER (and possibly other features), and 10 test cases with queries that contain UNION; and all of the queries contain at least two triples and have at least one answer. Note that there is a tool for transforming SPARQL queries into this format relatively easily.[8] We also have filters that ensure that the extracted queries are diverse and do not contain near-duplicates as generated by bots, for example. In fact, it turned out that the majority of such queries can be recognized by comparing the beginnings of the textual representations of the queries for equality.

The LSQ format capturing different query characteristics allows us to extract relevant sets of queries from possibly large query logs. However, in the end, we are only interested in the SPARQL queries. That is, if the user has a SPARQL query set of reasonable size for which tests should be created, they can also use this set and hence skip the query extraction phase. Note that this option also leaves the user the possibility to apply different query extraction approaches proposed in the literature, such as [19], or to use the queries from other benchmarks.

2. Data Extraction. The sheer number of triples given as input often makes it impossible to include all the relevant data from the endpoint since the test cases should be of reasonable size. On the other hand, the tests should not be too simplistic (i.e., with data covering only some of the situations modeled in the query, such as the one given for Q in the introduction). We therefore do not only take a subset of the relevant data that is restricted in size (i.e., the maximal size is specified by the user) but also ensure that it reflects the variability of the possible answers. More specifically, we extract data describing different situations (if available) depending on the shape of the query and covering the possible types of solutions described in the SPARQL specification:

- Q_1 UNION Q_2: data leading to (1) *compatible* solutions to subqueries Q_1 and Q_2 (i.e., solutions that map shared variables to the same term), (2) solutions to Q_1, and to (3) solutions to Q_2.
- Q_1 OPTIONAL Q_2: data leading to solutions as in (1)–(3), but we additionally ensure in (3) that the solutions to Q_2 are incompatible to the ones from (2). Q_1 MINUS Q_2 and Q_1 FILTER(NOT)EXISTS Q_2 are treated in the same way.

---

[8] http://aksw.github.io/LSQ/.

```
SELECT ?name ?description_en ?musician WHERE {
 ?musician skos:subject cat:German_musicians .
 ?musician foaf:name ?name .
 OPTIONAL {
  ?musician rdfs:comment ?description_en .
  FILTER (LANG(?description_en) = 'en') . } }
```

```
dbpedia:Laith_Al-Deen
rdfs:comment   "Laith Al-Deen, born February 20, 1972 in Karlsruhe,
Germany, is a German language pop musician."@en ;
skos:subject   ns3:German_musicians ;
foaf:name      "Laith Al-Deen"@de .

dbpedia:Kettcar   rdfs:comment   "Kettcar is an indie pop music band
based in Hamburg, Germany."@en ;
skos:subject   ns3:German_musicians ;
foaf:name      "Kettcar"@en .

dbpedia:Lou_Bega skos:subject   ns2:German_musicians ;
foaf:name      "Lou Bega"@en , "Lou Bega"@de ;
rdfs:comment   "Lou Bega je německý zpěvák latinskoamerické hudby, jenž
se proslavil zejména díky písni Mambo No. 5."@cs ,
"Lou Bega ist ein deutscher Latin-Pop-Sänger."@de ,
"David Lubega (born April 13, 1975), also known as Lou Bega ... ."@en .
```

```
<http://gen/0> <http://www.w3.org/2004/02/skos/core#subject>
<http://dbpedia.org/resource/Category:German_musicians> .
<http://gen/0> <http://xmlns.com/foaf/0.1/name> <http://gen/1> .
```

Fig. 3. Example DBpedia query Q_{ex}, data D_{ex}, and additionally generated data D_{gen}.

- Q_1 FILTER E: data leading to (1) solutions to Q_1 and for which E is true, and (2) solutions to Q_1 and for which E is false.

If Q_1 or Q_2 again contain such patterns, then we consider all combinations. The extraction is done using SPARQL CONSTRUCT queries describing the situations.

Example 1. For query Q_{ex} in Fig. 3, abstracted Q_1 OPTIONAL $\{Q_2$ FILTER $E\}$, we look for data about German musicians covering all the following situations.

- There is a comment in English
  (i.e., there are compatible solutions to Q_1 and Q_2 yielding that E is true; they are merged into a solution to Q_{ex}).
- There is a comment that is not in English
  (i.e., there are compatible solutions to Q_1 and Q_2 yielding that E is false; the former represents a solution to Q_{ex}).

- There is no comment – then the language filter is irrelevant for the result (i.e., there is a solution to Q_1 but none or no compatible one to Q_2 FILTER E; the former represents a solution to Q_{ex}).

The data we have extracted from DBpedia is also shown in Fig. 3. Observe that we did not retrieve data for the last case; there is no musician without comments. On the other hand, our consideration of various situations makes that the data may also contain approximate answers; for instance, comments in different languages.

Again, the data does not have to be extracted from an endpoint, the user also can provide it directly. Nevertheless, independent of where the data comes from, and as the example also demonstrates, we cannot assume that we have all the different kinds of data. In fact, the portion of the provided data matching a query usually only covers a few of the possible situation; in Sect. 4, we show this in more detail. To tackle this problem, we generate synthetic data for the remaining cases and integrate it with the real data.

3. Data Generation. For those of the above cases where data is not provided but which could arise theoretically, we generate synthetic data. We use Kodkod[9], a SAT-based constraint solver for extensions of first-order logic with relations to construct the dataset we target. In a nutshell, we encode every situation we consider for a given query into a formula Q in relational logic and represent the answers over the unknown data D in a relational logic formula $Ans(Q, D)$ as proposed in [5]. Our final formula is then the equation $Ans(Q, D) = \neg\emptyset$, requiring the answer set to be non-empty, and can be solved by Kodkod, yielding a dataset D as intended (i.e., satisfying Q); $\neg$ reads "not" and $\emptyset$ denotes the empty set.

Example 2. For query Q_{ex}, we consider amongst others the formula $Q := Q_1' \wedge \neg(Q_2' \wedge E')$; $\wedge$ reads "and", and X' denotes the relational logic translation of X. It represents the last case in Example 1 partly, namely that there is no compatible solution to Q_2 FILTER E. Our data D_{ex} from DBpedia contains no answers to Q because there is an English comment for all the musicians, and hence $Ans(Q, D_{ex}) = \neg\emptyset$ is not satisfied. If we consider the data to be a variable D_{gen}, then Kodkod can find and generate it as a solution to the equation $Ans(Q, D_{gen}) = \neg\emptyset$. Such data is shown in Fig. 3 (bottom).

The generated data is then added to the real data. Note that, in theory, data generated in this way would be sufficient for testing since the generation systematically considers the relevant test cases based on the queries' features. However, our generator currently does not yet cover all possible features because Kodkod is lacking full datatype support (e.g., for filters on dates, QED does not generate triples with different dates relevant for the filter); hence the real data may add important test cases. Also observe that, if there are many situations for one query, the numbers of triples to be considered can become large, but QED can be configured to generate smaller data files, for single situations. Further, there are

---

[9] http://emina.github.io/kodkod/index.html.

```
[ a rs:ResultSet ;
  rs:resultVariable "musician" , "description_en" , "name" ;
  rs:size            "5"^^xsd:int ;
  rs:solution [
   rs:binding [ rs:value <http://dbpedia.org/resource/Laith_Al-Deen> ;
    rs:variable "musician"] ;
   rs:binding [ rs:value "Laith Al-Deen, born February 20, ..."@en ;
    rs:variable "description_en"] ;
   rs:binding [ rs:value "Laith Al-Deen"@de ;
    rs:variable "name"] ] ;
  rs:solution [
   rs:binding [ rs:value <http://dbpedia.org/resource/Kettcar> ;
    rs:variable "musician"] ;
  rs:binding [ rs:value "Kettcar is an indie pop music band ...."@en ;
   rs:variable "description_en"] ;
  rs:binding [ rs:value "Kettcar"@en ;
   rs:variable "name"] ] ;
  rs:solution [
   rs:binding [ rs:value <http://dbpedia.org/resource/Lou_Bega> ;
   rs:variable "musician"] ;
   rs:binding [ rs:value "David Lubega (born April 13, 1975), ...."@en ;
   rs:variable "description_en"] ;
   rs:binding [ rs:value "Lou Bega"@de ;
   rs:variable "name"] ] ;
  rs:solution [
   rs:binding [ rs:value <http://dbpedia.org/resource/Lou_Bega> ;
   rs:variable "musician"] ;
   rs:binding [ rs:value "David Lubega (born April 13, 1975), ...."@en ;
   rs:variable "description_en"] ;
   rs:binding [ rs:value "Lou Bega"@en ;
   rs:variable "name"] ] ;
  rs:solution [
   rs:binding [ rs:value <http://gen/0> ;
   rs:variable "musician"] ;
   rs:binding [ rs:value <http://gen/1> ;
   rs:variable "name"] ] ; ] .
```

Fig. 4. The solutions to the example query Q_{ex} over the union of data D_{ex} and D_{gen} from Fig. 3.

special cases where the query (and the corresponding formulas) is unsatisfiable or where we cannot integrate all the generated data because the formulas for different situations contradict each other. We ignore the former cases and then generate no data at all. In the latter cases, we generate multiple datasets greedily: we initially consider the maximal dataset (integrating both the extracted and the generated data) and split it iteratively until there are no contradictions anymore.

Example 3. It is safe to ignore a query Q MINUS Q since it has no answers, over any data. The second case is more subtle, but can be illustrated with the query:

```
SELECT ?a WHERE { :s1 :p :s2 . OPTIONAL { :s2 :p ?a . }}
```

For any dataset, it either retrieves no answers (if the data does not contain the triple :s1 :p :s2), one answer in which ?a is not bound (if the data contains :s1 :p :s2 but no triple starting with :s2 :p), or answers where ?a is bound (the data contains the triple :s1 :p :s2 and some starting with :s2 :p). Here, we generate a dataset that contains the triple :s1 :p :s2 and one starting with :s2 :p, and a dataset including :s1 :p :s2 but no triple starting with :s2 :p.

4. Answer Generation. For all queries and the corresponding data, we include the answers. However, we do not rely on a standard endpoint to retrieve the answers since we do not have correctness guarantees for those. Therefore we again use Kodkod to generate the answers similar as the data. More specifically, for each dataset, so far consisting of a query Q and data D (comprising extracted and generated data), Kodkod can generate a set of answers A such that the equation $A = Ans(Q, D)$ is satisfied. Note that the correctness of the system implementing the declarative semantics has been verified with the W3C tests.

Example 4. Figure 4, for instance, shows that every answer to Q_{ex} over D_{ex} has a binding for each ?name, ?description_en, and ?musician, but the answer to Q_{ex} over D_{gen} is missing the optional binding for ?description_en.

The created test suite is in the format of the W3C tests: a machine-readable custom format that relies on manifest files specifying the single test cases, each of which comes with one file for each, the query, the data, and the result, as depicted for the example query Q_{ex} in Figs. 3 and 4. The queries are in SPARQL, the others in Turtle format.

Discussion

We regard guidelines **R1-R3** from Sect. 2, compare the tests to those of the W3C, and discuss possible extensions.

QED indeed allows to generate diverse and extensive datasets for SPARQL query evaluation based on real queries and data. Since the input queries and data, and also the query features in focus can be selected arbitrarily, and the tests are of reasonable size, the system is highly generic and can be used in various scenarios by a wider community. QED does not only allow the integration of other approaches (e.g., for query extraction); since the Java implementation is kept simple, easy to handle, and open source, it is also further customizable. Finally, the system design follows best practices: we rely not only on existing queries and data, but integrate the LSQ approach and adopt the format of the W3C compliance tests. Note that the latter allows testers to reuse existing infrastructure (originally created for the W3C tests) to directly run the tests generated with QED. We also verify that the query answers are correct.

In the initial version, we concentrate on the SELECT query form and on evaluation tests. The standard also specifies the forms ASK, CONSTRUCT, and DESCRIBE.

Since the `ASK` form only tests whether or not a query pattern has a solution, our implementation for `SELECT` can easily be adapted. The `CONSTRUCT` query form, which returns a single RDF graph specified by a graph template, would require a slightly more elaborate extension of QED. The `DESCRIBE` form is irrelevant for common tests since it returns information that is to be determined by the query service applied and hence cannot be tested in a general fashion.

Further, our approach to make the data reflect several possible situations relevant for the considered query is currently only applied with operator features (e.g., `OPTIONAL` and `UNION`). There are other, rather intricate features, such as property paths or complex filter conditions, whose consideration during diversification would certainly benefit applications, but which need to be handled carefully. Note that queries with these features are included, but we do not extract or generate data that additionally includes approximate answers w.r.t. these features.

Next to query evaluation tests, the W3C test suite includes syntax and protocol tests. The former test if syntactically (in)correct queries yield exceptions or not, and we plan to consider them in the future, either by using the parse error property of LSQ or by integrating a SPARQL parser into QED. The others are however out of the scope of our work, whose goal is to generate realistic and extensive datasets for SPARQL query evaluation. Nevertheless, we do not suppose our datasets to represent complete compliance tests covering the whole range of SPARQL. They should rather be considered as additional tests tailored to the queries and data used in practice.

4   Dataset Examples

In this section, we first describe a test case that showed a bug in Jena and Virtuoso and thus demonstrates that the comprehensive consideration of various situations is critical for compliance testing. Then we give an overview of example test suites generated based on queries over and data from DBpedia and Wikidata.

A Test Case

The following query over DBpedia nicely illustrates that there are often various possibilities for situations in the data that lead to answers to given queries.

```
SELECT ?name ?musician ?band WHERE {
 ?musician foaf:name ?name .
 OPTIONAL { ?musician foaf:member ?band . }
 MINUS {
  ?x foaf:homepage "some bad page" .
  OPTIONAL { ?x foaf:member ?band . } } }
```

For this query, QED generated the below two triples (amongst others) describing a situation where the optional parts of the query do not match any data.

```
<http://gen/0> <http://xmlns.com/foaf/0.1/name> <http://gen/1> .
<http://gen/2> <http://xmlns.com/foaf/0.1/homepage>
"some bad page" .
```

Since the domains of mappings from the two corresponding query patterns to the triples are disjoint, the MINUS does not remove the binding to the first triple from the set of solutions. However, in our evaluation, both Jena and Virtuoso did not present this binding as a solution.[10]

This example query illustrates the importance of considering all ways of satisfying a query, as discussed in Sect. 3. QED also generated multiple other datasets embodying different ways of satisfying this query, in which the domains of the two sides of the minus are not disjoint. An example is the following.

```
<http://gen/0> <http://xmlns.com/foaf/0.1/homepage>
"some bad page" .
<http://gen/0> <http://xmlns.com/foaf/0.1/member> _:BX5FX3A .
<http://gen/0> <http://xmlns.com/foaf/0.1/name> <http://gen/1> .
```

In this case, both optional clauses bind ?band to the same value and the systems correctly answered the query. Since SPARQL semantics is complex, our systematic exploration is an effective way of building a robust set of tests in an automated way.

Test Suites

Tables 1 and 2 show statistics about exemplary, generated test suites.[11] Since the DBpedia log queries primarily only cover the most common SPARQL features, we also consider the example queries that come with the Wikidata SPARQL endpoint[12], which have been formulated carefully and are rather diverse [4].

For DBpedia, we filter the DBpedia queries that are provided by the LSQ endpoint as described in Sect. 3.[13] Here, we look for queries that contain at least one of the following features: FILTER, MINUS, OFFSET, OPTIONAL, UNION, and hence create a relatively small and simple dataset in the style of the W3C tests. In the tables, the queries are grouped by the maximal set of the considered features which they contain. It can be seen that the queries are generally rather small (i.e., they only contain a few triple patterns), that there are usually several possible situations, but that the latter are only partly covered by DBpedia.

---

[10] In Jena, the bug has been solved by now (see https://issues.apache.org/jira/projects/ JENA/issues/JENA-1633).

[11] The datasets can be found in the GitHub repository of QED.

[12] https://www.wikidata.org/wiki/Wikidata:SPARQL_query_service/queries/ examples.

[13] The LSQ format also specifies characteristics such as the number of answers to the query, which is only useful if we also consider the DBpedia data considered with the generation of the query set. Alternatively, we could have applied the LSQ framework to generate LSQ-formatted queries for the current DBpedia version.

Table 1. Statistics about the datasets generated for DBpedia; Qs = total number of queries, TP = avg. number of triple patterns, Sit = avg. number of situations, Cov = avg. share of situations covered in source data, Triples1 = avg. number of triples in the extracted data, Triples2 = as Triples1 but including generated data (averages are per query); FI = Filter, MI = Minus, OF = Offset, OP = Optional, UN = Union.

Features	Qs	TP	Sit	Cov (%)	Triples1	Triples2
FI	7	3	2	28	1	8
MI	1	3	3	100	5	15
OF	1	4	1	100	4	11
OP	4	4	12	37	6	14
UN	5	6	18	48	7	14
FI,OP	7	3	14	6	2	10
FI,UN	4	3	10	52	8	13
FI,OF,OP	1	8	4374	0	12	21
FI,OP,UN	1	4	18	0	0	4

Hence, our data generation helps to create test cases with diverse data that are of reasonable size though.

For Wikidata, we consider the example SELECT queries given and only ignore those that yield parse exceptions or contain the SERVICE feature (i.e., we do not apply the LSQ-based filtering). Table 2 shows that they contain more features and often several in combination. Due to space constraints, we focus on the seven most frequent and interesting features; specifically, we ignore DISTINCT and LIMIT, which occur in many example queries, and MINUS, VALUES, and MIN, which occur in only one query. In six cases, the generator tool could not cope with the filter condition (i.e., there is no generated data although Cov is < 100%).

Nevertheless, especially the coverage of uncommon features differentiates our datasets from the existing ones, which mostly cover only the most common features. Also the currently still sparse usage of the newest SPARQL features (see, e.g., [4]) is a strong reason for generic frameworks like QED, which enable users to update their datasets if new queries or data become available. Finally, our diverse and realistic examples are special in the light of the most popular existing benchmarks, which usually still rely on artificial queries and/or data.

5 Related Work

The importance of SPARQL can easily be estimated by the attention payed to system development, evaluation, and optimization. There are numerous (generators for) datasets for SPARQL query evaluation. We have described the specifics of compliance tests and the tests proposed by the W3C in the introduction. Recall that the latter are nearly exhaustive in terms of the SPARQL feature combinations covered, but they contain artificial data only partly capturing the situations that could arise in practice.

Table 2. Statistics for the datasets for the Wikidata example queries; BI = Bind, FI = Filter, HA = Having, OP = Optional, SQ = Subquery, UN = Union, RE = Regex.

Features	Qs	TP	Sit	Cov (%)	Triples1	Triples2
	16	2	1	96	4	13
BI	2	4	1	100	8	8
FI	16	3	3	82	16	23
HA	1	1	1	100	2	2
BI,FI	6	3	4	86	15	17
BI,RE	1	1	2	100	4	12
FI,OP	14	3	9	51	19	24
FI,SU	1	1	2	0	0	7
BI,FI,OP	1	6	54	70	206	206
BI,OP,UN	1	3	9	100	26	26
FI,OP,SU	1	10	144	14	75	75
FI,OP,UN	1	7	108	86	430	440
BI,FI,OP,UN	1	8	36	97	165	165
BI,FI,RE,SU	1	4	16	62	43	43
FI,HA,OP,UN	1	7	252	13	191	191

All other benchmarks we are aware of focus on performance issues such as scalability. Most popular are the Lehigh University Benchmark (LUBM) [10], the Ontology Benchmark (UOBM) [13], the Berlin SPARQL Benchmark (BSBM) [3], SP2Bench [20], the DBpedia Sparql Benchmark (DBPSB) [14], the Waterloo Stress Testing Benchmark (WSTB) [1], and the BioBenchmark [24]. LUBM and its extension UOBM both integrate ontologies and hence also allow for evaluating reasoning. However, they only contain conjunctive queries and generators for artificial data; this also holds for WSTB. BSBM and SP2Bench also rely on data generation, but the queries contain some SPARQL features, though only a few of all possible ones. The queries in DBSP and BioBenchmark are similar to the latter but the data is real. Note that, with all of the benchmarks the queries are either fixed or generated based on a rather small set of templates. In a certain way, they are also domain-specific since each of the benchmarks focuses on a particular domain. In contrast, QED allows for generating tests for any domain. Also, apart from LUBM and UOBM, none of the benchmarks contains or considers the answers to the queries.

FEASIBLE [19] is an approach for mining SPARQL queries from logs for benchmarking and based on clustering similar queries and selecting prototypes. It is an alternative to our query extraction and, as outlined in Sect. 3, could be integrated with QED.

SPARQL query federation approaches are evaluated using benchmarks such as SPLODGE [9], FedBench [21], or LargeRDFBench [18]. They differ from the general benchmarks in that the queries span several data sources, the data is considerably larger in size (this often is also the case for the answers), and the evaluation focuses also on factors such as average source selection time and number of endpoint requests. SPLODGE is an approach for generating federated queries, but only conjunctive queries. FedBench comprises real data and queries but especially the latter are simple and cover only few SPARQL features. LargeRDFBench is similar to our approach since it contains several real datasets, including queries covering different SPARQL features. Apart from the number of sources they span and basic graph patterns they contain, the queries are comparable to the ones we extracted from DBpedia (see Sect. 4), in terms of complexity and variety. However, the simple queries are taken from standard benchmarks and hence less interesting; the more complex queries are from the life sciences domain and hand-crafted by the developers – and thus fixed –, whereas QED can be applied to extract new and diverse query sets for arbitrary domains. Also, the data (and answer) sets are much too large for the use cases we target and not tailored to the queries as ours. Note, however, that LargeRDFBench also allows for evaluating the correctness of the results.

6   Conclusions

In this paper, we have presented the SPARQL QED framework, which allows generating datasets for SPARQL query evaluation systems based on real-world queries and data. We have proven its value by generating tests that revealed bugs in Jena and Virtuoso, two popular endpoints. Beyond standard compliance testing, we have outlined other applications that could make use of the generated datasets. In contrast to the commonly used performance benchmarks, QED thus does not only help to make query answering systems adapt to common usage scenarios, and thus to make them more robust, but it also allows to develop and tune useful add-ons, such as query-by-example systems. This is further supported by the fact that QED is highly customizable and easy to handle. To the best of our knowledge, datasets as the ones generated by QED do not exist yet. Nevertheless, the current, initial version of QED only integrates a portion of the general approach behind the system. We have sketched possible extensions regarding the supported query forms, features, and kinds of tests in the paper. Support for ontology-based queries would be also an interesting extension.

Acknowledgments. This work is partly supported by the German Research Foundation (DFG) in the Cluster of Excellence "Center for Advancing Electronics Dresden" in CRC 912.

References

1. Aluç, G., Hartig, O., Özsu, M.T., Daudjee, K.: Diversified stress testing of RDF data management systems. In: Mika, P., et al. (eds.) ISWC 2014, Part I. LNCS, vol. 8796, pp. 197–212. Springer, Cham (2014). https://doi.org/10.1007/978-3-319-11964-9_13
2. Buil-Aranda, C., Hogan, A., Umbrich, J., Vandenbussche, P.-Y.: SPARQL web-querying infrastructure: ready for action? In: Alani, H., et al. (eds.) ISWC 2013, Part II. LNCS, vol. 8219, pp. 277–293. Springer, Heidelberg (2013). https://doi.org/10.1007/978-3-642-41338-4_18
3. Bizer, C., Schultz, A.: The berlin SPARQL benchmark. Int. J. Semantic Web Inf. Syst. 5(2), 1–24 (2009)
4. Bonifati, A., Martens, W., Timm, T.: An analytical study of large SPARQL query logs. PVLDB 11(2), 149–161 (2017)
5. Bornea, M., Dolby, J., Fokoue, A., Kementsietsidis, A., Srinivas, K., Vaziri, M.: An executable specification for SPARQL. In: Cellary, W., Mokbel, M.F., Wang, J., Wang, H., Zhou, R., Zhang, Y. (eds.) WISE 2016. LNCS, vol. 10042, pp. 298–305. Springer, Cham (2016). https://doi.org/10.1007/978-3-319-48743-4_24
6. Diaz, G.I., Arenas, M., Benedikt, M.: SPARQLByE: querying RDF data by example. PVLDB 9(13), 1533–1536 (2016)
7. Erling, O.: Virtuoso, a hybrid RDBMS/graph column store. IEEE Data Eng. Bull. 35(1), 3–8 (2012)
8. Fariha, A., Sarwar, S.M., Meliou, A.: SQuID: semantic similarity-aware query intent discovery. In: SIGMOD 2018, pp. 1745–1748 (2018)
9. Görlitz, O., Thimm, M., Staab, S.: SPLODGE: systematic generation of SPARQL benchmark queries for linked open data. In: Cudré-Mauroux, P., et al. (eds.) ISWC 2012, Part I. LNCS, vol. 7649, pp. 116–132. Springer, Heidelberg (2012). https://doi.org/10.1007/978-3-642-35176-1_8
10. Guo, Y., Pan, Z., Heflin, J.: LUBM: a benchmark for OWL knowledge base systems. J. Web Sem. 3(2–3), 158–182 (2005)
11. Lehmann, J., Bühmann, L.: AutoSPARQL: let users query your knowledge base. In: Antoniou, G., et al. (eds.) ESWC 2011, Part I. LNCS, vol. 6643, pp. 63–79. Springer, Heidelberg (2011). https://doi.org/10.1007/978-3-642-21034-1_5
12. Lissandrini, M., Mottin, D., Velegrakis, Y., Palpanas, T.: X2q: your personal example-based graph explorer. In: PVLDB 2018 (2018)
13. Ma, L., Yang, Y., Qiu, Z., Xie, G., Pan, Y., Liu, S.: Towards a complete OWL ontology benchmark. In: Sure, Y., Domingue, J. (eds.) ESWC 2006. LNCS, vol. 4011, pp. 125–139. Springer, Heidelberg (2006). https://doi.org/10.1007/11762256_12
14. Morsey, M., Lehmann, J., Auer, S., Ngonga Ngomo, A.-C.: DBpedia SPARQL benchmark – performance assessment with real queries on real data. In: Aroyo, L., et al. (eds.) ISWC 2011, Part I. LNCS, vol. 7031, pp. 454–469. Springer, Heidelberg (2011). https://doi.org/10.1007/978-3-642-25073-6_29
15. Potoniec, J.: An on-line learning to query system. In: ISWC 2016 Posters & Demonstrations Track (2016)
16. Rafes, K., Nauroy, J., Germain, C.: Certifying the interoperability of RDF database systems. In: Proceedings of the 2nd Workshop on Linked Data Quality (2015)
17. Saleem, M., Ali, M.I., Hogan, A., Mehmood, Q., Ngomo, A.-C.N.: LSQ: the linked SPARQL queries dataset. In: Arenas, M., et al. (eds.) ISWC 2015, Part II. LNCS, vol. 9367, pp. 261–269. Springer, Cham (2015). https://doi.org/10.1007/978-3-319-25010-6_15

18. Saleem, M., Hasnainb, A., Ngonga Ngomo, A.C.: LargeRDFBench: a billion triples benchmark for SPARQL endpoint federation. J. Web Sem. (2017)
19. Saleem, M., Mehmood, Q., Ngonga Ngomo, A.-C.: FEASIBLE: a feature-based SPARQL benchmark generation framework. In: Arenas, M., et al. (eds.) ISWC 2015, Part I. LNCS, vol. 9366, pp. 52–69. Springer, Cham (2015). https://doi.org/10.1007/978-3-319-25007-6_4
20. Schmidt, M., Hornung, T., Lausen, G., Pinkel, C.: SP^2 Bench: a SPARQL performance benchmark. In: ICDE 2009, pp. 222–233 (2009)
21. Schmidt, M., Görlitz, O., Haase, P., Ladwig, G., Schwarte, A., Tran, T.: FedBench: a benchmark suite for federated semantic data query processing. In: Aroyo, L., et al. (eds.) ISWC 2011, Part I. LNCS, vol. 7031, pp. 585–600. Springer, Heidelberg (2011). https://doi.org/10.1007/978-3-642-25073-6_37
22. Thompson, B.B., Personick, M., Cutcher, M.: The bigdata® RDF graph database. In: Linked Data Management, pp. 193–237 (2014)
23. Wilkinson, K., Sayers, C., Kuno, H.A., Reynolds, D., Ding, L.: Supporting scalable, persistent semantic web applications. IEEE Data Eng. Bull. **26**(4), 33–39 (2003)
24. Wu, H., Fujiwara, T., Yamamoto, Y., Bolleman, J.T., Yamaguchi, A.: Biobenchmark toyama 2012: an evaluation of the performance of triple stores on biological data. J. Biomed. Semant. **5**, 32 (2014)

ToCo: An Ontology for Representing Hybrid Telecommunication Networks

Qianru Zhou[1(✉)] ⓘ, Alasdair J. G. Gray[2] ⓘ, and Stephen McLaughlin[2] ⓘ

[1] University of Glasgow, Glasgow, UK
Qianru.Zhou@glasgow.ac.uk
[2] Heriot-Watt University, Edinburgh, UK
{A.J.G.Gray,S.McLaughlin}@hw.ac.uk

Abstract. The TOUCAN project proposed an ontology for telecommunication networks with hybrid technologies – the TOUCAN Ontology (ToCo), available at http://purl.org/toco/, as well as a knowledge design pattern `Device-Interface-Link (DIL)` pattern. The core classes and relationships forming the ontology are discussed in detail. The ToCo ontology can describe the physical infrastructure, quality of channel, services and users in heterogeneous telecommunication networks which span multiple technology domains. The DIL pattern is observed and summarised when modelling networks with various technology domains. Examples and use cases of ToCo are presented for demonstration.

Keywords: Linked data · Semantic web · Ontology ·
Hybrid telecommunication network · Knowledge based system

1 Introduction

The rapid growth in telecommunication services has resulted in today's network infrastructure being increasingly heterogeneous and complex [1–10]. State of the art network physical infrastructure is extremely complex, consisting of *routers, gateways, bridges, router servers, switches, firewalls, NATs, etc.* For traffic control, there are *packet shapers, packet sniffers, scrubbers, load balancers, etc.* Many of these devices differ from each other in relatively subtle ways. To compound matters, there are a variety of operators and equipment vendors for telecommunication networks, e.g., *HUAWEI, SAMSUNG, THREE, O2, CISCO, ERISSON, etc.*, who each develop and construct their own mechanisms and own versions of *configuration, description documents, technical specification, and software systems* all for devices with a similar functionality. Current *standardisation documents* of networks are also problematic. Multiple solutions and standards exist with limited differences. For example, there is a significant number of competing IETF RFCs (the proposals for internet technical standard documentation) providing solutions to similar questions [11–13].

This growing complexity coupled with the increase in telecommunication services requires the construction of a suitably abstracted knowledge base which is

© Springer Nature Switzerland AG 2019
P. Hitzler et al. (Eds.): ESWC 2019, LNCS 11503, pp. 507–522, 2019.
https://doi.org/10.1007/978-3-030-21348-0_33

universally accepted and machine interpretable [3–10,14,15]. Current knowledge bases for telecommunication networks management are problematic [2,16,17]. Most of them are defined for a specific protocol and focused on a single network layer. Consequently, when a situation arises which is out of the scope of the protocol or when the protocol is replaced or updated, then these knowledge bases are not appropriate.

Through the use of Semantic Web technologies, telecommunication networks can be described with all of their complexity and associated relationships. Thus allowing network administrators to operate at an abstract level removed from the technical details of configuration. Computer-processable semantics would also allow telecommunication network application developers to collect, reason about, and edit the network and the data transmitted.

In this paper we propose and develop an OWL formal-structured ontology – TOUCAN Ontology (ToCo) to describe the resources available in telecommunication networks with heterogeneous technologies. The ontology has 84 concepts, 39 object properties, and 54 datatype properties. To develop a well-structured and formal ontology, we propose a knowledge pattern to describe networks in various kinds of technology domain, namely a `Device-Interface-Link` (DIL) pattern, which forms the top-level of the ToCo ontology.

The contributions of this paper are threefold. The main contribution is the ToCo ontology. The domain definition of ToCo is introduced in Sect. 2. An outline and the key modules of ToCo are presented in Sect. 3. The second contribution is the DIL pattern based on which ToCo is built. DIL pattern identifies and provides an important insight into the abstract and recurring knowledge pattern in networks with different technology domains. With the DIL pattern, the ontology developing processes for networks will be made clearer and more efficient. The third contribution is the examples of ToCo, describing networks with various technologies, and the use cases in which ToCo is used (Sect. 4). This is followed by a conclusion (Sect. 5).

2 Background and Requirements

2.1 Background

This ontology development is part of an ongoing project – The TOUCAN project[1], which is a five-year EPSRC project exploring an technology agnostic, future-proof infrastructure and service management for networks with heterogenous technologies. The project is initiated by the University of Bristol, University of Edinburgh, Heriot-Watt University, and Lancaster University, with network experts in various technology domains (optical network, LiFi network, WiFi network, and computer network, respectively). One of the tasks of TOUCAN project is to use semantic web technologies to develop an knowledge base for networks with heterogenous technology domains.

---

[1] TOwards Ultimate Convergence All Networks (TOUCAN), Grant No. EP/L020009/1.

When developing ToCo, the 7-step ontology developing methodology discussed in [18] was adopted, due to its iterative approach which is suitable for modelling an ever-changing domain such as telecommunication networks. The evaluation of ToCo is carried out through use cases and problem-solving methods, as in [18].

Ontologies that have been proposed for telecommunication network are numerous in the literature [3–10,19–22]. The most popular ones are summarised below.

Network Description Language [23]: NDL is the first description language to describe computer networks. It provides several sub-ontologies that can be used for that purpose: a *topology sub-ontology* that describes the basic interconnections between devices, a *layer sub-ontology* to describe technologies, a *capability sub-ontology* to describe network capabilities and a *domain sub-ontology* for creating abstracted views of networks and a *physical sub-ontology* that describes the physical aspects of network elements, like a component in a device [23].

Ontology for 3G Wireless Network [3]: This ontology is proposed for wireless network transport configuration. It consists of two sub-ontologies, domain ontology and task ontology [3].

Mobile ontology [4]: Proposed for the SPICE Project, the Mobile Ontology has directed considerable effort towards ontology standardisation [4]. It is proposed as a scalable solution with several pluggable sub-ontologies: services, profile, content, presence, context, communication resources sub-ontology.

Ontology for Optical Transport Network (OOTN) [19]: OOTN is an ontology for optical transport networks based on ITU-T G.805 and G.872 recommendations. It is a computational optical ontology [19].

Ontology adopted in "OpenMobileNetwork" [21]: "OpenMobileNetwork" is a linked Open Dataset for Mobile Networks and Devices. It also developed an open source platform that provides semantically enriched mobile network and WiFi topology resource in RDF [21]. The ontology adopted is published online[2] and is efficient and mature for the description of mobile network topologies. However, that also limits the ontology to the specific scenario (describing WiFi topology). For example, it cannot describe optical backbone networks or LiFi.

2.2 Research Gap

As stated above, the ontologies proposed for network management are numerous. However, they are designed for specific tasks. There is no single "best" approach for the domain of network management. They are not yet able to provide a universally accepted knowledge base for telecommunication networks with hybrid technologies. There are three main reasons for this:

---

[2] http://www.openmobilenetwork.org/ontology/.

- First, many network description ontologies are proposed for some particular applications, rather than for the overall network resources.
- Second, the evaluation of ontology is problematic. Although many evaluation theories have been put forward [24,25], few reports detail how to carry out the evaluation step by step. Generally speaking, for network description ontologies, there are two approaches to evaluation. One is to discuss with experts in the specific field, the other is to apply it in a real-world application. To the best of our knowledge, very few use cases have been carried out in practice. Thus, it is difficult to determine if one particular ontology is superior to any other.
- The final reason lies in the ever-changing nature of communication technology. For example, wireless communication technology changes generation almost every decade. New technologies keep arising, and it is difficult to develop a standard vocabulary to describe them.

3   TOUCAN Ontology

The ToCo ontology, available at http://purl.org/toco/, is constructed into 8 modules, namely, Device, Interface, Link, User, Service, Data, Time, Location. These modules and their key relationships are shown in Fig. 1. The full ontology consists of 84 concepts, 39 object properties, and 54 datatype properties.

The namespaces used in this paper are written as the prefixes shown in Table 1. The ToCo has been formally published with a creative commons license[3]. The design and logic have been scanned and checked by ontology pitfall scanner (OOPS)[4].

The ontology is able to describe the physical infrastructures of the hybrid telecommunication networks, including devices, interfaces, and links in networks of all technology domains in current telecommunication system. Quality of communication service can also be described, such as bandwidth, data rate, package loss, delay, etc., to give a detailed representation for the performance of a certain link. Finally, concepts of services provided by the telecommunication networks, and the users being served, are also included, as they are part of the telecommunication system.

ToCo holds an inclusive view of the telecommunication networks: *"devices with interfaces through which can connect."* Ontology engineering is at its heart a modelling endeavour [26]. During the modelling process, networks with different access technologies are observed to have been repeating structurally similar knowledge patterns, termed here as the Device-Interface-Link (DIL) pattern[5]. The set of classes and relations that jointly form the Device-Interface-Link pattern are shown in Fig. 2. ToCo is built around this pattern. The pattern is developed based on the minimal ontological commitment to make it reusable for applications in variety of network technology domains.

---

[3] https://creativecommons.org/licenses/by-sa/4.0/.

[4] http://oops.linkeddata.es/.

[5] Published on http://ontologydesignpatterns.org/.

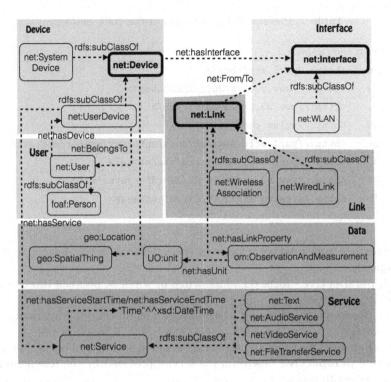

Fig. 1. The ToCo ontology, key concepts and relations, split by modules. The modules are divided by blocks with different colours. The central concepts are brought out by the DIL pattern.

The following Sect. 3.1 describes the details of the `device`, `interface`, `link`, `user`, `data`, and `service` classes. Examples are given for each class to demonstrate its application, interaction with other classes.

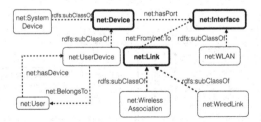

Fig. 2. The Device-Interface-Link Pattern (central concepts in bold).

ToCo can be seen from six perspectives:

A device perspective - focus on the devices in the network and their properties;

Table 1. Prefixes and namespaces of the ToCo ontology.

Prefix	Namespace
net	`<http://purl.org/toco/>`
xsd	`<http: //www.w3.org/2001/XMLSchema#>`
geo	`<http://www.w3.org/2003/01/geo/>`
foaf	`<http://xmlns.com/foaf/spec/>`
om	`<http://purl.oclc.org/net/unis/ontology/sensordata.owl/>`
UO	`<http://purl.obolibrary.org/obo/uo.owl>`
rdf	`<http://www.w3.org/1999/02/22-rdf-syntax-ns#>`
rdfs	`<http://www.w3.org/2000/01/rdf-schema#>`

An interface perspective - focus on the interfaces on the devices, and their properties;

A link perspective - focus on a link, wired or wireless, between two interfaces, and its properties;

A user perspective - focus on a user of a user equipment, her information and properties;

A data perspective - focus on the data measured or observed out of a property;

A service perspective - focus on the service provided by the telecommunication system to users.

3.1 Ontology Perspectives

Device. A device (`net:Device`) is the device in the physical infrastructure of the telecommunication networks, with the ability of transmit and/or receiving signals in the form of electromagnetic wave (based on the frequency, could be microwave, millimeter wave, optical wave, etc.). Based on the function and

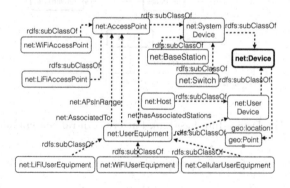

Fig. 3. Ontology view focusing on Devices.

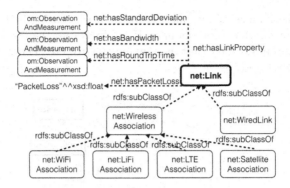

Fig. 4. Ontology view focusing on Links.

role played in the telecommunication networks, devices can be divided into system device (`net:SystemDevice`) and user device (`net:UserDevice`). Moreover, the devices in networks of a specific technology domain are subclasses of the device (`net:Device`), for example, in wired network, there are hosts (`net:Host`) and switches (`net:Switch`); in LTE network, there are base stations (`net:BaseStation`) and user equipment (`net:UserEquipment`); in WiFi and LiFi networks, there are access point (`net:AccessPoint`), which can be further divided into WiFi access point (`net:WiFiAccessPoint`) and LiFi access point (`net:LiFiAccessPoint`). The ontology view of Device is shown in Fig. 3.

Link. Link (`net:Link`) is one of the most important concepts in telecommunication networks. The principal obligation of the telecommunication network is to establish a link and maintain the quality of the link. A link could be a wired cable (`net:WiredLink`), or a cluster of wireless connections (`net:WirelessAssociation`). Please note that `net:WiredLink` and `net:WirelessAssociation` are disjoint with each other, i.e., a link cannot be both at the same time.

The properties of links determine the quality of a communication, for example, bandwidth (`net:hasBandwidth`), data rate (`net:hasDatarate`), transmit power (`net:hasTxpower`), receive power (`net:hasRecpower`), etc. An example of describing the bandwidth of a Link is shown below.

```
ex:link_1 a net:Link ;
net:hasBandwidth ex:link_1_bw .
ex:link_1_bw a
om:ObservationAndMeasurement ;
net:hasValue "50"^^xsd:float ;
net:hasUnit UO:0000325 .
```

It describes the fact that a link link_1 has a bandwidth of 50 MHz. The ontology view of Link is shown in Fig. 4.

Interface. The important information for network routing is described as the properties of an interface, for example: IP address (net:hasIP), MAC address (net:hasMAC), antenna gain (net:hasAntennaGain), etc. The ontology view of Interface is shown in Fig. 5.

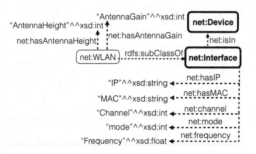

Fig. 5. Ontology view focusing on Interface.

User. The user information in telecommunication networks is covered, e.g., user id, name, join_date, home_country, home_town, etc. As the user is a human in real life, parts of the foaf ontology[6] is reused. The main relationship between User is with the UserEquipment:

net:User net:hasDevice net:UserDevice.

Some main concepts of User are shown in Fig. 6.

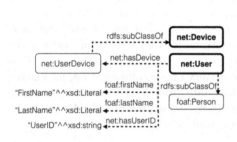

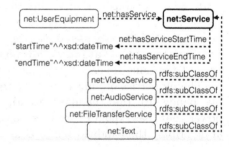

Fig. 6. Ontology view focusing on User.

Fig. 7. Ontology view focusing on Service.

---

[6] http://xmlns.com/foaf/0.1/.

Data. All the observation and measurement data, location and time information are described in the data module. General information, such as location, time, measurement, have previously been modelled by ontologies. Popular ontologies are reused here to describe the data. For example, the Units Ontology (UO)[7] is reused to describe the units of the data [27]. The SENSEI[8] observation and measurement ontology[9] is reused here to describe the observation results and measured data in telecommunication system. Location information are described with WGS84 ontology[10].

Service. The service module describes the details of telecommunication services, e.g., voice session, video session, document transmission. Some concepts of the service module is shown in Fig. 7.

4 Examples and Use Cases of ToCo

Examples are provided to demonstrate how networks within different technology domains are described with ToCo. From small-scale telecommunication networks such as vehicle-to-vehicle networks, smart home devices, to large-scale networks such as satellite networks can all be described with ToCo. The examples include: three network resource description examples for WiFi, LiFi, and computer network, respectively, two examples of network management task execution driven by ToCo, and a SDN flow description example.

4.1 Examples on Network Resource Description

To describe the information of a WiFi network, a simplified schema of a WiFi network is shown in Fig. 8. The x-axis and y-axis denote the longitude and latitude of a planar graph. The circles with different colours represent WiFi access points (circles in blue) and user equipments like phones, laptops (circles in red), with the area of circles denotes the cover range of signal. If the centre of a red circle is in range of the blue circle, it means this user equipment is in the range of the WiFi access point. Some of the main triples are shown in the example in Listing 1.1.

```
ex:wifi20 a net:WiFiAccessPoint ;
    net:driver "nl80211"^^xsd:string ;
    net:hasWLAN ex:wifi20-wlan1 ;
    net:ssid "wifi"^^xsd:string ;
    net:stationsInRange ex:sta1, ex:sta2, ex:sta3,
        ex:sta4, ex:sta5, ex:sta6 ;
    net:hasAssociatedStations ex:sta1 ;
```

---

[7] http://purl.obolibrary.org/obo/uo.owl.

[8] A project of EU, http://www.sensei-project.eu/.

[9] http://purl.oclc.org/net/unis/ontology/sensordata.owl.

[10] http://www.w3.org/2003/01/geo/wgs84_pos/.

```
    geo:location ex:wifi20_location .
ex:wifi20_location geo:alt   "0.0"^^xsd:float ;
    geo:lat "50.0"^^xsd:float ;
    geo:long "50.0"^^xsd:float .

ex:sta1 a net:WiFiUserEquipment ;
    net:hasWiFiWLAN ex:sta1-wlan0 ;
    net:hasName "sta1"^^xsd:string ;
    geo:location ex:sta1_location .

ex:sta1_h1 a net:WiFiAssociation ; net:from ex:sta1 ;
    net:to ex:h1 ; net:hasBandWidth ex:sta1_h1_bw .
ex:h1_sta1_bw a om:ObservationAndMeasurement ;
    net:hasUnit UO:0000325 ; net:hasValue "51.5"^^xsd:float .
```

Listing 1.1. Part of the RDF knowledge graph for a WiFi network. The knowledge of the stations in range, stations associated, location of a WiFi access point, and the bandwidth of the wireless link between the WiFi access point and a user device "sta1" is described.

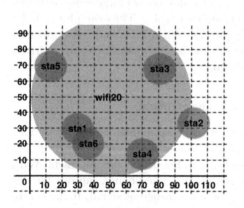 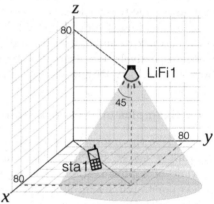

Fig. 8. The schema of a WiFi network with one access point "wifi20" and six mobile stations "sta1" to "sta6".

Fig. 9. A schema of a LiFi network with one access point and one mobile station.

Figure 9 shows a three-dimensional coordinate where a LiFi access point "LiFi1" and a user device "sta1" are located. The information of access point, such as, the half intensity angle, optical transmitted power, mobile stations in range, and location is represented in the Listing 1.2, as well as the information of the association between "LiFi1" and "sta1", such as distance, bandwidth, incident angle, and radiance angle.

```
ex:LiFi1 a net:LiFiAccessPoint ;
    net:hasGainOfOpticalFilter "1"^^xsd:int ;
    net:hasHalfIntensityAngle "45.0"^^xsd:float ;
    net:hasOpticalTransmittedPower "0.3"^^xsd:float ;
    net:hasRespansivity "1"^^xsd:float ;
    net:stationsInRange ex:sta1 ;
    geo:location ex:LiFi1_location .

ex:sta1 a net:LiFiUserEquipment ;
    net:hasFieldOfView "90"^^xsd:float ;
    net:hasGainOfConcentrator "1"^^xsd:float ;
    net:hasLiFiWLAN ex:sta1_wlan0 ;
    geo:location ex:sta1_location .

ex:sta1_wlan0 a net:WLAN ;
    net:hasWirelessAssociation ex:sta1_ap1 .

ex:sta1_ap1 a net:LiFiAssociation ;
    net:hasDistance "9"^^xsd:float ;
    net:hasIncidentAngle "15"^^xsd:float ;
    net:hasRadianceAngle "27.5"^^xsd:float ;
    net:hasBandwidth ex:sta1_ap1_bw .
ex:sta1_ap1_bw a om:ObservationAndMeasurement ;
    net:hasValue "5"^^xsd:float ; net:hasUnit UO:0000325 .
```

Listing 1.2. Part of a RDF knowledge graph for a LiFi. The knowledge about the half intensity angle, optical transmitted power, mobile stations in range, and location of a LiFi access point is represented, as well as the knowledge of the association between "LiFi1" and "sta1", such as distance, bandwidth, incident angle, and radiance angle.

To describe a wired computer network, some examples of the triples are shown in the Listing 1.3. Knowledge about the interfaces, e.g., IP address, MAC address, and link information such as bandwidth are described.

```
ex:s1 a net:Swtich ;
net:hasInterface ex:s1_eth0 , ex:s1_eth1 , ex:s1_eth2 .

ex:h1 a net:Host ;
net:hasInterface ex:h1-eth0 , ex:h1-eth1 , ex:h1-eth2 .

ex:h1-eth0 a net:Interface ; net:hasIP "10.0.0.1" ;
        net:hasMAC "f6:8a:d8:0b:6d:e7" ;
        net:isIn ex:h1 .

ex:s1_eth1 net:hasLink ex:s1_h1 .
ex:s1_h1 a net:WiredLink ; ex:hasBandwidth ex:s1_h1_bw .
ex:s1_h1_bw a om:ObservationAndMeasurement ;
        net:hasValue "50"^^xsd:float ;   net:hasUnit UO:0000325 .
```

Listing 1.3. Part of the RDF knowledge graph of a computer network, describing the knowledge about the interfaces and links, e.g., IP address, MAC address, and bandwidth.

Another example relates to the software defined network (SDN). SDN is about making decisions on how a flow (or a connection) is transmitted across the whole network. Thus, `Flow` is the key concept in SDN. ToCo is able to describe the properties of the `Flow`, as shown in the Listing 1.4.

```
ex:s1 net:hasFlow ex:s1_flow1 .
ex:s1_flow1 a net:Flow ; net:idleTimeout 0 ; net:tableId 0 ;
        net:flags 0 ; net:hardTimeout 0 ; net:priority 0 ;
        net:cookie 2 ; net:hasAction  ex:s1_flow2_action0 .

ex:s1_flow2_action0 a net:Output ; net:toPort ex:s1_port1 .
```

Listing 1.4. Part of the knowledge graph of a Flow in SDN. The information of a Flow is mainly described.

4.2   Examples on Network Management Task Execution with ToCo

With the knowledge base generated by ToCo, semantic queries can be designed to answer high level network management questions such as, "Which switch is host1 connected to?", "Find me the hosts in the network that are blocked from the others." or even more complicated one such as "Find me all the hosts connected to switch_1 and switch_3, if they are not host_3 or host_5," as shown in Algorithm 1.

```
SELECT ?port2 ?macAddr1 ?port4 ?macAddr2
WHERE {
    ?p1 net:isIn net:s1. ?l1 net:from ?p1; net:to ?p2. filter (?p1 != ?p2).
    ?p2 net:isIn ?h1. ?h1 rdf:type net:Host. filter(?h1 != net:h3). ?p2 net:hasMAC
?macAddr1.
    bind(strafter(str(?p2), "http://purl.org/toco/") as ?port2)
    ?p3 net:isIn net:s3. ?l2 net:from ?p3; net:to ?p4. ?p4 net:isIn ?h2.
    ?h2 rdf:type net:Host. filter(?h2 != net:h5)
    ?p4 net:hasMAC ?macAddr2. filter (?p3 != ?p4). }
    bind(strafter(str(?p4), "http://purl.org/toco/") as ?port4)}
```

Algorithm 1: SPARQL query to get all the hosts of switches "s1" and "s3" and their port number except the host "h3" and "h5".

The query in Algorithm 1 has been used in one project to build firewalls between customer selected hosts. For example, by passing the query result of Algorithm 1 to a firewall building function, we can build a firewall between switches "s1" and "s2", while the communication between hosts "h3" and "h5" (which are in the domain of "s1" and "s2" respectively) is not affected.

Another example for flow consistency detection in SDN is provided in Algorithm 2 [28]. To accomplish an autonomic network management system, the system needs to be self-aware. Thus, it should be able to learn what is happening inside, detect changes, decide what to do, and fix the problem itself. In SDN,

```
SELECT DISTINCT ?in_port ?to_port
WHERE {
  ?s a net:Switch; net:hasFlow ?f.
  ?f a net:PathFlow; net:inPort ?in_p; net:hasFlowAction ?a. ?a net:toPort ?to_p.
  ?p1 a net:Interface; net:isIn ?s; net:hasInterfaceName ?in_p; net:isUP ?isUp1.
  ?p2 a net:Interface; net:isIn ?s; net:hasInterfaceName ?to_p; net:isUP ?isUp2.
  filter (?isUp1 = "false"^^xsd:boolean || ?isUp2 = "false"^^xsd:boolean)}
```

Algorithm 2: SPARQL query for automatic flow update. A non-empty result returned by the query denotes that there are inconsistent flows.

flows are adopted to route packets to/from specific port. If a port accidentally fails, the flows related (the flows with instructions to send packet from/to this port) should be revised (stop sending packets to this failed port) correspondingly.

4.3 Use Cases

ToCo has been used in several applications for autonomic network management and disaster response. These use cases are: a network autonomic management system "SEANET" [28], a network policy-based management application "ReasoNet" [29], a shipwreck early detection use case "lost silence" [30], and "SARA" [31], a resource allocation application in post-tragedy situation.

SEANET [28] is a technology independent, knowledge-based network management system. The ToCo ontology and the DIL pattern are the key to the success of SEANET. It adopts the ToCo ontology as the language to build the knowledge base for telecommunication networks, and use SPARQL to query over the knowledge base. A technology-independent API is also provided by SEANET to implement autonomic network management tasks for customers without knowledge of semantic web or telecommunication network.

A policy based SDN network management approach "ReasoNet" [29] leads by researchers from Lancaster University, U.K., adopts concepts of ToCo to model their knowledge base on Ryu controller (a SDN controller). It can support network knowledge inference and integrity/consistency validation. Two popular control applications, a learning switch application and a QoS-oriented declarative policy engine, are presented to demonstrate the scalability which is comparable with current SDN network operation systems.

In lost silence [30], a methodology was illustrated to detect shipwreck incidents immediately (with the delay in the order of milliseconds), by processing semantically annotated streams of data in cellular telecommunication systems. In lost silence, live information about the position and status of phones are encoded as RDF streams, adopting part of the concepts of ToCo's Device module. The approach is exemplified in the context of a passenger cruise ship capsizing. However, the approach is readily translatable to other incidents. The evaluation results show that with a properly chosen window size, such incidents can be detected efficiently and effectively.

5 Conclusions

We developed the ToCo ontology, for hybrid telecommunication networks. ToCo is able to describe the devices, interfaces, and links inside the telecommunication system, and the measurement of the link properties (or in other term, channel QoS), without technology specificity. The information of users and services are also represented. ToCo also covers the main part of the SDN properties.

   While modelling the knowledge in networks, an ontology design pattern, the DIL pattern, has been observed and summarised. It provides a simple and efficient insight into the structure of ontologies for all kinds of linked devices, making the ontologies modelling process efficient, by avoiding some repetitive work.

   Eight physically separated modules are arranged in ToCo, focusing on different aspects, namely, Device, Interface, Link, User, Service, Data, the key modules of ToCo are Device, Interface, Link. The demonstrations conducted on four networks with different technologies have shown that ToCo is able to described these networks. Concepts from existing ontologies are reused, e.g., foaf for user presentation, wgs84 for location.

   ToCo is currently used in a number of projects. It is evaluated mainly based on the feedback from the projects. As the telecommunication network technologies are experiencing rapid developing, the ToCo ontology will keep evolving at the mean time. Now ToCo has been published via Github, thus it is open to public edition via Github pull requests, the authors are in charge of the edit inspection. We are open to more suitable approaches of the ontology publication and evolving in the future.

Acknowledgement. This research was supported by the EPSRC TOUCAN project (Grant No. EP/L020009/1).

References

1. Shenker, S., Casado, M., Koponen, T., McKeown, N.: The future of networking, and the past of protocols (2011)
2. Rexford, J.: The networking philosopher's problem, vol. 41, pp. 5–9. ACM (2011)
3. Cleary, D., Danev, B., O'Donoghue, D.: Using ontologies to simplify wireless network configuration. In: FOMI (2005)
4. Villalonga, C., et al.: Mobile ontology: towards a standardized semantic model for the mobile domain. In: Di Nitto, E., Ripeanu, M. (eds.) ICSOC 2007. LNCS, vol. 4907, pp. 248–257. Springer, Heidelberg (2009). https://doi.org/10.1007/978-3-540-93851-4_25
5. Devitt, A., Danev, B., Matusikova, K.: Ontology-driven automatic construction of bayesian networks for telecommunication network management. In: FOMI (2006)
6. De Vergara, J.E.L., Guerrero, A., Villagrá, V.A., Berrocal, J.: Ontology-based network management: study cases and lessons learned. J. Netw. Syst. Manage. **17**(3), 234–254 (2009)
7. Guerrero, A., Villagrá, V.A., de Vergara, J.E.L., Berrocal, J.: Ontology-based integration of management behaviour and information definitions using SWRL and OWL. In: Schönwälder, J., Serrat, J. (eds.) DSOM 2005. LNCS, vol. 3775, pp. 12–23. Springer, Heidelberg (2005). https://doi.org/10.1007/11568285_2

8. Guerrero, A., Villagrá, V.A., de Vergara, J.E.L., Sánchez-Macián, A., Berrocal, J.: Ontology-based policy refinement using SWRL rules for management information definitions in OWL. In: State, R., van der Meer, S., O'Sullivan, D., Pfeifer, T. (eds.) DSOM 2006. LNCS, vol. 4269, pp. 227–232. Springer, Heidelberg (2006). https://doi.org/10.1007/11907466_20

9. Strassner, J., et al.: The design of a new policy model to support ontology-driven reasoning for autonomic networking. J. Netw. Syst. Manage. 17(1–2), 5–32 (2009)

10. Xiao, D., Xu, H.: An integration of ontology-based and policy-based network management for automation. In: IEEE ICIEA 2006, pp. 27–27 (2006)

11. Clark, D.D.: Policy routing in internet protocols, Technical report, Internet Request for Comments 1102 (1989)

12. Braun, H.-W.: Models of policy based routing, Technical report (1989)

13. Steenstrup, M.: An architecture for inter-domain policy routing (1993)

14. Benyon, D.: Information and data modelling. McGraw-Hill Higher Education (1996)

15. Dijkstra, F., Andree, B., Koymans, K., van der Ham, J., et al.: Introduction to ITU-T recommendation, p. 805 (2007)

16. Houidi, Z.B.: A knowledge-based systems approach to reason about networking. In: ACM HotNets, pp. 22–28 (2016)

17. Fallon, L., O'Sullivan, D.: Using a semantic knowledge base for communication service quality management in home area networks. In: IEEE NOMS 2012, pp. 43–51 (2012)

18. Noy, N.F., McGuinness, D.L., et al.: Ontology development 101: A guide to creating your first ontology (2001)

19. Barcelos, P.P., Monteiro, M,E., Simões, R.D.M., Garcia, A.S., Segatto, M.E.: OOTN-an ontology proposal for optical transport networks. In: IEEE ICUMT 2009, pp. 1–7 (2009)

20. Poveda Villalon, M., Suárez-Figueroa, M.C., García-Castro, R., Gómez-Pérez, A.: A context ontology for mobile environments (2010)

21. Uzun, A., Küpper, K.: Openmobilenetwork: extending the web of data by a dataset for mobile networks and devices. In: ACM ICSS 2012, pp. 17–24 (2012)

22. Guizzardi, G., Wagner, G.: Using the unified foundational ontology (UFO) as a foundation for general conceptual modeling languages. In: Poli, R., Healy, M., Kameas, A. (eds) Theory and Applications of Ontology: Computer Applications, pp. 175–196. Springer, Dordrecht (2010). https://doi.org/10.1007/978-90-481-8847-5_8

23. Ham, J.J., et al.: A semantic model for complex computer networks: the network description language (2010)

24. Gómez-Pérez, A.: Evaluation of ontologies. Int. J. Intell. Syst. 16(3), 391–409 (2001)

25. Brank, J., Grobelnik, M., Mladenić, D.: A survey of ontology evaluation techniques

26. Clark, P., Thompson, J., Porter, B.: Knowledge patterns. In: Staab, S., Studer, R. (eds) Handbook on Ontologies, pp. 191–207. Springer, Heidelberg (2004). https://doi.org/10.1007/978-3-540-24750-0_10

27. Gkoutos, G.V., Schofield, P.N., Hoehndorf, R.: The units ontology: a tool for integrating units of measurement in science. In: Database 2012 (2012). bas033

28. Zhou, Q., Gray, A., McLaughlin, S.: SeaNet: Semantic enabled autonomic management of software defined networks. (manuscript under review)

29. Rotsos, C., et al.: Reasonet: inferring network policies using ontologies. In: NetSoft 2018 (2018)

30. Zhou, Q., McLaughlin, S., Gray, A., Wu, S., Wang, C.: Lost silence: an emergency response early detection service through continuous processing of telecommunication data streams. In: Web Stream Processing Workshop, ISWC, Joint Proceedings of WSP and WOMoCoE, pp. 33–47 (2017)
31. Zhou, Q., Gray, A., McLaughlin, S.: Sara: semantic access point resource allocation service. In: IEEE WD (2019)

A Software Framework and Datasets
for the Analysis of Graph Measures
on RDF Graphs

Matthäus Zloch[1]([✉]), Maribel Acosta[2]([✉]), Daniel Hienert[1], Stefan Dietze[1,3],
and Stefan Conrad[3]

[1] GESIS - Leibniz-Institute for the Social Sciences, Mannheim, Germany
{matthaeus.zloch,daniel.hienert,stefan.dietze}@gesis.org
[2] Institute AIFB, Karlsruhe Institute of Technology, Karlsruhe, Germany
maribel.acosta@kit.edu
[3] Institute for Computer Science, Heinrich-Heine University Düsseldorf,
Düsseldorf, Germany
{stefan.dietze,stefan.conrad}@uni-duesseldorf.de

Abstract. As the availability and the inter-connectivity of RDF
datasets grow, so does the necessity to understand the structure of the
data. Understanding the topology of RDF graphs can guide and inform
the development of, e.g. synthetic dataset generators, sampling methods, index structures, or query optimizers. In this work, we propose two
resources: (i) a software framework (Resource URL of the framework:
https://doi.org/10.5281/zenodo.2109469) able to acquire, prepare, and
perform a graph-based analysis on the topology of large RDF graphs,
and (ii) results on a graph-based analysis of 280 datasets (Resource URL
of the datasets: https://doi.org/10.5281/zenodo.1214433) from the LOD
Cloud with values for 28 graph measures computed with the framework.
We present a preliminary analysis based on the proposed resources and
point out implications for synthetic dataset generators. Finally, we identify a set of measures, that can be used to characterize graphs in the
Semantic Web.

1 Introduction

Since its first version in 2007, the Linked Open Data Cloud (LOD Cloud) has
increased by the factor of 100, containing $1,163$ data sets in the last version of
August 2017[1]. In various knowledge domains, like Government, Life Sciences,
and Natural Science, it has been a prominent example and a reference for the
success of the possibility to interlink and access open datasets that are described
following the Resource Description Framework (RDF). RDF provides a graph-
based data model where statements are modelled as triples. Furthermore, a set of
RDF triples compose a directed and labelled graph, where subjects and objects
can be defined as vertices while predicates correspond to edges.

---

[1] http://lod-cloud.net/.

© Springer Nature Switzerland AG 2019
P. Hitzler et al. (Eds.): ESWC 2019, LNCS 11503, pp. 523–539, 2019.
https://doi.org/10.1007/978-3-030-21348-0_34

Previous empirical studies on the characteristics of real-world RDF graphs have focused on general properties of the graphs [18], or analyses on the instance or schema level of such data sets [5,14]. Examples of statistics are dataset size, property and vocabulary usage, data types used or average length of string literals. In terms of the topology of RDF graphs, previous works report on network measures mainly focusing on in- and out-degree distributions, reciprocity, and path lengths [2,8,9,21]. Nonetheless, the results of these studies are limited to a small fraction of the RDF datasets currently available.

Conducting recurrent systematical analyses on a large set of RDF graph topologies is beneficial in many research areas. For instance:

Synthetic Dataset Generation. One goal of benchmark suites is to emulate real-world datasets and queries with characteristics from a particular domain or application-specific characteristics. Beyond parameters like the dataset size that is typically interpreted as the number of triples, taking into consideration reliable statistics about the network topology, basic graph and degree-based measures for instance, enables synthetic dataset generators to more appropriately emulate datasets at large-scale, contributing to solve the dataset scaling problem [20].

Graph Sampling. At the same time, graph sampling techniques try to find a representative sample from an original dataset, with respect to different aspects. Questions that arise in this field are (1) how to obtain a (minimal) representative sample, (2) which sampling method to use, and (3) how to scale up measurements of the sample [13]. Apart from qualitative aspects, like classes, properties, instances, and used vocabularies and ontologies, also topological characteristics of the original RDF graph should be considered. To this end, primitive measures of the graphs, like the max in-, out- and average-degree of vertices, reciprocity, density, etc., may be consulted to achieve more accurate results.

Profiling and Evolution. Due to its distributed and dynamic nature, monitoring the development of the LOD Cloud has been a challenge for some time, documented through a range of techniques for profiling datasets [3]. Apart from the number of datasets in the LOD Cloud, the aspect of its linkage (linking into other datasets) and connectivity (linking within one dataset) is of particular interest. From the graph perspective, the creation of new links has immediate impact on the characteristics of the graph. For this reason, graph measures may help to monitor changes and the impact of changes in datasets.

To support graph-based tasks in the aforementioned areas, first, we propose an open source framework which is capable of acquiring RDF datasets, efficiently preparing and computing graph measures over large RDF graphs. The framework is built upon state-of-the-art third-party libraries and published under MIT license. The proposed framework reports on network measures and graph invariants, which can be categorized in five groups: (i) basic graph measures, (ii) degree-based measures, (iii) centrality measures, (iv) edge-based measures, and (v) descriptive statistical measures. Second, we provide a collection of 280 datasets prepared with the framework and a report on 28 graph-based measures per dataset about the graph topology also computed with our framework. In this work, we present an analysis of graph measures over the aforementioned collection. This analysis involves over 11.3 billion RDF triples from nine knowledge domains, i.e., Cross Domain, Geography, Government, Life Sciences, Linguistics, Media, Publications, Social Networking, and User Generated. Finally, we conduct a correlation analysis among the studied invariants to identify a representative set of graph measures to characterize RDF datasets from a graph perspective. In summary, the contributions of our work are:

- A framework to acquire RDF datasets and compute graph measures (Sect. 3).
- Results of a graph-based analysis of 280 RDF datasets from the LOD Cloud. For each dataset, the collection includes 28 graph measures computed with the framework (Sect. 4).
- An analysis of graph measures on real-world RDF datasets (Sect. 5.1).
- A study to identify graph measures that characterize RDF datasets (Sect. 5.2).

2   Related Work

The RDF data model imposes characteristics which are not present in other graph-based data models. Therefore, we distinguish between works that analyze the structure of RDF datasets in terms of RDF-specific and graph measures.

RDF-Specific Analyses. This category includes studies about the general structure of RDF graphs at instance, schema, and metadata levels. Schmachtenberg et al. [18] present the status of RDF datasets in the LOD Cloud in terms of size, linking, vocabulary usage, and metadata. LODStats [5] and the large-scale approach DistLODStats [19] report on statistics about RDF datasets on the web, including number of triples, RDF terms, and properties per entity, and usage of vocabularies across datasets. Loupe [14] is an online tool that reports on the usage of classes and properties in RDF datasets. Fernández et al. [8] define measures to describe the relatedness between nodes and edges using subject-object, subject-predicate, and predicate-object ratios. Hogan et al. [12] study the distribution of RDF terms, classes, instances, and datatypes to measure the quality of public RDF data. In summary, the study of RDF-specific properties of publicly available RDF datasets have been extensively covered and is currently supported by online services and tools such as LODStats and Loupe. Therefore, in addition to these works, we focus on analyzing graph invariants in RDF datasets.

Graph-Based Analyses. In the area of structural network analysis, it is common to study the distribution of certain graph measures in order to characterize a graph. RDF datasets have also been subject to these studies. The study by Ding et al. [6] reveals that the power-law distribution is prevalent across graph invariants in RDF graphs obtained from 1.7 million documents. Also, the small-world phenomenon, known from experiments on social networks were studied within the Semantic Web [2]. More recently, Fernández et al. [8] have studied the structural features of real-world RDF data. Fernández et al. also propose

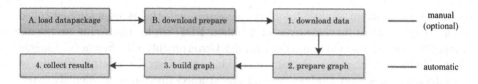

Fig. 1. Illustration of the semi-automatic process pipeline. Steps 1–4 include download, data and graph preparation, and graph analysis. Steps A and B are manual and optional preparation steps, described in Sect. 4.1.

measures in terms of in- and -out degrees for subjects, objects, and predicates and analyze the structure of 14 RDF graphs from different knowledge domains. Most of these works focus on studying different in- and out-degree distributions and are limited to a rather small collection of RDF datasets. Moreover, the work by Flores et al. [9] analyze further relevant graph invariants in RDF graphs including h−index and reciprocity. The work by Flores et al. applied graph-based metrics on synthetic RDF datasets. Complementary to these works, we present an study on 280 RDF datasets from the LOD Cloud and analyze their structure based on the average degree, h-index, and powerlaw exponent.

3   A Framework for Graph-Based Analysis on RDF Data

This section introduces the first resource published with this paper: the software framework. The main purpose of the framework is to prepare and perform a graph-based analysis on the graph topology of RDF datasets. One of the main challenges of the framework is to scale up to large graphs and to a high number of datasets, i.e., to compute graph metrics efficiently over current RDF graphs (hundreds of millions of edges) and in parallel with many datasets at once. The necessary steps to overcome these challenges are described in the following.

3.1   Functionality

The framework relies on the following methodology to systematically acquire and analyze RDF datasets. Figure 1 depicts the main steps of our processing pipeline of the framework. In the following, we describe steps 1–4 from Fig. 1.

Data Acquisition. The framework acquires RDF data dumps available online. Online availability is not mandatory to perform the analysis, as the pipeline runs with data dumps available offline. For convenience reasons, when operating on many datasets, one may load an initial list of datasets together with their names, available formats, and URLs into a local database (see Sect. 4.1). One can find

configuration details and database init-scripts in the source code repository[2].
Once acquired, the framework is capable of dealing with the following artifacts:

- Packed data dumps. Various formats are supported, including `bz2`, `7zip`,
  `tar.gz`, etc. This is achieved by utilizing the unix-tool `dtrx`.
- Archives, which contain a hierarchy of files and folders, will get scanned for
  files containing RDF data. Other files will be ignored, e.g. `xls`, `txt`, etc.
- Any files with a different serialization than N-Triples are transformed (if necessary). The list of supported formats[3] is currently limited to the most common ones for RDF data, which are N-Triples, RDF/XML, Turtle, N-Quads,
  and Notation3. This is achieved by utilizing *rapper*[4].

Preparation of the Graph Structure. In order to deal with large RDF
graphs, our aim is to create a as much automated and reliable processing pipeline
as possible that focuses on performance. The graph structure is created from an
edgelist, which is the result of this preparation step. One line in the edgelist
constitutes one edge in the graph, which is a relation between a pair of vertices,
the subject s and object o of an RDF triple. The line contains the predicate p
of an RDF triple in addition, so that it is stored as an attribute of the edge.
This attribute can be accessed during graph analysis and processing. To ease the
creation of this edgelist with edge attributes, we utilized the N-Triples format,
thus, a triple s p o becomes s o p in the edgelist. By this means, the framework
is able to prepare several datasets in parallel.

In order to reduce the usage of hard-disk space and also main memory during
the creation process of the graph structure, we make use of an efficient state-of-
the-art non-cryptographic hashing function[5] to encode actual values of the RDF
triples. For example, the RDF triple

```
<http://data.linkedopendata.it/musei/resource/Roma>
    <http://www.w3.org/2000/01/rdf-schema#label> "Roma" .
```

is turned into the hashed edgelist representation

```
43f2f4f2e41ae099 c9643559faeed68e 02325f53aeba2f02
```

Besides the fact that this hashing strategy can reduce space by the factor
of up to 12, compared to simple integer representation it has the advantage
that it facilitates the comparison between edgelists of different RDF datasets.
One could examine which resource URIs are the most frequently used across all
datasets. The framework provides a script to de-reference hashes, in order to
find a resource URI for the vertex with maximum degree, for instance.

Graph Creation. As graph analysis library we used *graph-tool*[6], an efficient
library for statistical analysis of graphs. In *graph-tool*, core data structures and

---

[2] Resource URL of the framework: https://doi.org/10.5281/zenodo.2109469.
[3] https://www.w3.org/standards/techs/rdf#w3c_all.
[4] raptor2-util library, http://librdf.org/raptor/rapper.html.
[5] xxhash, https://github.com/Cyan4973/xxHash.
[6] graph-tool, https://graph-tool.skewed.de/.

algorithms are implemented in C^{++}/C, while the library itself can be used with Python. *graph-tool* comes with a lot of pre-defined implementations for graph analysis, e.g., degree distributions or more advanced implementations on graphs like PageRank or clustering coefficient. Further, some values may be stored as attributes of vertices or edges in the graph structure.

The library's internal graph-structure may be serialized as a compressed binary object for future re-use. It can be reloaded by *graph-tool* with much higher performance than the original edgelist. Our framework instantiates the graph from the prepared edgelist or binary representation and operates on the graph object provided by the *graph-tool* library. As with dataset preparation, the framework can handle multiple computations of graph measures in parallel.

3.2   Graph Measures

In this section, we present statistical measures that are computed in the framework grouped into five dimensions: basic graph measures, degree-based measures, centrality measures, edge-based measures, and descriptive statistical measures. The computation of some metrics are carried out with *graph-tool* (e.g., PageRank), and others are computed by our framework (e.g., degree of centralization).

In the following, we introduce the graph notation used throughout the paper. A graph G is a pair of finite sets (V, E), with V denoting the set of all vertices (RDF subject and object resources). E is a multiset of (labeled) edges in the graph G, since in RDF a pair of subject and object resources may be described with more than one predicate. E.g. in the graph { s p1 o. s p2 o }, E has two pairs of vertices, i.e. $E = \{(s, o)_1, (s, o)_2 \mid s, o \in V\}$. RDF predicates are considered as additional edge labels, which also may occur as individual vertices in the same graph G. Newman [15] presents a more detailed introduction to networks and structural network analysis.

Basic Graph Measures. We report on the total number of vertices $|V| = n$ and the number of edges $|E| = m$ for a graph. Some works in the literature refer to these values as size and volume, respectively. The number of vertices and edges usually varies drastically across knowledge domains.

By its nature, RDF graphs contain a fraction of edges that share the same pair of source and target vertices (as in the example above). In our work, m_p represents the number of parallel edges, i.e., $m_p = |\{e \in E \mid count(e, E) > 1\}|$, with $count(e, E)$ being a function that returns the number of times e is contained in E. Based on this measure, we also compute the total number of edges without counting parallel edges, denoted m_u. It is computed by subtracting m_p from the total number of edges m, i.e., $m_u = m - m_p$.

Degree-Based Measures. The degree of a vertex $v \in V$, denoted $d(v)$, corresponds to the total number of incoming and outgoing edges of v, i.e., $d(v) = |\{(u, v) \in E \text{ or } (v, u) \in E \mid u \in V\}|$. For directed graphs, as is true for RDF datasets, it is common to distinguish between in- and out-degree, i.e.

$d_{in}(v) = |\{(u, v) \in E \mid u \in V\}|$ and $d_{out}(v) = |\{(v, u) \in E \mid u \in V\}|$, respectively. In social network analyses, vertices with a high out-degree are said to be "influential", whereas vertices with a high in-degree are called "prestigious". To identify these vertices in RDF graphs, we compute the maximum total-, in-, and out-degree of the graph's vertices, i.e., $d_{max} = max\ d(v)$, $d_{max,in} = max\ d_{in}(v)$, $d_{max,out} = max\ d_{out}(v)$, $\forall v \in V$ respectively. In addition, we compute the graph's average total-, in-, and out-degree denoted z, z_{in}, and z_{out}, respectively. These measures can be important in research on RDF data management, for instance, where the (average) degree of a vertex (database table record) has significant impact on query evaluation, since queries on dense graphs can be more costly in terms of execution time to evaluate [17].

Another degree-based measure supported in the framework is $h-$index, known from citation networks [11]. It is an indicator for the importance of a vertex, similar to a centrality measure (see Sect. 3.2). A value of h means that for the number of h vertices the degree of these vertices is greater or equal to h. A high value of a graph's $h-$index could be an indicator for a "dense" graph and that its vertices are more "prestigious". We compute this network measure for the directed graph (using only the in-degree of vertices) denoted as h_d and the undirected graph (using in- and out-degree of vertices) denoted as h_u.

Centrality Measures. In social network analyses, the concept of *point centrality* is used to express the importance of nodes in a network. There are many interpretations for the term "importance" and so are measures for centrality [15]. Comparing centrality measures with fill p shows that the higher the density of the graph the higher centrality measures it has for the vertices. Point centrality uses the degree of a vertex, $d(v)$. To indicate that it is a centrality measure, the literature sometimes normalizes this values by the total number of all vertices. We compute the maximum value of this measure, denoted as $C_{D,max} = d_{max}$. Another centrality measure computed is PageRank [16]. For each RDF graph, we identified the vertex with the highest PageRank values, denoted as PR_{max}.

Besides the point centrality, there is also the measure of *graph centralization* [10], which is known from social network analysis. This measure may also be seen as an indicator for the type of the graph, in that it expresses the degree of inequality and concentration of vertices as can be found in a perfect star-shaped graphs, that is at most centralized and unequal with regard to its degree distribution. The centralization of a graph regarding the degree is defined as:

$$C_D = \frac{\sum^{v \in V}(d_{max} - d(v))}{(|V| - 1) * (|V| - 2)} \qquad (1)$$

where C_D denotes the graph centralization measure using degree [10]. In contrast to social networks, RDF graphs usually contain many parallel edges between vertices (see next subsection). Thus, for this measure to make sense, we used the number of unique edges in the graph, m_u.

Edge-Based Measures. We compute the "density" or "connectance" of a graph, called *fill* denoted as p. It also can be interpreted as the probability that an edge is present between two randomly chosen vertices. The density is computed as the ratio of all edges to the total number of all possible edges. We use the formula for a directed graph with possible loops, accordance to the definition of RDF graphs, using m and m_u, i.e. $p = m/n^2$ and $p_u = m_u/n^2$.

Further, we analyze the fraction of bidirectional connections between vertices in the graph, thus pairs of vertices forward-connected by some edge, which are also backward-connected by some other edge. The value of *reciprocity*, denoted as y, is expressed as percentage, i.e. $y = m_{bi}/m$, with $m_{bi} = |\{(u,v) \in E \mid \exists (v,u) \in E\}|$. A high value means there are many connections between vertices which are bidirectional. This value is expected to be high in citation or social networks.

Another important group of measures that is described by the graph topology is related to paths. A path is a set of edges one can follow along between two vertices. As there can be more than one path, the *diameter* is defined as the longest shortest path between two vertices of the network [15], denoted as δ. This is a valuable measure when storing an RDF dataset in a relational database, as this measure affects join cardinality estimations depending on the type of schema implementation for the graph set. The diameter is usually a very time consuming measure to compute, since all possible paths have to be computed. Thus we used the `pseudo_diameter` algorithm[7] to estimate the value for our datasets.

Descriptive Statistical Measures. Descriptive statistical measures are important to describe distributions of some set of values, in our scenario, values for graph measures. In statistics, it is common to compute the *variance* σ^2 and *standard deviation* σ in order to express the degree of dispersion of a distribution. We do this for the in- and out-degree distributions in the graphs, denoted by σ_{in}^2, σ_{out}^2 and σ_{in}, σ_{out}, respectively. Furthermore, the *coefficient of variation* cv is consulted to have a comparable measure for distributions with different mean values. cv_{in} and cv_{out} are obtained by dividing the corresponding standard deviation σ_{in} and σ_{out} by the mean z_{in}, and z_{out}, respectively, times 100. cv can also be utilized to analyze the type of distribution with regard to a set of values. For example, a low value of cv_{out} means constant influence of vertices in the graph (homogeneous group), whereas a high value of cv_{in} means high prominence of some vertices in the graph (heterogeneous group).

Further, the type of *degree* distribution is an often considered measure of graphs. Some domains and datasets report on degree distributions that follow a power-law function, which means that the number of vertices with degree k behaves proportionally to the power of $k^{-\alpha}$, for some $\alpha \in \mathbb{R}$. Such networks are called scale-free. The literature has found that values in the range of $2 < \alpha < 3$ are typical in many real-world networks [15]. The scale-free behaviour also applies to some datasets and measures of RDF datasets [6,8]. However, to reason about whether a distribution follows a power-law can be technically challenging [1],

---

[7] https://graph-tool.skewed.de/static/doc/topology.html#graph_tool.topology.pseudo_diameter.

and computing the exponent α, that falls into a certain range of values, is not sufficient. We compute the exponent for the total- and in-degree distributions [1], denoted as α and α_{in}, respectively. In addition, to support the analysis of power-law distributions, the framework produces plots for both distributions. A power-law distribution is described as a line in a log-log plot.

Determining the function that fits the distribution may be of high value for algorithms, in order to estimate the selectivity of vertices and attributes in graphs. The structure and size of datasets created by synthetic datasets, for instance, can be controlled with these measures. Also, a clear power-law distribution allows for high compression rates of RDF datasets [8].

3.3 Availability, Sustainability and Maintenance

The software framework is published under MIT license on GitHub (see Footnote 2). The repository contains all code and a comprehensive documentation to install, prepare an RDF dataset, and run the analysis. The main part of the code implements most of the measures as a list of python functions that is extendable. Future features and bugfixes will be published under a minor or bugfix release, v0.x.x, respectively. The source code is frequently maintained and debugged, since it is actively used in other research projects at our institute (see Sect. 6). It is citable via a registered DOI obtained from Zenodo. Both web services, GitHub and Zenodo, provide search interfaces, which makes the code also be web findable.

Table 1. Processed datasets. Number of datasets, average and maximum number of vertices (n) and edges (m) in RDF graphs per knowledge domain.

Domain	Maximum		Average		# datasets
	n	m	n	m	
Cross domain	614,448,283	2,656,226,986	57,827,358	218,930,066	15
Geography	47,541,174	340,880,391	9,763,721	61,049,429	11
Government	131,634,287	1,489,689,235	7,491,531	71,263,878	37
Life sciences	356,837,444	722,889,087	25,550,646	85,262,882	32
Linguistics	120,683,397	291,314,466	1,260,455	3,347,268	122
Media	48,318,259	161,749,815	9,504,622	31,100,859	6
Publications	218,757,266	720,668,819	9,036,204	28,017,502	50
Social networking	331,647	1,600,499	237,003	1,062,986	3
User generated	2,961,628	4,932,352	967,798	1,992,069	4

4   RDF Datasets for the Analysis of Graph Measures

We conducted a systematic graph-based analysis with a large group of datasets which were part of the last LOD Cloud 2017[8], as a case study for the framework introduced in the previous Sect. 3. The results of the graph-based analysis with 28 graph-based measures, is the second resource[9] published with this paper. To facilitate browsing of the data we provide a website[10]. It contains all 280 datasets that were analyzed, grouped by topics (as in the LOD Cloud) together with links (a) to the original metadata obtained from DataHub, and (b) a downloadable version of the serialized graph-structure used for the analysis. This section describes the data acquisition process (cf. Sects. 4.1 and 4.2), and how the datasets and the results of the analysis can be accessed (cf. Sect. 4.3).

4.1   Data Acquisition

Table 1 summarizes the number of processed datasets and their sizes. From the total number of 1,163 potentially available datasets in last LOD Cloud 2017, a number of 280 datasets were in fact analyzed. This was mainly due to these reasons: (i) RDF media types statements that were actually correct for the datasets, and (ii) the availability of data dumps provided by the services. To not stress SPARQL endpoints to transfer large amounts of data, in this experiment, only datasets that provide downloadable dumps were considered.

To dereference RDF datasets we relied on the metadata (so called datapackage) available at DataHub, which specifies URLs and media types for the corresponding data provider of one dataset[11]. We collected the datapackage metadata for all datasets (step A in Fig. 1) and manually mapped the obtained media types from the datapackage to their corresponding official media type statements that are given in the specifications. For instance, rdf, xml_rdf or rdf_xml was mapped to application/rdf+xml and similar. Other media type statements like html_json_ld_ttl_rdf_xml or rdf_xml_turtle_html were ignored, since they are ambiguous. This way, we obtained the URLs of 890

Table 2. Runtime for the different stages in our graph-based analysis for selected datasets. All files needed to be transformed from RDF/XML into N-Triples.

Dataset name	m Edges	t_1 Preparation	t_2 Graph creation	t_3 Graph analysis
colinda	100,000	2.26 s	0.67 s	3.62 s
organic-edunet	1,200,000	25.81 s	8.62 s	16.95 s
uis-linked-data	*10,300,000	203.05 s	61.01 s	26.13 s

* Compressed archive with multiple RDF files.

---

[8] http://lod-cloud.net/versions/2017-08-22/datasets_22-08-2017.tsv.

[9] Resource URL of the datasets: https://doi.org/10.5281/zenodo.1214433.

[10] http://data.gesis.org/lodcc/2017-08.

[11] Example: https://old.datahub.io/dataset/⟨dataset-name⟩/datapackage.json.

RDF datasets (step B in Fig. 1). After that, we checked whether the dumps are available by performing HTTP HEAD requests on the URLs. At the time of the experiment, this returned 486 potential RDF dataset dumps to download. For the other not available URLs we verified the status of those datasets with http://stats.lod2.eu. After these manual preparation steps the data dumps could be downloaded with the framework (step 1 in Fig. 1).

The framework needs to transform all formats into N-Triples (cf. Sect. 3.1). From here, the number of prepared datasets for the analysis further reduced to 280. The reasons were: (1) corrupt downloads, (2) wrong file media type statements, and (3) syntax errors or other formats than these what were expected during the transformation process. This number seems low compared to the total number of available datasets in the LOD cloud, although it sounds reasonable compared to a recent study on the LOD Cloud 2014 [4].

4.2   Execution Environment

Operating system, database installation, dataset, and client software reside all on one server during analysis. The analysis was made on a rack server Dell PowerBridge R720, having two Intel(R) Xeon(R) E5-2600 processors with 16 cores each, 192 GB of main memory, and a 5 TB main storage. The operating system was Linux, Debian 7.11, kernel version 3.2.0.5.

The framework was configured to download and prepare the RDF data dumps in a parallel manner, limited to 28 concurrent processes, since transformation processes require some hard-disk IO. Around 2 TB of hard-disk space was required to finish the preparation. The analysis on the graphs require more main memory, thus it was conducted only with 12 concurrent processes. As serialized binary objects all 280 datasets required around 38 GB. Table 2 depicts examples of times for dataset preparation and analysis in our environment.

4.3   Availability, Sustainability and Maintenance

The results of the analysis of 280 datasets with 28 graph-based measures and degree distribution plots per dataset can be examined and downloaded via the registered DOI (see Footnote 9) The aforementioned website (see Footnote 9) is automatically generated from the results. It contains all 280 datasets that were analyzed, grouped by topic domains (as in the LOD Cloud) together with links (a) to the original metadata obtained from datahub and (b) a downloadable version of the serialized graph-structure used by the time of analysis (as described in Sect. 3.1).

As an infrastructure institute for the Social Sciences, we will regularly load data from the LOD Cloud and (re-)calculate the measures for the obtained datasets. This is part of a linking strategy, where linking candidates for our datasets shall be identified[12]. Datasets and results of future analyses will be made available to the community for further research.

---

[12] https://search.gesis.org/research_data.

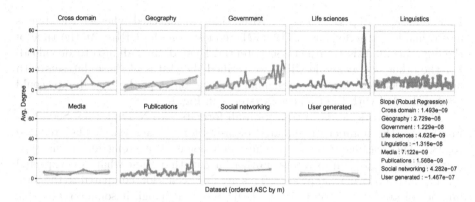

Fig. 2. Average degree z. The x-axis is ordered by the number of edges m. The slope of trend lines is computed by robust regression using *M-estimation*.

5   Preliminary Analysis and Discussion

This section presents some results and observations about RDF graph topologies in the LOD Cloud, obtained from analyzing 280 datasets with the framework, as described in the previous Sect. 4. The interested reader is encouraged to look-up single values in the measures section of one dataset on the website of the project (see Footnote 10). In the following, we present our main observations on basic graph measures, degree-based measures, and degree distribution statistics.

5.1   Observations About Graph Topologies in the LOD Cloud

Basic Graph Measures. Figure 2 shows the average degree of all analyzed datasets. Among all domains but Geography and Government, it seems that the average degree is not affected by the volume of the graph (number of edges). Datasets in the Geography and Government domains report an increasing linear relationship with respect to the volume. Some outliers with high values can be observed across all domains, especially in Geography, Life Sciences, and Publications. The highest value over all datasets can be found in the Life Sciences domain, with 63.50 edges per vertex on average (*bio2rdf-irefindex*). Over all observed domains and datasets, the value is 7.9 on average (with a standard deviation of 1.71). Datasets in Cross Domain have the lowest value of 5.46 (User Generated domain has even 4.81, but only few datasets could be examined).

Degree-Based Measures. Figure 3 shows the results on h-index. We would like to address some (a) domain-specific and (b) dataset-specific observations.

Regarding (a), we can see that in general, the h-index grows exponentially with the size of the graph (note the log-scaled y-axis). Some datasets in the Government, Life Sciences, and Publications domains have high values for h-index: 8,128; 6,839; 5,309, respectively. Cross Domain exhibits the highest

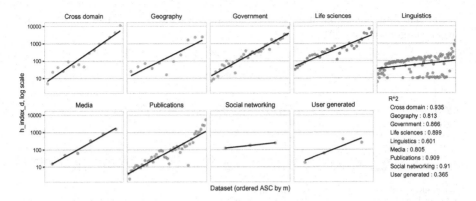

Fig. 3. h-index. The x-axis (log scale) is ordered by the number of edges m. Each plot has the same range for the x-axis. R^2 measures how well the regression fits. The closer to 1 the better the prediction.

h−index values on average, with *dbpedia-en* having the highest value of 11,363. Repeating the definition, this means that there are 11,363 vertices in the graph with at least 11,363 or more edges, which is surprising. Compared to other domains, datasets in the Linguistics domain have a fairly low h-index, with 115 on average (other domains at least 3 times higher).

Regarding (b), dataset-specific phenomena can be observed in the Linguistics domain. There seems to be two groups with totally different values, obviously due to datasets with very different graph topology. In this domain, *universal-dependencies-treebank* is present with 63 datasets, *apertium-rdf* with 22 datasets. Looking at the actual values for these groups of datasets, we can see that *apertium-rdf* datasets are 6x larger in size (vertices) and 2.6x larger in volume (edges) than *universal-dependencies-treebank*. The average degree in the first group is half the value of the second group (5.43 vs. 11.62). However, their size and volume seems to have no effect on the values of h-index. The first group of datasets have almost constant h-index value (lower group of dots in the figure), which is 10x smaller on average than that of datasets of *universal-dependencies-treebank* (upper group of dots). This, obviously, is not a domain-specific, but rather a dataset-specific phenomenon.

Degree Distribution Statistics. Researchers have found scale-free networks and graphs in many datasets [6,15], with a power-law exponent value of $2 < \alpha < 3$. We can confirm that for many of the analyzed datasets. As described in Sect. 3.2, it is generally not sufficient to decide whether a distribution fits a power-law function just by determining the value of α. Exemplary plots created by the framework for graphs of different sizes are presented in Figs. 4a and b. These graphs reveal a scale-free behaviour with $2 < \alpha < 3$ for their degree distribution. Figure 4c is an example for a degree-distribution not following a powerlaw function. For a detailed study on the distributions please find plots for all analyzed datasets on the website of our project (see Footnote 10).

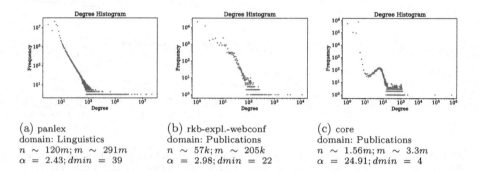

(a) panlex
domain: Linguistics
$n \sim 120m; m \sim 291m$
$\alpha = 2.43; dmin = 39$

(b) rkb-expl.-webconf
domain: Publications
$n \sim 57k; m \sim 205k$
$\alpha = 2.98; dmin = 22$

(c) core
domain: Publications
$n \sim 1.56m; m \sim 3.3m$
$\alpha = 24.91; dmin = 4$

Fig. 4. Exemplary plots created by the framework for datasets of different sizes. Please note the double-logarithmic axes. $dmin$ is the position on the x-axis from which the data may fit a power-law function.

Looking at the actual data for all datasets, we could observe that, in general, values for exponent α and for d_{min} vary a lot across domains. Furthermore, many datasets exhibit a scale-free behaviour on the total-degree distributions, but not on the in-degree, and vice-versa. It is hard to tell if a scale-free behaviour is a characteristic for a certain domain. We came to the conclusion that this is a dataset-specific phenomenon. However, the Publications domain has the highest share of datasets with $2 < \alpha < 3$ for total- and in-degree distributions, i.e., 62% and 74%, respectively.

5.2 Effective Measures for RDF Graph Analysis

Regarding the aforementioned use case of synthetic dataset generation, one goal of benchmark suites is to emulate real-world datasets with characteristics from a particular domain. Typical usages of benchmark suites is the study of runtime performance of common (domain-specific) queries at large scale. Some of them have been criticized to not necessarily generate meaningful results, due to the fact that datasets and queries are artificial with little relation to real datasets [7]. Recent works are proposing a paradigm shift from domain-specific benchmarks, which utilize a predefined schema and domain-specific data, towards designing application-specific benchmarks [17,20]. We have observed such discrepancies in the Linguistics domain, for instance (cf. Sect. 5.1). For both approaches, the results of our framework could facilitate the development of more accurate results, by combining topological measures, like the ones that can be obtained by the framework presented in this paper, with measures that describe statistics of vocabulary usage, for instance.

One may come to the question, which measures are essential for graph characterization. We noticed that many measures rely on the degree of a vertex. A Pearson correlation test on the results of the analysis of datasets from Sect. 4 shows that n, m, m_u, and m_p, correlate strongly to both h-index measures and to the standard descriptive statistical measure. The degree of centralization and degree centrality correlates with d_{max}, $d_{max,in}$, $d_{max,out}$. Both findings are intuitive. Measures that do almost not correlate are fill p, reciprocity y, the pseudo-diameter δ, and the power-law-exponent α (cf. Fig. 5). Hence, regardless of the group of measures and use case of interest, we conclude that the following minimal set of graph measures can be considered in order to characterize an RDF dataset: n, m, d_{max}, z, fill p, reciprocity y, pseudo-diameter δ, and the power-law-exponent α.

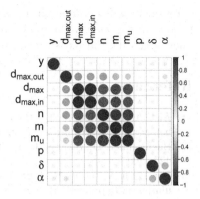

Fig. 5. Measure correlation

6   Conclusions and Future Work

In this paper, we first introduce a software framework to acquire and prepare RDF datasets. By this means, one can conduct recurrent, systematical, and efficient analyses on their graph topologies. Second, we provide the results of the analysis conducted on 280 datasets from the LOD Cloud 2017 together with the datasets prepared by our framework. We have motivated our work by mentioning usage scenarios in at least three research areas in the Semantic Web: synthetic dataset generation, graph sampling, and dataset profiling. In a preliminary analysis of the results, we reported on observations in the group of basic graph measures, degree-based measures, and degree distribution statistics. We have found that (1) the average degree across all domains is approximately 8, (2) without regard to some exceptional datasets, the average degree does not depend on the volume of the graphs (number of edges). Furthermore, (3) due to the way how datasets are modelled, there are domain- and dataset-specific phenomena, e.g., an h-index that is constant with the size of the graph on one hand, and an exponentially growing h-index on the other.

We can think of various activities for future work. We would like to face the question what actually causes domain- and dataset-specific irregularities and derive implications for dataset modelling tasks. Further, we would like to investigate correlation analyses of graph-based measures with measures for quality of RDF datasets or for data-driven tasks like query processing. For this reason, the experiment will be done on a more up-to-date version of datasets in the LOD Cloud. In the next version we are planing to publish a SPARQL endpoint to query datasets and measures from the graph-based analyses.

References

1. Alstott, J., Bullmore, E., Plenz, D.: powerlaw: a python package for analysis of heavy-tailed distributions. PloS one **9**(1), e85777 (2014)
2. Bachlechner, D., Strang, T.: Is the semantic web a small world? In: ITA, pp. 413–422 (2007)
3. Ben Ellefi, M., et al.: RDF dataset profiling - a survey of features, methods, vocabularies and applications. Semant. Web J. **9**(5), 677–705 (2018)
4. Debattista, J., Lange, C., Auer, S., Cortis, D.: Evaluating the quality of the LOD cloud: an empirical investigation. Semant. Web J. **9**(6), 859–901 (2018)
5. Auer, S., Demter, J., Martin, M., Lehmann, J.: LODStats–an extensible framework for high-performance dataset analytics. In: ten Teije, A., et al. (eds.) EKAW 2012. LNCS (LNAI), vol. 7603, pp. 353–362. Springer, Heidelberg (2012). https://doi.org/10.1007/978-3-642-33876-2_31
6. Ding, L., Finin, T.: Characterizing the semantic web on the web. In: Cruz, I., et al. (eds.) ISWC 2006. LNCS, vol. 4273, pp. 242–257. Springer, Heidelberg (2006). https://doi.org/10.1007/11926078_18
7. Duan, S., Kementsietsidis, A., Srinivas, K., Udrea, O.: Apples and oranges: a comparison of RDF benchmarks and real RDF datasets. In: ACM SIGMOD, pp. 145–156. ACM (2011)
8. Fernández, J.D., Martínez-Prieto, M.A., de la Fuente Redondo, P., Gutiérrez, C.: Characterising RDF data sets. JIS **44**(2), 203–229 (2018)
9. Flores, A., Vidal, M., Palma, G.: Graphium chrysalis: exploiting graph database engines to analyze RDF graphs. In: ESWC Satellite Events, pp. 326–331 (2014)
10. Freeman, L.C.: Centrality in social networks: conceptual clarification. Soc. Netw. **1**(3), 215–239 (1979)
11. Hirsch, J.E.: An index to quantify an individual's scientific research output. Proc. Nat. Acad. Sci. U.S.A. **102**(46), 16569–16572 (2005)
12. Hogan, A., Harth, A., Passant, A., Decker, S., Polleres, A.: Weaving the pedantic web. In: LDOW (2010)
13. Leskovec, J., Faloutsos, C.: Sampling from large graphs. In: SIGKDD, pp. 631–636 (2006)
14. Mihindukulasooriya, N., Poveda-Villalón, M., García-Castro, R., Gómez-Pérez, A.: Loupe - an online tool for inspecting datasets in the linked data cloud. In: ISWC Posters & Demonstrations (2015)
15. Newman, M.E.J.: Networks: An Introduction. Oxford University Press, New York (2010)
16. Page, L., Brin, S., Motwani, R., Winograd, T.: The pagerank citation ranking: bringing order to the web. Technical report, Stanford InfoLab (1999)
17. Qiao, S., Özsoyoglu, Z.M.: RBench: application-specific RDF Benchmarking. In: SIGMOD, pp. 1825–1838. ACM (2015)
18. Schmachtenberg, M., Bizer, C., Paulheim, H.: Adoption of the linked data best practices in different topical domains. In: Mika, P., et al. (eds.) ISWC 2014. LNCS, vol. 8796, pp. 245–260. Springer, Cham (2014). https://doi.org/10.1007/978-3-319-11964-9_16

19. Sejdiu, G., Ermilov, I., Lehmann, J., Mami, M.N.: DistLODStats: distributed computation of RDF dataset statistics. In: Vrandečić, D., et al. (eds.) ISWC 2018. LNCS, vol. 11137, pp. 206–222. Springer, Cham (2018). https://doi.org/10.1007/978-3-030-00668-6_13
20. Tay, Y.C.: Data generation for application-specific benchmarking. PVLDB Challenges Vis. 4(12), 1470–1473 (2011)
21. Theoharis, Y., Tzitzikas, Y., Kotzinos, D., Christophides, V.: On graph features of semantic web schemas. IEEE TKDE 20(5), 692–702 (2008)

In-Use Track

The Location Index: A Semantic Web Spatial Data Infrastructure

Nicholas J. Car[1]([✉])[iD], Paul J. Box[2][iD], and Ashley Sommer[1][iD]

[1] Land & Water, CSIRO, Brisbane, QLD, Australia
[2] Land & Water, CSIRO, Sydney, NSW, Australia
{nicholas.car,paul.j.box,ashley.sommer}@csiro.au

Abstract. The Location Index (LocI) project is building a national and authoritative, also federated, index for Australian spatial data using Semantic Web technologies. It will be used to link observation and measurement data (social, economic and environmental) to spatial objects identified in any one of multiple, interoperable, datasets. Its goal is to improve efficiency and reliability of data integration to support government decision making.

Keywords: Linked Data · Spatial Data Infrastructure · Social architecture · Semantic Web · Python · Australia

1 Introduction

The Location Index (LocI) is the spatial one of three data 'spines' (the others being *business* and *people*) the Australian government is creating to better enable reliable machine linking, integration and processing of government data with the goal of improving policy advice. LocI will enable government agencies to better geospatially integrate and analyze data across government portfolios and information domains.

Almost all government data contain some location information, because 'everything happens somewhere'. Data on service delivery to citizens, business productivity, population demographics, transport infrastructure, grants programs, and weather & climate all contain information about location. Similarly, location information is almost always contained in new and emerging 'big data' streams such as sensor technologies embedded in just about everything around us. Information from these sources will become increasingly important as we transform towards digital government services.

Joining data for analysis requires the ability for objects represented in multiple data sets to be identified uniquely and unambiguously. For example, data for Australian businesses is collected and identified using a unique Australian Business Number (ABN). This well-governed identifier is used across multiple data sets (Fig. 1).

© Springer Nature Switzerland AG 2019
P. Hitzler et al. (Eds.): ESWC 2019, LNCS 11503, pp. 543–557, 2019.
https://doi.org/10.1007/978-3-030-21348-0_35

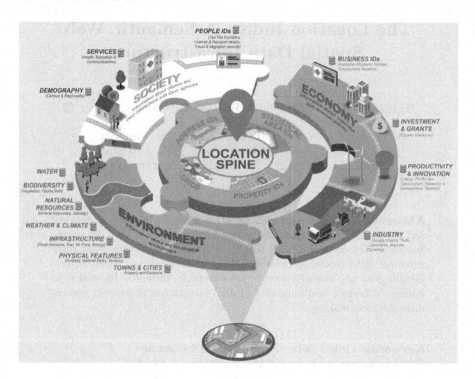

Fig. 1. A project brochure image of LocI the Location Spine's position with respect to Australian government *Environment, Society* and *Economy* data

Spatial features (features that exist in geographic space; e.g. local government areas, properties, rivers) can often have multiple identifiers. For example, a Local Government Area may have one identifier in the Australian Bureau of Statistic's Australian Statistical Geographic Standard, another in Commonwealth administrative data and yet another in State data sets. As very few spatial features have well governed identifiers, it is not possible to use them to join data sets together with certainly. This lack of shared unique identifiers means that every user must address integration challenges every time data are joined. These processes are often manual and unrepeatable, and do not add value to the data assets.

So far, it distributes three major Australian spatial datasets as Linked Data: the Geocoded National Address File (GNAF), the Australian Hydrological Geospatial Fabric (Geofabric) and the Australian Statistical Geography Standard (ASGS). These distributions draw from authoritative non-Semantic Web datasets and are converted to Linked Data using ontologies based on their particulars and also generic upper ontologies for multi-dataset consistency. All objects modelled by the various ontologies – from whole datasets to individual dataset objects and also the ontologies themselves – are assigned persistent HTTP URIs managed as part of Australian government interoperability efforts.

The project has also delivered 7 dataset crosswalks – Linksets – which join spatial objects with spatial relations. LocI implements stand-alone Linksets to ensure crosswalks are able to be independently governed.

Several Linked Data-specific clients are currently deployed or under development: an identifier downloader, a query builder and data processor. These are being built in response to challenges around the use of spatial data as a mechanism for integrating other data. These capabilities will offer LocI end users new ways of working. Also under development are RDF validation and inference tools.

This project and its products are an evolution of earlier work done to deliver Linked Data identifiers for spatial data in Australia known as the Spatial Identifiers Reference Framework (SIRF) [5]. For LocI, Linked Data was again chosen as a technical approach due to its perceived ability to deliver open data in a consistent and application-independent way across the Internet. Semantic Web modelling was chosen due to its multiple available, interoperable and modern models.

LocI is also investing heavily in the design of inter-departmental 'social architecture' (enabling social and institutional mechanism) to enable the continued generation of Linked Data and on-going infrastructure maintenance.

Section 2 follows detailing LocI project requirements, then Sect. 3 addressing governance issues, Sect. 4 describing the LocI systems and Sect. 5 mentioning some project tools developed. Finally a short concluding note is given in Sect. 6.

2 Requirements

2.1 Initial Datasets

LocI is required to deliver an interoperable set of foundational Australian spatial data products initially consisting of three major datasets created by different agencies:

- **Australian Statistical Geography Standard** (ASGS)
  - published by the Australian Bureau of Statistics (ABS)[1]
  - contains a hierarchy of approximately 500,000 geographies with which to aggregate census statistics
  - available via a series[2] of public Web Feature Service (WFS)[3] services
- **Australian Hydrological Geospatial Fabric** (Geofabric)
  - owned by the Australian Bureau of Meteorology (BoM)[4]

---

[1] http://www.abs.gov.au/.

[2] There are 6 WFS instances that supply data for this product. The WFS for the `asgs:MeshBlock` class is available at https://geo.abs.gov.au/arcgis/services/ASGS2016/MB/MapServer/WFSServer.

[3] http://www.opengeospatial.org/standards/wfs.

[4] http://www.bom.gov.au/.

- contains 35,000 surface hydrology features (lakes, rivers, catchments) data extracted from survey maps and remotely sensed digital elevation models. Of prime importance are the hierarchy of hydrological catchments which are monitored by river and stream gauges
    - available via a single, public, WFS[5]
- **Geocoded National Address File** (GNAF)
    - published by PSMA Australia Ltd. (PSMA)[6]
    - contains at least one entry for every one of the approx. 14.5 million street address in Australia as well as address aliases and relations (units within lots; addresses within localities)
    - available as a down-loadable database[7]

A fourth dataset, the **Australian Place Names Gazetteer** (PNGaz)[8] is an additional dataset that is partially deployed within the LocI project.

2.2 Future Datasets

The project has identified many more datasets to be added in future phases of LocI:

- national or state cadastral datasets
- irrigation areas and other socio-environmental administrative areas
- electoral boundaries and other social geographies
- electrical energy use data

Preparation for these datasets has been commenced but, as of the date of this publication, none have yet been incorporated into the published set.

2.3 Data Governance

Establishing appropriate institutional arrangement to sustain LocI has been identified as a priority activity. An analysis of existing spatial data supply chains and current governance arrangements for spatial and Linked Data domains is being undertaken. This will be used to inform the co-design of future state of trusted spatial Linked Data supply chains with cross-departmental identifier governance arrangements. This is to ensure that LocI-published datasets (together with their constituent spatial features) are seen to carry the authority, and therefore trust, of the original non-Linked Data datasets. This will assist in the adoption process as authority, persistence and trust are necessary precursors for community adoption. To this end, while technical delivery of the three core datasets as Linked Data products was mostly conducted by Australia's research

---

[5] The original WFS is http://geofabric.bom.gov.au/documentation/ however it's been re-implemented for updated functionality.

[6] http://www.psma.com.au/.

[7] https://data.gov.au/dataset/geocoded-national-address-file-g-naf.

[8] http://www.ga.gov.au/placename. This dataset is a Geoscience Australia product.

agency, CSIRO, the approval to publish the products was gained from the original owner agencies. Section 3 details some of the institutional arrangements in place to assist with LocI system management and data publication.

The requirement to implement trust-ensuring measures stems previous projects (SIRF, [5]) lessons where Linked Data versions of products where not operationalised as they lacked user perceived legitimacy/authority.

2.4   Data Delivery

In addition to delivering spatial data as Linked Data online, LocI also delivers spatial data object identifiers for offline use within secure Australian government data analysis systems, such as the Multi-Agency Data Integration Project (MADIP)[9] and Business Longitudinal Analysis Data Environment (BLADE)[10].

3   Identifier Governance

LocI resources are designed to be identified both authoritatively and persistently by HTTP URIs. All LocI data publishers have previously joined the Australian Government Linked Data Working Group (LDWG)[11] which is a technical advice group made of members from both Australian Commonwealth and State governments. The LDWG has a semi-formal mandate to advise on Linked Data matters and manages the use of the domain linked.data.gov.au for Linked Data URIs. The persistence of this domain, which is agency-neutral, is currently protected by a Memorandum of Understanding[12] between Linked Data-publishing agencies and the technical owner of the domain, the Australian Digital Transformation Agency[13]. Continued persistence of this domain is critical for LocI's long-term stability and more formal governance arrangements are being explored through the social architecture component of LocI.

The LDWG formalises how and what URIs may be requested with *Guidelines*[14] based on academic and government URI management work [6,13] and adjusted over 5 years of operation in Australia to their current form. The current guidelines require multi-agency URI proposal submission, review and acceptance, based on the publication standard ISO11179 [9]. For the LocI project, URIs have been created for datasets, linksets and ontologies using `dataset`, `linkset` & `def` namespace path segments, for example, http://linked.data.gov.au/dataset/geofabric for the Geofabric dataset (see below).

---

9   http://www.abs.gov.au/websitedbs/D3310114.nsf/home/Statistical+Data+
    Integration+-+MADIP.
10 http://abs.gov.au/websitedbs/D3310114.nsf/home/Statistical+Data+Integration+-
    +Business+Longitudinal+Analysis+Data+Environment+(BLADE).
11 http://www.linked.data.gov.au.
12 http://www.linked.data.gov.au/governance.
13 https://www.digital.gov.au.
14 http://www.linked.data.gov.au/governance.

4 Architecture

LocI has developed component architecture as shown in Fig. 2. Few central systems are implemented compared with predecessors such as SIRF [5] and, instead, datasets are distributed and published independently while they may also be cached for particular client use. This is to ensure LocI datasets are able to be used individually or in any combination and not just as originally demonstrated in this first LocI project phase.

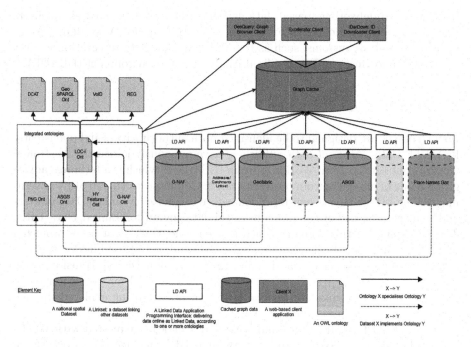

Fig. 2. Major LocI architectural components

4.1 Ontologies

The over-arching "LocI Ontology"[15], shown in Fig. 2, is used to structure LocI data for governance purposes and specializes multiple well-known ontologies to convey familiar data patterns: DCAT [7], VoID [2] and GeoSPARQL [11]. All LocI datasets must be published as DCAT's `dcat:Distribution` objects related to conceptual `dcat:Dataset` objects representing the original (likely non-RDF) datasets. Spatial elements within all LocI datasets must be `geo:Feature` objects published in `reg:Registers` and are expected, but not required, to relate to `geo:Geometry` objects. Instances of `void:Linkset` – a specialised `void:Dataset`

---

[15] http://linked.data.gov.au/def/loci.

for the *"description of RDF links between [other] datasets"* [2] – are published that join LocI datasets and, when published, must contain provenance information at the link level, which was not originally supported by VoID. The LocI ontology overview diagram is shown in Fig. 3.

Each LocI dataset is published according to at least one specialised Web Ontology Language (OWL) [14] ontology to convey the the specifics of the data it contains, e.g. the Geofabric models its contents using the HY_Features ontology. The three published LocI datasets to date, and the partly published PNGaz, have their specialized ontologies indicated in Table 1.

Table 1. LocI datasets and the ontologies used to publish them

Dataset	Ontology & Namespace	Notes
ASGS	ASGS Ontology http://linked.data.gov.au/def/asgs	A purpose-built ontology based on the original dataset's data model
Geofabric	HY Features Ontology [4] https://www.opengis.net/def/ appschema/hy_features/hyf/	An Open Geospatial Consortium domain ontology which informed the generation of the Geofabric product so there is natural alignment
GNAF	ASGS Ontology http://linked.data.gov.au/def/gnaf also ISO19160-1:2015 Address ontology (ISO19160) http://linked.data.gov.au/def/ iso19160-1-address	The first: a purpose-built ontology, the second: an OWL implementation of ISO19160-1:Address [1] updated and published by this author (Car)
PNGaz	Place Names Ontology http://linked.data.gov.au/def/ placenames	A purpose-built ontology based on the original dataset's data model

In addition to the LocI Ontology for governance, a "GeoSPARQL Extensions Ontology"[16] has also been created to describe spatial relations not well handled in existing ontologies[17]. So far properties for transitive spatial overlaps, spatial within/contains inverse and spatial resolution have been modelled with more likely to be added.

---

[16] https://github.com/CSIRO-enviro-informatics/geosparql-ext-ont.

[17] Recent discussion within the Spatial Data on the web Interest group (see the email archive: https://lists.w3.org/Archives/Public/public-sdwig/2018Nov/0085.html) has failed to provide simple existing mechanisms for this and though an extension to GeoSPARQL or a new general-purpose spatial ontology have been proposed, these will not be timely for LocI.

4.2   Dataset Publication

LocI datasets have been modelled as `dcat:Distribution` instances of their underlying `dcat:Dataset` objects delivered in both Linked Data and SPARQL service [8] forms. These forms are seen as *information-equivalent* to the non-Linked Data versions, even though significant gains are to be had from their substantially altered formats and availability.

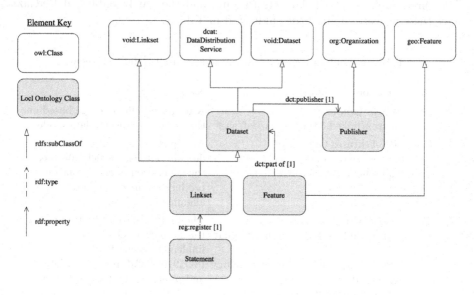

Fig. 3. Major LocI ontology classes and their relationships

Dataset publication as Linked Data here means their distributions are not only available in RDF but also HTML with web pages for the overall dataset objects, each major register of objects within datasets (as a Registry Ontology[18] `reg:Register` objects) and each object within datasets. The Geofabric dataset's *River Region 9400216* object is shown in Fig. 4. The various dataset, register and object representations are available via URIs derived from the namespace URI of the dataset and formats can be requested in different formats as per HTTP Content Negotiation as well as via specialised Query String Arguments. Examples of the URIs for the GNAF are given in Table 2.

Linked Data URIs for spatial objects can also be used offline and also other online, non-Linked Data systems, such as OGC Web Feature Services (WFS)[19]. Spatial object's information can be accessed via their URIs and reprocessed to be delivered according to the WFS standard allowing for more traditional Geographic Information Systems use.

---

[18] The Registry Ontology, http://purl.org/linked-data/registry.
[19] https://www.opengeospatial.org/standards/wfs.

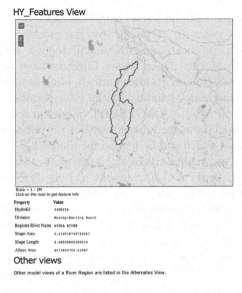

River Region 9400216

HY_Features View

Scale = 1 : 2M
Click on the map to get feature info

Property	Value
HydroID	9400216
Division	Murray-Darling Basin
Register River Name	AVOCA RIVER
Shape Area	0.410018749726263
Shape Length	6.48500000100019
Albers Area	4073060704.63587

Other views

Other model views of a River Region are listed in the Alternates View.

Fig. 4. A River Region object's HTML landing page from the Geofabric dataset

Objects in datasets may be published according to multiple ontologies, for example, the GNAF's `gnaf:Address` instances, are published according to both the GNAF Ontology, ISO16160 (see above) and also Schema.org[20]. RDF (and sometimes HTML) representations conforming to these ontologies are available independently by requesting a particular *view* of a resource, selected from a list of available *views*. This allows for ways of obtaining LocI objects conforming to particular standards and aligns with new W3C work to standardize Content Negotiation by Profile [12]. Views and URIs for a `gnaf:Address` object are as shown in Table 3.

As required at LocI project establishment, URIs acting as identifiers for all LocI dataset's elements are available for download for use in offline environments. To facilitate this, client software for the dataset's publication as Linked Data has been written[21]. This allows for the extraction of all element's URIs via the registers containing them and for their delivery in either Comma Separated Values or Microsoft Excel formats. All LocI datasets may be downloaded in this way at any time with this or any other client software, however a static copy of the dataset's register's first 1,000 items is also available for demonstration purposes due to the large sizes of full downloads: https://github.com/CSIRO-enviro-informatics/loci-dataset-download.

---

[20] https://schema.org.
[21] https://github.com/CSIRO-enviro-informatics/pyldapi-client.

4.3   Linkset Publication

LocI publishes multiple links between spatial datasets. Since these links sometimes take effort to generate (typically by geo-processing) and the results are often not shared, publication of them will reduce analyst task duplication. As of the date of this paper, seven Linksets have been published, see https://github.com/CSIRO-enviro-informatics?q=linkset. They have been produced using various methods including spatial intersections using GIS software, database processing, SPARQL CONSTRUCT queries and data conversion from offline data. Unlike LocI datasets, Linksets are not yet published as Linked Data, only as RDF resources which can be loaded for use within RDF databases.

The Addresses/Catchments Linkset[22] links `gnaf:Address` objects in the GNAF to `geofabric:ContractedCatchment` objects in the Geofabric and was produced using spatial intersections. This Linkset contains as many individuals (links) as the total number of `gnaf:Address` objects (14.5M) and in RDF Turtle form is a file of approximately 1 GB in size. It is also delivered as size-reduced Comma Separated Values file (0.5 MB).

In RDF form, this Linkset' structure extends on the basic VoID Linkset structure by using reification to associate further facts with each link. Where in VoID, each link is a regular triple (*subject, predicate, object*), here each triple's information is published as an `rdfs:Statement` object containing not only a *subject, predicate* and an *object* but also a `loci:hadGenerationMethod` property which indicates how it was produced by providing a shortcut to an object containing instructions. Each published Linkset contains extensive methodology notes and a register of LocI Linkset creation methods will be published in time.

So far, Linksets are published to crosswalk all LocI datasets and all versions of them. In time, multiple Linksets between the same datasets will be published to allow for different crosswalking methodologies to be selected for use by clients.

Table 2. GNAF dataset Linked Data URIs

Resource	URI	Format
GNAF Dataset (`dcat:Distribution`)	http://linked.data.gov.au/dataset/gnaf?_format=text/turtle (or `Accept: text/turtle`)	RDF
`gnaf:Address` Register (`reg:Register`)	http://linked.data.gov.au/dataset/gnaf/address/ http://linked.data.gov.au/dataset/gnaf/address/?_format=text/turtle	HTML RDF
`gnaf:Address` object	http://linked.data.gov.au/dataset/gnaf/address/GAACT714845933 http://linked.data.gov.au/dataset/gnaf/address/GAACT714845933?_format=text/turtle	HTML RDF

---

[22] http://linked.data.gov.au/linkset/bhafqv.

Table 3. *views* for a GNAF `gnaf:Address` object

View	URI
GNAF Ontology	http://linked.data.gov.au/dataset/gnaf/ address/GAACT714845933 (default) http://linked.data.gov.au/dataset/gnaf/ address/GAACT714845933?_view=gnaf
ISO19160	http://linked.data.gov.au/dataset/gnaf/ address/GAACT714845933?_view=iso19160
schema.org	http://linked.data.gov.au/dataset/gnaf/ address/GAACT714845933?_view=schemaorg

4.4   Data Validation

At present LocI only performs basic data validation however when caches of data from Datasets and Linksets are made for client consumption in mid-2019, SHACL [10] constraint language templates will be created for the LocI Ontology and GeoSPARQL Extensions ontology and other upper-ontologies with which to validate instance data. For this task, we have provisioned a new stand-alone SHACL validator tool (see RDF Validator below).

Given that LocI operations require data to conform to multiple ontologies, some of which may be in a derivation hierarchy, the power to model such dependencies and validating artefacts related to ontologies using the new Profiles Ontology [3] is being tested for use.

It is expected that 3rd parties may want to contribute datasets and Linkets to the pool of LocI resources and, when they do, validation systems will need to be in place. For this, tooling has been developed, see *RDF Validator* below.

4.5   Graph Expansion

Graph expansion – generation of inferred knowledge from ontological rules – is expected to be important for LocI as new business rules are added on top of the total data holdings in the forms of ontological axioms. So far inference data has not been published by LocI but both small- and large-scale interencing capability is currently under test (see *OWL Reasoners* below).

4.6   Clients

While data owners and system maintainers will publish ontologies, datasets and linksets, validate data and expand graphs, LocI end users will most likely not perform these actions. Data analysts and government policy advisers are expected, at least initially, to use specialised Linked Data clients and Linked Data-supplied element landing pages (see Fig. 4). Extensive stakeholder engagement is currently underway to ascertain client tooling requirements and, so far, 3 clients for LocI are currently being designed to meet discovered needs:

1. *IderDown*
   (a) for offline environment identifier use, see Sect. 4.2
2. *Genquery*
   (a) point-and-click browsing visual graph explorer for LocI ontologies, establishing paths joining classes and creating SPARQL[23] queries based on the paths to execute against RDF data
3. *Excelerator*
   (a) a data re-apportioning tool, uses dataset crosswalks (Linksets) to reapportion tabular data

4.7   Graph Caches

LocI works directly with the Linked Data APIs, SPARQL services or downloadable forms of the Datasets & Linksets or with cached graphs of content for performance reasons. Clients are built to prefer public access, where possible, ensuring open data principles are honored/maintained. Cached graphs of some/all LocI information will likely also be available as LocI assets for general use, depending on provisioning costs.

So far, the cached graph test are storing approx. 50M objects (all Dataset & Linkset objects) with approx. 40 triples per object, so approximately 2 billion triples. The feasability of supporting open access to this resource has not yet been determined.

5   Tools

LocI has built and extended a number of tools to achieve its data publication so far. A non-exhaustive list follows.

pyLDAPI - Linked Data API
LocI has tested and extended the Python Linked Data API, pyLDAPI[24], which has been added to Python's rdflib[25] family of RDF manipulation tools. In addition to the content negotiation by profile supported by this tool (see Sect. 4.2), the mechanics it uses to list objects' available views by providing an *alternates view* for every object it delivers, are informing the design of *Content Negotiation by Profile* [12].

pyLDAPI deployed for the GNAF with internal components shown and in relation to all the other parts of the total dataset, is given in Fig. 5.

---

[23] See https://www.w3.org/TR/sparql11-overview/ for all SPARQL documents.
[24] https://pypi.org/project/pyldapi/.
[25] https://github.com/RDFLib/.

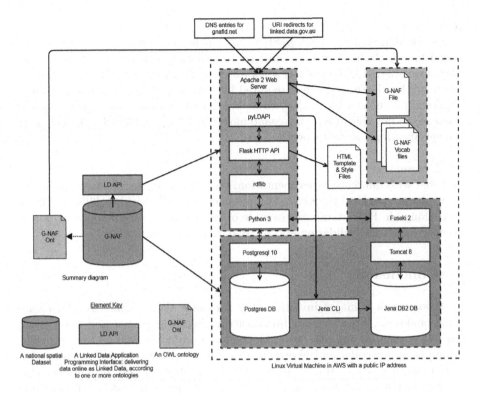

Fig. 5. Components within the GNAF dataset's Linked Data delivery system

pyLDAPI client
The pyLDAPI client software[26] was created for LocI and is being extended to act as a general-purpose Linked Data Registry harvester.

Persistent ID systems
LocI's precursor SIRF [5] and the LDWD's persistent ID services were used a custom "PID Service" tool[27] which LocI has now replaced with web server proxy tools. These tools[28] are extremely simple and rely only on a common web server[29] and its redirect module for operation. PID establishment is assisted by a series of redirection testing scripts which validate all deployed redirects. Redirect routing and API responses are tested multiple times a day to ensure all LocI assets perform.

---

[26] https://github.com/CSIRO-enviro-informatics/pyldapi-client.
[27] https://www.seegrid.csiro.au/wiki/Siss/PIDService.
[28] https://github.com/AGLDWG/pid-proxy.
[29] http://httpd.apache.org/.

RDF Validator

A new SHACL validator tool, pySHACL[30] has been created and it too has been added to the Python's rdflib. Until the completion of this tool, there was no freely available SHACL validator software available for mainstream programming languages like Python which is required for integration within mainstream web architectures such as those likely to be able to be implemented by non-research agencies. So far, this tool is the second most feature-complete SHACL tool, after the specification's author's own.

OWL reasoners

To assist with inference experimentation, the LocI team has updated, published as a software package the OWL-RL inferencing tool[31], within rdflib. It will be used alongside RDF databases capable of various forms of inference. It is also necessary for RDF validation and pySHACL depends on it.

6   Conclusions

LocI represents a major investment in Semantic Web technologies to create a national-scale, Spatial Data Infrastructure bridging spatial and observation data. It is a 2nd or 3rd generation Linked Data project benefiting from previous attempts in Australia and elsewhere to create a distributed yet interoperable collections of spatial datasets with accessible spatial objects. It is implementing new technical and social mechanisms to overcome issues such as fragmented data governance and lack of authority, leading to poor adoption of Linked Data outside of research agencies. Critically, the project is being implemented collaboratively with operational data delivery agencies (including ABS, GA and DoAWR), to ensure alignment with individual organisational drivers, buy-in at the early stages of development, and capacity uplift, to ensure a smooth path to transition these prototype capabilities to their eventually organisational homes. Many new yet simple tools have been developed to allow for Linked Data work in common web infrastructures to further ease the path to adoption.

LocI has delivered its expected milestones to date (dataset delivery as Linked Data and Linkset generation) and the next test (by mid 2019) is full client testing. Subsequent years (2020, 2021) will see LocI stabilise operational systems and grow the pool of datasets.

It has also redeveloped Linked Data API tooling now deployed 7+ times, client tooling deployed 3 times, the most feature complete, open source SHACL validator[32] and an update version of OWL-RL, thus the project greatly contributes to supporting Linked Data capacity generally.

---

[30] https://pypi.org/project/pyshacl/.

[31] https://pypi.org/project/owlrl/.

[32] See the SHACL implementation report.

References

1. ISO 19160–1:2015 addressing - part 1: Conceptual model. ISO Standard, Geneva, Switzerland
2. Alexander, K., Cyganiak, R., Hausenblas, M., Zhao, J.: Describing Linked Datasets with the VoID Vocabulary. W3C Working Group Note, World Wide Web Consortium, March 2011. https://www.w3.org/TR/void/
3. Atkinson, R., Car, N.J.: Profiles ontology. W3C First Public Working Draft, World Wide Web Consortium, December 2018. https://www.w3.org/TR/2018/WD-dx-prof-20181211/
4. Atkinson, R.: HY features ontology. Technical report, Open Geospatial Consortium, September 2018. https://github.com/opengeospatial/NamingAuthority/tree/master/definitions/appschema
5. Atkinson, R., Box, P., Kostanski, L.: Spatial Identifier Reference Framework (SIRF): A Case Study on How Spatial Identifier Data Structures can be Reoriented to Suit Present and Future Technology Needs, p. 24. International Cartographic Association, Dresden, Germany, June 2013. https://publications.csiro.au/rpr/pub?pid=csiro:EP139320
6. Hyland, B., Ghislain Atemezing, B.: Best Practices for Publishing Linked Data. W3c working group note, World Wide Web Consortium, March 2014. https://www.w3.org/TR/ld-bp/
7. Gonzalez-Beltran, A., Browning, D., Cox, S., Winstanley, P.: Data Catalog Vocabulary (DCAT) - revised edition. W3C Recommendation, World Wide Web Consortium, November 2018. https://www.w3.org/TR/vocab-dcat-2/
8. Gregory Todd Williams: SPARQL 1.1 Service Description. W3c Recommendation, World Wide Web Consortium, March 2013. http://www.w3.org/TR/sparql11-service-description/
9. International Organization for Standardization / IEC: ISO/IEC 11179, Information Technology - Metadata registries (MDR). ISO Standard, International Organization for Standardization / IEC (2004). http://metadata-standards.org/11179/
10. Knublauch, H., Kontokostas, D.: Shapes Constraint Language (SHACL). W3C Recommendation, World Wide Web Consortium, July 2017. https://www.w3.org/TR/shacl/
11. Perry, M., Herring, J.: OGC GeoSPARQL - A Geographic Query Language for RDF Data. OGC Implementation Standard OGC 11–052r4, Open Geospatial Consortium, September 2012. http://www.opengis.net/doc/IS/geosparql/1.0
12. Svensson, L.G., Atkinson, R., Car, N.J.: Content Negotiation by Profile. W3C First Public Working Draft, World Wide Web Consortium, December 2018. https://www.w3.org/TR/2018/WD-dx-prof-conneg-20181211/
13. Villazón-Terrazas, B., Vilches-Blázquez, L.M., Corcho, O., Gómez-Pérez, A.: Methodological guidelines for publishing government linked data. In: Wood, D. (ed.) Linking Government Data, pp. 27–49. Springer, New York (2011). https://doi.org/10.1007/978-1-4614-1767-5_2
14. W3C: OWL 2 Web Ontology Language Document Overview, (Second Edition). Technical report, World Wide Web Consortium (2012). http://www.w3.org/TR/owl2-overview/

Legislative Document Content Extraction Based on Semantic Web Technologies
A Use Case About Processing the History of the Law

Francisco Cifuentes-Silva[1,2(✉)] and Jose Emilio Labra Gayo[1(✉)]

[1] Department of Computer Science, University of Oviedo, Oviedo, Asturias, Spain
francisco.cifuentes@weso.es, labra@uniovi.es
[2] Biblioteca del Congreso Nacional de Chile - BCN, Valparaíso, Chile
https://www.bcn.cl

Abstract. This paper describes the system architecture for generating the History of the Law developed for the Chilean National Library of Congress (BCN). The production system uses Semantic Web technologies, Akoma-Ntoso, and tools that automate the marking of plain text to XML, enriching and linking documents. These documents semantically annotated allow to develop specialized political and legislative services, and to extract knowledge for a Legal Knowledge Base for public use. We show the strategies used for the implementation of the automatic markup tools, as well as describe the knowledge graph generated from semantic documents. Finally, we show the contrast between the time of document processing using semantic technologies versus manual tasks, and the lessons learnt in this process, installing a base for the replication of a technological model that allows the generation of useful services for diverse contexts.

Keywords: Linked Open Data · Legal information systems ·
Legal domain · Legal Knowledge Base · Automatic markup ·
Semantic Web

1 Introduction

The legal and legislative scenario has benefited greatly from the development of technologies that allow automating tedious tasks, such as the allocation of metadata or the marking of documents, which are nevertheless essential tasks for the construction of products that allow consulting, information synthesizing and extracting knowledge that resides in archived repositories. Indeed, the OASIS standard Akoma-Ntoso (AKN) provides electronic representations of parliamentary, normative and judicial documents in XML[1] using semantic markup and annotation of textual documents through Linked Open Data (LOD). The main motivation to employ Semantic Web Technologies in this context is the reuse

---

[1] http://docs.oasis-open.org/legaldocml/ns/akn/3.0.

© Springer Nature Switzerland AG 2019
P. Hitzler et al. (Eds.): ESWC 2019, LNCS 11503, pp. 558–573, 2019.
https://doi.org/10.1007/978-3-030-21348-0_36

of data in various products and services, and the implementation of a Legal Knowledge Base (LKB) for public access. In 2011, the BCN started a project to automate the elaboration of the History of the Law, a perfect scenario to use an open interoperability standard, given the public nature of the data. An initial exploration of the use of LOD was described in [8], where we described how it can be used to publish legal norms. In this paper, we present the History of the Law project: the generation process, the key tools and strategies adopted for its elaboration and the results that have been obtained integrating Semantic Web technologies in the production process.

2   History of the Law and Parliamentary Labor Projects

A *History of the Law* (HL) is the collection of all the documents generated during a law's legislative processing; since the initiative that gives life to the bill, until its discussion in the Congress, the reports of the parliamentary committees that studied it and the transcripts of the debates in the sessions rooms, gathering their traceability [9] within the legislative process.

The HL allows someone to collect the so-called *spirit of the Law*, allowing its interpretation in a precise way in relation to the scope and sense that was given to the norm when it was legislated. This legal instrument is particularly useful both for judges when preparing judgements and for lawyers when they use certain rules to support their arguments. Similarly, the *Parliamentary Labor* (PL) is a compilation of all the legislative activity carried out by a parliamentarian during the exercise of his office, such that it has been registered in printed media belonging to the legislative power, such as a parliamentary motion, a session journal or a commission report.

In Chile until 2011, both products were made by legal analysts, only for specific requests, and by processing manually each document related to a Law.

For the electronic and automated elaboration of both documentary collections, it is required to have a granular database, which registers all the documents of the legislative process where any reference to bills or parliamentarians is made, allowing later to extract and recover selectively, what was discussed around a bill that will become law, as well as what a certain legislator has said in any context. For this reason, AKN has been used for the construction of this LKB, since it allows the addition of semantic marks on the text, which in turn allow the precise identification of the location of parliamentary interventions, the presence of debates around a bill, the processing phases, and many other types of metadata.

2.1   Production Workflow

To carry out document processing, business processes have been designed that were implemented in a workflow environment. These processes divide and systematize the necessary tasks of planning, execution and quality assurance (QA), among others. A simplified outline of our process is presented in the Fig. 1.

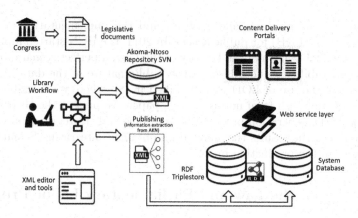

Fig. 1. Processing of legislative documents in BCN

The most relevant business processes implemented in the system are the *Documents' entry* process and the History of the Law generation process. The first, allows to enter and mark multi-purpose documents, such as the session log, which may contain references to various laws, as well as the parliamentary interventions in session that will give life to the PL. Among the most important tasks of the process are automatic marking and manual editing of XML, the passage through QA and the document publication. The latter will be reflected in the PL of each assistant to the session processed. The second process, allows to create a chronological record of a bill, which contains all the documents in which the published law will be discussed. Among the most important tasks of the process are the entry of specific documents, marking (automatic, manual and XML editing), publication of marked documents and publication of the HL as a dossier.

3   Software Environment

In this section, we present the most relevant elements of the system. An overview of the whole system has also been presented at [7] with a less technical focus.

3.1   Linked Open Data

The architecture of the system is based on the use of Linked Open Data, with the goal to establish a natural interoperability mechanism that enables sharing the public information that is generated. The project adopted Linked Data best practices [6] such as the use of URIs for identifiers within the system, a Linked Data frontend to access RDF resources[2], dereferenceable URIs modeling, reuse of existing vocabularies such as Dublin Core, SKOS, RDFS, FRBR[3], FOAF,

---

[2] https://code.google.com/archive/p/weso-desh/.

[3] http://purl.org/vocab/frbr/core.

GeoNames[4] and GEO[5]; the implementation of multiple ontologies in RDF that allowed to shape the published datasets, and the publication of the data through a public SPARQL endpoint[6]. The query in Fig. 2 can be executed in the SPARQL endpoint for getting the RDF, AKN and plain text representation of session documents.

The first proof of concept was the publication of an ontology and a dataset extracted from the legal database Leychile[7] as LOD, exporting basic metadata and relationships among norms and allowing the real definition of a graph with approximately 300,000 norms equivalent to 8 million RDF triples [8]. Later, a set of ontologies and datasets were published[8] for representing several domains, among others the HL and PL project, an entity dataset (people, organizations, etc.) used for entity linking, another ontology and dataset of geographical units, and an ontology to describe complex metadata related to the legislative business which is used for RDF publication documents marked in AKN. At this moment, in addition to what was mentioned before, the LOD database stores the RDF triples generated from the approximately 24,000 published AKN documents, as well as other datasets, such as the National Budget data, surpassing 28 million RDF triples in total (mid-November 2018).

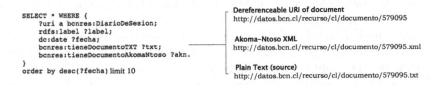

Fig. 2. SPARQL query for getting session documents in RDF, AKN and TXT

3.2 Automatic XML Marker

This tool[9] transforms a plain text document without format into an XML document based on Akoma-Ntoso schema. This problem has already been addressed using several approaches like machine learning [2], making use of visual properties of the text [5], looking for patterns associated with the content [4] or a combination of rules [1]. We defined three ways of approaching the problem, being the third a hybrid approach:

– **Knowledge engineering approach:** in this approach, the solution is based on the manual implementation of rules or ad-hoc algorithms, which are developed by a human specialist, a so-called *knowledge engineer*. The degree of precision and effectiveness of this type of solutions is limited by the quantity and

---

4 http://www.geonames.org/ontology.
5 http://www.w3.org/2003/01/geo/wgs84_pos.
6 http://datos.bcn.cl/sparql.
7 https://www.leychile.cl.
8 https://datos.bcn.cl/es/ontologias.
9 A test tool of the Automatic XML Marker can be found in http://bcn.cl/28n7h.

quality of the implemented rules so improvements in the tool will be directly related to manual adjustments and modifications. In our implementation, the techniques used with this approach, both for the detection of structural elements and entities identification in the text, were the application of regular expressions and exact matching. For this reason, for the implementation of structural marking through this approach, analysis and verification of at least a sample of the documents to be processed is required, as well as that they share some norms in the writing which can be identified and subsequently codified and integrated. In the case of entity recognition with this approach, it will be necessary to obtain a complete list of entity descriptors, names, labels and their variants.

- **Machine learning approach:** The main idea is that there is a set of documents previously marked or labeled by humans, structurally and/or their entities, which are randomly divided into a training set and one of tests in a proportion generally varying from 60% training - 40% testing to 90% training - 10% testing, depending on the number of elements available for training. The training documents are delivered as input to different classification algorithms based on the application of pattern recognition techniques (some of them being used as Hidden Markov Models - HMM, Naive Bayes - NB, Conditional Random Fields - CRF or Neural Networks) [12]) obtaining as a result a classification model that is used to mark the sources of testing documents. The quality check of the classifier is given by metrics such as Accuracy, Precision, Recall and F-Measure [3] that result from quantitatively and exhaustively comparing the results of manual labeling with those of automatic labeling.

  In practice, the marking components that most use this approach are mainly entity recognizers, and there is currently a wide range of off-the-shelf open source products that provide functionality, among which are the Stanford NER[10], spaCy[11] and OpenNLP[12].

- **Hybrid approach:** this is the one that we use in production, trying to capture the strengths of each approach to support the other's tasks. In this way, the most complex tasks of structural marking are carried out under the focus of knowledge engineering supported by recognition of entities (machine learning approach). In the same way, the recognition of entities is carried out only for certain structural sections, improving the efficiency and precision of the marking, and limiting it to the exclusively necessary.

In HL, given the complexity and detail of the marking of the different types of legal documents in which multiple tasks coexist, such as the detection and disambiguation of named entities, structural recognition of parts of the document

---

[10] https://nlp.stanford.edu/software/CRF-NER.shtml.

[11] https://spacy.io/usage/linguistic-features#section-named-entities.

[12] https://opennlp.apache.org.

and specific formatting, this function is implemented by four components specific orchestrated in a pipeline through HTTP Web services which are described below.

Named-Entity Recognizer: The task of Named Entities Recognition (NER) is to perform two fundamental functions: firstly identifying mentions of proper names or 'entities' presents in the text, for example dates or figures written in narrative prose, which can be composed of one or more words and secondly to identify the type of entity which the acknowledged name refers to.

We use the Stanford NER software implemented by a CRF classifier which, due to its probabilistic nature, delivers the input text marked with the recognized entity, associated with the possible types of entities (see Table 1 list of types) and its score of confidence in the match, being the type with highest score of the list that will be assigned as the one recognized for the entity. As a training corpus, text of session documents was used, composed of 64,727 words, which depending on the case were associated to their type by means of a label. Regarding the evaluation of the model in production, 10 fold cross-validation (90% training - 10% testing) was used, which reports that the NER manages to detect on average 97% of the entities present in the text and correctly assign the type of entity in 89% of cases. For the integration of the tool in the system, its functionality is provided by an HTTP Web service programmed in Java that receives plain text by POST and delivers the text with entities marked in XML.

Table 1. Types recognized by NER and number of entities in the Knowledge Base

Named-Entity type	Example	Total in LKB
Person	Salvador Allende Gossens, Sebastián Piñera Echenique	5.139
Organization	Ministerio de Salud, SERNATUR	2.848
Location	Valparaíso, Santiago de Chile	1.251
Document	Ley 20.000, Diario de Sesión N° 12	732.497
Role	Senador, Diputado, Alcalde	428
Eventos	Nacimiento de Eduardo Frei Montalba, Sesión N° 23	14.389
Bill	Boletín 11536–04, Prohibe fumar en espacios cerrados	12.737
Date	27 de febrero de 2010, el próximo año, el mes pasado	20.632

Mediator: This tool assigns the URI associated with an entity mentioned in the text performing the task of *Entity Linking* or *Disambiguation*. It is based on an RDF-based LKB which can be accessed through a SPARQL endpoint that stores information about basic descriptions (such as names or descriptors of text, dates or others) and more complex structures such as periods of membership or occurrence of events, all associated with entities of the types described in Table 1. For its operation, the mediator must load in memory pairs of (URI, label) that are queried to the triplestore via SPARQL and indexed internally. Once deployed, the job of linking or disambiguation is performed by text similarity algorithms based on Apache Lucene, comparing the input text with the tags that are associated with a map indexed in memory. Its simplest form of use is to send via REST a label by parameter, with which the mediator will return a list of suggestions in JSON with the structure (uri, label, score) ordered in a decreasing way by score. Some parameters can be added to improve their accuracy, such as the type of entity or a session ID. Additionally, it was implemented with another operating option in which an XML file with recognized entities is sent as input. The mediator will return an XML file in which it will add the URI and label attributes in each entity, establishing the URI with the highest score calculated for each case, as long as this value is greater than or equal to a threshold, which can also be configured. Although tools similar to this one such as DBpedia Spotlight [13], AGDISTIS [16] or KORE [10] are becoming more common (and almost all developed after our tool), there are three characteristics that make the mediator fits our use case:

- **Use of context information:** To improve the precision of the tool, it is possible to assign context data that allow to delimit the set of possible alternatives when selecting the URI for each label to be identified. Since this tool is used to disambiguate entities in documents of the National Congress, some of the context data that can be provided and that in turn are useful are: the date of the session, the chamber of the document, the number of the session or the legislature. A simple example in the use of context information is to narrow the list of URIs of possible people to recognize only those who are in the exercise of their position on a specific date and camera. If context information is sent to the mediator, it will generate a session ID that will be stored and associated with the context data and that will have to be used when using that specific data. Additionally, this ID will allow learning services to be used, given that if the tool assigns a wrong ID, it is possible to feed it back with the correct value, and as a result, upon being consulted again, the answer will be given by the feedback value.
- **Filters and association heuristics:** they are programmatic classes that implement logic to narrow the search results. These filters allow to increase the accuracy in URI assignment, allowing to limit the list of candidates according to criteria such as if on some date X is talking about a father or a son (political families are a common phenomenon), if a person is alive on the date that is being processed or if a person X belongs to a specific chamber.
- **Specialized Web Services:** within these are the assignment service to full document, which receives an XML document returning all the entities recognized in it, making it possible to optimize the number of requests; the reindexing options by type of entity, the feedback services, and the services that allow obtaining suggestion lists with or without session ID.

Structural Marker: We define as structural detection of text the task of identifying groups of consecutive strings that in the view of a human reader correspond to elements such as: titles, subtitles, paragraphs, sections (groups of paragraphs under the same title or subtitle) and other structures such as enumerations and lists. Additionally, given the context of application in documents containing parliamentary debate, a special type of structural element called Intervention (speech) will be defined, in which what is spoken by a person is described, and can be composed of one or more consecutive paragraphs. Then, we define the structural marker as the tool that performs the task of performing structural detection by adding marks to the text that indicate the beginning and end of each structural element. For our case, the marks added to the output of the text processing are in XML.

The main strategy used for the detection of structural and hierarchical sections in text documents is through the combined use of regular expressions and the application of rules that encapsulate programming logic that is applied when a certain regular expression is detected in the text. This solution is especially practical in the context of the documents generated in the National Congress, since there are usually some drafting rules that are standardized. In this way, the tool allows to identify structural sections of first, second and third level of document, sequences of elements based on numbered and unnumbered lists (even nested), as well as participations of parliamentarians. As the documents to be processed are mainly political debates, the main element to be recognized in the document is a block called *participation*. It is a block composed of one or more speeches in which an actor who moderates the session (usually the President of Chamber), an actor who owns the participation (who fundamentally speaks) and, eventually, some other actor who interrupts. In this composite block, it must be automatically identified which of the speakers is the participation author, wherewith an analysis of the discourses was necessary in order to detect the underlying structures of participation and be able to implement a rule with automaton characteristics. This particular implementation was needed given that in structural terms, participation is specific because it lacks a conventional structure of title and body, and it is included in other recognized structural sections of the debate. At the technical level, the structural marker receives plain text with or without entities as input. With this text, an object of type DocumentPart is generated that contains a property with all the text and an empty list of DocumentPart objects (sub-parts). The main idea is that depending on the type of document and the depth level of the DocumentPart object, an executor runs specific rules. In this way, each rule receives the text of a DocumentPart object and returns all the DocumentPart objects that can be consistently identified by adding them to the sub-parts list, so the last task of the process will be to serialize the object in XML.

XML Converter to Akoma-Ntoso: This component performs the task of transforming the XML resulting from the structural marking processes, entity recognition and entity linking, which we will call raw XML, in AKN format. The resulting version of this process will comply with the standard, and consequently is editable by tools such as LIME[13], Legis Pro[14], AT4AM[15], Bungeni[16], xmLegesEditor[17] or LEOS[18].

For the conversion process from raw XML to AKN, we initially tried XSLT, however, the XSLT style sheets to perform some operations such as identifying references to entities and grouping them in the header, a fundamental practice in AKN, were highly complex. Likewise, given the high variability of documents structure, we finally opted for a programmatic approach which takes the input XML file, generates a representation similar to a DOM, and traverses the XML node tree by converting each raw node to text in AKN XML. For this, each type of raw node can be implemented as a class that encapsulates the logic associated with the different types of AKN node, allowing to perform operations such as searching for specific expressions in internal nodes or their attributes.

3.3   Publishing

Each law has a life cycle that, in general, originates with a bill, then it is discussed, processed, published and with the passage of time, changing the cultural and political context, is explicitly or tacitly derogated from total or partial, ending its cycle. It is just before this last state, when the law is still in force and has maximum relevance. During the period of validity, the Law remains static, so that once having been published it does not change. In this way, both the Law and its HL can be filed, published and made available to the public. For this reason, at the end of the background collection and processing of documents that are part of HL, a publication process is run, which generates a physical file that is stored in a repository and archived by library specialists who index its content as part of the legal database. For this, every document associated with the HL must pass two final stages: quality control and document publication.

Quality Assurance: To ensure the consistency and correctness of HL products, QA processes have been implemented before a document is finally published. A QA analyst will exhaustively verify the work done in the previous phase and decide if it can be published or if, in case of some error having been found, it must be processed again. The QA process for the documents (such as session logs) is translated into a change of state in the workflow where a visual inspection is made using the XML editor of the document, checking things like the correct assignment of entity URIs, the correct metadata assignment and the verification of a well-formed document structure, for this reason it does not require an implementation other than the visualization of the document being edited. Regarding the QA process for HL publication, it is implemented using a combination of

---

[13] http://lime.cirsfid.unibo.it.

[14] https://xcential.com/legispro-xml-tech/.

[15] https://at4am.eu.

[16] https://github.com/bungeni-org.

[17] http://www.ittig.cnr.it/lab/xmlegeseditor.

[18] https://ec.europa.eu/isa2/solutions/leos.

SPARQL queries to the RDF triplestore and relational queries to the system database in specialized user interfaces. In the HL case, the triplestore is queried in all bill processing and a preliminary view of the HL is generated based on the documents described therein.

AKN2RDF: Once the AKN files have been annotated both automatically and manually and have successfully passed the QA phase, the publication process is performed which extracts the knowledge expressed in the document in the form of RDF triples and tuples for a base of query data. This process, packaged as a web service, implements a parser that traverses the XML tree of the AKN document, looking for the predefined structures within the different document sections. At the technical level, each type of document implements a collection of small data extractors per each document section, which are encapsulated in a specific class. In this way, classes that have the same behavior in different documents can be reused, and otherwise specific implementations can be made to require it.

3.4 Content Delivery

The BCN has made available to the public the portals of History of the Law[19] and Parliamentary Labor[20]. Both Web portals are built on a LKB supported by the extraction of information available in the documents generated in the National Congress. From a technological point of view, the portals have been developed using open source technologies (such as TYPO3 CMS, Python, Varnish, Java, Apache Lucene) and are mounted on a layer of REST web services that connect to both the RDF triplestore and a relational database depending on the case, offering in both cases search functions and data export to formats such as PDF, DOC and XML. A practice adopted is that the URIs of the parliamentary profiles are based on the same identifiers that form the URIs of people in the RDF triplestore.

4 Results

The growth of LKB BCN is a direct result of the publication and transformation of AKN XML documents to RDF, which has been carried out in four phases or data entry projects, where each one has been mainly oriented to the processing of session's documents associated with specific years intervals since 1965 until today. Table 2 describes the RDF triples that are obtained by type of document, evidencing that the largest contribution of triples is given by documents of the Chamber of Deputies. In terms of size, related to RDF triples obtained from session's documents we have around 14.250.000 RDF triples counted in November 4th of 2018 in our LKB.

---

[19] https://www.bcn.cl/historiadelaley.
[20] https://www.bcn.cl/laborparlamentaria.

Table 2. Description of RDF triples generated by document type

Dataset		RDF triples by document						
Document type	Total docs.	Min.	1st Qu.	Median	Mean	3rd Qu.	Max.	Stdev.
Debate Senate	3.614	35	665	1.001	1.097	1.353	6.883	668,67
Debate Chamber of Deputies	4.298	35	1.166	1.640	1.788	2.199	11.771	961,42
Bills	2.514	37	109	308	689	864	15.934	1055,93
Others types	13.942	37	40	40	49,78	40	15.720	245,68
Total	24.368							

Another perspective of the data generated is the number of triples by type of document published in the LKB per year (of document), which is shown in Fig. 3. Except for the period from September of 1973 to March of 1990, when in Chile the dissolution of the National Congress was carried out due to a period of 'non-democracy', this chart allows us to visualize a long-term upward trend, it may seem surprising that the growth of triple RDFs is not always greater than in previous periods.

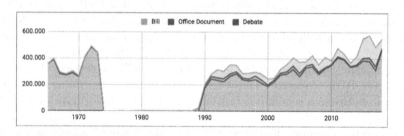

Fig. 3. RDF triples generated yearly by document type

Looking for an explanation, the Fig. 4 shows the attendance to the sessions of the parliament and the total of sessions per year adding the data of both chambers. Although both sets of data are part of the LKB, the sessions are created in RDF from a Web service provided by the opendata.congreso.cl portal, and the assistance is extracted from the documents published in AKN. In this case, a direct relationship between the number of sessions and attendance is shown, which could partially explain the RDF triples generation losses of the Fig. 3. An interesting thing about these data is that there seems to be some relationship between the number of sessions and the existence of elections (parliamentary or presidential), which may explain the differences between years regarding the number of triples generated by type of document. With regards to user queries registered by Google Analytics for the Content Delivery portal of History of the Law, between November 2016 and November 2017, 331,481 visits were received with an average browsing time of 2 min and 11 s. One year later between November 2017 and November 2018, the number of visits is approximately 476,241 and the average browsing time is 2 min 26 s, which represents an increase in visits of 144,760 equivalent to 43.6%, and an increase in the average time on the page of 15 s equivalent to 11.4% of additional time.

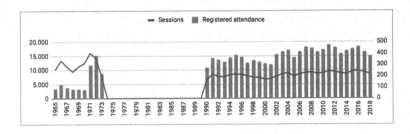

Fig. 4. Session attendance registered in Akoma-Ntoso documents by year

A final aspect to be analyzed is the time necessary to carry out the main marking operations associated with legislative documents. For this, the values provided by the literature referring to manual and semi-automatic marking of legal documents were taken as a baseline, which were compared with the usage statistics associated with the journal entry process, generated from the History of the Law system. Specifically for the comparison, data of document marking, transitions and status changes of the work orders (WO) registered in the production workflow were used, taking into account only those WO executed correctly (without errors during the process, whether or not they were resolved), and that they were not suspended explicitly or implicitly. Under these conditions, 2,625 WOs of entry were obtained, for which the information is summarized in Table 3. For purposes of comparison with the results described in [14], an estimate was made based on random sampling of session's documents, which considered that a document has on average 60 pages of content, which was calculated by the number of average document characters (180,000) divided by the average number of characters that has approximately one page (3,000). With this data, and considering that the extension of the document is linearly increased with the number of marks and ultimately, the human analyst's work, the times obtained in Table 3 will be divided by 3, given that the values described as baseline, are based on a 20 page document. Under these considerations, it is possible to construct the Table 4, which shows differences in the estimation of marking times between what is presented in the literature and what is obtained by analyzing process data.

5   Discussion

The comparison in Table 4 shows that our automatic marker generates more marks, which results in marginally less manual processing time and more references per document. Additionally, it is shown that the average time used for

Table 3. Statistics for markup related to entry document process, all time in minutes

	Markup from plain text						Markup from existent XML					
	Min	1st Q.	Med.	Mean	3rd Q.	Max.	Min	1st Q.	Med.	Mean	3rd Q.	Max.
Total structural marks	0	10	23	503,6	665	2.468	0	6	10	11,14	15	40
Total reference marks	0	14	30	33,6	46	525	0	20	32	33,49	44	173
WO Creation time	0,0	0,91	1,13	2,22	1,75	125,16	0	0,80	1,18	3,17	2,28	89,03
Automatic markup time	0.0	0.31	0.51	0.67	0.76	16.86	0.0	1.26	1.73	2.15	2.41	31.51
QA automatic markup time	0.0	0.58	1.08	3.74	1.88	296.7	0.0	0.97	1.35	4.26	2.31	303.35
Manual markup time	0.0	29.8	71.3	98.1	135.1	581.4	0.0	42.06	80.17	109.01	144.21	593.62
QA manual markup time	0.08	6.22	15.35	19.93	30.91	59.85	0.10	8.70	20.07	21.59	31.76	59.97
Publishing process time	0.08	0.40	0.86	1.85	2.03	29.68	0.06	0.73	1.18	1.76	2.00	29.56

Table 4. Statistics for markup related to entry document process, all time in minutes

		Baseline		Usage statistics	
		Manual markup	With automatic tools	From plain text	Process from XML
20 pages document	Average minutes	120	75	42.16	47.34
	Average references	10	10	11.2	11.16
60 pages document	Average minutes	360	225	126.49	142.03
	Average references	30	30	33.6	33.49

processing obtained by usage statistics is less than that described in the baseline, which may be due to the analyst's greater expertise (much more practice in marking), as well as to a more advanced environment of tools to support the marking.

At the beginning of the HL project, a pilot phase of document entry was developed, where differences in the documents marking implementation were experienced with respect to the current one. This could explain what is shown in Fig. 4 where, during the 1965–1973 period, it is observed that assistance is much less recorded between the years 1965 to 1969, very different from what happens since 1971 to 1973. From a technical point of view, although the initial idea of the project was to build the whole system natively in RDF using LOD (for both frontend and backend), during the development of the first prototypes associated with the Content Delivery portals, different approaches were tested for consulting and obtaining structure and texts associated with both HL and PL:

The first approach considered the implementation of SPARQL queries on a dataset modeled by an ontology with several classes and properties that extended from others (rdfs:subPropertyOf, rdfs:subClassOf), defining in turn properties' domains and ranges, which in practice meant that the dataset had fewer specific RDF triples while many others had to be inferred. The reasoner used was the same provided by the Virtuoso database. When testing this approach, it was discarded because it required high running times for simple and complex queries, with some cases where the process didn't finish.

A second approach tested was to generate and add *a priori* to the dataset all those RDF triples that were inferred in the previous approach, which eliminated the query time devoted to inference. In this case, it was actually possible to reduce the queries execution time by getting them to finish, however, the response times were still too high for the implementation of a production system, even more so considering the HL and PL which are composed of a large number of documents. For example, when generating a dossier of PL in Word or PDF, it can have over 10,000 pages of text. The problem became even greater when it was necessary to add a search filter to the SPARQL query to perform searches within the text of *participations*, which is a common use case, and for which the database was not prepared to be specialized in RDF and not in text indexing.

The third approach which was finally adopted was the use of RDF and SPARQL only to give access to specific parts of the database, such as the procedural structure of a bill, to establish a basis for universal identifier data (URI) common to all BCN systems, as well as to provide access to the community to public information generated in the National Congress, but not to access the text of interventions or metadata associated with them. For these purposes, both a relational database and a text index were implemented using Apache Lucene.

While the first two approaches mentioned above are empirical evidence of the computational complexity associated with complex SPARQL queries [15], it is possible that, having used other approaches such as Linked Data Fragments [17] or even a better query decomposition [15] and/or a scheme of greater redundancy of the service, could have allowed a system based on RDF. Indeed, newer experiences like Wikidata [11] suggest that it is possible to solve highly complex problems. Nevertheless, for the text search task, a tool is required that allows searching and efficiently retrieving over the entire dataset.

Another practical learning from this experience is that there are performance problems in users' browsers when they must edit large documents with many metadata marked on text. We mention this consideration because in our case it was difficult and even impossible to edit documents with more than 100 pages that were marked with a high level of detail (marking of all entity types for all structural sections). In order to correct such inconvenience, the level of detail of marking was reduced only to those structural sections that would later be extracted, and in the same way, only to those entity types of interest for the generation of products.

6   Conclusions

This work allows to validate the use of Semantic Web technologies for implementing systems oriented to the development of products based on semantic marking of texts, in the legislative context, and at the same time, to make available the information extracted as LOD. In addition, when comparing statistics of use about human work in tasks of document markup realized on the implemented architecture, versus the data established in the literature, it is possible to establish that, based on the statistics of our system, the time of human work necessary to carry out the editing and marking of documents are smaller than defined as baseline.

We consider that the experience gained in the development of the HL and PL project within BCN has been overall positive. The use of LOD (data and shared models using RDF and HTTP) and particularly dereferenceable URIs, has allowed to interoperate between internal websites, and in turn, to replicate the interoperability standard in new developments such as the portal of the National Budget[21], which also publishes a knowledge graph over HTTP.

Acknowledgements. We wish to thank David Vilches, Eridan Otto, and Christian Sifaqui by their contribution to the development of the HL project, that was funded by the Library of Congress of Chile. The described research activities were partially funded by the Spanish Ministry of Economy and Competitiveness (Society challenges: TIN2017-88877-R).

References

1. Abolhassani, M., Fuhr, N., Gövert, N.: Information extraction and automatic markup for XML documents. In: Blanken, H., Grabs, T., Schek, H.-J., Schenkel, R., Weikum, G. (eds.) Intelligent Search on XML Data. LNCS, vol. 2818, pp. 159–174. Springer, Heidelberg (2003). https://doi.org/10.1007/978-3-540-45194-5_11
2. Akhtar, S., Reilly, R.G., Dunnion, J.: Automating XML markup using machine learning techniques. J. Systemics Cybern. Inform. **2**(5), 12–16 (2004)
3. Baeza-Yates, R., Ribeiro-Neto, B.: Modern Information Retrieval: The Concepts and Technology Behind Search, vol. 82. Pearson Education Ltd., Harlow (2011)
4. Bolioli, A., Dini, L., Mercatali, P., Romano, F.: For the automated mark-up of Italian legislative texts in XML. In: Legal Knowledge and Information Systems (Jurix 2002), pp. 21–30. IOS Press (2002)
5. Burget, R.: Automatic document structure detection for data integration. In: Abramowicz, W. (ed.) BIS 2007. LNCS, vol. 4439, pp. 391–397. Springer, Heidelberg (2007). https://doi.org/10.1007/978-3-540-72035-5_30
6. Bizer, C., Hartig, O.: How to Publish Linked Data on the Web - Half-day Tutorial at the 7th International Semantic Web Conference (2008)
7. Cifuentes-Silva, F.: Service-Oriented Architecture for automatic markup of documents. An use case for legal documents. In: IFLA 2014, Lyon, p. 10 (2014)

---

[21] https://www.bcn.cl/presupuesto.

8. Cifuentes-Silva, F., Sifaqui, C., Labra-Gayo, J.E.: Towards an architecture and adoption process for linked data technologies in open government contexts. In: Proceedings of the 7th International Conference on Semantic Systems - I-Semantics 2011, pp. 79–86 (2011)

9. Gacitua B.R., Aravena-Diaz, V., Cares, C., Cifuentes-Silva, F.: Conceptual distinctions for traceability of history of law. In: Rocha, A. (ed.) 11th Iberian Conference on Information Systems and Technologies (CISTI). IEEE (2016)

10. Hoffart, J., Seufert, S., Nguyen, D.B., Theobald, M., Weikum, G.: KORE: keyphrase overlap relatedness for entity disambiguation. In: Proceedings of the 21st ACM International Conference on Information and Knowledge Management (2012)

11. Malyshev, S., Krötzsch, M., González, L., Gonsior, J., Bielefeldt, A.: Getting the most out of Wikidata: semantic technology usage in Wikipedia's knowledge graph. In: Vrandečić, D., et al. (eds.) ISWC 2018. LNCS, vol. 11137, pp. 376–394. Springer, Cham (2018). https://doi.org/10.1007/978-3-030-00668-6_23

12. Martinez-Rodriguez, J.L., Hogan, A., Lopez-Arevalo, I.: Information extraction meets the semantic web: a survey. Semant. Web J. (2018)

13. Mendes, P.N., Jakob, M., García-Silva, A., Bizer, C.: DBpedia spotlight: shedding light on the web of documents. In: Proceedings of the 7th International Conference on Semantic Systems, I-Semantics 2011, pp. 1–8. ACM, New York (2011)

14. Palmirani, M., Vitali, F.: Legislative XML: principles and technical tools. Technical report, Inter-American Development Bank (2012)

15. Pérez, J., Arenas, M., Gutierrez, C.: Semantics and complexity of SPARQL. ACM Trans. Database Syst. **34**(3), 16:1–16:45 (2009)

16. Usbeck, R., et al.: AGDISTIS - graph-based disambiguation of named entities using Linked Data. In: Mika, P., et al. (eds.) ISWC 2014. LNCS, vol. 8796, pp. 457–471. Springer, Cham (2014). https://doi.org/10.1007/978-3-319-11964-9_29

17. Verborgh, R., Vander Sande, M., Colpaert, P., Coppens, S., Mannens, E., Van de Walle, R.: Web-scale querying through Linked Data fragments. In: Proceedings of the 7th Workshop on Linked Data on the Web. CEUR Workshop Proceedings, vol. 1184 (2014)

BiographySampo – Publishing and Enriching Biographies on the Semantic Web for Digital Humanities Research

Eero Hyvönen[1,2(✉)] , Petri Leskinen[1] , Minna Tamper[1] ,
Heikki Rantala[1] , Esko Ikkala[1,2] , Jouni Tuominen[1,2] ,
and Kirsi Keravuori[3]

[1] Semantic Computing Research Group (SeCo), Aalto University,
Espoo, Finland
eero.hyvonen@aalto.fi
[2] HELDIG – Helsinki Centre for Digital Humanities, University of Helsinki,
Helsinki, Finland
[3] Finnish Literature Society (SKS), Helsinki, Finland
http://seco.cs.aalto.fi
http://heldig.fi

Abstract. This paper argues for making a *paradigm shift* in publishing and using biographical dictionaries on the web, based on Linked Data. The idea is to provide the user with enhanced reading experience of biographies by enriching contents with data linking and reasoning. In addition, versatile tooling for (1) biographical research of individual persons as well as for (2) prosopographical research on groups of people are provided. To demonstrate and evaluate the new possibilities, we present the semantic portal "BiographySampo – Finnish Biographies on the Semantic Web". The system is based on a knowledge graph extracted automatically from a collection of 13 100 textual biographies, enriched with data linking to 16 external data sources, and by harvesting external collection data from libraries, museums, and archives. The portal was released in September 2018 for free public use at http://biografiasampo.fi.

1 National Biographical Dictionaries on the Web

Biographical dictionaries, a historical genre dating back to antiquity, are scholarly resources used by the public and by the academic community alike. Most national biographical dictionaries follow the traditional form of combining a lengthy non-structured text, often written with authorial individuality and personal insight, with a structure supplement of basic biographical facts, such as family, education, works, and so on. Biographies are an invaluable information source for researchers across the disciplines with an interest in the past [22].

A well-known example of a biographical dictionary is the Oxford Dictionary of National Biography (ODNB)[1] with more than 60 000 lives. It was published

---

[1] http://global.oup.com/oxforddnb/info/.

© Springer Nature Switzerland AG 2019
P. Hitzler et al. (Eds.): ESWC 2019, LNCS 11503, pp. 574–589, 2019.
https://doi.org/10.1007/978-3-030-21348-0_37

online in 2004, and since then many dictionaries have opened their editions on the Web. These include USA's American National Biography[2], Germany's Neue Deutsche Biographie[3], Biography Portal of the Netherlands[4], The Dictionary of Swedish National Biography[5], and National Biography of Finland[6] [2] (NBF). There are also lots of "who is who" services describing living persons.

ODNB and other early adopters of web technology started the paradigm shift in publishing and using biographical dictionaries on the Web. This paper argues for making the next paradigm shift, i.e., to *publishing and using biographical dictionaries as Linked Data on the Semantic Web*. We present the new in-use system "BIOGRAPHYSAMPO – Finnish Biographies on the Semantic Web" based on the National Biography and other biographical databases of the Finnish Literature Society[7] interlinked with related data repositories. The idea is to (1) transform textual biographies into Linked Data (LD) by using language technology and knowledge extraction, to (2) enrich the data by linking it to internal and external data sources and by reasoning, to (3) publish the data as a LD service and a SPARQL endpoint on the web [10,13], and to (4) create end-user applications on top of the service, including data-analytic tools and visualizations for distant reading [33] of Big Data, i.e., for Digital Humanities (DH) research [9].

Today, national biography collections on the Web are used in the following traditional way: a search box or a more detailed search form is filled up specifying the person(s) whose biographies are searched for. After pushing the search button, a list of hits is shown that can be opened by clicking for close reading. BIOGRAPHYSAMPO challenges this traditional approach of publishing and using biographical dictionaries in the following ways: (1) Data from multiple biographies is provided. (2) The data is enriched by harmonizing and combining it with additional data sources, such as metadata from memory organization collections. (3) The data is enriched by reasoning for enhanced reading experience and for knowledge discovery. (4) Data-analytic and visualization tools for biographical [30] and prosopographical research [37] are provided.

In the following, the knowledge extraction process for textual bios is first described (Sect. 2), as well as the underlying event-based data model, datasets, and LD service (Sect. 3). After this, the system is considered from the end users's perspective by presenting seven application views included in the portal (Sect. 4). In conclusion (Sect. 5), the proposed paradigm change is analyzed from a Digital Humanities research perspective and related works are discussed.

2   Creating the Knowledge Graph

Knowledge Extraction. The biographies in dictionaries often have two sections: the beginning is written in terms of normal full sentences, and in the end

---

[2] http://www.anb.org/aboutanb.html.
[3] http://www.ndb.badw-muenchen.de/ndb_aufgaben_e.htm.
[4] http://www.biografischportaal.nl/en.
[5] https://sok.riksarkivet.se/Sbl/Start.aspx?lang=en.
[6] http://biografiakeskus.fi.
[7] https://www.finlit.fi/en.

there is a concise, semi-formal summary, explicating the major events, achievements, and other biographical data about the biographee [39]. An example of the semi-formal descriptions for the architect *Eliel Saarinen* is given below:

Gottlieb Eliel Saarinen S 20.8.1873 Rantasalmi, K 1.7.1950 Bloomfield Hills, Michigan, Yhdysvallat. V rovasti Juho Saarinen ja Selma Maria Broms. P1 1898 - 1902 (ero) Mathilda Tony Charlotta Gylden (sittemmin Gesellius) S 1877, K 1921, P1 V agronomi Axel Gylden ja Antonia Sofia Hausen; ...
URA. Arkkitehtitoimisto Gesellius, Lindgren & Saarinen, perustajajäsen, osakas 1896-1907; Arkkitehtitoimisto Eliel Saarinen, johtaja 1907–1923; ...
TEOKSET. Arkkitehtitoimisto Gesellius, Lindgren, Saarinen: Tallbergin talo. 1896-1898, Luotsikatu 1, Helsinki; Pariisin maailmannäyttelyn 1900 paviljonki. 1898-1900, Pariisi;

The semi-formal expressions here have uniformity in structure that can be used effectively for pattern-based information extraction: First, the person's given and family names are mentioned and after that the fields of birth and death information are separated with S for birth, and K for death. These fields contain the time and place of the event. A field beginning with V contains the information about the person's parents with the father followed by the mother, their names, occupations, and possible places and times of birth and death. Likewise, fields beginning with P, or if several $P1$, $P2$ etc., carry the information of possible spouses indicating the year of marriage, and the spouse's years of birth and death. There are also descriptions of person's life time events related to education, career (*URA*), or achievements (*TEOKSET*). For the knowledge extraction of the semi-formal part, rules based of regular expressions were used.

The pipeline for the free text part was built using pre-existing NLP tools [34]. The process consists of linguistic analyses (such as tokenization and morphological tagging) and converting the document structures and the linguistic data into RDF. The NLP Interchange Format (NIF)[8] [11] supplements the RDF representation with a Core Ontology that provides classes and properties to describe the relations between texts and documents. This provides flexibility and structure to divide a document into paragraphs, titles, sentences, and words that can be complemented with structural metadata supplied by NIF and linguistic information, such as lemmas and part-of-speech (POS) tags from NLP tools. In addition to the NIF format, the commonly used CIDOC CRM ISO standard, Dublin Core Metadata[9], and a custom namespace are used to supply classes and properties for describing document metadata.

BIOGRAPHYSAMPO automatically creates a narrative life story for each of the 13 100 protagonists in the biographies. [34] This story is enriched in the following ways: (1) Links to external biographies of the person are created for additional information and for using the linkage as a criterion for faceted search and determining target groups in prosopography. (2) The data is enriched from additional external sources, such as collection data from museums, libraries, and archives. For example, if there is a painting by an artist in a collection, the corresponding artistic creation event can be added as an entry in the biographical timeline of the protagonist. (3) The data is enriched by reasoning. For example, persons

---

[8] http://persistence.uni-leipzig.org/nlp2rdf/specification/core.html.
[9] http://dublincore.org/documents/dcmi-terms/.

with similar life stories are determined for recommendation links, family relations and egocentric networks between persons are explicated, and serendipitous
relations between entities such as persons and places are discovered.

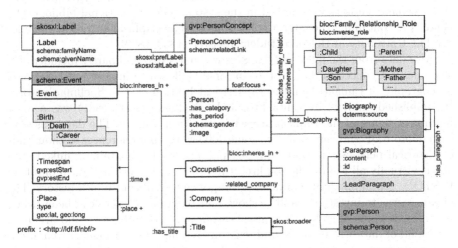

Fig. 1. BIOGRAPHYSAMPO data model uses *owl* and *skos(xl)* standards, namespace
bioc refers to Bio CRM [36], *schema* to schema.org, *geo* to W3C Basic Geo, and *gvp*
to Getty vocabulary.

3   Data Model, Datasets, and Data Service

The data model used is depicted in Fig. 1. The central class in the middle is:
Person. The life of a person instance is described essentially in terms of different
kind of events (s)he participated in different roles in time and place (on the left
side of the figure). For the human reader, links to biographical texts are provided
(on the right). However, based on the machine understandable RDF data, the
reading experience can be enhanced by providing the end user with additional
information related to the biographies and with tools for analyzing the lives and
biographies as texts in different way, as will be shown in the following sections.
The data model is an extension of CIDOC CRM [5,26] called Bio CRM see [36].

The core data includes the biography collections listed in Table 1, edited and
maintained by the Biographical Centre of the Finnish Literature Society (SKS).
These biographies have been written by 977 scholars from different fields. The
largest collection, the National Biography of Finland, was first published online
in 1997 and later on as a 9500 page book series of ten volumes and a separate
index [2]. All bios in Table 1 are available via a national web service[10].

The core datasets are linked not only internally but also enriched with links to
the external data sources of biographies listed in Table 2 according to the Linked

---

[10] http://kansallisbiografia.fi.

Data 5-star model[11]. The links were created by comparing names and birth years and were included in our data service for additional information of persons. In addition, the data sources are used as a search facet for filtering out persons described in different data sources. In comparison to our earlier prototype [19], two new datasets were linked in the system: (1) The national bibliography Fennica[12], containing the largest collection of bibliographical entries in Finland. (2) The University of Helsinki student register (1853–1899)[13].

Also data from the following datasets was harvested and partly included: (1) The open art collection data of the National Gallery of Finland[14]. (2) National bibliography of Finland Fennica. (3) Critical Edition of J.V. Snellman's works [1], published online[15] by Edita Ltd. J. V. Snellman (1806–1881) was a most prominent figure of the Finnish history in the 19th century. The data was converted into RDF and contains, e.g., some 3000 works and references to thousands of historical persons. (4) Booksampo semantic portal[16], containing linked data about virtually all Finnish fiction literature. (5) The Finnish historical ontology HISTO[17], containing linked data about important events of Finnish history. The idea here was to investigate and to show, how biographical data can be enriched by different kinds of collection contents from museums, libraries, and archives. This kind of data was instrumental, e.g., in creating the relational search application perspective of the portal [20] (to be presented in more detail later on).

Table 1. The biographies of the Finnish Literature Society. The National Biography and the Finnish Clergy datasets contain semi-formal summaries.

Dataset name	# of people
National Biography of Finland	6478
Business Leaders	2235
Finnish Generals and Admirals 1809–1917	481
Finnish Clergy 1554–1721	2716
Finnish Clergy 1800–1920	1234
Sum	13144

BIOGRAPHYSAMPOData Service serves 13 144 biographies from which some 125 000 events, 51 937 family relations, 4953 places, 3101 professions, and 2938 companies were identified and extracted. There are also over 26 000 links to the 16 linked external datasets and services, and tens of thousands of relations

---

[11] http://5stardata.info/en/.
[12] http://data.nationallibrary.fi/bib/me/CFENNI.
[13] https://ylioppilasmatrikkeli.helsinki.fi/1853-1899/.
[14] https://www.kansallisgalleria.fi/en/avoin-data/.
[15] http://snellman.kootutteokset.fi/.
[16] http://kirjasampo.fi.
[17] https://seco.cs.aalto.fi/ontologies/histo/.

Table 2. External data sources (person pages) linked to the BIOGRAPHYSAMPO.

Data source	# of links	Description
Wikipedia	6316	http://fi.wikipedia.org
Wikidata	6505	http://www.wikidata.org
Fennica	4007	National Bibliography of Finland
BLF	1084	Biografiskt Lexikon för Finland
BookSampo	715	Finnish fiction literature LD service
WarSampo	288	World War II, LOD service and portal
ULAN	213	Union List of Artist Names Online
VIAF	2475	Virtual International Authority Files
Geni.com	5320	Family research and family tree data
Home pages	43	Personal web sites
Parliament of Finland	631	Members of Parliament 1917–2018
University of Helsinki Registry	379	Students and faculty in 1853–1899
Sum	28197	

extracted from external sources. The data contains ca. 10 million triples, and there is a separate graph of over 100 million triples representing the texts linguistically.

To evaluate the knowledge extraction pipeline (cf. Sect. 2), a test set of 135 events was manually checked with promising results: 99% of the generated data were actual events of a person's life, and 98% of events had a correct time period. We filtered out the snippets having a timespan outside of person's living years. The snippets were also linked to our place ontology with a precision of 98%, and a recall of 77%. False positives occurred in cases, e.g., when a company has the same name as a place. In some cases, lemmatizing a place name caused a wrong basic form, and the event did not get linked to the correct place.

The data is provided using the "7-star" Linked Data Finland platform[18] [16]. The service is based on Fuseki[19] with a Varnish Cache[20] front end for resolving URIs and serving LD in different ways. A larger vision behind our work is that by publishing openly shared ontologies and data about historical persons for everybody to use, future interoperability problems can be prevented before they arise [12]. At the moment, all data has been opened for the public to read freely. Negotiations for opening the data service as well are underway.

The data service can be used as a basis for Rich Internet Applications (RIA). A demonstration of this is the BIOGRAPHYSAMPO Portal, where *all* functionality is implemented on the client side using JavaScript, only data is fetched from the

---

[18] See http://www.ldf.fi for more details.
[19] http://jena.apache.org/documentation/serving_data/.
[20] https://www.varnish-cache.org.

server side SPARQL endpoints. In below, new ways of using the biographical linked data in the portal are presented from the end-user's point of view.

4   New Ways for Studying Biographies

The BIOGRAPHYSAMPO Portal is not just one monolithic application, but a collection of thematic interlinked *application perspectives* to the underlying data. Different perspectives are needed [15,28] in order to address different end-user information needs properly. The portal includes seven perspectives that can be selected in the front page of the system or at any situation in the menu bar: (1) *Persons.* Faceted search view for filtering and finding biographies. (2) *Places.* Searching biographical events projected on interactive maps. (3) *Life maps.* Life events and trajectories from birth to death of person groups visualized on maps. (4) *Statistics.* Various histogram and pie chart statistics of filtered person groups. (5) *Networks.* Analyzing networks of person groups. (6) *Relations.* Finding serendipitous connections between persons and places with natural language explanations. (7) *Language.* Tools for analyzing the language used in biographies.

Many perspectives of the portal support the prosopographical research method [37, p. 47] that consists of two major steps. First, a target group of people that share desired characteristics is selected for solving the research question at hand. Second, the target group is analyzed, and possibly compared with other groups, in order to solve the research question. To support prosopography, BIOGRAPHYSAMPO employs faceted search for filtering out target groups. Once the group has been determined, various generic data-analytic tools and visualizations can be applied to it. In below, the major functionalities of the portal's perspectives are explained from the end user's view point.

Fig. 2. Home page of Eliel Saarinen (1873–1950).

1. Persons. The basic use case in biography collections is to find a person's biography to be read. In addition to supporting traditional name string based search, the Persons view features a full-blown faceted search engine on top of a SPARQL endpoint. Here properties, such as profession, place of birth, place of education, working organization, and other criteria can be used for filtering down persons of potential interest. After each facet category selection, the hit counts on all facets are calculated, so that the user never ends up in a "no hits" situation. Furthermore, the hit counts on the facets provide useful statistical information about the distributions of biographies along the orthogonal facets. The distributions can also be visualized as interactive pie charts by a click on a special symbol. The faceted search engine was implemented by developing a new version of the Faceter tool [23].

BIOGRAPHYSAMPO generates for each person in the system a global "home page" for enhanced reading experience by enriching data from various interlinked data sources and by reasoning. After finding a person of interest, the system provides the user with an enriched reading view of his or her life based on (1) data linking and (2) reasoning. Figure 2 shows as an example the home page of Eliel Saarinen (1873–1950), a prominent Finnish architect. The page contains six tabs providing different biographical views of the person, here two pages based on the NBF, data at the Linked Data Finland service, a genealogical family tree and home page by the Geni.com service, and the Finnish Wikipedia article. The entry is linked to seven external data sources on the web. On the right, recommendation links to related biographies are given, e.g., to similar biographies based on their linguistic content.

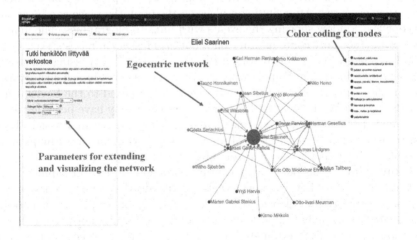

Fig. 3. Egocentric network analysis of Eliel Saarinen.

On the top of Fig. 2, there are five tabs for data-analytic views of Saarinen. For example, Fig. 3 presents his egocentric network based on the links between the bios in the NBF, with a coloring scheme indicating persons of different types.

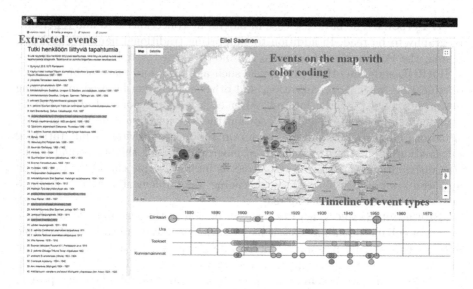

Fig. 4. Spatiotemporal visualization of the events in Eliel Saarinen's life.

The depth and other parameters of the network can be controlled by the widgets on the left. In Fig. 4, another tab visualizes the international events of four types of Saarinen's life on a map and a timeline for a spatiotemporal analysis.

2. Places. BIOGRAPHYSAMPO also provides the user with a map search view in which the events extracted from the biographies are projected on the places where they occurred. After finding a place on the map, the place can be clicked. This opens a window showing the events with links to biographies. The maps in this view are not only contemporary ones but also historical maps served by the Finnish Ontology Service of Historical Places and Maps[21] [21], using a historical map service[22] based on Map Warper[23]. Many events of Finnish history took place in the eastern parts of the country that was annexed to the Soviet Union after the Second World War. Old Finnish places there may have been destroyed, placenames have been changed, and names are now written in Russian. Using semi-transparent digitized historical maps on top of contemporary maps solves the problem by giving a better historical context for the events.

3. Life Maps. This perspective contains two kind of prosopographical tools: (1) *Event maps* show how different events (births, deaths, career events, artistic creation events, and accolades) that a target group of people participated in are distributed on maps. (2) *Life charts* summarize the lives of persons from a transitional perspective as blue-red arrows from the birth places (blue end) to the places of death (red end).

---

[21] http://hipla.fi.

[22] http://mapwarper.onki.fi.

[23] https://github.com/timwaters/mapwarper.

The prosopographical tools and visualizations in BIOGRAPHYSAMPO can be applied not only to one target group but also to two parallel groups in order to compare them. For example, Fig. 5 compares the life charts of Finnish generals and admirals in the Russian armed forces in 1809–1917 when Finland was an autonomous Grand Duchy within the Russian Empire (on the left) with the members of the Finnish clergy (1800–1920) (on the right). With a few selections from the facets the user can see that, for some reason, quite a few officers moved to Southern Europe when they retired (like retirees today) while the Lutheran ministers tended to stay in Finland. The arrows are interactive. For example, by clicking on the peculiar upper arrow to the east, one can find out that this arrow was due to general Gustaf A. Silfverhjelm's (1799–1864) biography, where one can learn that he was promoted to become a chief cartographer in western Siberia.

4. Statistics. The statistical application perspective includes histograms showing various numeric value distributions of the members of the group, e.g., their ages, number of spouses and children, and pie charts visualizing proportional distributions of professions, societal domains, and working organizations.

5. Networks. The networks perspective is used for visualizing and studying networks among the target group. The networks are based on the reference links between the biographies, either handmade or based on automatically detected mentions. The depth of the networks can be controlled by limiting the number of links, and coloring of the nodes can be based on the gender or societal domain of the person (e.g., military, medical, business, music, etc.).

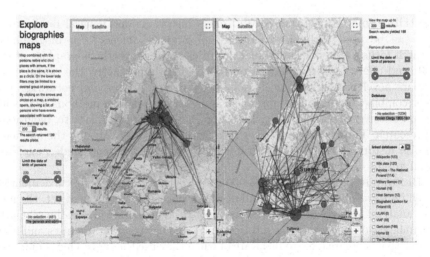

Fig. 5. Comparing the life charts of two target groups, admirals and generals (left) and clergy (right) of the historical Grand Duchy of Finland (1809–1917).

6. Relations. To utilize reasoning and knowledge discovery, an application perspective for finding "interesting/serendipitous" [3] connections in the biographical knowledge graph was created. This application idea is related to relational search [27,35]. However, in our case a new knowledge-based approach was developed to find out in what ways (groups of) people are related to places and areas. This method, described in more detail in [20], rules out non-sense relations effectively and is able to create natural language explanations for the connections. The queries are formulated and the problems are solved using faceted search. For example, the query "How are Finnish artists related to Italy?" is solved by selecting "Italy" from the place facet and "artist" from the profession facet. The results include connections of different types (that could be filtered in another facet), e.g., that "Elin Danielson-Gambogi received in 1899 the Florence City Art Award" and "Robert Ekman created in 1844 the painting 'Landscape in Subiaco' depicting a place in Italy".

7. **Language.** The biographies can be analyzed by using linguistic analysis, providing yet another different perspective for studying them. Both individual biographies as well as groups of them can be analyzed and compared with each other as in prosopography above. For example, it turns out that the biographies of female Members of the Parliament (MP) frequently contain words "family" and "child", but these words are seldom used in the biographies of male MPs. The analyses are based on the linguistic knowledge graph of the texts.

Re-using the Data. The application perspectives above were implemented by only modifying the way the data is accessed using SPARQL.

5   Discussion

Contributions. BIOGRAPHYSAMPO offers historians and general public tools that can be used without experience in computer science. For biographical research focusing on one individual, it enriches the in-depth biographies of the NBF and offers several visualization tools. Most importantly, the portal gives scholars novel prosopographical tools for analyzing groups and networks. The tools combine quantitative approach and distant reading methods [32] with the qualitative approach, often based on close reading, typical to biographical research. The system also offers new possibilities for analyzing the language Finnish historians use in the biographies of people of different gender, age, and social groups.

BIOGRAPHYSAMPO has had 43 000 distinct users during its first five months, which indicates interest in this kind of web services. However, as of yet, the new data analytic features of the portal have not been evaluated in real-life scholarly research. We do know that the datasets and tools have certain premises and limitations that scholars have to be aware of when they use the tools. One should pay close attention to the following questions: (1) *Who created the datasets and to what end?* The core data in BiographySampo comes from biographical databases created in projects carried out by the Biographical Centre of the Finnish Literature Society in co-operation with several learned societies: the Finnish Historical Society, The Finnish Economic History Association, and the Finnish Society of Church History. This good, academically sound information has been enriched with web resources such as Wikipedia and genealogical sites like Geni.com where everyone can contribute. In BiographySampo, the source of information is always indicated – it may not be of interest to most users, but for scholars it is essential. (2) *How was the biographical collection constructed?* When it comes to biographical collections such as the NBF, the construction of the collection and the process and criteria of inclusion and exclusion of historical persons is vital information. Without understanding the process, we cannot understand who the real subject of our analysis is when we work with the datasets and tools.

There are two types of bios in BIOGRAPHYSAMPO: Firstly, there are historical groups that have been recognized by their members and outsiders as a distinct group in a given time in history, e.g., the Lutheran ministers of the Diocese of Turku in the dataset Finnish Clergy 1554–1721. The dataset includes them all and thus makes true prosopographical research possible. This is where BiographySampo is at its very best. Ministers are an especially interesting group from the point of view of networks, as the vocation often went down from grandfather to father to son, and ministers often married the daughters of other clergy families. Secondly, there are groups created by historians. For example, the National Biography of Finland, or indeed of any given country, is an artificial group. In their lifetime the biographees were not connected and certainly did not identify with each other. In network analysis, for example, the egocentric network of Blanche de Namur, the Swedish queen Blanka (1318–1363), includes Albert Edelfelt (1854–1905) who lived 500 years later, because he depicted the queen in his famous painting, not because he was in the social network of the queen.

The biographies of NBF cover one thousand years and include, e.g., all Swedish kings who ruled Finland, a witch burned at stake in the 17th century, a 18th century prostitute, the first female professor in Finland, and the software engineer Linus Torvalds, the father of the Linux operating system. What all these people from different times and different walks of life do have in common is that they have been chosen by a large and authoritative group of Finnish scholars to form a biographical representation of the history of the Finns. Some of them were eminent in their own times, some represent an important group or a phenomenon, many were pioneers in their own fields.

The statistical or linguistic analysis of these artificial groups therefore tells us not about the past itself, but about the values and preferences of Finnish historians around the turn of the millennium. As an example, we compared above the language used in the biographies of male versus female Members of Parliament (MP). The results tell us very little about the MPs and their work, but illustrate how Finnish scholars emphasize different issues when writing about the work of male and female biographees.

More work is underway in developing BIOGRAPHYSAMPO tools and data to be better understood by the users doing serious historical research. More background information on the datasets and the collections they are based on is needed in order to make transparent how the tools process the information. Historians are trained in source criticism and used to work with complicated documents. Digital Humanities resources should take this into account and help scholars understand and critically evaluate the tools they are offered.

Related Work. Aside publishing biographical dictionaries in print and on the web, representing and analyzing biographical data has grown into a new research and application field. In 2015, the first Biographical Data in Digital World workshop BD2015 was held presenting several works on studying and analyzing biographies as data [4], and the proceedings of BD2017 contain more similar works [6]. In [25], analytic visualizations were created based on U.S. Legislator registry data. The idea of biographical network analysis is related to the Six Degrees of Francis Bacon system[24] [24,38] that utilizes data of the Oxford Dictionary of National Biography. However, in our case faceted search can be used for filtering and studying target groups. The work was influenced by the early Semantic NBF demonstrator [14] and its follow-up prototype [19], whose software has been applied also to a historical register of students [18] and to the U.S. Legislator data [29]. However, BIOGRAPHYSAMPO extends these systems into several new directions in terms of the DH tooling provided, such as faceted network analysis views, relational search, and text analysis views for studying the language of the biographies. Also more heterogeneous datasets are used.

Extracting Linked Data from texts has been studied in several works, cf. e.g. [8]. In [7] language technology was applied for extracting entities and relations in RDF using Dutch biographies in the BiographyNet. This work was part of the larger NewsReader project extracting data from news [31]. This line of research is similar to ours, based on the idea of extracting RDF data from unstructured biographical texts. However, BiographyNet focuses more on challenges of natural language processing and managing the provenance information of data from multiple sources, while our focus is on providing the end user with intelligent search and browsing facilities, enriched reading experience, and easy to use data-analytic tooling for biography and prosopography. Here BIOGRAPHYSAMPO employs the "Sampo" model [17], where the data is enriched through a shared content infrastructure by related external heterogeneous datasets, here, e.g., collection databases of museums, libraries, and archives, a critical edition, genealogical data, and various biographical data sources and semantic portals online. BIOGRAPHYSAMPO is a member in the Sampo series of semantic portals including also CultureSampo (2009), TravelSampo (2011), BookSampo (2011) (2 million users in 2018), and WarSampo (2015) (230 000 users in 2018), and NameSampo (tens of thousands of users in 2019).

Acknowledgements. Thanks to Business Finland for financial support and CSC – IT Center for Science, Finland, for computational resources.

---

[24] http://www.sixdegreesoffrancisbacon.com.

References

1. Snellman, J.V.: Kootut teokset 1–24. Ministry of Education and Culture, Helsinki (2002)
2. Suomen kansallisbiografia 1–10. Suomalaisen Kirjallisuuden Seura, Helsinki (2003)
3. Aylett, R.S., Bental, D.S., Stewart, R., Forth, J., Wiggins, G.: Supporting serendipitous discovery. In: Digital Futures (Third Annual Digital Economy Conference), 23–25 October 2012, Aberdeen, UK (2012)
4. ter Braake, S., Fokkens, A., Sluijter, R., Declerck, T., Wandl-Vogt, E. (eds.): BD2015 Biographical Data in a Digital World 2015. In: CEUR Workshop Proceedings, vol. 1399 (2015)
5. Doerr, M.: The CIDOC CRM–an ontological approach to semantic interoperability of metadata. AI Mag. **24**(3), 75–92 (2003)
6. Fokkens, A., ter Braake, S., Sluijter, R., Arthur, P., Wandl-Vogt, E. (eds.): BD2017 biographical data in a digital world 2017. In: CEUR Workshop Proceedings, vol. 2119 (2017)
7. Fokkens, A., et al.: BiographyNet: extracting relations between people and events. In: Europa baut auf Biographien, pp. 193–224. New Academic Press, Wien (2017)
8. Gangemi, A., Presutti, V., Recupero, D.R., Nuzzolese, A.G., Draicchio, F., Mongiovì, M.: Semantic web machine reading with FRED. Semant. Web J. **8**(6), 873–893 (2017)
9. Gardiner, E., Musto, R.G.: The Digital Humanities: A Primer for Students and Scholars. Cambridge University Press, New York (2015)
10. Heath, T., Bizer, C.: Linked Data: Evolving the Web Into a Global Data Space. Synthesis Lectures on the Semantic Web: Theory and Technology, 1st edn. Morgan & Claypool, Palo Alto (2011). http://linkeddatabook.com/editions/1.0/
11. Hellmann, S., Lehmann, J., Auer, S., Brümmer, M.: Integrating NLP using linked data. In: Alani, H., et al. (eds.) ISWC 2013. LNCS, vol. 8219, pp. 98–113. Springer, Heidelberg (2013). https://doi.org/10.1007/978-3-642-41338-4_7
12. Hyvönen, E.: Preventing interoperability problems instead of solving them. Semant. Web J. **1**(1–2), 33–37 (2010)
13. Hyvönen, E.: Publishing and Using Cultural Heritage Linked Data on the Semantic Web. Morgan & Claypool, Palo Alto (2012)
14. Hyvönen, E., Alonen, M., Ikkala, E., Mäkelä, E.: Life stories as event-based linked data: case semantic national biography. In: Proceedings of ISWC 2014 Posters & Demonstrations Track, pp. 1–4. CEUR Workshop Proceedings, vol. 1272 (2014)
15. Hyvönen, E., et al.: CultureSampo - Finnish culture on the semantic web 2.0. Thematic perspectives for the end-user. In: Museums and the Web 2009. Archives and Museum Informatics, Toronto (2009)
16. Hyvönen, E., Tuominen, J., Alonen, M., Mäkelä, E.: Linked data Finland: A 7-star model and platform for publishing and re-using linked datasets. In: Presutti, V., Blomqvist, E., Troncy, R., Sack, H., Papadakis, I., Tordai, A. (eds.) ESWC 2014. LNCS, vol. 8798, pp. 226–230. Springer, Cham (2014). https://doi.org/10.1007/978-3-319-11955-7_24
17. Hyvönen, E.: Cultural heritage linked data on the semantic web: three case studies using the Sampo model. In: VIII Encounter of Documentation Centres of Contemporary Art: Open Linked Data and Integral Management of Information in Cultural Centres Artium, 19–20 October 2016, Vitoria-Gasteiz, Spain (2016)

18. Hyvönen, E., Leskinen, P., Heino, E., Tuominen, J., Sirola, L.: Reassembling and enriching the life stories in printed biographical registers: Norssi high school alumni on the semantic web. In: Gracia, J., Bond, F., McCrae, J.P., Buitelaar, P., Chiarcos, C., Hellmann, S. (eds.) LDK 2017. LNCS (LNAI), vol. 10318, pp. 113–119. Springer, Cham (2017). https://doi.org/10.1007/978-3-319-59888-8_9
19. Hyvönen, E., Leskinen, P., Tamper, M., Tuominen, J., Keravuori, K.: Semantic national biography of Finland. In: Proceedings of the Digital Humanities in the Nordic Countries 3rd Conference (DHN 2018). CEUR Workshop Proceedings, vol. 2084, pp. 372–385 (2018)
20. Hyvönen, E., Rantala, H.: Knowledge-based relation discovery in cultural heritage knowledge graphs. In: Proceedings of the 4th Digital Humanities in the Nordic Countries Conference (DHN 2019). CEUR Workshop Proceedings (2019)
21. Ikkala, E., Tuominen, J., Hyvönen, E.: Contextualizing historical places in a gazetteer by using historical maps and linked data. Proceedings of DH 2016, pp. 573–577 (2016)
22. Keith, T.: Changing Conceptions of National Biography. Cambridge University Press, Cambridge (2004)
23. Koho, M., Heino, E., Hyvönen, E.: SPARQL Faceter–Client-side Faceted Search Based on SPARQL. In: Joint Proceedings of the 4th International Workshop on Linked Media and the 3rd Developers Hackshop. CEUR Workshop Proceedings, vol. 1615 (2016)
24. Langmead, A., Otis, J., Warren, C., Weingart, S., Zilinski, L.: Towards interoperable network ontologies for the digital humanities. Int. J. Humanit. Arts Comput. **10**(1), 22–35 (2016)
25. Larson, R.: Bringing lives to light: biography in context. Final project report, University of Berkeley (2010). http://metadata.berkeley.edu/Biography_Final_Report.pdf
26. Le Boeuf, P., Doerr, M., Ore, C.E., Stead, S. (eds.): Definition of the CIDOC Conceptual Reference Model, Version 6.2.4. ICOM/CIDOC Documentation Standards Group (CIDOC CRM Special Interest Group) (2018). http://www.cidoc-crm.org/Version/version-6.2.4
27. Lohmann, S., Heim, P., Stegemann, T., Ziegler, J.: The RelFinder user interface: interactive exploration of relationships between objects of interest. In: Proceedings of the 14th International Conference on Intelligent User Interfaces (IUI 2010), pp. 421–422. ACM (2010)
28. Mäkelä, E., Ruotsalo, T., Hyvönen, E.: How to deal with massively heterogeneous cultural heritage data–lessons learned in CultureSampo. Semant. Web J. **3**(1), 85–109 (2012)
29. Miyakita, G., Leskinen, P., Hyvönen, E.: Using linked data for prosopographical research of historical persons: case U.S. Congress Legislators. In: Ioannides, M., et al. (eds.) EuroMed 2018. LNCS, vol. 11197, pp. 150–162. Springer, Cham (2018). https://doi.org/10.1007/978-3-030-01765-1_18
30. Roberts, B.: Biographical Research. Understanding Social Research. Open University Press, London (2002)
31. Rospocher, M., et al.: Building event-centric knowledge graphs from news. Web Semant. Sci. Serv. Agents WWW **37**, 132–151 (2016)
32. Schultz, A., Matteni, A., Isele, R., Bizer, C., Becker, C.: LDIF - linked data integration framework. In: Proceedings of the 2nd International Workshop on Consuming Linked Data (COLD 2011). CEUR Workshop Proceedings, vol. 782 (2011)
33. Shultz, K.: What is distant reading? New York Times, 24 June 2011

34. Tamper, M., Leskinen, P., Apajalahti, K., Hyvönen, E.: Using biographical texts as linked data for prosopographical research and applications. In: Ioannides, M., et al. (eds.) EuroMed 2018. LNCS, vol. 11196, pp. 125–137. Springer, Cham (2018). https://doi.org/10.1007/978-3-030-01762-0_11

35. Tartari, G., Hogan, A.: WiSP: weighted shortest paths for RDF graphs. In: Proceedings of VOILA 2018. CEUR Workshop Proceedings, vol. 2187, pp. 37–52 (2018)

36. Tuominen, J., Hyvönen, E., Leskinen, P.: Bio CRM: a data model for representing biographical data for prosopographical research. In: Proceedings of the Second Conference on Biographical Data in a Digital World 2017 (BD2017). CEUR Workshop Proceedings, vol. 2119, pp. 59–66 (2018)

37. Verboven, K., Carlier, M., Dumolyn, J.: A short manual to the art of prosopography. In: Prosopography Approaches and Applications. A Handbook, pp. 35–70. Unit for Prosopographical Research (Linacre College) (2007)

38. Warren, C., Shore, D., Otis, J., Wang, L., Finegold, M., Shalizi, C.: Six degrees of Francis Bacon: a statistical method for reconstructing large historical social networks. Digit. Humanit. Q. **10**(3) (2016)

39. Wu, Y., Sun, H., Yan, C.: An event timeline extraction method based on news corpus. In: 2017 IEEE 2nd International Conference on Big Data Analysis, pp. 697–702. IEEE (2017)

Tinderbook: Fall in Love with Culture

Enrico Palumbo[1,2,3]($\boxtimes$) (iD), Alberto Buzio[1], Andrea Gaiardo[1],
Giuseppe Rizzo[1](iD), Raphael Troncy[2](iD), and Elena Baralis[3]

[1] LINKS Foundation, Turin, Italy
{enrico.palumbo,alberto.buzio,andrea.gaiardo,
giuseppe.rizzo}@linksfoundation.com
[2] EURECOM, Sophia Antipolis, France
raphael.troncy@eurecom.fr
[3] Politecnico di Torino, Turin, Italy
elena.baralis@polito.it

Abstract. More than 2 millions of new books are published every year
and choosing a good book among the huge amount of available options
can be a challenging endeavor. Recommender systems help in choosing
books by providing personalized suggestions based on the user reading
history. However, most book recommender systems are based on collaborative filtering, involving a long onboarding process that requires to
rate many books before providing good recommendations. Tinderbook
provides book recommendations, given a single book that the user likes,
through a card-based playful user interface that does not require an
account creation. Tinderbook is strongly rooted in semantic technologies, using the DBpedia knowledge graph to enrich book descriptions
and extending a hybrid state-of-the-art knowledge graph embeddings
algorithm to derive an item relatedness measure for cold start recommendations. Tinderbook is publicly available (http://www.tinderbook.
it) and has already generated interest in the public, involving passionate readers, students, librarians, and researchers. The online evaluation
shows that Tinderbook achieves almost 50% of precision of the recommendations.

Keywords: Recommender systems · Books · Knowledge graphs ·
DBpedia · Embeddings

1 Introduction

In recent years, the explosion of information available on the Web has made ever
more challenging the task of finding a good book to read. In 2010, the number
of books in the world was more than one hundred millions[1] and approximately
2,210,000 new books are published every year[2]. At the same time, a survey shows

---

[1] https://www.telegraph.co.uk/technology/google/7930273/Google-counts-total-
number-of-books-in-the-world.html.

[2] https://en.wikipedia.org/wiki/Books_published_per_country_per_year.

© Springer Nature Switzerland AG 2019
P. Hitzler et al. (Eds.): ESWC 2019, LNCS 11503, pp. 590–605, 2019.
https://doi.org/10.1007/978-3-030-21348-0_38

that in the US, a reader typically reads 4 books in one year[3] and a study shows that most readers typically give up on a book in the early chapters[4]. These figures show the importance and the complexity of the process of selecting a book to read among the enormous amount of available options. Recommender systems (RS) have provided a great deal of help in this task, using algorithms that predict how likely it is for a user to like a certain item, leveraging the history of the user preferences. Most of the existing book recommender systems are typically based on collaborative filtering, which suffers from the cold start problem [1], and are thus based on long onboarding procedures, requiring users to log-in and to rate a consistent number of books (Sect. 5). On the other hand, content-based recommender systems suffer the risk of overspecialization, i.e. tend to recommend over and over again similar types of items [14]. Hybrid recommender systems combine the best of collaborative filtering and content-based similarity and are able to provide good recommendations even when user ratings are few [1]. Knowledge graphs provide an ideal data structure for such systems, as a consequence of their ability of encompassing heterogeneous information, such as user-item interactions and item-item relations in the same model. Besides, knowledge-aware recommender systems have also the advantage of being able to naturally leverage Linked Open Data [4], which provide a rich database of item descriptions and model item-item relations with semantic properties [10].

In this paper, we describe Tinderbook, a book recommender system based on knowledge graph embeddings that provides book recommendations given a single book that the user likes. To achieve this, we extend a state-of-the-art knowledge graph embeddings algorithm [15] to compute item-to-item recommendations using a hybrid item relatedness measure. In Sect. 2, we describe the recommendation algorithm, the dataset and the experimental validation of the methodological choice. In Sect. 3, we provide a high-level description of the TinderBook end-user application. In Sect. 4, we report the results obtained during the online experiment with users. In Sect. 5, we compare TinderBook with existing competing applications. In Sect. 6, we discuss the main findings and lessons learned from the deployment of the application into a production environment, as well as the future work and possible improvements of the application.

2 Recommendation Algorithm

2.1 Definitions

Definition 1. *A knowledge graph is a set $K = (E, R, O)$ where E is the set of entities, $R \subset E \times \Gamma \times E$ is a set of typed relations between entities and O is an ontology. The ontology O defines the set of relation types ('properties') Γ, the set of entity types Λ, assigns entities to their type $O : e \in E \to \Lambda$ and entity types to their related properties $O : \epsilon \in \Lambda \to \Gamma_\epsilon \subset \Gamma$.*

---

[3] https://www.irisreading.com/how-many-books-does-the-average-person-read/.

[4] https://www.nytimes.com/2016/03/15/business/media/moneyball-for-book-publishers-for-a-detailed-look-at-how-we-read.html.

Definition 2. *Users are a subset of the entities of the knowledge graph, $u \in U \subset E$. Items are a subset of the entities of the knowledge graph, $i \in I \subset E$. Users and items form disjoint sets, $U \cap I = \emptyset$.*

Definition 3. *The property 'feedback' describes an observed positive feedback between a user and an item. Feedback only connects users and items, i.e. only triples such as $(u, feedback, i)$ where $u \in U$ and $i \in I$ can exist.*

Definition 4. *Given a user $u \in U$, the set of candidate items $I_{candidates}(u) \subset I$ is the set of items that are taken into account as being potential object of recommendation.*

The problem of top-N item recommendation is that of selecting a set of N items from a set of possible candidate items. Typically, the number of candidates is order of magnitudes higher than N and the recommender system has to be able to identify a short list of very relevant items for the user. The goal of the Tinderbook application is that of recommending books to read, given a single book that the user likes. In a more formal way, we need to define a measure of item relatedness $\rho(i_j, i_k)$ which estimates how likely it is that the user will like the book i_k, given that the user likes the book i_j. The item relatedness $\rho(i_j, i_k)$ is used as a ranking function, i.e. to sort the candidate items $i_k \in I_{candidates}(u)$ given the 'seed' item i_j. Then, only the top N elements are selected and presented to the user.

2.2   Approach

The approach to define the measure of item relatedness $\rho(i_j, i_k)$ is based on entity2rec [15]. entity2rec builds property-specific knowledge graph embeddings applying node2vec [13] on property-specific subgraphs, computes user-item property-specific relatedness scores and combines them in a global user-item relatedness score that is used to provide top-N item recommendations. In this work, we extend entity2rec to a cold start scenario, where user profiles are not known and item-to-item recommendations are needed. To this end, we apply entity2rec to generate property-specific knowledge graph embeddings, but then, we focus on item-item relatedness, rather than on user-item relatedness. Property-specific item-item relatedness scores are then averaged to obtain a global item-item relatedness score that is used as a ranking function (Fig. 1). We define:

$$\rho_{entity2rec}(i_j, i_k) = avg(\rho_p(i_j, i_k)) \tag{1}$$

where $\rho_p(i_j, i_k) = cosine\_sim(x_p(i_j), x_p(i_k))$ and x_p is the property-specific knowledge graph embedding obtained using node2vec on the property-specific subgraph. We compare this measure of item relatedness with that of an ItemKNN [20], which is a purely collaborative filtering system. The relatedness between the items is high when they tend be liked by the same users. More formally, we define:

$$\rho_{itemknn}(i_j, i_k) = \frac{|U_j \cap U_k|}{|U_j \cup U_k|} \tag{2}$$

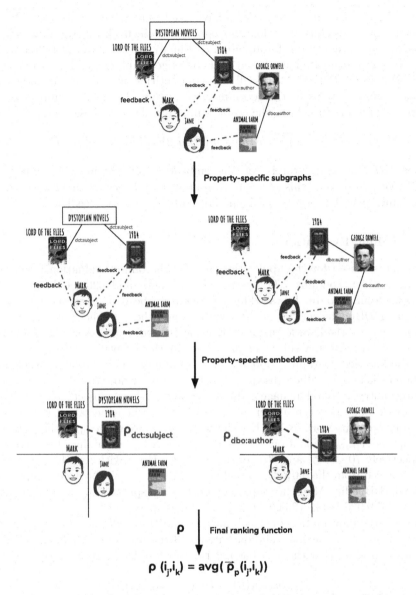

Fig. 1. The knowledge graph represents user-item interactions through the special property 'feedback', as well as item properties and relations to other entities. The knowledge graph allows to model both collaborative and content-based interactions between users and items. In this figure, 'dbo:author' and 'dct:subject' properties are represented as an example, more properties are included in the experiments. Property-specific subgraphs are created from the original knowledge graph. Property-specific embeddings are computed, and property-specific item relatedness scores are computed as cosine similarities in the vectors space. Finally, property-specific relatedness scores are averaged to obtain a global item-item relatedness score.

where U_j and U_k are the users who have liked item i_j and i_k respectively. We also use as a baseline the MostPop approach, which always recommends the top-N most popular items for any item i_j. Finally, we compare entity2rec with a measure of item relatedness based on knowledge graph embeddings built using RDF2Vec [18]. RDF2Vec turns all DBpedia entities into vectors, including the books that are items of the recommender system. Thus, we simply use as a measure of item relatedness the cosine similarity between these vectors:

$$\rho_{RDF2Vec}(i_j, i_k) = cosine\_sim(RDF2Vec(i_j), RDF2Vec(i_k)) \qquad (3)$$

where $RDF2Vec(i_j)$ stands for the embedding of the item i_j built using RDF2Vec. Note that this is a purely content-based recommender such as the one implemented in [19], as DBpedia does not contain user feedback.

2.3   Offline Evaluation

The dataset used for the application and for the offline evaluation is Library-Thing[5], which contains 7,112 users, 37,231 books and 626,000 book ratings ranging from 1 to 10. LibraryThing books have been mapped to their corresponding DBpedia entities [8] and we leverage these publicly available mappings to create the knowledge graph K using DBpedia data. As done in previous work [17], we select a subset of properties of the DBpedia Ontology[6] to create the knowledge graph: ["dbo:author", "dbo:publisher", "dbo:literaryGenre", "dbo:mediaType", "dbo:subsequentWork", "dbo:previousWork", "dbo:series", "dbo:country", "dbo:language","dbo:coverArtist", "dct:subject"]. We create a 'feedback' edge between a user and a book node when the rating is $r \geq 8$, as done in previous work [8,17]. For the offline evaluation, we split the data into a training X_{train}, validation X_{val} and test set X_{test} containing, for each user, respectively 70%, 10% and 20% of their ratings. Users with less than 10 ratings are removed from the dataset, as well as books that do not have a corresponding entry in DBpedia. After the mapping and the data splitting, we have 6,789 users (95.46%), 9,926 books (26.66%) and 410,199 ratings (65.53%).

We use the evaluation protocol known as AllUnratedItems [22], i.e. for each user, we select as possible candidate items all the items present in the training or in the test set that the user has not rated before in the training set:

$$I_{candidates}(u) = I \setminus \{i \in X_{train}(u)\} \qquad (4)$$

We use standard metrics such as precision (P@k) and recall (R@k) to evaluate the ranking quality.

$$P(k) = \frac{1}{|U|} \sum_{u \in U} \sum_{j=1}^{k} \frac{hit(i_j, u)}{k} \qquad (5)$$

---

[5] https://www.librarything.com.

[6] https://wiki.dbpedia.org/services-resources/ontology.

$$R(k) = \frac{1}{|U|} \sum_{u \in U} \sum_{j=1}^{k} \frac{\text{hit}(i_j, u)}{|\text{rel}(u)|} \tag{6}$$

where the value of *hit* is 1 if the recommended item i is relevant to user u (rating $r \geq 8$ in the test set), otherwise it is 0, $rel(u)$ is the set of relevant items for user u in the test set and i_j are the top-k items that are recommended to u. Items that are not appearing in the test set for user u are considered as a miss. This is a pessimistic assumption, as users typically rate only a fraction of the items they actually like and scores are to be considered as a worst-case estimate of the real recommendation quality. In addition to these metrics, which are focused on evaluating the accuracy of the recommendation, we also measure the serendipity and the novelty of the recommendations. Serendipity can be defined as the capability of identifying items that are both attractive and unexpected [12]. [11] proposed to measure it by considering the precision of the recommended items after having discarded the ones that are too obvious. Equation 7 details how we compute this metric. *hit_non_pop* is similar to *hit*, but top-k most popular items are always counted as non-relevant, even if they are included in the test set of user u. Popular items can be regarded as obvious because they are usually well-known by most users.

$$SER(k) = \frac{1}{|U|} \sum_{u \in U} \sum_{j=1}^{k} \frac{\text{hit\_non\_pop}(i_j, u)}{k} \tag{7}$$

In contrast, the metric of novelty is designed to analyze if an algorithm is able to suggest items that have a low probability of being already known by a user, as they belong to the long-tail of the catalog. This metric was originally proposed by [23] in order to support recommenders capable of helping users to discover new items. We formalize how we computed it in Eq. 8. Note that this metric, differently from the previous ones, does not consider the correctness of the recommended items, but only their novelty.

$$NOV(k) = -\frac{1}{|U| \times k} \cdot \sum_{u \in U} \sum_{j=1}^{k} \log_2 P_{\text{train}}(i_j) \tag{8}$$

The function $P_{train} : I \rightarrow [0, 1]$ returns the fraction of feedback attributed to the item i in the training set. This value represents the probability of observing a certain item in the training set, that is the number of ratings related to that item divided by the total number of ratings available. In order to avoid considering as novel items that are not available in the training set, we consider $\log_2(0) \doteq 0$ by definition.

The offline experiment simulates the scenario in which the user selects a single item he/she likes i_j (so-called 'seed' book) and gets recommendations according to an item-item relatedness function $\rho(i_j, i_k)$, which ranks the candidate items i_k. We iterate through the users of the LibraryThing dataset, and for each user we sample with uniform probability an item i_j that he/she liked in the training set. Then, we rank the candidate items $i_k \in I_{candidates}(u)$ using $\rho_{entity2rec}(i_j, i_k)$, $\rho_{itemknn}(i_j, i_k)$, $\rho_{RDF2Vec}(i_j, i_k)$ and MostPopular, and we measure P@5, R@5, SER@5, NOV@5. The results show that entity2rec obtains better precision, recall and serendipity with respect to competing systems (Table 1).

Table 1. Results for different item-item relatedness measures. entity2rec provides more accurate recommendations with respect to pure collaborative filtering such as ItemKNN and to the Most Popular baseline. It also scores better with respect to the content-based RDF2Vec, although RDF2Vec has the best novelty. Scores can be considered as without error, as the standard deviation is negligible up to the reported precision.

System	P@5	R@5	SER@5	NOV@5
entity2rec	**0.0549**	**0.0508**	**0.0514**	11.099
itemknn	0.0484	0.0472	0.0463	12.2
RDF2Vec	0.0315	0.0288	0.0311	**13.913**
mostpop	0.0343	0.0256	0.007	8.4525

3   Application

In this section, we describe the Tinderbook application.

3.1   Session

A complete usage session can be divided in two phases (Fig. 2):

1. **Onboarding:** the user lands on the application and gets books that are sampled with a chance that is proportional to the popularity of the book. More in detail, a book is sampled according to:

$$p(book) \sim P^+(book)^{\frac{1}{T}} \tag{9}$$

where P^+ is the popularity of the book, which is defined as the fraction of positive feedback (ratings $r \geq 8$) obtained by the book in the LibraryThing dataset. T is a parameter called "temperature" that governs the degree of randomness in the sampling. $T \rightarrow 0$ generates a rich-gets-richer effects, i.e. most popular books become even more likely to appear in the extraction. On the contrary, when T grows the distribution becomes more uniform, and less popular books can appear more often in the sampling. The user has to discard books (pressing "X" or swiping left on a mobile screen) until a liked book is found. The user can get additional information about the book (e.g. the book abstract from DBpedia) by pressing on the "Info" icon.

Fig. 2. A complete session of use of the application. The user selects a book that she likes, gets book recommendations based on her choice and provides her feedback. User can get info about the book by pressing on the "Info" icon.

2. **Recommendations**: after the user has selected a book ("seed book"), she receives five recommended books based on her choice, thanks to the item-item relatedness $\rho_{entity2rec}$ (see Sect. 2.2). The user can provide feedback on the recommended books using the "thumbs up" and "thumbs down" icons, or swiping right or left. The user can again get additional information about the book (book abstract from DBpedia) by pressing on the "Info" icon.

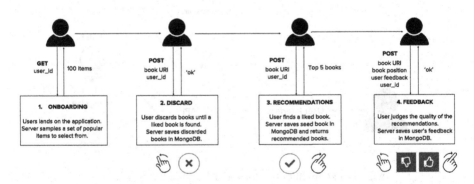

Fig. 3. Tinderbook interactions and corresponding API calls. In 1. ONBOARDING, books are sampled with a chance proportional to their popularity, as described in Eq. 9. In 2. DISCARD, the user goes through proposed books until he/she finds a liked book. In 3. RECOMMENDATIONS, the user receives five book recommendations related to his/her chosen book. In 4. FEEDBACK, the user judges the quality of the recommendations.

The graphical user interface of Tinderbook aims to engage users using playful interaction on popular like/dislike interaction [7]. The graphical representation of cards and a slot-machine-like interaction engage the users into an infinite swipe left and right loop as the popular Tinder interface [3]. We choose to adopt digital cards interface for Tinderbook because it can be applied to a variety of contexts and, combined with ubiquitous swipe gesture, can alleviate information overload and improve the user experience aspect of apps[7]. Moreover, Tinderbook can further leverage engagement data, i.e. each individual user-swipe interaction, to get insights on users' satisfaction in the usage of the application. The interactions of the user with the application are described in Fig. 3.

3.2 Architecture

The overall architecture is presented in Fig. 4. DBpedia is the main data source for the application. DBpedia is queried to get book title, author and abstract. Google images is queried to retrieve thumbnails for images, using the book title and author extracted from DBpedia to disambiguate the query. The model is a key-value data structure that stores item-item similarities as defined in Eq. 1 and it is used to get the five most similar books to the chosen book. MongoDB is used to store the discarded books, seed books, and the feedback on the recommended books ("thumbs up" or "thumbs down"), in order to evaluate the application in the online scenario (Sect. 4). Book metadata are collected once for all the books at the start of the server and kept in memory to allow faster recommendations.

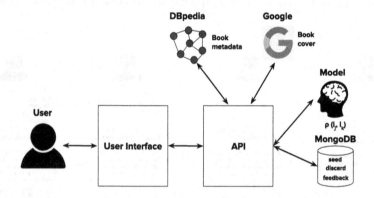

Fig. 4. The architecture of the Tinderbook application.

4   Online Evaluation

Tinderbook has been deployed on Nov 22nd, 2018. In this section, we report the results of usage data collected for two weeks, going from Nov, 22nd to Dec, 6th (Table 2). To evaluate the application, we have defined a set of Key Performance

---

[7] https://www.nngroup.com/articles/cards-component/.

Indicators (KPIs), which are specific to the online scenario, in addition to the metrics defined in Sect. 2.2. In the online experiment, we define the recommendation as a 'hit' if the user provides positive feedback ("thumb up" or swipe right), and as a 'miss' if the user provides negative feedback ("thumb down" or swipe left) in the recommendation phase. Recall cannot be measured in the online experiment, as we do not have a test set to measure $rel(u)$.

Definition 5. *We define* **completeness** *as the average percentage of rated books per session, given that the user has entered the recommendation phase.*

Definition 6. *We define* **discard** *as the average number of discarded books in the onboarding phase.*

Definition 7. *We define* **dropout** *as the percentage of users who leave the application during the onboarding phase.*

Definition 8. *We define* **seed popularity** *as the average popularity of the seed books.*

Definition 9. *We define* **recommendation time** τ *as the average time required to provide the list of recommended books in the recommendation phase.*

In the first week, we have experimented an onboarding phase with a temperature parameter set to $T = 0.3$. In the second week, we have increased this temperature to the value of $T = 1$. As described in Sect. 3, the temperature T governs the degree of randomness in the popularity-driven book sampling of the onboarding phase. The first effect observed as a consequence of the increase in temperature in the onboarding phase was the fact that less popular books were chosen during the onboarding phase. In Fig. 5, we represent the distribution of seed books falling in the top x% popular items for $T = 0.3$ and $T = 1$. The picture shows that $T = 1$ has made less popular books appear more frequently in the choices of the users in the onboarding phase with respect to the initial configuration $T = 0.3$. However, it is worth noticing that most seed books are still concentrated among the most popular books (80% in the top 20% popular books). The change of temperature has also had effects on the other KPIs. In order to compare the two different onboarding configurations $T = 0.3$ and $T = 1$, we have measured the KPIs mean values and standard deviations and run a statistical test to assess whether the observed differences were statistically significant or not. More specifically, we have run a Welch's t-student test [24] with a confidence value of $\alpha = 0.05$, only $p < \alpha$ are considered as statistically significant. As shown in Table 3, the onboarding configuration $T = 1.0$ decreases the average popularity of the seed books in a statistically significant way. This leads to the fact that users have to discard more items before finding a liked book in the onboarding phase, as it can be noticed by the increase of the average number of discarded books. However, the number of dropouts does not increase in a statistically significant way, meaning that we cannot say that this fact is pushing users to get bored during the onboarding and leave the application more easily. In fact, it shows that users are engaged enough to keep using the application even if they have to discard more books in the onboarding. Interestingly, the configuration with $T = 1.0$ is also increasing the novelty, meaning that less popular books also appear more often in the recommendations. Overall, we can claim that $T = 1.0$ is the best configuration for the application, as it leads to more novelty without significantly increasing the number of dropouts.

Table 2. Total usage stats for the online experiment for the whole experiment (22 Nov–6 Dec), for $T = 0.3$ configuration only (22nd Nov–29th Nov) and for the $T = 1$ configuration only (30th Nov–6th Dec).

	All	T = 0.3	T = 1
tot. # seeds	470	358	112
tot. # feedback	1,936	1495	441
tot. # discarded books	3,668	2263	1405

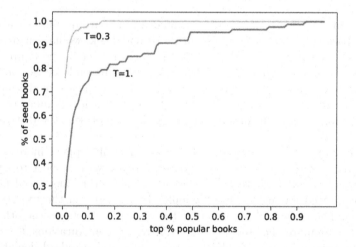

Fig. 5. Showing how different values of the temperature affect the popularity of the books chosen as "seeds" for the recommendations in the onboarding phase. In both cases, seeds are strongly concentrated among the most popular books. However, in the case of $T = 0.3$ the effect is stronger, with all of the seeds falling into the top 20% most popular books. In the case of $T = 1$, roughly 80% of the seed books fall into the top 20% most popular books.

The recommendation time is very short, roughly 12 ms, as it involves accessing values from a key-value data store, which can be done in unitary time. More specifically, we measure $\tau = 12.4 \pm 0.3$ ms across the whole experiment.

Table 3. Online evaluation results. KPIs for the $T = 0.3$ configuration only (22nd Nov–29th Nov) and for the $T = 1$ configuration only (30th Nov–6th Dec). Welch's t-student test is used to compare the KPIs with a confidence value $\alpha = 0.05$.

	$T = 0.3$	$T = 1$	p value	Significant
P@5	0.497368 ± 0.026381	0.495833 ± 0.052701	9.79E–01	no
SER@5	0.417105 ± 0.024892	0.437500 ± 0.047382	7.07E–01	no
NOV@5	8.315443 ± 0.176832	10.095039 ± 0.347261	2.30E–05	yes
completeness	0.903947 ± 0.018229	0.937500 ± 0.025108	2.86E–01	no
discard	6.321229 ± 0.663185	12.544643 ± 2.070238	2.09E–03	yes
dropout	0.131285 ± 0.019150	0.178571 ± 0.039930	2.45E–01	no
seed pop	0.002626 ± 0.000060	0.000835 ± 0.000086	2.74E–48	yes

5   Competing Systems

Existing book recommender systems are typically based either on content-based or collaborative filtering [2]. In Fig. 6, we report a comparison of TinderBook with existing book recommender systems. The first point that makes TinderBook stand out from competitors is the recommendation algorithm, a hybrid approach based on knowledge graph embeddings. In the past years, several works have shown the usefulness of knowledge graphs for recommender systems, and more specifically, of Linked Open Data knowledge graphs [10]. More in detail, knowledge graphs are often used to create hybrid recommender systems, including both user-item and item-item interactions. For instance, in [9], the authors use hybrid graph-based data model utilizing Linked Open Data to extract metapath-based features that are fed into a learning to rank framework. Recently, some works have used feature learning algorithms on knowledge graphs, i.e. knowledge graph embeddings for recommender systems, reducing the effort of feature engineering and resulting in high-quality recommendations [16–18,21,25]. In particular, entity2rec [15], on which TinderBook is based, has shown to create accurate recommendations using property-specific knowledge graph embeddings.

The second point that makes TinderBook stand out is the Graphical User Interface (GUI) and the quick onboarding process, with no necessity of log-in or account creation. Card-based GUI are a great way to deliver information at a glance. Cards help avoid walls of text, which can appear intimidating or time-consuming and allow users to deep dive into their interests quicker. Many apps can benefit from a card-based interface that shows users enough necessary information to make a quick maybe/no decision [5]. Cards serve as entry points to more detailed information. According to Carrie Cousins, cards can contain multiple elements within a design, but each should focus on only one bit of information or content [6]. A famous example of card-based GUI is that of the dating application Tinder, and according to Babich: "Tinder is a great example of how utilizing discovery mechanism to present the next option has driven the app to emerge as one of the most popular mobile apps. This card-swiping mechanism is curiously addictive, because every single swipe is gathering information - cards connect with users and offer the best possible options based on the made decisions" [3].

Finally, TinderBook leverages DBpedia [4] and this allows to leverage a wealth of multi-language data, such as book descriptions, without the cost of creating and maintaining a proprietary database.

	RECOMMENDATION MODE			USER PROFILING		USER EXPERIENCE		
	RECOMM. APPROACH	MIN # BOOKS FOR RECCOM.	FEEDBACK MODE	MANDATORY LOGIN	INFO REQUIRED	BOOK DESCRIPTION	WEB	MOBILE (OPTIMIZED)
goodreads	collaborative filtering	20	rating	✓	user data, favourite genres	✓	✓	✓
WHAT SHOULD I READ NEXT?	collaborative filtering	1	✗	✗	book liked	✗	✓	✓
LibraryThing What's on your bookshelf?	collaborative filtering	10	rating	✓	book ratings & liked	✗	✓	✗
whichbook	content-based filtering	0	✗	✗	book tags	✓	✓	✗
BookBub	human recommendation	0	like	✓	user data, favourite genres, favorite authors	✓	✓	✓
YOURNEXTREAD.COM	collaborative filtering	1	like & dislike	✗	book ratings & liked	✓	✓	✗
Readgeek	collaborative filtering	2	rating	✓	book ratings & liked	✓	✓	✓
TINDERBOOK	Hybrid filtering	1	like & dislike	✗	book liked	✓	✓	✓

Fig. 6. Comparison of existing book recommender systems.

6   Conclusions and Lessons Learned

In this paper, we have described TinderBook, a book recommender system that addresses the "new user" problem using knowledge graph embeddings. The knowledge graph is built using data from LibraryThing, containing book ratings from users, and DBpedia. We have explained the methodological underpinnings of the system, reporting an offline experiment showing that the entity2rec item relatedness based on knowledge graph embeddings is outperforming a purely collaborative filtering algorithm (ItemKNN) as well as a purely content-based system based on RDF2Vec. This is in line with the claim that hybrid recommender systems typically outperform purely collaborative and content-based systems. Then, we have provided a high-level description of the application, showing the typical usage session, the architecture and how user interactions are mapped to server API calls. We have reported the main findings of the online evaluation with users, showing that providing less popular books in the onboarding phase improves the application, increasing the novelty of the recommendations while achieving almost 50% of precision. We have also discussed how TinderBook stands out from competing systems, thanks to its recommendation algorithm based on knowledge graph embeddings, its easy onboarding process and its playful user interface.

Semantic technologies play a fundamental role in TinderBook. DBpedia has allowed to create the knowledge graph for the recommendation algorithm, connecting books through links to common entities and complementing the collaborative information coming from LibraryThing ratings with content-based information. Furthermore, DBpedia has enabled to obtain rich book descriptions (e.g. abstract), without the cost of creating, curating and maintaining a book database. The multilinguality of DBpedia will also be a great advantage when, in the future, we will extend TinderBook to multiple languages. On the other hand, using DBpedia data has some pitfalls. The first one is the data loss during the mapping, as only 11,694 out of a total of 37,231 books (31.409%) in the LibraryThing dataset are mapped to DBpedia entities[8]. The second one is that, in some cases, the information in DBpedia resulted to be inaccurate. For example, during some preliminary tests, we have noticed that in many cases the thumbnail reported in the 'dbo:thumbnail' property is far from ideal to represent accurately the book (see Jurassic Park novel[9]), and we had to rely on Google to find better book covers. The loss of coverage and the data quality issues are relevant ones, and they open the question of whether the use of other knowledge graphs might give better results. Finally, it has to be noted that in our specific case, the cost of building the knowledge graph has been strongly mitigated by the re-use of existing DBpedia mappings. The generalization of this approach to a new dataset would require also this effort.

In spite of these challenges, users generally give positive feedback about the application, saying that it is fun to use and that recommendations are accurate. So far, it has been used by passionate readers, librarians, students and researchers, and has been promoted through the personal network of its creators, word-of-mouth, as well as popular social media. Although we do not have a precise number, we estimate that, only during the online evaluation of two weeks, more than 100 users have used the application. Some of the complaints that we have received from users is that recommendations lacked diversity or novelty. Thus, we will keep gathering data from the application and as a future work, we will try to improve other dimensions of the recommendation quality such as the diversity and the novelty, as most of the work so far has been done in optimizing the accuracy of the recommendations in an offline setting.

---

[8] https://github.com/sisinflab/LODrecsys-datasets/tree/master/LibraryThing.
[9] http://dbpedia.org/page/Jurassic_Park_(novel).

References

1. Adomavicius, G., Tuzhilin, A.: Toward the next generation of recommender systems: a survey of the state-of-the-art and possible extensions. IEEE Trans. Knowl. Data Eng. **17**(6), 734–749 (2005)
2. Alharthi, H., Inkpen, D., Szpakowicz, S.: A survey of book recommender systems. J. Intell. Inf. Syst. **51**(1), 139–160 (2018)
3. Babich, N.: Designing card-based user interfaces (2016)
4. Bizer, C., Heath, T., Berners-Lee, T.: Linked data-the story so far. In: Semantic Services, Interoperability and Web Applications: Emerging Concepts, pp. 205–227 (2009)
5. Cai, T.: The tinder effect: swipe to kiss (keep it simple, stupid!) (2018)
6. Cousins, C.: The complete guide to an effective card-style interface design (2015)
7. David, G., Cambre, C.: Screened intimacies: tinder and the swipe logic. Soc. Media+ Soc. **2**(2) (2016)
8. Di Noia, T.: Recommender systems meet linked open data. In: Bozzon, A., Cudre-Maroux, P., Pautasso, C. (eds.) ICWE 2016. LNCS, vol. 9671, pp. 620–623. Springer, Cham (2016). https://doi.org/10.1007/978-3-319-38791-8_61
9. Di Noia, T., Ostuni, V.C., Tomeo, P., Di Sciascio, E.: SPRank: semantic path-based ranking for top-n recommendations using linked open data. ACM Trans. Intell. Syst. Technol. (TIST) **8**(1), 9 (2016)
10. Figueroa, C., Vagliano, I., Rocha, O.R., Morisio, M.: A systematic literature review of linked data-based recommender systems. Concurrency Comput. Pract. Experience **27**(17), 4659–4684 (2015)
11. Ge, M., Delgado-Battenfeld, C., Jannach, D.: Beyond accuracy: evaluating recommender systems by coverage and serendipity. In: 4th International Conference on Recommender Systems (RecSys), pp. 257–260 (2010)
12. de Gemmis, M., Lops, P., Semeraro, G., Musto, C.: An investigation on the serendipity problem in recommender systems. Inf. Process. Manage. **51**(5), 695–717 (2015)
13. Grover, A., Leskovec, J.: node2vec: scalable feature learning for networks. In: 22nd International Conference on Knowledge Discovery and Data Mining (SIGKDD), pp. 855–864 (2016)
14. Lops, P., de Gemmis, M., Semeraro, G.: Content-based recommender systems: state of the art and trends. In: Ricci, F., Rokach, L., Shapira, B., Kantor, P.B. (eds.) Recommender Systems Handbook, pp. 73–105. Springer, Boston (2011). https://doi.org/10.1007/978-0-387-85820-3_3
15. Palumbo, E., Rizzo, G., Troncy, R.: Entity2rec: learning user-item relatedness from knowledge graphs for top-n item recommendation. In: 11th International Conference on Recommender Systems (RecSys), pp. 32–36 (2017)
16. Palumbo, E., Rizzo, G., Troncy, R., Baralis, E., Osella, M., Ferro, E.: Knowledge graph embeddings with node2vec for item recommendation. In: European Semantic Web Conference (ESWC), Demo Track, pp. 117–120 (2018)
17. Palumbo, E., Rizzo, G., Troncy, R., Baralis, E., Osella, M., Ferro, E.: Translational models for item recommendation. In: Gangemi, A., et al. (eds.) ESWC 2018. LNCS, vol. 11155, pp. 478–490. Springer, Cham (2018). https://doi.org/10.1007/978-3-319-98192-5_61
18. Ristoski, P., Rosati, J., Di Noia, T., De Leone, R., Paulheim, H.: RDF2Vec: RDF graph embeddings and their applications. Semant. Web J. **10**(4) (2019)

19. Rosati, J., Ristoski, P., Di Noia, T., de Leone, R., Paulheim, H.: RDF graph embeddings for content-based recommender systems. In: CEUR Workshop Proceedings, vol. 1673, pp. 23–30 (2016)
20. Sarwar, B., Karypis, G., Konstan, J., Riedl, J.: Item-based collaborative filtering recommendation algorithms. In: 10th International World Wide Web Conference, pp. 285–295 (2001)
21. Shi, C., Hu, B., Zhao, X., Yu, P.: Heterogeneous information network embedding for recommendation. IEEE Trans. Knowl. Data Eng. 357–370 (2018)
22. Steck, H.: Evaluation of recommendations: rating-prediction and ranking. In: 7th ACM Conference on Recommender Systems, pp. 213–220 (2013)
23. Vargas, S., Castells, P.: Rank and relevance in novelty and diversity metrics for recommender systems. In: 5th ACM Conference on Recommender Systems, pp. 109–116 (2011)
24. Welch, B.L.: The generalization of student's problem when several different population variances are involved. Biometrika $34(1/2)$, 28–35 (1947)
25. Zhang, F., Yuan, N.J., Lian, D., Xie, X., Ma, W.Y.: Collaborative knowledge base embedding for recommender systems. In: 22nd International Conference on Knowledge Discovery and Data Mining (SIGKDD), pp. 353–362 (2016)

Using Shape Expressions (ShEx) to Share RDF Data Models and to Guide Curation with Rigorous Validation

Katherine Thornton[1(✉)], Harold Solbrig[2], Gregory S. Stupp[3],
Jose Emilio Labra Gayo[4], Daniel Mietchen[5], Eric Prud'hommeaux[6],
and Andra Waagmeester[7]

[1] Yale University, New Haven, CT, USA
katherine.thornton@yale.edu
[2] Johns Hopkins University, Baltimore, MD, USA
solbrig@jhu.edu
[3] The Scripps Research Institute, San Diego, CA, USA
gstupp@scripps.edu
[4] University of Oviedo, Oviedo, Spain
labra@uniovi.es
[5] Data Science Institute, University of Virginia, Charlottesville, VA, USA
daniel.mietchen@virginia.edu
[6] World Wide Web Consortium (W3C), MIT, Cambridge, MA, USA
eric@w3.org
[7] Micelio, Antwerpen, Belgium
andra@micel.io

Abstract. We discuss Shape Expressions (ShEx), a concise, formal, modeling and validation language for RDF structures. For instance, a Shape Expression could prescribe that subjects in a given RDF graph that fall into the shape "Paper" are expected to have a section called "Abstract", and any ShEx implementation can confirm whether that is indeed the case for all such subjects within a given graph or subgraph.

There are currently five actively maintained ShEx implementations. We discuss how we use the JavaScript, Scala and Python implementations in RDF data validation workflows in distinct, applied contexts. We present examples of how ShEx can be used to model and validate data from two different sources, the domain-specific Fast Healthcare Interoperability Resources (FHIR) and the domain-generic Wikidata knowledge base, which is the linked database built and maintained by the Wikimedia Foundation as a sister project to Wikipedia. Example projects that are using Wikidata as a data curation platform are presented as well, along with ways in which they are using ShEx for modeling and validation.

When reusing RDF graphs created by others, it is important to know how the data is represented. Current practices of using human-readable descriptions or ontologies to communicate data structures often lack sufficient precision for data consumers to quickly and easily understand data representation details. We provide concrete examples of how we

---

The original version of this chapter was revised: By mistake the chapter was originally published non open access. The correction to this chapter is available at https://doi.org/10.1007/978-3-030-21348-0_40

© The Author(s) 2019
P. Hitzler et al. (Eds.): ESWC 2019, LNCS 11503, pp. 606–620, 2019.
https://doi.org/10.1007/978-3-030-21348-0_39

use ShEx as a constraint and validation language that allows humans and machines to communicate unambiguously about data assets. We use ShEx to exchange and understand data models of different origins, and to express a shared model of a resource's footprint in a Linked Data source. We also use ShEx to agilely develop data models, test them against sample data, and revise or refine them. The expressivity of ShEx allows us to catch disagreement, inconsistencies, or errors efficiently, both at the time of input, and through batch inspections.

ShEx addresses the need of the Semantic Web community to ensure data quality for RDF graphs. It is currently being used in the development of FHIR/RDF. The language is sufficiently expressive to capture constraints in FHIR, and the intuitive syntax helps people to quickly grasp the range of conformant documents. The publication workflow for FHIR tests all of these examples against the ShEx schemas, catching non-conformant data before they reach the public. ShEx is also currently used in Wikidata projects such as Gene Wiki and WikiCite to develop quality-control pipelines to maintain data integrity and incorporate or harmonize differences in data across different parts of the pipelines.

Keywords: RDF wd:Q54872 · ShEx wd:Q29377880 · FHIR wd:Q19597236 · Wikidata wd:Q2013 · Digital preservation wd:Q632897

1   Introduction

The RDF data model is a core technology of the Semantic Web. RDF is used to integrate data from heterogeneous sources, is extensible, flexible and can be manipulated with the SPARQL query language [9].

The need to describe the topologies, or shapes, of RDF graphs triggered the creation of an early version of Shape Expressions (ShEx 1) and the formation of a World Wide Web Consortium (W3C) Working Group—the Data Shapes Working Group—in 2014 [15]. Its task was to recommend a technology for describing and expressing structural constraints on RDF graphs. This has led to SHACL [8]–another shape-based data validation language for RDF–and further development of ShEx.

We provide an overview of ShEx, discuss implementations of the language, and then consider use cases for the validation of RDF data. The use cases we present consist of two types. For the first type, which is domain-specific, we provide an overview of how ShEx is being used for validation in medical informatics. For the second type, which is domain-generic, we provide examples that involve validation of entity data from the Wikidata knowledge base. We analyze workflows and highlight the affordances of multiple implementations of ShEx.

2   Shape Expressions

The Shape Expressions (ShEx) schema language can be consumed and produced by humans and machines [9] and is useful in multiple contexts. ShEx can be used

in model development, both for creating new models as well as for revising existing ones. ShEx is helpful for legacy review, where punch lists can be created for
existing data issues that need to be fixed. ShEx is useful as documentation of
models because it has a terse, human-readable representation that helps contributors and maintainers quickly grasp the model and its semantics. ShEx can be
used for client pre-submission, when submitters test their data before submission to make sure they are saying what they want to say and that the receiving
schema can accommodate all of their data. ShEx can also be used for server
pre-ingestion, through a submission process that checks data as it comes in, and
either rejects or warns of non-conformant data.

ShEx's semantics have undergone considerable peer review. [2] compares it
with SHACL and discusses stratified negation and validation algorithms. [23]
analyzes the complexity and expressive power of ShEx. With extensions like
ShExMap [16], ShEx can generate an in-memory structure of the validated RDF,
from which it is possible to operate, much like XSLT does for XML. Some experimental ShEx 1 extensions translated from RDF to XML[1] and JSON[2] [15]. To
date, there are three serializations and five implementations that are actively
maintained. We will discuss three of the implementations in this paper.

2.1   ShEx Implementations

shex.js for Javascript/N3.js. The shex.js[3] JavaScript implementation of
ShEx was used to develop the ShEx language and test suite[4] and is generally
used as a proving ground for language extensions. It was used to develop Gene
Wiki[5], WikiCite[6] and FHIR/RDF schemas [21]. The online validator[7] was used
to develop and experiment with all of these schemas. In addition, the FHIR/RDF
document production pipeline used its REST interface, and the Gene Wiki and
WikiCite projects used its command line interface to invoke it in node.js. The
development of the Gene Wiki schemas uses several branches of shex.js that are
aggregated into a single "wikidata" branch[8].

Shaclex. Shaclex[9] is a Scala implementation of ShEx and SHACL. The library
uses a purely functional approach where the validation is defined using monads
and monad transformers [11]. The validator is defined in terms of a simple RDF
interface (SRDF) that has several implementations. Two implementations are

---

[1] http://w3.org/brief/NTAx.
[2] http://w3.org/brief/NTAy.
[3] http://github.com/shexSpec/shex.js.
[4] https://github.com/shexSpec/shexTest.
[5] https://github.com/SuLab/Genewiki-ShEx.
[6] https://github.com/shexSpec/schemas/tree/master/Wikidata/wikicite.
[7] https://rawgit.com/shexSpec/shex.js/master/doc/shex-simple.html.
[8] https://rawgit.com/shexSpec/shex.js/wikidata/doc/shex-simple.html.
[9] http://labra.weso.es/shaclex/.

based on RDF models that can be created using Apache Jena[10] or RDF4J[11]. Another implementation of the simple RDF is based on SPARQL endpoints, so the validator can be used to validate the RDF data that can be accessed through those endpoints. By leveraging Apache Jena or RDF4J libraries, the Shaclex library can take as input RDF defined in all the serialization syntaxes that they support, e.g. Turtle, RDF/XML, JSON-LD, or RDF/JSON. Shaclex also has an online demonstrator, available at http://shaclex.validatingrdf.com/.

PyShEx. PyShEx[12] is a Python 3 implementation of the ShEx[13] specification. It uses the underlying model behind the ShEx JSON format (ShExJ)[14] as the abstract syntax tree (AST), meaning that ShEx schemas in the JSON format can be directly loaded and processed. PyShEx uses the PyShExC parser[15] to transform ShEx compact format (ShExC) schemas into the same target AST. PyShEx is based on the native Python RDF library – the rdflib[16] package – meaning that it can support a wide variety of RDF formats. PyShEx can also use the sparql_slurper[17] package to fetch sets of triples on demand from a SPARQL endpoint. An example of PyShEx can be found at https://tinyurl.com/ycuhblog.

2.2   Interoperability

The three implementations above offer a consistent command line and web invocation API. These same parameters can be embedded in "manifest" files, which store a list of objects that encapsulate an invocation. The shex.js and shaclex implementations offer a user interface allowing a user to select and execute elements in the manifest. In addition to agreement on the semantics of validation, this interface interoperability makes it trivial to swap between implementations, e.g. depending on immediate platform and user interface preferences.

3   Use Cases

We present use cases that encompass two distinct models for validation. In the first use case, validation is performed on clinical data in an institutional context. In the second group of use cases, validation is performed via the Wikidata Query Service, a public SPARQL endpoint maintained as part of the Wikidata infrastructure.

---

[10] https://jena.apache.org/.
[11] http://rdf4j.org/.
[12] https://github.com/hsolbrig/PyShEx.
[13] http://shex.io/shex-semantics/.
[14] https://github.com/hsolbrig/ShExJSG.
[15] https://github.com/shexSpec/grammar/tree/master/parsers/python.
[16] http://rdflib.readthedocs.io/en/stable/.
[17] https://github.com/hsolbrig/sparql_slurper.

3.1   Domain-Specific ShEx Validation in Medical Informatics

The Yosemite Project [29] started in 2013 as response to a 2010 report by the President's Council of Advisors on Science and Technology [14] calling for a universal exchange language for healthcare. As part of its initial efforts, this project released the "Yosemite Manifesto"[18], a position statement signed by over 100 thought leaders in healthcare informatics which recommended RDF as the "best available candidate for a universal healthcare exchange language" and stating that "electronic healthcare information should be exchanged in a format that either: (a) is in RDF format directly; or (b) has a standard mapping to RDF".

Around the same time as the Yosemite Project meeting, a new collection of standards for the exchange of clinical data was beginning to gather momentum. "Fast Healthcare Interoperability Resources (FHIR)" [4] defined a modeling environment, framework, community and architecture for the REST oriented access to clinical resources. The FHIR specification defines some 130+ healthcare and modeling related "resources" and describes how they are represented in XML[19] and JSON[20]. One of the outcomes of the Yosemite project was the formation of the FHIR RDF/Health Care Life Sciences (FHIR/HCLS) working group[21] tasked with defining an RDF representation format for FHIR resources.

ShEx played a critical role in the development of the FHIR RDF specification. Prior to its introduction to ShEx, the community tried to use a set of representative examples as the basis for discussion. This was a slow process, as the actual rules for the underlying transformation were implicit. There was no easy way to verify that the examples covered all possible use cases and that they were internally self-consistent. Newcomers to the project faced a steep learning curve. The introduction of ShEx helped to streamline and formalize the process [21]. Instead of talking in terms of examples, the group could address how instances of *entire* FHIR resource models would be represented as RDF. Edge cases that seldom appeared received the same scrutiny as did everyday usage examples. The proposed transformation rules could be implemented in software, with the entire FHIR specification being automatically transformed to its ShEx equivalent.

ShEx allowed the participants to finalize discussions and settle on a formal model and first specification draft in less than three months. A formal transformation was created to map the (then) 109 FHIR resource definitions into schemas for the RDF binding. This transformation uncovered several issues with the specification itself as well as providing a template for the bidirectional transformation between RDF and the abstract FHIR model instances. The documentation production pipeline was additionally extended to transform the 511 JSON and XML examples into RDF, which were then tested against the generated ShEx schemas. [21] These tests both caught multiple errors in the transformation software and

---

[18] http://yosemitemanifesto.org/.

[19] http://hl7.org/fhir/xml.html.

[20] http://hl7.org/fhir/json.html.

[21] https://www.w3.org/community/hclscg/.

uncovered a number of additional issues in the specification itself, ensuring that the user-facing documentation was accurate and comprehensive. In early 2017, the FHIR documentation production framework, written in Java, switched from using the shex.js implementation to natively calling the Shaclex implementation. As a testament to the quality of the standard, both implementations agreed on the validity of all 511 examples. The first official version of the FHIR RDF specification was released in the FHIR Standard for Trial Use (STU3) release [5] in April of 2017.

3.2 Domain-Generic ShEx Validation in Wikidata

What Wikipedia is to text, Wikidata is to data: an open collaboratively curated resource that anyone can contribute to. In contrast to the language-specific Wikipedias, Wikidata is Semantic Web-compatible, and most of the edits are made using automated or semi-automated tools. This 'data commons' provides structured public data for Wikipedia articles [19] and other applications. For each Wikipedia article–in any language–there is an item in Wikidata, and if the same concept is described in more than one Wikipedia, then Wikidata maintains the links between them.

In contrast to language-specific Wikipedias, and to most other sites on the web, Wikidata does not assume that users who collaborate have a common natural language [7]. In fact, consecutive editors of a given Wikidata entry often do not share a language other than some basic knowledge about the Wikidata data model. Using ShEx to make those data models more explicit can improve such cross-linguistic collaboration.

Wikidata is hosted on Wikibase, a non-relational database maintained by the Wikimedia Foundation. The underlying infrastructure also contains a SPARQL engine https://query.wikidata.org that feeds on a triplestore which is continuously synchronized with Wikibase. This synchronization–which occurs in seconds–enables data in Wikidata to be available as Linked Data almost immediately and thus becoming part of the Semantic Web. Basically, Wikidata acts as an "edit button" to the Semantic Web and as an entry point for users who otherwise do not have the technical background to use Semantic Web infrastructure. While Wikidata and its RDF dump are technically separate, they can be perceived as one from a user perspective. Content negotiation presents either the Wikibase form or the RDF form, creating a sense of unity between the two. For instance, https://wikidata.org/entity/Q54872 (which identifies RDF) points to the Wikibase entry at https://www.wikidata.org/wiki/Q54872, while http://www.wikidata.org/entity/Q54872.ttl will provides the Turtle representation and http://www.wikidata.org/entity/Q54872.json a JSON export.

The Wikidata data model [28] currently consists of two entity types: **items** and **properties** (a third one, for lexemes, is about to be introduced). All entities have persistent identifiers composed of single-letter prefixes (Q for items, P for properties, L for lexemes) plus a string of numbers and are allotted a page in Wikidata. For instance, the entity Q1676669 is the item for *JPEG File Interchange Format, version 1.02*. Properties like *instance of* (P31) and *part* *of* (P361) are used to assert *claims* about an item. A claim, its references and qualifiers form a *statement*. Currently, Wikidata's RDF graph comprises about 5 billion triples (with millions added per day), which reflects about 500 million statements involving about 50 million items and roughly 5000 properties.

Besides serving Wikipedia and its sister projects, Wikidata also acts as a data backend for a complex ecosystem of tools and services. Some of these are general-purpose semantic tools like search engines or personal assistants [1], while others are tailored for specific scientific communities, e.g. Wikigenomes [18] for curating microbial genomes, WikiDP for digital preservation of software [26], or Scholia [13] for exploring scholarly publications. Through such tools, communities that are not active on Wikidata can engage with the Wikidata RDF graph. ShEx can facilitate that.

Non-ShEx Validation Workflows for Wikidata. Wikidata uses constraints for validation in multiple ways. For instance, some edits are rejected by the user interface or the API, e.g. certain formats or values for dates cannot be saved. Some of the quality control also involves patrolling individual edits [20].

Most of the quality control, however, takes place on the data itself. Initially, the primary mechanism for this was a system of Mediawiki templates[22], similar to the infobox templates on Wikipedia. These templates express a range of constraints like "items about movies should link to the items about the actors starring in it" or "this property should only be used on items that represent human settlements" or a regular expression specifying the format of allowed values for a given property. For more complex constraints, some SPARQL functionality is available through such templates. In addition, an automated tool goes through the data dumps on a daily basis, identifies cases where such template-based constraints have been validated, and posts notifications on dedicated wiki pages where Wikidata editors can review and act on them[23]. This template-based validation infrastructure, while still largely functional, has been superseded by a parallel one that has been built later by having dedicated properties[24] for expressing constraints on individual properties or their values or on relationships involving several properties or specific classes of items. For instance, P1793 is for "format as a regular expression", P2302 more generally for "property constraint", and P2303 for "exception to constraint" (used as a qualifier to P2302). This way, the constraints themselves become part of the Wikidata RDF graph. This arrangement is further supported by dedicated Mediawiki extensions[25], one of which also contains a gadget that logged-in users can enable in their preferences in order to be notified through the user interface if a constraint violation has been detected on the item or statement they are viewing. Reading through the reports generated by constraint violation systems supports inspection on a per-property basis. This system of validation requires community members to

---

[22] https://www.wikidata.org/wiki/Category:Constraint_templates.

[23] https://www.wikidata.org/wiki/Wikidata:Database_reports/Constraint_violations.

[24] https://www.wikidata.org/wiki/Help:Property_constraints_portal.

[25] https://www.mediawiki.org/wiki/Wikibase_Quality_Extensions.

create and apply constraint properties on each of the Wikidata properties, of which there are more than five thousand. Constraints have not yet been added to all properties.

ShEx is a context-sensitive grammar with algebraic operations while Property Validation is a context-free. Unlike in ShEx Validation, where properties have context-sensitive constraints, Property Validation constraints must be permissive enough to permit all current or expected uses of the property. For example, a ShEx constraint that every human gene use the common property P31 "instance of" to declare itself an instance of a human gene MUST NOT be expressed as a property constraint as P31 is used for 56,000 other classes. Of course Property Validation is additionally problematic because the author of a constraint may not be aware of its use in other classes. ShEx allows us to write schemas that describe multiple properties, their constraints, their permissible values in combinations for which there are not yet property constraints created in Wikidata's infrastructure. This allows us to test conformance to schemas that describe features that may not yet be relevant for the Wikidata community, but may be necessary for an external application.

Generic ShEx Validation Workflow for Wikidata. One issue with the existing template-based constraint and validation mechanisms for Wikidata is that they are usually very specific to the Wikidata platform or to the tools used for interacting with it. ShEx provides a way to link Wikidata-based validation with validation mechanisms developed or used elsewhere. Getting there from the RDF representation of the Wikidata constraints is a relatively small step.

Efforts around the usage of ShEx on Wikidata are coordinated by WikiProject ShEx[26]. The ShEx-based validation workflow for Wikidata consists of:

1. writing a schema for the data type in question, or choosing an existing one;
2. transferring that schema into the Wikidata model of items, statements, qualifiers and references;
3. writing a ShEx manifest for the Wikidata-based schema;
4. testing entity data from Wikidata for conformance to the ShEx manifest.

Initially, Wikidata may be missing some properties for adequately representing such a schema. Such missing properties can be proposed and, after a process involving community input, created. Once they appear in the Wikidata RDF graph, ShEx can be used to validate the corresponding RDF shapes.

At present, the ShEx manifests for Wikidata are hosted on GitHub, but they could be included into the Wikidata infrastructure, e.g. through a dedicated property similar to *format as a regular expression* (P1793).

---

[26] https://www.wikidata.org/wiki/Wikidata:WikiProject_ShEx.

4   ShEx Validation of Domain-Specific Wikidata Subgraphs

4.1   Molecular Biology

In 2008, the Gene Wiki project started to create and maintain infoboxes in English-language Wikipedia articles about human genes [6]. After the launch of Wikidata in 2012, the project shifted from curating infoboxes on Wikipedia pages towards curating the corresponding items on Wikidata [12]. Since then, Gene Wiki bots have been enriching and synchronizing Wikidata with knowledge from public sources about biomedical entities such as genes, proteins, and diseases, and are now regularly feeding Wikidata with life science data [3]. To date, there are items about ~24k human and 20k mouse genes from NCBI Gene[27], 8,700 disease concepts from the Disease Ontology[28], and 2,700 FDA-approved drugs.

The Gene Wiki bots are built using a Python framework called the Wikidata Integrator (WDI)[29]. This platform is using the Wikidata API and does concept resolution based on external identifiers. The WDI is openly available.

Validation Workflows for Gene Wiki. In the Gene Wiki project, the focus is on synchronizing data between Wikidata and external databases. After the data models used by these external sources have been translated into Wikidata terms and the missing properties created, one or more exemplary entities from the sources in question are chosen and manually completed on Wikidata. Upon reaching consensus on the validity of these items and their data model, a bot is developed to reproduce these handmade Wikidata entries. Once the bot is able to replicate the items as they are, more items are added to Wikidata. This is done gradually to allow community input; first 10 items, then 100, then 1000 and finally all. During the development of a bot, it is run manually (at the developer's discretion). Upon completion of development, the bots are run from an automation platform where the sources are synchronized regularly[30].

ShEx has its value in both the development phase and the automation phase. During development, ShEx is used as a communication tool to express the data model being discussed. For instance, https://github.com/SuLab/Genewiki-ShEx/blob/master/genes/wikidata-human-genes.shex contains the data model of a human gene as depicted in Wikidata (note the many uses of the comment sign "#"). Currently, data-model design is done in parallel by writing ShEx and drawing graphical depictions of these models. We are currently working towards creating ShEx from a drawn diagram.

After completion of the bot, ShEx can be used to monitor for changes in the data of interest. This is either novel data, disagreement or vandalism. Regularly, all Wikidata items on a specific source/semantic type are collected and tested for inconsistencies.

---

[27] https://www.ncbi.nlm.nih.gov/gene/.
[28] http://disease-ontology.org/.
[29] https://github.com/SuLab/WikidataIntegrator.
[30] http://jenkins.sulab.org.

4.2   Software and File Formats

Metadata about software, file formats and computing environments is necessary for the identification and management of these entities. Creating machine-readable metadata about resources in the domain of computing allows digital preservation practitioners to automate programmatic interactions with these entities. People working in digital preservation have a shared need for accurate, reusable, technical and descriptive metadata about the domain of computing.

Wikidata's WikiProject Informatics[31] collaboratively models the domain of computing [25]. Until now, members of the Wikidata community have created items for more than 85,000 software titles[32] and more than 3,500 file formats[33].

Schemas for software items[34] and file format items[35] in Wikidata have been created and entity data was tested using the ShEx2 Simple Online Validator (see Footnote 7). In order to use ShEx, we created manifests for software items[36] and file format items[37]. These manifests contain a SPARQL query for the Wikidata Query Service Endpoint that gathers all of the Wikidata items one wishes to test for conformance. The online validator accepts the manifest and then tests the entity data pertaining to each item against the schema for conformance. It provides information about conformance status and error messages.

The ability to validate subgraphs of Wikidata pertaining to the domain of computing allows us to quickly get a sense of how other editors are modeling their data by identifying Wikidata items for which the entity data graph is not in conformance with our schema. This allows us to communicate detailed information about data quality metrics to other members of the digital preservation community. Outputs of validation from ShEx tools provide evidence we can incorporate into our data quality metrics. This allows us to communicate with precision and accuracy, which then allows us to build trust with members of the community who are unfamiliar with the work processes of the knowledge base that anyone can edit.

4.3   Bibliographic Metadata

WikiCite is an effort to collect bibliographic information in Wikidata [24]. Launched in 2016, it is concerned with developing Wikidata-based schemas for publications – such as monographs, scholarly articles, or conference proceedings – and with the application of such schemas to Wikidata items representing publications and related concepts (e.g. authors, journals, publishers, topics). While

---

[31] https://www.wikidata.org/wiki/Wikidata:WikiProject_Informatics.
[32] https://github.com/emulatingkat/SPARQL/blob/master/software/software
Count.rq.
[33] https://github.com/emulatingkat/SPARQL/blob/master/fileFormat/ffCount.rq.
[34] https://tinyurl.com/y46lotsy.
[35] https://tinyurl.com/y3spaw87.
[36] https://tinyurl.com/yxmugpvl.
[37] https://tinyurl.com/y6h5at4a.

these schemas are mature enough to be encoded in a range of tools used for interacting with the WikiCite subgraph of Wikidata, they are still in flux, and using ShEx—especially with an interoperable set of implementations and graphic and multilingual layers on top if it—could help coordinate community engagement around further development. At present, the WikiCite community is curating around 15 million Wikidata items about ca. 700 types of publications[38], which are linked to each other through a dedicated property *cites* (P2860) as well as with other items, e.g. about authors, journals, publishers or the topics of the publications, and with external resources. Several hundred properties are in use in these contexts, the majority of which are for external identifiers.

The usage of ShEx in WikiCite is currently experimental, with tests being performed via the ShEx2 Simple Online Validator. Drafts of ShEx manifests exist for a small number of publication types like conference proceedings or journal articles as well as for specific use cases like defining a particular subset of the literature, e.g. on a specific topic. One such literature corpus is that about the Zika virus[39]. In this context, a ShEx manifest has been drafted[40] that goes beyond the publications themselves and includes constraints about the way the authors and topics of those publications are represented. It is currently being tested, compared against the existing non-ShEx validation mechanisms and developed further. Other use cases include curating the literature by author (e.g. in the context of working on someone's biography), by funder (e.g. for evaluating research outputs), or by journal or publisher (e.g. in the context of digital preservation).

5   Discussion

5.1   Novelty of Validation of RDF Data Using ShEx

RDF has been "on the radar" for the healthcare domain for a number of years, but always as a speculation: "If we could figure out how to build it, maybe they would come". ShEx proved to be the key that enabled actual action, and it moved RDF from a topic of discussion to an active implementation. ShEx provided a formal, yet (relatively) easy to understand view of what the RDF associated with a particular model element would look like. It provided a mechanism for testing data for conformance, as well as a framework for *assembling* the elements of an RDF triple store into pre-defined structures. ShEx has the potential to define a unifying semantic for multiple modeling paradigms – in the case of FHIR, ShEx is able to represent the intent of the FHIR structure definitions model, constraint language and extension model in a single, easy to understand idiom. While it is yet to be fully explored, ShEx has exciting potential as a data mapping language, with early explorations showing real promise as an RDF transformation language [16]. The validation workflows introduced above for the

38 http://wikicite.org/statistics.html.
39 https://www.wikidata.org/wiki/Wikidata:WikiProject_Zika_Corpus.
40 https://tinyurl.com/yyf42sal.

Wikidata cases are the first application of shapes to validate entity data from Wikidata. The impact of software frameworks that support validation of entity data is an important improvement in the feasibility of ensuring data quality for the Wikidata ecosystem and facilitating cross-linguistic collaboration. Wikidata data models are defined by the community and the knowledge base is designed to support multiple epistemological stances [27]. Wikidata contributors may model data differently from one another. ShEx makes it possible to validate entity data across the entire knowledge base, a powerful tool for data quality.

5.2   Uptake of ShEx Tooling

ShEx schemas are highly re-usable in that they can be shared and exchanged. The fact that ShEx schemas are human readable means that others can understand them and evaluate their suitability for reuse. ShEx schemas can also be extended. The ShEx Community Group of the W3C[41] maintains a repository of ShEx schemas[42] published under the MIT license that others are free to reuse, modify, or extend to fit novel use cases. We recommend that ShEx manifests be licensed as liberally as possible, so as to facilitate and encourage their usage. The Gene Wiki team led the way with workflows for the validation of entity data in Wikidata. An example of the uptake of ShEx tooling is that the Wikidata for Digital Preservation community modeled their validation workflow on that of the Gene Wiki team. We demonstrate the portability of these workflows for additional domains covered by the Wikidata knowledge base. Once a domain-based group has created ShEx schemas for the data models relevant for their area, others can follow this model to develop a validation workflow of their own.

5.3   Soundness and Quality

The ShEx test suite (see Footnote 4) consists of 1088 validation tests, 99 negative syntax tests, and 14 negative structure tests and 408 schema conversion tests between ShExC, ShExJ and ShExR. Work described in [2] provides efficient validation algorithms and verifies the soundness of recursion. [23] identifies the complexity and expressive power of ShEx. The comprehensive ShEx test suite (see Footnote 4) ensures compliance with these semantics. These projects used ShEx because it (1) has many implementations to choose from (2) has a well-engineered and tested, stable, human-readable syntax (3) is sound with respect to recursion. On the other hand, using ShEx poses new challenges about best practices to integrate the validation step into the data production pipeline, the performance of the validation for large RDF graphs and the interplay of ShEx with other Semantic Web tools like SPARQL, RDFS, or OWL.

---

[41] https://www.w3.org/community/shex/.

[42] https://github.com/shexSpec/schemas.

5.4 Availability

The ShEx Specification is available under the W3C Community Contributor License Agreement[43]. In addition to the specification itself, the ShEx community also created a Primer[44] that provides additional explanation and illustrative examples of how to write schemas. All of the software tools we describe are available under an open source license which is either the MIT or the Apache license. The developers of these software frameworks have made them available for anyone to reuse [10,17,22]. Contributing to open specifications and releasing software tools under free and open licenses lowers barriers to entry for others who might like to explore, test or adopt ShEx. The use cases we present are evidence of how ShEx validation is applicable to different domains. Extending it to additional domains is the goal of a dedicated initiative in the Wikidata community, the aforementioned WikiProject ShEx.

6 Conclusion

The ability to test the conformance of RDF graph data shapes advances our ability to realize the vision of the Semantic Web. Validating RDF data through the use of ShEx allows for the integration of data from heterogeneous sources and provides a mechanism for testing data quality that has been adopted by communities in different domains. Using ShEx in data modeling phases allows communities to resolve ambiguity of interpretation that can arise when using diagrams or natural language. Through a data modeling process using ShEx, these differences are resolved earlier in a workflow, and reduce time spent fixing errors that could otherwise arise due to different understandings of model meaning. Using ShEx to validate RDF data allows communities to discover all places where data is not yet in conformance to their schema. From the validation phase, a community will generate a punch list of data needing attention. Not only does this allow us to improve data quality, it defines a practical workflow for addressing non-conformant data. Consumers of RDF data will benefit from the work of data publishers who create ShEx schemas to communicate the structure of the data. The use cases presented here demonstrate the viability of using ShEx in production workflows in several different domains. ShEx addresses the challenges of communicating about the structure of RDF data, and will facilitate wider adoption of RDF data in a broad range of data publishing contexts.

Acknowledgements. We would like to thank the members of the W3C Shape Expressions Community Group for insightful conversations and productive collaboration. We would also like to thank the members of the Wikidata community. This work was supported by the National Institutes of Health under grant GM089820. Portions of this work were also supported in part by NIH grant U01 HG009450.

---

[43] https://www.w3.org/community/about/agreements/cla/.
[44] http://shex.io/shex-primer/.

References

1. Bielefeldt, A., Gonsior, J., Krötzsch, M.: Practical linked data access via SPARQL: the case of Wikidata. In: Proceedings of the WWW 2018 Workshop on Linked Data on the Web (LDOW 2018). CEUR Workshop Proceedings. CEUR-WS.org (2018)
2. Boneva, I., Labra Gayo, J.E., Prud'hommeaux, E.: Semantics and validation of shapes schemas for RDF (2017)
3. Burgstaller-Muehlbacher, S., et al.: Wikidata as a semantic framework for the Gene Wiki initiative. Database (Oxford) 2016 (2016)
4. HL7: Welcome to FHIR. https://hl7.org/fhir/
5. HL7: WFHIR release 3 (STU). https://hl7.org/fhir/STU3/index.html
6. Huss, J.W., et al.: A gene wiki for community annotation of gene function. PLoS Biol. **6**(7), e175 (2008)
7. Kaffee, L.A., Piscopo, A., Vougiouklis, P., Simperl, E., Carr, L., Pintscher, L.: A glimpse into Babel: an analysis of multilinguality in Wikidata. In: Proceedings of the 13th International Symposium on Open Collaboration, OpenSym 2017, pp. 14:1–14:5. ACM, New York (2017). https://doi.org/10.1145/3125433.3125465
8. Knublauch, H., Kontokostas, D.: Shapes Constraint Language (SHACL). W3C Recommendation, June 2017. https://www.w3.org/TR/shacl/
9. Labra Gayo, J.E., Prud'Hommeaux, E., Boneva, I., Kontokostas, D.: Validating RDF Data. Morgan & Claypool Publishers, San Rafael (2017)
10. Labra Gayo, J.E.: SHACLex: Scala implementation of ShEx and SHACL, April 2018. https://doi.org/10.5281/zenodo.1214239
11. Liang, S., Hudak, P., Jones, M.: Monad transformers and modular interpreters. In: Proceedings of the 22nd ACM SIGPLAN-SIGACT Symposium on Principles of Programming Languages, POPL 1995, pp. 333–343. ACM, New York (1995). http://doi.acm.org/10.1145/199448.199528
12. Mitraka, E., Waagmeester, A., Burgstaller-Muehlbacher, S., Schriml, L.M., Su, A.I., Good, B.M.: Wikidata: a platform for data integration and dissemination for the life sciences and beyond. bioRxiv (2015). https://doi.org/10.1101/031971
13. Nielsen, F.Å., Mietchen, D., Willighagen, E.: Scholia, Scientometrics and Wikidata. In: Blomqvist, E., Hose, K., Paulheim, H., Ławrynowicz, A., Ciravegna, F., Hartig, O. (eds.) ESWC 2017. LNCS, vol. 10577, pp. 237–259. Springer, Cham (2017). https://doi.org/10.1007/978-3-319-70407-4_36
14. President's Council of Advisors on Science and Technology (PCAST): Report to the President Realizing the Full Potential of Health Information Technology to Improve Healthcare for Americans: The Path Forward (2010). https://obamawhitehouse.archives.gov/sites/default/files/microsites/ostp/pcast-health-it-report.pdf
15. Prud'hommeaux, E., Labra Gayo, J.E., Solbrig, H.: Shape expressions: an RDF validation and transformation language. In: Proceedings of the 10th International Conference on Semantic Systems, pp. 32–40. ACM (2014)
16. Prud'hommeaux, E., Mayo, G.: ShExMap (2015). http://shex.io/extensions/Map/
17. Prud'hommeaux, E., et al.: shexSpec/shex.js: release for zenodo DOI (Version v0.9.2), April 2018. https://doi.org/10.5281/zenodo.1213693
18. Putman, T.E., et al.: Wikigenomes: an open web application for community consumption and curation of gene annotation data in Wikidata. Database 2017, bax025 (2017). https://doi.org/10.1093/database/bax025
19. Sáez, T., Hogan, A.: Automatically generating Wikipedia info-boxes from Wikidata. In: WWW 2018 Companion: The 2018 Web Conference Companion, Lyon, France, 23–27 April 2018. ACM (2018)

20. Sarabadani, A., Halfaker, A., Taraborelli, D.: Building automated vandalism detection tools for Wikidata. CoRR abs/1703.03861 (2017). http://arxiv.org/abs/1703.03861

21. Solbrig, H.R., et al.: Modeling and validating HL7 FHIR profiles using semantic web Shape Expressions (ShEx). J. Biomed. Inform. **67**, 90–100 (2017)

22. Solbrig, H.: PyShEx - Python implementation of Shape Expressions (Version v0.4.2), April 2018. https://doi.org/10.5281/zenodo.1214189

23. Staworko, S., Boneva, I., Labra Gayo, J.E., Hym, S., Prud'hommeaux, E.G., Solbrig, H.R.: Complexity and expressiveness of ShEx for RDF. In: 18th International Conference on Database Theory, ICDT 2015. LIPIcs, vol. 31, pp. 195–211. Schloss Dagstuhl - Leibniz-Zentrum fuer Informatik (2015)

24. Taraborelli, D., Dugan, J.M., Pintscher, L., Mietchen, D., Neylon, C.: WikiCite 2016 Report, November 2016. https://upload.wikimedia.org/wikipedia/commons/2/2b/WikiCite_2016_report.pdf

25. Thornton, K., Cochrane, E., Ledoux, T., Caron, B., Wilson, C.: Modeling the domain of digital preservation in Wikidata. In: iPRES 2017: 14th International Conference on Digital Preservation (2017)

26. Thornton, K., Seals-Nutt, K., Cochrane, E., Wilson, C.: Wikidata for digital preservation (2018). https://doi.org/10.5281/zenodo.1214319

27. Vrandečić, D.: Wikidata: a new platform for collaborative data collection. In: Proceedings of the 21st International Conference Companion on World Wide Web, pp. 1063–1064. ACM (2012)

28. Wikidata: Datamodel (2015). https://www.mediawiki.org/wiki/Wikibase/DataModel

29. Yosemite: About the Yosemite Project (2013). http://yosemiteproject.org

Correction to: Using Shape Expressions (ShEx) to Share RDF Data Models and to Guide Curation with Rigorous Validation

Katherine Thornton, Harold Solbrig, Gregory S. Stupp,
Jose Emilio Labra Gayo, Daniel Mietchen, Eric Prud'hommeaux,
and Andra Waagmeester

Correction to:
**Chapter "Using Shape Expressions (ShEx) to Share RDF Data
Models and to Guide Curation with Rigorous Validation" in:
P. Hitzler et al. (Eds.): *The Semantic Web*, LNCS 11503,
https://doi.org/10.1007/978-3-030-21348-0_39**

By mistake this chapter was originally published non open access. This has been corrected.

The updated version of this chapter can be found at
https://doi.org/10.1007/978-3-030-21348-0_39

Author Index

Acosta, Maribel 523
Aebeloe, Christian 3
Auer, Sören 427
Ayala, Daniel 397

Bandara, Madhushi 412
Baralis, Elena 590
Behnaz, Ali 412
Berberich, Klaus 162
Bilenchi, Ivano 298
Borrego, Agustín 397
Box, Paul J. 543
Buron, Maxime 19
Buzio, Alberto 590

Car, Nicholas J. 543
Cataldi, Mario 101
Chaudhuri, Debanjan 225
Cifuentes-Silva, Francisco 558
Conrad, Stefan 523

d'Amato, Claudia 68
Darmon, David 116
Debruyne, Christophe 270
Desmontils, Emmanuel 255
Di Caro, Luigi 101
Di Sciascio, Eugenio 298
Dietze, Stefan 523
Dolby, Julian 491
Duan, Shangfu 36

Elbassuoni, Shady 52
Emani, Cheikh Kacfah 209
Ercan, Gonenc 52
Ezeiza, Jon 379

Fanizzi, Nicola 68
Faron-Zucker, Catherine 116
Farzanehpour, Mehdi 379
Fathalla, Said 427
Fauceglia, Nicolas 283
Fernández-Izquierdo, Alba 443
Ferré, Sébastien 84

Ferrod, Roger 101
Frasincar, Flavius 363

Gaiardo, Andrea 590
Gandon, Fabien 116, 194
Gao, Huan 36
García-Castro, Raúl 443
Garcia-Duran, Alberto 459
Gazzotti, Raphaël 116
Gentile, Anna Lisa 131
Gliozzo, Alfio 283
Goasdoué, François 19
Gonçalves, Rafael S. 146
Gramegna, Filippo 298
Gray, Alasdair J. G. 507
Gruhl, Daniel 131
Gupta, Dhruv 162

Haralambous, Yannis 209
Hernández, Inma 397
Hienert, Daniel 523
Hildebrandt, Marcel 179
Hose, Katja 3, 52
Huang, Hai 194
Hyvönen, Eero 574

Ikkala, Esko 574

Janke, Daniel 475
Joblin, Mitchell 179
Juric, Damir 330

Kamdar, Maulik R. 146
Kassawat, Firas 225
Keravuori, Kirsi 574
Kharlamov, Evgeny 314
Khodadadi, Mohammad 330
Koutraki, Maria 346

Labra Gayo, Jose Emilio 558, 606
Lacroix-Hugues, Virginie 116
Lamparter, Steffen 314
Lange, Christoph 427

Lehmann, Jens   225
Leskinen, Petri   574
Lewis, Dave   270
Li, Hui   459
Liu, Bing   36
Liu, Ye   459

Manolescu, Ioana   19
McLaughlin, Stephen   507
Mehta, Akhil   179
Mietchen, Daniel   606
Mogoreanu, Serghei   179
Mohamed, Sameh K.   240
Montoya, Gabriela   3
Moore, Jonathan   330
Moreau, Benjamin   255
Mugnier, Marie-Laure   19
Musen, Mark A.   146

Niepert, Mathias   459
Nováček, Vít   240

O'Sullivan, Declan   270
Onoro-Rubio, Daniel   459

Palumbo, Enrico   590
Pandit, Harshvardhan J.   270
Perrin, Matthieu   255
Poveda-Villalón, María   443
Prud'hommeaux, Eric   606

Qi, Guilin   36

Rabhi, Fethi A.   412
Rantala, Heikki   574
Ristoski, Petar   131
Rivero, Carlos R.   397
Rizzo, Giuseppe   68, 590
Rosenblum, David S.   459
Rossiello, Gaetano   283

Ruiz, David   397
Ruta, Michele   298

Sack, Harald   346
Savković, Ognjen   314
Schifanella, Claudio   101
Scioscia, Floriano   298
Semeraro, Giovanni   283
Serrano-Alvarado, Patricia   255
Skubella, Adrian   475
Solbrig, Harold   606
Sommer, Ashley   543
Staab, Steffen   475
Stoilos, Giorgos   330
Strötgen, Jannik   162
Stupp, Gregory S.   606
Sunder, Swathi Shyam   179

Tamper, Minna   574
Thon, Ingo   179
Thornton, Katherine   606
Thost, Veronika   491
Tresp, Volker   179
Troncy, Raphael   590
Tuominen, Jouni   574
Türker, Rima   346

Urbani, Jacopo   379

Waagmeester, Andra   606
Wallaart, Olaf   363
Wartak, Szymon   330
Welch, Steve   131

Zeinalipour-Yazti, Demetrios   162
Zhang, Lei   346
Zheng, Yalung   379
Zhou, Qianru   507
Zloch, Matthäus   523

Printed in the United States
by Baker & Taylor Publisher Services